WINDS OF

DESTRUCTION

WINDS OF

DESTRUCTION

The autobiography of a Rhodesian combat pilot

P.J.H. Petter-Bowyer

30° South Publishers

Published in 2005 and reprinted in 2013 by:
30° South Publishers (Pty) Ltd.
16 Ivy Road
Pinetown 3610
South Africa
email: info@30degreessouth.co.za
website: www.30degreessouth.co.za

Designed & typeset by Kerrin Cocks
Cover design by Kerrin Cocks
Printed in South Africa by Pinetown Printers (Pty) Ltd, Pinetown,
KwaZulu-Natal

ISBN 978-0-954849-03-0

Contents

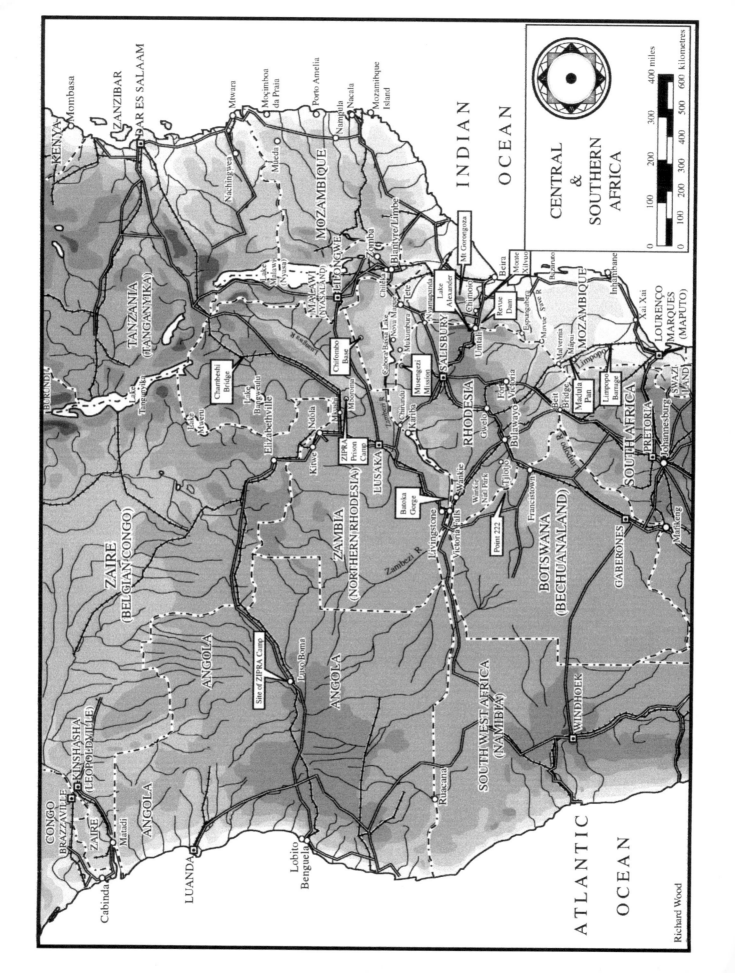

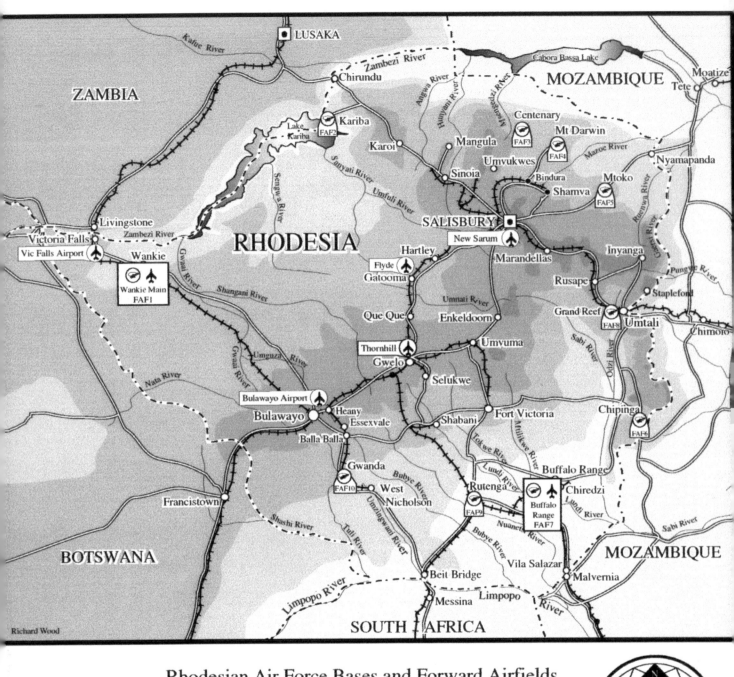

ZAMBIA

LUSAKA

Kafue River

Zambezi River

Chirundu

MOZAMBIQUE

Moatize

Tete

Cabora Bassa Lake

Kariba
FAF2

Lake Kariba

Karoi

Mangula

Centenary
FAF3

Mt Darwin

FAF4

Mazoe River

Nyamapanda

Sengwa River

Sanyati River

Umfuli River

Umvukwes

Sinoia

Bindura

Shamva

Mtoko
FAF5

Ruenya River

Livingstone

Victoria Falls

Vic Falls Airport

Zambezi River

RHODESIA

SALISBURY

New Sarum

Gwaai River

Wankie

Wankie Main
FAF1

Shangani River

Hartley

Flyde
Gatooma

Marandellas

Inyanga

Rusape

Staplefond

Pungwe River

Odzi River

Gaesi River

Umguza River

Que Que

Umnati River

Enkeldoorn

Grand Reef
FAF8

Umtali

Chimoro

Nata River

Gwaai River

Thornhill
Gwelo

Umvuma

Sabi River

Bulawayo Airport

Selukwe

Bulawayo

Heany
Essexvale

Shabani

Fort Victoria

Chipinga
FAF6

Balla Balla

Tokwe River

Mtilikwe River

Lundi River

Gwanda

FAF10

West
Nicholson

Bubye River

Rutenga

FAF9

Buffalo Range

Buffalo
Range
FAF7

Chiredzi

Lundi River

Sabi River

Francistown

Shashi River

Umzingwani River

Tuli River

Nuanetsi River

Bubye River

Vila Salazar

MOZAMBIQUE

BOTSWANA

Beit Bridge

Malvernia

Limpopo River

Messina

Limpopo River

SOUTH AFRICA

Richard Wood

Rhodesian Air Force Bases and Forward Airfields

FAF1 = Forward Airfield

Flyde = Rhodesian Air Force Base

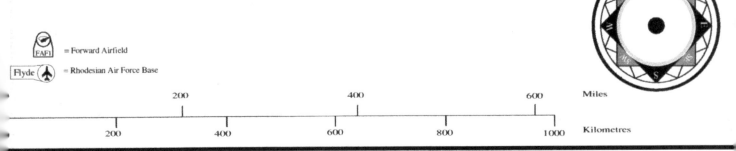

| | 200 | | 400 | | 600 | Miles |

| | 200 | 400 | 600 | 800 | 1000 | Kilometres |

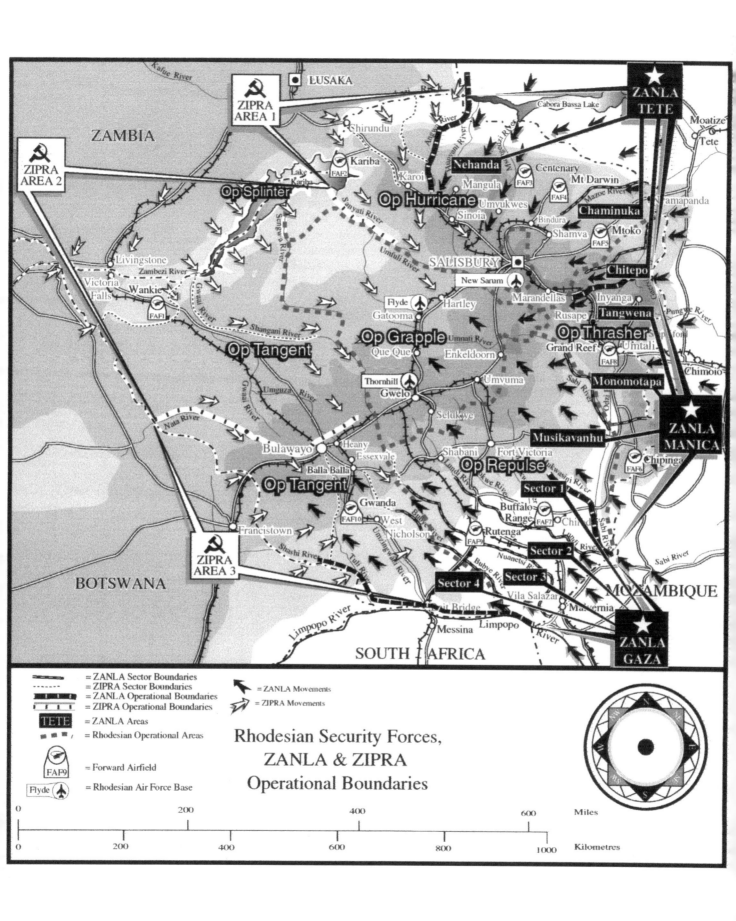

ZIPRA
AREA 1

ZANLA
TETE

ZAMBIA

ŁUSAKA

Kafue River

Moatize
Tete

Chirundu

Cabora Bassa Lake

ZIPRA
AREA 2

Kariba

FAF2

Nehanda

Karoi

Centenary

Mt Darwin

FAF3

Namapanda

Op Splinter

Lake
Kariba

Mangula

FAF4

Chaminuka

Op Hurricane

Umvukwes

Bindura

Mtoko

Livingstone

Zambezi River

Sinoia

Shamva

FAF5

Victoria
Falls

Wankie

Sanyati River

SALISBURY

Chitepo

FAF1

Sengwa River

Gwaai River

Umfuli River

New Sarum

Marandellas

Inyanga

Tangwena

Shangani River

Flyde
Gatooma

Hartley

Rusape

Op Thrasher

Pungwe River

Op Tangent

Op Grapple

Umniati River

Grand Reef

Umtali

Que Que

Enkeldoorn

FAF8

Chimoio

Umguza River

Thornhill
Gwelo

Umvuma

Sabi River

Monomotapa

Gwaai River

Selukwe

ZANLA
MANICA

Nata River

Musikavanhu

Bulawayo

Heany
Essexvale

Shabani

Fort Victoria

FAF6
Chipinga

Op Tangent

Balla Balla

Op Repulse

Sector 1

Buffalo
Range

Gwanda

FAF10
West
Nicholson

Lundi River

FAF7

Chiredzi

Francistown

Shashi River

Rutenga

FAF9

Sector 2

Sabi River

BOTSWANA

ZIPRA
AREA 3

Tuli River

Umzingwani River

Nuanetsi R.

Sector 4

Sector 3

Vila Salazar
Malvernia

MOZAMBIQUE

Limpopo River

it Bridge

Messina

Limpopo

River

ZANLA
GAZA

SOUTH AFRICA

= ZANLA Sector Boundaries

= ZIPRA Sector Boundaries

= ZANLA Operational Boundaries

= ZIPRA Operational Boundaries

= ZANLA Movements

= ZIPRA Movements

TETE = ZANLA Areas

= Rhodesian Operational Areas

FAF9 = Forward Airfield

Flyde = Rhodesian Air Force Base

Rhodesian Security Forces,
ZANLA & ZIPRA
Operational Boundaries

0   200   400   600   Miles

0   200   400   600   800   1000   Kilometres

Foreword

I WILL NOT PRETEND THAT I have known Group Captain Peter John Hornby Petter-Bowyer, affectionately known as 'PB', as long as some have. After both having left our beloved Rhodesia, we lived in the same town, Durban, for years without encountering each other. Given my work on the history of Rhodesia, and my service in the Rhodesian Regiment and the Rhodesian Intelligence Corps, I knew his reputation, of course, indeed the awe in which this modest-to-a-fault airman was held within the ranks of the Rhodesian Security Forces. If our paths did not cross in daily life, I made it my business to interview him about what I knew of his achievements.

What PB presents us with in this book is a unique account of Rhodesia from the prosperous post-Second World War years to her death-throes in 1980. Unique because it is seen not just through the eyes of a pilot, because PB was seldom desk-bound, rarely flying a 'Mahogany Bomber' at headquarters, but through those of a Renaissance man, the proverbial man of great knowledge. PB's restless, inquiring mind never allowed him just to perform the task required of him. He was not what the Army thought of the typical pilot, homeward bound to clean clothes, a warm bed, fine food and the girls and the beer.

If PB was flying, he was thinking. Thinking about his aircraft. He was not an engineer but he would be responsible for many modifications of his aircraft, much to the irritation of a few of the technical staff. If he was bombing, he was thinking about the bomb, its purpose and whether it was achieving it. So it would be PB who would mastermind the invention and production of Rhodesia's remarkable range of bombs. He did not do this alone, but his inquiring, inventive mind was the inspiration. The Rhodesian Air Force was condemned by circumstance to fly aircraft which elsewhere were obsolete, but the best had to be made of them, and not just by a high level of flying competence. The aging Canberra bomber (designed by PB's cousin, William 'Teddy' Petter) was Rhodesia's bomber equipped with a range of standard NATO bombs. PB soon saw ways to make it more effective even if metal fatigue would reduce the number of available Canberras. PB enhanced the humble air-to-ground rocket and gave the Hunter a formidable blast bomb, among other weapons. When a helicopter pilot, PB would enhance the Alouette III's refuelling ability, and assist in improving its weaponry.

It was not just a fascination with technology that marks the man. PB is not just an inventor; he was an inspiring and resourceful leader of the school that did not ask his pilots to do anything he would not do, and he would be the one doing it longer. Beginning with his helicopter days in the latter half of 1960s, PB was a leading counter-insurgency tactician. It was PB who realised that one could track from the air. Better than that, alone among the pilots, he realised that there were telltale signs, not just tracks, which betrayed the presence of his enemy. His self-imposed social anthropological research led him to become Rhodesia's leading air-recce pilot when commanding No 4 Squadron. When PB appeared overhead in his stuttering Trojan, everyone in the ground forces knew something was about to happen, that the whereabouts of the quarry was about to be known. His training led to others acquiring this skill, and one at least bettered him, but it was PB who had the vision. He would carry that vision into every task that he performed.

I commend to you not just this inspiring pilot's tale, but the man himself.

Professor J.R.T Wood
Durban, South Africa

Author's Note

WHILE RESEARCHING MY FAMILIES' backgrounds I ran into difficulties that forced me to rely entirely on faded memories of aged relatives because no written legacies exist. So in 1984 I started recording my own life's story with the simple objective of leaving a permanent record, in hopes that my family would record their own historical narratives for successive generations to build upon. But then in January 2000 I was persuaded by Rhodesian friends to expand on what I had recorded, to meet a need for at least one Rhodesian Air Force story told at an individual level. Consequently this book is not an historical account of the most efficient air force of its day; nor does it cover important subjects that did not involve me either directly or indirectly. Nevertheless, my experiences are unique and sufficiently wide-ranging to give readers a fair understanding of the force I served, and reveal something of the essence of Rhodesia and her thirteen-year bush war.

In 1980, the long struggle to prevent an immensely successful country from falling into the hands of political despots, particularly Robert Gabriel Mugabe and his goons, was lost at political level. This was because of relentless international pressure against the white government of Ian Smith in favour of 'immediate' black-majority rule. Britain's ruling parties had not only failed to uphold promises of independence for Rhodesia, they totally disregarded every warning of the calamity that would befall the country and its people if 'one man—one vote' was prematurely forced into effect. Now, after more than twenty-five years in power, Robert Mugabe's ZANU (PF) has exposed Britain's disastrous folly and proven that Rhodesian fears were well founded. Too late to prevent the appalling mess that exists in modern-day Zimbabwe, our efforts to preserve responsible government have now been fully justified.

However, upon gaining power, Robert Mugabe and his ZANU (PF) cohorts became paranoid about the security of their personal positions. This led to the implementation of laws that ensured white Zimbabweans were denuded of personal weapons, military paraphernalia and any Rhodesian documentation that might be used against ZANU Having handed in my own weapons in 1980, I took the precaution of destroying all my diaries. This book reveals some of the reasons why such hasty action was taken but I have lived to regret dumping twenty diaries into the septic tank of our Salisbury home. In hindsight I realise that I should have buried them deep for later recovery. Nevertheless, the consequence of my error is that *Winds of Destruction* is, for the most part, written from memory. I offer no excuse for inevitable errors in detail that the ageing mind may have created, because the essence of this book is correct. Nor do I make any apology for naiveté on political issues, as military personnel in my time were strictly apolitical and this may show in my personal opinions.

During the great wars men left their families for months or years at a time. In Rhodesia this was not the case. Typically, many soldiers, airmen and policemen were in the field for periods of six weeks or more and returned home to rest and retraining for no more that ten days before returning to the bush. This cycle imposed incredible strains on men and their families. A two-year stretch in action and six months at home might have been easier to bear because short-duration homecomings tended to cause higher stress levels. From an environment of 'blood and guts' a serviceman was expected to instantly revert to the tranquillity and comforts of home life without being able to share his experiences and fears with his loved ones. The family on the other hand, though forced to living a life without 'dad', expected him to be the relaxed and fatherly character of a stable family from the very moment he came home. They had no idea of his harboured secrets and built-up tensions. In reality 'dad' could not reconcile himself to the normality he encountered away from 'the sharp end' and probably drank too much with his friends after a day of retraining. He then became subdued, even difficult, in the last couple of days before returning to the bush. Misunderstandings caused too many marriages to fail or left deep-seated problems in those that survived. Mine survived thanks to my beloved wife Beryl who guided our children through the tough times.

It is for these reasons that I dedicate this book to my wife Beryl, my daughter Debbie, my son Paul, and to all those wonderful wives and widows of Rhodesian servicemen who kept the home fires burning and sustained our will to fight on for our country.

My thanks go to my friend, Air Marshal Sir John Baird, retired Surgeon General to Britain's armed services and Queen's Physician, for very kindly reading my draft work, which helped eliminate many obvious typographical errors. Thank you Sir John. Special thanks also go to Professor Richard and Carole Wood for reading my first draft and giving me the encouragement and direction I needed to complete this book.

Peter Petter-Bowyer ('PB')
Norfolk, England

Chapter

1

A short history of the Rhodesian Air Force

AT THE CONCLUSION OF THE Anglo–Boer War all seven Southern Rhodesian military units, which had participated with the British forces, were disbanded. However, in 1914 at the outbreak of the Great War in Europe, the Rhodesia Regiment was re-established. It served with distinction and remained in force until it was again disbanded in 1920.

A Territorial Force was formed in 1927 with 1st and 2nd Battalions of the Rhodesia Regiment based at Salisbury and Bulawayo. At the outbreak of World War II in 1939 the regular members of these battalions, together with a disproportionately large component of volunteers, were absorbed into British units in many theatres.

A Territorial Force Air Unit had been formed in 1935 and operated out of the commercial airport at Belvedere on the south-western edge of Salisbury City. Six Hawker Hart twin-seater fighter aircraft were received from the RAF in 1937 to add to an existing small communications flight. Combat pilot training commenced immediately, resulting in the first Rhodesian wings presentation to six pilots on 13 May 1938. Later in the year they were to prove themselves by flying the next batch of Hawker Harts from Britain to Southern Rhodesia.

With war clouds looming over Europe, the Territorial Force members of the Air Unit were called up for full-time service in August 1939 and by the end of the month the aircraft were on the move. Ten pilots (among them Lieutenant E.W.S. Jacklin, later to become the first post-war Chief of Air Staff) and eight aircraft left Salisbury on 27 August to fly to Nairobi—constituting the only aerial force available to Imperial Authorities in East Africa.

Nairobi proved to be merely a staging post on the route north, for within two or three days all the Rhodesian aircraft had been moved to the Northern Frontier District on the Abyssinian border. On 19 September 1939, the Air Unit officially became the Southern Rhodesian Air Force, and the flights on service in Kenya were designated No 1 Squadron of that force.

In April 1940, all Southern Rhodesian Air Force personnel were absorbed into the Royal Air Force and No 1 Squadron was redesignated No 237 (Rhodesian) Squadron. As a tribute to its preparedness, it was allowed to adopt the motto 'Premium Agmen in Caelo' (The First Force in the Sky).

By November 1941, No 237 Squadron was equipped with Hurricanes and was embroiled in the seesaw battles with the Afrika Korps and the Luftwaffe. In February 1942, it was ordered back to Ismalia in the Canal Zone before travelling yet farther east.

The next year was spent covering the Iraq/Persia sector with the squadron operating from such bases as Mosul, Kermanshah and Kirkuk. In March 1943, it returned to the Canal Zone where its role changed from army co-operation to fighter reconnaissance, flying Spitfires. A long spell of operations across North Africa followed, during which the squadron moved progressively westward.

But with the war obviously coming to an end, the squadron was gradually losing its all-Rhodesian nature. It became increasingly difficult to replace personnel who had completed their operational tour, and after two more moves to Italy and France the squadron was eventually disbanded in 1945.

But 237 was not the only unit to operate as a 'Rhodesian' squadron with the Royal Air Force. In 1940, No 266 Squadron was officially designated a 'Rhodesian' unit and the decision was made that aircrew from Rhodesia should be posted to it. The following year, No 44 Squadron of bomber command followed suit. In addition to the Rhodesians who fought in these squadrons, there were obviously many more who played their part in other Air Force units and in other theatres of operations.

During the six years of war, the total number of Rhodesians in Air Force uniform stood at 977 officers and 1,432 other ranks. Of these, 498 were killed—a proportion of one man in every five who went to war. But one further casualty of the war was the Rhodesian Air Force itself—certainly as far as Rhodesia was concerned. No 1 Squadron of the Southern Rhodesian Air Force had been turned into 237 Squadron that had then been disbanded. Further, the training element of the old SRAF had been absorbed into the Royal Air Force and had become the nucleus of the huge Rhodesian Air Training Group. But in doing so, it had lost its identity.

It was not, however, a situation that was to last long, and the vacuum was soon to be filled. In the immediate post-war period, men trickled back to Rhodesia after being demobilised from the British services. Some of them joined the Southern Rhodesia Staff Corps, generally at very low ranks, and it was from this nucleus that the Air Force was to arise again.

Many of the ex-Air Force members of the Staff Corps itched to re-establish military aviation, but prospects were far from promising. There was no money, there were no aircraft, and even the original SRAF buildings had been appropriated for use by new immigrants and for various government departments. However, the enthusiasts cajoled and persuaded, and eventually attracted to their cause Sir Ernest Guest, then Minister of Defence, and Colonel S. Garlake, Commander of Military Forces in Southern Rhodesia. The result was the provision of £20,000 sterling and the instruction to form an air unit. The financial grant was woefully inadequate, but there were almost limitless reserves of enthusiasm and resourcefulness to call upon.

Under the leadership of Lieutenant-Colonel E.W.S. Jacklin, the dozen or so officers and men of the unit set about acquiring some aircraft. The Royal Air Force contributed a war-surplus Anson light transport aircraft, and then a major salvage exercise started. The men went on forays through the old RAF maintenance depots and even scrap dumps. Tools, raw materials, spares, supplies and even trained personnel filtered through to the little unit at Cranborne from all over the country. Eventually, using basic tools and equipment, the unit had rebuilt six scrapped and abandoned Tiger Moths.

On 28 November 1947, the Government Gazette No 945 carried the notice establishing the Air Force as a Permanent Unit of the Rhodesian Staff Corps, and this was the beginning of the Southern Rhodesian Air Force to come. The six rebuilt Tiger Moths were joined by six Harvard trainers purchased from the Rhodesian Air Training Group, and later twelve more Harvards were obtained from South Africa at nominal prices.

The work paid off in progressive expansion—more ex-Air Force personnel joined the unit, and gradually a varied selection of aircraft was acquired. By 1951, a Leopard Moth, a Dakota, Rapides, Ansons and Austers had been collected from a variety of sources, and the unit operated a small regular element with one active auxiliary squadron—No 1 Squadron.

By this time the Berlin Blockade, the clamping of the Iron Curtain across Europe and the onset of the Korean War had made it obvious to all that the preservation of peace was to be more a matter of armed preparedness than of wishful thinking. So once again the Southern Rhodesian Government made a contribution to the defence of the Commonwealth—this time it was in the form of two fighter squadrons.

From Britain twenty-two Spitfire Mk22 aircraft were successfully ferried out in spite of dire predictions and a certain amount of betting from a number of aviation experts. Full-time training was then re-introduced in the form of the 'Short Service' training scheme.

Spitfire Mk22.

In 1952 the Air Force moved from Cranborne to Kentucky Airport, which subsequently became the huge airfield jointly used by New Sarum Air Force Station and Salisbury International Airport. This was the first permanent home of the Air Force, and it was the first time that it had occupied buildings and facilities specifically designed for its purposes.

Increased obligations to the RAF and the need to modernise became issues in making the decision to withdraw the Spitfires from service. Painful though it was for all concerned, single-seater De Havilland Vampire FB9 jets replaced the much-loved Spitfires. Later T11 two-seater jet trainers were added.

In addition to the Vampire fighter/bombers, expansion continued with the acquisition of Provost piston-engined trainers. Seven more Dakotas and two Pembrokes were acquired to replace the Ansons and Rapides, and further aircrew and technicians were recruited. By the beginning of 1956, the Air Force boasted four active squadrons, two Vampire fighter squadrons, a transport squadron and a flying training squadron.

Africa was now being subjected to the first of many political changes leading up to the withdrawal of the colonising nations. The Federation of Rhodesia and Nyasaland was formed in 1953 and, in its turn, caused some major changes within the Air Force.

The title was changed to Rhodesian Air Force, with Queen Elizabeth conferring the 'Royal' prefix. As the Royal Rhodesian Air Force, the unit forsook its army ranks and khaki uniforms and adopted ranks and uniforms similar to those of the Royal Air Force.

But the major change of the Federal inception was one of scope and responsibility. From being a minor, self-contained force, preoccupied with territorial defence, the RRAF was now responsible for the defence of the Federation as a whole and was also to acquire wider responsibility as a part of the Royal Air Force's potential in the Middle East.

At the conclusion of the Second World War, the RAF retained its RTG airfield, Thornhill, where flying training on Harvards continued. This was the largest and best-equipped RTG airbase sited close to the Midlands town of Gwelo. It remained an active RAF base until its closure in 1955 when it was taken over by the Royal Rhodesian Air Force.

With ever-increasing commercial flights in and out of Salisbury Airport, Group Headquarters decided to reduce congestion at the jointly used facilities by moving all Air Force training to Thornhill. Initially this was only possible for piston operations, using existing grass runways. Two years of work during 1956 and 1957 were needed to build a tar macadam runway with taxiways, concrete hard standings and a modern control tower, incorporating radar, before jet training could commence.

In line with RAF practice, the RRAF pilot-training scheme was known as a Short Service Unit (SSU). Successful applicants for pilot training were inducted as officer cadets for a two-year training course. Failure at any point in training resulted in the immediate release of a student with no obligation on either side. However, students who gained their wings and had completed advanced-weapons training had the option of either applying for a medium-service commission or returning to civilian life. Air Headquarters was under no obligation to accept those who applied for medium service.

No 1 SSU was inducted in 1952 with successive intakes occurring at six-monthly intervals. Tiger Moths, Harvards and Spitfires served the training needs initially until Provosts and Vampires replaced them. In 1956, the intake frequency was reduced to one intake a year when No 9 SSU was the first to undergo Basic Flying School (BFS) training at Thornhill.

At the conclusion of BFS in December 1956, No 9 SSU had to move to New Sarum for the Advanced Flying Training

(AFS) on Vampires because Thornhill was not yet ready to accommodate jets. The first course to undergo BFS, AFS and OCU (Operational Conversion Unit) at Thornhill was No 10 SSU. This was the course I attended.

Younger days

AT 13:15 ON 2 JUNE 1936, Doctor Ritchken's regular lunchtime break was interrupted to attend to my mother who was in labour at the Lady Chancellor Maternity Home in Salisbury. No complications occurred with my birth and I was declared to be a strong and health baby.

My father and mother were both from England. Dad was born in Southampton and Mum in Brighton. Dad came from a long line of naval pilots who brought many thousands of ships safely down Southampton's Water. Not surprisingly Dad had hoped to join the Royal Navy but he was rejected for being unable to differentiate between purple and mauve. So, in 1923 at the age of 17 he set out to see the world as a hired hand on a steam-powered cargo ship. In New York he explored the big city, wearing the only clothes he possessed—a rugby jersey and shorts. After roaming the seas he found New Zealand to be the right place to stay ashore and to try and settle down.

He did well as a lumberman. He also worked on sheep farms and played a good deal of rugby in his free time. There he met his lifelong friend, Alan Martin, who later became my godfather. Alan interested Dad in opportunities being offered by the British Government in far-off Southern Rhodesia; so they moved to Africa together.

Dad was christened Paul Charles Petter Bowyer. The third Christian name was in fact his mother's maiden name. The Petters were, and still are, well known for their internal-combustion engines and other engineering successes. For instance, William Petter was designer and chief engineer of Britain's Canberra bomber, Lightning interceptor and Gnat trainer. Prior to this, William's father had designed the famous short-field aircraft, Lysander, which gave such excellent service to special agents and the French Resistance during World War II.

In New Zealand Dad's banking affairs were getting muddled up with another Bowyer. All efforts to rectify the situation failed until Dad hyphenated his name—to become Petter-Bowyer. Though this resolved his problem and fitted a fashion for double-barrelled names in those times, the surname has presented its difficulties over the years.

When I joined the Royal Rhodesian Air Force my surname was short-circuited. Nobody could pronounce Petter-Bowyer correctly so I became known as 'PB'. It is the name Bowyer that seemed to cause problems to many until I explained that my ancestors were men who equated to modern-day artillery-fire controllers. In their own day the Bowyers trained and controlled groups of bowmen in battle. During critical stages when British and enemy forces were closing on each other, it was the bowyers who gave bowmen their orders on aiming angle, draw strain, lay-off and release, for each volley of arrows launched against rapidly changing enemy formations. When BOW of the arrow launcher replaces BOUGH of the tree or BOY of youth, my surname comes out okay!

Dad was six-foot tall, good-looking and immensely strong. Not long after arriving in Rhodesia he attended a country fair at Penhalonga in the east of the country. Late in the evening he was walking past an ox-wagon where an elderly man asked for his assistance. Dad was happy to comply by lifting a large blacksmith's steel anvil from the ground onto the deck of the wagon. When he had done this he became aware of shouted congratulations and slaps on his back from a group of people he had not noticed until then. The elderly man also congratulated him and with great difficulty pushed the anvil off the wagon. He then invited Dad to lift the anvil back onto the wagon, this time for a handsome cash prize that none of many contenders had won. Dad tried but no amount of cheering and encouragement helped him even lift the anvil off the ground.

Mum moved with her parents to Southern Rhodesia in 1914 when she was four years of age. Her father was controller of the Rhodesian Railways storage sheds in Salisbury. He, together with Mum's mother, ran a dairy and market garden on their large plot of land, one boundary of which bordered the bilharzia-ridden Makabusi River, south of the town.

Mum attended Queen Elizabeth School in Salisbury where she acquired a taste for the high-society lifestyle of her friends, though this was not altogether to the liking of her middle-class father. She was christened Catherine Lillian Elizabeth but became known as Shirley because of her striking resemblance to a very beautiful and well-known, redheaded actress of the time. This nickname stuck to Mum for life; and she loved it. Her maiden name, Smith, on the other hand did not suit the image Mum desired. However, that all changed when she married Dad in early 1935.

Dad enjoyed the company of many male friends at the Salisbury City Club. It was from there that he went to register my birth following a lunchtime session to celebrate the birth of his first-born son. I guess he must have been fairly tipsy because he added an extra name to the ones he had agreed with my mother. To Peter John he added another family name, Hornby. In consequence, three of my names link me to family lines in sea, rail and air.

Two years after my birth my brother Paul Anthony (Tony) was born. Together we enjoyed a carefree childhood in the idyllic surroundings of the Rhodesian highveld. Our westward-facing home was set high on a ridge overlooking rolling farmlands,

My parents wedding day photograph was taken in my grandparents' garden. Dad's best man, Alan Martin (later my godfather), is left of Dad. To the right of my mother are her parents and sister Roma. Her brothers John and Bill are the two youngsters seen here.

Mom, Dad and I.

with the city of Salisbury and its famous *kopje* (Afrikaans for hill) clearly visible beyond the multi-coloured msasa trees and bushlands. From here our parents enjoyed breathtaking sunsets as they took their after-work 'sundowner' drinks on our spacious verandah.

Both Mum and Dad worked. Dad had his own heavy-transport business, Pan-African Roadways, and Mum was personal secretary to the Honourable John Parker who headed up the Rhodesian Tobacco Association. So, with the exception of weekends, Tony and I were left from about 07:00 until 17:30 in the autocratic care of our African cook, Tickey. Tickey was the senior man over Phineas (washing and ironing), the housekeeper Jim (sweeping, polishing and making of beds), two gardeners and, during our younger years, someone to watch over our every move. Such a large staff was commonplace in Southern Rhodesia in those days.

Tickey was a fabulous cook. Mum had taught him everything he knew but Tickey had a knack of improving on every dish he learned though the names of some gave him difficulty. For instance, he insisted on calling flapjacks "fleppity jeckets" because the common name of the African khaki weed, black jacks, had stuck in his mind as "bleckity jeckets".

We had more black friends than white for many years and we really enjoyed their company. Together we hunted for field mice and cooked them over open fires, before consuming them with wild spinach and *sadza* (boiled maize meal—the staple diet of the African people). Only people born in Africa will understand why Tony and I enjoyed these strange meals, squatting on our haunches out in the bush, just as much as roast beef and Yorkshire pudding taken at the dinner table!

Whenever possible, we limited our lunch intake to keep enough space so as to be able to join our African friends for *sadza*, gravy and whatever they produced as *muriwo* (supporting relish). Meat was usually cooked extensively to give it a burnt surface from the barely wet base of a three-legged cooking pot set over a small fire. Once the meat was ready, spinach, tomatoes and onions might be added and cooked until well done. On a separate fire a larger pot was used to boil water before mielie-meal was added in small quantities and stirred continuously with a mixing paddle until the texture was just right. All participants in the meal would then wash their hands in a communal bowl and squat on haunches in a circle around two and sometimes three bowls of food.

Only one hand was used to scoop up a lump of boiling hot *sadza* that was then manipulated into the shape of a rugby ball, sufficient in size for three mouthfuls. Severe burning of fingers was avoided by knowing exactly how to use the side of the index finger during pick-up, immediately followed by quick thumb and finger movements to change the point of contact of the steaming lump. The end of the lump was then dipped in the relish for each bite, following strict observance of sequence to ensure that everyone had equal share. All the time someone within the circle would be talking. These were noisy affairs with much laughter. There is no such thing as silence during an African meal. Tony and I loved every moment of those far-off but never forgotten delights.

A gravel road running behind our spacious gardens served the line of homes built along the ridge on which we lived. Across this road lay various fruit and cereal farms and a big dairy farm. Beyond these lay a large forested area, full of colourful msasas and other lovely indigenous trees, through which ran two

rivers. The larger of these was the Makabusi in which Tony and I were forbidden to swim because of bilharzia. Needless to say we swam with our mates whenever our wanderings brought us to the inviting pools bounded by granite surfaces and huge boulders. Being laid up in bed with bilharzia seemed a more attractive option than attending school. But try as we did, we failed to pick up the disease.

Ox wagons were still in use on the farms. This gave ample opportunity to try our hands at the three functions of leading the oxen, wielding the long whip and manning the hand-crank that applied brakes on downhill runs. The black men whose job it was to do these things were amazingly accommodating and never seemed annoyed by our presence.

When old enough to do so, Tony and I rode bicycles to David Livingstone School some four miles from home. I neither liked nor disliked school, but dreaded the attention of bullies who cornered me on many occasions. Dad told me one day that all bullies had one thing in common—they were very good at meting out punishment but cowardly when receiving it. Dad also told me that to accept one good hiding was better than receiving many lesser ones. I got the message and waited until the biggest and meanest of the bullies cornered me in an alley. I climbed into him with everything I had. He tried to break free but I pursued him with vigour until I realised that he was crying like a baby. Not only was I left alone from then on, I assumed the role of protector for other bullyboy victims. The attention I received from the girls was very confusing but strangely pleasing!

Tony and I were blessed with angelic singing voices and were often asked to sing for our beloved grandparents. We took this all for granted until one day we attended a wedding in the Salisbury Anglican Cathedral. After the service I got to talk

with one of the choirboys. From him I learned that he had just been paid two shillings and sixpence, the going rate for singing at weddings. That added up to a lot of ice-creams; so Tony and I joined the Anglican Cathedral choir that very week. Dad was horrified when he learned his sons had joined the Anglican choir, though he never said why. Mum thought it a good idea.

The organist and choirmaster were Mr Lillicrap and Mr Cowlard respectively—names that caused much amusement and some confusion for us. Nevertheless they were good at their work and taught us a great deal about singing. But going to church was a totally new experience for me because the nearest I had come to knowing about God arose from questions I had asked some years earlier when driving past one of Rhodesia's famous balancing granite rock formations.

I asked Mum how the rocks had been placed in such precarious positions. When she told me that God had put them there I wanted to know how many Africans He had used to lift such massive rocks so high. I'm sure she gave me a sensible answer but it obviously went right over my head. Dad on the other hand planted information in my small mind, and it stuck. He told me that all of God's tools are invisible. Some that we know and take for granted include gravity, magnetism, light, sound, radio waves and electricity, simply because we can measure them. However, those tools of God that we know about but cannot measure, such as our powers of thought and love, are substantially less in number than those of His tools about which we know absolutely nothing. These are the ones that control the stars, the air above, the rocks, trees and grasses on the surface as well as the oceans and the depths of the earth. Strangely, with all he said, including something about God's dwelling-place, heaven, Dad did not mention Jesus. This is why the Anglican experience was entirely new to me.

While World War II was raging in Europe, Dad was in Air Force uniform in Rhodesia. Like all Rhodesians, Dad wanted to get to where the action was but the Royal Air Force needed his expertise in transport, right where he lived. This was to support the Rhodesian component of the vast British Empire scheme established to train badly needed aircrews. Dad was disappointed, embarrassed even, but Tony and I saw him as a star and revelled in the situations that the war had brought into our lives.

One of the RAF's Rhodesian Air Training Group (RATG) stations, Cranborne, was just out of view from our house behind the carpet of intervening trees. However, the Harvard Mk2 training aircraft would come into view immediately after take-off. These noisy machines filled the air around us with their ever-changing sounds all day and night as they ploughed around the circuit.

With so many aircraft flying so many hours it was inevitable that mishaps occurred both at and beyond the airfield. On occasions, engine failures and student errors caused crash landings on and beyond the airfield. Some of the crashed machines came down where Tony and I could get to inspect

them. Harvards, which still fly in many clubs around the world today and remained in service with the South African Air Force right up until 1996, possess amazingly strong airframes. Those that came down in the bush and farmlands around our home had all ploughed through trees before coming to rest. Though buckled and bent, not one machine we saw had shed wings or tail planes. The unique smell of those crashed aircraft was too wonderful and we clambered in and out of the cockpits at every opportunity. Sharing ultra-thick dry sandwiches and lukewarm tea with RAF guards and salvage crews added to memories that remain clearer to me today than yesterday's happenings.

My mother's three brothers all went off to the war in Europe. John Smith was an air gunner on Halifax bombers and was posted missing after the second 1,000-bomber raid into Germany. His body, along with those of his crew, was never found.

Eric Smith was killed in a most unfortunate accident while leading his Spitfire squadron back to Britain at the cessation of hostilities in Italy. This was a cruel loss considering he had survived many months of offensive action in the Desert and Italian campaigns.

Eric Smith.   *John Smith.*

Bill Smith, incensed by the loss of his brother John, lied about his age to get into the Fleet Air Arm at age seventeen and saw active service in the latter stages of the war. Later he joined the auxiliary force in Rhodesia, which became the Southern Rhodesia Air Force. Dad's only brother, Steven Bowyer, left his gold mining occupation in Rhodesia to join the RAF as mid upper gunner on Halifax and Lancaster bombers. He survived many missions, including the one on which Guy Gibson died

Tony and I could not fully comprehend the loss of two uncles. Even though we had known and loved both of them, we did not understand the enormous pain their deaths had brought to Mum and our grandparents. We only comprehended the glamour of our Dad in uniform, bringing home many high-ranking officers and gracious ladies to the Sunday swimming parties for which he and Mum were renowned.

Towards the end of the war Dad lost his arm in a freak accident. As Officer Commanding the RATG motor transport fleet, he had visited Thornhill airbase near Gwelo and was on his way to Heany airbase near Bulawayo. Along the way he realised that he still had a document that he should have left at Thornhill. As he was approaching a bridge on a steep downward slope he spotted an RAF truck, still some way off, coming towards the bridge from the opposite side. Dad crossed the bridge and pulled over just short of a point where the road commenced a right-hand sweep. He put out his arm and was waving down the oncoming driver with a view to handing him the document for delivery to Thornhill.

Unbeknown to Dad, the airman driver had been drinking and panicked when he recognised his CO's staff car. Instead of slowing down, he accelerated. The truck drifted on the corner and passed Dad's car in a mild broadside with the tail sufficiently off-line for the extended number plate to rip Dad's arm off just above the elbow.

The truck roared off into the distance, leaving Dad with not a soul around. He could not easily get the severed arm into the vehicle because it was hanging outside the door on a substantial section of skin. He leaned out with his left hand and managed to bring the arm inside. Blood was spraying everywhere in powerful spurts bringing Dad to the realisation that he would be dead in less than a minute if it continued. The door panel of his American Dodge was made of compressed hardboard. Through this panel he managed to drive the exposed bone and press the flesh tight up against the surface to stem the blood flow. He then drove like the wind for Heany. On arrival at the main gate, the duty provost marshal failed to understand Dad's frantic calls to lift the security boom. Instead he ambled to the car, looked inside and keeled over in a faint. Dad had no option—he smashed through the boom and drove straight to Station Sick Quarters where he kept his hand on the horn until help arrived. Shocked and now in pain some forty minutes after the accident, he surprised the doctor and staff by not only remaining conscious but for being fully articulate.

Reverting to me—the matter of what I wanted to do in life came early. Having passed through the usual stage of wanting to become a driver of the beautiful Garret steam engines that Tony and I loved to watch labouring up the long hill from Salisbury station or racing fast in the opposite direction, I settled for surgery. When I was about nine years old, the war having just ended, Dad and Mum told me that they had booked a place for me at Edinburgh University for 1954.

When I turned eleven and Tony was nine, our secure little world fell apart. We woke one morning to discover that Mum had left Dad. We loved our parents dearly and simply could not understand why things could not go on as before. In a relatively short time, in a blur of insecurity, uncertainty and confusion, Tony and I learned that Mum and Dad were divorced and that we were going to a boarding school in the Vumba Mountains near Umtali, as founder members of Eagle Preparatory School.

When we checked into this brand-new school we found ourselves with another twenty youngsters ranging in age from nine to twelve.

Frank Carey and his small staff had come from the Dragon School in Oxford, England, to establish Eagle School. He intended to emulate a style of teaching he knew and believed in. Our environment was wonderful so Tony and I settled in easily, and quickly regained lost confidence. The style of teaching was quite different from that we had known and new subjects, including Latin, French and trigonometry, were brought in immediately.

Group Captain Berrisford-Pakenham.

In our first year at Eagle, Mum remarried and moved with her husband, Group Captain Berrisford-Pakenham, to farm in Mkushi in Northern Rhodesia. Dad had bought a farm and lime-works near Cashel Valley in the foothills of Rhodesia's eastern border mountains. Tony and I alternated our school holidays between Mum and Dad, which was fine for a while but we both hated being away from Mum for such long periods.

On return to school at the beginning of the second year we learned that Dad had married Joan Shevill who had a daughter of my age and a son of Tony's age. Jennifer and John were in boarding at Umtali High and Umtali Junior schools, respectively. Our first holiday with the new family on Moosgwe Farm went well, though we were all a bit uncertain of each other. Thereafter relations became strained because Tony and I were only present on alternate holidays and because my stepmother loathed my mother, whom she never ever met.

Visits to Mum were too wonderful for words. Much of this had to do with the fact that our stepfather, Berry, had gained our absolute trust by never interfering in matters that did not concern him, but always giving sound advice and clear answers to any question we asked.

Berry had served with the British Border Regiment where he had risen to the rank of colonel. He then switched to the RAF, accepting a considerable loss in seniority simply because he wanted to fly. In the RAF he rose to the substantive rank of group captain. To have achieved the same level of rank in two substantially different forces was a remarkable achievement considering he was only forty-two when he retired from service and immigrated to Rhodesia.

The ranch on which Berry and Mum farmed, in partnership with two other ex-servicemen, was vast (36,000 acres) and absolutely beautiful. Apart from running big herds of Afrikaner and Red Poll cattle, large quantities of tobacco were grown and cured. We lived in pole and *dagga* (mud) thatched houses for many months with communal kitchen and dining hall constructed in like manner. Peter, Michael and Marcus Gordon, though younger than Tony and me, were good friends who, like us, enjoyed living in the crude accommodation so much more than the brick homes that came later.

During the 1949 Christmas holidays with Dad we learned that Tony and I would not be returning to Eagle School but were moving to government schools in Umtali. We were heart-sore about leaving the Vumba, which had been a happy place. Had the reason for moving—money—been explained to us, it would have been much easier to understand why we had to step-down, in line with our stepsister and stepbrother.

We moved to Umtali High School in January 1950. I boarded in Chancellor House, whereas Tony went to the junior school and boarded in Kopje House. From the outset I enjoyed Umtali High School, which catered for boys and girls. Unfortunately the subject levels I had reached at Eagle School were substantially higher than the grade into which I was first placed. I was immediately moved up a grade but, again, I had covered its levels. Any thought of elevating me further was rejected because I would have been two years younger than the youngest member. My brother was in a far worse position for having to stay at junior school.

By the time new subject matter came my way I was fourteen years old and had been in a state of idleness for over a year. Somewhat bewildered, I found myself struggling to learn for the first time in my life. Nevertheless, I managed to pass all examinations and moved up another grade with Jennifer, my stepsister. But instead of remaining in the upper academic stream, as expected, we were both placed in what was know as Form 4-Removed where subject levels were slightly lower than those being taught to some of our previous classmates, now in Form 4A. I did not understand this, but accepted that I would have to do another year at school before writing the Cambridge Certificate examination. Good results in these examinations qualified one for a Matric Exemption, which was crucial for acceptance into Edinburgh University.

On the 2 June 1952, my sixteenth birthday, the whole family attended a dance at the Black Mountain Hotel in the small village of Cashel. Any occasion at the Black Mountain Hotel was great fun, but this particular night turned out to be a depressing one for me. It brought about another substantial turnabout in my life. Dad chose that night to take me out into the cold night air to tell me that, with immediate effect, I was being taken out of school.

Schooling for Rhodesian whites was mandatory to the age of sixteen, so I could not have been removed before that day. But now Dad was telling me that my headmaster, Mr Gledhill, had told him that I was wasting my time at school and that I had no chance of gaining the all-important Matric Exemption needed for Edinburgh. Though totally shaken, I accepted Dad's word, never realising that he was acting under direction from my stepmother who had absolute control over him. Another thing I did not realise at the time was that money was the root of the problem. I can only guess that Dad, who had used up most of his financial reserves to buy his farm and implements, was wholly responsible for Tony and me, whereas my stepmother, who was financially better off, following the death of her first husband, took care of Jennifer and John.

I worked with Dad on his farm, Curzon, which he had bought after selling Moosgwe and its lime-works. All was fine for a short while before things went horribly wrong. My stepmother decided I was too big for my boots for daring to offer a suggestion on how to improve the surface of the tortuous roadway leading up to the farmhouse set on the edge of a high ridge.

My self-confidence was already sub-zero when I was told I would be going to work for Freddie Haynes on his cattle ranch, Tom's Hope, near Cashel. Dad said this had been arranged to give me experience under the care of a successful rancher. Later my stepmother let slip the real reason. She hoped that Freddie, an Afrikaner, would subject me to a hard time to 'sort me out'. As it happened, Freddie and his English wife Sayer, together with his old father Hans Haynes, were very kind and I learned a great deal from them.

A strange thing happened whilst we were dipping cattle in the foul-smelling brown liquid of the deep plunge dip-tank through which the cattle had to swim regularly for tick control. Old man Hans Haynes had an Australian-style stock whip in his hand and, with a huge grin on his face, he told me that I could use the whip on him if I dived into the dip-tank and swam its full length. Being an Englishman I was certain this old-timer Afrikaner was inferring that I lacked the guts to meet such a challenge. Without hesitation I stopped the flow of cattle and dived into the tank. When I emerged from the slippery ramp at the far end I was choking and my eyes were burning badly.

The horrified herdsmen rushed to me with buckets of clean water, which they splashed on my face and poured all over my sodden clothing. When I regained control of my sight and caught my breath I went to the stunned old man and demanded his whip. This he gave me, then stood back expecting to be lashed. I smiled and handed the whip back before running off as fast as I could to a nearby dam to clean myself in an attempt to stop the awful burning that was consuming me from my head to my toes.

When she saw that I was sopping wet, unable to walk normally and reeking of dip, Sayer Haynes, who was a qualified nurse, became furious with Freddie and his father. She ordered me to undress and take a shower before inspecting my body in detail and applying dressings to awkward areas that were already raw and peeling. I stayed in bed for almost a week and was spoiled by everyone. The old man kept saying he was really sorry; that he had absolutely no idea that I would respond so rapidly to a challenge he claimed was made in jest.

Freddie Haynes had many outbuildings behind his beautiful home, with superb stables and all manner of implements and goods in storerooms. I asked him if I could use some of the poles and timber lengths stacked in one storeroom to build shelving in others so that I could get order into the hundreds of items that were in disarray. He welcomed the suggestion and was very pleased with the final result. In consequence of this, Freddie told my father that I was very good with my hands and implied that I should be in an occupation that would fully utilise this talent. For the first time in his presence, I broke into tears when Dad suggested to me that I should become an apprentice carpenter and joiner. Embarrassed by this emotional breakdown, I reminded Dad how I had always told him I wanted to use my hands for surgery.

Being the only young person on the ranch, I missed contact with my own age group. So, having given Dad's suggestion some thought, the idea of going to town for an apprenticeship became more attractive. I moved to the Young Mens' Club in Umtali and commenced my apprenticeship with Keystone Construction early in 1953. I got on well with everyone and did well in learning crafts that included cabinet-making, machining, joinery and site construction. I was able to see my brother Tony regularly, which was great, but I recall the envy I felt whenever he went off on his holidays to be with Mum and Berry.

Late in the winter of 1956, I ran from my work place to watch four Venom jet fighter-bombers of No 208 RAF Squadron. They were on a goodwill tour of Rhodesia and Umtali was one of the many centres the jets visited so to excite thousands of gawking citizens. All they did was a simple high-speed tail-chase inside the mountains ringing the town. But the sight and sound of those machines immediately decided me that the Air Force life was for me.

Right away I looked into joining the Royal Rhodesian Air Force but soon recognised two major problems. The maximum age for trainee pilots was 21 and a Matric Exemption was mandatory. For reasons I cannot recall, I made an appointment to see the company MD, Mr Burford. I wanted to tell him about my wish to be an Air Force pilot, notwithstanding the fact that this appeared to be an impossibility.

Of small build, dapper and very well spoken, Mr Burford

always struck me as being too refined and gentlemanly for the world of construction. In his always-courteous manner he treated me in a gentle, fatherly manner. Before I could tell him of my hopes, he was telling me that the Board of Directors had decided to take me off the bench and get me cracking in quantity surveying—as a first step to management and later, maybe, to become an active shareholder in the company. I should have been pleased by such news but it all went straight over my head because it in no way fitted with what I had come to talk about, and I told Mr Burford so.

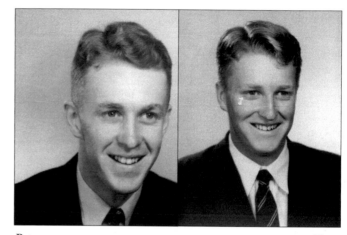

Peter.   *Tony.*

I told him of my original dream to become a surgeon and all that had happened to bring me to being an apprentice in his company. From the moment I mentioned having been taken out of school prematurely I detected agitation in Mr Burford's face. Before I could get to the matter of joining the Air Force, he cut in to say he could not accept that my withdrawal from school had been based on academic limitations considering the results of my NTC examination reports, all of which he had seen. Without further ado, and in my presence, he telephoned my old headmaster. Mr Gledhill told Mr Burford emphatically that he had not told my father that I was wasting my time at school. He said, however, that he would update his memory from my records and phone back.

While awaiting the call, I told Mr Burford that I had lost all desire to become a surgeon and that, although I desperately wanted to join the Royal Rhodesian Air Force, I was faced with major problems. Firstly, I had no Matric Exemption Certificate and, secondly, application for the next pilot intake was already in train. If I failed to get into the force on the current intake, I would be too old for the next one.

Mr Burford could not reconcile my original desire to be a lifesaver through surgery with my current wish to become an airborne killer. I told him I did not see things that way and that I considered both professions were for the protection of life. Nevertheless he tried to get me back to thinking surgery and even offered financial assistance and accommodation with his brother who happened to live in Edinburgh. This conversation was broken short by the return call from Mr Gledhill.

The headmaster repeated that he had at no stage given my father any reason to withdraw me from school—quite the opposite. On file was a copy of a letter from him to my father urging my immediate return to school. On the basis of my overall examination results, Mr Gledhill said that I would have passed Cambridge Certificate and almost certainly would have gained the all-important Matric Exemption. Mr Burford then asked Mr Gledhill if he would be prepared to repeat that in writing, to which Mr Gledhill gave an affirmative reply. Mr Burford also asked if his letter could be addressed to Royal Rhodesian Air Force Headquarters, for me to include in my application for pilot training. Again Mr Gledhill acceded and, true to his word, the letter was in my hands the next day.

Through Mum and Berry I had met the Northern Rhodesian politician Roy Welensky at his home in Broken Hill. This happened long before he became Prime Minister of the Federation of Rhodesia and Nyasaland. But now as Sir Roy Welensky, heading the Federal Government, he gladly provided me with the written character reference required by the Air Force Pilot Selection Committee.

Having filled in all forms, I rode out to Dad's farm on my AJS 500-single motorbike to get his signature of parental approval. Dad was happy to do this but, while searching for a pen, my stepmother interrupted, "Not over my dead body will you sign that application form." That stopped Dad dead in his tracks. I could not believe what I had heard nor could I understand why Dad would not stand up for me in what he had first supported.

Why was I being stopped from doing something that would be good for me and without cost to family? The sad look on my father's face told the whole story. I deliberately rode off gently rather than expose my incredible pain and anger by storming off at high speed.

Although, up until this time, my stepmother had done all in her power to crush me, I shall be eternally grateful to her for giving Tony and me two fantastic sisters. In years to come, Brigid and Mary married Jock McSorley and Doug Palframan whom Tony and I both consider the greatest and most lovable brothers-in-law any man could wish for.

Everything was complete, but for Dad's signature—I even considered forging it but changed my mind. Instead I returned to Mr Burford for advice and this resulted in a consultation with his lawyer. The lawyer pointed out that the unsigned signature block read PARENT/LEGAL GUARDIAN. He drew a line through LEGAL GUARDIAN and told me to send the forms to Northern Rhodesia for my mother's signature. Mum signed the form in spite of her deep concerns, having lost two brothers to flying with her only surviving brother already serving as a pilot in the Royal Rhodesian Air force.

Mine was one of over 350 applications received for No 10

SSU (Short Service Unit) training. Of these only thirty-five applicants were accepted for the final pilot selection process at New Sarum airbase. I was lucky to be one of these and even luckier to be one of the eighteen candidates to receive instructions to report for pilot training on 3 January 1957.

Chapter

2

Ground Training School

REPORTING FOR SERVICE MUST BE much the same for everyone. I am certain most recruits suffer intense apprehension and a sense of awkwardness while seeking out anyone in civilian clothing looking as unsure and awkward as they feel. I was delighted to find David Thorne whom I had met some months before during the pilot selection process. Together we felt more confident and were soon gathering in our new course mates.

All Rhodesian schoolboys had undergone Army Cadet training at school and the annual cadet camps at Inkomo Barracks. So we instinctively responded to the bellowed command "Fall in". Before us was the Station Warrant Officer (SWO) Bill Holden, a large ruddy-faced ex-British Royal Marine. Having welcomed us into the RRAF and, following a few words on what we were required to do over the next two days, sixteen men in civvy clothing were doubled-off to sign up for service.

Thereafter, we went to Station Equipment section where we drew uniforms and our flying kit, then doubled to the Officers' Mess single quarters to check into our billets; two cadets to a room. By midday we were being drilled in our unpressed and uncomfortable new uniforms and stiff shoes. The SWO gave all commands in the typical Army way but otherwise he acted somewhat differently to the drill sergeants we had previously known. He used no bad language and acted in a formal yet non-threatening manner.

We were released to our billets in the late afternoon to find all members of No 9 SSU awaiting our arrival. They immediately set out to subjugate us, a recognised prerogative of the senior course. Since they only had two nights before we would be at Thornhill and beyond their clutches, 9 SSU decided to make both nights sheer hell for us.

This course had been at Thornhill for their training and, like us, had only been subjected to the attentions of their predecessors—No 8 SSU—for two nights when they attested for service. The consequence of this was that they had little idea of how to handle a junior course.

The first 'directive' issued was that every one of 10 SSU was to have all his hair shaved off. For a short while they thought they had us under control until it came to cutting Gordon Wright's hair.

Gordon stood back and said, "There is no way I am taking this. If you want to cut my hair you will have to force it on me."

From me they received a similar response, which was again repeated by Ian Ferguson. The senior course recognised that someone was going to get hurt if they pressed the issue and found a feeble way of doing away with the mandatory haircut. They decided instead to leave things be until we had showered and dressed for dinner.

In the Officers' Mess, under guidance of young officers who had recently gained their commissions, 9 SSU first challenged 10 SSU to a schooner race. This is a drinking competition involving an equal number of competitors facing each other in two rows. 9 SSU needed six junior officers to match our number.

In a schooner race each contender is given a full tankard of beer and an umpire verifies this. Upon instruction from the umpire, the first two opposing contenders at one end of the line commence drinking their beer as fast as possible with everyone else chanting "down, down, down". Once a contender has emptied the contents of his tankard down his gullet, he inverts the tankard onto his head, giving signal to the next in line to start downing his beer. The first team to have all tankards inverted on heads is the winner.

For my course there was no chance whatsoever of winning such a race as none of us was a drinker. Most of us had not even started to drink by the time our opposition was through, but we were compelled to down the beer anyway. Having done so, we were committed to a second and then a third race. Even before the third race started every member of 10 SSU was reeling about, most giggling and one ran off to throw up.

We were then subjected to a number of humiliating activities that were of little consequence until it came to the 'communal trough'. This was an oversized chamber pot filled with beer. Our course was to remain out of sight until called forward, singly, to the circle of baiting officer cadets and junior officers. There, each of us had to lift the pot from the floor, take four large mouthfuls and place the pot on the floor for the next in line. There was great cheering and jeering from our baiters as each of us was called forward to take his turn.

Sergeant McCone.   *Flight Lieutenant Parish.*

My time came and as I lifted the pot I saw two turds floating in the beer. Instinctively the pot was lowered until I realised that they were in fact two over-cooked sausages. I took four gulps and put the pot down. The very last of our number failed the test when he puked directly into the pot. At this point our course turned as one and walked away. Commands to return to order were met by somewhat drunkenly uttered "force us if you can" challenges.

We were left alone. 9 SSU had failed miserably to subjugate us and we remembered this when, one year later, 11 SSU became our juniors in very different circumstances.

Our flight to Thornhill next day was by Dakota. My uncle, Flight Lieutenant Bill Smith, whom I have already mentioned, skippered this aircraft. Before the flight Bill had told me to keep our relationship to myself for my own good. This I did. Once airborne he invited all members of the course to go up to the cockpit in pairs where he explained instrument layout and answered many questions. The flight ended all too soon with our arrival in dispersals at Thornhill.

A truck drove up to the aircraft and its driver, a sergeant in Army uniform with a small dog, instructed us to load our kit onto the vehicle. Having done this the sergeant told us to fall in. He then introduced himself in a gentle manner as Sergeant McCone and even told us the name of his canine companion. He said he was our Drill Instructor (DI) for the duration of the course and welcomed us to Thornhill—all very soothing.

We expected to be told to climb onto the truck to be driven to our quarters. Not so! The DI's quiet voice suddenly switched to that of an Army drill instructor. We were moved off at the double, our standard speed when moving from point to point … for months to come. As we turned to run past a hangar, Sergeant McCone gave the thumbs-up signal to a man, the actual driver of the truck, who had been waiting out of sight.

We ran to our quarters and saw that Thornhill was a neatly laid-out station, with tree-lined roads. Other than a handful of brick buildings, most were constructed of corrugated iron. All the roofs were red and the walls cream. We ran past the guardroom then over the main Gwelo–Umvuma road and rail line running parallel to Thornhill's long southern boundary fence.

This led us into the large married quarters, which we could see were all brick-under-tile homes set in well-treed grounds. We then wheeled into the driveway of No 1 Married Quarters and were brought to a halt in front of the verandah where Flight Lieutenant Parish stood waiting to address us.

He introduced himself as the Officer Commanding Ground Training School (OC GTS), responsible for all our activities during the first four months of our Initial Training School (ITS) phase. He said that once flying training commenced in May, we would fall under OC 4 Squadron for the Basic Flying Training School (BFS) but he would continue to be responsible for all our ground schooling throughout our two years of training. We were told that Vampires were scheduled to arrive at Thornhill for the Advanced Flying School (AFS) in January 1958), twelve months hence.

The house before which we stood rigidly to attention was being used as the temporary Officers' Mess. Four houses back from the Mess were our quarters. Flight Lieutenant Parish read out our names and the number of the house to which each of us was allocated. It being Sunday, we were instructed to go to our quarters, sort out our kit and return to the Mess for lunch in casual attire. The afternoon was free.

I shared a house with David Thorne, Bill Galloway and Robin Brown. How he had managed it I cannot recall, but Dave Thorne's MG was parked outside the house. He invited us to accompany him for a look around Gwelo town, some four miles away.

During my apprenticeship in Umtali I had met, and thereafter dated, Pat Woods. For over two years we did everything together and spent much time exploring the mountainous eastern districts on my AJS 500 motorcycle. Her family always made me feel very welcome in their home.

When Pat went off to Teachers' Training College in Grahamstown, South Africa, I felt pretty lost riding alone down back roads and through forests. Then one day a tubby blonde female who was at college with Pat told me that Pat was having a gay old time with the college boys in Grahamstown. I was shaken but, believing what I had heard, immediately wrote to Pat terminating our association. Pat made many attempts to get me back, but I stubbornly refused.

Because I had been very distressed over Pat, I vowed to myself that I would not get involved with a woman until I had completed pilot training. Looking back on events it still amuses me that I met my wife-to-be during that very first visit to Gwelo on that very first day at Thornhill, not that I realised this at the time.

Gwelo was the fourth largest town in Rhodesia and on this Sunday it appeared to be deserted. Having driven around a while we spotted a place called the Polar Milk Bar and dropped in for milkshakes. The pretty redhead with a big smile behind the counter was very pleasant and introduced herself as Beryl. Once I had received my drink, I went to a table and looked out of the window onto the dismal street while my three course mates engaged Beryl in conversation.

About two weeks had passed when we heard that a major dance was to take place in Gwelo. Dave, Bill and Robin were keen to go but needed to find dates for the occasion. They decided Beryl was the person to help and that I, being the oldest member in our house, should do the talking. Even knowing that I had no desire to find a date or to go to the dance, they cajoled me into helping them.

We went to the Polar Milk Bar but found another lady there instead. Cleo Pickolous told us that Beryl Roe was a hairdresser friend who had been standing in for her on the afternoon we had met, so she gave us directions to Beryl's home. Mr and Mrs Roe met us at the front door and seemed to be incredibly pleased to see us. I was taken through to the lounge to talk to Beryl while my younger mates stayed in the sun lounge chatting with her folks.

Beryl, whom I judged to be about twenty-six years of age, seemed mildly perplexed by my request to find dates for my three course mates—yet not asking her for a date myself. Nevertheless, she was helpful and all was duly arranged. We left and I thought no more about the matter.

Our day at Thornhill started at 5:30 a.m. with a walk to the Mess for coffee, after which the week's course commander, a duty we all took in turn, formed us up. We then doubled off to collect weapons for morning drill, which commenced at 6 a.m. Sergeant McCone was always standing to attention awaiting our arrival, his dog sitting patiently close by. Without fail, he consulted his wristwatch as we came to a halt in front of him. For a solid hour we responded to his bellowing and binding which, happily, reduced in proportion to improvements in our standards of drill and dress. At 7:30 we handed in our weapons and were always ravenously hungry by the time we had run back for an excellent breakfast.

With the exception of Ian Ferguson, all my course mates were either directly out of school or had gained Matric Exemption twelve months earlier. So, from Day One I realised that my premature removal from school, with three years out of an academic environment, would present major challenges for me. My problem areas were essentially mathematics, English grammar and spelling. The practical subjects of engines, airframes, instruments, radio, airmanship, meteorology, navigation and so on, were fine.

The pass mark required for every examination paper was 70%, providing the average for all subjects was over 75%. I met these criteria at the end of each month, but only just. Many years passed before I gained access to my personal training file at Air HQ and found that Flight Lieutenant Parish, insofar as my weak subjects were concerned, likened me to a tube of toothpaste: "Press Petter-Bowyer here and a bulge appears in a different place."

We were in our sixth week of training when I broke my right ankle on our way to morning drill. As with most days, the dawn was quite splendid. All colours of the rainbow painted the early morning cirrus stratus, adding a special dimension to the crisp, clean, highveld air. I diverted attention for just a moment to look at the sky while we were running next to the service railway line that brought fuel trains into Thornhill. In so doing I failed to see the displaced rock that twisted my ankle.

In agony I was taken to SSQ where the doctor found that a section of bone had broken away from my heel and was being held apart from its rightful place by the ligament of the calf muscle. After treatment and with my leg in a plaster cast, I was ordered to bed for one week. Of all the members of my course, I was the least able to handle a full week off lectures. I feared that my misfortune might result in my failing ITS, even though Dave Thorne did his best to keep me abreast of what was being covered.

I had been laid up for a couple of days when Flight Sergeant Reg Lohan, the Officers' Mess caterer, came to my room to say that a young lady had called and would be visiting me that afternoon. I went into a cold sweat believing Pat Woods had tracked me down again and I lay wondering how I was going to a handle this unhappy situation.

When Beryl Roe breezed into my room with Flight Sergeant Lohan, I was very relieved. She was an easy person to relate to and we discussed all sorts of things without any loss for words or subjects. Flight Sergeant Lohan sent us a tray with tea and cakes, which Beryl said was "so sweet of him." Then the guys came back from classes and, without consulting me, they suggested to Beryl that we all go to the cinema that evening. Beryl accepted and persuaded me to go along. What an awful night! I was in agony with my foot on the floor, so Beryl insisted I lift it, plaster cast and all, onto her lap. We both agonised through the show and I was happy when the evening came to an end. Thereafter Beryl and I saw each other regularly, but

Back row: Scrubbed, Ian Ferguson, Murray Hofmeyr, Peter Petter-Bowyer, Ian Law.
Centre: Scrubbed, Scrubbed, Scrubbed, Dave Thorne, John Barnes, Scrubbed.
Front: Eric Cary, Gordon Wright, Keith Corrans, Scrubbed, Bill Galloway.

PB and Beryl at Great Zimbabwe.

Auv Raath, PB and Dave Thorne.

only after she had shown me her passport to prove that she was nineteen years old and not twenty-six as I had thought.

On my twenty-first birthday we got engaged, before attending a dining-in at the Mess. Arranged by my course mates and Flight Sergeant Lohan to celebrate my coming-of-age it turned out to be an engagement celebration as well. So much for having nothing to do with women before completing pilot training!

Our Commanding Officer was Squadron Leader Doug Whyte—a superb individual who enjoyed the respect of everyone who ever met him.

He came to lecture us about the dangers of 'crew-room bragging', a real killer in any Air Force. With the aid of photographs taken of a fatal flying accident in the Thornhill Flying Training Area the previous year, the Squadron Leader pressed home his message to us. With our flying training about to commence he urged us all to exercise responsibility towards each other and never to brag or challenge others into unauthorised flying activities. The death of 9 SSU Officer Cadet Nahke had been the direct result of a crew-room bragger's challenge to a tail-chase. In a steep turn, Nahke had probably entered the bragger's slipstream and paid an awful price for his inexperience. The loss of a valuable aircraft and the unnecessary pain caused to a grieving family was simply too high a price to pay for sheer stupidity. The CO's message was firmly embedded in all of us.

Two of our numbers were 'scrubbed' on the grounds of poor officer-potential and fourteen of us passed on to the BFS (Basic Flying School) phase. During the two weeks preceding BFS we had spent most of our free time in Provost cockpits learning the various routines and emergency drills that we were required to conduct blindfold. During this time we anxiously awaited news of who our personal flying instructors would be.

Basic Flying School

WE KNEW ALL OF THE instructors by sight and for weeks had heard the exciting sound of the Provosts on continuation training as instructors honed up their instructional skills.

One instructor had the reputation of being an absolute terroriser of student pilots, so we all feared being allocated to this strongly accented South African, Flight Lieutenant Mick McLaren. Murray Hofmeyr and I were the unlucky ones and everyone else breathed a sigh of relief.

Mick McLaren.

The Percival Provost had replaced the Mk2 Harvards as the basic trainer and was quite different in many ways. The most important difference was that the Provost had side-by-side seating as opposed to the tandem arrangement of the Harvard. This permitted a Provost instructor to watch every movement his student made, which was not possible in the Harvard because the instructor's instrument panel obstructed view of the front cockpit.

A single Leonides air-cooled, nine-cylinder radial engine powered the Provost's three-bladed propeller. At sea level this engine developed 550 hp at 2,750 rpm Thornhill was 4,700 feet above sea level and the maximum power available at this level was reduced to about 450 hp, equating to the power developed by the Harvard's Pratt and Whitney motor at the same height.

Whereas the Harvard had retractable main wheels, the Provost's undercarriage was fixed, making an otherwise neat airframe look unsightly in flight. Apart from the cost of retractable wheels, the fixed undercarriage of the Provost prevented *ab initio* students from making the expensive error of landing with wheels up, as happened to many students flying aircraft with retractable gear.

The Harvard employed hydraulics to operate undercarriage, brakes and flaps. Toe pedals on the rudder controls activated the wheel brakes. However, there are penalties for using hydraulics. They incur high costs, high weight of hydraulic oil and the reservoir in which to house it, as well as hefty pipelines to deliver pressure to services with duplicated pipes to recover hydraulic fluid back to the oil reservoir.

The Provost designers opted for pneumatics to reduce cost and weight. By using compressed air there is only need for a single lightweight delivery line to each service point and a lightweight accumulator tank to store compressed air. But the advantages of using pneumatics presented difficulties to pilots insofar as control of brakes was concerned.

Wheel braking was effected by pulling on a lever, much like a vertically mounted bicycle brake lever affixed to the fighter-styled hand grip on the flight control column. The position of the rudder bar determined how the wheel brakes would respond. If, say, a little left rudder was applied, braking was mainly on the left wheel and less on the right. The differential increased progressively until full left rudder gave maximum braking on the left wheel only. With rudder bar set central, both wheels responded equally to the amount of air pressure applied by means of the brake lever.

Attainment of proficiency in handling brakes was of such importance that, before flying started, the instructors spent time with their students simply taxiing in and out of dispersals. The ground staff revelled in watching brand-new students trying to control their machines, even drawing men off the line from other squadrons.

Every aircraft of any type exhibits different characteristics to others of its own kind, which is why many Air Forces allocate an aircraft to an individual pilot or crew. No brake lever on Provosts, whether student's or instructor's side, felt or acted the same. They varied from a spongy, smooth feel, which was best, to those sticky ones that would not yield to normal pressure and then snap to maximum braking with the slightest hint of added pressure. The instructors knew which aircraft had sticky brake levers and it was these that they preferred for initial taxi training. Once a student was proficient on the ground, the flying began.

Firing a cordite starter cartridge started the Provost engine. Raising a handle set on the floor between the seats did this. At its end was a primer button that injected fuel into the engine during the three revolutions given by the cartridge starter motor. Learning engine start-up, particularly when the engine was hot, was quite a business largely because of a tendency to over-prime and flood the cylinders. 'Duck shooting' was the term used by technicians when pilots fired more than two cartridges. Years later electric starter motors were introduced, making matters much easier.

The first hurdle in any student's training is to get to his first solo flight. The Air Force insisted that a student had to be prepared for every possible error that he 'might' encounter when flying without the protection of an instructor. Apart from the need to take off and land proficiently, a student had to act instinctively and correctly in the event of an engine failure or if he stalled (flying too slowly to produce sufficient lift on the wings) at any stage of flight.

Instructors seated: F/O Saunders, Flt Lt McLaren, Flt Lt Edwards, Sqn Ldr Whyte (CO), F/O Myburgh, F/O Hudson and F/O Bradnick.

Early morning preparation of Provosts at Thornhill, 1957— for the day's flying.

Full stall, if not corrected early enough results in the uncontrolled, downward spin that killed so many pilots during World War I. In those early days pilots did not understand that pulling back as hard as possible on the elevator control maintained the stalled condition and hence the spin. So far as I know, one pilot chose to limit the duration of his spinning death descent by pushing forward on his control column and, to his utter amazement, the spinning ceased and he was back in control of an aircraft that was flying normally again. Preparing for the fundamental control actions needed to recover from

spins was bad on the stomach but it needed to be practised ad nauseam.

From the very first flight, many, many spinning and incipient spin (the first stage of spinning) recoveries were practised, together with simulated forced landings. Limited aerobatics also acquainted the student with the sensations of 'G' and inverted flight. Most students returned from their flights feeling pretty ill. I remember only too clearly how the combination of fuel vapour and the flick-turn of every spin manoeuvre made me feel sick, causing my instructor to regularly ask me if I was all right to continue.

Harvards.

Murray Hofmeyr (Hoffy) could not understand why I was not having a tough time with Mick McLaren because he was going through absolute hell. We soon learned why. Mick McLaren established that Hoffy, who hailed from Mossel Bay in South Africa, could neither ride a bicycle nor drive a car, yet here he was learning to fly a 450 hp machine. No wonder he was struggling under the toughest of our instructors. None of us had been aware of this but the course was instructed to have Hoffy both riding and driving within a week. Determined to protect one of our number, we had Hoffy ready on time and his flying difficulties immediately diminished.

I did not find the glamour in flying that I had dreamed of. It was hard work, stressful and made one feel bloody awful. This changed somewhat on 22 May when my flying time totalled thirteen hours and twenty-five minutes. I had radioed the Control Tower reporting being down wind for a roller landing when Mick McLaren transmitted again to say we would be making a full-stop landing.

When I had pulled off the runway to conduct routine post-landing checks, Mick McLaren called the Tower and asked for a fire jeep to collect him. With this he unstrapped and climbed out onto the wing with his parachute still on. There he turned back to secure the seat straps and said to me, "Well done Petter-Bowyer, you are on your own. Taxi back to runway 13—use my callsign—once around the circuit—I will see you back at the Squadron." He unplugged the pigtail lead that connected his mask microphone and earphones to the radio intercom, and disappeared from sight.

Murray Hofmeyer.

PB in dispersals after first solo.

I experienced no sense of euphoria or achievement until I was in the air. The empty seat next to me emphasised the fact that I had reached an important milestone. Suddenly I was enjoying what I was doing. On final approach for landing I could see the fire jeep near the runway threshold and knew Mick McLaren was watching me closely. I did not let him down. I made the smoothest of landings.

A little earlier our Squadron Commander, Flight Lieutenant Ken Edwards, had sent John Barnes solo with thirty minutes less flying time than me. Only Flight Lieutenants Ken Edwards and Mick McLaren were qualified to send students solo. This

was a distinct advantage to their own students because, when other instructors decided that their students were ready, one of these two senior instructors had to conduct the solo test; an added strain on any student trying to make it past his first hurdle.

By the time the last solo flight had been flown our numbers had reduced to twelve, two having been scrubbed for not possessing pilot qualities. But now came the solo party!

Wing Commander Archie Wilson had just taken over from Squadron Leader Whyte as Commanding Officer at Thornhill. He dropped in on our party some time after it had started. Since none of us was used to alcohol, we were already pretty tipsy on the champagne we had been drinking liberally as we toasted each other with nonsensical speeches. In consequence I can only recall two events.

One was Gordon Wright offering the Wing Commander a drink and, having handed it to him, putting his arm around the new CO's neck before loudly welcoming him to Thornhill. Gordon, oblivious to the furious look on the Wing Commander's face, pressed on with his welcoming statement. Fortunately, he did not resist Flight Lieutenant Edward's not-so-gentle removal of his arm from around the CO's neck. The second memory is of later in the evening. I was standing on top of a table next to an open window playing my piano accordion when I decided to sneak a pee through the open window. This didn't work out too well! I lost my balance and fell headlong through the window into the dark night.

For a while flying became very pleasant because aerobatics and some low flying gave breathing space between the ongoing spinning, forced landings and never-ending circuits and landings. For every two flights with one's instructor, there was a solo. The stress had subsided and stomachs had become used to the sensations of flight and the stench of fuel. But ahead of us was the next, and by all accounts, most challenging hurdle—instrument flying.

For instrument-flying training, many aircraft employed an arrangement of canvas screens set around a pilot to prevent him from peeping outside the cockpit. Such an arrangement with side-by-side seating was dangerous because it would blank off an instructor's vision on the port side of the aircraft, thereby limiting his ability to keep a good lookout for other aircraft.

The Provost's designers overcame the problem with a unique solution. They fitted a robust, amber screen that resided, out of view, between the instrument panel and the engine firewall. For instrument-flight training it was drawn up and locked in place to cover the whole forward windscreen. Swivelled amber panels that came up with the main screen covered the side panels. Finally, sliding panels on the canopy catered for lateral vision. When all screens were in place the instructor continued to have complete freedom of vision though the world appeared to him as if wearing yellow sunglasses.

The student wore a pair of heavy goggles, such as those used by motorbike riders; but a clear vision lens was replaced by one of blue Perspex. Within the cockpit everything looked like the blue moonlight scene of an old movie but the amber screen became ivory black. Only the sun could be seen though this arrangement, which was so effective that direct viewing of the sun was quite safe.

For the first fifteen minutes or so 'under the hood' I suffered a high level of claustrophobia. The combination of tight parachute and seat straps, a tight-fitting oxygen mask and large, tight-fitting goggles in a small world of blue, made me battle for breath. However, by the time my instructor had taxied the long distance to the runway, I had acclimatised and was quite settled.

In the learning phases, Instrument Flying (IF) was every bit as difficult as I had expected, particularly in the small blue world devoid of any external references. From the outset I suffered from vertigo which most pilots experience in varying degrees. I was badly affected by this problem; and it never improved throughout my flying days. I simply had to believe that my instruments were right and accept that my senses were wrong. It took a lot of effort and absolute faith in the instruments to master the weakness.

Once I had become reasonably proficient on a full panel of flight instruments and had started to gain confidence, Mick McLaren covered the primary instrument with a plastic stick-on vehicle licence disc holder. Loss of the artificial horizon introduced a new and infinitely more difficult dimension to flight control, but again, practice made this progressively easier. Then a second disc was applied to remove the directional indicator from view, compounding the difficulties because the magnetic compass was awkward to read and was subject to a host of errors, even in straight and level flight.

In the latter part of every flight, my instructor would take over control and put the aircraft through a series of harsh manoeuvres to confuse my understanding of what the aircraft was doing. I tried to use sunlight moving through the cockpit from ever-changing directions, but this confused me more than it helped. Mick McLaren would then say, "You have control" which meant I had to get the aircraft back into straight and level flight in the shortest time possible. Each flight then concluded with a limited panel let-down on the Non-Directional Beacon (NDB) that then flowed into a radar talk-down to landing on a full panel of instruments.

Full panel flying seemed easy compared to limited panel flying, which constituted most of the time spent on IF. A spell of bad weather with eight-eighths cloud (no blue sky) gave opportunity to fly without the amber screen and blue goggles. I could not believe how easy it was to fly instruments under these conditions, but then it was back to the world of blue for many flights to come.

One morning my instructor lined up on the runway for a standard instrument take-off. As I powered up and released the brakes, he began criticising me and kept thrusting his finger at the directional indicator. When I eased the aircraft

off the ground, I lost heading a bit—for which he cursed me in a manner I had not known before. For the entire flight I was given hell for everything I did and the names I was called would not pass censorship. My whole world seemed to fall apart as I battled to satisfy my instructor's non-stop demands, so it was a great relief to get back on the ground.

As Flight Lieutenant McLaren and I were walking back to the crew room he asked, "What went wrong with you today?" I could not answer and dared not look at him because I was too close to tears. He obviously saw the quiver on my chin and said, "Tomorrow will be better. Have a cup of tea, then come and see me in my office for debriefing."

The next morning I was horrified to see the Flight Authorisation Book had me down for IF with Flight Lieutenant Edwards, our OC I immediately came to the conclusion that this was a scrub check. When the time came, I was called to his office for a pre-flight briefing, but all he said was "Go and pre-flight the aircraft and get yourself strapped in. I will be with you shortly."

When Ken Edwards climbed into his seat I could not get over the size of the man. His left arm was against mine whereas my instructor's arm was always clear. He started the engine and commenced taxiing to the runway before telling me to relax. "Take this as just another IF flight," he said. From then on he only told me what he wanted me to do next. The unusual attitudes I was asked to recover from were so much easier than Mick McLaren's. The routine NDB and radar let-down were fine and we were back on the ground in less than the usual hour. As we taxied back to dispersals Ken Edwards said, "Well done, you have passed your instrument-rating test." I was over the moon.

I had had absolutely no idea that this had been a rating test or that my instructor had deliberately set me up for it. By baiting me continuously the previous day, Flight Lieutenant McLaren had satisfied himself that I would not fall to pieces under duress, so he was quite sure I would fly a good test.

It was great to be the first of my course to gain a White Card instrument rating. Some of my fellow students struggled

Ronnie Thompson.

with instrument flying and our number had reduced to ten students by the time the last IF test was flown. For the two weeks between my test and the last student passing his, I was flying two solo sorties for every one flown with my instructor. Flying was now becoming really enjoyable!

One of the students who failed to make it

through the IF phase was Ronnie Thompson. He was very depressed and embarrassed by his failure. However, upon his return to civilian life, he followed his passion for wildlife and became a game warden with Rhodesian National Parks. In a career that continues today, Ronnie proved himself to be a top-line ranger and an enthusiastic promoter of wildlife. Over the years he has featured in many wide-ranging wildlife topics on radio, TV and press.

Having achieved instrument flight proficiency, it was time to move on to night flying, which was great. The fairyland of coloured lights covering Gwelo town and Thornhill reminded me of the 1947 visit to Rhodesia by King George VI, Queen Elizabeth and the two princesses. For that royal visit Salisbury had been transformed into a dream world of coloured lights, with thousands of flags and portraits of the Royal Family. The colours, sights and sensations of the occasion are indelibly printed in my mind and night flying always induces recall of that special occasion.

Daytime navigation commenced at the same time as night flying. Now, after many years of flying and having flown with many civilian-trained pilots, I look back and recognise the excellence of Air Force instruction given from day one. Simple matters such as looking over one's shoulder to ensure a town or other landmark was in the right relative position for one's heading to next destination may seem obvious, but this insured against misreading the compass or Directional Indicator. Typical and sometimes deadly errors of steering, say, 315 degrees instead of 135 degrees, are thus avoided.

Initially our navigation was conducted on 1:1,000,000-scale maps that, by the nature of their small scale, provide limited topographical information when compared to the abundance of visible features along every flight path. Though this made map-reading for students difficult, it also helped to ensure that maps were read sensibly. Too often man-made features such as roads, railways, bridges, power lines and water storage dams appearing on our maps printed some years earlier were either no longer in use, had altered course or could not be seen at all. There were also many clearly visible landmarks that were not shown at all. So the need to ignore all but God-made natural features was repeatedly drummed into us.

Ever-improving navigational aids, which have become commonplace for present-day pilots, did not exist in Rhodesia in the 1950s. Non-Directional Beacons (NDBs) sited at a few main airfields were only reliable (when they worked) close to their locations. So reading the ground with one's Mk1 eyeballs and using map, clock and compass correctly was essential. The ability to identify correctly those riverlines drawn on our maps and interpret ground contouring and high features accurately, particularly at low level, became one of the hallmarks of Rhodesian Air Force pilot proficiency in the years to come.

Night navigation presented different problems, especially when the summer months laid a heavy haze across the country. Dead reckoning and the ability to interpret distances and

angles to the lights of towns and mines were of paramount importance. The atmosphere at night with dimly illuminated instruments always thrilled me. Some nights were as dark as a witch's heart, whereas full moonlight made ground visible at low level. My favourite night-flying condition was when the moon illuminated towering, flashing thunderclouds that sent brilliant lightning strikes to the ground. The dangers one would face in the event of engine failure on any night were deliberately pushed to the back of one's mind.

General flying continued between night and navigational flights and on occasions solo students were flying every airborne aircraft. Sometimes this was a pretty dangerous situation because, at that time, we had all logged about 140 flying hours.

I cannot recall where I learned that the Royal Air Force consider there are specific danger periods in the average military pilot's career. These are when overconfidence tends to peak—around 50, 150, 500 and 1,500 hours. We were in the second danger period and the warnings given to us by Squadron Leader Whyte, concerning crew-room bragging and challenges, were all but forgotten. It was Eric Cary who always sought to challenge.

Eric was an outstanding sportsman who revelled in any one-on-one sport such as squash, for which he was then the Rhodesian champion. He also liked to pit his skills against other pilots and it was he who challenged me to meet him at a pre-arranged site in the flying area for a 'dog fight' to see which of us could outmanoeuvre the other.

On arrival at the appointed area I was astounded to find all six students gathered in what can only be described as a bloody dangerous situation with everyone chasing everyone else. The greatest potential for mid-air collision probably came from Hoffy who repeatedly climbed above the rest of us then dived straight through the pitching and circling mêlée.

We had not yet started formation flying but coaxed each other into giving it a go anyway. I shudder when looking back at what we did. We had not yet learned that the lead aircraft maintains steady power and that station-holding is the responsibility of those formatting on the leader. During one illegal formation flight, I could not understand why I could not hold a steady position on Bill Galloway who was 'leading'. Once back on terra firma, Bill said he had been adjusting power to help me stay in position. The result was that I repeatedly overtook or fell back, with wing tips passing, oh so close!

Because there was no senior course to discipline or shove us around one of our instructors, Flying Officer Rex Taylor, had been appointed as Disciplinary Officer. He was a real little Hitler from time to time, but only in working hours. One day he instructed me to have John Barnes report to his office when John returned from flying. Since I would be flying by the time John landed, I wrote a notice for him on our crew-room board. I made the mistake of writing the instructor's first name with surname instead of rank and surname. Flying Officer Taylor saw this and all hell broke loose. I owned up to the instructor and attempted to draw his wrath on me. He would have none of it, saying we all needed bringing down a peg or two.

It was a hot day and we were ordered to form up in two rows in full flying gear with masks clipped up to our faces. Flying Officer Taylor came to each student in turn and personally pulled the parachute harnesses so tight that we were really bent

Flying Officer Rex Taylor.   *Flight Lieutenant Mac Geeringh.*

The Queen Mother is seen here with AVM Jacklin, Major-General Garlake and Wing Commander Taute before presenting wings to 9 SSU.

forward and could not straighten our legs. Then in two files he set us off at the double.

Hard-standings for the jets were still being constructed and a vast area was covered with row upon row of decomposed granite piles waiting to be levelled and compacted. Over these endless mounds we were forced to double. Though falling and sliding on the soft heaps and totally exhausted, we were driven for what seemed a lifetime. Fortunately Flight Lieutenant Edwards arrived on the scene and called a halt to the agony. Most of us reported to SSQ for treatment to raw groins and shoulders.

It was round about this time that the senior course, 9 SSU received their wings from Queen Elizabeth, the Queen Mother, at New Sarum.

When regular formation training started, the BFS phase was drawing to a close. We were all looking forward to our final cross-county flight with night-stop and a party with the townspeople of Gatooma because, immediately it was over, we would then be off on three weeks' Christmas leave.

A final cross-country with night-stop at one of Rhodesia's towns was a way to celebrate the completion of BFS and it also brought the Air Force into closer contact with Rhodesian citizens. As with any town in the country, the people of Gatooma went out of their way to give us a great party and treated us to superb food and anything we wished to drink. My course was still mostly teetotal though we did justice to the huge spread of food. The instructors and supporting ground staff were less interested in the food than joining the local drinking fraternity, for which they suffered the next day on a particularly bumpy ride home in the back of a Dakota.

I had asked Beryl to pick me up at Thornhill when I passed over on return from Gatooma. She would recognise my return by my changing engine revs up and down a couple of times over her house. However, I stupidly dived for a low-level pass over her house then climbed steeply to enter the Thornhill circuit. Considering I was behind the Air Traffic Controllers' field of view, I was surprise that, almost immediately, Thornhill Tower broadcast "Aircraft flying low level over Riverside identify yourself." I owned up immediately but on entering the Squadron crew-room I received instruction to get dressed and report immediately to the Station Commander.

Wing Commander Wilson had seen operational service with the RAF during the war and, thereafter, became a prime mover in re-establishing the Southern Rhodesian Air Force. Many stories of this stocky, softly spoken and immensely strong man had reached our ears. One was that he preferred direct disciplinary action to conventional military processes. It was rumoured that, rather than give a man the option of court martial, he took offenders out of sight behind a hangar and laid them low with a couple of mighty blows. Because I was engaged, the CO had asked Beryl and me to baby-sit his two daughters on a few occasions while he and his wife Lorna attended official functions. Within his home it was hard to believe that this man could be anything but a gentle person. Nevertheless, I was very nervous when I reported to his secretary who wheeled me straight into the CO's office.

I marched up to the front of Wing Commander Wilson's desk and saluted. He sat looking me in the eye for a moment then came straight to the point by saying he'd happened to be visiting the control tower and while ascending the stairway had spotted an aircraft climbing steeply from low level. "Was that you?" he asked. I said it was. With no further ado he asked, "Do you elect to be tried by court martial or will you accept my punishment?" I accepted his punishment though I feared it more than a court martial. But I was not marched off to the back of a hangar.

Instead, Wing Commander Wilson said, very quietly, that I was to forfeit Christmas leave and be on duty as the Station Orderly Officer for twenty-four hours a day until my course mates returned from their leave twenty-one days hence. I could neither make nor receive private telephone calls and was disallowed any visitor for the whole period. This punishment was far worse than being taken behind the hangar because I had been looking forward so much to taking Beryl to Norrhodia to meet my mother and stepfather.

I was depressed and lonely when I started my rounds as Orderly Officer. However, Flight Lieutenant Mac Geeringh the Senior Air Traffic Control Officer, who had been something of a father to my course, came to see me on the first night. He let me know that he had been to see Beryl and had told her of a back entrance into Thornhill which, if used after midnight, would allow her to visit me undetected. He considered forfeiture of leave and being Orderly Officer without break was sufficient punishment. He felt being denied visitors as well was too harsh because, in effect, Beryl was being punished too. Mac had persuaded Beryl to visit me daily and said he would accept responsibility if the CO found out.

Beryl's nightly visits were wonderful and she always arrived with hot coffee and sandwiches. Her parents could not understand why Beryl was going to bed very early and why her Dad's car, a Vauxhall Cresta, appeared to be parked in a slightly different position each morning. Nevertheless, Beryl and I got away with the secret visits, or so we thought.

When, in 1967, Air Vice-Marshal Archie Wilson interviewed me upon my promotion to Squadron Leader, he let me know just how much he knew of my many misdemeanours over the years. The first of these was Beryl's nightly visits to me. With a twinkle in his eye he said he would have been disappointed, for Beryl's sake, had I not disobeyed his 'no visitor' ruling.

When the guys came back from leave, it was good to be off permanent duty and return to flying, even though we had to continue on Provosts for another two months because the Vampires were away on their first detachment to RAF Aden.

Whereas most of the pilots, technicians and aircraft of No 1 Squadron were involved, Group HQ had decided to withhold moving the balance of the squadron to Thornhill until one week before the detachment was due back from Aden.

Far from being disappointed by the delayed jet conversion,

my course saw possibilities opening up for involvement in future overseas deployments. I was given Flying Officer Alan Bradnick as my instructor for the period, which I found refreshing. He smiled easily and spoke a lot in flight.

Apart from consolidating on general flying standards, it was a pleasure flying with little if any pressure. However, an unfortunate flying accident marred an otherwise easy-going period. It involved a mid-air collision.

Four aircraft were practising formation with emphasis given to slick formation changes. At the time of the incident Bill Galloway was flying lead with his instructor, Flying Officer Mike Saunders. Gordon Wright was with Flying Officer Alan Bradnick as No 4.

The formation was in echelon starboard in which Bill would have been nearest camera and Gordon farthest away.

Lead called "Box, Box go," whereupon No 3 and No 4 initiated a drop in height and moved left to their new positions. In this, No 3 moved to echelon port (nearest camera) and No 4 moved to line astern behind and below the lead aircraft. Flying conditions were typically bumpy and Gordon had moved too far forward. Unfortunately his aircraft rose as the lead aircraft dropped and his propeller chopped off the lead's elevators.

No 4 fell back out of harm's way but the lead Provost pitched nose down and, with no elevator to control pitch, settled into a moderately steep dive from which there was no hope of recovery. Flying Officer Mike Saunders jettisoned the canopy and ordered Bill Galloway to bail out immediately but he stayed with the aircraft to steer it away from a built-up area in order to crash in open veld. Only when very low did Mike abandon the aircraft. His parachute opened in the nick of time and he suffered a very heavy landing with the fireball from the stricken aircraft very close by.

Advanced Flying School

THE ARRIVAL OF VAMPIRES FROM Aden is indelibly embedded in my memory. The fellows who had remained in Salisbury while most of 1 Squadron were away in Aden were now at Thornhill with all the ground equipment and one Vampire T11. Everyone at Thornhill, including the wives of the squadron guys, assembled on the flight lines to welcome the boys back.

The first formation of four in echelon starboard came in low and fast to make a formation break. Lead banked sharply pulling up and away from the group. Nos 2, 3 and 4 followed suit at two-second intervals. This manoeuvre placed the aircraft on the downwind leg, equally spaced for a stream landing off a continuous descending turn to the runway.

No war film ever impressed me as much as those screeching jets taxiing to their parking positions. All aircraft closed engines as one with the pilots climbing down from their machines. They had just completed the last legs from Dar es Salaam via Chileka in Nyasaland, so large patches of sweat substantially marked their flying suits and Mae West survival vests. Removal of bone domes, incorporating inner headgear with oxygen mask and headphones, revealed untidy, wet and flattened hair. Their glistening faces, deeply marked by the pressure

lines of masks and huge grins made the pilots look really macho. A further three formations arrived and soon the place was full of jet aircraft and happy people.

We had been practising our cockpit drills on the side-by-side Vampire T11 trainer for some time. So we were well and truly ready when allocated to our instructors the very next day. Mine was Flight Lieutenant John Mussell whom I had not seen before his arrival from Aden.

Learning to fly a jet was totally different to what I expected. Flight Lieutenant Mussell was easygoing and talkative, the nose wheel design made taxiing so much easier than the propeller-driven 'tail-dragger' Provost, the engine sounded quiet inside the closed cockpit and take-off was a dream—though controls were noticeably heavy.

This first flight in a jet was on a cloudy day with intermittent bursts of sunlight. I was amazed by the speed once airborne, with stratus clouds zipping fast overhead. Once through, the fluffy white structures fell away rapidly as the Vampire made its seemingly effortless climb. Flight seemed so quiet and smooth with only a gentle background hissing from the high-speed airflow and a muffled rumbling from the Goblin jet engine embedded in the airframe behind us.

On this first sortie I not only experienced stalling, spinning and steep turning but was given an introduction to jet aerobatics. All seemed easier than flying a Provost, though two situations were trying. Firstly, steep turning and aerobatics brought about much higher 'G' loadings than I had known before. The Provost's 4.5 Gs was now replaced by up to 6 Gs so I found turning my head very difficult and raising an arm required considerable effort.

A pair of Vampires.

The second difficulty concerned jet engine handling, which did not compare with a Provost's instant response to throttle movement. The Vampire's Goblin engine had to be handled very gently in the low rpm regions because rapid application of throttle would flood the engine and cause it to flame out. Once engine speed reached 9,000 rpm, the throttle could be advanced quite rapidly.

Back in the Thornhill circuit things changed a great deal. I simply could not get through all the pre-landing checks on the downwind leg before it was time to commence the continuous descending turn onto the runway. Going around again also required speeds of action that had me sweating. Within a few sorties I was coping well and could not understand why I had been so hard pressed in the first place. My whole course agreed that flying the Vampire T11 was not only great fun it was much easier to handle than the propeller-driven, 'tail-dragger' Provost.

Flying at high altitude was not only wonderful in itself; it induced a sense of awe from the sheer vastness of the air mass and the beauty surrounding me. By day the colour of the sky varied from the stark dark blue above to the light smoky blue of the far-off horizon. The sheer whiteness and gentle contours of clouds contrasted greatly with the blue above and the motley browns and greens of hills, trees, fields, rivers, dams and open veld far below.

On dark nights it seemed as if the stars had multiplied both in number and brightness and they appeared so close that one felt it possible to reach out and touch them. Although acrobatics were disallowed at night, I enjoyed diving for speed then pitching up to about sixty degrees before rolling the aircraft inverted. Once upside down, I allowed the aircraft to pitch gently at zero G as I gazed at the stars imagining myself to be flying in space with the stars spread out below me. The majesty of this was greatly enhanced by the wonderful sensations that accompany weightlessness.

My greatest joy came on those rare occasions flying in full moonlight between towering cumulonimbus clouds whose huge structures were illuminated in dazzling lightning displays of immeasurable beauty. In such surroundings one feels very small, but cosy and safe within the compact cockpit, while sensing God's immeasurable power all around.

The Royal Rhodesian Air Force possessed more Vampire FB9 single-seater aircraft than Vampire T11s. 'FB' denotes fighter-bomber and 'T' trainer. Whereas a Vampire T11 was fitted with two Martin Baker ejector seats, each incorporating parachute and emergency pack, the FB9 lacked this comforting luxury. Its single seat, just like the Provost, was known as a bucket seat.

A pilot had to strap on his parachute before climbing into the FB9 cockpit and, on entry, the parachute upon which the pilot sat fitted into the 'bucket' of the seat. When flying long-range sorties, particularly over water, a survival pack was included between the pilot's buttocks and his parachute. The only similarity between this arrangement and the permanent survival pack, upon which a pilot sat in an ejector seat, was the immense discomfort of sitting on a hard, lumpy pack. Any flight of more than an hour usually ended with a pilot emerging from his cockpit rubbing a sore, numb bum.

Because of the Vampire's twin-boomed tail arrangement, with the tail plane set between the booms, a major collision hazard existed for any pilot having to abandon his aircraft in flight. The Vampire FB9 had such a bad reputation for RAF pilots being killed when abandoning stricken aircraft that the fitment of ejector seats had been considered. However, cost for modification was so high that the RAF withdrew Vampire FB9s from service and replaced them with up-rated single-seater Venom fighter-bombers fitted with ejector seats. (These were the aircraft I had seen over Umtali that excited me so much, causing me to join the Air Force.) Due to a lack of Federal defence funds, our Air Force took on refurbished FB9s from Britain at very low cost, fully accepting the risks involved in operating them.

Not only were FB9s without ejector seats, they had a very bad reputation for their habit of stabilising in a spin. In this situation, recovery to normal flight was impossible and the aircraft simply kept spinning until it hit the ground. In consequence, intentional spinning of the FB9 was disallowed. The T11, however, was cleared for spinning when an instructor was present. Yet, even though the twin fins of T11s had an improved profile and larger surface area to make spin-recovery more certain, there were some occasions when this aircraft would not respond to pilot recovery actions.

Such was the case on 8 January 1957 when Rob Gaunt of No 9 SSU was on an instructional flight with Flight Lieutenant Brian Horney. They were forced to jettison the canopy and eject when their T11 failed to respond to spin recovery within the prescribed eight revolutions. The strange thing was that, once they had ejected, the aircraft recovered into wings level flight and continued downward in a powerless glide to its destruction.

All members of my course were pretty apprehensive about flying the FB9, having learned how naughty the aircraft could

Vampire FB9.

be. At the same time we had reason to look forward to flying this type because we had been told it was much like flying a Spitfire without the visual limitations given by a long nose and forward-set wings. Nor was an FB9 pilot troubled by the gyroscopic swing and high torque problems that arose from the Spitfire's huge propeller and immensely powerful, high-response piston engine.

I was the first of my course to fly solo in the T11 having flown a solo test with Flight Lieutenant Colin Graves, the Squadron Commander. This was not a once-around-the-circuit affair, but a full hour including aerobatics. When I taxiied into dispersals a reporter, who had come to cover the first ever jet solo at Thornhill, photographed me. Dave Thorne had done such a good job with the reporter that I was saved an interview and an hour later Dave himself made his first solo flight. Following my first solo, I flew a further three solos and a dual flight before moving to the FB9.

Peter after solo flight in a T11.

The FB9 cockpit presented difficulties for the first flight. When seated in a T11 it was only possible to see the head of a tall man standing six feet forward of the nose of the aircraft. In an FB9, in identical circumstances, the visual freedom given by the low stubby nose was such that one could see the entire man, right down to his shoes. This gave a first-flight student the problem of judging the aircraft's attitude for climbing and steep turning, having become used to judging aircraft attitude by references to the T11's high nose.

Flight Lieutenant Mussell had briefed me on what to expect in flight and emphasised that his main concern was that I should not pitch too high and slide the tail booms along the runway during take-off and landing. Preparation for this was very simple. When I was strapped in and ready for engine start-up, eight men put their weight on the tail booms to bring the tail protection slides into contact with ground, thus raising the nose beyond normal take-off and landing attitude.

Once I was satisfied that I would remember this position,

Note the differences in the angle from pilot's head to aircraft nose between FB9 (foreground) and T11.

by using the gun-sight glass as my reference, the nose wheel was set down again and I was ready for my first-ever flight in a single-seater aircraft.

On take-off I was immediately aware that the lighter FB9 accelerated better than the T11. At 85 knots I eased back on the control column to lift the nose wheel and noticed the elevator was lighter than the T11 and the aircraft became airborne earlier than I expected. I retracted the undercarriage and the speed mounted normally but then settled at 130 knots instead of the normal 180 knots climbing speed. Clearly my climbing attitude was way too steep. But it was not until I had reached 15,000 feet that I achieved the correct climbing speed when the nose seemed to be so far below the horizon that I felt I should be descending. Levelling off at 30,000 feet was really strange. I put the nose down quite a bit, then some more, then some more but the aircraft kept on climbing. By the time I achieved level flight, using flight instruments, I was at 33,000 feet. For a long while I maintained level flight, looking around to get a feeling for aircraft attitude while enjoying the newfound freedom of excellent forward vision and the ability to see over both sides of the cockpit.

I rolled the aircraft inverted and pulled through gently back to level flight at 390 knots IAS (Indicated Airspeed). Again I really had to force the nose attitude way down to stop climbing. Having done this I went into a series of aerobatics using the wing tips for attitude reference. By the time I was ready to come back to base, I had acclimatised to an aircraft that was every bit as pleasant to fly as I had hoped. Circuits and landings presented no difficulty and I was a very happy young man as I climbed down from the cockpit in time to watch Dave Thorne preparing for his first FB9 flight. I gave him thumbs-up with both hands and, even though he had his mask on, I could see the huge smile in his eyes.

No 11 SSU had arrived at Thornhill and were involved in their GTS phase. My course, being the senior course, was expected to give the 'new boys' a tough time. This we did. Although not obvious to us at the time, the purpose of a senior course giving its juniors a hard time was to weld the individuals of that course into a unified group.

When sixteen youngsters from different backgrounds, with varying characters and levels of ability are put together, they remain sixteen individuals until forced to turn to each other for mutual support. Fear of air combat and a deep hatred for the Nazi enemy automatically welded the youngsters who trained for World War II. In Rhodesia there was no such enemy or fear, so we deliberately set ourselves up as the enemy by inducing situations of discomfort, even hatred, which soon turned the juniors towards each other.

The Vampires were not due to return to Aden until early 1959. However, trouble broke out in the Middle East following the military overthrow of Iraq's pro-west ruler, King Faisal. Americans landed in Beirut and Russia warned of a possible world war. In support of British deployments to face these situations No 1 Squadron, less the instructors, was on its way at short notice for its second tour to Aden.

For us ground school, square-bashing and PT continued routinely until we learned that our drill instructor Sergeant McCone had met with a bad vehicle accident and would be off line until after our training was completed. We were told that an instructor from the Army's School of Infantry near Gwelo would be taking his place.

Regimental Sergeant-Major Ron Reid-Daly's first command drew a quiet "Oh boy!" from Ian Ferguson who was next to me. His commands were the loudest I have ever heard; his posture was ramrod-stiff and every movement he made was impossibly precise. We had come to believe that we were pretty smart in our drill but Sergeant-Major Reid-Daly did not see it this way. For at least six weeks he gave us absolute hell and we hated every moment of his nitpicking and abuse. With his nose almost in contact with anyone who had not executed a movement to his liking, he would scream such threats as "If you don't stop turning like a fucking ballerina, I will tear your bloody arm off and smash your silly little face with its soggy end ... sir."

Whenever the wind exceeded 15 knots, and that was often, the sadistic sergeant-major chose to put us through formation colours drills. For 'colours' we were given a wooden pole to which was affixed a heavy blanket. The wind drag on this arrangement was enormous and very tiring. Strong gusts would either propel the lighter fellows forward or backward bringing about a flurry of abuse from our instructor. But all the time we were getting better at everything and suddenly the pressure eased. We were then introduced to silent drill in which no word of command was given. Following fixed patterns of movement we moved as one and became very proficient at it. Yet for all the practice, 10 SSU was the only course not to display its silent drill skills during the Wings Presentation Parade. Sword of Honour for the best student was another aspect that was bypassed on the day we received our wings.

Ron Reid-Daly, who in the 1970s established and commanded the famed Selous Scouts, became a good friend of mine. Looking back on the period he had been sent to drill Nos 10 and 11 SSUs, he told me how horrified he had been when ordered to get over to Thornhill to train a bunch of 'Brylcreem boy' officer cadets. He remembered giving us a hard time and said that nothing he tried ever dented our spirit or determination to succeed. He found this both amazing and pleasing. His attitude towards the Air Force changed to one of respect and this was greatly enhanced during Rhodesia's long bush war.

When we started instrument flying, students were switched among the Vampire instructors. I was fortunate to fly with Flight Lieutenants Colin Graves (Squadron Commander), Chris Dams and Brian Horney. Most of our general training sorties were flown solo. On one of these, a long-range navigation flight, I passed out from the lack of oxygen. The oxygen-control box on the instructor's side of the cockpit had been set to high flow but I had not noticed this during my pre-engine start-up checks. On the last leg to base, flying over an area known as the Somabula Flats, I became aware of great noise and high vibration which awakened me to the fact that the aircraft was in a steep descending spiral turn, flying at critical Mach. This is when supersonic shock waves develop on sections of a sub-sonic aircraft's airframe, causing high drag with severe vibration. My mind was confused as I recovered from a situation I had not seen coming. In this dozy state, I dropped undercarriage, instead of activating the dive brakes as I had intended, and put out a call to Thornhill Approach. I was told later that my speech sounded like that of a very drunk man.

By the time the aircraft was in level flight at fairly low level, I was not too far from Thornhill and decided to leave the gear down. The landing was normal and, apart from minor distortion on one of the main-wheel 'D' doors, no damage had occurred. Nevertheless I received one hell of a rocket for not having seen the high-flow selection on the instructor's oxygen-control box and for not noticing my depleted oxygen tank reading before suffering hypoxia.

Shortly after this, Wing Commander Wilson flew me on progress checks and Squadron Leader Dicky Bradshaw conducted my instrument flying test, which was successfully flown on Wednesday, 6 August 1958. This was a day I can never forget!

Beryl and I had been engaged for fourteen months at this

stage. Apart from Beryl's objections to sex before marriage, her mother had planted a notion in our minds that made us decide to get married in secret. Beryl had turned twenty-one two days before, so parental consent was not an issue and we both believed we could keep our marriage secret.

Marriage day—what a hat! What a haircut!

Immediately after my IF test we motored to Bulawayo on the pretext of visiting my brother Tony, who was there on secondment for Territorial Army training. In reality, we had an appointment to be married in the Magistrate's Court. At three o'clock we were ushered into a room with the magistrate and his assistant. A moment or two later two people, who worked in the Magistrate's Court, came in to act as witnesses. One of these was a girl from Gwelo. She immediately recognised and greeted Beryl. In so doing she had blown our secret out of the water even before the marriage had taken place! But there was no way out of the situation.

Having been officially pronounced man and wife we visited friends of Beryl's folks who lived in Bulawayo. This was part of our cover plan but it turned out to be a bad mistake. The family cat took to Beryl in a big way and nothing would induce the long-haired creature to leave her alone.

Beryl had become a chronic bronchial asthmatic as a young girl, which led her parents to move from Britain to the drier climate of Rhodesia. For the most part she had been fine throughout her latter teens but certain irritants, one of which was cats' hair, could trigger a severe asthmatic attack. Beryl struggled for breath all the way back to Gwelo and any idea of consummating our marriage on our wedding night was lost. I had to get her home to her parents and bed. Then, back in my own single-quarter room I lay on my back and, looking at the ceiling, asked myself aloud "What have you done PB? Have you just destroyed your own future and made Beryl's uncertain?"

Two days passed before Beryl's mother made singsong utterings about a little bird having told her a secret. Though she would not tell Beryl what this secret was, it was quite clear that she had heard about our marriage. So we felt compelled to come clean with the folks, who both took the news very well. The Air Force would be another matter! Nevertheless, I decided I had to let Wing Commander Wilson know right away

When I went to the CO's personal secretary to make an appointment for the following day, her face lit up and away she rushed to the CO's office. The next moment she called out, "Officer Cadet Petter-Bowyer, the CO will see you now." I went cold because I had not yet worked out what to say, but it was very obvious to me that the secretary was tapped into Gwelo's gossip network.

I had absolutely no feeling below my waist. My upper body seemed to glide through the door into the CO's office and it stopped automatically in front of his desk. An involuntary salute occurred and I could not speak until the CO asked me what my business was. "Sir, I have come to let you know that I married Beryl last week. I need to tell you this before anyone else does." The Wing Commander's face told it all. He was dumbfounded and seemed not to know what to say or do. Then he rose from his chair, came around the desk and extended his hand saying, "Let me be the first to congratulate you."

Archie Wilson was well known for his handshake and many stories have been told of the agony suffered by many an unprepared hand. Those who knew him well made quite certain that they put their hand in rapidly to avoid his snap-action vice-grip from trapping their fingers. I was taken by surprise because his hand trapped my fingers so fiercely that all feeling returned to my legs and I was in such pain that I found myself almost on tiptoes. There was silence between us as he looked me directly in the eye, maintaining his grip on my severely graunched fingers.

"I did not have to get married, sir," I said in a high-pitched voice. Whereupon the CO let go and said he was relieved to hear this. He invited me to take a seat as he returned to his own. Then, rubbing his chin and looking blankly at his desk, he remained silent. I piped up again, this time in a normal voice, and told him why I had got married. He seemed impressed by

Beryl's attitude to premarital sex and understood my response to this.

Very quietly he told me that I was to continue as normal and he would handle Group HQ in his own time. I was instructed to let the members of my course know my situation and ask them to keep my news to themselves. I found my course mates at Station Equipment Section drawing their wings and pilot officer-rank braid for our forthcoming Wings Parade.

Two days later Wing Commander Wilson conducted my final handling test for wings. I passed and together with my ten colleagues received my wings on 19 August 1958 from Sir Roy

This photograph was taken just before I went to see the CO. Left to right: Ian Law, PB, Gordon Wright, Eric Cary, Murray Hofmeyr, John Barnes, Bill Galloway, Ian Ferguson, Dave Thorne and Keith Corrans.

PB receiving his wings from Sir Roy Welensky.

Welensky, the Prime Minister of the Federation of Rhodesia and Nyasaland. There was no presentation of the Sword of Honour for the best student on 10 SSU but Dave Thorne was presented a book by OC Flying to acknowledge the fact that he attained the best all-round position on our course.

This was quite a day for Bill Galloway to receive his wings and promotion to acting pilot officer because it was his 21st birthday. The Wings ball that evening was the first such occasion for the Royal Rhodesian Air Force at Thornhill, the forerunner of many to follow.

Operational Conversion Unit

ON 10 SEPTEMBER, MY COURSE moved into the Operational Conversion Unit (OCU) phase, which was the final stage of our two-year course. This was by far the most interesting period of training, during which we learned to use our aircraft as weapons platforms.

First Flight Lieutenant Ted Brent taught me to fire 20mm cannons, He and his wonderful wife Di were to become very close friends to Beryl and me. Ted was a gentleman through and through and his manner appealed to me from the moment I met him. On the ground and in the air his instructional techniques were very detailed and polished, which made learning a pleasure. In flight, he suggested corrections to my dive angle and aiming errors in a manner that helped me bring my strikes to target without ever making me feel pressurised or foolish.

Flight Lieutenant Frank Mussell (John's elder brother) was a good Pilot Armament Instructor (PAI) too, though his superior manner somewhat undermined the confidence I thought was needed between instructor and student, particularly during advanced training. Frank introduced me to the delivery of 60-pound rockets. Next, I flew with a very different instructor who had come from the RAF.

Flight Lieutenant Sandy Mutch, then the Flight Commander heading weapons training for No 1 Squadron, was bulldoggish in appearance and during his pre-flight briefings. In line with his personality he was very harsh in aircraft handling. He instructed me in low and high dive-bombing. When I made attacks, he had the nasty habit of grabbing the controls when my flight line was not to his liking and pressing his bomb-release button before I could press mine. This had never occurred with my other instructors so I was pleased that my solo bombing results were better than during instruction.

Having said this, I must say how grateful we were when Sandy persuaded Group HQ to let our course accompany elements of No 1 Squadron to Nairobi for that city's annual Royal Agricultural Show. Aerobatic and formation displays were to be given at the show by the Royal Rhodesian Air Force in conjunction with displays by the RAF.

We were very excited at the prospect of flying Thornhill to Chileka in Nyasaland, then to Dar es Salaam in Tanganyika and onward to Nairobi in Kenya. Such an opportunity had not been given to any previous training course. But, unfortunately for Sandy Mutch, the inclusion of No 10 SSU resulted in dramas that disallowed future courses from enjoying flights beyond the Federation's borders.

Twelve Vampires, in three formations of four aircraft, left Thornhill at hourly intervals. This allowed formations refuel at each destination before the arrival of the next. I was in the second formation that passed through Chileka and arrived in Dar es Salaam as planned. We had refuelled and were about to fly on to Nairobi when we received instructions to hold over in Dar es Salaam for the night.

I cannot say why this was really necessary, but it was good news for Keith Corrans, Bill Galloway and me who had not visited this part of the world before. It was extremely hot and humid and our stay, though pleasant, was somewhat dampened by the fact we could not swim in the inviting, clear-blue sea because of vast numbers of bluebottle-type jellyfish in the water and on the beaches.

The flight ahead of us had struck a snag between Dar es Salaam and Nairobi when Dave Thorne's FB9 canopy disintegrated at 33,000 feet. It punctured the hydraulic reservoir, resulting in Dave getting red hydraulic fluid all over his flying suit. Dave immediately switched over to emergency oxygen but, though in no danger of passing out, he was freezing cold with no option other than to continue with the formation because he had insufficient fuel to complete the journey at a warmer level. Behind us, one of the third formation's aircraft was found unserviceable at Chileka, forcing an overnight stay in Blantyre to await spares from Thornhill.

All aircraft finally assembled at RAF Eastleigh (Nairobi) where a replacement canopy was fitted to Dave's FB9. When all the aircraft were declared serviceable, we set off for the bright lights of Nairobi. In town I met up with Dave Thorne who had borrowed his aged Kenyan aunt's Rolls Royce shooting brake to impress a bevy of pretty girls he had in tow.

I saw Dave again the following day when we met in the Nairobi Show Grounds, the venue of the Royal Agricultural Show. An hour before the flying displays were due to start, Dave disappeared into the gents' toilets and remained there for an hour beyond the time the flying displays had ended. He then returned to the girls with his hair dampened and his face lined with pseudo headgear pressure marks. Those of my course who witnessed this did not let on to the excited girls that Dave had not been part of the formation; though we were most amused by the antics that certainly succeeded in impressing the girls.

That night I met Flight Lieutenant Booth of the RAF who had given a single-aircraft display in a Canberra B6, following a solo aerobatic display by an RAF Javelin. He offered to take me along for his display the following day; an opportunity I immediately accepted. At the appointed time I checked in with him in my flying kit. The correct oxygen mask was fitted to my helmet and I was briefed by the navigator on when and how I must move from rear ejector seat to the fold-down 'Rumbold' seat next to the pilot and back to the ejector seat for landing.

As soon as we were clear of the airfield, the navigator moved from his ejector seat to his bomb-aiming position on a bed in the aircraft nose. I followed, folded down the Rumbold seat, and strapped in next to Flight Lieutenant Booth. I had to stretch my neck to see over the right lip of the large domed canopy, but otherwise was able to take in the immense beauty of the famous Rift Valley where we descended for a few practice low-level barrel rolls. These went well and I remained firmly in my seat as we pitched and rolled high over the top and back into low-level flight.

On call from the ground controller at the Show Grounds, we positioned for the display. This initially involved very low-level turns with bomb bay opening and undercarriage lowering for the crowds to view at close range. We cleared for the RAF Javelin and waited to come in for the barrel roll that required the Canberra to invert as it passed over the crowd, because their view of the sky was limited by high trees surrounding the arena.

As the Javelin cleared we were close in and commenced the barrel roll. All seemed fine until Flight Lieutenant Booth said he had started the roll too late. At this point he rolled faster to the inverted and pushed forward on his control column. The navigator, snorting and swearing, was thrown into the wiring and other paraphernalia in front of the pilot's instrument panel. The emergency hydraulic pump handle dislodged and hit me in the face while I hung in my lap strap with my shoulder pressed hard against one of the canopy's jettison bolts. The two parachute packs of the rear-ejector seats broke loose and deployed their silk 'chutes all over the rear cabin.

As the aircraft passed the inverted position, the nose pitched very steeply and I was absolutely certain we were going to crash into the ground. However, the roll rate was increased with full rudder and the aircraft pitched out of the dive ever so close to the treetops. Fortunately, the ground beyond the Show Grounds dropped away somewhat; otherwise we would have been history. Loud abuse from the navigator and endless apologies from the skipper continued all the way to landing and for some time beyond.

After a splendid stay in Nairobi, our return to Rhodesia went fine until the third formation arrived at Chileka. I was standing with other pilots on the balcony of the Chileka Airport bar and watched the standard formation break that extended the line of aircraft for the usual descending turn to land. Unfortunately, however, Gordon Wright as No 3 was a bit too tight and slow when, in the final stages of his approach, he hit slipstream from the aircraft ahead. The FB9 impacted the ground about sixty metres short of the raised shoulder of the runway.

No 4 had seen the problem coming and powered up for an overshoot before Gordon's aircraft bounced from its first impact point, clearing the rising ground and impacting ground again in a broadside at runway level. A huge cloud of red dust marked the aircraft's passage but smothered it from our view as it slid to a halt on the lip of a storm-water drain. Another three feet and Gordon would almost certainly have lost his legs. As it was, he was lucky to get away with a badly damaged ego, which he showed by throwing his helmet down in frustrated anger. The aircraft was quite severely damaged and was transported to New Sarum by road for repair, and flew again. But it took a long time for people in Air HQ to forget Gordon's error.

Back at Thornhill we resumed our weapons training. I continued flying with Frank Mussell and Ted Brent and also flew with three new instructors whom I can only describe as salt-of-the-earth individuals and good PAIs (Pilot Armament Instructors) too. Flying Officers Peter McLurg, Randy du Rand and Justin Varkevisser had totally different characters but were pleasant instructors and great marksmen to boot.

The accurate delivery of air weapons takes considerable understanding, practice and in-built skills. Speed, firing range, angle of attack, allowance for gravity drop and wind lay-off, all have to be spot on. For the likes of myself this needed great effort and practice. However, there were those few pilots whose actions and judgement were instinctive. Justin Varkevisser was one of the few. He was deadly accurate with any weapon he delivered. Largely because of his teaching and example, a number of future pilots acquired his unique abilities.

Apart from delivery of air weapons, we were introduced to new operational flying requirements. Formation tail-chases were necessary to experience the effects of opening and closing speeds when climbing and descending as we learned how to loosen and tighten turns to open and close on potential enemy aircraft. Quarter attacks from high level onto lower flying aircraft were easy enough to fly, but holding the centre graticule of the gyro gun-sight on the target aircraft, while matching its wing-span by twisting the range controller on the throttle to cater for rapidly closing distance, was another matter altogether. Apart from Justin, the only pilot I remember doing this with comparative ease was Randy du Rand whose gun-sight camera records gave him 'kills' off most of his attacks.

This is a short section of one of Randy's camera records. The lack of clarity in these gun-sight shots was typical of those days, but the outer ring of diamond-shaped spots can be seen to match the target's wing-span. This matching determined the range of the target.

We flew a great deal of high- and low-level battle formation, usually in flights of four aircraft. This involved aircraft flying a wide 'finger four' pattern (as per tips of fingers on a spread hand) which allows all pilots flying about 500 meters apart to detect incoming enemy aircraft on other aircraft within the formation.

I enjoyed flying 'bandit', either solo or as a pair, and seeing a 'friendly' formation commence its attack. Response to this resulted in a call such as "Red, bandit four o'clock high—break", whereupon our formation would disintegrate into tight defensive turns and manoeuvre for a counter-attack or break away to 'safety'.

During the OCU phase Eric Cary was challenging me, among others, to the odd meeting out in the flying area. Stupidly I agreed rather than risk being considered a wet fish. One of Eric's favourite challenges involved flying fast, at ultra-low level, one beside the other, directly towards the base of a high Selukwe mountain range. At the last moment the aircraft were pitched into a climb to avoid collision below the ridge, then rolling inverted as soon as safely possible. From here each aircraft would be allowed to pitch at zero G, still inverted, until diving back towards low ground on the opposite side of the mountain.

Eric Cary.

The idea was to establish who rolled right side up first. Needless to say I was always first out and on most occasions I watched Eric's aircraft shadow closing on his inverted aircraft before he rolled right side up close to the treetops. It was quite clear to me that Eric's flying ability and judgement, even when inverted, was much better than mine and I was more than happy to acknowledge this.

The normal speed for the commencement of a loop was 280 knots or higher. Eric boasted that he had succeeded in looping a T11 off an entry speed of only 180 knots. I took the bait! The problem was that my next solo flight, on 25 November 1958, was in an FB9. Nevertheless I decided to give it a go. The cloud base at Thornhill was about 1,500 feet with some clear patches between cumulus clouds. I had to climb to 20,000 feet before reaching cloud tops. Between Selukwe and Shabani there was no cloud to speak of, just what I needed!

I started my trial with an entry speed of 220 knots intending to reduce speed thereafter in ten-knot steps. Using full power all the way round, I managed to coax the aircraft over the top of the first three loops. The fourth attempt was initiated at 190 knots but just before the top of the loop the aircraft stopped pitching, fluttered gently, then hammer-stalled out. Deciding that I must pitch more rapidly until past the vertical, I tried again. Much the same happened, but the stall developed into a gentle upward spin that slowed as the aircraft flopped into downward flight then, even with controls centralised, it went into a tight right-hand spin.

Recovery action was taken and the aircraft responded normally. This was my first experience of the FB9's forbidden manoeuvre. I decided to try once more pulling around as tightly as I dared. This time a spin developed, going vertically upwards so I centralised controls and throttled right back to await the flop back into downward flight. Instead, the aircraft attitude held until the flight direction reversed in a tail-slide with a big puff of black smoke passing the cockpit from behind, just before the aircraft hammered into a vertical dive.

As the speed built up I advanced the throttle gently, but there was no response from the engine. A glance at the JPT (jet pipe temperature) showed that the engine had flamed-out during the tail-slide. I set up a powerless glide at 160 knots with the HP (high-pressure) fuel cock closed. I pressed the re-light button and advanced the HP cock slowly. The JPT rose immediately but then fell back to zero. I closed the HP cock again and made a call to Thornhill Approach who controlled all aircraft operating beyond the Thornhill circuit.

"Approach this is Papa 1. I have flame-out at 21,000 feet, attempting re-light. Over."

Flight Lieutenant Rex Earp-Jones replied, "Roger Papa 1. Out."

Whereupon I switched off all electrics, including the radio, to preserve power for another attempt at starting the engine after the prescribed one minute had elapsed, to clear the engine of unburned fuel. Low engine rotation on the rpm gauge was from the windmilling effect of airflow through the engine.

I was about thirty nautical miles from base when I entered cloud, heading for home. It felt strange to be flying on instruments in the glide without the familiar rumble from the engine. The second attempt to re-light met with no response at all and I realised I might have to go all the way to the runway without power. I was not concerned about this and never doubted I would make it safely to Thornhill, providing the cloud at base was not too low.

I switched the old-fashioned valve radio on and, as it came to life, I heard Rex Earp-Jones calling, "Papa 1, this is Approach. Confirm you are on practice forced landing. Over."

I replied, "Approach, Papa 1. Negative, I have flame-out but engine not responding to re-light. Will try again. Out."

Apparently all hell broke loose on the ground but I did not know this because I had switched off the radio again for another unsuccessful attempt to re-light. By this time I was descending through 13,000 feet at a gentle 1,600-feet per minute when I noticed first signs of the odd break in the cloud below me. I switched the radio on again and told Rex Earp-Jones I was committed to a 'dead-stick' landing.

At around 9,000 feet I saw Guinea Fowl School a little to the rear and a section of the Umvuma road ahead, so I knew I was home and dry. Approach instructed me to change channel to Thornhill Tower Control. When I checked in on the Tower frequency the unmistakable voice of OC Flying, Squadron Leader Dicky Bradshaw replied. He immediately turned my confidence to doubt. Strangely he was calling me PB and not Papa 1. He said he could yet not see my aircraft but told me to bail out NOW if I had any doubts about making the runway. I replied that I had the necessary height, whereupon he said he had me visual. Then he told me to get my gear down immediately, but I knew this was too early and held back.

I selected wheels-down on his second insistence as I lined up on a high downwind leg. The gear flopped out but did not lock. This required me to pump vigorously on the emergency hydraulic handle with my right hand until I had three green lights to prove the wheels were locked for landing. I commenced the turn onto finals and pumped like mad to get flaps down. These were coming down way too slow so there was nothing for it but to dive off height and make a flat approach to wash off excess speed. I overdid this slightly because the aircraft only just reached the runway and stalled onto the concrete threshold. But the aircraft and I were safely home.

When called into OC Flying's office, I told my story exactly as it had happened but without mentioning Eric Cary's challenge. Squadron Leader Bradshaw was furious with me for attempting aerobatics below recommended speeds, particularly with my limited experience, and more so for pressing on after dangerous loop failures. He gave me a stern lecture on the need to show more responsibility and ended by telling me I had done well to bring the aircraft home, considering the cloud situation. He also said that the technicians had already reported finding a fault with the re-light ignition system.

The last time Eric challenged me was to fly formation aerobatics that were not included in our OCU training. I was leading when I hand-signalled for a barrel roll 'left'. A barrel roll is the combination of roll and loop. With Eric on my left, I entered a gentle, diving turn to the right then commenced pitching up and rolling left. When I had almost reached the top of the barrel roll I looked upward through the canopy to seek the horizon and was horrified to see a mirror image of my own aircraft closing on me. It was only a split second before the aircraft crossed right next to mine, but in that moment I saw Eric's up-turned face visor and noticed the two white scribble pads on the laps of his overalls. How we missed I do not know, but I wanted no more of this nonsense.

I lost Eric by breaking away to low level and headed straight for home. Before Eric could say a word to me back at base, I told him that a flying challenge was one thing, but I had no time for outright stupidity and would no longer indulge in any further unauthorised flying.

After my flame-out experience someone told me that air incidents tend to come in threes. This was the case with me and all three occurred in the same week. The second incident involved total electrical failure in an FB9 during a short night cross-country training flight from Thornhill to Glencova, Buhera and return.

A continuous blanket of stratocumulus of about 1,000 feet in depth covered most of the Midlands. Very soon after becoming airborne, I was above this cloud in brilliant moonlight with vast cumulus formations widely spread and towing above the low cloud. These formations, together with the moon and stars above, always gave me the feeling of drifting through an immense fairyland. The low stratus cleared about ten minutes out and I could see the lights of Fort Victoria and Mashaba off to the right of track.

Having turned north from my first turning point, the cockpit lights flickered twice then failed, as did my radio. Although the moonlight was bright I could not read my instruments or see anything within the cockpit. I switched on the battery-powered emergency lights and started to consult my map to work out a heading to steer for home. While I was doing this, the emergency lights were fading rapidly, before petering out completely. I could not believe this was happening to me!

Next, I took out my pencil torch from its purpose-made pocket on the shoulder of my flying suit, but it would not stay on. While I was trying to get it to work, the back shot off and the batteries tumbled out of reach onto the cockpit floor. Now I was really up a creek without a paddle and a horrid clammy fear spread through my body. Try as I did, I could not remember the course I had been steering on the first leg nor could I bring to mind the layout of Rhodesia. Fortunately I remembered what time I expected to land back at Thornhill and by moonlight could read my Air Force wristwatch clearly.

My position was changing rapidly as I battled to fathom out a heading to steer for Thornhill. It probably only took a minute but it seemed like an eternity as I dithered to come to a firm decision to steer a true heading of 290 degrees. Strangely that decision had a calming effect as I looked east to find the distinctive star pattern of Orion's Belt.

This very distinct star group consists of three evenly spaced and equally bright stars set in a straight line (the belt), with another line of lesser stars on the south side (the sword) that points to the centre of the three bright stars. If a line is taken from the southernmost of the lesser stars through the northernmost of the bright stars and extended to the horizon, this is True North in the period December to January. I turned port to align with True North.

Using my port wing and the nose as reference I assessed where 290 degrees was, selected a star on that line and turned to head for this star. No cumulus formation appeared to lie directly in the path between my destination and me and, odd though it may seem, I was certain that I would arrive directly over Thornhill with plenty of fuel to spare.

Approximately three minutes before my expected time overhead Thornhill I noticed that stratocumulus lying in the shadow of a cumulonimbus mass was glowing from a lighted area beneath it. This I knew must be Gwelo, and Thornhill would be at the edge nearest to me. Not daring to change power from the 9,500 rpm I had set for cruise I pitched the nose down to a comfortable descent angle and turned the trim wheel progressively forward to cater for the increasing speed. The aircraft was correctly trimmed and the speed was stable by the time I was over the illuminated cloud.

A twenty-degree turn to port was then established. Around and around the lighted area I went in the descent, with the aircraft passing in and out of the moon's shadow until the entire orbit at a lower level was in the shadow of the huge cloud. Flight was smooth and I had frozen both hands on the spade grip of the control column to prepare for the blind passage through cloud.

Entry came in an unexpected rush. It was slightly turbulent and I held my breath when I heard the speed increasing. I dared not move a muscle for what seemed like a long time with the noise of the airflow steadily rising. As suddenly as the aircraft had entered cloud in a controlled manner, it exited fast and steep with about ninety degrees of port bank. The lights of town were so close as I rolled right to pull out of the dive, breathing like a racehorse, only to shoot straight back into cloud. I pressed forward hard and emerged out of cloud and turned left again to stay over the lights of the town.

Still hyperventilating, I cruised at low level around and around the town attempting to orient myself on the landmarks of Gwelo. Nothing fitted until I noticed a high mast on the edge of the town. I must have done at least six turns before I realised that this high mast fitted Que Que, not Gwelo. Now I knew I was about seven minutes away from base and felt certain I would get there with some fuel to spare.

The aircraft had settled into a steady trimmed state and I had regained control of my breathing as I swept around at about 280 knots in relative safety with Que Que town about 500 feet below me and the lighted cloud base 100 feet above. I knew this would change the moment I set course for base but there was no time to spare.

Knowing that the road from Gwelo ran right next to the mast on entry into Que Que, I was able to establish the line of the main road by the lights of vehicles approaching Que Que from Gwelo. I rolled out along the road line and flew straight into blackness. Barely sufficient moonlight was illuminating stratus to help me keep wings level, but the cloud base itself was indistinct. For about a minute all seemed well until vehicle lights were lost as I entered cloud. I pushed out gingerly and, as I saw vehicle lights again, I also saw, way off, the faint glow of Gwelo lighting the low cloud base. Suddenly the glow was lost and I knew I had dropped below high ground along this route so I pulled up smartly, saw the glow momentarily and lost it as I entered cloud, yet again.

Deep breathing set in once more as I eased down. Out of cloud the glow came back brighter and even the cloud base became more distinct. From here on I was safe. When the actual lights of Gwelo were visible I could work out where Thornhill lay. I picked up the moving tail-light of a Vampire on final approach for runway 13. This helped me find the runway lights but I could see I was closing on the Vampire very rapidly.

Only when I was sure of making the runway did I throttle right back and selected undercarriage down when the reducing speed sounded right. With no flap and rolling onto the runway much too fast, I held to the extreme right edge of the runway to overtake the Vampire I had seen on finals. Having turned off the runway I taxied to dispersals where a marshaller, waiting for the aircraft behind me, was surprised to see another Vampire, with no lights, roll into view in the illuminated dispersal area.

In response to the marshaller's signals, I made the first turn towards the hard-standing and had just commenced the second turn when the engine quit. The marshaller, thinking I had deliberately closed down the engine, was visibly annoyed as he moved over to bring in the next aircraft.

Flight Lieutenant Colin Graves was in the T11 that taxied in behind me. Squadron Leader Dicky Bradshaw had recalled him from his sortie because the Air Traffic Controllers at Thornhill, Salisbury and Bulawayo had been unsuccessful in their attempts to establish communications with me. Radar contact with an aircraft, presumed to be mine had been seen flying some distance to the north-east of Thornhill, was lost in the vicinity of Que Que.

Colin's relief at seeing me was obvious and he had not seen my unlit aircraft overtake him on the runway. I told him I had experienced total electrical failure, followed by emergency light failure and the disintegration of my pocket torch before he noticed that my hands and body were shaking. He arranged some very sweet black coffee for me and made me sit down in his office while he made calls to ATC and OC Flying to let them know I was safe. In listening to what he had to say to OC Flying, I realised that I had survived a freak situation.

When Colin had listened to the whole story he asked me why I had not diverted to Salisbury Airport. Everyone attending night-flying briefing, including me, had heard that Salisbury would be free of cloud. I felt such a fool but had to admit that in my state of near-panic I had given this obvious solution to my problem no thought whatsoever. What a way to build up experience!

The third incident occurred when Bill Galloway and I were in the flying area, flying pairs-formation exercises. Another formation of four Vampires had taken off about forty minutes after us. We were both flying FB9s and had already descended to low-level on return to base when warned that two heavy thunderstorms were merging into one massive storm so rapidly, that Thornhill would be engulfed in torrential rain before we could get down.

There was insufficient fuel to divert to another airfield, so we were instructed to hold off for about fifteen minutes when the storm was expected to clear. Bill was leading and immediately

reduced power to 6,500 rpm to conserve fuel. Had we been warned of the storms two minutes earlier we would certainly have remained at high altitude where a lower fuel-consumption rate would have allowed us to divert to Bulawayo.

We orbited a little away from the edge of the dark rain line nearest to the end of runway 31 until it became clear to us that the storm was moving so slowly that we would be out of fuel before it cleared. So Bill requested that the runway lights be switched on to maximum brightness for a landing in rain. He then lined up on two references he assured me were on a direct line with the runway.

We had both lowered undercarriage and flaps when Bill disappeared from my view into heavy rain. I entered it about five seconds later. Visibility through the FB9's armour-glass was poor in such heavy rain, but out of the corner of my eye I saw the rail and road pass under the aircraft and picked up the blur of runway lights a little to my left. Having landed, I could just make out a large white blob of spray ahead with Bill's wing tips showing on each side. Seeing this, I instinctively moved to raise the flaps to reduce any damage from the high-pressure spray coming off the main wheels. As I did so, my nose wheel collapsed and the aircraft skidded along the runway noisily in a steep nose-down attitude. When the aircraft came to a halt, I advised the controllers that my nose wheel had collapsed on landing and that I was on the extreme right-hand side of the runway, well clear of the centre line.

Fire engines emerged out of the gloom as I climbed out onto the runway. The tarmac surface was so close that I did not have to await extrication of the fuselage footstep for the usual climb down to ground. Having pulled the canopy closed, I ran across to the nearest fire vehicle in heavy rain. When I looked back at the FB9, my heart sank. Not only had the nose wheel collapsed, both main wheels were partially retracted and pressed against the runway surface. Flight Sergeant Jimmy Dumas, the senior fire-fighter, followed me back to the aircraft. I slid the canopy open and we both looked in to see the positions of the flap and undercarriage levers. Both were fully down.

Jimmy Dumas took me back to the control tower, which was halfway along the runway and set back about 300 metres. No sooner had I climbed the steps up to the third storey and into the actual control tower than Wing Commander Wilson came running up the steps and it stopped raining. He passed me not saying a word and set about ensuring the safe return of the airborne formation.

Watching the CO go about his business with the two controllers at their consoles, I wondered where I stood. My FB9, now clearly visible, was lying on its belly because of my own error. Added to this were my secret marriage, hypoxia, flame-out and electrical failure at night—all so close together that I felt the CO might give up on me now.

Flight Lieutenant Mac Geeringh, the ever-helpful friend to students, took me aside. Mac had originally served with the South African Air Force and had seen service in Korea where the loss of a nipple on his chest bore witness to one of the injuries he sustained when his Mustang fighter-bomber struck a landmine on a taxiway. He asked me what had happened.

I told Mac how I went to raise flaps but obviously moved the undercarriage lever instead. The downward forces when the fuselage dropped onto the runway would have brought my arm down and reset the undercarriage lever into the 'down' position.

Without hesitation Mac Geeringh told me not to say a word about this. "Just say the undercarriage collapsed on landing. Say not a word about lifting flap. Too much has happened to you already. Take no chances."

Although I understood what Mac was saying—and why—I decided to repeat to the CO exactly what I had told Mac. I am glad I did.

Wing Commander Wilson knew that the undercarriage lever should have locked the moment the weight of the aircraft was on the wheels. He told me not to be too concerned for the moment because he had initiated a technical investigation to establish why the micro-switch in the undercarriage bay failed to energise the lock plunger on the undercarriage-operating lever. The answer to the CO's queries was given by the STO (Senior Technical Officer) very promptly. He reported that the micro-switch on the port oleo worked normally until subjected to high-pressure water spray.

Notwithstanding the technical defect, I felt very embarrassed about this incident because I had been taught never to tamper with flap or undercarriage controls on the ground. Not long

after this, Keith Corrans, flying with his instructor John Mussell, made an unavoidable wheels-up landing in a TII because of a punctured port wheel jamming the undercarriage in the retracted position. I have to say that when I saw this aircraft lying on its belly on the runway, I did not feel quite so bad about my cock-up, even though mine had been caused by my own piloting error.

Shortly after this our operational conversion was complete and all ten members of my course were offered a Medium Service Commission for regular service in the Royal Rhodesian Air Force. Nine of us accepted. Ian Ferguson opted to return to his first love, farming. This meant that No 10 SSU, with a 90% return on training costs, became the most fruitful of any SSU course ever trained by the Royal Rhodesian Air Force.

Beryl and I went on Christmas leave to Northern Rhodesia where Mum and Berry met Beryl for the first time. We had collected my grandmother on our way through Salisbury and returned her there, having enjoyed a magnificent time at Mkushi.

Keith's T11 belly-landing.

Chapter

3

No 1 Squadron

ON 3 JANUARY 1959 WE returned from Christmas leave and I was very pleased to learn that I had been posted to No 1 Squadron together with Dave Thorne, Eric Cary, Bill Galloway and Keith Corrans. Before being split up to go our various ways, my course was summoned to Wing Commander Wilson's office to take commissioning oaths and sign a ten-years' Medium Service contract. (On completion of ten years, one could apply for permanent service.)

Only after this had been done did the CO tell Group HQ about my marriage. As expected, he got one hell of a rocket for withholding this information for five long months. The next day I was called to his office again to be told that I would be called to Group HQ in the near future for an interview with the Chief of Air Staff, Air Vice-Marshal Ted Jacklin. In the meanwhile I was to get on and establish myself as a useful squadron pilot.

No 1 Squadron was a regular-sized squadron in terms of its fifteen pilots but was very short staffed on the technical side with only thirteen technicians led by a frosty, no-nonsense old timer Scot, Flight Sergeant Jimmy Stewart, who was the NCO in charge of all technical matters.

Flight Lieutenant Colin Graves commanded the squadron with Bob Woodward (ex-RAF Central Flying School) and Flying Officer Norman Walsh as his flight commanders. Three of the PAIs who had instructed my course on weapons, Randy du Rand, Justin Varkevisser and Peter McClurg, remained with No 1 Squadron. Basil Green, Eddie Wilkinson, Ted Stevenson and Mike Reynolds made up the balance of our numbers.

Frank Mussell, Ted Brent and Brian Horney had been posted off the squadron to join other pilots for a conversion onto Canberra bombers at RAF Bassingborne in the UK.

Sandy Mutch also left the squadron for a staff position in Group HQ.

Thornhill worked different hours to both Group HQ and New Sarum. The aircrew workday commenced at 06:30 in the station briefing room where OC Flying covered any non-routine events. This was followed by that day's meteorological forecast given by the resident meteorologist, Mr Harvey Quail. Thereafter everyone went about his normal business and regular work ceased at 13:30.

Everyone was free to do his own thing in the afternoon. For the most part this involved sports followed by a few drinks in the all ranks Sports Club or within individual messes. A pilot's life in those days seemed to be more like being on permanent holiday than working for a living.

Interview with Commander

I HAD BEEN DREADING MY INTERVIEW with the Air Force Commander, which occurred on 3 February 1959. Having been authorised to fly myself to New Sarum in a T11 for the occasion, I was pleased to be approached by Mike Reynolds who wanted a lift to attend to private business in Salisbury. We landed at New Sarum a whole hour ahead of my 10:00 appointment and Mike raced off immediately saying he should be back at lunchtime.

Because I was so nervous about the interview, Beryl had

approached a chemist friend who gave her a small white tranquilliser tablet and a larger one to offset drowsiness induced by the first. These were to be taken thirty minutes before my interview.

Ten minutes before due time I reported to Group Captain Harold Hawkins. This large, good-looking man was much gentler than I had expected. He told me to relax and said, "The old man is going to give you a going over like you will never have to face again. But don't worry, all will be fine." 'Harry the Hawk', as he was known, was not to know that I was so relaxed by the tranquilliser tablet I had taken twenty minutes earlier that my fears were all but gone.

AVM Jacklin.

At precisely 10 o'clock I was ushered into the Chief of Air Staff's office. I had only seen this revered man once before at our Wings Parade and the Wings Ball that followed it. Having saluted him I remained at attention in front of his desk. Looking me straight in the eye, the CAS started off in a quiet voice with the words, "So you are the puppy who chose to disobey Air Force regulations and undermined the standards of my Air Force!" His voice rose steadily as he lectured me on his intolerance to indiscipline and had resorted to thumping his desk with his fist to emphasise points by the time he had come to shouting his words.

The tranquilliser's effects on me made everything seem quite unreal. I was taking in the words and the scene thinking: 'He is really having to work at raising his anger.'

The next moment the Commander started to cough and reached into a drawer for a small container from which he inhaled spray. Later I learned that he was an asthmatic but at that moment he was red-faced and struggling for breath. I remained dead still knowing instinctively that I would be doing the wrong thing to offer help. The CAS was still struggling to

breathe when I said, "Sir, may I tell you my story." He nodded and signalled me to sit down.

By the tine I had finished telling him how and why I had married Beryl, the CAS had fully regained his composure. His first words were very reassuring. "Son, I am so pleased you did not have to get married and that your wife is not pregnant now. I hate shotgun marriages in my force."

For over forty minutes AVM Jacklin, all the time referring to me as "son", told me all about his plans and dreams for "my Air Force". He ended up by saying I was to take six weeks' paid leave so that Beryl and I could put our lives into good order.

The Commander then telephoned Mr Lionel Harris of Bannett and Harris, a well-known, high-quality furniture shop in Salisbury, and requested that he attended to our needs; the Air Force would stand guarantor to Beryl and me. He told me I was to ensure that we set out in our married life with the best-quality furniture and a good clean home. Today, over forty years on, we still have much of the furniture we bought from Bannett and Harris in 1959 and Beryl has always kept a very clean home.

I was about to leave his office when the Commander asked me how I had come up from Thornhill. Still a bit tranquillised I unthinkingly said I had flown up in a Vampire. This news sent the Commander through the roof.

Knowing that I must have been pretty stressed ahead of this interview, he could not understand why I had not been flown up by one of the squadron pilots. When I revealed that Mike Reynolds had hitched a lift with me, Group Captain Hawkins was called in and told to change the flight authorisation for Reynolds to captain the return flight to Thornhill. As I marched out, Air Vice-Marshal Jacklin was already on the phone to Wing Commander Wilson. I felt really bad about my CO having to take another blasting from CAS because he had done more to protect me than I deserved or expected.

Beryl and I found a lovely apartment in Shema's Flats in Gwelo that we furnished to our liking. Beryl's dad helped us with half the money to buy a second-hand Vauxhall Velox so we were well set and happy by the time I returned to duty and Beryl to her hairdressing job.

Air Force life was idyllic. Flying was a joy and the squadron crew room was a happy place. There was always a great deal of chatter, leg pulling, reading or playing cards, Scrabble and other games. One day we acquired a chess set. Those who had not played the game before chose to ignore it. Two of these were Justin Varkevisser (Varky) and Randy du Rand, but when I came in from a sortie one morning, I was surprised to find these two playing each other at chess. I moved closer and was astonished to see that Varky had Randy's king off the board. "You cannot do that," I told Varky. "The king never leaves the board." Other pilots gathered and were amused to hear Randy say, "You play to your rules and we will play to ours!"

Eddie Wilkinson had a dog named Pickles who followed him everywhere. Pickles was allowed into the squadron

Varky, Peter McLurg, Randy and Dave Thorne.

Pembroke landing at New Sarum.

building where his presence was hardly noticed because he was very well behaved. The one thing that amazed us all about this dog was that he was only noticed when Eddie went out to his aircraft or taxiied into dispersals. He would follow his master right through the pre-flight inspection then move off the hard-standing to watch Eddie taxi out towards the runway. Pickles would not be noticed again until he leapt up and ran out to the flight line to meet Eddie as he taxied in. Only a dog could differentiate between the many Vampires Eddie flew. They all sounded the same to us!

Nyasaland emergency

THE FEDERATION OF RHODESIA AND Nyasaland was facing opposition from black leaders who wanted the three territories of the Federation to be dissolved and independence bestowed upon each under 'black governments'. Rioting broke out in Nyasaland and blood had been spilled before the Police and Army moved in to quell the unrest. Nos 3 and 4 Squadrons (Dakotas, Pembrokes and Provosts) were dispatched to the troubled region immediately and No 1 Squadron was put on standby. Then on the first day of April we deployed to Chileka Airport near Blantyre.

The Dakotas and two Pembrokes were still engaged in positioning ground forces around the country and Provosts had already flown missions in active support of Police and Army units serving as airborne observers and laying tear-gas screens when needed.

The Vampires were only there to 'wave the flag', uphold the spirits of the 'goodies' and undermine the confidence of the 'badies'. Ours should have been a very soft number but the

first flag-waving flight was a pretty hairy experience for me. A formation of six Vampires was to expose our presence in and around Zomba, the seat of government.

Norman Walsh led the formation of six aircraft. We took off from Chileka Airport in pairs under 'chiparoni' conditions of low cloud with drizzle (known to Rhodesians as *guti* and normal wet weather in Britain). Because we entered dense stratocumulus shortly after take-off, Norman instructed us to hold a particular heading until above the cloud where we would link up. I was No 2 in the second pair and saw Norman and his No 2 as soon as we came into clear air in a cloud valley with higher banks to right and left of our flight line. We linked up and I became No 4 on Norman's lead. The third pair reported being above cloud but could not see our formation. After orbiting for about three minutes Norman decided that link-up would not occur and instructed the unseen pair to return to Chileka.

The cloud opened about twenty kilometres northwest of Zomba sufficiently to allow for a visual descent. Norman picked up the main road from Lake Nyasa to Zomba and flew us fast and low in tight battle formation along the road just below thickening low cloud. I was slightly stepped up in the starboard outer position where I could see the three aircraft as well as the reaction of people along the road. Most had not seen jets at close range before and were diving for cover as Norman swept over them.

The northern slopes of Zomba mountain suddenly appeared out of the gloom, its base reaching down to the main road. This forced both of us on the starboard side to step higher and steepen the echelon angle, placing me at cloud base close against the mountainside.

As the outskirts of Zomba came into view I suddenly saw a heavy cable at such close range that I had to make a violent break to port to avoid it. I then had to repeat the manoeuvre in the reverse direction so as not to lose sight of the other aircraft, now on my right side. It became so dark over Zomba town, in moderately heavy rain, that Norman considered it unwise to make the planned orbits of the town, so he led us straight back to Chileka Airport.

On the ground we learned that the line I had so nearly hit was an old hawser cable that used to transport timber from the

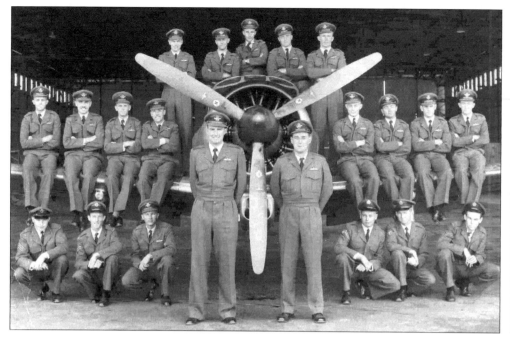

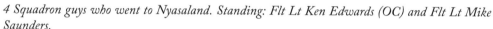

4 Squadron guys who went to Nyasaland. Standing: Flt Lt Ken Edwards (OC) and Flt Lt Mike Saunders.

Pregnant Beryl: a happy consequence of the Nyasaland Emergency.

top of Zomba mountain down to its base. Norman expressed his relief that the third pair had been dropped because, with six aircraft, the unmarked hazard may have proven fatal.

For the next few days the weather was good and we flew a number of sorties over troubled areas. We got to see much of truly beautiful Nyasaland and crystal-clear Lake Nyasa that, like Lakes Albert, Kivu and Tanganyika, is a water-filled section of the Great Rift Valley running down the eastern side of Africa.

Mount Mlanje, the highest feature in the territory, was surrounded by a vast spread of well-manicured tea estates having lines of magnificent acacia trees that acted as protective windbrakers. Norman was leading as usual when he turned our formation of four FB9s towards the mountain for a zoom climb up a well-defined gully running from the base of the mountain to its summit. Full power was applied as we commenced the ascent in loose line astern. I was No 3 and soon became concerned when the mountain seemed too steep and high because I was dropping back from the two aircraft climbing ahead of me. Keith Corrans flying No 4 passed on my right side waving at me as he flew by.

I had suspected that my FB9's engine was shy on power during each formation take-off over the previous few days, but now I knew for sure that it was not performing like those of the three aircraft racing away from me. Soon all three aircraft disappeared from view as they pitched over the rounded summit that was still a long way ahead.

I was considering lowering undercarriage for what looked like an unavoidable stall onto the rough rising ground but by using a small degree of flap; I managed to wallow past the

mountain climbers' resthouse at the summit. Falling ground allowed a slow acceleration to safe flying speed and I re-established visual contact with the formation descending some two miles ahead.

For pilots and technicians of the jet and transport squadrons, life at Chileka Airport was comfortable, with pleasant tented accommodation and the airport restaurant and bar at our permanent disposal. On the other hand, No 4 Squadron's crews were split up at three forward airfields where conditions were not so easy; but at least they were seeing action in close support of the Army and Police.

For the men operating the Provosts, accommodation and food was pretty basic with little to occupy the long hours between sorties. It was during such a lull that Frank Gait-Smith, sitting in a camp chair and having lost interest in all the over-read magazines, watched a black woman bearing a bucket of water on her head cross the grass runway at Kota Kota. In a bored voice, and speaking to nobody in particular, he observed that, "Absence surely makes the blacks grow blonder!"

I was instructed to take my underpowered FB9 back to Thornhill and was granted permission to stay over for the night before returning with a replacement aircraft. A few weeks after this we learned that Beryl was pregnant and nine months after that one night stay-over our daughter Deborah was born.

One morning there was quite a commotion as police vehicles came onto the airport apron and pulled up to the open doors of a waiting Dakota. A number of black men emerged from the vehicles and were ushered into the Dakota. I noticed that one of them was small and still wearing pyjamas and dressing gown. This was Doctor Hastings Banda who was on his way to Gwelo Prison. The Nyasaland Emergency was over and we returned to base having been away for only twenty-one days.

The need to prepare aircrew to survive many days in the bush brought about a series of 'bush survival exercises'. The first of these was run in August after our return from Nyasaland. Half of 1 Squadron's pilots were flown to Binga airfield on the south bank of the Zambezi River, soon to be lost below the waters of Kariba Dam. Many crocodile basking points were evident right next to the runway markers.

A famous hunter cum game-ranger, Mr Cockroft, conducted the course that included a very long and strenuous hike to the Amanzituba Vlei area climbing from the hot bush-covered flats through a rugged range into the cooler highveld. Close encounters with two black rhino induced high adrenaline flow but otherwise we all enjoyed moving through bushveld that supported a full spread of African wildlife totally unaffected by human intrusion.

On completion of our bush hike we were pretty exhausted and very much enjoyed swimming in the therapeutic waters of a hot spring pool. I believe it is still there, close to the Kariba shoreline.

Standing: Eddie Wilkinson, PB and Eric Cary. Centre: Basil Green, Dave Thorne, Peter McClurg and Bill Galloway. Squatting: Keith Corrans.

Canberra bombers

NEGOTIATIONS BETWEEN THE FEDERAL GOVERNMENT and the British Government had been ongoing since September 1956 concerning our participation in Britain's defence undertakings in Africa and the Middle East. The Federal Prime Minister, Sir Roy Welensky, considered the acquisition of Canberra bombers important to the Federation for fuller support to the Baghdad Treaty signatories. Though this was opposed by a number of Federal politicians, negotiations with Britain for the on-take of the bombers continued.

The Suez Crisis delayed communications on the issue until Mr Duncan Sandys, the British Minister of Defence, wrote a letter to Sir Roy Welensky dated 13 August 1957 to say that 18 RAF Canberra B2 bombers had been earmarked for refurbishment for the RRAF. In light of today's prices, the cost to the Federal Government of £18,310,000 for eighteen jet bombers seems remarkable. At the same time, plans were being made for RRAF Vampires to spend time in Aden to foster good relations with Britain's Middle East Command and to prepare for situations of limited and global war. When ready to do so, RRAF Canberras would also participate.

The first flight of four Canberra B2 bombers, led by Squadron Leader Charles Paxton, arrived at Thornhill where they were met by a large welcoming crowd including the Air Force Commander, every man on station and many wives with their children.

This lovely-looking aircraft held special interest for me because my second cousin, William Petter, had designed it. His father had designed the famous WW II 'behind the lines' short-field workhorse, the Lysander, and William followed in his father's footsteps. He designed a bomber that all the recognised aircraft manufacturers refused to take on. In desperation he eventually approached the English Electric Corporation who had not until then been involved directly in the production of aircraft.

Canberra B2 bombers at Thornhill.

In this group photograph taken in front of a Canadair, my uncle Squadron Leader Bill Smith (seated 7th from left) was OC of the transport squadron. Future OCs are Peter Barnett (seated 6th from left), George Alexander (seated 9th from left) and Mike Gedye (squatting 2nd from left).

Subject to design modifications to incorporate English Electric in-house technology, William Petter's bomber was taken on and become Britain's first jet bomber and a great success for the manufacturer.

As chief design-engineer for the company, William was also instrumental in designing the prototype of the Lightning interceptor. Later he designed a low-cost fighter that became the Folland Gnat.

Not only had the Royal Rhodesian Air Force strike power increased with the addition of Nos 5 and 6 (Canberra) Squadrons, No 3 (Transport) Squadron's lift capacity was substantially enhanced with the addition of four Canadairs (DC4 M-2 Argonaut) aircraft, each powered by four Merlin engines. The Federation was establishing a fair-sized balanced Air Force and there were rumours that we would be getting Hunter GF9s in the near future. All of this was very exciting for the likes of myself!

The Colin Graves tragedy

AFTER THE FIRST CANBERRAS ARRIVED, No 1 Squadron was preparing a formation aerobatic team to participate at the 'Elizabethville Air Show'. The reason for the Belgian invitation to our Air Force to participate in their great show at Elizabethville in the Katanga Province of the Congo is lost to me. Nevertheless the Vampires were to put on a formation aerobatics display and the newly acquired Canberras were to give solo and formation demonstrations.

As Squadron Commander Colin Graves led a formation team of four aircraft with Mike Reynolds No 2, Peter McClurg No 3, and Randy du Rand No 4. Norman Walsh was one of two reserve pilots and, though I led him on a couple of pairs formation aerobatic practices, I only recall him flying with the initial team of six on a couple of occasions. Then the team was reduced to four because of Vampire power limitations.

Colin had taken his team out into the flying area for some days before he felt ready to come to the airfield to have his prepared sequence viewed and evaluated. The results were pleasing and we all felt good about having such a team to show off Rhodesian talent. Most Air Forces around the world boasted national aerobatics teams of which the Black Arrows team (Hunters) of the RAF was closest to us by association.

However, there was an enormous gap between handling demands on pilots flying formation aerobatics on Hunters and those doing the same in Vampires. The Vampire's power margins were really too small and engine response too slow for formation aerobatics, placing unusually high demands on pilots to hold a steady station in all manoeuvres. Typically a jet suited to formation aerobatics would have at least 25% power reserve and rapid response engines. The Vampire at best had 10% reserve with relatively poor thrust response to throttle.

The old Control Tower, soon to be demolished, incorporated an outside balcony that served as a perfect place from which to watch Colin's team go through its routines. Together with others, I was on this balcony on 6 May 1959 waiting for another

Vampires.

Old Control Tower.

in a series of display practices when I happened to notice that Wing Commander Wilson was joining us.

Colin had completed a barrel roll running across our front from east to west before leading the formation in a long sweeping climb to starboard during which the aircraft, all FB9s, changed from finger four to box formation. In this pattern and still in the turn, the formation kept coming around descending to gain speed for a loop directly in front of us.

Before the aircraft reached the top of the loop Randy du Rand, as No 4, had fallen back two aircraft lengths from his correct position. Immediately Wing Commander Wilson crossed the platform at a run and went racing off down the stairway. Most of us saw this out of the corner of the eye but thought nothing of it because our attention was focused on the formation.

In the descent Randy's aircraft moved forward but overshot slightly, his nose coming under the leader's tail plane as the formation swept through the bottom of the loop. As the aircraft pitched into the climb Colin's aircraft dropped in turbulence and his tail plane was removed as it smashed through Randy's canopy. This created a shower of flashing debris that seemed to stop dead in mid-air with the aircraft passing on. Without its tail plane, Colin's aircraft pitched down from its shallow climb into a shallow dive then rolled inverted and disappeared from view behind a line of gum trees on Thornhill's western boundary. A huge angry red fireball enveloped in black smoke rose into view a couple of seconds later.

We were staring in disbelief when I pointed to Wing Commander Wilson's speeding staff car. How he had sensed what was coming we could not say but from the start he had been heading directly for the crash site.

That the much-loved and respected Colin Graves was dead there could be no doubt and one was left wondering how the decision not to fit life-saving ejector seats could be justified on the basis of high costs. Compared to the loss of this experienced officer and father of two young children it seemed such a petty issue. But then our attention was drawn from the tragedy to a new situation. Randy, though still flying, was in mortal danger.

The impact with Colin's tail plane had shattered Randy's canopy. The thick armoured glass of his windscreen, still encased in its battered frame, had been pushed past the gunsight and lay across Randy's arms fully exposing his head and upper body to high-speed airflow. This might have been tolerable had the visor on Randy's helmet not been shattered too. Fortunately his oxygen mask was still in place and prevented Randy from an air drowning.

With blood being driven into his eyes by the airflow, Randy could not see a thing. Fortunately he did not lose consciousness, his mask and earphones continued to function and he could still move throttle and control column. Peter McLurg had seen the collision right next to him but instantly lost Colin's aircraft when it pitched out of sight. Like Mike Reynolds, Peter moved away slightly but he kept his eye on Randy whose aircraft was climbing.

Peter knew that Colin had ploughed in and, closing his mind to this horror, switched his full attention to Randy who reported that he was blind. Peter moved in and became Randy's eyes by calling his climb angle and telling him which way to roll to keep wings level. Holding formation on Randy, Peter asked him to start throttling back and continued informing Randy of his flight attitude, speed and engine rpm.

Randy du Rand.   *Peter McLurg.*

Randy considered bailing out but Peter McLurg insisted he was safer where he was and assured Randy he would guide him in for a safe landing. After discussion, Randy agreed that a wheels-up landing on the large open expanses of cut grass was safer than attempting to bail out or risking a blind landing on the relatively narrow tarmac runway. By this time Randy, now flying at reduced speed, could see just enough to hold formation on Peter.

All attention was on the two dots descending towards the airfield. Anyone not knowing of the drama in the air would not have guessed that the pilot of one aircraft could hardly see. Everything looked normal except for the fact that the aircraft were not aligned with the main runway. On short finals Randy's descent suddenly increased towards high-tension power-lines running between the railway and the airfield boundary fence. He responded to Peter's urgent "Pull up—check—hold it— descend—close throttle—start rounding out—a bit more— touch down now!"

Peter McLurg was overshooting as Randy's aircraft bellied onto the grass. High friction pitched the aircraft nose down, lifting the tail so high it remained visible above flying debris and a great cloud of red dust. Having travelled about 200 metres, the aircraft went into a slow turn and was lost to view in dust before it came to rest facing back along the line of torn-up grass. A staff car seen tearing across the grass paddock from the Tower disappeared into the dust cloud. When it cleared

we could see Randy being helped out of his wrecked cockpit by the one and only Mac Geeringh; ever ready to help anyone in trouble.

An inspection of the crash site suggested that Colin had deliberately rolled his stricken aircraft to avoid crashing into a particular house. The engine had buried itself into the ground but three of the 20mm cannons broke loose and somersaulted ahead of airframe wreckage. In another house, a Rhodesian Railways man was fast asleep in his bed, having come off night duty. He was awakened by the loud noise of one cannon smashing through his window and driving sideways through a large wardrobe. It had passed just a couple of inches above his body. Two other cannons passed either side of the man's two small children who were playing in the driveway. These came to rest at the back of his garage, one each side of his unscathed car. These were lucky people but Colin was not the only casualty that day. An old man seeking to give assistance died of a heart attack before reaching the crash site.

Prior to the accident, a routine medical examination showed that one of Randy's eyes had become weaker than the other, but not to the extent that he could not pass the compulsory six-monthly flying fitness test. When he had fully recovered from the accident, it was established that the bang he had received on his head might have been the reason his faulty eye had returned to normal.

Air shows

FOLLOWING THE DEATH OF COLIN we received a new squadron commander. Squadron Leader Sandy Mutch's posting to No 1 Squadron brought our OC's rank into line with the other squadrons. He took over leadership of Colin's formation aerobatic team and had it ready in time for the 'Elizabethville Show'.

After this there were air shows in Broken Hill and Lusaka in Northern Rhodesia and a number of others in Southern Rhodesia. Each involved flying displays by all squadrons. My involvement with other junior officers was manning static displays of aircraft and equipment. It happened to be a very pleasant task because spectators showed so much interested in the aircraft. When the flying started I could watch every display from start to finish because all spectators were doing the same. There were two particular displays that stick in my mind. They were given by Canberra and Vampire FB9 solo routines, both at Broken Hill.

Squadron Leader Charles Paxton flew the Canberra. Like most bombers, this aircraft was not stressed for aerobatics even though, without the encumbrance of bombs and long-range fuel tanks, it could perform lovely-looking loops and barrel rolls.

Charles opened his display with a high-speed pass followed by loops and barrel rolls. Next came tight turns at very slow speed so that spectators could see bomb doors opening for a close look into the bomb bay. In the next turn undercarriage was lowered to show the sequencing of wheel doors and gear, again at close range. Two more turns were made with bomb doors closing and wheels retracting before full power was applied in the last turn which developed into a thunderous sounding steep climb-out followed by a powerless and silent descending turn back towards the crowd.

Still holding crowd attention, Charles whispered past the crowd flying slowly with full flap and wheels down. At this point John Mussell opened his display with an ultra low-level,

Charles Paxton (right) seen here with his navigator, John Digby (centre) and 'Numpie' Phillips, Station Adjutant.

high-speed pass under the Canberra, flying in the opposite direction then pulled up into the loop that opened his sequence. John Mussell had flown the FB9 solo aerobatic display for some time before Bob Woodward arrived from the RAF with his own polished version of low-level aerobatics flown in a T11.

Bob, who had been the top solo aerobatist in RAF Central Flying School in the mid 1950s, flew a close-in compact display at relatively slow speed that only pilots could appreciate because of the flying skills involved. John Mussell on the other hand flew to please the public. Flat out at full power he provided the noise and speed expected by all civilian spectators.

John's run under the Canberra was so low that many people standing two or more rows back heard but did not see the FB9 flash by. The crowd loved the noisy surprise, which resulted, according to the newspapers, in two of Broken Hill's pregnant ladies being carted off to the maternity home ahead of schedule.

Because he was so fast, John's first loop took him almost out of sight before he came down in a forty-five degrees inverted dive. Leaving his roll-out very late, he entered a second loop with plenty of crowd-pleasing speed and noise. He continued on with his sequence for about five minutes, throwing in every aerobatic manoeuvre before making a slow roll along the viewing line at very, very, low level as only John could do. He then pulled up sharply into a vertical climb intending to execute a left-hand stall turn, again high up.

John Mussell.

I do not recall what went wrong. The aircraft was pivoting around its left wing when suddenly it started a rotation. This tightened as the aircraft descended. When John had done more than six turns in an ever-tightening spin, it seemed he would not recover from the dreaded condition for which the FB9 had such a bad reputation. It was obvious that John would have trouble bailing out and I had a picture in my mind of what he was experiencing up there as the crowd clapped and cheered this 'spectacular manoeuvre'. When it looked as if there was no hope, the aircraft snapped out of the spin and John stole the show by continuing his noisy display as if nothing untoward had happened. The crowd certainly did not realise how close they had come to witnessing a disaster!

On return to Thornhill there was a fuss over the Canberra that Charles Paxton had been flying. Many of the rivets in the fin and rear fuselage had popped, indicating that the aircraft had exceeded its structural limitations. Though the damage was easily repaired, Canberra pilots were immediately banned from making any aerobatic manoeuvre.

Standing: Officers of No 1 Squadron at the time Sandy Mutch assumed command. From left to right: Eric Cary, Keith Corrans, Mike Reynolds, Ted Stevenson, Eddie Wilkinson, Peter McLurg, Bob Woodward, Sandy Mutch, Norman Walsh, Randy du Rand, Justin Varkivisser, Basil Green, Dave Thorne, Bill Galloway and PB. Kneeling is Warrant Officer Jimmy Stewart whose incredibly small team of dedicated technicians maintained an ongoing 90% daily line availability of sixteen Vampires; the equivalent of one and a half aircraft per man. The man sitting second to the right of Jimmy, on secondment from the RAF, was used to at least three men per aircraft.

Flypasts

NO 1 SQUADRON WAS OFTEN INVOLVED in formation flypasts for a variety of special occasions. In the latter half of my first year on the squadron I was included in formation flypasts over parades held for the Queen's Birthday, the Governor-General of the Federation inspection of forces and the Battle of Britain Commemoration Parade. Little preparation was required for formating pilots but the formation leaders had to practise for the split-second accuracy needed to pass over a parade bang on time. This was much more difficult to achieve than was apparent to observers on the ground.

The first requirement was to know the exact order of parade, the height and 'time zero' for the first formation to be overhead. Also needed were timings and heights for those following. Time Zero inevitably coincided with the last note of the Royal Anthem. The parade would remain at the 'Present' until the last formation noise had abated sufficiently for the parade commander's voice to carry to all units on parade.

An Air Force officer on the ground (air co-ordinator) had to time parade rehearsal so that he would be in a position to give the formation leaders a running commentary on what was happening on the parade ground with a countdown to 'Zero'.

Formation leaders would usually fly a reverse pattern from the parade ground to their intended holding point to establish precisely how many minutes and seconds it took to fly the route. Having established this, they would then fly their intended path a few times to prove their timings for the actual parade when they would be leading whole formations.

Out of sight and hearing of the parade each formation flew a racetrack pattern in its assigned waiting area, well separated by height and distance for safety's sake. Each leader knew how long it would take from any position in his racetrack pattern to get to the parade ground on time and on correct heading. But seldom did the timings of the practice match those of the official parade. This made a formation leader's job a very tricky business.

The problems in getting timings right were almost always due to unexpected actions by the reviewing officer. This is

Formation of six Vampires.

the sort of information from the Air Force co-ordinator that formation leaders dreaded, but had to be prepared for:

"No sight of the Reviewing Officer's car yet—already running five seconds late—Oh! Here he comes—he is driving slower than expected—pulling up behind dais now—56 seconds—Governor General climbing out of the car—51 seconds—Oh boy, he has turned to the crowd and not the dais—moving to greet someone on the front seats—still talking—looks like he might move now—yes—51 seconds—climbing steps now—taking position—35 seconds—presenting arms—Royal salute—28 seconds."

The leaders of slow aircraft faced the greatest difficulties when this type of thing happened because, to make the distance, they would have been running in, even before the reviewing officer's car came into view. Having reduced speed to meet the first five-second delay they then faced the unexpected problem of the reviewing officer turning to greet someone giving no option but to go into a 180-degree turn. But how tight? How long before the reviewing officer moves to the dais? Problems such as these were greater for a leader of cumbersome Dakota formations than for leaders of smaller nimble aircraft such as the Provosts. For the helicopters that came later this was a piece of cake.

When helicopters led flypasts Provosts, Dakotas, Vampires, Canberras and Hunters followed them in that order. I recall the reviewing officer of one parade in Bulawayo making so many changes to his briefed routine that the helicopters, Provosts and Dakotas passed over the parade at the same time; one formation stepped closely above the other. Happily the spectators thought this was intentional and were suitably impressed. Just a few seconds further delay would have had the aircraft passing in reverse order before the Royal Anthem had been played out.

Formation leaders were generally cool characters who always considered pilots' difficulties formating on them. Sandy Mutch, being a highly excitable character, was not one of

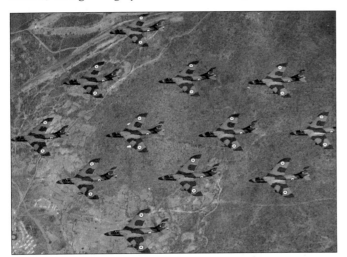

In four years' time we would see twelve-ship Hunter formations such as this.

these and being led by him was usually bloody dangerous. For example, we were doing a six-machine Vampire flypast for a parade in Luanshya in Northern Rhodesia when Sandy became uncertain of his position. At a very late stage he suddenly saw the parade area at ninety degrees to his left and without any warning banked sharply. I was the second aircraft on the port side where I had to roll rapidly and pull away to avoid collision with the inside aircraft, whose pilot had been forced to do the same. My breakaway put me well outside the formation forcing me to close rapidly, so rapidly in fact that I was banking steeply to check closing speed as the formation passed over the parade. In this case the observers could not possibly have been impressed.

It must be said however that the standard of leadership and of formation flying in general improved noticeably as the Air Force increased in size and experience.

Aden detachment

IN LATE SEPTEMBER 1959 WE learned that No 8 Squadron of the RAF was to be temporarily detached from Aden to Cyprus and that No 1 Squadron was to fill in for the month of November.

Preparatory to going on the squadron's third trip to Aden, I passed my Green Card Instrument Rating test and gained a First Line Servicing Certificate. The squadron's entire weapons allocations for the balance of the financial year was made available for intensified weapons training and emphasis was given to formating in cloud.

Two days before our departure, a Canadair set off from New Sarum to drop technical staging parties and Air Traffic Controllers at three airfields along our route, and to take the detachment technicians to Aden. On its return, the Canadair recovered the staging parties.

Our route to Aden was via Chileka, Dar es Salaam and Mogadishu. The legs, Chileka to Dar es Salaam and on to Mogadishu, were flown in almost continuous cloud, which I found very hard going because, whilst in cloud, I suffered continuously from 'the leans'. Flying No 4 in a tight-finger four-starboard position I felt as if we were in a continuous steep left-hand turn orbiting over one spot. When cloud density allowed me to see the lead aircraft it was not so bad, but on many occasions the cloud was so dense that I could see no more than the red wing-tip of Mike Reynold's aircraft, on which I was formating. Coming out of cloud and being able to see all the aircraft was a great relief.

At Dar es Salaam my whole canopy and front windscreen

misted up on short finals, forcing me to roll back the canopy on touch down so that I could see the edge of the runway to hold line up. As soon as the aircraft was rolling slow enough I undid my straps and stood on the rudder pedals looking over the top of the windscreen to taxi into dispersals in blistering hot conditions.

Our pre-positioned ground crews, shirtless, bathed in sweat and smiling as always, brought superbly cold bottles of Coca-Cola to each pilot. Refuelling and aircraft turn-round for my formation was very slick and had been completed just before the next formation of four taxiied in.

We stayed overnight in Dar es Salaam but once in the air-conditioned hotel few of our number ventured out into the oppressive heat. Following an early breakfast, we were ready to return to the airport. Early though it was, the air was muggy and we were all sweating in our flying overalls even before climbing aboard a steamy airless bus.

One was supposed to be airborne with gear raised before turning on the Vampire's Godfrey air-conditioning unit. However, it was so hot that I am sure I was not the only pilot who rolled the air-conditioner control wheel to maximum cold as soon as we were at full power on the take-off run. The inrush of cold air provided instant relief and allowed me to enjoy the sight of endless palm trees stretching across the vast land that sank away from the climbing formation. Zanzibar Island was in full sunshine as we passed it, still in the climb. Brilliant colours varying from deep blue water to light turquoise over shallow coral reefs contrasted strongly with Persil-white beaches of mainland and island. It looked just as spectacular as the glossy travel magazines showed it. But the view was short-lived.

Back in cloud all the way to Mogadishu, I again suffered the sensation of that damned continuous left turn. About ten minutes out of Mogadishu we picked up the unmistakable and most comforting voice of Flight Lieutenant Peter Cooke. He had pre-positioned at Mogadishu Airport, which ran parallel and close to the beach, with his portable device that gave him the directions he would give us to steer to reach the airfield. Peter told us that the cloud base was down to 500 feet over the airfield that was covered by thin sea mist, but he thought that the cloud base was somewhat higher and visibility better out at sea. Having heard this, Bob Woodward changed heading with the intention of breaking cloud over water east of Mogadishu.

At around 1,500 feet above sea level the descent rate and flying speed had been reduced when we passed through particularly dense cloud and encountered a patch of severe turbulence. Mike Reynolds, upon whom I was formating, lost visual contact with the leader's wing-tip and immediately pulled up and out of my sight. I broke starboard and reverted to instruments.

In reply to Mike's call Bob gave his heading, speed, power settings and rate of descent. Mike said he would add five degrees to leader's heading to ensure safe separation and I advised Bob that I had added ten degrees. Peter McLurg in the meanwhile had managed to hold station on Bob's port wing.

When Bob broke out he broadcast that, because of dark and murky conditions, he had not seen the sea surface until he was dangerously low and was now turning for Mogadishu. I commenced my turn onto the heading Peter Cooke gave Bob, my descent rate having been reduced from 500 feet per minute to 300 fpm.

Even though I was switching my attention rapidly from instruments to what lay ahead, no distinctive cloud base or horizon came into view. At 300 feet I levelled off on instruments in what looked like smoky-grey cloud when I saw a small fishing boat that appeared to be suspended on its white wake in the grey murk where sea and cloud blended as one. Shortly thereafter I picked up dull white sand dunes directly ahead and in a moment I passed over the beach and runway. Gingerly I eased my way around to land fairly close behind Mike whom I had not seen until I rolled out on runway line-up. Fortunately there was no recurrence of canopy misting when I throttled back. Once out of the cockpit in hot humid air, the technicians plied us with ice-cold Cokes that we gulped down whilst rubbing sore butts and exchanging individual accounts of our hairy arrival.

Mogadishu's runway was not suited to a full-formation take-off so we took off for the last leg in pairs. Once airborne, Bob reduced power and levelled off until Mike and I had come up on his starboard side. As soon as our climb was established, we entered cloud and remained there throughout the climb to 29,000 feet.

Soon the cloud gave way to cirrus and then cleared completely. It was a joy to open out into battle formation and feel relaxed after flying hundreds of miles in cloud. Below us was endless desert, which I was seeing for the first time in my life. The barren land of sand and rocks supporting a few clumps of brown scrub looked so uninviting that I found myself wondering why so much blood had been shed for this vast desolate land called Somalia.

The desert seemed to go on forever until we reached the mountainous region in the north. We crossed the coast at Berbera with Djibouti visible on our left. Out over the Gulf of Aden a surprisingly large number of vessels, trailing long wakes, headed to and from the Red Sea. Our descent commenced long before the Arabian coastline was visible.

When Aden Bay and the distinctive mass of Mount Shamsham came into view we remained in loose formation, long enough to take a look at the peninsula on which Mount Shamsham, Aden town and the suburb of Crater stood separated from the mainland by a narrow isthmus.

Across the entire width of this isthmus lay the runway of RAF Kormaksar with beach and sea at both ends. The only road linking the mainland to Aden ran right across the centre of the runway with RAF buildings spread out over a large area on the Aden side. Apart from the sea, everything looked just as dismal to me as the brown African desert behind us.

We ran in along the runway in echelon starboard for a

standard formation break onto downwind. Whilst in the descending turn for landing, I noticed that the water was shallow for some distance out into Aden Bay. Later I was told that sharks favoured this particular patch, but in all the landings I made thereafter I never spotted one.

The moment I switched off the air-conditioner on landing I became aware of the heat and high humidity that had me sweating during the long taxi run to dispersals. The Commanding Officer of RAF Kormaksar and our ever-cheerful, shirtless sweating technicians welcomed us. The CO then led us to our poorly lit, dull-looking crew-room.

Next we were shown the aircrew changing-room. The stench from the sweat-stained flying overalls hanging on lines of hooks was overpowering. My first impression was that our RAF counterparts were not up on their hygiene but within a week I realised that our kit looked and smelled the same.

It was late afternoon so we were taken to our billets to settle in and clean up. We then went to the 'Jungle Bar' adjoining the Officers' Mess. This was a large area under a trellised canopy covered by creepers where one could sit and enjoy a drink in good company under coloured lights with a gentle breeze coming from banks of electric fans. The RAF officers insisted that this was a cool time of the year and suggested we try Aden in July when sweat ran so freely that one only needed to urinate every third day, no matter how much one drank.

Our accommodation was good; four men sharing a room with plenty of fans and decent ablutions. Apart from the Jungle Bar, there was a large air-conditioned bar where drinks were served at amazingly low prices, Aden being a duty-free port.

It was in this bar that I first acquired a taste for beer because it was inexpensive and I found it to be the most effective thirst quencher. I enjoyed the fact that the beer did not intoxicate me at sea level as it did in Rhodesia at 5,000 feet. Presumably the high rate at which one's body sweated had a part to play in this.

Some distance from base, beyond Aden town on the southern end of the peninsula was the Tarshayn Officers' Club where we could take a swim in the sea in safety behind rusty pole-borne shark nets. The beach was clean, the water crystal-clear and tepid but the sun made daytime swimming so unpleasant for me that I only swam at night. Most of my visits to this club were with Bob Woodward who did not seem to be too popular with the other squadron pilots. I never did get to know why because I got on well with him. Bob, a thickset man of medium height, displayed amazing agility by frequently executing a string of seemingly effortless flick-flack somersaults along the beach.

All travel to Aden town and the club was by taxi. The cost was not high but the driving habits of the Arab drivers were maddening. No Arab driver I met could cruise at a constant speed. It was a case of foot on accelerator to speed up and foot off to slow down. The continuous forward and rearward force on one's body, about every three seconds, sometimes turned annoyance into hysterical laughter. Vehicle maintenance was poor and only when the hooter failed was a vehicle considered seriously unserviceable because it was used constantly, even on deserted stretches of road.

The only driver I encountered who could cruise was a fellow from India who had spent time in Britain. He complained about Aden drivers. He said that in India nobody obeyed the rules of the road so every driver knew where he stood. In Britain everyone obeyed the rules so, again, everybody knew precisely where they stood; but in Aden some obeyed and others did not which made driving plain dangerous.

There was a peculiarity about shopkeepers in Aden; they could spot a Rhodesian way off and would start shouting, "Hello Rhodesia. Hello Rhodesia, come see my shop." How they distinguished us from the RAF people we could not tell. Our clothing was the same as our RAF counterparts, we wore the same wristwatches and sandals yet even ex-RAF Brits serving in the RRAF were immediately identified as Rhodesians.

One particular shopkeeper called Smiley gained most of our business because he had the best shop in town. I was there one afternoon when the most beautiful woman I have ever seen, even to this day, came gliding through the door. Dressed in white and obviously Eurasian, everything about this tall lady was so absolutely perfect that I wondered if I was looking at an angel. Moments later, her husband dressed in white slacks and jacket, came in. He was impossibly handsome and so neat despite the heat that I felt doubly sure that God had sent down His angels—but why to Aden?

When the couple, whose English-speaking voices and accents matched their looks, left the shop to return to their ship, I could not remember why I had come into the shop. Smiley, realising I was in a tizzy over the couple, laughed and told me that they were film stars from India who stopped over in Aden from time to time on their many sea cruises to the USA and Europe.

Having been brought back to earth, I remembered that I had come to buy something to take home to Beryl. One item I bought was an elaborately painted, hand-operated sewing machine called a Lion, a direct copy of the Singer sewing machine. Yvonne Stajer, Beryl's sister, eventually took this machine to Canada where it is still rated as a good collector's item.

Smiley talked me into looking at some special German brassières that he said were tops in women's underwear. Knowing no better, I took him at his word and looked at them; but I had no idea what size to take. He was gesturing cup size with his hand when I noticed an RAF wife in the shop who was about Beryl's build. Much to my embarrassment Smiley called the woman over and I left with two pairs of bras and a set of seven knickers embroidered for every day of the week. When I gave these to Beryl she laughed, saying the knickers would not fit a ten-year-old; but she said nothing about the bras. For years they remained amongst her underclothing until, I guess, she found someone to give them to, unused!

We were instructed to attend an Officers' Dining-in Night that was quite unlike any I had known in Rhodesia. There were four RAF squadrons on base together with all the supporting services; so about a hundred officers sat down in full mess dress at superbly laid tables. Even before the main course was over, large quantities of salt tablets, ever present in bowls on the dining tables, were being thrown up into the fast rotating overhead fans that propelled them around the room like shotgun pellets. Next came little balls that exploded when thrown at any surface offering moderate resistance. Hilarious laughter, flying tablets, bangs and smoke filled a room that seemed more like a Goon Show set than a gathering of Her Majesty officers. I must say we Rhodesians found it great fun, probably because such behaviour would never have been condoned at home.

We received our flight briefings in the Station Operations Room where the air-conditioning was so cold that having to return to the hot air outside was like walking into a blast furnace. Doctors had told us that going from cold into the heat was more likely to bring on flu than moving from hot to cold, but none of us was any worse off for the twice daily Ops Room visits.

The first briefing was for those of us who were new to the Aden Protectorate. This was for an orientation cruise up the eastern coast to the Oman border, along the northern border with Saudi Arabia, down the western border with Yemen then out to Pemba Island in the Red Sea.

Along the route the features we would use in the following days were pointed out. Radar-controlled anti-aircraft guns along the Yemeni border presented a threat which necessitated both height and distance separation, which we plotted on our maps as we cruised by.

The sheer height of the rugged mountains running along the north and west region impressed me more than I had expected. Steep slopes with tumble-down rocks and narrow ravines running into dry twisting wadis gave way to lush green agricultural strips between the mountains' edge and the dry desert. Beyond the green, the dry watercourses followed haphazard lines that dissipated and were lost on barren sand. Clusters of mud-structured buildings were on every prominent hill adjacent to the green belts. Building on mountain foothills was to gain relief from high day temperatures and freezing cold air that settled over the desert floor at night.

When we were issued with our maps, we were instructed to mark the boundaries of 'Prescribed Areas'. The governor-general of Aden had to sanction these as 'No Go Areas' for all living souls, animals included. Any sign of life within a Prescribed Area demanded immediate offensive action with air weapons best suited to terrain and target.

Along with our maps, we were issued with cards in English and Arabic that the RAF nicknamed 'gooly chits'. In the event of coming down beyond secure locations, a pilot was to hand his gooly chit to the first person he encountered. The chit offered a £10,000 sterling reward for returning a pilot, alive,

to any British authority. However, there was a problem with this. The Yemeni Government offered twice this amount for any British serviceman brought in, whether dead or alive. We heard some terrible stories about mutilated bodies of downed pilots being dragged for all to see through the streets of Sana, capital of Yemen.

Some specially trained Army and Air Force men assigned to roam within and beyond the Prescribed Areas were employed to find the locations of the communist-backed terrorists who were waging a war of independence against Britain. These specialists were also highly trained to conduct forward air control (FAC) of strikes by bombers and fighter-bombers against enemy targets.

We had been told of these individuals who spent long, dangerous periods in the desert turning them into pretty strange characters who needed to return to base from time to time to regain some level of sanity in safe and civilised surroundings. I saw two of these men whose skin was almost black where their Arab clothing had not given their otherwise white skin protection from the sun. They were on recall for six weeks of total rest and recuperation. They seemed to stick to themselves and their eye movements and physical actions made it clear that they were 'different'.

From time to time the special agents, known as Air Liaison Officers (ALO), called for strikes within Prescribed Areas and sometimes as punitive actions against headmen who were known to be assisting terrorists. It was easy enough to respond to calls for air actions against terrorists, but punitive strikes against headmen required a great deal of preparation. When any headman had been identified as having assisted terrorists, the British Governor-General had to approve punitive action before it was taken.

If this involved an air strike, photo-reconnaissance was flown to positively identify the headman's house and pamphlets were airdropped or hand-delivered to every person in or near the headman's village. This was to allow the headman time to empty his home and to let his people know the British were going to punish him for being a bad lad for having helped terrorists. The pamphlets told everyone the day and time that the headman's house was to be destroyed and suggested were they should go for their own safety. The venue chosen was invariably a high position to give everyone a good view of the event.

Such an occasion occurred whilst we were there and I witnessed the event when Varky and Randy were tasked to destroy a three-storey house that was separated from neighbours by very narrow streets. To cater for the flight path of 60-pound. squash-head rockets, only one direction of attack was possible.

The ALO identified the ridge on which he and a large gathering of people were assembled, and we could see them all clearly. Varky's salvo of four rockets scored direct hits on the house. To start with, the combined effect of the explosions seemed to have taken out the entire village until the huge dust-cloud drifted off to expose a heap of rubble where the headman's house had stood. Only a small portion of the bottom storey, at the rear of the downed house, remained above street-level. I thought there was no more to be done, but Randy fired a pair of rockets with such accuracy that no damage extended across the road and no portion of the house remained standing.

The ALO said everyone, including the headman, was very impressed but the headman's immediate neighbours were very disappointed that they would not be able to claim for damages from the British Government.

We had only been in Aden ten days when I was tasked to accompany Flight Lieutenant Buster Web of the RAF, who was to be the RAF's Air Liaison Officer (ALO) to an Army convoy travelling from Aden to Dhala in the mountains. My job was to assist Buster and learn something about British Army–Air Force co-operation.

The Royal Rhodesian Air Force had trained Buster but, together with Barry Raffel, Cyril White, Bernard du Plessis, Roy Morris and Doug Bebbington, he had left Rhodesia on completion of his SSU course to join the RAF. The latter four officers were destined to rejoin the RRAF but, at that time, they were all flying Venoms on No 8 Squadron. Why Buster had remained behind in Aden when the rest of his squadron was in Cyprus, I cannot say. I only remember him saying he was not too keen about the Dhala route, which he referred to as 'ambush alley'.

An Army Arab levy drove the open Land Rover in which Buster and I travelled behind the armoured vehicle carrying the convoy commander who headed the long line of vehicles. Numerous armoured vehicles and covered trucks stretched back about two kilometres. Our drive started by crossing the centre of the main runway at Kormaksar, this being the only route from Aden to the interior. Once through Shaykh 'Uthman we entered the open desert which was hot, dusty and boring.

In the late afternoon, camp was established about five kilometres short of the mountain range that ran square across our route. The extreme cold of the desert and the loud incessant crackling and chatter on the Army radio network made it seem a very long night.

Before sunrise we had coffee and set off on a road along the bed of a steep-sided gently winding wadi (watercourse) running through mountains for most of the remaining distance to Dhala. At the end of this wadi the road left the watercourse to climb up the southern side of a steep mountain face known as the Dhala Pass. On the opposite side, high rough mountain faces overlooked the narrow roadway all the way to the high plateau where the village of Dhala stood. This was the section that gave the route the name 'Ambush Alley'. The entire wadi line and, more especially the pass itself, offered perfect terrain for terrorist ambushes. They could hide in strength amongst rocks and scrub, attack from behind excellent cover, then melt into the rugged countryside behind.

We had been running up the wadi for about an hour when the lead vehicle came to an abrupt halt and the commander leapt out onto the road. Behind us all vehicles bunched up and stopped as soldiers ran to take up defensive positions under a barrage of loud commands. Buster went forward to the Army commander to establish what was going on. I saw the Army commander pointing to the right mountain ridge as they talked. Buster then shouted to me, "Call Air." I had absolutely no idea what the fuss was about nor did I know how to call up aircraft because I had not been told how to. So, having heard RAF pilots use a callsign in jest, I transmitted, "Pig's Arse, Pig's Arse, this is Dhala ALO. Do you read? Over."

To my surprise and great delight I received an immediate reply. I said where we were and two Venoms arrived overhead in less than a minute, by which time Buster had returned to our vehicle. He told the Venom pilots that one soldier had been hit. This may have been a lone sniper but there was no way of knowing if more terrorists were about. The jets made passes along the ridges even though there was virtually no hope of seeing bandits in that rough country. The real value of the Venom presence was to dissuade anyone from taking on the stationary convoy.

A large-calibre musket round had passed through the side of one of the convoy trucks, ripped away half of a soldier's right buttock, and lodged in the seat between two soldiers sitting opposite him. Buster requested the lead Venom to call in a Twin Pioneer transporter to uplift the casualty back to base.

For almost an hour we waited for the Pioneer. I did not hear or see this twin-engined high-wing light transport aircraft until it was already rolling along the floor of the wadi. It was amazing to see that it had landed on unprepared ground then picked up the casualty without stopping engines. Immediately the Pioneer took off in a reverse run of no more than 200 metres. Its pilot told Buster on radio that his casualty was all smiles because he knew he would be flying back to Britain before the day was out. "Wait till the morphine wears off, most of the poor bugger's arse is missing."

The rest of the trip to Dhala was uneventful and we spent a pleasant evening with the OC of the Army company we had come to relieve and return to Aden. I was amused to hear the amiable posh-speaking Army major progressively revert to his natural Cockney accent as gins and tonic took effect. The next morning we were on the road again and reached Aden that evening following a disappointingly trouble-free trip.

On the 16th November 1959, I flew wingman to Varky on a call to strike a specific location near the base of the deep Wadi Adzzh that ran through the highest mountain range northeast of Aden and close to the Saudi border. Terrorists were reported by an ALO to be based up at this specific spot. We ran east along the mountain ridge with Wadi Adzzh on our starboard side. As Varky came abreast of the target location he called "Turning in live" and rolled right into a steep dive down the deep valley. Smoke was streaming from his guns as I followed about 1,500 meters behind him. His strikes were concentrated and easy to see.

When Varky broke off his attack and pulled up left, I started firing all four 20mm cannons with my sight set high above the target. I had not fired all four cannons together before and revelled in the noise, airframe shudder and the sight of my very first rounds exploding right on target. I was impressed by the length of time the firing continued before all four guns stopped as one.

I then turned hard to port pulling up sharply to align with the short eastward leg of the wadi. The only route out was straight ahead and over the top of the mountain, because the wadi turned ninety degrees south followed by ninety degrees east that was way too tight a route to follow. As soon as the aircraft was angled for the summit, I realised I was in deep trouble because my speed seemed insufficient to make the ridge ahead. The Mlanje mountain experience in Nyasaland immediately came to mind and my breathing went into overdrive.

Full power had been applied the moment I pulled out of the attack, so all I could do was aim for the crest and pray. After an agonisingly slow climb, the mountain face was cleared by no more than ten feet and my FB9 was very close to stalling. Having passed the crest in a fifty-degree climb, I was able to allow the aircraft to pitch down to twenty degrees nose-down to regain flying speed. This was achieved very close to the ground on the plateau beyond the ridge, but I was able to breathe normally again. Varky was miles ahead of me turning starboard for base. By turning inside him I caught up quickly enough, but said nothing to Varky about my close shave with the mountain until we were back on the ground.

In the crew-room I learned that when firing all four cannons the usual speed build-up was severely curtailed, necessitating 7,500 rpm to be set to ensure adequate acceleration throughout the dive, particularly where such a steep climb-out was necessary. I had nearly lost my life for want of such simple yet vital information that I should have been given during my OCU. Immediately the other junior pilots were briefed on this matter.

The very next day I returned to Wadi Adzzh on a routine armed patrol, this time with Randy du Rand. I ran my eye along the path I had flown the previous day, then along the wadi's passage south then east to where it broke out onto the desert floor. At this point I saw two camels standing close to a crude single-floor mud building on the desert floor tight up against the base of the mountain. Immediately I turned in to attack the building knowing that terrorists alone were in this area. Four Squash-head rockets were launched and I pulled up really hard to clear the mountain under which the target was sited. When I looked back, I saw the camels running south into the desert but could see nothing of the house because of the dust from the explosions. After one orbit the dust had drifted away and I could see that the house had been flattened but, in almost childish enthusiasm, I turned in again to attack the

immediate surrounds with cannon fire. This time I had set the appropriate power and cleared the mountain with ease. So far as I recall, someone on the flat desert had shot at Randy and whilst I was doing my thing he was trying to find the man to give him a 'snot squirt'.

When we returned to base I reported my strikes to the operations staff. The RAF Squadron Leader in charge of the Operations Room consulted the map and told me that I had taken on a target just outside the 'Prescribed Area'. For some reason the area's eastern boundary had been extended along the wadi's south leg straight out into the desert. In consequence the final east leg of the wadi opening to the desert plus the eastern corner of the mountain range lay outside of the official 'no go area'.

I was really worried that I had made this error but the Squadron Leader, who was not a particularly friendly type, told me not to be concerned. He had no doubts that the target was legitimate. But he gave me hell for not killing the camels with my cannons instead of wasting ammunition on a worthless piece of real estate. He emphasised the need to have taken out these animals because they constituted vital transportation for terrorists. The thought of killing animals with cannon fire appalled me, but this requirement had not been spelled out strongly enough in earlier briefings.

Set in the old extinct volcanic crater of Shamsham mountain was the Arab town called Crater. We were all advised not to visit this potentially dangerous place that was strictly off limits to all servicemen during the hours of darkness. Nevertheless, Eric Cary and I were keen to make a visit to Crater town and went there by taxi one Thursday afternoon.

Once through the mountain tunnel leading into the crater, we entered a world of strange sights, sounds and smells. We walked around the narrow streets that bustled with folk moving to-and-fro into open-sided shops and amongst hundreds of street vendors selling an amazing assortment of herbal drugs, vegetables and cooked food. The smells were very inviting but the swarms of flies crawling over prepared food and vendors' faces dissuaded us from trying anything.

It was late afternoon when we turned back for the tunnel where the taxi rank was sited. Soon enough we realised that we were lost but unable to communicate with those around us. Panicking somewhat in fast fading light, we eventually picked up our bearings quite close to the taxi rank. It was then that I spotted a man following a short distance behind wearing a thick belt in which was tucked a superb ghambia (curved Arabian fighting knife) with a magnificent jewel-studded black handle showing prominently above the belt-line.

When I drew Eric's attention to the weapon, the man slowed to a crawl, his face twisting noticeably into a menacing expression. He continued to move towards us as Eric dived into an open-sided shop urging me, under his breath, to get off the street but I remained mesmerised. Next moment the shopkeeper was calling even more urgently saying I must not, under any circumstances, look at the weapon again. Feeling rather foolish I went in and pretended to be interested in a stack of rubber mats.

Out of the corner of my eye I saw the man walking slowly by. When he had gone, the shopkeeper who spoke good English told us that there were problems with that specific individual and his bejewelled ghambia. Firstly he was a renowned terrorist who was in town because it was 'market day' and secondly, it would have been incumbent upon the man, by custom, to give me his knife had I continued to admire it. In return however, I would be compelled to give him something of equal worth; but I was in no position to do this. Failure to produce a reciprocal gift simply meant forfeiture of one's life. Having been given such sobering information, Eric and I were escorted by the shopkeeper to a taxi, but not before he pressurised us into buying unwanted items from his shop.

These experiences lead us to ask questions about what the shopkeeper had said concerning 'market day'. We were told that, in the strange world of British and Arab relations, Thursday was a day when fighting stopped to allow friend and foe to go to market in safety. A recurring ceasefire existed from midnight Wednesday to midnight Thursday. Whether this very strange arrangement was true, or not, I still cannot say. Nevertheless, my impression of Arabs, developed from stories I had heard before and during the visit to Aden, was not good at all. Any doubts I had then had been totally removed by the goings-on at the RAF's crude air-weapons range which lay about ten kilometres to the north of RAF Kormaksar. This range was nothing like ours at Kutanga with its beautiful trees and wild game. It was just an area of desert sand set against the beach.

During weapons training Arabs ran about in the danger area where spent cartridge casings fell from the aircraft. The RAF Range Safety Officers were not too concerned because no amount of effort had succeeded in stopping those people from collecting spent cartridge cases that they sold over the border to Yemeni gun-makers.

The kinetic energy of a spent 20mm cartridge case reaching ground at speed was lethal. The Arab collectors knew this only too well, but it did not put them off. RAF officers said that when a collector was killed, others would rush to grab the dead man's bag, dig out the spent cartridge from head or body, and continue collecting as if nothing had happened.

On any air weapons range there is need for clearly visible targets for pilots to aim at and to measure their accuracy. Old vehicles make good targets because non-explosive practice weapons pass through a vehicle leaving it intact and reusable. Hundreds of hits could be taken before a vehicle fell to bits. But in Aden such a target would be stolen the first night it appeared. Laying down white lime as a marker was a waste of time because the mark disappeared under sand thrown up by just a few strikes. In fact a single 60-pound rocket falling short could totally obliterate a freshly laid lime marker. So, the

RAF armourers decided to overcome the problem by building a huge pyramid using old forty-four-gallon drums encased in concrete. This target took a week to build and was guarded day and night for another week to ensure that the concrete had set. However, it only took the first unguarded night for Arab thieves to destroy the entire arrangement and abscond with every single drum. The remaining concrete rubble, rejected as worthless by thieves, was then bulldozed into a heap and used for a while as a viable target.

In the last week of our detachment I managed to arrange a flight in an RAF photo-reconnaissance Meteor with Flight Lieutenant Munroe. He let me aerobat the twin-engined jet and showed me how to stall-turn the aircraft using power on the outside engine to make the manoeuvre very easy. Next I flew with Flight Lieutenant Morris in a Hunter T7 and experienced supersonic flight for the first time. Going supersonic at height was a bit of an anti-climax but low-flying the Hunter at high speed was really fantastic—though I found the servo-driven controls almost too light and sensitive. One had only to think about a manoeuvre and it seemed to occur instantly.

Having been away from my pregnant wife for four weeks, I was pleased when the time came to return home to a land of sanity. It was even more pleasing to learn that Varky and I were to fly in the RAF Shackleton that would provide search and rescue cover for No 1 Squadron's formations between Aden and Nairobi in Kenya. The formations were to route via Addis Ababa in Ethiopia and then on to Nairobi. At Addis Ababa, the jet pilots experienced the horrors of having to let down through cloud that was lower than the mountains surrounding the national airport.

Apart from the joy of flying low-level in the four-engined bomber-cum-maritime-surveillance Shackleton, it meant that neither Varky nor I would be flying from Nairobi to Thornhill in the back of a Rhodesian Air Force Dakota. The old DC3 made most pilots flying as passengers airsick; a situation that never failed to amuse our strong-stomached technicians.

When we arrived back in dispersals at Thornhill, the whole station was gathered to welcome us home. I was one of the sweat-stained pilots who climbed down from his aircraft wearing Mae West with mask and helmet pressure lines under wet, dishevelled hair. But I was too busy seeking out Beryl to savour the glamour I had witnessed two years earlier when, as a student pilot, I watched pilots returning from the first Aden detachment.

At the end of December I took leave to be with Beryl for the arrival of our first-born child. Towards the middle of January it became obvious that the baby was in a breach position and the decision was taken by Doctor Deuchar to make a caesarean delivery on 14 January.

Deborah Anne was perfect in every way with not a single blemish on her nine pound, six ounce body. Beryl handled the operation like a star, her private ward full to bursting with many flowers and cards from family, friends and clients. It was a special time for both of us.

Chapter

4

No 2 Squadron

ON RETURN TO DUTY I was told that I had been posted, together with Dave Thorne and Keith Corrans, to a re-formed No 2 Squadron. This squadron was to handle all future student training on both piston and jet aircraft. Dave and I were to become instructors on Provosts, Keith on Vampires. The prospect of instructing so early in our careers was both disappointing and pleasing. The disappointment came from having to leave the easygoing lifestyle of an operational squadron; the pleasure was in being considered worthy to become instructors.

Flight Lieutenant Bob Woodward being an ex-RAF Central Flying School instructor was a natural choice to command No 2 Squadron with Flight Lieutenant Chris Dams as his second-in-command.

For the first two months we did very little flying and instructor training was limited to groundwork. This left us with a fair amount of time on our hands, which we occupied in other interests. One of these was fashioning aerobatic model aircraft from balsa wood. Bob Woodward introduced this rather dangerous hobby that involved high-speed launching of

Sitting (left to right): Roy Morris, Keith Corrans, Dave Thorne, Basil Myburgh, Bob Woodward (OC), Chris Dams (Flt Cdr), Pat Meddows-Taylor, Mark Smithdorff and PB. Back Row: Technicians who are named in this book are, from left: Taffy Dowell (2nd) Jimmy Stewart (Sqn WO centre) and Don Annandale (7th) Note: the efficiency of Rhodesian technicians is again amply illustrated in this photograph. One tech for every pilot seems ridiculous. In any other air force this number would not have been less than 3 to 1.

these gliders, fashioned to resemble well-known jet aircraft. A five-metre length of heavy elastic line propelled the small aircraft at initial speed somewhere in the region of 250 knots. One man held one end of the elastic with arm stretched high above his head whilst the launcher walked backwards holding the model aircraft. When the elastic was at full stretch some twenty-five metres from the launcher, he made sure wings were level and released the model. Usually the aircraft passed well above the launcher's head as the aircraft pitched up into a high loop.

One of my gliders, fashioned to look like an RAF Lightning interceptor, failed to climb when Randy du Rand, visiting from No 1 Squadron, was holding the elastic for me to launch. The aircraft failed to climb immediately and its heavily leaded nose struck the peak of Randy's Air Force cap, splitting it in two and leaving Randy with a nasty blue lump on his forehead.

Another activity involved building a ladies' bar in the grounds of the Officers' Mess. The Officers' Mess of RAF times was in the middle of the Married Quarters but the Ministry of Education had commandeered it as a school for retarded children. It was known as Glengary School. The RAF Sergeants' Mess had been damaged by fire in RAF days and, when refurbished in mid-1958, it became the Officers' Mess. Close by in the garden of this mess was a building that had become completely overgrown by scrub and bramble.

Bob and I cut our way through the vegetation to find out what this building was all about. We discovered that it had once been a billiard room that had also suffered fire damage though the walls and roof remained sound. With the blessings of Group Captain Jock Barber, who was Station CO at the time, we set about refurbishing the building.

In a remarkably short space of time the entire structure and its surrounds took on a new look. Because of my experience in carpentry, it fell to me to build a decent-size bar, construct requisite shelving and install comfortable wall seats. Upon its completion, Bob requested all officers on Station to make submissions from which to select a name for the ladies' bar. Over a hundred names were offered and one of my submissions was chosen. From then on the ladies' bar was known as 'The Grog Spot'; a name that became well known to thousands of military and civilian visitors who enjoyed its special atmosphere and superb parties.

Death of Jack Roberts

JACK ROBERTS OF NO 11 SSU had only served on No 1 Squadron as a staff pilot for six months when, on 1 July 1960,

he was reported overdue from a low-level, cross-country flight. An air search was about to be mounted when a telephone call was received from a ranch south of Belingwe mountain. The rancher reported that the sight of a wheel bouncing past him at high speed had shaken him and his trailer-load of workers. When he located the wheel he realised it must have come from an aircraft. In fact it had travelled an incredible distance from Belingwe mountain peak where Jack Roberts had met his death.

The Board of Inquiry into this incident established that Jack, flying an FB9, had encountered low cloud on his first leg from Thornhill but had left the decision to climb above it a fraction too late. His aircraft impacted a vertical rock face a mere three feet from the summit of Mount Belingwe and disintegrated.

The four 20mm Hispano cannons remained deeply embedded in the rock face but most of the airframe debris, including the engine and undercarriage, passed over the summit. The Army kindly provided fifty territorial trainees from Llewellin Barracks to assist our technicians recover the scattered wreckage.

There were no helicopters available in those days so there was no way around the long climb up the mountain to recover every piece of wreckage which had to be manhandled or dragged down the difficult slope. Fortunately very heavy items, such as engine, main planes and undercarriage, were near the foot of the mountain and were accessible to four-wheel drive vehicles. The four cannons could not be extracted from the rock and were left in situ. They are probably still embedded there to this day!

Sabotage

IN OCTOBER 1960 THERE WAS a great deal of political manoeuvring by black organisations seeking the dissolution of the Federation of Rhodesia and Nyasaland. Because this caused much industrial unrest in Southern Rhodesia the Federal Government decided to get a message to all the black folk by air-dropping leaflets, as most of the people in the remote areas did not have radios.

Nos 2, 3 and 4 Squadrons were tasked to fly Provosts, Dakotas and Pembrokes to do the drops. Each aircraft was allocated a specific area to ensure full coverage of the country without overlaps. I had to cover a sector to the north and east of Gwelo before returning to the industrial area of Gwelo at 5 p.m. when workers would be streaming into the streets from the factories.

Flight Lieutenant Charlie Tubbs, the Senior Air Traffic

Controller at Thornhill, asked if he could accompany me on this four-and-a-half-hour sortie. With thousands of leaflets in bundles behind our seats and tucked in every accessible, safe location we set off with Charlie, an ex-RAF pilot, making the take-off. Once airborne he asked me if he could try his hand at landing on return to base. I agreed he could.

Charlie did most of the flying to allow me to map-read and record every village with the number of leaflets dropped as we moved from place to place in a pre-planned pattern. Our final drop was over the black townships of Gatooma. We then turned for Gwelo remaining at low level. The Provost was purring along when I turned to Charlie and said, "Isn't it amazing how reliable engines are nowadays. Here we are flying along, never worrying that the fan might fail on us." Charlie was horrified. "Don't say that, you might regret your words."

We arrived at Gwelo's industrial area on time. The canopy was rolled back and we had just commenced dropping leaflets when the sight and stench of smoke preceded severe vibration from a faltering engine. The canopy was rolled forward then immediately re-opened because of blinding, foul-smelling smoke in the cockpit. When the engine quit I was already aiming for the zigzag roof of the Bata Shoe Factory just ahead of us because there were too many power lines about and the roadways were crowded.

I put out a hurried 'Mayday' call to Thornhill Approach just as we were about to touch down on the factory roof. But happily the engine powered up again just long enough to allow us to wallow past the factory to the edge of the disused wartime RAF base, Moffat Airfield. The engine then quit completely and I was able to put down quite smoothly in very high grass. As the aircraft sliced through the grass, I prayed we would not strike any hidden antheaps or antbear holes that were common to this area. Blindly we rolled over rough ground for some distance before emerging smack bang on a grass runway that had recently been trimmed by the Gwelo Gliding Club.

When we climbed down from the aircraft Charlie's hands were shaking as he groped for his cigarettes. After a couple of hard drags Charlie said in a stern voice, "You promised to let me try my hand at landing," whereupon we both burst into near-hysterical, relieved laughter.

This was the first of a number of incidents involving sabotage of Royal Rhodesian Air Force aircraft. A 30mm steel ball bearing had been introduced into the engine casing and had settled at the rear of the number six-cylinder piston. There it had banged away with every revolution of the engine until eventually it broke through the piston head. Once the piston was holed, the whole engine casing became highly pressurised, forcing all the engine's oil to dump to atmosphere through the crankcase breather pipe.

Two days later another Provost suffered engine failure for the self-same reason. I think it was Flight Lieutenant Ken Edwards who put down safely with no damage to the airframe in Seke Reserve near New Sarum. An inspection of all the Leonides engines revealed that another four engines contained loose 30mm ball bearings.

The next incident involved a Canberra. Flight Lieutenant Ozzie Penton, a man of small build, was conducting his pre-flight inspection when he came to the port engine where, with fingers around the shroud, he could pull up as he jumped just high enough to check the lower turbines of the jet engine. He noticed something unusual and called a tall technician over to take a close look. There, between the line of static vanes and the first impeller blades, lay a socking great bolt that had obviously been placed there to damage the engine on start-up.

Initially it was believed that the sabotage was by black hangar staff acting for the Zimbabwe African Peoples' Union who continued to create unrest throughout the land. But then an incident occurred which made it obvious that ZAPU agents were not involved.

One of the black hanger workers at New Sarum called the Warrant Officer in charge of No 3 Squadron to come and inspect the undercarriage of a Dakota. He told the WO that when he was cleaning the aircraft's oleos the wheel axle retainer nuts did not feel right, even though they looked normal. The WO soon established that the nuts were indeed visually normal but felt wrong. They had perfect shape, threads and all, but had been fashioned from compressed paper and glue, sanded smooth and painted silver.

Though never proven, it was concluded that one or more of a number of RAF technicians on secondment to our Air Force were acting against our interests, possibly for MI6 in London. The seconded men returned to Britain shortly after these incidents and others that involved two Canadairs of No 3 Squadron. These incidents are covered later.

With ongoing unrest in the Shona areas, there was concern for the safety of the tribal chiefs who had become targets of youths stirred to action by ZAPU. Ground-to-ground communication with soldiers protecting the chiefs and their families were so poor that it became necessary for the Air Force to overfly all chiefs' kraals twice daily. To assist the pilots, each army protection unit laid out a white sheet on the ground. If nothing was overlaid on the sheet all was well. If, however, the unit had a problem, three orange strips could be laid on the white sheets in any one of a number of patterns set out in a booklet to convey their situation to the pilots who passed these on to local Army commanders. The flights were long and generally enjoyable, though I couldn't help worrying that my aircraft engine might have been sabotaged again.

Flying Instructors School

THE FLYING INSTRUCTORS SCHOOL (FIS) was, for me, a real drag. The need to fly very accurately was not so much the problem as the patter (what one needed to say whilst demonstrating to a student). I found this tedious, boring and somewhat confusing.

Bob Woodward would teach me a patter sequence in one style, but for the same sequence Chris Dams gave it differently. Soon enough it became obvious that the other QFIs (Qualified Flying Instructors) were giving different versions of patter that suited their own personalities and flying experience.

Every aspect of instructing was repeated and repeated ad nauseam with QFIs and between student instructors. My problem, as I saw it, was how I was going to satisfy Bob Woodward during progress tests and the all-important final test. Near the end of the course Flight Lieutenant Dickie Dives, an ex-RAF Central Flying School officer serving as an Air Traffic Controller at Thornhill, flew with me and gave me his brand of patter, encompassing every exercise in the book. I believe I learned more from Dickie Dives in two hours than in all the 150 hours I had flown with other QFIs and fellow students. I cannot say if Dickie was a good instructor for others, but he certainly made everything so much clearer and easier for me, just when I needed it. Thanks to him, I passed my final test without stress because I had learned to ignore parrot-fashioned patter and use the words that suited mood and action.

The flying side of our FIS commenced at the beginning of August 1960 and was completed in time for the commencement of the BFS for No 14 PTC (Pilots Training Course).

For those who watch for sequential numbering it will be obvious that Nos 12 SSU and 13 SSU are missing and that SSU had given way to PTC. This was partly due to political thinking and partly to superstition.

The Federal Government had become disenchanted with the Short Service Commission arrangements because too-high a proportion of trained pilots had opted to leave the force on completion of expensive 'free training'. Furthermore, most of them had taken up employment with airlines and moved beyond the borders of the Federation, thereby breaking their undertakings to be immediately available in times of need.

It was decided instead that all future student pilots would sign up for two years of training followed by a mandatory ten years' Medium Service Commission. In the event of a student's failure at any stage, Air HQ's only obligation was to offer him alternative training as navigator, technician or administrator. This new scheme was renamed Pilots Training Course (PTC) as prefix to the course number.

12 SSU should have commenced training in 1959 but, because no training occurred that year, the number was dropped. Considering that superstition for the number '13' might present difficulties, Group HQ, by now Air HQ operating from Dolphin House in Salisbury, decided to bypass it. No 14 Pilot Training Course (PTC) started their ground training at the beginning of January 1961 and came to 2 Squadron for the BFS in May.

Paul Mark

SIX MONTHS PRIOR TO THIS, on the 30 November 1960, Beryl came to fetch me at the usual knock-off time of 1.30 pm She was seven-and-a-half months' pregnant with our second child and was in absolute agony. With difficulty I got her into the passenger seat and drove her straight home. Getting her to the living room was a major effort.

She could not sit properly as pains in her abdomen were overwhelming her. Beryl's gynaecologist, Doctor Deuchar, who happened to live directly across the road from us, came to Beryl's aid immediately. He was not happy with what he saw and called Doctor Comline to come over urgently. Together the doctors concluded that Beryl was suffering from kidney failure necessitating immediate hospitalisation and the removal of her baby to save her life. I was taken aside and told that, following the operation, Beryl should be fine but the baby's chances of survival were not good.

I took time off work next day to look after Debbie and was playing with her whilst awaiting a call from the hospital. It was 9 am on 1 December when Debbie took her first faltering steps unaided; but the occasion was all but lost because I was so concerned for Beryl and baby.

A few minutes later Doctor Deuchar phoned to say Beryl would be fine and that our little boy had been transferred to Gwelo's Birchenough House Nursing Home. Not twenty minutes later, when I was dressing for a visit to the nursing home, I received a call from a Church of England padre. Very clumsily he asked in what names he should christen the baby who was not expected to survive another hour. Completely taken aback I blurted out "Paul Mark."

By the time I reached the nursing home the padre had left and the matron took me through to see my son. He was in an incubator and seemed fine enough to me until matron pointed out that he was breathing by stomach action with no signs of normal rib-cage movement. Five days passed after his birth before the doctor said Paul would be fine because his breathing had normalised. But nineteen vital days elapsed after his birth before Beryl was allowed to hold her baby.

Death of Eric Cary

ON THE 9 FEBRUARY 1961, I was instructed to get over to OC Flying Wing, post-haste. When I walked into Squadron Leader Dicky Bradshaw's office I saw Tol Janeke standing in flying overalls by the side of his desk looking pale and shaken.

OC Flying, seated behind his desk, looked more stern than usual. In a quiet steady voice he said, "PB I have bad news for you. Your coursemate Eric Cary has crashed and I want you to go and find the site to guide the doctor and fire vehicles to it." I was given brief details and set off to the squadron where Flying Officer Pat Meddows-Taylor said he would accompany me. We were airborne when Squadron Leader Frank Mussell, flying a Canberra, told me he had located the crash site on the south bank of the Umniati River, upstream from the bridge on the main road to Salisbury. He said there was no need for a grid reference, as I would see the rising smoke from some distance.

When we reached the crash site we saw that impact had occurred in a disused cattle kraal where the aircraft disintegrated. Wreckage of varying sizes littered the crash line for over a kilometre to a stream. Beyond this lay the still-flaming magnesium wheels and the smouldering engine.

We had been flying around for a couple of minutes before noticing a lone black male who was waving at us frantically and pointing to the top of a large tree just off to the left side of the debris line. We concluded this might mean Eric's body was lodged in the tree but the foliage was too dense for us to confirm this.

After an age we spotted the far-off dust trails from a red fire Jeep and white ambulance. I could not raise the fire Jeep because, as I learned later, it had radio failure. Pat unstrapped and stood up (highly illegal) to make himself visible to the lead driver. By flying over his vehicle and waggling my wings I gave the fireman changes of direction to avoid difficult ground and Pat kept emphasising these changes with hand signals, a difficult thing to do in the powerful slipstream.

When, eventually, the vehicles arrived at the crash site Doctor Dorber came up on the radio, loud and clear. He had not responded to our calls to the fire Jeep "not wanting to interfere". The mind boggles! Anyway we asked him to drive over to the large tree where we suspected Eric's remains might be. There was no sign of the black man by now as he had obviously given us up when we flew off out of his sight to guide the vehicles.

Having reached the tree, the doctor confirmed Eric's body was there and appeared complete save for the loss of a leg that was soon discovered near by. It was almost unheard of in a crash of this nature for a pilot's entire body to be available for burial considering the location of a Vampire's engine.

Tol Janeke was tried by court martial following this accident and was found guilty of contravening Air Force Regulations for unauthorised low flying outside the prescribed training area. His punishment of eighteen months' deferred promotion was probably harsh in the circumstances. Eric had persuaded his junior to follow him on a low-level inspection of the Umniati River to establish if the water level was suitable to repeat a canoeing trip he and Tol had made down the same river the previous year.

Eric led the downstream reconnaissance. At the road bridge on the main road leading to Salisbury he turned to fly back up the river. Then by waggling his wings, so as not to give away his position to Thornhill Approach Control, Eric passed lead to Tol.

As Tol was about to pass, Eric in typical fashion did a slow roll that did not work out as so many had before. In the second half of the roll the aircraft scooped and so ended a very capable young pilot's life.

After his military funeral our course held a private party as a send-off to Eric.

Left to right: Gordon Wright, Murray Hofmeyr, Bill Galloway, PB, Keith Corrans, Dave Thorne, John Barnes and Ian Law.

First students

AT THIS TIME NO 14 PTC had completed the GTS phase and were ready to commence flying training on Provosts. I was allocated Officer Cadets Doug Pasea and Terry Ryan and set about putting my instructor training into practice.

Teaching a student who knew nothing about flying seemed easy, though I soon realised I was 'pattering' just what I had been taught but without the pressure of practising it on someone more experienced than myself.

Doug Pasea learned quicker than Terry Ryan and I considered

Terry Ryan, PB and Doug Pasea.

him fit for solo after about twelve hours. Bob Woodward who, for reasons I never established, disliked Doug Pasea even taking him on his solo test. Unbeknown to me Bob had already decided that Pasea was not going to pass BFS, no matter what! Doug was not only 'failed' on this test, Bob also disallowed him the benefit of further training with a second solo check; so I pleaded with Chris Dams to intervene. This he did, but to no avail! Having 'failed' BFS, Doug Pasea was sent to Britain to train as a Canberra navigator. He did splendidly and became an outstanding officer who gained respect throughout the force.

When Terry Ryan was reaching maximum hours allowed for solo he was taken on a progress check by Bob Woodward. Though not a patch on Doug Pasea as a pilot, he was sent solo off this very sortie. I was pleased for Terry Ryan's sake but very displeased at losing Doug Pasea. This was my first experience of unfair prejudice by a senior officer against a junior. Unfortunately I would see close friends suffer from this human failing in the years ahead.

In June I was given Officer Cadets Tony Smit and Keith Clarke in exchange for Terry Ryan. Tony Smit was under threat of being scrubbed and his instructor had suggested that a change of instructor might be helpful. Keith's instructor asked for the change on the grounds of incompatibility, but he gave me no difficulties. But I was very conscious of the fact that Tony Smit was the same age as me, the maximum age for student pilots having been elevated from twenty-one to twenty-four.

A couple of hours with Tony showed me that he had the potential but lacked concentration and was trying to 'fly by numbers' (meaning he was not yet using natural senses and every muscle in his body was as tight as an over-wound spring). Tony's problem with flying reminded me of my father-in-law's problem with dancing. Whether waltz, quick-step or tango he always moved his feet to his loudly whispered "one two three— one two three—one … "

I gave Tony a very hard time even though it was not in my nature to do this. Determined not to have another of my pupils fail, I drove him mercilessly. Then it dawned on me that, in my early stages of learning to fly, I had overcome the natural tendency to tense up by deliberately relaxing the muscles of my buttocks. This I had been taught by my father as a youngster learning to ride horses. By repeatedly telling him, "Relax your butt," Tony's main problem of tensing was overcome and soon enough he started to fly well.

Tony, five years later.

For me Tony's success has been something of a private triumph because he went on to give excellent service in Rhodesia and in the South African Air Force. He also qualified on a large number of aircraft types, including WWII fighters and bombers and became a member of the Confederate Air Force in the USA. However my success with Tony turned out to be a problem because I lost good students in exchange for difficult ones. In consequence I gained the questionable reputation of being a hard-arsed instructor, like Mick McLaren.

Fire Officer

DURING 1961 I WAS APPOINTED Station Fire Officer over and above my flying duties and found Flight Sergeant Jimmy Dumas and his crew of fire-fighters easy men to work with. My job was to ensure that their training was brought to the highest standard and that they were adequately equipped to deal with aircraft accidents and domestic fires.

Within a week of my appointment, and by prior arrangement

with Air Traffic Control, I called for a practice 'fire rescue' of Sergeant Taffy Dowell and me from the cockpit of our Provost, which I had stopped in the middle of the runway after landing.

What an experience this turned out to be! Taffy and I, still strapped into our seats, were slumped forward holding our breath and simulating unconsciousness as black firemen climbed up to 'rescue' us. One big strong guy put his feet on the canopy rails then, placing his hands under my arms, nearly dislocated my shoulders because I was still firmly held down by the seat harness.

Flight Sergeant Dumas shouted instructions to release the harness, which in itself was a fiasco. Finally I was lifted clear and inadvertently dropped head first off the trailing edge of the wing before flopping onto hard tarmac. Taffy suffered similar mishandling and we were both lucky to get away with a few scratches and bruises.

Right away I decided to polish up on rescue training but to use firemen, complete with parachutes and helmets, in place of aircrew. Under my supervision they practised crew rescue, ad nauseam, from Provosts, T11s, FB9s and Canberras until procedures and techniques were slick and safe.

Canberra belly-landing

SQUADRON LEADER CHARLIE GOODWIN WAS the Senior Technical Officer at Thornhill. One morning he came rushing into the squadron asking to be taken up for an in-flight inspection of a Canberra whose right main undercarriage refused to respond to pilot selections. He wanted a Provost rather than a Vampire and I was instructed to make the flight.

Squadron Leader Frank Mussell was flying the Canberra in question. He reduced speed to 120 knots to allow me to come into close formation directly under his right wing. It was immediately clear that the 'D' door had closed out of sequence ahead of the main wheel which was pressed hard against the outside of the 'D' door. The nose wheel and left main wheel were extended and locked down correctly.

A Canberra's undercarriage was controlled by sequence valves which were designed to lift the main wheel into its bay then close the 'D' door under the wheel to provide continuity to the wing surface for high speed flight. In this case the 'D' door sequenced before undercarriage and there was no way of overcoming the problem by selecting undercarriage-down because the sequence valve was trying to open the 'D' door first but it was held fast by the stronger hydraulic jack of the undercarriage. The history of sequence-valve failures on RAF Canberras was known to Charlie Goodwin who told Frank Mussell that he had no option but to tuck away the other wheels and land the aircraft on its belly.

For a landing of this nature it was necessary to burn off fuel to the lowest level possible, preparatory to a high-friction belly slide along the tarmac runway. The period required to burn off the fuel gave ample time for every person in camp to get up to the flight lines to join many excited spectators awaiting the event.

Frank put the aircraft down very gently. A magnificent dense plume of white sparks fanned upwards from the Canberra which, holding a straight course, slid along the hard surface for about 1,200 metres before coming to rest, wings still level. When jacked up, the undercarriage was lowered and the aircraft was towed away for inspection. The damage, mainly to bomb doors, was considerably less that expected and the aircraft was declared fit for a one-time, wheels-down flight to New Sarum.

At New Sarum, Master Technician Les Grace and his crew in the Stressed Skin Section of the Aircraft Servicing Flight repaired the Canberra in quick time. Les was a superb, softly spoken man who always wore a smile and had a great deal to talk about. He was also a good listener. His skills and those of the men he taught were proven hundreds of times over. They not only beefed up airframes and mainplanes of aircraft to meet operational stresses their designers had never considered, they also repaired aircraft damaged in accidents and in later years by enemy action. The work done was so perfect that only an expert eye could detect the sites of these repairs.

Practical jokers

AS WITH ANY FORCE THE RRAF had its fair share of practical jokers. Keith Kemsley was the best known at Thornhill, though I heard it said he was better at giving than in receiving.

Hi-fi was new to Rhodesians and John Mussell seemed to be the most knowledgeable man on station about the technicalities and strange terms introduced with the equipment. Woofers and tweeters sounded more like Goon Show terms than serious electronic ones. Nevertheless John was a relatively wealthy bachelor who only bought the very best of equipment on the market. Keith was well aware of this when he met up with a Gwelo salesman of recently imported Hi-fi equipment. Keith asked the young man if he would be interested in coming over for dinner with him and his wife Pat so that he could meet a pilot who was looking for the tops in Hi-fi.

The salesman accepted the invitation keenly before Keith

told him that John Mussell was a great guy who was suffering some level of deafness from flying jets. "You will find he shouts loudly. Do not be embarrassed by this, just shout back. John has plenty of money so it's worth your while."

Keith then asked John if he would be interested in coming over to his house where he and Pat had a Hi-fi fundi visiting for dinner. John leapt at the opportunity and accepted Keith's warning that; "This guy is so into powerful speakers that he has become very deaf. Ignore the fact that he shouts and simply shout back."

John got to Keith and Pat's home first. When the salesman arrived, Keith shouted introductions whereupon his guests responded more loudly and were immediately immersed in a shouted technical conversation. Keith, battling to keep a straight face, asked them to sit down and excused himself on the pretext of having to give Pat a hand in the kitchen. From there Keith heard the shouted conversation mounting in volume, just as he had hoped.

After some time John turned his head away and muttered something to himself in a low voice. Immediately the salesman asked, "What was that?" in an equally low voice. Keith's game was up; not that it spoilt a pleasant evening. But John left the Kemsley home determined to get his own back on Keith. He consulted Flight Lieutenant 'Porky' MacLaughlin on how best to do this.

In the meanwhile Keith continued with his practical jokes, many of which were aimed at his beloved wife. The story goes that he sent Pat to the hardware store where she was instructed to ask the salesman for 'a long wait'. She got it all right, but had given the salesman hell for bad service before realising that her husband had set her up. On another occasion Pat was told to buy a pint of white-on-purple polka-dot paint. "Remember, white on purple—not purple on white." Again, Pat had been set up. When, however, Keith asked her to get a real item - a two-pound ball-and-claw steel-shafted hammer—Pat thought the description sounded too much like another of Keith's pranks. Consequently he was not too pleased that his instruction had been ignored because he really needed the hammer for a job he intended to do that very day.

Then one Friday afternoon, at the very moment all Government departments closed down for the weekend, Keith and Pat received a hand-delivered registered envelope from the Registrar of Births, Marriages and Deaths. The enclosed document stated that, due to some error in paperwork at the time of their marriage they had never, in effect, been officially married. This meant that in the eyes of the law their children were illegitimate. An early visit to the offices of The Registrar of Births, Marriages and Deaths was strongly recommended to put matters to right.

Keith and Pat were beside themselves with concern for the entire weekend, just as John and Porky had hoped. Keith arranged a flight to Salisbury to be at the Registrar's office the moment its doors opened on Monday morning. He presented the letter to the receptionist and waited while the appropriate file was being sought from registry. A puzzled attendant kept appearing and disappearing, saying the file reference group seemed correct but that the final digit corresponded to a file that could not be located. Eventually the penny dropped and Keith realised that the joke against him had been so well prepared that even the Registrar's Office had been fooled.

John enjoyed this experience so much that he decided to pull a fast one on all officers at Thornhill. We received an official-looking questionnaire purporting to have come from Air Headquarters. It started with the usual Rank, Name, Number, Date of Birth, Date of Attestation etc. and required individual Flying Log Book records be broken down into components that required hours of work. The spaces to be filled were such that little space was given where the entry would be long and large spaces for entries requiring little space; typically Government! However, the questions went on and on and even asked for domestic details including such things as how many pets one kept, their names and food brands.

It only fooled those who were in the habit of filling in forms as they read each question. Those of us who read through the questionnaire first, smelled a rat and threw it into the waste bin. Unfortunately, two senior officers who had little time to spare put in a lot of work before realising a prankster had caught them out. There was hell to pay.

Before an official investigation could progress too far, John Mussell owned up to being the one who had prepared, printed and issued the questionnaires. For his troubles he received a severe reprimand and had to replace all the paper that had been wasted.

When my course reported to New Sarum for the pilot selection process in 1956, we all noticed that the cover flap on one toilet seat in the ablution block of the officers single quarters had been elaborately painted with a poem set inside a floral wreath. As I recall it, the poem started with the words "In loving memory of Mike Saunders who did'st on … "

Mike Saunders was well known for naughty deeds right from the start of his flying career. He was a junior pilot when he went into a toilet and waited there until the other three adjoining ones were occupied. At this point he lit a short fuse affixed to a commercial detonator. As soon as the fuse was burning, Mike dropped it into the toilet and flushed. He expected the water to transport the fuse and detonator into the external sewerage pipe where detonation would pressurise the system and blow the contents of the toilet bowls upward onto the bare butts of his unsuspecting mates.

Mike's plan failed. The fuse and detonator were too heavy for the water to carry over the bowl's water trap. The flush was complete before detonation occurred, shearing the toilet bowl at floor level. Mike's error cost him all the repair expenses and his colleagues rubbed this in with the painted remembrance wreath and poem on the new wooden seat.

Some time during the '60s, Alex Roughead had become a

menacing pyromaniac. He revelled in explosives and set many traps for his mates. One of his pranks involved substituting a small wad of magnesium cotton in place of the filament of a broken light bulb. Upon entering their own rooms his friends would receive quite a fright and become temporarily blinded when they switched on the main light. He had done this at New Sarum so many times that all of his friends had learned to look away and expect a bang when they switched on ceiling lights.

Alex decided he should change the position and set up a larger charge on a bedside light. Having heard nothing during the night nor received any abuse at the breakfast table next morning, he felt disappointed. So he went to inspect the bedside light he had doctored and found it as he had left it. Alex switched on the light, but nothing happened. He could not understand this. Next he went to the main electrical board in the passageway where he found a thermal breaker had dropped out. As he switched it on an almighty explosion occurred.

Alex returned to his friend's smoke-filled room to discover that the bedside cabinet, light and most of the bed had been destroyed. Huge black burn marks covered two walls and the ceiling. Realising that his friend might have been killed or badly hurt if the thermal switch had not tripped out the previous night, Alex abandoned pyrotechnic trapping.

Unrelated to Air Force were stories of a commercial pilot serving with Central African Airways before that airline became Air Rhodesia. He had been trained by Air Force and delighted in teasing old ladies and brand-new airhostesses. Walking backwards from the flight deck, drawing out two lengths of string, he would come to an old lady and hand her both strings requesting that she fly the aircraft whilst he slipped off to the loo.

Targeting a new hostess on her first flight he gathered up all the salad on his lunch plate and placed it inside an airsick bag. With the connivance of the skipper, he rang the service bell for the hostess. When she arrived on the flight deck she found the second Dickey doubled up and noisily puking into the sick-bag. He turned and apologised for asking her to take the bag from him. As the hostess reached for the bag the captain grabbed it saying, "I love my salad warm" whereupon he hand-scooped salad into his mouth. The hostess, with hand over mouth, left the cabin retching.

On another occasion this naughty pilot dug a hole in the paper plate on which his lunch had been served. He undid his fly and pulled the head of his twin through the hole and set salad neatly around it. When the new hostess responded to the cockpit service bell, he pointed to the centre of the salad pile and asked, "What's the meaning of serving this with my salad?" The panicking hostess apologised, took the fork from the plate and stabbed the offending item, which promptly bled profusely as cries of agony emitted from its owner. Not surprisingly, this pilot became more circumspect in future pranks.

The impending arrival of Hunters meant we had urgent need for more pilots.

15 PTC

WITH THE INTRODUCTION OF CANBERRAS and the impending arrival of Hunters, the RRAF was running short of pilots. Following the 1960 break in pilot training, it was decided to make this up in 1961. No 15 PTC was brought forward to mid-1961 to follow close behind 14 PTC, which was then midway through BFS.

When 14 PTC moved on to Vampires, I was allocated three 15 PTC students. They were Officer Cadets David Hume, Doug Patterson and Bruce McKerron. Patterson did not do well. I put him up for a scrub check and he returned to Civvy Street. McKerron was a cocky young fellow who was too

Officer Cadets David Hume, Doug Patterson and Bruce McKerron.

familiar for my liking, but once he knew where he stood he did well and I enjoyed teaching him.

Hume came from Umtali where I had known his parents and brother Peter before I joined the Air Force; but I had only noticed young David in passing.

From his very first gentle flight Dave Hume was airsick and sortie after sortie had to be cut short to get the honking cadet back on the ground. It was obvious to me that David had potential and should make a good pilot, so long as the airsickness problem could be overcome. Feeling sure his was not a physical problem, I set out to cure him.

Most of the students had flown about eight hours but Dave Hume had less than half of this time. As usual, he reached for his 'honk packet' twenty minutes into the flight. Once he had heaved up, I told him to tighten his seat belt and hold tight to see what he must eventually endure if he was to become a pilot. For about fifteen minutes I conducted non-stop aerobatics with lots of positive and negative 'G', plenty of fuel fumes and a couple of naughty flick rolls that even made me feel a bit queasy. When I stopped, Dave had half his face in the honk packet and his knees were up by his ears as he wretched noisily and repeatedly, but with nothing coming from his stomach. Back on the ground he staggered back to the crew-room bathed in sweat and so pale I became worried that I might have overdone things. When he eventually recovered I said to him, "Hume, you have experienced and survived much harsher flying than you will face at any stage of your flying training. What you have to go through to reach solo is very, very gentle, so stop worrying about your stomach and let's get on with the job." Dave never had a moment's trouble from then on and went solo with time to spare. He eventually gained the Sword of Honour as best student when he and his course members received their wings.

Some time after the last solo had been flown I was given Officer Cadet Harold Griffiths, due to 'non-compatibility' with his first instructor. He had joined the ground-training phase of his course late because, as a member of the Churchill School Pipe Band, Griffiths (Griff) had been given special dispensation by Air HQ to accompany the band on a tour of Scotland. His introduction to flying with the RRAF was unusual and might have put a lesser man right off flying as a career.

The Churchill School Pipe Band was well known to all Rhodesians for its excellence in Scottish piping dress and drills. So their invitation to participate at the Edinburgh Festival was wholly supported and the RRAF undertook to fly the band to Scotland and back.

OC 3 Squadron, Squadron Leader Harry Coleman, captained the aircraft with Flight Lieutenant Bill Smith as his co-pilot. They were in for a tough trip because the work of professional saboteurs showed up again. Just prior to crossing the Zambezi River on the northbound leg, the port outer engine had to be closed down due to total loss of oil pressure. This necessitated turning back to Salisbury where a standby

Canadair was available to resume the long flight to England. Two engines on this replacement aircraft also suffered the selfsame problem as the first. Fortunately these both occurred in the UK costing much wasted time and money. The aircraft eventually returned to New Sarum safely and disgorged a very relieved bunch of pipers.

Each of the three Rolls Royce Merlin engine failures occurred when high-pressure oil hoses fractured. The replacement engines acquired and fitted in England were fine. But back in Rhodesia all Canadairs had been grounded to find out why relatively new, high-quality hoses had failed.

This led to the discovery that some hoses, all in different locations on affected engines, had been cut with a fine blade right up against the steel sleeve of a coupling. The cuts ran all the way around the lip of the coupling, penetrating two of the three braided reinforcement layers. The cut lines were so fine that they were undetectable until subjected to severe bending. The saboteurs knew their business because it would have been impossible for any technician conducting a routine pre-flight inspection to see the cuts.

Returning to Harold Griffiths. His first instructor had passed him to me because of his cocky attitude. I had to agree that Griff seemed to be a bit too sure of himself, but I experienced no difficulties and found him to be a good student who learned quickly and flew well. In time to come Griff and his lovely wife Linda became special family friends.

Fire-fighting cock-up

THORNHILL WAS OPENED TO THE public one Saturday for static displays of aircraft and equipment, flying displays, guard-dog displays and, horror of horrors, a fire-fighting demonstration.

As Station Fire Officer I had to arrange a meaningful display involving a fuel fire sufficient in size to radiate enough heat to force spectators to keep a respectable distance. For this, a three-foot barrier in sheet metal was erected and filled with plenty of old tyres, rags and half drums of aviation fuel. Immediate upon ignition, huge flames shot up to considerable height with masses of flame, heat and boiling black smoke.

First and second rehearsals by the fire section had the flame extinguished in quick order and Flight Sergeant Dumas assured me that his men would do even better on the day of the show. I had my doubts because experience had shown me that success in practice, with no hitches, often results in cock-ups and major embarrassment.

At the appointed time, with everyone's attention focused by

the public address system, Flight Sergeant Dumas walked up to the tank and initiated the fire. Spectators had moved back from the intense heat as the main Rolls Royce fire tender arrived and firemen commenced connecting their hoses. Immediately my doubts turned to concern because I could see that the black firemen, with so many spectators watching them, were overacting in typical African fashion.

As the fire hoses were rolled out to their correct positions, Flight Sergeant Dumas signalled the tender to provide foam. Seconds passed before a tiny trickle of liquid emerged from the nozzles where firemen stood braced for the pressure that failed to come.

The flames got bigger and hotter with spectators taking a few more paces backwards. Some of the hose tenders left their stations to seek out possible kinks in the line when suddenly full pressure came through to the nozzles. This threw the men who had remained at the nozzle ends straight into the air before the hoses broke loose and whipped around showering white foam over everything but the fire.

When the foam-soaked men regained control of their hoses and placed the gushing foam where it was intended, the fire went out. I was deeply embarrassed by such an appalling demonstration, but the crowd roared, "Encore! Encore!"

Congo crisis

DURING A VISIT TO SOUTH Africa, the then British Prime Minister, Harold Macmillan, had made his famous 'winds of change' speech in Cape Town. I can remember telling Beryl that he should have used the words, 'WINDS OF DESTRUCTION' because we could already see that the dismantling of the British Empire was doing no good at all to those African states that had been granted independence. Infrastructures were collapsing and ordinary peoples' standards of living were declining whilst the political 'fat cats' got fatter and military coups became order of the day. But it was not only Britain's Empire that was being given away.

In mid-1960, chaos and savagery broke out in the Belgian Congo when the Government of Belgium handed control to unprepared black politicians. New names appeared in the papers—Lumumba, Kasavubu, Bomboko, Mabuto and Tshombe being the most prominent ones. Large numbers of soldiers of the Force Publique, who had previously been highly efficient and disciplined under white Belgian officers, were suddenly leaderless and refused to take orders from any black politician.

Throughout the country the gendarmerie broke loose from their barracks with their weapons and went off on a spree of looting, rape and murder. The outrages, particularly against missionaries and nuns, were widespread and unbelievably cruel in nature. Seeking to escape the confusion and threat to their lives, thousands of white refugees fled into Northern Rhodesia.

Initial RRAF involvement was limited to the air transportation of distraught refugees from Ndola to Salisbury where huge transit facilities were established. After the last of the refugees had left, mainly bound for Belgium, the situation settled for a while but then it went from bad to worse.

Moise Tshombe, who was President of the Provincial Government of Katanga Province, attempted to take the initiative to regain control of the situation in his province. Realising that the Central Government had lost control he sought to save copper-rich Katanga that, by virtue of its socio-economic and geographical position, could stand alone.

Having gained some semblance of control, Tshombe declared Katanga independent which had the effect of drawing Katangese gendarmerie to his cause. Along with this came many white volunteers and mercenary officers to head the newly formed Katangese Army.

Tshombe was known to be pro-West whilst Patrice Lumumba, head of Central Government in Leopoldville, was pro-communist. A United Nations force was sent to Congo to help restore order and for reasons known only to himself, Kasavubu—President of the Congo—had Lumumba arrested. Lumumba was half dead through maltreatment by the time he was dumped off at Elizabethville, in spite of Tshombe's refusal to accept him on Katangese soil. Lumumba was murdered by Katangese villagers soon thereafter with Tshombe becoming the scapegoat for his demise. With UN attention now focused on Katanga there existed a threat to peace in Northern Rhodesia and the Federation.

Federal troops and the RRAF were called to readiness though at no time was there any question of entering Katanga or any other part of Congo. Considerable political manoeuvring ensued and at one point it appeared as if Tshombe's own initiatives might succeed. It was agreed that provinces would be given autonomy whilst Kasavubu's Central Government retained a neutral stance on purely provincial matters. However, as has become common in African politics, Kasavubu ignored an agreement made at Tananarive in Malagasy and had Tshombe arrested at Qoquilhatville, the venue for a meeting intended to ratify the Tananarive Agreement. Tshombe was later released.

Following this, a real tragedy developed when the so-called 'peace-keeping force' of the United Nations was used with the aim of returning Katanga to the control of Central Government. Yielding to a multiplicity of communist and non-aligned demands, Tshombe's voice of democracy was ignored and the UN, whose real character became fully revealed, systematically blocked all his efforts.

The true colours of this world body were exposed again

when, acting behind a screen of western press outcries at the building of the Berlin Wall, the UN implemented the most shameful abuse against the freedom-seeking Katangese people. Irish, Indian, Swedish and Ghurkha troops used appalling armed force. The Katangese soldiers were not willing to meekly surrender their arms however, so the bloody conflict that then ensued threatened to spill over the Federal border and the RRAF moved two squadrons forward to Ndola.

A full-scale UN offensive launched at 04:00 on Wednesday 13 September 1961. As a direct consequence, just four days later, the secretary-general of the United Nations, Dag Hammarskjold, died in an air tragedy whilst approaching to land at Ndola Airport for talks with Tshombe who was waiting there to meet him. Had Dag Hammarskjold lived, it is conceivable that some sense might have been brought into the UN's Congo policy. Instead the situation worsened.

Following a tenuous ceasefire the UN force under Brigadier Raja of the Indian Army launched a second offensive against the Katangese. This opened at 13:45 on 5 December. Canberra bombers of the Indian Air Force and Saab fighters of the Swedish Air Force bombed and strafed the Katangese airbase at Kolwezi the next day. All-out war had been initiated against Katanga whose crime had been to seek independence under its western-oriented, multi-national government. For its part, the UN sought nothing short of all-out control by the ultra-left Central Government.

Incredibly this whole tragedy was largely USA-inspired for its own greedy interests in Congo's minerals. In fact, successive US governments fully supported their corruptible puppet, Mabuto Sese Seko and for many years ignored his tyrannical rule and blatant corruption against his people just so long as US interests in Congolese minerals were met.

Pilot training at Thornhill was temporarily suspended when all the instructors were attached to No 1 Squadron to make up pilot numbers for Vampire operations. For me this was a most welcome break from instruction. No 3 and No 4 Squadrons had already been operating out of Ndola and northeastern Zambia for some days when we arrived.

A Central African meteorological condition known as the ITCZ (Intertropical Convergence Zone) develops in the summer months when warm moist 'Congo air' converges with the cool air masses driving up from the south. This creates a deep belt of rainy weather with low cloud that can persist for many days and nights.

The ITCZ usually moved between central Congo and Southern Rhodesia's southern border. During the time we were at Ndola for 'the Congo Crisis', however, the ITCZ remained almost stationary over Katanga and the northern sectors of Northern Rhodesia. This made flying difficult and even dangerous, as proven when the over-tired aircrew of Dag Hammarskjold's DC6 aircraft crashed in line with, but way short of Ndola's active runway.

The crash site was discovered the following morning by one of the Provost pilots sent out to search for the missing DC6. The aircraft had been heard by all of us in the early hours of the morning as it passed over Ndola Airport on its procedural NDB let-down. But on the inbound leg for landing the pilot flew into a 100-foot-high forested ridge five miles from the airfield. Inspection of the crash site, where a number of local charcoal producers lived within the forest, showed that the aircraft had met with the trees, wings level, in a shallow descent. Had the cloud base not been so low, the crew would have picked up the lights of Ndola and arrived safely. Instead the aircraft descended below the check height given on the International let-down chart for Ndola. However, a United States Air Force Jeppesen manual, found clipped open at the Ndolo (Congo) section, happened to be 1,000 feet lower than Ndola (Northern Rhodesia).

Dave Thorne and I, flying Vampire FB9s, operated as a pair for the entire period of our stay. Our task, along with those of other Vampires and a couple of Provosts based at Ndola, was to make the RRAF's presence known along the western Katangese border and keep an eye open for any trans-border movement of refugees and foreign armed forces. All flying had to be conducted under persistent low cloud, which in places was no more than 100 feet above the trees. This made map reading particularly difficult on our small-scaled 1:1,000,000 maps.

Beyond the built-up areas, tarmac roads and railway lines linking the Copper Belt towns there existed nothing but a sea of magnificent tall trees that stretch for hundreds of miles in every direction. A few dirt roads were marked but no physical features existed to define the international boundary line. In consequence we strayed across the border on occasions, once with Dave leading us as far beyond it as the rail-line just east of the UN-occupied base at Kolwezi. This was some forty nautical miles north of where we thought we were. Fortunately the weather was so bad that we seemed not to have been noticed.

A second deep penetration occurred with me leading. We had come upon a large convoy of vehicles at the border post of Kasumbuleza. Having orbited to identify vehicle types and numbers I rolled out to fly along the roadway leading to the Northern Rhodesian town of Bancroft. We had flown some distance when Dave Thorne radioed "Cheeky!" at the same moment I saw the black smoke ahead caused by fighting in Elizabethville. We did a smart turn about and retraced our route to Kasumbuleza.

It was only then that I realised that the road, power-lines and hills on the right side of the road from Kasumbuleza to Elizabethville looked exactly the same as those from Kasumbuleza to Bancroft. Considering there was no sun to give an automatic sense of direction, I had been remiss in relying on hills, road and power-lines without also checking my compass heading.

When out of radio range of Ndola Approach, we often switched over to the Elizabethville Approach Control frequency to listen in on UN aircraft chatter. We had heard

'Tiger formation', four Indian Air Force Canberras, a couple of times before something unusual occurred one morning.

We had just switched over to listen to UN natter when Tiger Leader came up on Elizabethville Control, "Tiger, check-in." Spontaneously the usual "Tiger 2"—"Tiger 3"—"Tiger 4" check-in occurred. But this time it was immediately followed by "Tiger 5"—"Tiger 6"—"Tiger 7"—"Tiger 8"; all in typically Indian accents.

The formation leader, showing annoyance transmitted, "Tiger, do not be playing foolishly, check-in," whereupon Tigers three to four were followed smoothly by the phantom Tigers 5 to 8. The leader obviously realised someone was interfering so he instructed his formation to QSY (change frequency) to their operational channel.

Next day Tiger Leader was bringing his formation back to base. Having come onto the Elizabethville Approach Control frequency the formation checked in normally and, sure enough, the phantom Tigers 5 to 8 checked in too. The leader ignored the interference and asked Elizabethville Approach for a QDM (heading to steer to base) whereupon the Approach Controller, another Indian voice, asked Tiger Lead for an unmodulated transmission. This is a radio transmission with no voice inclusion that allows the directional sensing apparatus to receive a smooth (unmodulated) carrier wave on which to sense.

As Tiger Leader transmitted, screeching in our headphones told us that a second aircraft was transmitting at the same time. The approach controller told Tiger his transmission had been blocked and asked for another unmodulated transmission. Again the screeching of an overlaid transmission disallowed the controller from establishing a heading for Tiger Lead to steer. His directional indicator needle would have been flicking randomly around its 360-degree dial.

This situation repeated itself a few more times before Tiger 2 told his leader he was low on fuel and breaking away for an independent recovery to base. In a relatively short time the obviously angry Canberra leader was on his own, the other Canberras having also broken formation. Two days later we heard Tiger Formation once more showing that all Canberras had made it safely back to base. By this time the 4 Squadron pilot responsible for interfering with Tiger Formation had been exposed and given a flea in the ear. He did not interfere with Tiger Formation again.

The Katangese forces were fighting the UN forces with all they had and one colourful French pilot's exploits came to our notice. We knew him as Max and I only met him once. He operated a Twin-Dornier out of a small bush strip, Kipushi, whose 1,000-foot runway was half-inside Northern Rhodesia and half-inside Katanga Province. Most nights Max got airborne for his one-man air war against the UN. Crudely applied green and brown poster paint seemed to handle the rainy weather remarkably well and the camouflage effect was excellent. He employed crudely made bombs that were hand-

dropped through an opening cut in the floor of his aircraft. Using the gas flame that emitted from its high stack at the Union Minière copper-smelting plant near Elizabethville, Max made timed runs to drop two bombs off each pass across the blacked-out UN airbase. He ignored ineffectual searching ground fire and made run after run against unseen aircraft on the ground. His efforts were well rewarded; in particular the destruction of a UN Globemaster was high return for such crude and inexpensive effort.

When he could, Max drank at bars in Elizabethville where UN forces were present. What guise he employed I cannot say but his objective was to find out how his bombing had affected the UN air effort and to glean whatever other information he could. In doing this he befriended a helicopter technician who agreed to take him onto the airbase and show him over a small Bell helicopter. Max's casual questions were answered and he found out how to start the machine. He then awaited an opportunity to steal it.

When the right moment came, Max started the engine and, never having flown a helicopter before, heaved the Bell into the air and wobbled and swayed into forward flight. There were no difficulties with the low-level bolt to the border and Kipushi airstrip. But landing a helicopter is no simple matter as Max found out when his attempt to hover for the landing ended in a big mix-up as rotor blades beat the airframe to destruction. Max survived the experience and was airborne again that same night in his Dornier to bomb UN planes.

On 18 December the instructors were released from Ndola to return to normal duties. Most of the flight back to Thornhill was in bright clear skies, which was wonderful after the awful weather around Ndola. However, this changed as we approached Thornhill where we had to make independent radar approaches through torrential rain in severe thunderstorms. Bulawayo and Salisbury were experiencing similar conditions so there were no question of a diversion. Flight Lieutenant Ron Vass directed me by radar to the point where I was handed over to the Precision Radar Controller whose voice I recognised as that of Squadron Leader Bat Maskell. Without hesitation I requested to be passed to Flight Lieutenant Mac Geeringh. As always Mac guided me right onto the runway whose lights I did not see until Mac instructed me to look up for touch-down.

Having just settled down in the crew-room with a cup of coffee, I received a call from OC Flying who asked why I had insulted Squadron Leader Maskell by asking for Mac for the final radar talk-down. I explained that there had been no intention of insulting anyone but that a few weeks earlier on an instrument let-down in clear sky conditions my student, reacting correctly to Bat Maskell's directions, would have reached ground well to the right of the runway. The experience had badly affected my confidence in him. Mac Geeringh, on the other hand, had a very reassuring voice and a special way of coaxing a pilot down the glide slope. For me, this had always ended up smack on the runway centre-line. Considering the weather conditions during this let-down I needed this confidence. OC Flying was satisfied, I heard no more about the matter and my personal relationship with Bat seemed unaffected.

The return to Provosts and instruction after jet flying seemed boring but it had its rewards because Dave Hume, Griff and Bruce McKerron were coming along well. But then I was very annoyed when told I would be losing my best student, Dave Hume, to take on Officer Cadet Dave Becks whose instructor had engineered a direct swap of students.

Gwelo Gliding Club

OUR METEOROLOGIST, HARVEY QUAIL ALWAYS provided very accurate forecasts of weather conditions until his deep involvement with the Gwelo Gliding Club, which he founded, seemed to rob him of his forecasting talent.

Harvey Quail.

In 1962 he persuaded me to join his club as its Chief Flying Instructor. I accepted the position on condition that all flying members were grounded until they had undergone full instruction in spin recoveries with a Bulawayo instructor who owned a Tiger Moth. This was because, in 1961, two learner pilots had inadvertently entered spins and died because they had not been taught how to avoid or recover from this flying hazard. I would have preferred to do the instruction myself but our trainer, a Slingsby T31, was not suited for the purpose.

Every flight I ever made in a glider gave me special pleasure, even the simple instructional ones. I particularly enjoyed flying

high-performance, single-seater machines. So far as I was concerned, gliding could not be compared with powered flight. It possessed a magic all of its own and two particular flights stick in my mind.

Mrs Mungay (pronounced Mingay), a great enthusiast who was always on hand to make tea for anyone needing refreshment, asked me to take her up on a short jolly. We made a normal cable-winch launch in the Slingsby T31 tandem trainer for what was intended to be a simple circuit and landing. However, on this occasion we entered strong lift just before the normal cable-release point so I cut free and entered into a tight turn to hold the thermal.

The initial rate of climb was impressive and, amazingly, it kept increasing. The T31 was considered to be more like a streamlined brick than a performance glider but our thermal was so potent that we climbed with ease to 11,000 feet where it was bitterly cold.

Being in an open cockpit dressed in shorts and a light shirt did not concern me because I was concentrating on climbing as high as possible. However Mrs Mungay, using the old-fashioned voice tube shouted, "My fanny is frozen." I laughed and ignored her problem until at 11,600 feet she was pleading with me to get her back on the ground. I rolled out of the turn to break from the thermal but the aircraft just carried on climbing. A little short of 12,000 feet I placed the glider in a full sideslip that did the trick and we descended down through ever-warmer air until finally we were back on the ground.

Since there had been no intention to do more than fly one circuit, the aircraft had not been fitted with a barometric recorder to prove the height achieved. So there was no point in complaining that I might have been denied the opportunity to claim a world height record for a Slingsby T31, simply because my passenger's fanny was frozen.

My second memory is of a failed attempt to fly a Slingsby Swallow from Gwelo Gliding Club to the Salisbury Gliding Club. Progress was fine initially thanks to a starting height of 14,300 feet over Gwelo. But in the Redcliff area near Que Que I could find no thermals at all. In desperation I made for the Rhodesian Iron and Steel Company works to pick up lift around a smoke column rising from the factory. The acrid smoke made me cough and splutter and I experienced eye-watering burning of my eyes. As soon as I had sufficient height to make for Que Que I broke out into clean air. On two occasions I flew towards hawks soaring in weak thermal conditions but eventually I was forced to land in a farmer's field and await collection. Any hope of becoming a proficient high-performance glider pilot was short lived. Club life was robbing me of time I needed to spend with my family and the cost of gliding was becoming too high.

16 PTC

IN JULY 1962 NO 16 PTC commenced their BFS and I was allocated Officer Cadets Graham Cronshaw, Prop Geldenhuys and Chris Dixon. All three progressed normally and I made it known that I did not wish to have any of these students taken from me to satisfy any other instructor's will. This only worked for three and a half months before my favourite student, Prop Geldenhuys, was taken away. I was given Officer Cadet du Toit who had not been shaping up with his first instructor.

Graham Cronshaw, Prop Geldenhuys, PB and Chris Dixon.

I had a very soft spot for Prop Geldenhuys for more reasons than his good nature; we had experienced two serious incidents together. The first of these was when I was demonstrating recovery from engine failure on a short-field take-off.

A short take-off required full power against brakes before rolling and forcing lift-off at around 65 knots with a steep climb out. No recovery from engine failure was possible below 200 feet, which made me wonder why this exercise that I had demonstrated many times was considered necessary. Anyway, at 200 feet I chopped the engine and pitched the nose down sharply. Talking to Prop all the time, the airspeed was increased to 85 knots before the first of two attitude changes was made to reduce the descent rate and glide angle preparatory to a normal round-out for landing.

When I made the first check the aircraft attitude changed but the descent rate and angle remained unaltered. Full throttle was applied, but the engine did not respond and even full flap failed to prevent the aircraft from slamming heavily into the ground. This fully compressed the main wheel oleos that then forced us to rebound back into the air. Immediately the motor roared to full power, lifting the aircraft precariously with insufficient runway remaining to put down again safely. The Provost was staggering along when I realised the wings were badly distorted. Aileron control was all but lost, necessitating the use of rudder to lift the port wing. To achieve the correct climbing speed, the nose had to be depressed well below its normal climbing attitude because the distorted wings were now set at a higher than normal angle to the airframe.

I was still sorting myself out when Prop blurted out, "Sir, this wing is coming off." I looked down my side and could see that the wing root fairing had separated from the leading edge and that there were stress wrinkles on the mainplane. Obviously Prop's side looked the same but sun reflections on the ripples, from his perspective, must have given him an impression of imminent structural failure.

Having assured Prop we would be okay, I waited until we were above a safe bail-out height before telling him to be prepared to jettison the canopy and abandon the aircraft without hesitation if I told him to do so. Very limited aileron movement was available at each end of full application because the control cables had become slack within the distorted wings. Elevator and rudder control responses were normal so I continued climbing to 10,000 feet with a view to establishing the stalling speed and to conduct low-speed handling checks preparatory to a landing that I felt sure would be possible.

Bob Woodward came up to inspect our Provost and reported that, apart from severely bent wings, the port tyre had burst and the tail wheel had disappeared into the fuselage. He formated on me as I reduced speed to check my damaged aircraft's slow-speed handling characteristics. When it felt as if we were near to stalling, my airspeed indicator read 100 knots whereas Bob said his was reading 85 knots. We concluded this had something to do with changed geometry of the airframe.

The landing was fine, the wings did not come off but the burst wheel, even with a fair amount of right-wheel braking, pulled the aircraft into a wide turn before we came to a dusty halt.

In the hangar after replacement of the burst tyre. Note the increased wing-pitch angles outside of the undercarriage legs.

I had just climbed out of the cockpit onto the wing with my parachute slung over my shoulder when Group Captain Jock Barber drew up behind the aircraft in his staff car. Looking directly towards the CO, I took the normal step down from the trailing edge of the wing and nearly broke my neck and back when my foot met ground about two feet closer than usual because the trailing edge of the wing was so much closer to ground. This bad jolt, and possibly the high-impact landing, initiated spinal problems that were to plague me for twenty-four years until an orthopaedic surgeon eventually performed a successful lower lumber fusion in 1986.

Chris Dams and Dave Thorne conducted tests in which they discovered that the Leonides engine's response to full throttle application failed when rpm was reducing close to idling speed. This was taken to be the reason for my engine not giving full power at a critical moment. But it was the technicians who pinpointed the primary cause of the accident. The airspeed indicator on my side of the cockpit was over-reading by 10 knots. Had I been using the student's airspeed indicator, as I should have done when instructing, a costly accident would certainly have been avoided.

The second incident with Prop occurred during a take-off run. Prop had applied too much elevator when lifting the tail. Because the nose was too far down, I placed my hand on my control column and, easing back slightly, said "Not so much!", whereupon Prop applied full brakes, pitching the nose down violently. Fortunately my hand was already on the control column so I was able to yank back and prevent the propeller from digging into the runway. In so doing the aircraft was forced to stagger into flight prematurely.

I climbed and had turned down wind for a landing to have the tyres inspected when I noticed that Prop had his hand on the control column, still with brakes fully applied. A gentle tap on his arm made him let go. Even before lining up with the runway we could see the two lines of torn grass down the centre of the runway. They were later paced out at sixty-eight yards.

Prop explained that he thought we were already airborne when he applied the brakes; anyway we had been very fortunate. Had the propeller dug into the ground at speed and full power a serious situation might have resulted.

Pat Meddows-Taylor and Dave Thorne, seeing that I was somewhat shaken by the incident, offered me a cigarette. Not having smoked in my adult life I declined their offer; but both of them insisted I take a couple of puffs to calm me down. Foolishly I took the lighted cigarette and, under guidance, inhaled smoke. There was no coughing so I took another and then another drag before becoming dizzy.

The first incident with Prop Geldenhuys led to major spinal problems and the second one set me off on cigarette smoking; two awful afflictions that can be blamed on nobody but myself.

Officer Cadet Strnad, a student on 16 PTC, was one of the most troubled youngsters I had ever met. He was not my student and I only flew with him once on IF. Like the rest of his course, Strnad was not used to alcohol but, when he did drink, he became very weepy and needed to talk to anyone who would lend a sympathetic ear. In Beryl and me he found sympathy, not that either one of us could make sense of his ramblings until Beryl managed to get to the root cause of his distress. His father was practising incest on his sister who was a very unwilling participant. Not long after this Strnad, after his release from the RRAF, returned to South Africa where he murdered his father to protect his sister and then changed his name. He was imprisoned but later released when an Appeal Court judge ruled in his favour.

RAF Trappers

No 1 SQUADRON CONTINUED TO undertake annual detachments to Aden and the Canberras made their contribution to Middle East Commonwealth defence by training with RAF bombers based at RAF Akrotiri in Cyprus.

Canberras at RAF Akrotiri, Cyprus.

Although our Canberra pilots were Rhodesian-trained, most of the navigators had been recruited from the RAF and the South African Air Force. Rhodesian determination to turn in top results in all they did obviously rubbed off on the navigators because No 5 Squadron gave the RAF Canberra boys quite a hiding during annual bombing competitions. This seemed to intrigue the RAF hierarchy who, with the concurrence of our Air HQ, decided to look into Royal Rhodesian Air Force flying standards.

Central Flying School of the RAF ran a team of testing officers nicknamed 'The Trappers'. The team was comprised of highly rated instructors who roamed RAF squadrons testing other instructors as well as fighter, transport, bomber and helicopter pilots. When the Trappers arrived in Rhodesia to test our pilots, absolutely nothing was known of their presence or purpose until, unannounced, they appeared in every squadron crew-room.

Two testing officers came to 2 Squadron, one to test Vampire instructors and the other to test Provost instructors. Each selected three of us at random and I was one to be tested by Flight Lieutenant Grimson. He asked for pre-flight briefings on three nominated flight exercises prior to flying. In the air he tested my teaching techniques on the entire range of daytime exercises, excluding formation and navigation. In the Officers' Mess bar that evening I found him to be a very pleasant individual, quite unlike the austere Trapper I knew in briefing room and cockpit. He uttered not a word to anyone about his assessment of those he had tested and would not be drawn to express opinion of our flying standards.

From Central Flying School our Headquarters received detailed reports revealing that, with the exception of No 4 Squadron, RRAF flying standards were equal to those of the RAF. The report made recommendation that an instructor be posted to 4 Squadron with a view to bringing its pilots up to standard. I was selected for this task and was posted to New Sarum.

No 4 Squadron

JUST PRIOR TO MY LEAVING Thornhill, my very first student Terry Ryan, then serving with 4 Squadron, was killed whilst flying unauthorised low-level aerobatics to impress his friends who were visiting the Snake Park near Salisbury. Apparently he was attempting a left-hand stall-turn that went pear-shaped and the aircraft slammed belly first into the ground close to the main Salisbury road. This was a sad prelude to my arrival on the squadron whose commander was Squadron Leader Ozzie Penton. Until this time I had only known him as a short cocky man who flew Canberras and revelled in baiting navigators and pilots who were six foot and over. From pilots serving under him I learned that he was tops as a squadron commander.

Ozzie Penton had flown Spitfires during WWII and became one of the most colourful individuals in our force.

His small build, cocky attitude and loud voice were endearing characteristics of a man who shunned administrative posts and only wanted to fly aeroplanes.

He made me feel welcome the minute I reported for duty and insisted that my corrective instruction would start with him. He said that between the two of us we would raise squadron standards to the point where 4 Squadron would be the next winner of the Jacklin Trophy. This we succeeded in doing.

Ozzie receiving the Jacklin Trophy from AVM Raf Bentley. Upon his retirement from service, Air Vice-Marshal Ted Jacklin had given this floating trophy to Air HQ for presentation to the squadron adjudged to have turned in the best performance or made the greatest advances during each year.

Flight Lieutenant Ted Brent.

Ozzie claimed that he was the ugliest man in the force and established the 'Uglies Club' with Doug Bebbington as his first though somewhat unwilling member. When six-foot-tall Canberra navigator Flight Lieutenant Don Brenchley suggested to Ozzie that his looks qualified him for Uglies Club membership, Oz raised himself to everything of five foot four inches and answered Don with spaced words loudly spoken saying, "Not a bloody chance mate! We may be ugly but we do have our standards!" Had Don been a pilot or technical man this would have been different!

My task in bringing flying standards up to scratch was a pleasant one that required no more than two months of fairly intensive effort. Under Ozzie's unique style of leadership the squadron's discipline was tightened and already high spirits amongst air and ground crews soared.

Flight Lieutenant Ted Brent was both 'A' Flight Commander and Pilot Armament Instructor responsible for all weapons training. He arranged a ten-day weapons training camp at Kutanga Range for all pilots using all twelve Provosts on squadron strength. This was my first introduction to the delivery of weapons from a Provost.

I was very dissatisfied with the squadron's poor gunnery results and wondered what I could do about it. Then, upon close inspection of the .303 Browning machine-guns, I found that they whipped about in poorly designed wing mountings. This problem was the consequence of the manufacturer having to convert Provost T1 trainers to MkT52 in too great a hurry to meet contract deadlines. I knew exactly what needed to be done and asked my OC if I could fix the problem. Not only did Ozzie approve this; he turned the issue into an official instruction to be certain I received maximum assistance from the Station Armoury and other technical sections at New Sarum. Initial resistance to a pilot leading the technical work came from two technical officers but Ozzie, who took absolutely no nonsense from anyone, sorted this out.

The mountings I designed were manufactured and fitted and ground-firing tests showed a great improvement in the accuracy of the guns. More important than this, from my own point of view, was the fact that I had established close relations with all the technical officers and technicians with whom I dealt; all were really top-line operators.

A task Ozzie pinned on me was to become the RRAF's low-level aerobatist on Provosts; my first exhibition at an Air Show occurring at Lusaka on 26 May 1963. Of all the low-level aerobatists who ever flew for the Air Force, I was certainly the least enthusiastic. Nevertheless my display at Lusaka and many to follow went off well enough.

A couple of years later I was pleased to hand this task over to Spaz Currie, a gifted young pilot who not only flew better aerobatics than me, he enjoyed it. I flew with Spaz on low-level aerobatic instruction, but it was really Dave Thorne who had brought him to the standard of excellence for which Spaz became well known. Dave Thorne and I were rated above-average pilots but it seemed to me that, as instructors, we both had the gift of being able to teach others to fly better than ourselves.

Almost any person can be taught to fly an aircraft but few people are 'born pilots' possessing natural flying ability. Yet, every now and then there arise those who possess a God-given ability to handle aeroplanes with amazing precision. So far as I can recall the 'born pilots' of our force were Charlie Paxton, Colin Graves, John Mussell, Mark Smithdorff, Keith Corrans and Spaz Currie. Bob Woodward was rated as a top line aerobatist but when flying with him I found his control movements to be incredibly harsh.

The RRAF was somewhat under-manned for situations requiring deployment of squadrons into the field. To cater for this a Volunteer Reserve (VR) force was established under Group Captain Charles Green, himself a volunteer. He had seen service during WWII and distinguished himself when commanding 266 (Rhodesia) Squadron operating Typhoon fighter-bombers that specialised in ground-attack. As a consequence of his extreme aggression against German tank concentrations during General Patton's push in the Ardennes campaign, Charles was shot down and became a POW.

In the initial stages there were so many Rhodesian Greek volunteers that some of us nicknamed the VR 'The Hellenic Air Force'. Four VR officers were attached to 4 Squadron for orientation purposes, though none of them was Greek. They were Derrick Whelehan, Brian Patton, Derrick Purnell and Trevor Ruile. Their arrival coincided with my request to introduce flying exercises designed to hone pilot skills in low-level map-reading, powers of visual observation and mental retention. Our technicians were to be included in most exercises as were the four attached VR officers. Ozzie Penton's permission was enthusiastically given before he turned things around and, in typical Ozzie fashion, ordered me to do exactly what I had asked for. I set about preparing exercises for counter-insurgency operations even though I knew absolutely nothing about COIN operations. I had to rely entirely on my imagination and plan accordingly.

A points system was established for all these exercises which engendered a strong sense of competition amongst the participants, making the training seem more like a game than serious business. There were continuous variations introduced into the exercises, all flown at low level to simulate worst operating weather conditions.

A typical single flight task might be to: (1) find the most suitable site for float plane operations in clear water having a straight run of 800 yards within thirty nautical miles of nominated place; (2) identify features at grid references a,b,c and so on; (3) make a single pass on the bridge at grid reference so and so and have a sketch and written report on the bridge air-dropped to police station such and such.

The British South Africa Police were very helpful in providing observers at bridges, or any other place involving a single pass. Aircraft numbers were recorded and passed to the squadron so that anyone making more than one pass would be spotted and disqualified.

In the initial exercises there were wide variations in results but, with persistence, we reached a point where all results matched, thereby indicating that good standards in map-reading and recce observations had been achieved.

We returned to Kutanga for another weapons camp. The gunnery results improved unbelievably. Pilots who had previously scored around 15% hits were recording better than 60% and Ted Brent managed to score 100% on one of his solo flights. Air HQ was well pleased with the marked improvements in our gunnery, rocket and bomb results. This precipitated a visit to Kutanga by the Director General Operations, Group Captain John Deall.

During WWII at the tender age of twenty-three, John Deall relinquished his command of No 266 Squadron to take over a wing of Typhoon and Spitfire squadrons, including 266 Squadron. Later he returned to Rhodesia as a Wing Commander with five proven victories, a DFC, a DSO and the Netherlands Flying Cross.

Air Commodore John Deall.

Provost armament: Teargas canisters, 4-inch rockets with 60 lb. concrete practice heads, 24 lb. practice bombs (white concrete bodies), 28 lb. Mk1 fragmentation bombs, 250 lb. GP high-explosive bomb and a parachute container for emergency delivery of medical supplies and other small items. Not shown are belts of .303 Browning machine-gun ammunition and illuminating flares. Note the squadron building and hangar. These were built at Thornhill in 1940 for the RAF's RATG needs and were still in use beyond the '80s.

Though of small build, Johnny Deall was a giant in all respects and greatly revered by all ranks. He always remained cool, was softly spoken and had an ability to admonish men with very few words. By far the worst chiding I ever received from anyone came from John Deall in the mid-1970s when he was Chief of Air Staff in the rank Air Commodore. He called me to his office and, holding a draft paper in front of him, simply said, "I feel let down PB. I expected better of you!" I was floored and deeply embarrassed by the quietly spoken words. I received his apology the moment he realised that I was not the writer of the paper. Nevertheless, I left Johnny Deall's office feeling decidedly crushed.

John Deall had not flown for some years when, at Kutanga, he went up with Ted Brent to try his hand at firing rockets from a Provost; a far cry from Typhoons and Spitfires. After a couple of dummy runs he fired four rockets, one off each of four live passes. We were all stunned because he scored direct hits every time. When invited to try his hand again, Johnny declined saying he would be a fool not to quit whilst he was on top.

Warrant Officer Tommy Minks headed 4 Squadron's technical team, made up of a lively bunch of mischievous men. One of these was Marlow Sharp, a foul-mouthed ex-Fleet Arm type who delighted in taking the mickey out of pilots and using bad language to shock young ladies.

When our beaten-up old Bedford van arrived from Que Que with a bevy of girls escorted by the unmarried guys they were met by Ted Brent. Always the perfect gentleman, Ted

lifted the wet hessian screen that served as back door and dust trap. Then, one by one, he greeted each young lady and holding her hand helped her down the back step. Once inside the large marquee tent containing bar, food and chairs, Ted would satisfy himself that every lady was attended before retiring to his tent for a full night's sleep. It was in the marquee that I first witnessed Marlow Sharp's naughty antics.

Pilot Officer Henry Elliott had a reputation for snaffling the prettiest girls before any one of the other single fellows could make a move. However, on this particular evening, Marlow decided to turn things around. He went to a small group of girls, who he had seen sneaking looks at Henry, and said something along the lines, "Do not look now, but that good-looking pilot by the centre tent pole—such a pity about his malady. His ears are healed now. Only the deep holes behind the ears remain from where the disease started. It has moved down to his chest now, but do not be put off by that, he is well covered with special dressings so you will not smell the rotting skin." With that Marlow excused himself and left.

In no time at all every girl had learned about Henry's 'rotting flesh'. As it happened Henry had deep wells behind his ears and though these were part of his natural make-up, the girls had surreptitiously checked them out. Poor Henry could not figure out why his usual ability to attract girls was failing; each one he approached found reason to drift off somewhere else. Henry's weapons results over the following two days were pathetic until Marlow told him why the girls had avoided him. Henry's smile returned and his weapon scores improved.

Federal break-up

DURING MY TOUR ON 4 Squadron the Federation of Rhodesia and Nyasaland was dissolved by the British Government to meet black nationalist demands. Northern Rhodesia and Nyasaland, having originally been British protectorates, were both granted independence by Britain. Respectively, they were renamed Zambia and Malawi. Southern Rhodesia had been self-governing since 1923 and reverted to this status with her name reduced to Rhodesia. Britain had guaranteed that, for agreeing to the dissolution of the Federation, Rhodesia would be given full independence at the same time as Zambia and Malawi. Sadly however, the true nature of Britain's political expediency and its policy of appeasement, as witnessed in Chamberlain's dealings with Hitler, became fully revealed when black governments in Africa successfully pressurised Britain into reneging on this solemn undertaking. This was but the first of many broken promises and agreements that Rhodesians were to face throughout eighteen long years of communist-inspired political turbulence.

When it came to sharing out Federal assets one of the thorniest issues was the matter of what was to be done with the RRAF. The British Government realised that the Air Force, having been built into a well-balanced force, could not simply be split three ways—this was neither practical nor sensible. It was also recognised that the majority of the costs in creating the Air Force had been borne by the people of Southern Rhodesia who, in any event, were more capable of operating the Air Force than either Zambia or Malawi. An equally important consideration was the matter of its serving personnel who had either been born in Southern Rhodesia or had set up permanent homes there.

The only component of Air Force eventually affected by share-out was No 3 (Transport) Squadron. Six of the squadron's aircraft, four Dakotas and two Pembrokes, were allocated to Zambia. Nothing was given to Malawi.

Although the Federation was officially dissolved on 3 December 1963 the Royal prefix to Rhodesian Air Force was to remain until March 1970 when Rhodesia became a republic. In the meanwhile all members of the force were given three options before the break-up. These were to remain under their existing contracts, to join the Zambian Air Force with attractive incentives or, to leave the force permanently.

The latter option was disgustingly close to an invitation to quit the service because of the excellent terminal benefits offered. To placate those who remained in service, guarantees were given that men who accepted a 'golden handshake' would never be accepted back into the force. These guarantees were later ignored when Rhodesia needed experienced men in troubled times. Many were allowed to rejoin and, considering the times, this was perfectly acceptable to those who had remained. What was irksome, however, was that too many returnees were coerced into rejoining with the same rank and benefits they would have enjoyed had they not left.

Federation had been a great success yet its destruction had been forced on Rhodesia to appease black politicians bent on personal gain. Like my colleagues, I chose to ignore the dire warnings given by politicians and news media and simply put my head in the sand, got on with my work and hoped for the best. I was not alone because the majority of white Rhodesians ignored anything they preferred not to hear. Life had changed little after ten years of Federation. The beer was good, we still had the finest beef in the world and there was no shortage in any of life's comforts.

I recall that my biggest concern in those times was that Beryl had been incapacitated by chronic asthma for the ten months since we moved from Thornhill to Salisbury. Any amount of medical effort had been given to resolve her problem but nothing helped. Then, out of the blue, my father suggested we visit Leslie Shaw, the chiropractor. We were willing to try anything at that stage and despite our doubts paid him a visit. Beryl's asthma was so bad that she was hardly able to take four steps in succession over the short distance from our car to his rooms.

Leslie amazed us by saying that 90% of asthmatic problems stem from spinal misalignment. He asked me to wait for twenty minutes whilst he took Beryl off for X-rays of neck and spine to determine if her problems lay there. Happily they did and, after three further visits to Leslie Shaw over a period of ten days, he corrected Beryl's misaligned neck and upper spine. This put an end to Beryl's inhibiting asthmatic problems. Thanks to Leslie Shaw, and indirectly to my Dad, they have not recurred for the thirty-five years leading to this time of writing.

Return to Thornhill

FOLLOWING THE DISSOLUTION OF THE Federation, the RRAF found itself short on manpower, necessitating many adjustments. At the same time Salisbury Air Traffic Control was seeking a reduction in an existing high level of slow aircraft movements to improve safety and control in the face of ever-increasing volumes in jet traffic. This brought about the move of 4 Squadron back to Thornhill. At the same time Nos 5 and 6 Squadrons were amalgamated into No 5 Squadron and the Canberras moved to New Sarum. For a while, No 6 Squadron did not exist until it eventually took over 2 Squadron's role in pilot training for BFS and AFS with 2 Squadron retaining responsibility for weapons training only.

Beryl and I were pleased to be returning to Thornhill. However, the wind was taken out of my sails the moment the squadron taxiied into dispersals where the Station Commander, Group Captain Doug Whyte, met us.

Having welcomed our OC, Squadron Leader John Mussell, he came to me with a broad grin on his face to say he had both good and bad news for me. The bad news was that he was taking me from the squadron for an indefinite period to be his Station Administration Officer, a post that had hitherto not existed. The good news was that I would be doing a limited amount of flying, most of which would be developmental testing of locally manufactured weapons.

Doug Whyte had been Station Commander in the rank of squadron leader when Thornhill was taken over from the RAF in 1955 and he remained there until my course had reached solo stage on BFS in mid-1957. Now he was back in command

Group Captain Doug Whyte welcomes Squadron Leader John Mussell to Thornhill.

Doug Whyte.

of a much larger station and had many things he wanted doing to get things running his way. Working directly under him was fantastic and I did not miss flying as I thought I might. The tasks I was required to perform were clear-cut, wide-ranging and quick in coming. One of these was to prepare Kutanga Range for an air weapons demonstration for cabinet ministers, African chiefs, the

Army, the British South Africa Police and the press.

Kutanga Range was well known to every pilot who underwent weapons training because all had performed Range Safety Officers duties and all had enjoyed this task. Warrant Officer Nobby Clarke was the Range Warden who had a small permanent staff. One of these was John MacKenzie (Kutanga Mac), an excellent ranger who would later replace Nobby.

The Fire Section supplied a fire Jeep and crew who were housed on the range during their seven-day stints on range duties. Three domestic workers and six labourers with their wives and children lived on the range permanently whereas Nobby and John commuted daily to their homes in the town of Que Que.

A lone kudu at Kutanga Range.

Surrounded by large cattle ranches, Kutanga Range was more like a game reserve than an air-weapons range. It had large expanses of mopani bushveld and an abundance of small game, the largest species being kudu. About 3,000 acres of bush had been cleared eastward from the northern boundary fence to give visibility to widely dispersed targets. Though primarily intended for air-weapons training, Army used Kutanga for field gun, armoured car, mortar and jungle-lane training. The BSAP also used the range occasionally.

Sleeping accommodation existed for ten people and the large kitchen was able to handle many additional people whether on day visits or camping in tents. One tarmac runway and a grass runway catered for piston-engined aircraft and both could accept fully laden Dakotas. Three high, brick-under-iron roof structures, widely separated and known as quadrant huts, were used to take bearings of each rocket and bomb strike. The hut nearest the domestic area was the 'master quadrant hut' where the Range Safety Officer resided with radio communications to aircraft. Telephones linked it to the two secondary quadrant huts.

Two bearings were necessary to plot the position of each projectile's impact point. The Range Safety Officer took one bearing and received the second bearing from one or other of two secondary quadrant huts. The two bearings when applied to a plotting board gave the strike position. Each result was passed to a pilot by radio within ten seconds of his strike. When the datum lines of both quadrant huts were 'zero', a pilot was given one or other of the following calls: "Direct hit", "DH" or "Coconut". These were music to every pilot's ear but as often as not impact error would be given along the lines "six yards, four o'clock". Errors given at 12 o'clock were overshoots along the attack line whilst 6 o'clock errors were undershoots on the same line.

Six three-metre-square elevated frames, numbered and set in a line, were covered with cardboard for Provosts firing .303 guns. Individual scores were recorded by physically counting the number of stick-on patches used to cover fresh bullet holes. Vampire 20mm gunnery targets were the same except that the frames were covered with stretched hessian. Scoring was also by physical count but paint was used to daub fresh strikes.

Hunter strike.

The same gunnery targets could not handle Hunter 30mm shoots because a single strike on any section of the frame collapsed the target. Because of this, Hunter gunnery was done on the rocket target with reliance being placed on the Range Safety Officer's ability to judge effectiveness of each strike. Kutanga Mac was better at this than any pilot, so Hunter gunnery training was usually deferred on those rare occasions when Mac was not available.

The rocket and dive-bombing target was one and the same, sited about 800 metres from the master and closest secondary quadrant huts. The 'Bull's eye' aiming point was a simple circular pyramid of earth that was regularly covered with whitewash. This pyramid lay at the centre of a broad-lined circle whose radius was fifteen metres. The Canberra bombing target was

two-and-a-half kilometres from the master and farthermost secondary quadrant huts. It comprised a single, high pyramid of earth covered with white rocks to make target acquisition possible for the long distances involved in high and medium level bombing.

Weapons demonstration

THE DATE OF THE AIR-WEAPONS demonstration was set for 12 May 1964. The guest of honour was to be the Prime Minister, Mr Winston Field, whose Rhodesian Front (RF) Party had come to power following an overwhelming victory at the polls in December 1962. Well-known Federal personalities such as Sir Roy Welensky, Sir Godfrey Huggins and Edgar Whitehead had gone and a new breed of politicians was firmly in control.

Every RF minister had seen military service in WWII and many were farmers. With the RF still settling in to govern a country facing uncertain times, Rhodesian citizens' morale needed boosting. A demonstration of the country's air power was expected to be helpful in this regard, though Air HQ was aiming more at establishing itself with the new breed of politicians who appeared to understand the importance of balanced military strength.

With the able assistance of Warrant Officer Nobby Clarke, I established the lay-out of targets, seating design and location, a public address system, catering plans, parking areas for aircraft and cars and so on; all of which the CO approved. With Nobby's men and input from Thornhill's workshops, all targets and adequate spectator benches were constructed with time to spare. There was, however, a need for extra hands to mix mud and to hand-plaster pole and thatch structures that constituted some of the targets. I asked for and got all officer cadets of both courses then undergoing pilot training.

No 17 PTC, being the senior course, was hoping to give 18 PTC most of the hard graft but I scotched this by separating their tasks and locations during working hours. But, out of working hours, the members of 18 PTC had a pretty torrid time. Wherever this junior course went its members had to carry teddy bears, all having personal names. No matter who a junior cadet met, he was obliged to introduce his teddy by name, then introduce teddy to the individual. This and other demeaning impositions certainly had the desired effects. The juniors so hated their seniors that they had become welded into a unified group.

Beryl, Debbie and Paul came out to Kutanga to visit me one day and were taking tea when the junior course, having showered away mud from their bodies and dressed in clean clothes, came in for refreshments. They set themselves up in a line to introduce their teddies to Paul then Beryl and finally Debbie. I was amused to see that every teddy was being placed at Debbie's feet, all gifts for the little girl! Things changed when the senior course arrived. In reverse order each member of the junior course came to Debbie, apologised for his error, and retrieved his teddy, much to Debbie's disappointment.

Notwithstanding their clean clothing, the junior course was ordered to bury a three-foot snake that the senior course had killed out on the range. First a narrow vertical grave had to be dug. When the grave was ready we watched the solemn funeral procession for a snake being borne horizontally by every hand of the junior course to the site of its vertical burial. As they marched slowly along they sang a mournful dirge composed by the senior course, their dislike of their seniors showing clearly on every face.

Group Captain Whyte was very pleased when he flew to Kutanga to inspect the entire set-up but became annoyed when press photographers arrived, uninvited. They gave the CO a bit of a run-around wanting to film aircraft in their attack dives because this would not be possible on the day of the demonstration. The CO obliged by arranging for Nos 1 and 2 Squadrons to lay on a Hunter and a Vampire for the purpose. He then asked me to fly my Provost on both high- and low-level attack profiles. For the low-level profile the CO told me to make sure one particular photographer would be put off asking for anything else.

The 'particular' photographer was waiting as I descended to pass over him low and fast. I could see him all the way and hoped he would chicken out because my wheels were almost in contact with the ground during the final run of 300 yards to where he stood; but I was forced to pitch up very, very, close to him. Apparently he did not budge an inch when the propeller passed over him at about three feet. He simply swung the

Flight Lieutenant Ian Douglas Smith, North Africa 1942 .

camera around to film the aircraft climb away.

On the very day of the weapons demonstration we learned that a new man had replaced Winston Field as Prime Minister. None of us knew who Ian Smith was at that time and had no way of knowing how this WWII pilot would influence everything we did and thought.

However he did not attend the weapons demonstration because he knew that Winston

Field was really looking forward to the event, having been invited as guest of honour.

On a small knoll comfortable padded seats were set out for VIPs in the shadow of a secondary quadrant hut. Below this, row upon row of fixed wooden benches provided seating for the African chiefs and other guests.

AVM Bentley sitting with the chiefs and Civil Service observers.

The first demonstration was announced as four Provosts peeled over in line astern diving steeply, each to deliver eight British-made 28-pound fragmentation bombs against the closest target that was about 500 metres away. The loud crrrumping denotations of each cluster of bombs following close upon each other had all the African chiefs and African soldiers diving for cover with loud cries of fear. When the Provosts cleared, they all rose cheering, dusting themselves off, laughing loudly and slapping each other on the back.

For the next two hours ever-noisier attacks had the spectators enthralled, but none more than our black countrymen who, to the end, bubbled and babbled after every noisy airstrike. Following the last bang spectators were moving off for drinks and lunch when four Hunters came in from the rear of the stands flying very low close to supersonic speed. This gave everyone the greatest fright of all and even caused that 'particular' photographer to drop his camera. The entire demonstration had proved a resounding success.

Early weapons testing

WHILST PREPARING FOR THE WEAPONS demonstration, I was required to fly a number of tests for Wing Commander Sandy Mutch who was then Staff Officer Operations at Air HQ. Working for him was a private engineering company seeking to improve two locally manufactured weapons and develop a new one. Twenty-eight-pound fragmentation bombs and their equivalent practice units were undergoing tests to prove new impact and airburst fuses. My involvement in this was straightforward because these bombs had been in use for some time.

The use of locally designed and manufactured fragmentation and practice bombs resulted in considerable savings in both cost and foreign currency. The fragmentation bombs were specifically intended for Canberras but could be delivered by any weapon-carrying aircraft. Ninety-six of them could be dropped from a Canberra bomb bay in a rippled release from a locally designed and manufactured carrier device nicknamed the 'bomb box'. The practice bombs, which fired a small smoke marker charge on impact, were used for training by all the strike aircraft.

The Staff Officer Armaments, Squadron Leader Ken Gibson, and two assistant armourers had brought all the bombs and fuses to Kutanga Range. Use of a dedicated Provost piloted by me and operating out of Kutanga made loading, air releases and on-site inspection quick and simple.

Included for first tests were eight prototype sixteen-gallon napalm bombs that had not previously been used by the RRAF. Napalm was considered an excellent weapon for bush warfare but its use invariably attracted considerable criticism from a number of world bodies. In an attempt to disguise the real purpose of these units, they were referred to as 'frangible tanks', giving rise to the abbreviated term, 'Frantan'. The early Frantans comprised of three sections fashioned from 1.5mm mild steel sheeting. These were a short conical nose, a central cylinder incorporating filler cap and suspension lugs and a tail cone incorporating a fuse pocket. Welded together these formed the 1.8-metre-long Frantan. In early tests Frantans were filled with reject aviation gas and soap flakes that together produced a sticky gel. I was very concerned when I learned that the test units were fitted with modified phosphorus grenades to ignite the gel.

The use of phosphorous igniters was what concerned me more than the fuel gel, though I did not know why at the time. Four sorties were to be flown with two Fantans per sortie delivered singly at low-level onto open ground. All went well with the first three sorties though I was surprised by the high level of radiated heat on the back of my neck.

On the last sortie one of the Frantans refused to separate from the carrier even when high 'G' and excessive yawing was applied. There was nothing I could do but land with the 'hang up'. Having touched down and rolled along the grass runway for some distance the Frantan came away from the carrier, bounced up into the tail plane and ignited. A fiercely hot fireball engulfed the fuselage right up to the cockpit for just a moment but I rolled to the dispersal area none the worse for the experience. Apart from mild scorching of my neck, similar to sunburn, and blistered paint on the aircraft's rear fuselage, fin and tail plane no real harm had been done. Had the Frantan dislodged at slower speed the outcome might have been serious.

A close inspection of components revealed that the suspension lug, upon which the Frantan hung on the carrier hook, had been the cause of the hang-up. This was rectified and I flew many further Frantan tests after locally designed 'multi-directional inertia pistols' had been fitted to fire the flash-powder charge that assisted in bursting the tank to free and ignited gel.

During these trials I got to know Wing Commander Sandy Mutch better than before. Though still bulldoggish in manner, he listened to my opinions about our air weapons in general and grudgingly agreed that most were totally unsuited to the type of conflict we seemed headed for; counter-insurgency warfare. I committed these same opinions to writing and, through Group Captain Whyte, the paper was submitted to Air HQ.

The result was that the CO received a reply asking, "What does that puppy PB know about weapons effectiveness? Had he seen how 60-pound rockets destroyed German trains and how 1,000-pound bombs blew buildings to smithereens, he might be wiser." I knew very well that our weapons were effective in conventional warfare but nobody seemed interested in considering anything beyond the small fragmentation bombs and Frantans I had been testing for bush warfare. Twelve long years were to pass before I was taken seriously and, eventually, given authority to develop locally manufactured weapons that better suited our needs.

Deaths of Bruce McKerron and Henry Elliot

ON THE AFTERNOON OF 22 June 1964 I was returning to Thornhill from Salisbury cruising at 15,000 feet. Strictly speaking the Provost was not permitted to operate above 10,000 feet because the unpressurised cockpit was not equipped with oxygen. However, out of curiosity, I was establishing the aircraft's performance at that level. I suffered no ill effects and watched my nails continuously to make sure there was no bluing of the cuticles, an early sign of oxygen deficiency.

When I switched radio channel from Salisbury Approach Control to Thornhill, I was asked to divert to the Jet Flying Training Area. A mayday call had been received from Bruce McKerron who was flying an FB9 but nothing had been heard from him since. I made a long, full-powered descent directly towards a major feature named Umgulugulu where I intended to commence my search. Along the way I called Bruce repeatedly whilst scanning for any sign of smoke.

There was no reply and I saw no smoke. Over the massive granite dome of

In Royal Rhodesian Air Force colours, four of the five original Alouettes. Salisbury Airport is above the rotor mast of the nearest helicopter and New Sarum Airbase lies on the other side of the longest runway in Africa.

PB with Bruce during his BFS.

Umgulugulu, I looked down on the white painted numbers made by successive Pilot Training Courses. The smallest simply read '14 PTC' and each PTC number was larger than the preceding one. 18 PTC was the largest and whitest having recently been put there above the others.

I looked at 15 PTC, which was McKerron's course, and for some unaccountable reason sensed from it that Bruce was dead. It took me a while to spot the thinnest wisp of white smoke rising way back along the route I had just come. With nothing else to work on I flew to this point where a small fire was burning along a thin line of grass half way up the slope of a granite outcrop.

Looking back along the line of burnt grass I could see a black smudge on a flat rock surface at the base of the outcrop but could see nothing resembling aircraft wreckage. Then, a little way off, I noticed a group of men signalling wildly and pointing to a pyramid of newly cut branches. I made a slow low pass over six men who were all waving with one hand and pointing at the pyramid with the other. This, I was certain, was where the body of my ex-student lay so I returned to Thornhill

having passed the men again waggling wings to signify that I had seen them.

Our Alouette III helicopters had recently arrived in Salisbury and by pure chance one had just landed at Thornhill. I was asked to accompany Flight Lieutenant Rex Taylor and Doctor Kirk to the crash site. Not the best occasion for my first helicopter flight!

Upon landing we were met by four African males who all talked at the same time. In their own language I requested them to take down the branches to reveal Bruce's body that was covered by a brand-new raincoat whose owner made sure we knew this. He gladly accepted a £5 note to have it cleaned.

On removal of the coat we were met with a very dismal sight. Bruce's parachute was still strapped to his body, the 'D' ring still firmly set in its retainer pocket. Apart from Bruce's legs having being pushed into his torso, his head was flat and both blue eyes were bulging out. This was clearly the result of a very high-speed impact with ground. The thing that struck me immediately was that every joint in the right arm had dislocated and the arm lay out to twice its normal length. This could not possibly be attributed to ground impact. Rex agreed with me that Bruce had bailed out in a steep descent, probably a stabilised spin, and his right arm had caught the tail plane. With such damage to the arm we were certain that Bruce had been knocked unconscious and knew nothing thereafter.

Keith Corrans headed the Board of Enquiry whose findings concurred with our assessment. I remember how frustrated Keith was with the verbal evidence given by many Africans who claimed to have seen the aircraft come down. Not one story fitted another so Keith was forced to submit a report based on his reasoned assessment of events.

Exactly six months after this tragedy, one of Bruce McKerron's coursemates, Henry Elliot, died in another FB9 accident. He was returning to Thornhill from the Bulawayo area at night and was under Thornhill Approach Control. He was given a heading to steer and instructed to contact Radar Control when level at 6,500 feet. The radar controller observed the aircraft approaching on the correct heading before the blip disappeared off his screen.

Henry did not respond to Approach Control or radar calls

Henry Elliott.

so another Vampire was guided by radar to the point Henry's aircraft had last been seen. Immediately he arrived in the area the pilot located a fire making it clear to all that Henry had flown straight into the ground. We learned later that Henry had not been feeling well before this flight but, refusing to let this be known, went ahead with his navigational training flight instead of going to bed.

Henry Elliott had dated Beryl's sister Yvonne for some time but this changed and he was then courting a lovely girl. Wendy Miller was well known to Beryl and me so the CO requested that we go to her home to break the news to her. Wendy was in bed and had been asleep for some time when we woke her. This was my first experience of conveying bad news and it was every bit as hard to handle as I had imagined.

First terrorist action

FIVE MONTHS EARLIER ON 4 July 1964, when Americans were celebrating Independence Day, a brutal act heralded the start of terrorism and savagery in Rhodesia. A gang of thugs of the Zimbabwe African National Union (ZANU), styled the 'Crocodile Gang' and led by William Ndangana, set up a simple roadblock with rocks and tree branches on a mountain section of the Melsetter road. It was late at night when Petrus Oberholzer and his family, travelling in their VW Kombi, were forced to a halt.

As Petrus alighted from the vehicle he was attacked by some of the gang with knives and was mortally wounded. Other members of the gang were attempting to drag his wife and children from the vehicle but Petrus somehow managed to get back to the driving seat to bulldoze his way through the road obstruction. He drove a short distance before dying at the wheel. The vehicle impacted the low verge of the road and stalled to a halt just short of a steep drop off the mountain's edge. By this time all the doors had been locked from inside.

The terrified survivors knew the gang was back from their shouted abuses as they made an attempt to force open the doors. When this failed, the gang tried to light fuel streaming from the fuel tank damaged by the road obstruction. Thanks to wet matches and the timely approach of another car, the attack was broken off and the gang disappeared into the night.

Petrus Oberholzer was the first white man to die in an act of war since the Mashona Rebellion sixty-seven years earlier. The ZANU men responsible for his death were not yet armed with guns although these had become available to their Zambian-based rival ZAPU back in 1962. We knew that ZANU had started training in China in September 1962 so, considering the nature of the attack, it was feared that Mau Mau-styled operations might be opening up. These fears faded with time and armed offensives held off for twenty-one months.

Flying Wing Adjutant

IN AUGUST 1964 MY JOBS for Group Captain Whyte had been completed and I returned to flying instruction. My students were Officer Cadets Barry Roberts, Terry Jones, Blake Few and Steve Kesby. Teaching three of the students was straightforward but Blake Few suffered badly from airsickness.

I decided to apply on Blake Few the same treatment that had worked so well for Dave Hume. This time it was a dismal failure and I probably did Blake more harm than good because he continued to be sick, though less frequently. Nevertheless, this was enough to place his flying career in question. He transferred to Air Traffic Controller duties until, some years later, he returned to flying having overcome his motion sickness problem.

During the period of this course I flew two sorties with Officer Cadet Bill Buckle who I heard had the reach of an orang-utan. The average pilot had to undo his shoulder harness lock to reach over to the far side of the instrument panel to select two magneto switches for engine start-up. Bill could do this without unlocking shoulder straps, so far was his reach. Nobody could work out how he did it because he was a man of average height and his proportions were normal.

I had become bored with flying instruction and was longing

Barry Roberts, Terry Jones, PB, Blake Few and Steve Kesby.

for a posting. It came at the beginning of 1965 when I was moved to the newly established post of Flying Wing Adjutant. I was in this post for only nine months but enjoyed the break and was able to fly whenever I felt like doing so. I was also called upon to fly with Harold Griffiths and Brian Jolley who were undergoing instruction in the Flying Instructors School.

Deaths of Barry Matthews and Sandy Trenoweth

ON 24 MARCH 1965 ELEMENTS of 4 Squadron were returning from a short camp at Tjolotjo where they had been involved in an exercise with the Army. Leading a flight of four aircraft, Mike Reynolds climbed out straight ahead until all aircraft were airborne then turned back to bid farewell to the Army guys camping next to the runway. He ran in and executed a barrel roll at too low an altitude for the inexperienced pilots following behind. The next in line, Barry Matthews, attempted to follow Mike's manoeuvre but failed to make it through the bottom of the roll and slammed into the ground, belly down. The aircraft disintegrated and both Barry and Warrant Officer Sandy Trenoweth perished.

Sandy Trenoweth's distressed widow requested that Sandy's ashes be scattered from the air alongside the grass runway 13. In particular she asked OC Technical Wing for me to do this for Sandy's sake. I had liked Sandy very much but was somewhat surprised and flattered by Mrs Trenoweth's request.

With the urn containing Sandy's ashes prepared and lying in the empty bucket seat next to me, I settled on line with the runway and opened the canopy. Using my knees to hold the control column, I held the urn in both hands and put it out into the slipstream. Immediately I removed the lid, the slipstream started emptying the box but some of the light ash blew back into my eyes. When the urn was completely empty the canopy was closed but I was battling to see. For almost thirty minutes I remained at height giving the tears steaming from my eyes time to clear my vision for landing.

Rupert Fothergill

ON 8 AUGUST 1965 I was sitting at my Flying Wing Adjutant's desk when I received a distress call from National Parks Head Office in Salisbury. This was to say that a game-ranger had been gored by a rhino way up near Kariba Dam. Air Force assistance was needed to get morphine to the camp in which Rupert Fothergill had received first aid treatment but was in too much pain to face the long rough ride to the nearest hospital or airfield. A helicopter had been requested but this was going to take some time to reach him.

Having arranged a Provost with full overload tanks and collected morphine from Station Sick Quarters, I quickly fashioned a parachute and tested it to ensure a soft landing for the morphine and needles, which were neatly packed in sponge rubber. At the temporary game camp, I found the rhino pens where three of these large animals, disturbed by the Provost's presence, were running around in circles. A short distance away I saw the white sheets laid out as markers for the drop. The parachute deployed perfectly and waving bush hats and thumbs-up signals confirmed safe receipt of the morphine. Later, Peter Cooke with Dr Laidlaw arrived in an Alouette helicopter to fly Rupert to Salisbury Hospital.

How the rhino came to gore Rupert Fothergill I do not recall other than it was to be darted with a drug for capture and re-location to Wankie Game Reserve. Rupert Fothergill was leader of the much-publicised Operation Noah in which thousands of animals were rescued from certain death when the rising waters of Lake Kariba trapped them on newly formed islands that were going to disappear below water. Considering the nature of operations to capture panicking animals, it was surprising that Rupert was gored only this once and survived to continue his world-acclaimed work.

Posting to 3 Squadron

THORNHILL'S WORKING HOURS REMAINED 06:30 to 13:30, which gave everyone ample free time in daylight hours. Apart from boxing for Umtali High School and representing the school's first rugby team once, I had never excelled in any sport. My sports involvement was limited to golf once gliding became too expensive. Even in golf my participation with Dave

Thorne, Pat Meddows-Taylor and others was limited to one afternoon per week, so I looked to other activities to occupy spare time. Two of these were sewing and boat-building.

I had bought Beryl the latest in sewing machines, a Singer Slant-a-Matic, but she showed no interest in learning to use it. Rather that let the expensive machine lie idle, I decided to try my hand at making clothes for Debbie then Paul and did well in both. Without having taken a single lesson I progressed to day-dresses for Beryl and then to her eveningwear. The outcome of Beryl's evening dresses was very pleasing to both of us and led some wives to ask me to make dresses for them. Beryl would have nothing of this because of the way I handled her body during fittings. However, having satisfied myself that I could sew, I lost interest and thereafter only made curtains, box-pleated bedspreads and material coverings for furniture when pressed into doing so.

I built a mould for the sixteen-foot power catamaran that I designed. This was done in a large lean-to garage I had built for the purpose. I was doing well with my project but needed another eight weeks to make the fibreglass hulls when I learned that I had been posted to No 3 Squadron at New Sarum to fly Dakotas. My request for a delay so that I might complete the catamaran was turned down and I never did finish it.

My routine six-monthly flying medical examinations coincided with our arrival in Salisbury in mid-September 1965 when it was found that my hearing had been severely impaired by my job as Flying Wing Adjutant at Thornhill. I had become upper tone deaf from the continuous high-pitched screaming of Vampire engines whose noise was intensified by reflected sound off two walls in my second-storey office. I was grounded for six weeks with special plugs fitted in my ears until my hearing recovered to an acceptable level.

In late October I commenced the flying conversion to the Dakota but soon realised I was being held back for reasons that nobody would tell me. Instead of flying daily and going on my first solo on type in the usual ten days, I was flying every second day. When the day arrived for my first solo, which had already been recorded in the Flight Authorisation Book, I was told to report to OC Flying Wing. In his office Wing Commander Harry Coleman told me I was being withdrawn from 3 Squadron with immediate effect because I had been reallocated to helicopters. My disappointment at not making that solo flight was great because I really enjoyed my limited time on the famous old 'Gooney Bird'.

Helicopter training for the first RRAF pilots had been conducted in France. The South African Air Force then took over this role and our pilots were trained on French Alouette II and Alouette III helicopters operating out of Langebaan Air Base near Cape Town. Air HQ decided to establish if we could train our own pilots in Rhodesia as this would bring about considerable savings in time and foreign currency. Flight Lieutenant Mark Smithdorff had undergone some level of training as a helicopter instructor so it was decided that,

because I was an experienced instructor, he should try his hand at training me. If this worked out well, all future helicopter training would be undertaken in Rhodesia and I would become the squadron's second helicopter instructor. However, my training was only scheduled to begin in January 1966.

Catamaran.

Chapter

5

Unilateral Declaration of Independence

POLITICAL HARANGUING BETWEEN RHODESIA AND Britain had been ongoing since the granting of independence to Zambia and Malawi because Britain had failed to do the same for Rhodesia, despite her promises. Additionally, the British Government had undertaken not to interfere in Rhodesia's internal affairs and had endorsed the need to retain the tribal chiefs. But again, both of these important issues were conveniently forgotten.

In October 1964, many countries sent their observers to the biggest gathering of chiefs ever held in the country but Britain, supposedly the 'responsible power' for Rhodesia, refused to attend. Earlier, when the chiefs had sent a delegation to London to make their views known to the British Government, they were snubbed by Commonwealth Secretary Duncan Sandys and returned to Rhodesia deeply enraged by this discourtesy.

Realising that Britain had no interest or knowledge concerning the protocols and needs of the African people of Rhodesia, the chiefs gave their unanimous support to the RF to proceed to independence under the 1961 Constitution, which Britain had already ratified. Then, on 5 November, a referendum showed that 89% of the largely white electorate supported the chiefs' stance, thereby giving the RF authority to unilaterally declare Rhodesia's independence. The decision had not been an easy one but the ever-changing stance of the Conservatives made it crystal clear that they had absolutely no intention of holding to their word. This was the solemn promise to Rhodesia of independence in exchange for her co-operation in dissolving the Federation; despite such action being in conflict with the British Government's own recorded and declared principle that, "the Federation was indissoluble". If the Conservatives were bad news, the Labour Party's victory

in October was expected to make things worse, considering the rhetoric of pre-election speeches.

Just prior to coming to power, the new British Prime Minister Harold Wilson had made it known that the Labour Government "is totally opposed to granting independence to Southern Rhodesia as long as the Government of that country remains under control of the white minority." He had certainly misread things because Ian Smith's RF Party, the chiefs and the electorate were dedicated to the retention of 'responsible government'. It was from British politicians that racist definitions were generated; certainly not Rhodesia whose people had accepted the terms of the 1961 Constitution that underlined the undertaking of 'unimpeded progress to majority government'.

The track record of independent black governments in Africa made it clear to all Rhodesians that progress to black rule had to be handled with great care if the country was not to be reduced to a shambles by self-seeking despots. It was contended that we owed it to the black folk as much as to the whites to continue to build on the strong foundation of the country's existing infrastructures and wealth and to develop a healthy middle class from which future politicians, black and white, would emerge.

The possibility of Rhodesia declaring herself independent occupied Whitehall's attention to such an extent that veiled threats of dire action began to flow. That the governments of black Africa and the communist-dominated OAU were pressurising Britain was obvious because, in response to every move the RF made seeking fair play, the Labour Party, like the Conservatives before them, simply moved the goal posts. Rhodesia's need to take matters into her own hands to stymie the communist-orchestrated line was becoming more certain.

It was in these circumstances that I was attached as the Air Liaison Officer (ALO) to Army's 2 Brigade Headquarters at Cranborne Barracks, the old RAF wartime base. The military actions Britain was threatening and preparing for did not materialise, so the only real benefit of my presence at 2 Brigade was one of strengthening Army and Air Force relationships. This was my first full exposure to the Army and I enjoyed the experience very much. Brigadier Steve Comberbach and his staff went out of their way to make me feel comfortable in their midst and willingly provided answers to all my queries concerning their procedures that were, necessarily, very different from those of my own force. With much time on our hands Major John Smithyman treated me to a series of sound thrashings at chess.

During this period I managed to grab a ride in a helicopter with Ozzie Penton on a search for a large number of prisoners who had broken out of Salisbury Prison. The search ended up over a typical Rhodesian boulder-strewn hill of some twenty acres near Lake McIlwaine. Even when hovering close to the trees and boulders it was impossible for us to see any of the prisoners who were hiding under the boulders and in caves. It took dogs to flush them out eventually but the experience of rough country searches was something that I would become familiar with in time to come.

On 11 November 1965 I was instructed to get to the Officers' Mess at New Sarum before 11 o'clock. On arrival I found all officers assembled to listen to an important broadcast to the nation by the Prime Minister. On the dot of 11 o'clock, Ian Smith read Rhodesia's Unilateral Declaration of Independence (UDI). He ended the presentation with the words "God save the Queen".

The radio was switched off and not a word was spoken by the motionless gathering, everyone buried in his own thoughts.

Portrait photo.

Our loyalty to Her Majesty Queen Elizabeth II never faltered, though we all secretly worried that we would soon lose our royal title and with it the crown on badges and wings. When eventually this came to pass, I went to the trouble of visiting a photographer to have a portrait taken to remember my Queen's Commission. Many others did the same because British Royalty was deeply revered by all of us.

However, insofar as Her Majesty's Government was concerned, there was no respect whatsoever. Notwithstanding the unfairness of it all, we knew we were in for a torrid time from Harold Wilson's socialist government and, through this, the world at large.

Initial concern had been that Britain would take military action against us to 'restore' our country to British control. If this had happened, a modern-day disaster along the lines of the Anglo–Boer War would undoubtedly have resulted and South Africa may well have come to our aid, thereby creating a major war. A few Rhodesians may have scurried off to safety, but most of us would have fought with the blind courage and a determination that no British politician of those times would have expected. Unlike every one of our political leaders, the main Labour players had never heard a shot fired in anger.

Preparations were made for the most likely course of military action, a paratrooper assault on one or more of our main airfields. Thank God this never came because a kith-on-kin war would have been too awful. Later we heard that the Labour Party had come to realise that ordering British forces into action against their Rhodesian relatives might bring about their immediate undoing. There were even rumours that some well-known British Army units had made it absolutely clear that they would refuse to follow orders to act against Rhodesia.

Any doubts we had as individuals about the British Government's honesty were laid aside when Britain and America made threats of sanctions. Shortly thereafter, Rhodesian Hunter and Canberra engines inside Britain and those in transit for servicing by Rolls Royce were impounded, thereby creating an immediate and serious problem.

Just prior to this Group Captain Slade, the RAF Liaison Officer in Rhodesia, was recalled to Britain. On his return, he told the British press that our Air Force would grind to a rapid halt. He gave the jets, specifically the Hunter, three months and suggested that piston aircraft and helicopters would all be out of action within nine months. Our reaction to this was: "Not bloody likely, we'll show that pompous bastard that he is way off the mark." Group Captain Slade unwittingly did the RRAF a great favour by dispelling any remaining doubts about Britain's intention to destroy us and this engendered an overpowering will to surmount every difficulty that was laid in our path.

In addition to Britain trying to bring us to heel simply to remove pressure from the OAU, ZAPU and ZANU continued their preparations for war. In Rhodesia organisations of all descriptions set about overcoming sanctions even before they had been officially declared. Anti-British feeling ran high, particularly amongst those who had fought for Britain and the Empire during WWII. Even dedicated whisky drinkers dropped their favourite Scotch and local manufacturers benefited from British and American commodities being removed from housewives' shopping lists. Local manufacturers received full support for their products, even though these were sub-standard to start with. But in a relatively short time local substitutes improved and saved the country an absolute fortune in foreign currency. Familiar British trade names such as Heinz gave way to a host of Rhodesian producers including Cashel Valley products.

Hunter.

Rolls Royce engines

THE FIRST ROLLS ROYCE COMPONENT that came up for service was an Avpin (volatile liquid that ignites under pressure) powered starter motor for the Hunter engine. With care the starter motor was taken apart, serviced and reassembled. Only one 'O' ring needed replacing at a cost of six shillings and eight pence. The starter was back in service in one day, saving months in time and thousands of pounds in shipping and servicing costs. This, and many more experiences in the servicing of components, built up enormous confidence. But then came the Rolls Royce engines themselves.

In Air Force stores there were only a couple of reserve engines each for Hunters and Canberras. This meant that no time could be wasted when the first Hunter engine was removed for overhaul. It had to be stripped completely for an in-depth inspection of every component to determine what needed replacing. The engine then had to be rebuilt and test-

run. My recollection is that Chief Technicians Brian Fletcher and John Swait were initially baffled when having to split the heavy casings of the awkward-to-handle jet engine. A galley was noticed but it disappeared into the bowels of the beast and, being curved, there was no way of seeing where it went to, or what was at its end. A medical gastroscope was acquired and having been run down the galley revealed a bolt head at the end of, and in-line with, the galley. By trial and error a flexible wrench was fashioned at Station Workshops and a series of sockets were manufactured by Chief Technician Graham Harvey who, eventually, made one to fit the non-standard bolt head. Once the bolt was removed, the engine was successfully dismantled. Whereas the engine was found to be in pretty good shape, dust and small stone chips from high-speed air ingestion had pitted the leading edges of all impeller and turbine blades, as is normal with any jet engine. Reference numbers were taken from the highly specialised blades and passed to the 'sanctions busters' to source and procure. All replacement components and primarily seals were inspected, measured and referenced, again for the attention of 'sanctions busters'.

Like these RAF Hunters of No 8 Squadron seen over the Kariba dam wall on a visit in happier times, Rhodesia's Hunters just kept flying.

No component on the first engine gave cause for concern, so it was reassembled and satisfactorily test-run. It was then returned to service at 30% of its normal time between services to establish in-flight performance and gauge rates of wear and deterioration when the next major service was undertaken. The engine performed normally, giving confidence for the next engine strip-down. By the time the third Hunter engine was handed over to Engine Refurbishment Section (ERS), all essential spares had been acquired. Although these had been sourced at considerable cost the overall savings to Rhodesia, vis à vis the Rolls Royce route, were substantial. Just as important were the quick turn-around times that rendered our small reserve of engines adequate for our needs.

Canberra engines followed a similar path to that of Hunters and high levels of sophistication developed rapidly. First-class engine-handling rigs made maintenance technicians' work easier and safer. Purpose-made tools were manufactured in-house for difficult tasks such as the removal and replacement of turbine blades. Women were brought into ERS and did a wonderful job alongside the men. They all took great pride in turning out engines that ran more smoothly than those previously received from Rolls Royce. Much of this was due to purpose-built balancing rigs to trim each rotating assembly meticulously for vibrationless operation. Inadvertently the British Labour Government had made us more than self-sufficient and our jets were never limited for the want of engines.

Not long after receiving the Canberra B2 bombers, the Royal Rhodesian Air Force had asked Rolls Royce if compressed air could be used to start Canberra engines instead of the large cordite cartridges that powered starter motors. Rolls Royce considered the issue but assured our Air Force that this was an absolute impossibility. However, with the difficulties we faced after 1965, our technicians decided to do what Britain's top engineers had said was impossible. They not only succeeded in developing an adapter to make the cartridge starter function from high-volume-flow compressed air, they also retained starter motors' ability to use cartridges when operating from places where large compressed air bottles were unavailable. The system served us for fifteen years with enormous cost savings. A similar system was used to start the Hunter Avon 207 but was discarded because of the need to have an airline permanently fitted in the air intake.

No 7 Squadron

SQUADRON LEADER OZZIE PENTON WAS coming to the end of his tour as OC 7 Squadron when I joined him for the second time. He was to be replaced by John Rogers who was then undergoing his helicopter conversion with the South African Air Force.

On the last day of January 1966 I flew my first training flight in an Alouette III with Mark Smithdorff. I cannot say I enjoyed flying helicopters initially because it was so different from fixed-wing flying. In forward flight the aircraft felt and handled in typical fixed-wing fashion though the controls were very sensitive, almost too sensitive in fact.

Apart from the difficulties in learning to hover, I found descending turns with the speed falling off very disconcerting because I was expecting the helicopter to stall and flick over

like any fixed-wing aircraft would do. It took time to accept that all flying speed was in the fast-turning rotor blades. Once I had overcome the instinctive fear of stalling, helicopter flying became a little more enjoyable but learning continued to be hard work.

Kyle Dam.

Once I had flown solo and gained confidence from many entries into the tightest of landing places with high trees or rocks all around, helicopter flying became progressively easier. It took time for my brain to adjust to new flight sensations and make arms, legs and eyes co-ordinate automatically. Thereafter flying a helicopter became more enjoyable than fixed-wing. I found low-level map-reading particularly demanding and a great deal of practice was needed to master the art. Even at the relatively slow speed of 95 knots flying 100 feet above ground, the aircraft crossed over 1:50,000 scale maps very fast. The need to change maps quickly was made difficult by the fact it had to be accomplished with the left hand only because at no time could one let go of the cyclic control. With open doors the problem was compounded by air turbulence that could whip one's map through the rear door in a flash.

I could not get over the fact that Mark Smithdorff always had his map facing north no matter the direction of flight. Like all the other pilots, my map was turned to face in the direction of travel. If Mark tried this he became as confused as I did with the map the right way up when flying on any heading but north. Mark had another peculiarity. When writing on a blackboard, he would stand at its centre writing from left to centre with his left hand before transferring the chalk to his right hand and continuing uninterrupted in identical neat style towards the

Cargo slinging, hoisting slope landings on mountain ledges.

Melsetter village. Hopping from one pool to the next we emptied the trout into the cold water and saw them all swim off strongly. These fish survived and more trout were flown in for National Parks over time. By early 1970 all the pools within the Chimanimanis, both within Rhodesia and Mozambique, carried good populations of large trout.

On completion of basic training, I flew my Final Handling Test with Ozzie Penton who declared me ready for the Ops Conversion phase. My instructor, Mark Smithdorff, was one of nature's natural pilots who made everything look so simple. When he hovered, the helicopter remained absolutely static no matter how the wind gusted or how high the hover.

Cargo slinging, hoisting slope landings on mountain ledges, forced landing precisely on any point of my choice - all so smooth and unfussed yet always too good to be repeated with Mark's precision and ease. I was fortunate to have had such an instructor to prepare me for my final handling test.

The final test was conducted by Ozzie Penton who had been promoted to Wing Commander as OC Flying Wing at New Sarum. By this time Squadron Leader John Rogers had returned from South Africa.

Sinoia operation

right-hand edge of the board.

Mountain flying was by far the best part of training. On my first time out, Mark had arranged for us to route via Mare Dam in the Inyanga area to collect young breeder trout that we were to release into pre-selected pools in the Bundi Valley high up in the Chimanimani mountains. Rex Taylor had done this previously with fingerling trout but platanna frogs had devoured all of them. We were trying larger fish. There were about fifteen six-inch trout sealed in plastic bags that were half-filled with water and blown to capacity with oxygen. Each bag was in a cardboard box and about thirty-odd boxes filled the rear cabin. It was necessary to fly the one-hour leg directly to Chimanimani to limit damage that fish could cause each other.

The beauty within the mountain range astounded me because previously I had only seen the side of this range from

Squadron Leader John Rogers (left) takes command of 7 Squadron.

FOR BECOMING THE RRAF'S FIRST wholly trained helicopter pilot, I was made squadron standby pilot for the next seven days. Because of this I was the one called out following a report of terrorist activity near Sinoia. My flight technician for this trip was Ewett Sorrell. We set off for Sinoia not knowing more than an attempt had been made to blow down pylons on the main Kariba to Salisbury electrical power-line at a point just north of Sinoia town. Sinoia lay some sixty miles northeast of Salisbury on the main road to Zambia via Chirundu. The town served as the commercial hub and rail centre to large farming and mining communities in the region. It was also home to the Provincial Police HQ, which commanded a number of outlying police stations.

Superintendent John Cannon DFC was very pleased to see us on our arrival in his HQ building and invited us to lunch with his charming wife before getting to the business at hand. I had not met John before although I knew that he had served with distinction as a Lancaster pilot during WWII.

In his quiet, precise manner, which I came to know quite well over the next couple of days, John gave me a detailed briefing before we flew off to inspect the pylons against which sabotage had been attempted. The inspection revealed a very low standard of training by the ZANU men who had tried to knock out the country's power supply. They obviously knew nothing about pylon design or how to use explosive charges to shear steel structure. Damage at the points of detonation was so minor that no repair work was necessary. At some points scattered chunks of TNT showed that detonators had been thrust into the end of the Russian-made TNT slabs and not into the purple dots which clearly marking the location of primer pockets. All that ZANU had achieved was to show us that they intended to do harm.

John's information was that seven men known as the 'Armageddon Group' were one component of a group of twenty-one ZANU men who had entered the country together some ten days earlier from Zambia. This group was responsible for this job. Where the remaining fourteen men were John had no idea but he said they could not be too far away. All the same the Armageddon Group, having shown its hand, was the one we had to locate and destroy.

During the first afternoon at Sinoia I found that, for all my training, I had not been properly prepared for operations. To fit a helicopter into an opening in the trees with no more that six inches to spare was fine in training, yet here I nearly fell out of the sky when landing full loads of Police Reservists (PR—mostly portly farmers) and their equipment. The enormous reserve of power available from the Alouette's jet engine, small though it was, was sufficient to destroy the main-rotor gearbox if the calculated maximum collective pitch angle on the rotor blades was applied too long. I exceeded the gearbox limits during a number of landings by yanking on excess collective pitch to check the helicopter's descent for a soft landing. This necessitated the removal of a magnetic plug on the gearbox casing to check for telltale iron filings. Fortunately nothing was found, so no damage had been done. But it took a number

of exciting 'arrivals' on terra firma before I got the hang of making full-load landings safely, particularly on sloping ground.

Having established the right techniques I vowed to myself that, when I was instructing on helicopters, I would prepare future pilots better than I had been prepared myself. This in no way reflects on Mark Smithdorff's instructional abilities because mine was the first genuine operational deployment for a helicopter.

Tony Smit proved the difficulty some months later as seen in this crunch-up from his botched 'slope landing' in training.

Once the PR had been taken to their assigned locations I decided to take a look around the search area with Ewett Sorrell who had remained on the ground whilst I deployed the PR. It makes me shudder to think how, having first orbited suspect locations and old roofless buildings, we moved close in hovering to inspect every nook and cranny. Within six years this would have been suicidal and no pilot would have been so foolish as to think of terrorists simply as peasant farmers with guns.

During the early evening of 27 April, John Cannon received hot intelligence from Police General Headquarters in Salisbury to say that a 'Police source' was in contact with the Armageddon Group. This police undercover man, operating within the ZANU organisation, was due to meet up with the group near Sinoia the next day when the gang would be changing into black dress for their first planned attack against a white farmstead. The contact man was delivering some supplies and written instructions from ZANU HQ. He was not expected to be with the gang for more than ten minutes.

The contact was going to travel by car from Salisbury to Sinoia where he would be met by one of the gang at about 11 o'clock. He had been briefed to proceed along the main road to a point where the old strip road went left off the main road. Along this road he would find a member of the gang who would take him to the gang's night camp. He understood that the gang would be between the main road and the old strip road. For us this was a gift for both planning and execution of a classical police-styled cordon and search operation.

It seemed 'too good to be true' because the relevant sections of main road and strip road, each about one-and-a-half kilometres' long, formed an acute triangle with the Hunyani River forming its short base of about half a kilometre. The Hunyani River ran south to north on Sinoia town's eastern flank and both roads came to the river from the east. The only advantage the terrorist group would have was the heavy bush covering the entire area within this triangle. But the bush posed a real danger to the Police Reservists wearing their highly visible dark-blue fatigues.

Great secrecy was required concerning the police source. This contact man was not to be spoken about nor was there to be any indication of his being followed on the journey from Salisbury. I recommended that a helicopter should be employed to tail the contact vehicle all the way from Salisbury. The pilot would be able to do this and witness interception by the man from the Armageddon Group as well as the point at which the contact was taken into the bush. Just as important was the need for the helicopter pilot to let us know when the contact was clear of the target area. I assured John that a helicopter flying at great height would not upset the contact man or the terrorist group because it would appear too high and insignificant to constitute a threat to anyone.

Agreeing that this was a better option than attempting to follow the contact in another vehicle, John sought and gained PGHQ approval. I contacted Air HQ and arranged for the high-flying helicopter and also asked for three additional helicopters. These were to land at Banket, twelve miles from Sinoia, after the contact vehicle passed that village.

Murray Hofmeyer and Mark Smithdorff.

Hoffy, with Mark Smithdorff, had recently returned to Rhodesia from his Alouette conversion course in South Africa and had just completed a short OCU with Mark Smithdorff. I was told he would be following the contact vehicle.

Both John and I felt that the Army should conduct the operation, as a firefight seemed certain. The Commissioner of Police, Mr Barfoot, would have nothing of it. Notwithstanding the fact that the Armageddon Group was armed with automatic weapons and hand-grenades, he insisted we were dealing with law-breakers requiring armed Policemen and Police Reservists to kill or apprehend them; Army would only be involved if a state of war existed.

The dawn of 28 April 1966, like most Rhodesian mornings, was cool, bright and clear. Soon a stream of private vehicles started arriving at the Police Sports Club where men changed from civilian clothing into their dark-blue uniforms. These uniforms were intended to give high visibility for riot control but certainly not for bush warfare where the wearer presented an easy target to armed men in hiding.

Thick black ammunition belts set at various inclinations accentuated the corpulence of some amongst the PR, most being farmers and miners. They looked an unlikely bunch of fighters appearing too relaxed for the purpose of their gathering. In their clumsy uniforms the very wealthy and the poor were indistinguishable, their inbuilt courage hidden, as John Cannon arranged them into seven groups under regular police officers.

Nobody but John and I knew what was going on. We alone knew there were to be three groups each along both roadways and one for the river line. Alpha 1, 2 and 3 were nominated and allocated their vehicles, as were Bravo 1, 2 and 3 and Charlie 1. When this was done John Cannon told the expectant gathering that they were about to be involved in a cordon and sweep operation. Alpha would form one stop-line, Bravo the second line and Charlie the third one. Everyone knew there was at least one terrorist group in the area but when John told of the Armageddon seven in such a nearby triangle of ground, the level of excitement rose. His briefing was simple.

"At the word, 'Go', Alpha will move off along the main road dropping off Alpha 3 first, starting from the bridge, then Alpha 2 and finally Alpha 1, ending at the junction with the strip road. Bravo will do a mirror image of Alpha's deployment along the strip road to its junction with the main road. The officers are to shake out their men for even distribution along the entire length of both roads. Charlie is to proceed to both bridges, half the men to each, then walk in towards each other on the west bank of the river and shake out.

"When everyone is ready, a sweep is to commence from the east at the road junction. As the sweep line moves westward, the stop lines are to bunch up with every second man joining the sweep line."

After the briefing I walked the short distance to my helicopter parked by the HQ building. I checked in with Murray Hofmeyr who was following the police contact's vehicle, flying his helicopter at 6,000 feet above ground. All seemed to be going to plan when an Army Land Rover pulled up next to my helicopter. Major Billy Conn climbed out and came over to me to ask what was going on. I told him the story, including PGHQ's refusal to involve the Army.

Billy was on his way to Kariba and had popped in to see his old friend, John Cannon. He could not resist this opportunity for action and asked John if he and his sergeant could be fitted into the plan. John agreed and put them in with Bravo 2. A good choice as it happened!

All vehicles were assembled in two lines along a road running past the Police HQ building. I noted that the regular policemen and both Army men were armed with 7.62mm SLR assault rifles whereas the PR men were armed with an amazing mix of self-loading shotguns, .303 Enfield rifles, Sten-guns and the odd sporting rifle. All that was missing from this scene was a film director, huge movie cameras and a glamorous actress. It all seemed surreal but like everyone else around, I was pretty excited.

I heard Hoffy tell the other three helicopters they were cleared to land at Banket, the contact vehicle having passed there. Gordon Nettleton transmitted an acknowledgement. The time was 10.45 and I told Hoffy we were ready to roll. Only then did he let me know he was armed with an MAG machine-gun just in case there was need for such a weapon.

It seemed a long wait before Hoffy called; "The contact vehicle has been stopped at the road junction, Stand by." A moment later he said someone had climbed into the vehicle that was now proceeding slowly along the strip road. Next Hoffy said, "The vehicle has stopped and the occupants have gone into the bush on the south side, repeat south side, not north as expected."

This turned our planning upside down but I was pleased I had asked for extra helicopters. Having studied my map to consider possible changes to plan, I knew precisely what needed to be done. Hoffy in the meantime was moving very slowly westward still at 6,000 feet watching for the contact man's departure from the area. I asked him to get the other helicopters airborne for a circuitous route to avoid their sound reaching the gang. Their final approach to Sinoia was to be from the west. Fuel was already set out on the sports field.

John Cannon accepted my recommendation and quickly prepared his men for a reverse image of the first deployment plan. A power-line ran eastward from the strip-road bridge and crossed a north-to-south cattle fence line next to open farmland. This fence line ran from there to the junction of the main and strip roads. Bravo units would move up the strip road by vehicle, as planned. Using five helicopters, I would arrange for the deployment of Alpha units along the power-line and place Charlie along the farm fence. Charlie would no longer be a static line but would constitute the sweep line for a westerly drive.

This would have been easy enough if the police radios on the ground were compatible with those in our helicopters, as would have been the case with the Army. We had no means of communicating with any ground unit other than through John Cannon's radio room. All Alpha and Charlie units were instructed to get over to the sports field and prepare themselves for helicopter deployment. Way up in the sky the tiny dot of Hoffy's helicopter still moved very slowly westward as men hurried over to the sports ground. As soon as they were positioned, the three helicopters came in across town, landed and commenced refuelling.

I briefed my new OC Squadron Leader John Rogers, my 'A' Flight Commander Gordon Nettleton and Flying Officer Dave Becks on their tasks, I told them that I would take only one load of men and immediately commence a recce of the area. The first loads of six policemen per helicopter were aboard and all pilots were ready to start engines when Hoffy called to say the contact vehicle was clear and heading for Salisbury.

I led the way and deposited my load by the power-line nearest the river then climbed to orbit the area looking for signs of movement. A grassy vlei running both sides of a rivulet split the search area in two. It ran from the farmland almost to the Hunyani before crossing the strip-road 100 metres short of the bridge. The trees were fairly open along the edge of the vlei itself so I felt confident that I would see anyone attempting to cross from the northern bush area to even thicker bush on the power-line side of the vlei.

I noted that Bravo was in position along the strip-road and watched the helicopters as they raced back and forth placing down men and returning for more. Hoffy had refuelled and joined the other three helicopters who were all having difficulties finding landing spots along the power-line. Eventually all was in place and the sweep line started moving westwards from the fence. I flew over to see if the stops along the power-line had shaken out correctly but I could not find a soul until, to my horror, I found a disjointed line of men moving northward through the bush towards the vlei. The danger of these men converging on the correct sweep line was obvious so I asked John Cannon's radio room to instruct all Alpha units to hold their positions.

Dave Becks had refuelled and came to help me prevent Alpha and Charlie from bumping into each other. For over an hour Dave hovered at treetop level just ahead of the primary sweep line with his technician waving at men and pointing to those they were closing on. He did a great job and no policeman shot at another. Dave's noisy manoeuvring may have been the main reason the terrorists remained on the north side of the area. My presence over the vlei would also have limited them until I was forced to pop into Sinoia for fuel.

I returned with my technician and four PR who had been retained in reserve. Upon reaching the centre of the vlei I spotted a black man standing under a tree on its north side. He was dressed in dark slacks and a white shirt but did not appear to have a weapon nor show any sign of concern for my helicopter's presence. I was discussing this man with my technician when one of the PR spotted him too. Without warning, the PR started firing his Sten-gun at the figure, his rounds passing through the disc of the helicopter's rotor. Ewett Sorrel snatched the weapon smartly and gave the bewildered man a shouted lecture as I flew out of the area to dump the PR men out of harm's way on the Hunyani Bridge. When I returned to the vlei, the lone figure was still under the same tree. Although I had discounted him from being a threat I decided that Hoffy should get airborne with his machine-gun, just in case.

At the western end of the area I spotted another man crouching in long grass right in the centre of the vlei. Suddenly this guy, also wearing dark slacks and a white shirt, stood up and started shooting at my aircraft. I could not believe it at first, but the gun was pointing at us and clearly visible puffs of smoke were emitting from his weapon. I called Hoffy to come across to me with his machine-gun. The fellow stopped firing and crouched again to reload. Having done this he continued firing at my aircraft then, for reasons I did not appreciate immediately, he ceased firing and started running at high speed towards a ridge on the south side of the vlei. As he reached the edge of the vlei he disappeared in a cloud of dust created by gunfire from Hoffy's aircraft. It was only then that I realised an earlier dustless burst into the grass area had got him running. I had not seen the shadow of Hoffy's helicopter moving in opposite orbit to mine until now. So I broke away, found Hoffy above me, reversed from a right-hand to left-hand orbit and climbed above him to watch the action.

The terrorist had emerged from the dust cloud running even faster than before then disappeared from view in the dust of the third burst of fire. Again he emerged running up the ridge at super-Olympian speed. The fourth burst struck his weapon, sending it flying sideways out of his grip before he disappeared from view. He emerged beyond the dust staggering at walking speed before going down under the fifth and final burst. The Air Force had scored the first kill in a bush war that would continue for almost fourteen years and Hoffy's good-looking technician, George Carmichael, acquired the nickname 'Killer Carmichael'.

Hoffy was on his way back to Sinoia to stand by for any further call on him whilst I continued my recce around the area. Close to the point where the terrorist had fired at me, I picked up two persons standing together dressed in dark slacks and white shirts so I asked Hoffy to turn back. As I started to orbit these two characters looked up, their white faces shining in the sunlight. Fortunately for them Hoffy had not reached me before I told him that these were white men who were not supposed to be in the area. Later we learned that they were Police Special Branch officers, Bill Freeman and Dusty Binns, who had moved off the strip-road aiming to get a better view of what Hoffy had been firing at. They were the handlers of the Police 'contact' and had arrived after the sweep had commenced.

Through John Cannon's radio room I relayed a message to the man in charge of sweep line Charlie to watch for the man under the tree. They came up on him, declared him innocent and left him standing wide-eyed exactly where he was. Moments later PR elements of the sweep line opened fire on a

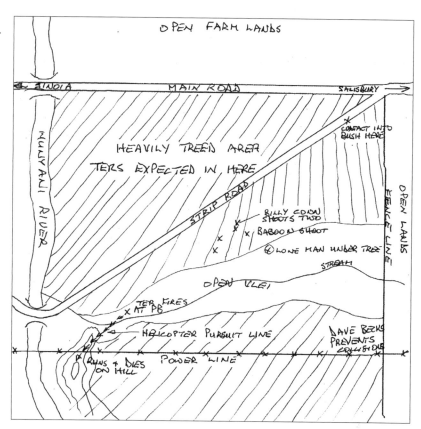

terrorist and, having killed him, gathered around his body in a manner one might only expect at a farmers' baboon shoot.

Fortunately, Major Billy Conn and his sergeant had joined the sweep line and were just off to the right of the bunched-up PR men. Billy screamed at the PR guys to spread out and move on, but they ignored his warning. It was then that two terrorists leapt to their feet, one in the act of throwing a grenade into the knot of PR men. Billy Conn's first round struck this terrorist in the heart causing him to let go of the grenade which went straight up then landed between the two terrorists, killing the second man before he had fired a shot. The PRs were shaken by the incident and there was no further bunching. The final three terrorists were taken out singly in quick succession, thus accounting for all seven of the Armageddon Gang.

Back at Sinoia John Cannon was elated with the success of the operation and let this be known when he addressed the participants at a debriefing in the Spots Club. The beer was running freely by the time all five helicopters departed for New Sarum and Major Conn and his sergeant continued their journey to Kariba. I submitted a detailed and scathing report to Air HQ saying that, whilst the operation had been 100% successful in accounting for all members of the Armageddon Group, it had in reality been a shambles. But for Dave Becks and Billy Conn, there would undoubtedly have been police casualties. Major difficulties in command and control due to non-compatibility of Air Force and Police radios would not have arisen if Army troops had been used. PGHQ were very displeased with this report and the Army loved it. Incredibly Air HQ chastised the squadron for "expending 147 rounds of precious 7.62mm ammunition to kill just one terrorist."

Today the ZANU government of Zimbabwe celebrates the start of its Chimurenga war on 28 April, the anniversary date of the 'Battle of Chinhoyi' where "a gallant force fought against impossible odds in which the Rhodesian enemy used thousands of Army troops and powerful helicopter gunships." What they conveniently forget is the expediency of their actions in committing the young men of the Armageddon Group before they had been given adequate training for their mission.

These unfortunate young men were launched way too early, simply to provide proof of ZANU's active involvement in Rhodesia simply to sweeten Organisation of African Unity (OAU) attitudes to their cause because, at the time, OAU only supported their rival ZAPU. Nevertheless, I personally agree with ZANU that 28 April 1966 was the true date of the commencement of the bush war in Rhodesia. Many historians give it as 22 December 1972, thereby ignoring all the offensive actions and combat-related deaths before this date.

Helicopter projects

JUST PRIOR TO THE SINOIA operation there had been embryonic moves to mount a side-firing MAG machine-gun to our Alouette helicopters. Ozzie Penton as OC Flying Wing had insisted that Hoffy take the MAG along with him even though no firing trial had been conducted. The actual fit was no more than a simple bipod fixed to the step on the port side of the cabin. There was no rigidity in this arrangement nor were there any means of ensuring that ejected cartridge cases and belt links were retained within the safety of the cabin. This was important because these loose items, if allowed to enter into the slipstream, could cause serious damage or total failure of the fast-spinning tail rotor. Hoffy had been lucky that none of the 147 cases and links had struck his tail rotor. All the same, I took it upon myself to design, build and test a decent mounting for a 7.62mm MAG machine-gun and to fit a gunsight suited to side-firing in forward flight. During the time of this project I also looked into changing the way we refuelled our helicopters

Throughout my training away from base and during the Sinoia experience, I found refuelling to be irksome and way too slow. We were using a hand-operated wobble pump that Africans called the '*kamena kawena*' pump. Loosely translated this meant 'for me, for you' in Chilapalapa; a bastardised language that continues to be the common lingo for multi-ethnic communications on South Africa's gold mines.

The *kamena kawena* Pump was packed in a large metal trunk stored next to the fuel tank behind the cabin's rear wall. To refuel, the pump had to be removed from the fuel-soaked trunk. It had then to be assembled by one member of the crew whilst the other rolled a drum of fuel to the aircraft, heave it onto its base and remove the sealed bung. The pump stack-pipe was dropped into the drum, the flexible pipe nozzle inserted into the helicopter fuel tank and hand pumping commenced. Even with technician and pilot taking turn in pumping, it was a tiring business. Once the drum was empty, the process was reversed; by which time one's hands and overalls were stained and stinking of fuel.

We only had eight helicopters and could ill-afford a slow turn-around and the physical stresses that repeated refuelling induced during intense operations. Too often a pilot needed to be briefed or debriefed between flights meaning that his technician had to do the entire refuelling job on his own; a situation of considerable embarrassment to many pilots. There had to be a simple way of overcoming this.

My contention was that the aircraft should be a slave unto itself. I started by testing the jet engine at idling rpm, when rotor blades were static, and found that six psi of air pressure could be continuously tapped from a P2 pressure plug located on the engine casing just aft of the compressor assembly. By using a compressed air cylinder with pressure regulated to six psi, it was easy enough to prove that, by pressurising a fuel drum, the fuel could be forced to flow up a pipeline into a helicopter's fuel tank. It was also established that a drum of fuel could be pumped more rapidly this way than by a *kamena kawena* pump. I then approached Shell and BP who supplied our fuel and was assured that pressurising a drum to six psi was entirely safe.

My Squadron Commander John Rogers and OC Flying Wing Ozzie Penton supported my intention to produce a prototype refueller, as did the Air Staff. However, I met with opposition from one senior officer of the technical staff at Air HQ. He told me how during WWII Spitfires had to be hand-refuelled from four-gallon jerry cans in the hot desert sun and, anyway, refuelling with engine running was totally unacceptable.

The strict rule of not running engines whilst refuelling with highly volatile aviation gas was fundamentally sound, but it did not seem to fit with the low volatility of non-atomised refined paraffin (or diesel). I simply could not believe my ears about the 'jerry can' coming twenty years after WWII. However, what I thought did not alter the fact that I had not gained official approval to proceed with the project.

So as not to implicate OC Flying or my Squadron Commander, I carried on in secret by designing and producing a pressure-refuelling pump. This could not have been done without the willing assistance of Master Technician Frank Oliver who ran Station Workshops and who did the necessary machine work out of working hours. The unit we produced was really quite simple. A pressure line from the P2 pressure plug (the six psi static pressure point) conveyed pressure air into a head on the stack-pipe. With the stack-pipe inserted into a drum the head sealed the drum's bunghole when a handle bar on its side was rotated through ninety degrees. The pressure air then forced fuel up the stack-pipe and into the helicopter fuel tank via a standard flexible hose. The effort required was minimal.

Both refuelling and gun-mounting projects were interrupted by a series of Police and Army ATOPs (Anti-Terrorist Operations) exercises that had obviously been generated by interest in the lessons learned during the Sinoia operation. One of these exercises was with the RAR (Rhodesian African Rifles) Battalion at Mphoengs close to our southwestern border. Apart from some interesting flying, this short detachment sticks in my mind because of an embarrassing incident. The RAR camp was set in heavy riverine bush where full blackout procedures were enforced. Screening inside the large Officers' Mess marquee allowed dim lights to be used at the bar and dinner table. It was in this mess that I first witnessed RAR's insistence on maximum comfort in the field. Because the Battalion Commander was present, the Battalion's silver and starched tablecloths were laid for all meals.

In the absence of moonlight I found it difficult to navigate my way through the bush to my tent. I was awaked to the call of nature one night and decided not to try and find my way to the loo but to spend a penny on what appeared to be an anthill under bush close to my tent. I was half way through my need when 'the anthill' moved and cursed in N'debele. I was deeply embarrassed, but the soldier who rose from under his wet blanket laughed when he realised what had happened. He called to his mates saying he had been "urinated upon by a Bru-Jop." Blue Job was the army nickname for Air Force people.

Just after this, during a period of flying training in the Chimanimani mountains, Mark Smithdorff and I met up with Major Dudley Coventry, commander of C Squadron Special Air Services. I had only seen this strongly built officer a few times at New Sarum when he and his SAS men were undergoing routine parachute training. In this Dudley stood out a mile because he wore glasses that were secured by thick Elastoplast strips to his nose and temples to prevent the windblast from removing his all-important visual aid.

At the Chimanimani Arms Hotel, we learned from him about SAS and its style of operations. He told us we would probably be seeing a number of young soldiers in the mountains undergoing an SAS selection process. The next morning on our way into the mountains we spotted SAS tents near the base of the mountains at Dead Cow Camp from which place the selection course was being conducted. Then, late in the afternoon, I was flying with my technician Butch Graydon when I spotted two men climbing the long slope of Ben Nevis. One virtually carried the other.

I landed on the steep slope right next to these two exhausted men and established that the man being assisted had broken his ankle some hours earlier. I asked the injured man to come aboard so I could fly him out for medical treatment. He refused point blank saying he would fail the SAS selection process if he did not get to the top of Ben Nevis and then complete the descent to Dead Cow Camp next day via a really tortuous route running down a very long and steep forested ravine. Not fully understanding the harshness of the SAS selection process, and using rank, I ordered the injured man to come aboard saying I would explain to his seniors that I had forced him into doing this. Reluctantly he boarded the aircraft, but his mate refused a lift saying he would be fine now that he no longer needed to assist his injured mate.

We flew down to Dead Cow Camp where I met Warrant Officer Bouch MCM for the first time. He struck me as a frosty old-timer who was not at all pleased with me for interfering with his selection course. I explained that, apart from the injured man's foot being in serious need of attention, I was concerned that his mate might also become a casualty when bringing the injured man down the mountain ravine. Fortunately, Major Coventry showed up. He accepted that I had acted in good faith and all was forgiven. Happily both the injured man and his mate were accepted into the SAS.

Nevada murder

AT 04:30 ON 25 MAY 1966, I received a call requiring me to report to the squadron with my bush gear. Since this was always ready and packed, I left home within ten minutes of the call. On arrival at the squadron I found our technicians, who lived on station, preparing four helicopters. At a short briefing in New Sarum Operations Room, Squadron Leader John Rogers, Gordon Nettleton, Ian Harvey and myself were instructed to fly to Nevada Farm just north of Hartley where a gang of terrorists had murdered a farmer and his wife.

Our arrival at Nevada Farm was at dawn. We went into the farmhouse where the naked body of Mr Viljoen lay sprawled on the floor close to his dead wife. Three exhausted Special Branch (SB) men lay fast asleep on the bed from which the couple had risen to investigate knocking on their bedroom door.

It appeared that Mr Viljoen had been reluctant to open the door to late-night callers because the bullets that cut him down had been fired through the door. Mrs Viljoen had obviously gone to her husband's aid only to be cut down too. The terrorists then broke down the door and stepped over the dead bodies. A baby sleeping in her cot in her parents' room was narrowly missed by bullets that remained embedded in the wall above and below her. Two other children sleeping in their own bedroom escaped injury. By the time reports of gunfire brought help to Nevada Farm, the terrorists had vanished into the night having first put the three children back to sleep and looted fridge and pantry of all foodstuffs.

All day long we deployed police and SB groups for miles around to search for leads on the whereabouts of the group responsible for these awful murders. Feelings ran high as more and more police, some with dogs, arrived and set up camp next to the farmstead. A police mobile canteen had been established by 7 am and from it we were able to snatch the odd cup of coffee and ultra-thick sandwiches between flights. In the evening, cold beers and a good meal were followed by welcome sleep. At daybreak a substantial breakfast, served by very friendly Police Reserve men and women, set us up for the day.

I was required to take six PR men to a position where the Umfuli River passes through the Mcheka-wa-ka-Sungabeta mountain range to guard a damaged helicopter. Gordon Nettleton had struck a tree with his main rotor blades whilst landing in the heavy bush that made this untamed area of countryside so beautiful. Fortunately, a technical inspection showed that Gordon's aircraft would be safe for a one-time unloaded flight back to Nevada for rotor blades to be changed. With Gordon's aircraft gone, the PR men I had brought in linked up with the ones from Gordon's aircraft and together they set off on a patrol, seeking leads on what had become known as the 'Nevada Gang'.

After dark Ian Harvey and I were required to return to uplift these same men because they reported having hot information. Landing in that general area by day was quite tricky, but finding the same location and landing in the dark could have presented major problems. As it happened, the PR had located an open ledge on the side of the Umfuli River making single-aircraft

Gordon Nettleton with Henry Ford, MD of the Salisbury-based company Rhotair that undertook all major works on our helicopters.

entries fairly straightforward for both Ian and myself.

Though not needed for this uplift, our OC decided to tag along flying very high above us. He did this in hope of picking up a campfire in the remote and unpopulated area. When we were already on our way back to base, John Rogers told us that he had located a fire close to a distinctive bend on the Umfuli River. Judging by its relative position to the river, his map showed it to be on a steep slope and he was certain this was where the terrorists were camping.

Back at Nevada Farm however, he became frustrated by the Police choosing only to react to ground-acquired intelligence and refusing to accept any lead given by a pilot. Two days later a cave with freshly burnt embers, at the precise location John Rogers had plotted on the police operations map, proved to have been occupied by the terrorist gang on the night in question.

Intelligence established that the Nevada Gang, comprising seven men, was a component of the twenty-one men who entered Rhodesia together then split up near Sinoia. The Armageddon Group had remained in the Sinoia area where it had been annihilated and the third group of seven had gone on to Salisbury. An ex-BSA policeman by the name of Gumbotshuma led the gang we now sought. He turned out to be a wily bird because he understood police thinking and tactics. In particular he understood the police cordon-and-search system and obviously knew how to exploit its weaknesses, as we were to find out.

Following discovery of the cave, ground leads indicated that Gumbotshuma and his men were currently camping on the side of the Mcheka-wa-ka-Sungabeta mountain, some way northeast of the cave. This section of the mountain range formed the western boundary of the Zowa African Purchase Land for black farmers. It was from a named farmer that the Nevada Gang was receiving succour. From his lofty perch Gumbotshuma could monitor all movements on the African farms below. Nevada Farm was only thirteen miles away and all roads leading into his area were visible to Gumbotshuma.

He watched the helicopters flying to the ridge behind him and knew that they were deploying men of the stop line. He watched the vehicles arriving at the base of the mountain and saw flanking men climb the mountain in two lines on either side of his position. After a long while, the sweep line at the base commenced its slow climb towards him.

All of the terrorists were closely grouped in a gully and moved slowly forward under directions given by Gumbotshuma. When the gap he was watching for seemed right, the gang tucked against one bank of the gully and listened as the closest men in the sweep line passed noisily by. Having been missed, Gumbotshuma knew the force would be uplifted from the ridge by helicopter and flown back to the waiting vehicles below. All he had to do was stay low until all the police returned to base.

There is a basic rule for aircrew concerning the consumption of alcohol. This is, 'eight hours between bottle and throttle'. It is easy enough to comply with if one or two drinks are taken before retiring to bed early. In the bush we would not consume any alcoholic beverage until we were certain there would be no need to fly that night. However, after the abortive sweep of the mountain all was quiet so the aircrew tucked into a couple of ice-cold beers before dinner and an early night.

We had consumed three beers apiece and were about to have our meal when Ian Harvey and I were instructed to grab our kit and get up to the police station at Zwimba. With three beers in an empty stomach, having not eaten since early morning, I was very concerned about flying on such a dark night. The act of lifting off into the black had the apparent effect of sobering me up completely and we arrived at Zwimba safely.

At Zwimba every policeman available had set off to investigate a report of a lone terrorist who had arrived at a farmer's house. We waited all night to be called forward but no call came. I remember how Ian Harvey curled up under the Charge Office counter and slept like a baby whilst my technician Jerry Hayter and I paced up and down until vehicles arrived at dawn with a wounded terrorist. His name was Abel Denga.

Abel had been shot through the stomach by an African police sergeant when he emerged from a hut next to the farmer's house and attempted to shoot the sergeant. Abel had been with the Nevada Gang during the unsuccessful sweep on the mountain the previous day. He said he knew where Gumbotshuma and the rest of his gang could be found some distance from the mountain. In response to questioning, he said he would be able to direct an airborne force to their present location.

Following first-aid treatment to his wound, I got airborne with Abel and five armed policemen. Ian followed with another six armed policemen. But it soon became clear that Abel had no idea where he was because we were being given haphazard changes in direction. The police believed he was deliberately misleading us, so we returned to Zwimba for the exercise to be conducted by road. This also turned into a wild goose chase because Abel was totally disorientated. He looked really washed out when the ground party returned, so we wrapped him up in blankets and placed him on a stretcher to fly him to Harare Hospital.

Jerry Hayter watched Abel throughout the flight and became concerned about his fast and weakening pulse. An ambulance was waiting at the hospital helicopter pad where two black female nurses took the stretcher from us and were about to put it in the ambulance. I requested that they return the stretcher to the helicopter as soon as possible. "Certainly," said the older of the two nurses, whereupon they rotated the helicopter stretcher to drop Abel face down onto their own ambulance stretcher. Jerry and I were incensed by this callous act but the older nurse simply said, "Bloody terrorist bastard," climbed into the ambulance and sped away towards the hospital. Having seen relatively kind treatment from the Police and SB, including the sergeant Abel had attempted to shoot, the attitude of these professional nurses seemed way out of place. Two days later we heard that Abel Denga had died.

From the hospital we flew the short distance back to New Sarum because I had been recalled to start my QHI (Qualified Helicopter Instructor) course. Back in the op area four terrorists were killed. Edmond Nyandoro who had received his training at Nanking Military College in China was captured and sentenced to death for his direct involvement in the Viljoens' murders. Gumbotshuma escaped back to Zambia following a long trek up the Hunyani River and the Tete Province of Mozambique. The third group of seven made a serious mistake in going to Salisbury. They were all apprehended when Police ground coverage teams detected their presence the moment they arrived in Harare Township.

Of the group of twenty-one men who entered Rhodesia, only Gumbotshuma escaped. Nevertheless, publicity arising from their activities suited ZANU perfectly. The loss of twenty men was of no concern to the politicos of ZANU whose only interest was to prove to the Liberation Committee of the OAU that the party was active inside Rhodesia.

Aiden Diggeden

MOST RHODESIANS KNEW OF A colourful young prisoner named Aiden Diggeden. He was a gentle rogue who claimed that no prison would ever hold him for long and, as I recall, he proved this three times. On one of these, Aiden escaped with two other white prisoners. I became involved in covering ground from Lake McIlwaine to the small settlement of Selous on the main road to Bulawayo. After a fruitless search of almost three hours I needed to refuel but no police station was prepared for helicopter operations in those times. Fortunately our Alouettes' engines could use Avtur, the correct jet paraffin, or diesel fuel, so I landed on the main road next to the Selous service station. Vehicles backed up either side of the helicopter until my technician and I pushed it to a diesel pump. This created consternation for the station attendant and drew crowds of people to watch proceedings until the diesel storage tank ran dry before the helicopter's tank was half full. Then new information came through to let us know the search had switched to another area; so we returned to base. Aiden was apprehended three days later.

On another occasion he triggered a countrywide manhunt that had been on the go for three days before Aiden was accidentally discovered hiding in a water reservoir set high above the main prison buildings. He had been waiting in there for everything to quieten down before making the escape he had planned.

Aiden was a man who could charm anyone including his

jailers and he used this gift to good advantage. He was also a gifted athlete. For some weeks, when out in the exercise yard, he would sprint to the high prison wall and run almost to its summit before executing a backward somersault to land neatly on his feet. He told his prison warders he was practising for the day he would reach the top of the wall, roll over it, and land next to the vehicle that would race him away to freedom. Believing the wall was too high, this latest leg-pull amused the warders who were used to being ribbed by Aiden. When the time was right however, Aiden did just as he said he would and managed to reach South Africa.

Helicopter projects continued

IN BETWEEN QHI FLIGHTS, THERE was time to continue with my two projects. With the aid of the Drawing Office and Station Workshops I produced a prototype mounting for side-firing machine-guns that incorporated an arrangement to arrest expended cartridge cases and links. Squadron Leader Rogers and I conducted firing tests that proved the mounting but highlighted the need for a suitable gun-sight. I managed to lay hands on a small French reflector sight that improved accuracy dramatically.

PB showing visiting Portuguese officers the MAG fit.

With minor modifications, the mounting was used for the next fourteen years though .303 Browning machine-guns, because of their higher rate of fire, later replaced the MAG

machine-guns. Because .303 Browning had a bad reputation for jamming, they were fitted in pairs.

Every pilot and technician on 7 Squadron was required to attain high proficiency on these side-firing guns. It took some doing, but Air HQ eventually agreed to the award of Air Gunners Wings to all technicians who met the laid-down standard of proficiency.

These embroidered cloth wings, displaying upward facing bullet set between two stubby wings (*second from left on the bottom row*), that were proudly worn above rank insignia on the left arm.

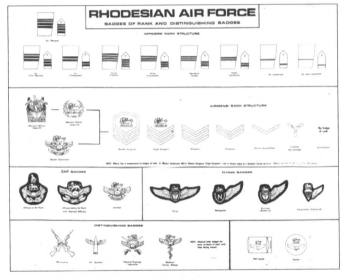

Badges of rank and distinguishing badges.

When the pressure refuelling pump had been proven in secret I told my Squadron Commander what had been done and why. Having witnessed a demonstration he gave me his unreserved approval for what had been achieved and even undertook to take the project on his own head to protect me from the inevitable repercussions that would flow from Air HQ. For this I was grateful but said I must take the responsibility, having intentionally hidden the developmental work from him. Nevertheless, Squadron Leader Rogers arranged for a high-level team of Air and Technical staff officers to visit the squadron.

Visiting from Air HQ was a team of four officers comprising the Director General Operations, Staff Officer Operations, the Director General of Supporting Services (DGSS) and Command Armament Officer. They went directly to Squadron Leader Rogers' office for discussions on subjects that differed from my OC's prime purpose, which was to demonstrate pressure refuelling.

The concrete helicopter pad was bare but for two full drums of Avtur. One stood upright and the other was on its side at the edge of the pad. Out of sight on the sports field were two waiting helicopters. One carried the conventional *kamena kawena* pump and the other was fitted with the lighter prototype pressure-refuelling unit.

When the visiting officers emerged from the OC's office they were invited by John Rogers to witness a short demonstration. As he approached the hangar door and saw only two fuel drums on the empty Helicopter pad, Group Captain Jimmy Pringle (DGSS), who had not been opposed to running an engine to refuel helicopters, immediately realised what was coming. He winked at me and whispered in my ear, "Naughty, naughty."

The two helicopters lifted into view and moved forward to the helicopter pad. The one with the *kamena kawena* pump landed well clear of the drum that lay on its side. The one with the pressure refueller landed next to the upright drum. Both pilots closed fuel cocks and stopped the rotors, but only the pilot with the *kamena kawena* pump closed down his engine. Both crews exited and removed their refuelling gear from the rear compartment. The pressure-refuelling pump was inserted into the drum the moment the bung had been removed and refuelling commenced before the technician of the second aircraft had rolled his drum to the helicopter. Pressure refuelling ended, the pump was back in its storage bay, and rotors were wound up to governed speed for lift-off six minutes after landing. At that moment, the pilot of the second aircraft had just started cranking the *kamena kawena* pump. He lifted off sixteen minutes after landing.

Squadron Leader Rogers and I received a bit of a blasting for unauthorised development and for using Station Workshops and materials without HQ approval. Otherwise, the Air HQ officers were convinced by the demonstration and gave authority to manufacture pressure pumps for each helicopter.

Some days after all helicopters had been equipped with the new pressure pumps, I was astounded to be told by Air HQ that, being a commissioned officer, I could expect nothing for my invention. I knew this without having to be told but, because the matter had been raised, I requested that Air Force take out a patent on the design. This request was made so that any financial benefit that might derive in the future could be passed to the Air Force Benevolent Fund that provided relief to servicemen in distress. I was assured this would be done.

Sanctions against Rhodesia were affecting our ability to buy certain spares and more so to procuring additional helicopters. A number of visits from Frenchmen of Sud Aviation as well as South African and Portuguese military people included inspections and demonstrations of the helicopter gun-mounting and pressure-refueller. Arising from French interests in the refuellers, it seems that the full data pack for the pressure equipment was handed to Sud Aviation in exchange for our urgent needs. That was fine, but no rites or royalty agreement was concluded because no patent existed.

When I learned about this, I was as mad as a snake for three reasons. Firstly, the French asked if our latest order for three new helicopters was to be with or without pressure refuellers. Secondly, we heard that the French had sold the refueller

design to the USAAF for use in Vietnam and finally, Air Force members with wives and children in need of special medical treatment outside the country could not expect the level of assistance from the Benevolent Fund that might have been possible had AIR HQ patented the refuelling system—as had been promised.

Accidental entry into Zambia

THE FRENCH HAD ALWAYS MADE it clear to all Alouette III users that this helicopter should not be flown at night or deliberately enter cloud. This was because, unlike fixed-wing aircraft, helicopters are inherently unstable and cannot be allowed to enter into any unusual flight attitude that could, in a matter of seconds, result in the aircraft breaking up in flight. However, because our Air Force seniors had not flown helicopters and believed that Rhodesian pilots were too well trained to worry about French opinions our helicopter pilots were committed to flying at night. For this they had to be wide-awake for every second in the air. We even had to practise daytime instrument flying under a hood arrangement and were tasked for hundreds of night training flights into every remote police station in the country.

We really needed every possible aid to reduce uncertainties and tension at night, whereas our aids were limited to standard flight instruments and VHF radio. My own experiences had shown me that navigation at night was particularly difficult and that there was urgent need for an instrument that would indicate the direction to fly to reach the point of destination. Such an instrument was already in service with South African Air Force helicopters. It was known as the Becker Homer.

A Becker Homer responded to incoming transmissions on any selected frequency. A needle on its indicator dial moved left or right of a centre-line marker in response to an incoming signal. Though the needle should have remained upright for a transmission emanating from directly ahead, it seldom did. Nevertheless, by asking the ground operator to give a long transmission it was possible in a turn to watch for the needle's swing across centre as the nose came to the direction to steer to the point of transmission.

I submitted a request for this equipment through my Squadron Commander and OC Flying Wing who both added their weight to the request. Though the Becker Homers were readily available in South Africa and were not expensive, nothing was forthcoming because bids for these instruments had not been included in the squadron's annual returns. Because of this, I got myself into a near-fatal situation.

I was at Thornhill participating in a School of Infantry exercise code-named 'Happy Wanderer' when, just after dinner one evening, I received instructions to get to Binga at first light with three MAG machine-guns and a large supply of ammunition and mortar bombs. A terrorist crossing of Lake Kariba had been detected and Army troops were on follow-up. A FASOC (Forward Air Support Operations Centre), two helicopters and two Provosts were already at Binga.

My technician Ewett Sorrell and I loaded the aircraft before I contacted Thornhill's Meteorological Officer who forecast an eight-knot headwind at 8,500 feet, which was my intended cruise altitude. We went off to bed at around 20:30. When we lifted off at 03:00 I took the precaution of making a run down the centre-line of the tarmac runway 31 to check that my directional indicator had been set correctly from the tiny, difficult-to-read, P2 magnetic compass. Coincidentally, the runway direction was the same as the heading to Binga.

Throughout the climb the haze level was unusually dense. At 8,500 feet haze density was such that it created a fairly distinct though false horizon at about forty degrees above the true horizon. Below the aircraft the night was as black as hell but above the haze line there were stars to help hold heading without continuous reference to instruments. At altitude I sensed that there was strong drift to port but I could not be certain of this because the ground was not visible to conscious sight. The sensation bothered me so much that I asked Ewett Sorrell if he was sensing the same thing. He said he was not.

At about eighty nautical miles, based on time, I picked up the faint greyish white ribbon of a riverbed that ran along track for a while then broke sharply left and was lost in the black. I took this to be the distinctive bend on the Gwelo River. This placed me on track and a little ahead on time. Despite the river check, the sensation of drift persisted. At about the halfway point a bush fire came up on our right side but it was impossible to establish the direction the smoke was blowing because the haze only allowed light from the circular line of flame to show through.

At 05:10 I called FASOC and was answered immediately, loud and clear, by Gordon Nettleton. I told him we were estimating Binga at 05.25 though we may be a little late because I had changed heading for Chete Island to offset the sensation of high but unproven drift. Even though the haze had reduced dramatically I could not see the lake at 05.30. It was then that Ewett Sorrell picked up the glow of town lights way off on our port side. I was dumbfounded thinking that this must be Wankie and that my sensations of drift had been correct after all. I called FASOC, but there was no reply.

The Alouette fuel gauge was calibrated by fuel weight from zero to 1,000 pounds. With cruising power set and flying at 8,500 feet there was sufficient fuel for a flight time of between two hours, fifty minutes and three hours. Before reaching zero fuel, a small light on the fuel gauge gave warning when only fifteen minutes of flying time remained. The light would flicker

for a while before burning brightly. It was from this point that the fifteen minutes was timed. When we saw the lights of the town the warning light flickered for the first time. Dawn was breaking but I knew I must get on the ground as soon as possible to await better light. An autorotative descent was made to conserve fuel and halfway down the descent the ground became vaguely visible. As we got closer, I saw that we were over very rough country with deep ravines that looked wrong. Even in the poor light conditions the rivers seemed to be running south when they should be flowing north. I had not seen the lake or the Zambezi River so put this matter out of mind as I eased on power to level off over one of the ridges. We spotted a small vlei deep in a valley and went in to land. On short finals, however, the fuel warning light came on steady at the very same moment that we picked up a herd of elephant right where we had to land. They cleared off quickly enough allowing us to put down in the long grass that reeked of the great brutes. After fifteen minutes waiting with curious elephants milling around us it became light enough to get airborne.

As we crested the ridge we saw farmlands directly ahead and set course for the closest farmstead. Close up the farm looked very dilapidated so we went on a little farther to one that looked much neater and landed in a paddock close to a fence. Just beyond the fence was the farmhouse from which smoke was rising lazily in the cold morning air. A couple of moving figures showed that the place was coming to life. I had a sneaking suspicion we were in Zambia but wondered how this could be since we had not seen the Zambezi River.

As a precaution I asked Ewett to remain in the helicopter cabin and prepare his rifle in case of trouble—what trouble I could not say. I walked forward of the helicopter and stopped at the fence to await a man who was coming towards me. Because I could not speak N'debele, I greeted the guy in the usual Shona way with the words "Mangwanani, mamuka se?" to which he replied "Tamuka! Mamuka wo?" I then asked him where the 'boss' was to which he replied "bwana ne dona vakaenda ku taundi." His use of the words *Bwana* and *Dona* really worried me. Even though the man spoke Shona, my guard was already up when I asked him for the direction to Binga. He had never heard of the place, so I asked where Livingstone was. He pointed in a southwesterly direction saying Livingstone was quite close. Quite close in African terms usually means a long way off!

I thanked the man and was about to turn round when, in English, he asked in a rude fashion "Where the hell you come from?" I told him we were on our way from Lusaka to Livingstone but the haze had been so bad that I was making sure I had not crossed the Zambezi into Rhodesia. He seemed satisfied and I turned to walk back to the helicopter as coolly as I could. My nonchalance was overdone because my foot slipped through the step and I nearly broke my leg between the two bars that formed it.

There was no time to rub my aching leg. Two others had

joined the man and all three were climbing through the fence to get a closer look at the helicopter. On selection of the engine starter switch the engine fired up but suddenly quit. I slammed back the fuel-flow lever to close the micro switch that had caused the motor to shut down. Then, hand-signalling the three approaching men to stay where they were, we had to wait an agonising thirty seconds before repeating the start-up sequence

As soon as the engine start sequence ended, I advanced the fuel-flow lever much faster than normal to wind up the rotors to governed speed before lifting off into backwards flight to prevent the men on the ground from seeing RRAF 503 painted on the belly of the helicopter. Suddenly the reverse airflow caught my unlocked door and flung it forward where it engaged with the lock that normally held the door open on the ground. I had not even strapped myself in but this made reaching the lock possible as I rotated the aircraft with rudder to turn it into forward flight. This caused the door to whip back and strike my elbow with great force.

Once strapped in and settled in the climb, I headed in the general direction of Livingstone Airport where I told Ewett we might have to take on fuel, at gunpoint if necessary. I scrabbled for my map case, found the appropriate 1:250,000 map and positively confirmed Senkobo and Kananga railway sidings ahead and right of our course. We already had a cumulative flying time of over five minutes since the warning light had first come on, which seemed to place Livingstone Airport beyond our reach, so I kept climbing at eighty knots seeking as much height as possible. Attempts to raise Victoria Falls Airport and the FASOC at Binga met with no response.

I was mildly concerned about RAF Javelin fighters that had recently been deployed to protect Zambia from imagined aggression from Rhodesia, but decided that they would not be able to respond to a call from the farm or from Livingstone Airport before we were safely out of Zambian airspace. The fuel warning light had been on for more than twenty minutes when we passed over Livingstone Airport at almost 11,000 feet. Below we could see the fuel storage depot and two fuel bowsers parked next to a building close by. The Zambezi River was still just out of reach if the engine quit but there was ample space to make a forced landing where the bowsers stood. A minute later we knew we were safe when the south bank of the Zambezi River was within our reach.

The flight line was altered to fly directly for the police station at Victoria Falls just three nautical miles ahead. At twenty-three minutes on warning light, I could see the small sports field by the police station and entered into an autorotative descent for a powerless landing on the sports field. We rolled onto the grass exactly where I intended at a little over walking speed. The engine was still running when I applied collective pitch to keep rolling towards the road where police usually dropped fuel for helicopters. We had not quite reached this point when the engine quit.

Squadron Leader Woodward was the duty officer who answered my telephone call to Air HQ. I had to tell him of our experience in veiled terms that he understood, having already learned from the FASOC at Binga that we were more than an hour overdue. Having shaken up the Police we took on fuel and flew off to Binga. Routing along the Zambezi Gorge, we established why we had not picked up the river in the dark. The water surface was completely covered by Kariba Weed (*Salvinia Auriculata*).

When I made contact with him, Gordon Nettleton told me that a Provost was on its way from Salisbury with a replacement helicopter pilot because I was to return to Salisbury with the same Provost and report to the Air Force Commander. Having not shaved and still dressed in flying overalls that smelled quite strongly of fuel, I felt awkward about being hustled from the flight line by Ozzie Penton to see Air Vice-Marshal Harold Hawkins.

Air Vice-Marshal Harold Hawkins.

When I entered his office the AVM had a 1:250,000 map laid out before him. He asked me to go through my experience and identify the farm at which I had landed. I told him the whole story and emphasised the sensation of drift, which I had tried to ignore after seeing the sharp bend of what I had taken to be the Gwelo River. In retrospect it was obvious this had in fact been the Shangani River whose line exactly matched the sharp bend of the Gwelo River. Though much further from Thornhill this landmark corresponded closely with the expected flight time to the Gwelo River bend.

There was no difficulty in pinpointing the farm we had bypassed and the one where we landed. Then AVM Hawkins told me that we had been very fortunate to give the first farm a miss. Special Branch had been to see him before me and had pointed out that this particular farm was ZAPU's 'Freedom Farm' where large numbers of trained and well-armed terrorists were in residence.

The Commander had been in contact with the RAF Air Liaison Officer in Zambia to apologise for the inadvertent landing of an RRAF helicopter in Zambia. He told the RAF officer that the pilot of the aircraft had been on a mercy mission and had strayed into Zambia in error. The Liaison Officer had acted in a very friendly way and told the AVM there was nothing to worry about; he would settle any political problems that might arise. None did!

I took the opportunity to emphasise to the AVM that had my helicopter been fitted with a Becker Homer I would have known that the FASOC transmission from Gordon Nettleton was coming from a point off to my right and that I would have turned starboard to reach Binga safely. The AVM took up the matter personally and Becker Homers were ordered.

Elephants and the minister

MARK MCLEAN WAS MY FIRST helicopter student. Flying with him made me realise how great it was to convert a fully qualified pilot to a new style of flying. Apart from the usual struggle to master precision hovering Mark progressed well through all phases of his operational conversion, most of which were done in high weight conditions. To end his course, I received authority to conduct what became known as the end of course 'around the houses' training flight. We started with three days in the Chimanimani mountains, which was both essential and enjoyable. All of our flying was broken down into short periods of intensive work with picnic and swim breaks in between.

From there we moved north along the mountainous border, then east via low country and the Zambezi River line stopping for fuel at police stations and Army bases along the route.

Mark was a keen photographer who often passed flight control to me so that he could take photos of places that caught his eye. It was late afternoon with the sun about to set behind the western Zambian escarpment when we passed a large herd of elephants spread along a stretch of sand and drinking at the Zambezi River's edge. Mark asked me to take control. Whilst he prepared his camera I took the aircraft into a long turn-about then ran close to the river

whose waters reflected the superb sunset. As we passed slowly by the herd set off eastwards creating an enormous dust cloud that glowed red in the sunset, adding another dimension to colours reflecting off the huge river. I turned around for Mark to photograph this magnificent sight through his open window then turned back again to reposition ahead of the herd.

We had moved about 200 metres when I noticed people standing on a bank towards which this herd was moving. Immediately I flew ahead of the elephants and came to a hover behind the group of white people to force the elephants to stop moving in their direction. The herd came to a dusty halt short of the group, so we broke away to let them enjoy the sight.

We continued on for a night landing at the Army camp on Kariba Heights where we spent an evening with the Brown Jobs. The rest of the trip was a resounding success and proved the value of taking new helicopter pilots through the widely varying situations that they would encounter during operations.

A few days after returning to New Sarum, I was ordered to report to the Air Force Commander. For the second time in seven weeks, I entered Air Vice-Marshal Harold Hawkins' office. The AVM asked me if I had been flying in the area of Mana Pools at around 18:30 on 9 September. I said I had. The AVM then told me that he had received an angry report from a Member of Parliament to say that we had endangered his life and those of his family and friends by driving elephants directly at them. I told the AVM what had happened and how we had deliberately stopped the jumbos before breaking away to let the people on the ground enjoy the animals at relatively close range. He said he was pretty fed up with complaints that came from the same handful of high and mighty people. More in jest than annoyance he told me to "run the blighters over next time."

Ian Harvey (wearing cap) and technicians taken during a mountain training rest period.

First helicopter engine failure

TRAGEDY WAS TO BECOME COMMONPLACE in a war that had started slowly. But on 12 October 1966 it struck the Special Air Service badly. The nation was shaken by news of the deaths of Warrant Officer Bouch MCM, Colour Sergeants Cahill MCM and Wright MCM and Chief Superintendent Wickenden who had been killed in an accidental explosion on the banks of the Zambezi River.

Officer Commanding SAS, Major Dudley Coventry, and these four men had been preparing canoes at the water's edge before crossing the river and proceeding to Lusaka to blow up ZANU Headquarters. The major had returned to vehicles parked above the high riverbank for some reason or other when an enormous explosion occurred. The force of the explosion was so great that, even with the protection of the bank, the major was knocked unconscious. He awakened to find his hair burning, his scalp peeled back off his skull and his hearing completely gone.

Regimental Sergeant-Major 'Bangstick' Turle of the Rhodesian Light Infantry heard the explosion from his base at the Chirundu road bridge that linked Rhodesia to Zambia. He set off without delay to investigate and found the blood-soaked major staggering along the road on his way to find help. Sergeant-Major Turle immediately called for a helicopter and was badly shaken by what he found below the bank on which the damaged SAS vehicles stood.

Mark Smithdorff piloted the helicopter sent to uplift the dead and convey Dudley to Kariba where a Dakota and doctor were standing by for his onward flight to Salisbury Hospital. Having just crossed the Chirundu tarmac road a terrific screaming noise came from the engine. Quick as a flash Mark turned back for the road and was in reach of it when the engine casing burst with a bang. He 'dumped collective' (reducing all main rotor-blade angles to zero) and made an expert forced landing through the narrow gap between trees overhanging both sides of the road.

Being deaf, Dudley Coventry had not heard the engine scream or the casing explode. He climbed out of the aircraft and turning to Mark asked in his usual polite manner, "What seems to be the problem old boy?" Pointing to the burst engine casing and using sign language Mark was able to answer the major's question. Two unhappy incidents in one day did not seem to get the major down. He was a really tough old bird.

In time to come we were often left wondering if Dudley Coventry had been blessed with the many lives of a cat. Much of what he did during his incredible life may never be told but, having survived many wounds and dangers, it seems quite

unfair that, in his old age in independent Zimbabwe, he was brutally bludgeoned to death by an intruder in his own home. I know of some of the close shaves he had but can only recall details of one.

This occurred on 26 May 1967 when Dudley was leading an SAS team in an armed roadblock above the escarpment on the Chirundu road some way south of where Mark Smithdorff's forced landing had occurred. Intelligence had picked up information that a particular pantechnicon, purporting to carry furniture, was entering Rhodesia from Zambia with a load of armed terrorists and war material.

The vehicle was duly identified and waved to a halt. The driver denied that he was transporting terrorists but refused to open the back doors. As the SAS moved to force them open, automatic fire initiated from inside the vehicle. This, together with intense return fire from the SAS, turned the pantechnicon's sides into sieve-like surfaces.

During the exchange, Dudley received a hit high up on his inner thigh. He dived for cover and dropped his pants. Satisfied that his manhood had not been affected, he ignored his heavy bleeding and continued firing into the vehicle. All the terrorists were killed and Dudley recovered from the strike that narrowly missed his femoral artery.

British military versus Labour Government

FOR SOME TIME THE ARMY had been involved in continuous border-control operations along the Zambezi River line. This involved what the Army referred to as 'side-stepping' between bases to check for tracks of terrorists crossing into Rhodesia. One day all callsigns moved left from one base to the next and returned along the same route the following day. Except for the odd senior officers' visits and casualty evacuations (casevac), the Air Force had little to do with Border ops in early times. The Hunter and Canberra boys also flew the river line on odd occasions, but for a very different reason.

The RAF Javelin squadron personnel were billeted in

Javelin.

chalets, which were modified cattle sheds in Lusaka's show grounds. The squadron leader commanding this British fighter squadron happened to be South African and, like every man under his command, he had a soft spot for Rhodesia. They made telephonic contact with our jet squadrons to offer our men best wishes and suggest that it would be fun to meet in the air. Our pilots needed no second invitation. On a few occasions Hunters or Canberras met the Javelins to fly along the Zambezi River in formation with crews waving and taking photographs of each other.

On the pretext of going on Christmas break to South Africa, a number of RAF guys took civilian flights to Salisbury, via Johannesburg (no passports were stamped). They were welcomed and, out of sight of prying eyes, given a great time. I have no idea if their desire to meet Ian Smith was fulfilled. But one can only guess that Harold Wilson and his Labour Party would have been horrified if they had known of these goings-on and especially that the Javelin boys had made it clear that they would never have responded to orders to make strikes against Rhodesians.

When, in August 1966, the British Government announced the withdrawal of the Javelin squadron, the Rhodesians gave the RAF fellows a grand farewell party at Victoria Falls. But it was not only the Royal Air Force that had a soft spot for Rhodesia; the Royal Navy seemed to have had similar sentiments.

When Ian Smith met for talks with Harold Wilson, first on HMS *Fearless* and later on HMS *Tiger*, one of his team was Flight Lieutenant Brian Smith, a Rhodesian Air Force communications officer. Brian received the highest possible co-operation from the Royal Navy, resulting in perfectly secure communications with Salisbury. By all accounts, Ian Smith himself was accorded greater respect and acknowledgement by all ranks than Harold Wilson.

We were aware that the British forces were violently anti-communist and sympathised with Rhodesia, but this did not apply to the British Government who seemed hell-bent on forcing us into a communist take-over. Sanctions were taking

Ian Smith and Harold Wilson aboard the HMS Fearless.

effect in so far as open trade was concerned but Rhodesia had turned towards South Africa and Portugal and our sanctions busters were becoming increasingly effective. For the ordinary man in the street not much had changed and support for Ian Smith and his RF party strengthened with every new threat from Whitehall.

A different way of thinking

IAN SMITH DESCRIBED THE BLACK folk of Rhodesia as the nicest and happiest people in all of Africa. I have no doubt that this was so because they needed no persuasion to report the presence of terrorists whenever and wherever they appeared. Through 1966 to 1972 very few of our black countrymen were even aware of the ZANU and ZAPU armed incursions and continued to lead normal lives.

Many amusing stories of these times can be told of our black countrymen and the way that they interpreted non-tribal issues. I give some short examples here.

What with a drought and one thing and another, an old man in the southwestern region near Kezi, was facing hard times. For hours he contemplated what he should do until he recalled being taught by missionaries many years before. "Ask and it shall be given unto you."

The old man decided to act on this and wrote a letter to God asking Him for £10 to overcome all his problems and promised never again to trouble Him if he received this help. When the letter was in an envelope the old man was in a quandary because he did not remember being given God's address. Deciding the post office people would know what to do, he addressed the stamped envelope 'TO GOD IN HEAVEN' and posted it at the Kezi Post Office.

The sorter of mail did not know what to do with the letter so took it to the postmaster who was a white man. The postmaster said he would handle the matter. At the end of his working day he drove to the local Roman Catholic mission and handed the letter over to the senior father who was so pleased by the writer's faith that he passed it all the way around the mission. A total of £5 was collected in silver that was reduced to a £5 note and mailed to the old man with an accompanying letter.

During the following week a second letter addressed 'TO GOD IN HEAVEN' arrived at the mission. In this the old man thanked God for the gift of £5 but suggested that, in future, God should not make any payment through the Catholic mission because they keep half of His gifts.

A terrorist was captured unhurt but in an emaciated state. He was armed with an SKS rifle and had plenty of ammunition.

His belly had been empty for days and the urine in his water bottle had turned to acid because he had failed to find water. Once he had been fed and his thirst had been quenched he was interrogated by Special Branch. He told SB that he was the sole survivor of a contact with the Army and had been trying to get back to Zambia. The matter of hunger and thirst came up and he was asked if he had seen any game. He said he had seen plenty of animals. When asked why he had not shot something to eat, he said, "I do not have a Government hunting licence!"

An old headman near Chipinga came with his people to inspect my helicopter—the first they had seen close up. The headman was delighted to be taken on a short goodwill flight around his own territory accompanied by his ten-year-old grandson. Having experienced flight for the first time in his life, the old man declared that he was now the possessor of untold knowledge. He understood cars, buses and tractors, all of which he had driven. He understood most mechanical things, having worked with ploughs, farm implements and dairy milking machines. He said he even understood jet airliners because he had seen them flying high in the sky. But there was one thing that really puzzled his mind. He could not understand how white men put whole sardines into a totally enclosed tin. When I told him how this was done and pointed out the solder lines around the crimped lid he was tickled pink but asked me to promise that I would keep this amazing secret to myself.

When we were operating in the Kanyemba area, I came upon some of the people of the two-toed tribe known as the Vadoma. Not all members of the tribe suffered the affliction, but all seemed to be resistant to the killer disease 'sleeping sickness' caused by tsetse flies that plagued that area of the Zambezi Valley. Every time I was bitten by one of these creatures I not only jumped at the sting but also came up in a red and painful swelling around the bite. When I asked a Vadoma chief how he put up with the tsetse fly menace, he said he suffered no problem. He always made certain that a person who was more attractive to the flies than himself stayed close to him, day and night.

My father was overseeing the monthly dipping of tribal cattle when a delegation of old men approached him driving three oxen before them. These animals had been castrated many moons back but the men had come to Dad to say they had made a big mistake; these beasts should never have been castrated. Would 'Mambo' please turn them back into bulls!

Amongst European traders there was always good-natured rivalry evidenced by notices and nonsensical poems affixed to shop windows. I cannot recall any that I saw but Maria Pickett, who lived in Gatooma, told me of one incident that typified the rivalry between people trading in similar lines. This involved two chemists whose premises were opposite one another on the main street in the middle of town. One altered his display window to promote a whole range of quality hand-soaps. Included was a poem that read, "I am young and full of hope—I wash my pussy with Coal-tar soap!" Seeing this, his rival responded by filling his window with all sorts of low-cost soaps and displayed them with the following message: "I am old and have no hope—I wash my cock with any old soap!"

FAC courses and smoke trails

AT THORNHILL THE HUNTER AND Vampire squadrons were running Forward Air Controller (FAC) courses for Army officers undergoing company and platoon commander training at the School of Infantry, Gwelo.

The FAC courses were primarily intended for situations of conventional warfare where the Army might need air strikes to be undertaken against a variety of targets, including tanks, other armoured vehicles and artillery. These courses were the foundation upon which the Army and the Air Force developed very special bonds between units and individuals. Most of the participating Army officers were majors, captains and lieutenants who became senior commanders in future operations.

Arising from the FAC courses, I thought that situations could arise in which helicopter pilots might also have to

PB, Rob Gaunt and Eddie Wilkinson seen here with Army officers of an early FAC course. Most of these officers were to become the mainstay of Army operations as excellent field commanders.

undertake airborne FAC tasks by directing jet pilots onto pinpoint targets. It occurred to me that if two helicopters could trail smoke from different directions towards a target, jet pilots would be able to visually extend the lines and strike the intersection point. With official approval to investigate this possibility I had special nozzles made to inject atomised oil into the combustion chamber of the jet engine. For weeks I worked on this with the willing assistance of the squadron's technicians, often covering the entire airbase in a cloud of white smoke.

When the nozzle design and method of pumping the fluid into the engine seemed right, airborne tests were conducted with a Canberra. The Canberra's crew could easily see the smoke trail from over twenty nautical miles but it soon became apparent that a helicopter's flight line and the smoke trail differed considerably, even in the gentlest of wind conditions. Since this was bound to lead jets into striking wrong positions the project was discarded.

Missing rhino

AIR HQ RECEIVED AN UNUSUAL request for help from a farmer living a few miles west of Salisbury. He ran game on his place. Included was a white rhino that had gone missing. I was tasked to find the animal and, if possible, drive it back to the farm. A pass up one of the boundaries revealed a break in the fence through which the rhino had escaped. Fairly high grass on the adjacent farm clearly revealed the line the rhino had taken and led me to the big fellow who was having a snooze under trees some five miles from the gap in the fence. The animal responded well to helicopter shepherding and trotted back to where the farmer and his workers had positioned to guide the animal through the broken section of fence.

However, when the rhino spotted the people ahead of him he became confused and gave me a run-around as I moved about trying to steer him in the right direction. The people on the ground waved hats and other objects to help but two of them only succeeded in getting knocked over by the rhino before I eventually came very close and forced him through.

The fun of helicopters

IT WAS UNUSUAL EVENTS SUCH as this that made helicopters so much more fun to fly than any fixed-wing machine.

Because of the helicopter's versatility, every opportunity was taken to reduce stresses and make a student's training a special experience. Intensive training was broken down into short periods with rest breaks taken in a variety of locations. This allowed students to meet a whole range of people, which was not possible when operating conventional aircraft.

Many of our training flights included tea and luncheon stops with farmers who were always delighted to have us drop in on their front lawns. Seldom was this done without forewarning and, in consequence, there were usually additional guests invited to join the helicopter crew for a swim and sumptuous meal.

Visiting Great Zimbabwe. Hotel out of sight to the right.

A number of officers at Air HQ considered such practices a misuse of helicopters. Fortunately, most recognised the true value of these stopovers because it saved many wasted flying hours. If two hours of actual flying training was to be done in two parts and a farm visit was taken in between, it saved the high cost of having to route to and from the training area twice. The second benefit was the all-important matter of generating good public relations for which the Air Staff received loads of good reports.

Police Reserve Air Wing

ANOTHER GROUP OF PEOPLE WE were getting to know in these times were pilots and observers of the Police Reserve Air Wing. PRAW had been established along the same lines as the Kenyan Police Air Wing that did such good work during the Mau Mau rebellion in Kenya.

PRAW operated privately owned aircraft ranging greatly in make and capacity. All crews were flying enthusiasts who longed to be employed in operational roles in preference to mundane transporting of passengers around the country. But their operational training was very limited and wholly geared to police needs and thinking.

One aspect of training that received an inordinate amount of attention was message dropping. All aircraft were fitted with radios for civil aviation communications but the police radio network was not compatible with these sets, hence the need for occasional message drops. To meet this shortfall, a message was inserted into a small weighted bag to which was attached a long thin red streamer. A ground party could easily follow the streamer when the bag was dropped, even in the thickest bush. The PRAW pilots however placed great emphasis on dropping a message at its recipient's feet.

I was called upon to lecture PRAW pilots on air operations in general but, because of the number of individuals involved, my lecture was given in two sessions. At question time during the first session a lawyer from Umtali, Dendy Lawton, raised the matter of message dropping in mountainous areas. I spelt out the immense dangers of flying at low speed close to any mountain and stressed the reason for having a long streamer to assist ground parties follow and find a message. Flight safety was the issue, not accuracy of the drop. In particular I said no drop should ever be made flying towards rising ground, irrespective of the wind direction.

During the second PRAW session Chipinga farmer, Bill Springer, raised the self-same question. He received the same answer and cautions I had given Dendy Lawton. Yet, incredibly, it was these two men who met their deaths making drops towards rising ground.

On 6 May 1967 Dendy Lawton ploughed into the side of a mountain and his observer, Bill Perkins (Perky), was thrown clear. When Perky staggered to his feet he saw that the aircraft was on fire with Dendy inside. Without hesitation he went into the aircraft to rescue his friend but was driven back badly burnt and Dendy perished. It took many months for Perky to recover from severe burns, though he eventually did so with surprisingly minor scarring.

Two years later, on 19 July 1969, Bill Springer was dropping supplies to ground troops monitoring the valley through which the Umtali to Beira road and rail line ran. In the process Bill flew into rising ground. How it came to be that Bill Perkins was there I do not remember. But Perky got into the aircraft and, with fuel pouring all over him, he managed to pull badly injured Bill Springer clear of the wreck.

Fortunately for Perky there was no fire this time but, unfortunately, Bill Springer lost his life. The bravery shown by Bill Perkins in knowingly going to a friend's aid in spite of a real danger of being burnt again is beyond description.

Perky (centre) with Hugh McCormick and John Blythe-Wood.

Chapter

6

Operation Nickel

BY MID-AUGUST 1967 I had completed helicopter conversions for Peter Nicholls, Hugh Slatter and Mick Grier before moving to Makuti where the RLI was engaged with incoming terrorist groups. They were also searching for arms reported cached in a cave.

Border Control units continued picking up small terrorist group infiltrations across the Zambezi east of Chirundu at a time when the Zambezi Valley floor was stinking hot and bone-dry. Soldiers were catching up and accounting for almost all terrorists whose water bottles were either empty or contained urine. The few terrorists that managed to reach local tribesmen above the escarpment were reported to the police who either captured or killed them. So ZANU was getting nowhere!

It was whilst I was with the RLI at Makuti, that the officers and men ripped sleeves off camouflage shirts and cut legs off camouflage trousers to counter the heat. All wore veldskoen boots (vellies) without socks because socks picked up irritating burs and sharp grass seeds. Most young farmers had rejected socks years before this for the same reason. In the cool of evening I noticed Army officers were wearing slacks and vellies but no socks. They nicknamed the bare skin of their ankles 'Makuti socks'; a name that stuck. Thereafter, vellies and Makuti socks were fashionable for most young Rhodesian men.

In 1967 the helicopter squadron was small. As usual for those times, technicians were almost equal in number to pilots and every one of them served as gunner-technician in the field.

The search for the hidden arms cache eventually led RLI to a site in the Vuti Purchase Area. It proved to have been the cache point but the equipment had been moved just before its discovery. All the same, it was interesting to explore the narrow cave whose deep bed of bat guano made one bounce as one walked. A ledge on one side of the cave was at the base of a vertical tunnel that led to another small ledge on the open side of the ridge above the cave. ZANU's keepers of arms had built a long stepladder that gave access to this opening so that they could survey all approaches; which is why they detected the RLI's approach in time to move their arms cache to safety.

My real interest in the cave was the huge quantity of bat guano that was much sought after by gardeners. Recognising the commercial value of this natural fertiliser I planned to do something about getting it to market when I could find time to do so. However, I obviously talked too much and lost out to one of 3 Squadron's VR pilots who had the time to set up camp and extract all the guano, which he sold in Salisbury. During later operations I located another cave off the Umfuli River in the Mcheka-wa-ka-Sungabeta range. This cave contained greater volumes of bat guano but I never did find the chance to capitalise on it.

I was still operating from Makuti when, on 14 August 1967, I received orders to get to FAF 1 (Forward Airfield 1). This was an established permanent Forward Airfield at Wankie Town. At the time FAF 2 was being developed at Kariba Airport. In time to come another eight such bases would be built. On arrival at FAF 1, I learned what the flap was about. A large group of terrorists (later established to be ninety-four men) had crossed the Batoka Gorge, downstream from Victoria Falls, during the night of 9 August and had covered a distance of almost seventy miles before Rhodesian forces made contact. The operation was codenamed Operation Nickel.

Most of the deep gorge below the Victoria Falls had been ignored in regular Border Control operations. This was partly due to a shortage of troops but more so because that stretch of the border was considered safe. The bone-dry, unpopulated rough country on the Zambian side of the Zambezi River plus steep-sided gorges and fast-flowing turbulent water with many crocodiles all appeared to form a perfect barrier. But this crossing awakened us to the fact that we had been focusing too much on ZANU's infiltration methods that involved the use of vehicles to reach the Zambezi River and fishermen's canoes to cross it.

ZAPU's Russian advisers had obviously studied our Border Control coverage and techniques and had selected the Batoka Gorge as being the last place we would expect a crossing to occur. Employing a system of ropes, pulleys and two rubber dinghies, men and equipment were ferried from north to south bank on and above the raging water.

The process started at sunset and was completed before dawn. The group rested up on the south bank until late afternoon then commenced the difficult climb up to the high ground. Avoiding all habitation, the group bypassed Wankie town then turned south to intercept the railway line. Terrorist presence was first reported from Matetsi Mission but the report gave no indication of numbers.

We were to learn that one third of the force comprised ZAPU men with the balance being South African ANC terrorists. There was significance in this, the largest crossing to date. It had been jointly planned and launched by James Chikerema who was deputy to ZAPU's leader and Oliver Tambo, the external leader of the SAANC. (ZAPU's leader, Joshua Nkomo, was in detention in Rhodesia.) A few days after hurriedly launching their joint force, they signed a military alliance that remained in effect throughout the Rhodesian war.

The force was four times larger than any ZANU group and all its men were substantially better trained. Mistakenly, Chikerema and Tambo considered their joint force to be strong enough to fight off any Rhodesian Security Force (RSF) it might encounter. The force was tasked to establish a safe passage through N'debele territory down the western flank of Rhodesia, right up to the Limpopo River, to give SAANC a permanent route to South Africa.

POWER STATION

The Batoka Gorge lay the same distance again from the bottom right hand corner of this aerial photograph as the distance to Victoria Falls (top left). Of interest in this picture are five ancient falls lines that have stepped back over millions of years. The next line in the existing falls is developing on the left side of Victoria Falls, as witnessed by a deepening cut known as The Devil's Cataract.

The whole group was resting in the shade of heavy riverine bush covering both sides of the small Inyatue River where they encountered surface water for the first time since leaving the Zambezi. Close to their position was the Inyatue railway bridge on the line from Victoria Falls to Bulawayo. Having followed the winter-dry riverbed, the terrorists had passed under the railway bridge before locating the shaded water point three kilometres farther upstream. Here they split the force either side of their entry tracks as a precaution against armed follow-up.

It was in response to a railway repair party's report that a mixed tracker-combat group of RAR and Police moved in. Led by Major Peter Hoskins it comprised twenty men, which was considered a strong force at the time. Tracks of many men led the Rhodesians along the river-line up to the railway bridge. The Rhodesians opened into extended line to cross the high railway embankment and continued forward until they encountered thick riverine bush. Concentrating on the bush ahead, they moved with caution until they came under fire at close range. The Rhodesian's were lucky not to suffer serious casualties immediately.

When after some time Major Hoskins attempted a flanking movement, Acting Corporal Davison and Private Karomi were killed and the major was wounded. He lay unable to move for something like ten hours before being dragged to safety by his daring Regimental Sergeant-Major, Aubrey Corb. Three separate firefights developed with the terrorists using searching fire on the line of men who, though pinned down, had crawled into cover. With so much fire in an environment of deep shade and brilliant sunlight, where visual penetration into the bush was less than three meters in most places, it proved impossible to detect actual points of enemy fire or judge the terrorist force disposition and strength. What was patently clear was that reinforcements were needed in a hurry.

Flight Lieutenant Mick Grier with Bob Whyte as his gunner brought these in then expended all their ammunition into the unseen terrorist positions before returned to FAF 1 to refuel and re-arm. A Provost flown by Prop Geldenhuys remained overhead the contact scene until after dark to serve as a radio relay (Telstar) back to Brigade HQ in Wankie. Since Peter Hoskins had been separated from his radio, there was concern for his safety. Before sunset one group of SF had led a lateral skirmish towards other SF with a view to consolidating defence and firepower. During this move, a radio was put out of action by machine-gun fire. Prop received a request for a replacement radio and was able to pick up the position of a white map laid out in an open patch of ground on the right flank where troops with the defunct radio had moved.

Bob Whyte, son of Group Captain Doug Whyte, had the replacement radio. Having dropped off troops, Mick Grier located the men waiting for the radio. As he landed the helicopter came under heavy fire. Mick lifted away immediately, but Bob Whyte had already leapt out onto the ground where

he immediately attracted terrorist fire that forced him to go to ground.

Lying on his belly in a small depression, Bob realised he was out of the terrorists' direct view but he could not move. Bob could see the troops who required the radio but he could not get to them. Bob's quandary was that he had a serviceable radio without an aerial and the troops with a serviceable aerial were just too far away to throw it to him.

Bob Whyte.

After some thought Bob reached into his flying overalls for a screwdriver, which he thrust against the radio's aerial jack point and tried a transmission to Mick Grier watching him helplessly from above. To Bob's amazement and relief, he received a reply and was able to make further transmissions when called upon to do so. The benefit of having a working radio outweighed the discomfort of receiving a sharp electrical belt down his arm each time he transmitted. With extra troops now available, covering fire was given for the troops to get to Bob.

The firefight continued until darkness fell but at some stage Inspector Phillips of the BSAP, who had come in with reinforcements, received a bullet wound to his head that would commit him to a wheelchair for life. Any ground movement attracted heavy fire from terrorists who everyone could hear talking Zulu, the same language as N'debele. RSM Aubrey Corb, who had also come in with the reinforcement force, called for but received no answer from Major Hoskins. Everything remained quiet so long as troops stayed in situ. Since movement or sound drew immediate enemy response, Aubrey Corb knew that Peter Hoskins, if still alive, would remain silent unless he was absolutely certain of friendly force positions. At about 22:00 the RSM was on high ground at the edge of the contact site. From this position he fired an Icarus flare knowing that

Peter Hoskins would recognise it as having come from an RAR position. Peter recognised the distinctive plume almost directly above him and immediately called from the darkness. During his descent to retrieve the major, Aubrey Corb accidentally discovered seriously wounded Inspector Phillips.

Apart from the blackness of the night, it was decided that casualty evacuation by Mick Grier in the only available helicopter was too dangerous because its landing light would undoubtedly attract enemy fire; so the alternate option of a motorised rail car was used to reach the remote area. But this involved carrying the casualties three kilometres from the contact area across rough ground on a pitch-black night. Major Hoskins insisted that Inspector Phillips be given the only available stretcher because he considered the policeman's condition to be more serious than his own. Hoskins himself was in deep trouble having been hit in the upper thigh right next to the femoral artery. He had managed to stuff fabric into the wound to stem the high flow of blood but had lost so much during his long wait that he was barely conscious during his ride on a crude makeshift stretcher.

At dawn the troops moved cautiously forward only to find that the terrorists had extricated themselves during the night. A sweep through the area revealed five dead terrorists with evidence that others had been wounded. Large quantities of Russian equipment, mislaid during the battle and silent withdrawal, lay scattered over a large area. Notwithstanding the withdrawal, there was no doubting we were involved with a new breed of fighters. The aggression and efficiency shown by ZAPU and SAANC at Inyatue revealed that they were both prepared and able to fight and were unlikely to turn back for Zambia as might be expected from experiences with ZANU. Rather, they would continue in a southerly direction through the Wankie Game Reserve or along its eastern boundary, which was the railway line.

By 10 am three extra helicopters were available and the trackers had found that the terrorists had not made a completely ordered withdrawal. An initial assessment was that they had become divided in darkness into three separate groups. One large group and a lesser one were heading southwards into the Wankie Game Reserve and a very small group of four had set off south-eastwards along the line of rail. An ambush was established near the railway village at Dett where the four terrorists were killed.

For two days, trackers cast ahead but were experiencing some difficulty in getting a clear lead on the biggest group because the terrorists had spread out employing anti-tracking techniques as they moved through open savannah terrain. The countryside was bone dry, so surface water had to be the key to locating them.

With the general southward movement there was need to relocate forces. No 1 Brigade HQ, commanded by Brigadier Godwin with his staff officers Majors 'Mac' Willar and 'Buttons' Wells-West, moved to Shapi Pan during the course

of the next day, 18 August. A FASOC, commanded by Flight Lieutenant Doug Butler, together with large quantities of drummed Avtur, was positioned next to Brigade HQ.

By the time our four helicopters arrived at Shapi Pans, Lieutenant Ian Wardle and his RAR tracker-combat team had been following spoor of the smaller group estimated to be for fifteen terrorists and twenty-four-hours old. The next morning Ian reported that he was passing Rhino Pens where National Parks nursed sick or hurt rhinos back to health. The terrorists had not seen water since leaving Inyatue and were moving down a line of water pans that were all baked white and bone dry.

Avtur drums.

A little later in the day I was returning from a deployment task when Brigadier Godwin requested that I divert to establish Ian's exact position because he had just reported being two hours behind the terrorists and about to enter a forested area. Having established Ian's location, I returned to Shapi Pans to refuel. Brigadier Godwin then asked me to return to Ian Wardle with a supply of water because Ian felt certain he was close to making contact.

I met Ian and his black soldiers in a tiny clearing deep inside the treed area. Everyone was drenched in sweat and, having filled water bottles and quenched their thirst, delighted in pouring cold water over their already soaking wet bodies. Watching these men made me wondered how the terrorists were faring having had no water since leaving Inyatue. Filthy dirty, unshaven and bubbling with enthusiasm, Ian said he would make contact in less than two hours and moved off at the head of his men. They were all out of sight before I had chance to wind up and lift off.

No sooner had we refuelled at Shapi Pans and settled down for a cup of tea when Buttons Wells-West ran over to say, "Get airborne chop, chop, Wardle called 'contact' on his HF radio.

We heard heavy firing during the transmission but have heard nothing since and cannot raise him. Please get over there and find out what is happening."

As I headed back with Bob Whyte, who I had taken on as my technician, I attempted, unsuccessfully, to raise Ian. We noticed heavy smoke rising from the bush way ahead and realised this was close to where we had last seen Ian. Even before we arrived overhead we saw that the fire was racing outwards spewing heavy black smoke. Already many hawks were heading towards it to feast on insects disturbed by the fire. Again and again I called but there was no response.

We had started an orbit over the already burnt-out area of the forest before a deep breathing and obviously excited Ian Wardle answered. I told him we had been very worried having heard nothing since his 'contact' call. "Hell, no sweat. We have killed most of the bastards but we think a few got away. It is safe here now. Come on down and take a look. I will have a couple of my men watch the chopper."

I passed on the good news to Brigade and found a big-enough gap in the trees close to where I saw Ian waving his map. The whole area was burnt out so the helicopter had to be placed on the ground very smartly to limit the swirl of black ash thrown up by rotor-wash. Ian and his men were black from head to toe. The whiteness of eyes and teeth and the pinkness of mouths surrounded by matt-black faces emphasised their huge grins. These were very happy guys who had come through a very noisy though short-lived experience. Ian couldn't wait to take us, step by step, through every action.

After their water break, the refreshed troops advanced in an echelon formation either side of trackers moving in heavy shade under high trees. Ian was next to the lead tracker when he detected movement under the trunk of a tree that had been pushed over by elephants. His eyes immediately focused on the unmistakable outline of the barrel and bipod of a Russian RPD machine-gun. He opened fire instinctively. The whole callsign joined in as terrorist movements were picked up over an area of no more than thirty meters square, centred on the point where Ian concentrated his fire. Suddenly, from this spot, a double explosion rocked the area and initiated a bush fire.

Retaliation from the terrorists was limited in the face of RAR's overwhelming firepower and most terrorists died immediately. When firing stopped the force swept cautiously forward. Moaning was heard before it turned to screams as one terrorist, his cloths on fire, emerged from behind another fallen tree. Ian dropped him with one shot and the sweep continued right through the area. When certain that there were no live terrorists around, Ian gathered his men for a site debrief. The men who had been on Ian's right during the firefight had spotted eight terrorists breaking as a group. They knew they had accounted for three, which Ian found lying some distance from the main group of eight dead men, but five had escaped.

Ian was preparing to continue with the follow-up on the survivors when Brigadier Godwin ordered him to prepare for uplift. A Provost pilot had reported the huge extent of the fire and it had been decided to deploy fresh troops ahead of the survivors who had headed off in a southerly direction, probably running ahead of the fast moving bush fire.

Ian had pushed his men almost ninety kilometres in less than forty-eight hours so, although Ian himself was disappointed at being pulled off, his men deserved a break after a job well done. In the Brigade Officers' Mess marquee that evening the brigadier invited Ian to recount events for the assembled RAR and Air Force officers. Like many of our Army officers, Ian Wardle's speech was somewhat affected but his briefing was graphic and amusing. About the burning terrorist incident, he said, "The man was screaming, burning and making a general nuisance of himself, so I shot him."

Wounded Major Hoskins' E Company of RAR was taken over by Major Ray Howden who, together with A Company under Major Taffy Marchant, established a forward base at Limpandi Dam near the southwestern corner of the game reserve. Murray Hofmeyr was attached to this base to facilitate troop deployments for operations along the Gwabazobuya River and the Botswanan border that formed a funnel through which the main terrorist group was expected to pass. From Shapi Pans two tracker combat units were deployed to locate and neutralise the five terrorists who had survived Ian Wardle's contact.

Out of the blue a South African Police (SAP) Alouette III helicopter arrived at Shapi Pans. The first thing I noticed about the SAP helicopter was that it was fitted with a Becker Homer, which we had not yet received. The South African Air Force pilot, Lieutenant 'Weasel' Wesley, was seconded to SAP to fly Police-owned helicopters. He told us that he had been sent from Katimo Mulilo in South West Africa and that additional SAP helicopters were to follow. This was because of South African ANC terrorists being involved with ZAPU.

For two days after Ian Wardle's contact, things were quiet at Shapi Pans, so I took opportunity to visit Paul Grobelaar's large mobile processing factory that handled all elephant and buffalo carcasses from a game-culling operation that was in progress in the Wankie Game Reserve. This unpleasant periodic slaughter of animals was necessary to control population growth but it needed Paul's support to ensure that no destroyed animal was wasted and that everything was put to good use.

Paul had a small Cessna 140, which he flew to locate small herds of around twenty elephants. Two game-rangers were then directed to the selected herd. They walked in from downwind to get right in amongst the herd before shooting the babies first as this had the effect of stopping the adults from running off. Taking out the adults necessitated fast shooting and rock-steady nerves whilst the great brutes were rushing around screaming in angry panic, often charging the men. Because of their marksmanship and knowledge of vital points from every angle, it was almost unheard of for a ranger to have to use a second shot to finish off a wounded jumbo. They really hated the task but insisted on doing the culling themselves. Because they loved the animals so much, they refused to leave it to other hunters. They dared not fail to eliminate every member of the selected group because any elephant escaping the slaughter would certainly induce panic in neighbouring herds.

Two baby jumbos that had been orphaned by ivory poachers roamed around the camp at Shapi Pans. They loved people and were a bit of a nuisance. Though small in elephant terms, they were amazingly powerful and would push one around seeking to be fed and scratched. Their interest in helicopters was a bit of a worry, but apart from leaving snotty marks on the vision panels they did no damage. Years later, in 1982, I saw these same two elephants. By then they were almost full grown at Ozzie Bristow's Lion and Cheetah Park near Harare (new name for Salisbury).

I had known and feared Willie de Beer from school cadet camp days at Inkomo Barracks where he was Regimental Sergeant-Major. Now retired from the Army and serving as a ranger with National Parks, Willie offered to take me on a buffalo-culling operation that, because of Op Nickel, was being done by day. Buffalo were normally culled at night using powerful searchlights in specially designed vehicles. The one we used had 40mm holes in its metal sides, showing how dangerous a buffalo bull's horns could be.

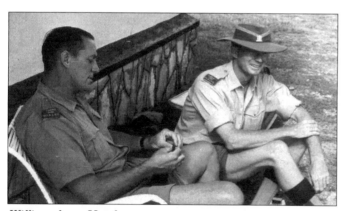

Willie and van Heerden.

A young ranger aged about thirty by the name of van Heeden drove the vehicle, with Willie and me sharing the front seat. Four black game-ranger-trackers were standing behind us holding a rail that ran around the rear section of the open vehicle. We were a long way southeast of Shapi Pans searching the sandy road for fresh buffalo spoor when one of the trackers pointed to the road and said there were boot tracks of someone moving in the opposite direction to ourselves. We stopped and without hesitation the tracker said that these had been made no more than two minutes earlier.

I recognised the sole pattern immediately. It was the well-known figure 8 pattern of boots issued to terrorists. Sand was still trickling at the edge of the spoor. Realising that we had

passed close to a terrorist who was obviously trying to make his way back to Zambia, I warned the rangers there was the possibility that other terrorists were with him walking off the line of road. We turned around and had only gone a short distance following the spoor when it moved left off the road into the bush.

Willie, ignoring my advice to keep moving, climbed out of the vehicle and followed the tracks a short distance armed only with a dart gun that was intended to anaesthetise buffalo. He shouted out to the unseen terrorist to surrender. Nothing happened so Willie returned to the vehicle. I recommended that I drive the vehicle and drop off the young ranger with one of the trackers in an ambush position once we were down the road and out of sight. This was agreed. When we had gone about 150 metres and had thick bush on our left, I moved the gear lever to neutral whilst maintained engine revs and applied gentle hand-braking. The two men dismounted and we continued on to Shapi to collect troops.

When we returned after sunset a dead terrorist lay on the road. He had appeared as soon as we left and had run across the road, waited a while, then run diagonally across to the other side. His next crossing would be straight towards the hidden ranger who stood up and called to the terrorist to surrender. The unfortunate terrorist raised his weapon but knew nothing of the .375 magnum bullet that removed one vertebra from his neck. Van Heeden said he had aimed for the neck because he understood it was important for identification purposes not to damage a face.

The young ranger was deeply concerned that he might be placed on a murder charge and was feeling guilty because the SKS rifle this man was armed with had only one round of ammunition in it. When studies of papers and a notebook in the terrorist's possession proved that he had been at Inyatue, the ranger accepted the legal situation but he remained shaken and depressed for having killed a human being.

On this same day, tracks of the five survivors from Ian Wardle's contact were found and followed into thick bush close to the National Parks southeastern border game fence. A call to the terrorists to surrender was answered with automatic fire. Under covering fire, the RAR officer crawled forward and lobbed in a phosphorus grenade. This single grenade spewed phosphorus over all five terrorists whose smouldering bodies were found close together during a sweep through the site.

Earlier in the day, an RAR patrol spotted two terrorists collecting water from Leasha Pan. Long-range fire was initiated too early when these two men spotted the troops. One broke north and the other south. The man who ran north was ignored by the troops but was killed later that day by the game ranger. Tracks of the second moved south and led RAR trackers to a resting place from which about sixty terrorists had departed in a hurry.

Disastrous twenty-four hours

TRACKERS MOVED FAST ALONG THE trail that showed the terrorists had moved at a run for a considerable distance through open scrubland. When the trackers reached the point where the terrorists had broken through the game fence, Lieutenant Nick Smith arrived to take command of the follow-up along with extra troops flown in by Hoffy.

Two helicopters from Shapi Pans (I was still out with Willie de Beer) joined Hoffy in deploying other troops under command of Lieutenant Ken Pierson. Ken's orders were to set up ambushes on the Nata River directly in line with Leasha Pan and the point the terrorists had crossed the game fence. It was dark when helicopters, flown by John Rogers and Ian Harvey, returned to Shapi Pans where Chris Dixon, who had recently arrived, joined them and me in a helicopter forward-lift of fuel for the following day.

All night long under a brilliant full moon we lifted fuel to a location just beyond the game fence close to a Botswanan border beacon known as Point 222. This was a frustrating job because we could only lift two drums of Avtur in our underslung cargo nets to Point 222 but then had to use one of these to get back to Shapi Pans for the next load. The net result of four helicopters flying throughout the night was that only twelve full drums of Avtur were available at the remote forward logistics base at dawn.

At the commencement of the fuel lift, Prop Geldenhuys flying a Provost at height provided communication between soldiers on the ground, Tac HQ and Brigade. The first sign of trouble came when Sergeant-Major Timitiya told Prop that Nick Smith had been shot and that he was under heavy fire. Nothing more was heard. Nick Smith failed to come up on the HF radio at the scheduled reporting time of 18.00 and there was no response to any call from Prop, the two companies or Brigade HQs. When Ken Pierson checked in on schedule, he reported having heard heavy firing from Nick Smith's area and said he could not raise Nick on VHF. Deep concern had already set in as Prop continued trying, unsuccessfully, to raise Nick. I remember how impressed I was by Prop's cool manner and efficiency in conveying what needed to be said.

Prop was then a PAI (Pilot Armament Instructor) on 4 Squadron, which amazed me because, as a past student of mine, he seemed too young to be doing such a responsible job. It took some time before it dawned on me that I had been just as young in similar circumstances.

More anguish was added to the night when Prop relayed the appalling news that Ken Pierson was dead. Ken had been shot by one of his own men when he moved from one ambush position to another. As dawn broke I flew from Point 222 to the Company HQ were Hoffy gave Bob Whyte and me a very welcome cup of coffee whilst we refuelled from his diminishing stock of Avtur. All he had in the way of food was tinned pilchards in tomato sauce. Having eaten nothing since breakfast the previous day, I was able to face the cold fish and hard ration biscuits in preparation for what promised to be a long day.

Front from left: Prop with 4 Squadron instructors: Pat Meddows-Taylor, Bill Jelley, Ken Edwards (OC), Nobby Nightingale, Rob Tasker and Justin (Varky) Varkivisser. Back: Chris Weinmann, Bill Buckle, Hugh Slatter (sitting on canopy rail), John Bennie, Mark McLean and Harold Griffiths.

At some time during the night John Rogers had flown Major Mac Willar from Shapi Pans to the Company HQ. Mac was still in discussion with the company commanders Ray Howden and Taffy Marchant when Ian Harvey called the ops room to say he had been attracted to the game fence by smoke rising from a small fire. Here he found some of Nick Smith's troops in a state of despair. They reported that they had run out of ammunition following contact with many terrorists in ambush but did not know what had happened to Nick Smith or Timitiya.

John Rogers and Hoffy lifted Mac Willar with troops and spare ammunition forward to link up with these men. By the time he arrived the rest of Nick Smith's troops, drawn by the earlier noise of Ian's helicopter, were also there. Mac moved off with the troops to the site of the ambush where he found the bodies of Nick Smith and Sergeant Major Timitiya. In the meanwhile, I had collected the one and only terrorist captured thus far. He was an SAANC man who had panicked during the firefight and had been found and arrested by locals living in a small tribal village about eight kilometres away.

Hoffy and I landed at the ambush site when trackers confirmed the area safe and terrorists well clear. They had left this position in the direction that should have taken them directly to the ambush positions Ken Pierson had prepared. I joined in on an inspection of the contact site that showed the terrorists had moved across open ground, which they had obviously selected as ideal killing ground for a prepared ambush. They then orbited in a wide left-hand circuit and set up a crescent-shaped ambush along the edge of a line of scrub overlooking the selected killing ground. Here they dug shallow shell-scrapes to await the arrival of troops they knew must be close by, because they had heard Hoffy's helicopter deploying Nick's callsign at the fence.

Site of ambush. The helicopters are parked in the 'killing ground' with the ambush line lying just beyond the tree belt. In white shirts are: SB officer, his assistant and the SAANC prisoner.

The terrorists may have been forced to initiate the ambush early when troops of the left echelon were about to bump the right side of their ambush line. By this time, however, Nick and Timitiya were abreast of the RPD machine-guns clustered at the centre of the ambush line. Nick was totally exposed with no cover at all whereas Timitiya was next to a lone tree. The firefight that ensued was intense and it was clear that Nick and Timitiya had used deliberately aimed conservative fire, whereas the other troops had expended their limited issue of ammunition. In retrospect the standard issue of two full magazines and only twenty rounds of reserve ammunition was way too little for situations such as this. It was a hard-learned lesson!

Clearly the eight dead terrorists, five with RPD machine-guns, in the centre of the ambush line had been taken out by deadly accurate fire from Nick and Timitiya. The tree that Timitiya had used to steady himself whilst firing his MAG machine-gun from the hip was riddled with bullet strikes high above his head with just one single graze mark from the round that struck him in the head. Most bullet strikes to his body had occurred after death. Judging from his line of spent cartridges, Nick had run directly towards the ambush line before he went down because, without any cover, outright aggression must have been his only option.

Of greatest concern was that Nick's VHF radio had been taken by the terrorists. Also taken was Nick's FN rifle, Timitiya's MAG and a number of packs which had been thrown off when the firing started. The capture of SF clothing by the terrorists posed a greater problem than the radio, because all spare batteries were still in the possession of one of the RAR survivors.

The bodies of two terrorists.

Only when the loss of the radio became known was Hoffy able to make sense of a VHF call he had received from an African male asking him to come and pick up wounded men. The caller had used the word 'helicopter' instead of the usual 'Cyclone 7' when a caller did not know a helicopter pilot's personal callsign. Hoffy had tried to get this caller to give him a locstat (grid reference) of his position. There was no reply so Hoffy got on with what he was doing.

There was plenty of evidence to show that a number of wounded terrorists had left the ambush site with the main body. Along the trail an RAR tracker detected drag marks leading to a clump of scrub off to one side of tracks that showed the group had been walking in single file. Here the bodies of two more terrorists were found. I popped in to take a photograph of these bodies on my way back to Point 222.

A sudden change in course by the terrorists, who had been heading directly for the RAR ambush sites on the Nata River, must have been induced by the sound of the gunfire that killed Ken Pierson. A tracker-combat group under Lieutenant Bill Winall picked up on the tracks from the Nata River at around 10 o'clock.

The SAP helicopter arrived at Point 222 where the pilot indicated he was keen to become involved. However, we could not task him until we were given instructions on how he, his technician and his aircraft were to be employed and what restrictions, if any, applied. Nevertheless, both pilot and technician were able to assist with the interrogation of the SAANC prisoner who could only speak Afrikaans and Xhosa. They established that an SAANC man was leading the group and that he would respond to radio calls in Afrikaans.

John Rogers piloted the SAP helicopter whilst the two South African men held the SAANC prisoner and monitored his VHF transmission as he attempted to get a response from the terrorist leader. John kept an eye on the Becker Homer hoping to get a direction, but no reply was made. In hopes that the terrorist leader was listening in on the radio, the prisoner transmitted a prepared message in Afrikaans and, using his own pseudonym, recommended that the leader should surrender because there was no chance of anyone surviving as he could see the Rhodesian security forces were determined to kill him and all his followers. We never did find out if those calls were received.

When I flew over to check on his progress at around 11:00, I noticed that Bill Winall had two police handlers with their dogs. His callsign was moving in single file through high dry scrub with the dogs following the trail, now heading east for the first time. Flying high so as not to give terrorists any specific indication of the follow-up, I did a survey of the ground ahead. On the line of movement, about six kilometres ahead of the troops, thick scrub gave way to open, treed savannah where ground rose gently to a flat crest before descending more steeply to the banks of the Tegwani River. On a section of this river bright-green trees lining both banks contrasted strongly with the otherwise drab brown countryside. Here I found surface water in the riverbed, the only water for miles around.

Having seen this, I flew off northeastward well away from the area before heading back across the line of the follow-up group. When I passed over Bill Winall's callsign, I was surprised to see how little progress had been made in the twenty minutes since I had plotted his last position. The line of men was moving very slowly in terrific heat and most noticeable was that the dogs were no longer leading but were trailing behind the troops.

At Point 222 I liaised with John Rogers and Major Mac Willar who had been gathering in new troops for deployment ahead of the terrorists. I told them of Bill Winall's last position and of the water in the Tegwani River. We agreed the terrorists must have reached the high ground from which they would certainly have seen the green trees along the Tegwani River. This would undoubtedly attract them, having been without water since leaving Leasha Pan. I suggested we try jet-strikes along the south bank of the river and this was agreed.

An Airstrike Request was processed through Flight Lieutenant Doug Butler's FASOC at Shapi Pans. We asked for a Hunter strike at 15:00 to be followed by a Canberra strike at 18:00. The reason for two strikes was that, if the terrorists had been caught in a Hunter strike, survivors would return to water and any kit they might have abandoned after about two hours believing that no further strike would occur. If on the other hand they had not yet reached the water when the Hunters struck, thirst would make them move to the inviting green trees feeling confident that no further air action would follow.

At 14:50 I passed high over Bill Winall and in veiled language told him that, "Cyclone One (Hunters) will be making a speculative strike, I repeat speculative, on a location ahead of you." It was necessary to use veiled speech knowing that the terrorists might be listening to me on the captured radio. Ten minutes later, on a different frequency, I talked the

Hunters onto the stretch of green trees on the south bank of the Tegwani. Four Hunters struck with 68mm rockets and 30mm guns exactly as instructed.

John Rogers' helicopter was without fuel so he commandeered the SAP half-full helicopter to control the Canberra strike. At 18:00 he talked two Canberras, each with ninety-six 28-pound fragmentation bombs, onto the target. On his way back to Point 222 he switched from the airstrike frequency and immediately received a frantic call from Bill Winall. Bill's callsign had been attacked by the terrorists and had suffered serious casualties. He had fought them off but did not know how far they were from his position.

John Rogers was too low on fuel to go to Bill's immediate assistance. At Point 222 all fuel drums lay empty and it was getting dark. The SAP helicopter as well as John's and mine were empty and it would be ages before Hoffy, Chris and Ian returned with fuel from Shapi Pans. In any event, any thought of going into Bill's location that night was discarded as any helicopter with its landing light on would be a sitting duck to the terrorists whose location was not known, but whose aggressive intentions had been demonstrated on three separate occasions.

Earlier in the day I had seen an old half-filled drum of dieseline at a disused road camp near the game fence some two kilometres north of Point 222. In darkness Bob Whyte and I pumped this fuel into our helicopter to get us to the Company HQ where only one full drum of Avtur remained. We had been airborne less than ten minutes when our fuel-filter warning light came on. This meant having to land immediately to clean the filter. Four further night landings in remote ground were necessary before we finally reached the company base. There we had to drain our fuel tank of all polluted dieseline before we could take on Avtur to get us to Shapi Pans to join in on another night of lifting Avtur to Point 222.

The Shapi Pans base was deserted except for a handful of full Avtur drums because Brigade HQ and FASOC had already departed for Tjolotjo. This small village lay east of the action and only half the distance to Bill Winall's position with operations moving that way. Shell & BP worked throughout the night transporting hundreds of drums of fuel from Bulawayo to Tjolotjo.

At midnight we lifted out the last of the fuel from Shapi Pans. Back at Point 222, after forty-two hours without sleep, the helicopter crews managed to get in four hours' rest. At first light we commenced lift-out of Bill Winall's dead and wounded to Tjolotjo where the Brigade HQ and FASOC were already established. This is when we learned the details of what had happened to Bill's callsign.

Bill had not yet reached the edge of the treed area at the base of the rising ground when I spoke to him about Cyclone 1. He realised Hunters would be striking but failed to take in my essential words "speculative strike, I repeat, speculative". Bill saw the Hunters and heard their strikes as his weary callsign continued its move to the area where trees provided welcome shade at the base of the rising ground. They reached this point before the Canberras' strike and Bill had told his callsign to rest and 'brew up'. Most men removed their boots and were sitting or lying down brewing tea. Unfortunately for Bill, he had come to the erroneous conclusion that we knew exactly where the terrorists were, hence the airstrikes. But he failed to follow fundamental soldiering procedures by not conducting a perimeter clearance patrol or even posting sentries.

At about the time Canberras were running in for their strike, Bill felt confident that all was well when, without warning, a black man in Rhodesian camouflage dress appeared out of the bush. In a loud voice he said, "Good evening gentlemen. I am a terrorist," whereupon he threw a grenade into the middle of the callsign as a wave of terrorists charged forward, lobbing grenades and lacing the area with automatic fire. In spite of being caught so badly off guard and suffering casualties, the callsign retaliated so fiercely that it drove off the attack, killing two terrorists in the process and wounding others.

Hoffy and Ian picked up the seriously wounded before I put down where a soldier signalled me to land. Two terrorist bodies were loaded on the cabin floor behind me. As I looked over my shoulder I noticed the bowels of one spilling out onto the cabin floor just as the stench of death reached me. Being squeamish, I started to retch. Bob Whyte saw this and came around the front of the helicopter, lighting a cigarette for me. As I drew on the fag it had the effect of multiplying the stench so I really had to force myself to regain control. Deliberately I took in very deep breaths of the foul-smelling air.

Whilst this was happening, a third body had been placed on top of the two dead terrorists. Only then did I realise it was an RAR soldier. The body of a white policeman, who I realised must be one of the dog handlers, was about to be loaded when I signalled the troops to wait for the next helicopter. I asked John Rogers who was waiting to come in behind me to uplift the policeman's body. As I got airborne I spotted a dead black dog lying about 100 metres from the troops. I passed John Rogers its location and requested him to uplift the dog too. Though he did this, John said later that the stench of the dead dog had been horrific. This Alsatian was Brutus whose handler survived the attack.

On the flight to Tjolotjo I could not take my mind off the dogs. There were specific issues that occupied my thoughts.

Firstly, the dogs had been pulling against their leashes for about two hours before losing scent or becoming too tired to work. Secondly, had the dogs been free to track untethered at their natural speed, they would have caught up with those terrorists in less than an hour. Thirdly, the dogs were totally pooped by the time the callsign stopped to rest so, with human scent all around them, they had no chance of detecting the terrorist group. And finally, I had found it very easy to see the dogs from the air.

From these simple facts, the idea came to me that by using

Terrain and temperature conditions were tougher on Winall's follow-up than for this training session on the highveld.

Bodies of Corporal Cosmos and three terrorists laid out.

a helicopter to follow one or more dogs along a trail, it would be possible to overhaul terrorists quickly. The question I asked myself was, "Could dogs learn to be controlled by radio from the air?" This had to be explored so I decided there and then to follow this up when I returned to base.

As I landed at Tjolotjo I took a really deep breath and held it as long as it took to bring the rotor blades to rest then leapt out into the fresh air. The RAR troops laid out the three bodies then complained bitterly about the body of Corporal Cosmos having been carried on top of dead terrorists. They found this to be extremely offensive. I apologised explaining how I had been retching instead of watching the loading of my helicopter. A huge N'debele sergeant told me I had nothing to apologise for. He and his men felt that "the troops who loaded the bodies should have known better than to lay Corporal Cosmos on top of terrorist scum."

From here on follow-up operations, which now included RLI troops, had the effect of fragmenting the terrorists, following a series of contacts in which one more RSF member was killed. Operation Nickel eventually wound up when it was clear that at least twenty terrorists had made good their escape into Botswana. Many years later, after Nelson Mandela's SAANC came to power in South Africa, someone on TV mentioned that Chris Hani, then leader of the SA Communist Party, had been one of those who escaped from Operation Nickel. Joe Modise, Nelson Mandela's first Minister of Defence, was another.

PB and Hoffy at the RAR Officers' Mess, Tjolotjo.

RAR Officers' Mess.

Thirty-three SAANC and ZAPU men were known to have been killed, thirty-four were captured and twenty-seven were unaccounted for which, although a military success, had cost Rhodesia dearly in that eight of our security forces had been killed and thirteen wounded. One RSF man lost for just over eight terrorists killed or captured was considered far too

high a price to pay. This was certainly a wake-up-call for the military.

There was a great deal of media coverage about the death of Spencer Thomas, the dog handler I had asked John Rogers to uplift. Spencer was a third-generation Rhodesian and his Alsatian Satan was missing, but not presumed dead. For two months Satan was lost until found by locals who lived many miles from where he had run from attacking terrorists. The scruffy and emaciated dog was returned to the Police Dog School where he quickly regained weight and his shiny coat.

Radio tracker dog project disallowed

BACK AT NEW SARUM I discussed the idea of using a radio-controlled tracker dog with the man in charge of the Air Force Dog Section. Warrant Officer Peter Allen was certain the concept would work. I then went to Wally Jefferies in the Radio Section and asked if he thought it possible to make a two-part, lightweight radio arrangement for fitment into a harness for a dog. One radio was to be a receiver with earphone on one frequency. The other was to be an open transmitter with microphone on a separate frequency. Wally had a storm of questions that I was able to answer before he told me, very cautiously, that he thought it possible.

Squadron Leader Rogers had already given me his approval in principle so it was just a matter of getting Air HQ's authority to explore the possibilities. The two most senior members of Air Staff immediately saw the advantage of speed tracking with helicopters and dogs. Both were especially interested in the possibility of wresting advantage from terrorists who might be lying in ambush. Except for the accidental death of Ken Pierson, most of our losses during Operation Nickel had come from ambush situations, hence the Air Staff interest. They realised that, if the tracker dog system worked, it would become essential to have additional airborne helicopters with troops for vertical envelopment of terrorists located by dogs.

With no objection from Air Staff, I put the same case to the Technical Staff. Here I found the same cynicism as when I had sought permission to develop pressure refuellers. The self-same officer who had spiked that request with his story about refuelling Spitfires from four-gallon Jerry cans spiked this project also. He asked, "PB, if we train elephants to fire machine-guns, will that interest you?" I said it certainly would but that this was not what I had come to discuss.

Any project requiring expenditure of money had to be wholly approved by both Air and Technical branches so the radio tracker dog plan, contested by only one officer, seemed to be doomed, at least for the time being.

Find Sherriff

ON 15 SEPTEMBER 1967, I flew to Sipolilo Police Station where Flight Lieutenant John Swart awaited me. He had been on a four-day exploration walk with Chief Superintendent Ted Sheriff in the northern section of the Umvukwes mountain range. They had become separated and big John's search for the older and equally big Ted had been fruitless, so he walked out to seek help. His main concern was that Ted may have fallen and incapacitated himself in rough country that was full of ridges and deep ravines.

The mineral-rich Umvukwes range, known as 'The Dyke', runs for over 150 kilometres in a near continuous mix of folded mountains and sharp ridge lines running from the southern Mcheka-wa-ka-Sungabeta mountain range to the high ground of the Zambezi escarpment between the Musengezi and Hunyani river exits into the Zambezi Valley. Within a northern section of this range known as the Horseshoe mountains there existed a unique species of palm trees known only to this area together with rare orchids and a great variety of birds. John and Ted's interest in these wonders of nature had been the reason for their exploration trip.

The helicopter is a truly amazing machine when it comes to searching for someone who wants to be found. John Swart directed me to the spot where separation had occurred. In less than five minutes we made a detailed search of the area that had taken John one whole day to cover. It took another five minutes of searching to find Ted at the bottom of a deep ravine next to a fast-flowing stream from which we winched him to safety. Apart from his embarrassment, the chief superintendent was none the worse for his experience.

Mountain flying

IN OCTOBER 1967, I CONDUCTED Terry Jones' helicopter conversion and finalised the mountain-flying phase Hugh Slatter needed for his helicopter instructor's rating. Mountain flying was a very important aspect in helicopter training because it prepared pilots to recognise and manage dangerous wind conditions, to judge distances when approaching to land on high ledges and peaks and to conduct mountain rescues using the cable winches that we called hoists.

Mountain-flying training, though potentially dangerous,

was great fun. Invariably our rest breaks included picnic lunches, trout fishing and naked swimming in icy mountain pools. For Hugh's training with technician Ewett Sorrell we commandeered Corporal Jerry Duncan of the Station Photographic Section to make pictorial records of helicopter operations in the mountains.

One photograph we wanted necessitated placing Jerry on an impossibly small slippery rock to show hoisting work against the backdrop of Martin's Falls.

In November John Rogers received notice that he would be leaving us. His disappointment at leaving helicopters was offset by his posting to command No 5 (Canberra) Squadron.

On the other hand, OC 1 (Hunter) Squadron, Squadron Leader Norman Walsh, was really distressed about his posting off Hunters to take command of helicopters. Like most pilots who had not flown helicopters, Norman looked upon these machines with disdain: "Bloody egg beaters! Not aircraft at all!" He was echoing a general view and did not believe me when I told him that he would come to enjoy flying Alouettes more than Hunters.

This photograph taken by Jerry Duncan shows Hugh Slatter on the cable operated by Ewett Sorrell with PB flying the helicopter.

Family in helicopter

IN THE LATTER HALF OF December and early January 1968 I was with the Army at Kariba for local training. Air HQ took advantage of this by having me take over FAF 2 so that the permanent OC could take long overdue leave. This gave me opportunity to get Beryl and the children to Kariba for the Christmas and New Year period. We stayed at the Cutty Sark Hotel on Lake Kariba where I was in continuous contact with FAF 2. Staying at the same hotel was Hugh Maude who had been one of Winston Churchill's wartime secretaries

Hugh Maude was a political friend of the Rhodesian Government and hated what the Labour Government was doing to destroy our country. He was enjoying a break from political work at Kariba and asked me to take him on a visit to FAF 2. Debbie and Paul already knew Hugh because of his friendship with my mother and Berry. So they asked him if they might accompany him in his chauffeur-driven car. Beryl and I in our own car were leading the way when we came upon 'George', a well-known elephant bull who was always close to Kariba Airfield.

George, charging our car.

George was browsing close to the roadside so I passed him and stopped well forward leaving plenty of room for Hugh's driver. The chauffeur obviously did not know too much about elephants because he stopped before reaching George. I told Beryl I did not like this and was signalling the chauffer to come forward when George decided it was time for fun. He

charged first towards us then turned for the other car.

The chauffeur reversed at great speed but George was moving faster. Only when the trunk of the screaming jumbo was over the car bonnet did George break away having enjoyed his naughty car-chasing habit. Five minutes later we arrived at FAF 2 and listened to simultaneously spoken stories from our two excited children. Hugh and his driver were noticeably quiet.

Next morning, on Christmas day, I received a call from FAF 2 to say that the SAP helicopter permanently based there was well overdue from a task it had been sent to conduct in the Chirundu area. Beryl and the children accompanied me to the airfield where they were to wait whilst I flew down to Chirundu to investigate the SAP helicopter situation.

My technician, Corporal Butch Phillips, and I were about to lift off when we saw the entire FAF contingent walking towards us with Beryl and the children in tow. The senior NCO came to my door and shouted, "Sir, you cannot pass up the opportunity to give your family a ride in the helicopter. Nobody here will say a word. Please take them along with you." I was going to refuse when I realised that Debbie and Paul had already been ushered aboard, their faces full of expectancy. I relented and Beryl came in to sit beside me.

By its very nature a helicopter is too easily misused. Some pilots had given rides to unauthorised persons, but this was the first and only time for me and it troubled me for ages until I felt certain I had got away with it. The children never breathed a word though they must have longed to tell their friends.

This, their first flight in any aircraft, started out under patches of low cloud on our route along a green valley in the high ground running

Family on Kariba Lake—Christmas 1967.

to open sky on the lip of the escarpment where the Zambezi River exits the Kariba Gorge. The spectacle was breathtaking as could be seen in the facial expressions of my family.

We had just descended to follow the river at low level when I spotted the SAP helicopter approaching up-river towards us. As I turned to climb back up the escarpment, the other helicopter came into loose formation adding more excitement for the children. Having been airborne for just a short time, I decided to fly another five minutes by routing back to the airfield through an area that carried plenty of wildlife. I was showing the various animals when eight-year-old Debbie pointed ahead saying she could see a rhino. Butch Phillips and I could not see the beast but Debbie kept pointing directly ahead. I held track for over three kilometres before seeing the rhino at the edge of bush that was yet another kilometre ahead. Debbie's eyesight amazed us all.

Training Norman Walsh

FLIGHT LIEUTENANT MIKE GRIER ACTED as OC of the squadron for the month between John Rogers' departure and Norman Walsh's arrival. There was need to get the new OC converted onto the helicopter in the shortest time possible and, as 'B' Flight Commander, the task fell on my shoulders. Norman's training started on 9 January 1968 and was completed in record time on 21 February.

Of all the pilots I instructed on helicopters, none was more frustrated by the learning process than 'steely-eye jet pilot' Norman Walsh.

Flight Lieutenant Mike Grier.

He simply could not understand why he could not control the Alouette III in the hover and muttered angry words to himself when the aircraft failed to respond to his bidding. During his second flight he was attempting to keep the aircraft stationary at about three feet but, as happened to all pilots, Norman was over-controlling on cyclic. The aircraft would pitch nose down and move forward, followed by over-correction so that the nose pitched up and the machine moved backwards before the next over-correction induced forward movement.

I had seen this all before and what Norman actually said as the aircraft seesawed back and forth, I do not remember. Nevertheless I had to switch off my microphone to conceal my laughter as aircraft pitching and Norman's frustration grew progressively worse. Hardly able to see through my tears, I took control, steadied the aircraft and handed it back to Norman. "It's all right for you," he grumbled, "you've had plenty of practice," and the over-controlling started all over again. By the end of this flight, Norman's brain started providing the right signals

Norman Walsh (left) with Peter Cooke and Cyril White—Centenary 1972. Those who knew him well will recognise Norman's habit of nibbling at the end of a pen or pencil.

and he was able to hover jerkily from point to point around the white-lined square we used to practise precision hovering.

As with my previous students, Norman's flying training was mostly at high weight. At the conclusion of the operational conversion phase the usual 'round the houses' exercise was flown. We started with mountain-flying at Chimanimani, then flew a series of legs via Army and Police positions up the eastern border, along the Zambezi to Victoria Falls then down to Bulawayo to conduct helicopter enplaning and deplaning training for the Police and Army. Every conceivable aspect of helicopter operations was practised along the route in widely varying terrain, temperature and altitude conditions. Because of his personal experience, Norman became a stalwart in supporting the need for this type of training. By now he had grown to love helicopters and in his dealings with the Air Staff he was able to convey that the final 'round the houses' flights, though great fun, served an all-important purpose in more fully preparing pilots for most operational situations. As had happened to me, Norman Walsh did not have long to wait for his first operation on helicopters.

Tracker dog project

BEFORE JOHN ROGERS LEFT THE squadron, he raised the subject of the radio tracker dogs. Though Air HQ approval had not been forthcoming, he suggested that I should look more deeply into the concept and not let it die. Encouraged by this, I arranged for trials to see if a dog could be taught to respond to radio instructions from his handler. Peter Allen decided to use his big Alsatian, Beau, for the purpose. This concerned me because Beau was well on in years and had been trained as an attack dog.

Thousands of Rhodesians had seen Beau in action at a variety of shows where he and Peter Allen were brought in by helicopter to demonstrate the 'arrest of a criminal'. Although the Air Force man acting the part of the criminal wore a protective sleeve on his arm to give protection against Beau's large teeth and powerful jaws, Beau was strong enough always to throw the man to the ground. This is why I felt we should be using a less aggressive animal.

Wally Jefferies made a small receiver that was inserted into a back harness made especially for Beau in the Safety Equipment Section. In less than one week Peter Allen had his dog obeying radio commands when Beau could neither hear Peter's normal voice nor see him. The next step was to work the dog along human trails laid by two persons. For this we had to add a transmitter in Beau's harness so that his 'out of sight' handler could hear Beau's breathing whilst also receiving his own transmissions to his dog.

First runs were made on thirty-minute-old scent trails over short distances. These were stepped up progressively to six-hour-old trails with longer runs. Beau did well but he always expected a good bite at the end of each run. Because of this, the men who laid the trail had to wait up a tree out of Beau's reach. Peter Allen's call, "Beau, come-come-come", always worked and Beau backtracked rapidly to receive his handler's applause and fussing.

When Beau was ready to be flown to the starting point of a trail, we fully expected teething problems. The plan was for Peter to climb out of the helicopter, with both Beau's and his own radios switched on, and run Beau on leash a short distance to be sure he had picked up the trail scent. Peter would then release his dog and, shouting above the noise of the helicopter, "Go Beau, go, go, go", remain static as he continued urging his dog by radio. On the helicopter's radio I could hear Peter's commands overlaid by the noise of the helicopter and Beau's breathing.

Peter had then to run back to the helicopter and jump in, all the time urging his dog, "Go Beau, go, go, go." We lifted vertically upwards to pick up Beau about 200 metres ahead. He wore a bright day-glo patch on his harness to make finding him in long grass easy. On the first two flight trials Beau started off well, but when the helicopter was over 300 feet high, he turned back to run in circles below the helicopter awaiting uplift. His love of helicopters was frustratingly obvious.

On the third try he managed to ignore the rising helicopter and had run over two kilometres with the helicopter orbiting above when he suddenly skidded to a halt to relieve his bowels. Having done this, he lost interest in the trail and, again, ran in circles barking madly for uplift. The fourth attempt was successful. Beau ran three kilometres and nearly caught one of the trail layers who managed to climb a tree in the nick of time. He then sat under the tree watching his 'quarry' until Peter called, "Beau come, come, come!" whereupon Beau ran towards the helicopter for uplift. No one was more pleased than Beau who leapt into the helicopter and licked me all over my face as I lifted into flight.

From now on Beau ran the trail each time but he always hoped for a good bite at the end of an ever-increasing trail distance. One thing we were trying to get him to do was go to ground when he had sight or direct scent of those he was tracking and bark just once. Amazingly Peter achieved this, thereby proving that even old dogs can learn new tricks. There were times when Beau really amused us by going to ground and hiding behind the smallest of bushes as he sounded once with more of a suppressed yelp that a bark. From the direction he pointed we were able to establish where his quarry was hiding.

We now knew that it was feasible to use a helicopter and one or more dogs to run down terrorists without sacrificing dogs in the process. Even on the hottest day Beau could cover fifteen kilometres in about forty minutes following a trail laid eight hours earlier. He tended to be slow initially where the scent was oldest then progressively increased speed as the scent became younger and stronger. Squadron Leader Norman Walsh had been on 7 Squadron for a while by the time we had achieved this. Right from the start he supported what we were aiming for and was impressed when he witnessed a run. As a result, he arranged for Wing Commander Dicky Bradshaw to fly with me to see Beau in action.

Dicky Bradshaw was convinced by what he saw and arranged for Director General Operations Air Commodore John Deall and Staff Officer Operations Wing Commander Sandy Mutch to visit 7 Squadron to see for themselves. They were both satisfied that the tracker dog concept should be progressed for operational employment.

Two days later Norman Walsh was instructed by HQ signal to give me a blast for the unauthorised stripping of A60 radios to make Beau's receiver and transmitter and for expending flying hours without Air Staff's knowledge. My OC showed me the signal but said nothing. Instead he visited Air HQ to state his opinion that senior technical staff officers, with no bush warfare knowledge whatsoever, were not paying close attention to the needs expressed by operational pilots and technicians. Squadrons were still feeling their way in preparing for intensification in the bush war that surely lay ahead. Norman contended that Air HQ's fullest support and co-operation was essential, particularly where squadron commanders had added support to sensible ideas intended to promote operational effectiveness.

Operation Cauldron

OPERATION CAULDRON WAS INITIATED BY National Parks game-ranger Dave Scammell who, when driving with African game-scouts below the Zambezi Escarpment, noticed boot prints of two persons crossing the main east–west access road. Right away Dave recognised that the prints were from terrorist issue figure 8 and chevron pattern boots. RLI troops were flown in and a tracker-combat team under Lieutenant Bert Sachse took control.

Squadron Leader Norman Walsh, John Barnes, Mark McLean and their technicians were called forward next day after Bert Sachse's callsign contacted a terrorist group, which took an awful pounding. During the follow-up on survivors, a major base was located near the Chiwore River resulting in a second punch-up on the same day as more RLI callsigns deployed. RLI gained further successes with survivors scattering in all directions. Continued follow-up operations resulted in the discovery of five well-established bases along the Chiwore River stretching from the Zambezi River southward for over eighty kilometres to a sixth base that was later found close to where the Angwa River exits the escarpment. The sixth base was still well short of the populated area the terrorists had sought to reach secretly.

About 250 ZAPU and SAANC terrorists had established this line of bases with more to follow after reaching the African population above the Zambezi Escarpment. Once established with the locals, they expected to create safe routes all the way through Rhodesia to South Africa—an aim that had failed in the west because of Operation Nickel. Again we had been caught off guard by ZAPU choosing a section of the Zambezi devoid of routine patrol coverage. We had absolutely no hope of covering every inch of our long border and had concentrated on ZANU's dependence on Zambian fishermen to help them cross the big river. In any case, ZAPU did not fit into our planning so far east.

Operation Nickel had taught ZAPU that regular food and water had to be guaranteed to transit men and material across unpopulated ground. To achieve this, all the camps were sited on fresh water pools along the Chiwore River's course where there was also an abundance of game for fresh meat all the way to the populated high ground. Each camp lay under heavy riverine cover to prevent detection from the air. Centuries-old elephant paths were used so as not to create new paths that might show up on aerial photographs or be seen by reconnaissance pilots, both considered by ZAPU to be the primary threat. Captured documents in good condition and neatly written recorded quartermasters' control of meat issued out to large numbers of men.

Underground tunnels and ammunition bunkers amazed the soldiers just as much as the enormous quantities of arms, ammunition, explosives and staple food supplies they contained. As it happened, the camps had only just been completed. If we had detected ZAPU's presence a few days earlier, over 100 ZAPU recruits who had portered stores and provided manual labour would also have been subjected to the RLI's attentions, but they had returned to Zambia. About 150 ZAPU and SAANC trained men remained in Rhodesia.

Apart from meat found hanging in the camps, the source of huge meat supplies was evident to our forces who came upon the rotting carcasses of elephants whose trunks had been removed but whose tusks remained firmly embedded in their sculls; certainly not the work of poachers! Buffalo with only hindquarters removed lay in grotesque attitudes attended by hyenas and vultures.

The rotting carcass of an elephant.

Control of Op Cauldron forces was through a Joint Operations Centre (JOC) established in the small farming town of Karoi. The JOC comprised senior Army, Air Force, Police and Special Branch officers. Also included was Internal Affairs in the person of the District Commissioner. A FASOC for fixed-wing aircraft operated from Karoi Airfield. A tactical HQ and forward base for the RLI and supporting helicopters lay ninety kilometres to the northeast at Dean's Camp sited on a small hill at the base of the Zambezi Escarpment. The camp had originally been a road construction site until it was taken over by the Department for Tsetse Fly Control. At this base dust and flies added to the discomfort of the Zambezi Valley's heat. With every helicopter take-off and landing Dean's Camp disappeared in a cloud of dust. Fortunately it was taken away quickly enough by the permanent gentle breeze but not before finding its way into every tent and building. Living conditions were rough for Norman Walsh, his helicopter crews and the small RLI command unit.

VHF communication difficulties in the vast expanses of the flat valley floor were overcome by placing a radio relay team on the high mountain feature, Chiramba-ka-doma. This mountain lay to the east of the terrorist camp line between ZAPU bases 4 and 5. Daily resupply of water, rations and radio batteries was made by helicopters whose pilots' mountain-flying training had fully prepared them for the turbulence and cloud interference encountered when flying into the tiny sloped patch at the summit of Chiramba-ka-doma. Callsign for the radio relay point was 'Cloud Base'.

The leader of the terrorist force was Hedebe who was known to be carrying over $1,000 on his person. This had every RLI soldier hoping he would get to him first; but Hedebe had other ideas and proved himself to be a slippery foe.

In the valley RLI continued to have short-duration contacts, killing and capturing many terrorists, which caused further disintegration of an already scattered force. Many individuals tried to make their way back to Zambia via the line of camps not realising they had become death traps. Many were killed in RLI ambushes at these camps and along the Zambezi River line. One ZAPU terrorist did not go the Chiwore River route but set off for Zambia in a northeasterly direction. After more than a week without food, this emaciated man stumbled into an SAS patrol somewhere near Kanyemba. Given normal Army field rations, he gulped these down then dropped dead. When Captain Brian Robinson had recovered from the surprise of the incident, he sent a signal to the Quartermaster General offering SAS congratulations for his unit's first confirmed kill. The QMG was not amused!

Everything was going RLI's way until, on 18 March 1968, contact was made at the Mwaura River with a large group led by Hedebe himself. Under Lieutenant Dumpy Pearce, troops of 3 Commando RLI were pinned down on the north bank by intensive fire coming down on them from heavy bush on the higher south bank. John Barnes with Senior Technician Monty Maughan arrived in their helicopter and put down 600 rounds of MAG fire into the position of the unseen enemy. Their intention was to draw attention to themselves and give the ground commander a chance to move his troops to a safer position. Since this had no effect whatsoever, and the troops remained pinned down, John called for heavy airstrike.

Meanwhile Mark McLean with Corporal Brian Warren came in at lower level to draw terrorist gunfire, which was returned in short measured bursts. Though the helicopter expended only 150 rounds of 7.62mm MAG ammunition, Mark's actions gave Dumpy Pearce the break he needed to move his men to safer ground. Then, under Mark McLean's directions, a pair of Vampires put in accurate strikes with 60-pound squash-head rockets and 20mm cannon fire before a Canberra checked-in preparatory to making an attack with ninety-six 28-pound Frag bombs.

Newly appointed OC of 5 Squadron, Squadron Leader John Rogers, had elected to fly the air task, much to the annoyance of his experienced Canberra crews. When he called one minute out, Mark passed low over the target to place down a

phosphorus grenade as a visual marker. The marker was on the terrorists' position but wind carried its white cloud away from target. The bomb-aimer concentrated his aim on this cloud with the consequence that bombs were released off target, some to explode near ground troops waiting in the 'safer ground'. Fortunately no one was seriously hurt.

Prior to Op Cauldron pilots usually flew without a gunner and carried six troops. From Cauldron onwards, it was unusual for pilots to fly without gun and gunner but this limited carriage to five troops (as in this photo where three soldiers and the gunner occupied the back bench). In 1973 it reduced to four, due to increased weight of soldiers' equipment. This allowed removal of the front centre seat (occupied by the seated soldier seen here) giving the gunner improved angles of traverse.

When the somewhat annoyed troops moved forward, no fire came down on them because the terrorists had pulled out. By the time they had swept through the abandoned area and established the direction of flight, it had become too dark to follow tracks. The following day the tracker-combat callsign was moving on a trail heading straight for the escarpment.

At the same time, a smaller callsign was following frothy pink splatters of blood from a single terrorist who obviously had a serious lung wound. By late afternoon they had not closed on this man but reported that spoor of two hyenas overlaid the tracks of the wounded terrorist. Believing the terrorist would not survive the night, the follow-up troops were uplifted for re-deployment to more important task.

It was probably five years later when I was asked by Special Branch if I remembered the Op Cauldron terrorist we had given up for dead because hyenas were following him; I certainly did. "Would you like to meet the man?" I was asked. It seemed unbelievable but I met the recently captured terrorist whose beaming face showed he was pleased to be alive following his second brush with our security forces. His story was amazing. No white man would have survived the ordeal he described.

He had been wounded in the attack made by Vampires. He panicked and ran off even before the main group under Hedebe left the contact site. All night and the next day, he struggled for breath as he made his way to the foot of the escarpment. In the late afternoon his attention was drawn to a helicopter coming from behind him. Only then did he see, for the first time, the two hyenas as the helicopter frightened them off. When the aircraft landed it was so close that he could see the rotor blades whirling above low scrub. He tried to get back to it for help but moved too slowly. As the helicopter rose into full view he waved madly trying to attract attention but he was not seen before the helicopter turned and disappeared.

The two hyenas then reappeared and stayed about thirty metres behind him as he commenced his breathless ascent of the steep escarpment. By then it was almost dark and he was too tired and breathless to continue. So he sat down and faced the hyenas as they moved left and right in short runs, each time coming closer. When they were no more than ten metres away he shot one but missed the other and chased it with a long burst from his AK-47 rifle. Overwhelmed by tiredness, he lay down to sleep; surely to die.

He was amazed when he awoke at dawn, wheezing and frothing with his clothing covered in freezing-cold, caked blood. But he was still alive! All day he struggled slowly up the steep escarpment until evening when he lay exhausted and wanting to die. Again he was amazed at the dawning of the third day. Still wheezing and frothing he struggled to his feet and wobbled on ever higher. By nightfall he had reached the high ground and was about to lie down when he noticed a light shining some way off. He noted its position by reference to a tree and went to sleep; again not believing he would survive the night. But, yet again, he awoke on the fourth day.

Taking a line on the tree and noting the relative position of the sun he plodded off. At around 10 o'clock he came to a farm store that sold goods to the local African people. He was recognised for what he was but told the superstitious storekeeper how he had been unharmed by hyenas; an omen the keeper should know was deadly to anyone reporting his presence.

Using his Rhodesian money he bought a large bottle of Dettol for his wound as well as something to eat and drink. He repeated his warnings of doom to anyone reporting him and returned to the bush. Under shade in good cover he cut a long thin stick and stripped the bark away. He then inserted the stick into the wound in his chest and manoeuvred the stick until it came through the exit hole on his left shoulder blade. Then, moving the stick in and out slowly in long strokes, he poured the undiluted Dettol into the entry point and down his shoulder into the large exit hole of his terrible wound. Having emptied the bottle and removed the stick he knew in his mind that he would heal. He settled down to eat and drink before falling into a deep sleep that lasted for at least two days.

The Special Branch man asked the terrorist to remove his shirt so that I could see his scars. The shiny black puckered scars and the dent caused by the loss of a section of shoulder blade showed how large the chunk of shrapnel from a Vampire rocket must have been. I asked the man, "Was it not very painful when you pushed the stick through your body? Didn't the Dettol burn like crazy?" He said that these were not a problem. "I was choking on neat Dettol blowing out of both holes and into my throat. It was the choking that nearly killed me!"

Returning to Op Cauldron itself. On 26 March 1968 three young Rhodesian Light Infantry soldiers were killed in two separate actions; all three happened to be under the age of eighteen. This caused such an outcry throughout the country that every soldier under eighteen years of age had to be withdrawn from operations. Most were in the field at the time and had to be gathered in by helicopters. Almost without exception they objected strongly and tried to lie their way out of having to return to base.

In the meantime Hedebe's group was already well south and closing with the farming area on the high ground above the escarpment. So a second forward HQ manned mainly by police reservists was established at Doma Police Station. This was called Red Base. When I arrived there my first tasks were in support of small teams of PATU (Police Anti-Terrorist Unit) who, using African game-trackers, were cross-graining for Hedebe's group along the northern most farms fence lines. Quite by accident I learned of shotgun traps set for wild pigs in maize fields where they did great damage to crops. Through the Police I arranged for the farmers to disarm all the gun-traps to safeguard PATU cross-graining patrols as well as the RLI tracker-combat group following Hedebe's trail.

Red Base was well organised by PATU who were all local farmers. With wives roped in, they provided excellent meals and a good bar service. Toilets and showers were pretty basic but they proved to be an absolute luxury for Norman Walsh and his technician when they flew up from the discomforts at Dean's Camp. Following a hot shower and a good meal, Norman prepared to return to flies and dust whilst grumbling at me for being "a sporny blighter with all the comforts".

On 2 April, I flew from Red Base to the tracker-combat group, now on lush high ground some five kilometres north of the east–west fence line running next to the maize fields from which gun-traps had been removed. I found the callsign of about 15 RLI men moving in shallow echelon formation across an open grass vlei with clumps of trees and small rock strewn hills ahead. As soon as I saw the lead trackers I also saw the well-defined trail that the terrorists had made through lush green grass. I followed this trail without difficulty to where it turned east just short of the fence line.

The trail meandered in and out of heavily treed patches until it reached the last group of trees with open grass vlei beyond. I could find no exit line and became confused by many trails that looked identical to the one I had been following. I did a fast low-pass next to the trees and noticed many small patches of upturned earth made by wild pigs digging for roots.

Realising that pigs were responsible for the multiple trails, I opened my search and picked up the terrorist trail running north into a line of small hills covered with large boulders and trees. The trail led through an open gully of short grass before it circled around and led back to boulder-strewn ground overlooking the open gully. This looked to me like a deliberate ambush set-up. I was absolutely certain Hedebe and his group was waiting here for the RLI troops, so I called for troops to be helicoptered in.

There was immediate reluctance on the part of the Army to use a small reserve of troops that had only just reached Red Base. So far as the local commander was concerned, responding to calls from the air was unproven, whereas the tracking callsign was still on fresh tracks and must, sooner of later, catch up with the terrorists. I guess Norman Walsh changed the Army's mind because troops were made available quickly enough.

John Barnes.

I remained over the spot whilst John Barnes and a second pilot flew in RLI troops of 3 Commando. My fuel warning light had come on, forcing me to leave the area as soon as I had shown John the terrorists' position. On my way back to Red Base, the troops called 'contact' and then I heard John Barnes voice being overlaid by his own MAG fire. John's gunner, Brian Warren, killed one terrorist and another three were killed by the RLI. Unfortunately the use of only ten RLI soldiers against more than twenty terrorists was insufficient to prevent Hedebe and most of his men from escaping. Nevertheless, the Army acknowledged that the terrorists had been in a very good ambush position and, had the Air Force not wrested the advantage from them, the tracker-combat group would almost certainly have suffered serious casualties.

Disappointed at having missed the action, I flew back to pick up the terrorist trail again, this time at Army's request. It proved successful and showed that the terrorist survivors had moved east through vlei grass before moving onto a well-worn cattle path running along the fence line. The direction having been established, I made a reconnaissance of the ground well beyond the farming area and returned to Red Base. John Barnes and I then flew an RLI ambush party to a likely site I had chosen well ahead of the terrorists. Here the only well-worn path for miles around crossed over a dry riverbed.

The soldiers remained in position until, at 10:00 next morning, the troop commander called for the ambush to be lifted. The soldiers were preparing their kit for helicopter recovery when Hedebe's group suddenly appeared, coming down the very path for which the ambush had been sited. The terrorists were just as surprised as the troops. Both sides opened fire simultaneously as the terrorists broke north and

disappeared into the bush. Neither side sustained casualties and Hedebe had survived his third encounter with RLI. Back in the valley contacts with small groups and lone terrorists continued on a daily basis. By 4 April it had become clear that Hedebe's group of around sixteen men constituted the only worthwhile objective when, much to my disappointment, I was recalled to base to continue helicopter instruction. Terry Jones replaced me.

Two days later the RLI killed most of Hedebe's group in a series of running actions. Four of these had holed up before being taken out with phosphorus grenades. After this action helicopters had to fly out the terrorist bodies because there was no road access into the contact areas. Prior to Op Cauldron we had always loaded terrorist bodies into the cabin. This created real problems because the helicopter's nose-down attitude in loaded flight caused blood from the bodies to flow to the rudder pedals and around the base of the instrument console. The corrosive effects of blood, though bad in itself, was made worse when water was used to clean up because diluted blood simply penetrated deeper into unreachable areas. Because of this, blood was allowed to dry so that most of it could be brushed or vacuum-cleaned away.

Whereas we continued carrying our own dead inside the cabins, there were so many more dead terrorists to carry that we were forced to reduce the blood spillage problem by carrying their bodies in underslung cargo nets designed to carry fuel drums.

The four terrorists killed by phosphorus were lifted by Flying Officer Terry Jones who was instructed to fly them to Karoi. Phosphorus is really naughty stuff and only burns when exposed to air. When in contact with human flesh, phosphorus burns until below surface where oxygen is denied by flesh closure over entry points. Terry Jones was blissfully unaware of the fact that, in flight, the airflow had opened the dead terrorists' wound points sufficiently to expose and re-ignite phosphorus that was then also burning the cargo net.

Because of turbulent flight conditions, Terry did not register the weight loss as all four bodies broke through the net. Only on approach to land at Karoi did his technician look down to see that the net was tattered, empty and trailing high. Terry reported the matter to JOC Karoi just before a somewhat irritated farmer phoned the JOC complaining that Air Force had just dropped four smoking bodies onto his front lawn. After being persuaded that this had been an accidental release, the farmer was pleased to hear that an Army truck was being dispatched to clean things up.

Op Cauldron was wrapped up when it was clear that Hedebe plus one member of his group had broken north and reached safety. sixty-nine terrorists were killed, on the basis of body counts, though many wounded were believed to have died and not been found. Fifty terrorists had been captured.

I was at Kanyemba on another unrelated operation some weeks later when a call was received from the Portuguese

Chef do Post at Zumbo to say he was holding Hedebe in his prison cell. One of our helicopters flew an SB man across the Zambezi to collect him. Like everyone else around, I was very disappointed when Hedebe climbed out of the Allouette. He had obviously taken a beating but otherwise was of medium height, scrawny and very ordinary in looks; nothing like the tough rebel leader we had pictured in our minds.

Apparently Hedebe had gone down the Angwa River and, once inside Mozambique, sought the help of locals to take him across the Zambezi River to the Zambian shore opposite Zumbo. This is where the Luangwa River, which separates Mozambique from Zambia, joins the Zambezi River. The people agreed to do this. When, however, Hedebe got into the canoe he was laid low with a blow to the head and was bound up because, unknown to Hedebe, the Mozambicans knew that they had a reward coming from the Chef do Post for handing over any live terrorist. When the locals told the Chef do Post of Hedebe's coming for help, the Chef do Post gave them hell for letting Hedebe walk to the river, saying he might have escaped. An old man responded by explaining that he could see no sense in carrying Hedebe to the river when he was fit to walk the long distance and wanted to go there anyway.

Some time after Op Cauldron there was a need to uplift large numbers of RAR and RLI soldiers from different locations and take them to their vehicle transport sited at a single pick-up point. At the time, there were four helicopters available for the task, mine being one. I elected to undertake the RAR uplift with another helicopter, and tasked the most junior pilots to do the RLI uplift. This was an entirely selfish decision!

All of the troops had been in the bush for many days without having bathed or changed their clothing. The use of deodorants was forbidden because even the lightest scent would give terrorists early warning of troop presence. It was for this reason that had I elected to collect RAR soldiers. Experience had taught me that the smell of white soldiers is appalling after only one week without a bath, whereas the smell of black soldiers, in equal circumstances, was much easier to tolerate.

The difference between black and white body odours was probably due to diet. For me the smell of unclean black men is similar to that of faintly rotting onions. With the passage of time, the intensity increases but the basic odour remains much the same. On the other hand, the smell of unclean whites varies from individual to individual ranging from stale, sour milk to rotten meat. Collecting RAR was fine because I knew exactly what to expect and each man entering the helicopter smelled the same as the next. With white soldiers, I found myself retching from the foul stench that changed as each man came aboard; and no batch smelled the same as another.

P. K. van der Byl

P. K. VAN DER BYL WAS a very colourful, eccentric minister in Ian Smith's Rhodesian Front Cabinet. Of South African aristocratic stock, he spoke with a very affected nasal accent in a style somewhat akin to Eton graduates. He did not wear underpants and dressed 'to the left' in a manner that confirmed his reputation for being well endowed.

Following the Vampire strikes against Hedebe's group, PK decided to visit the site. He was not really known to the men in the field at that time and his arrival at Karoi for his helicopter flight to site was quite an eye-opener because his dress was so appalling. Below his Australian bush hat he wore a pink shirt with bright-blue tie, khaki shorts with black belt, short blue socks and vellies. On return to Salisbury he appeared on national television properly attired in suit and tie. Speaking of his visit to the airstrike site and making grand gestures with his hands he told of seeing "Blood, blood everywhere!" In fact we knew the red fluid splattered about the area was mopani sap oozing from shrapnel wounds to the trees.

When the RLI and SAS got to know him better, PK became very popular with the soldiers. His ridiculous accent appealed to them just as much as his strange dress. He often requested to be taken on patrol so he could "shoot a terrorist" but asked that care be taken not to get him "lawst".

After one of his many field visits, he was flown back to Salisbury in a helicopter piloted by Peter Simmonds. Contrary to orders given Peter to take the minister to New Sarum, PK ordered Peter to drop him off where his servants would be awaiting him close to his home. When the helicopter landed in Salisbury Botanical Gardens, right next to the main road during rush hour, all vehicles came to a halt to watch the unbelievable sight of 'white-hunter PK', with elephant gun over shoulder, leading white-clad servants carrying baggage on heads.

After he became better known to the Air Force, he arrived by air at Thornhill to attend some official function or another in Gwelo. Station Commander Group Captain Ken Edwards offered the minister lunch in the Officers' Mess after his official function was over. PK said he had an awful headache and declined the offer. However, when he returned to Thornhill, he told Ken that he had changed his mind and would love to take up the earlier offer of lunch before flying back to Salisbury. Not surprisingly the caterers were in a bit of a tizzy for receiving such late notice but, as always, they presented a superb meal.

There were many officers and wives enjoying a Saturday lunchtime drink in the Grog Spot when John Digby walked in wearing P. K. Van der Byl's very smart Homburg hat. He had found this on the table in the entrance hall to the mess. "Surely the minister with his British Army background knows better that to leave his hat in the entrance hall of an officers' mess when its rightful place is in the cloak room!" Having said this, John placed the hat on my wife's head.

Beryl immediately sat on the bar counter and posing in an exaggerated manner made some statement in PK's affected accent. She was still doing this when Eddie Wilkinson whipped the hat from her head and, before he could be stopped, poured a full pint of beer into it causing instant loss of shape. Some officers took sips from the hat before it became the object of a roughhouse rugby match during which it shrivelled and shrunk into a shapeless mess. Once the match was over, the hat was unceremoniously driven down one of the horns of a kudu trophy hanging on the wall. When the minister was ready to leave, his headache immediately re-developed because he could not find his prized hat. Group Captain Edwards tore into the Grog Spot to see if anyone had seen it. Everyone pointed to the kudu horns.

PK took off for Salisbury in a thundering bad mood and John Digby phoned officers at New Sarum to brief them on what had happened. A whole group of them rushed off to find hats and gathered at Air Movements in time to meet the minister. As PK emerged from the Dakota, everyone doffed their hats in greeting. Unable to respond, the minister's annoyance and headache worsened. Fortunately he was humoured sufficiently to accept the offer of a drink in the mess where his headache dissipated before his departure for home in good spirits.

John Digby took all the Saville Row hat-maker's details from the destroyed hat and, through his brother in London, had a new Homburg made. When Terry Emsley was persuaded by John to present the new hat to PK, the minister vowed never again to leave it unattended in any place other than a hatbox in the boot of his car.

For all his eccentricities and flamboyance, PK was a bright politician who spoke fluent German. I heard it said that he very

cleverly saved Rhodesia many millions of dollars by 'confiding', very loudly, with a fellow passenger on a Lufthansa flight out of Germany. This was done to make sure that an agent, whether British or American I do not know, sitting behind him could hear his words. He knew the agent was trying to establish the purpose of his visit to Germany—and PK wanted to oblige. This was because he had just received confirmation from home that the new Rhodesian Mint had successfully started pumping out high-quality Rhodesian dollar notes. By boasting loudly about the German firm that was about to deliver Rhodesian currency through an agency he named, he triggered a UN action that blocked the deal. Thanks to PK, this 'UN sanctions-blocking success against Rhodesia' not only saved millions in foreign currency at UN expense, it highlighted another of the country's self-sufficiency triumphs.

Roland Coffegnot

SUD AVIATION'S CHIEF TEST PILOT, Roland Coffegnot, made his second visit to Rhodesia to discuss any problems we were experiencing with our Alouettes and to fly with instructors. Being Sud Aviation's test pilot for the Alouette III's, Roland knew the absolute limits of these machines, which made flying with him both enlightening and frightening.

The first thing he demonstrated to me seemed crazy. In the hover at about shoulder height he applied full rudder. The helicopter tail swung around with increasing speed and the nose pitched progressively downward until it seemed the main rotor blades were about to strike the spinning ground. At this point full opposite rudder was applied to stop the rotation, which caused the aircraft to shoot off into forward flight as if catapulted. It was nice to know this was possible but, not seeing any operational value in the manoeuvre, I never tried it myself.

Next, Roland asked me to hover. I was settled when, without warning, he slammed the fuel-flow cock closed. This was my first-ever powerless landing that worked out well enough, although touchdown was a bit heavy. Only then did Roland realise that I had no prior 'engine-off' experience, so he repeated the exercise twice. Next on his programme were three engine-off autorotations from height, which I enjoyed. This is when he told me

P. K. Van der Byl stood out in any situation—even in this official Parliamentary record circa 1976. His pose and dark glasses make PK easy to spot.

that, when instructing a student, I should always cut power when the student least expected it to happen.

He insisted that it was absolutely essential for an instructor to be quite certain that his students would automatically check the yaw that occurs with power loss and instinctively 'dump' the collective pitch lever to ensure minimal loss of rotor speed. Hesitation would be fatal. He then demonstrated and made me practise hair-raising, power-off, forced landings from the hover at 500 feet. When hovering below this height recovery from an engine failure was impossible.

Ten years after my flights with him, Roland Coffegnot is seen here during one of his regular visits to Rhodesia. From left to right: PB, Harold Griffiths, Roland, Graham Cronshaw and Air Commodore Norman Walsh.

At the moment the engine cut, it was necessary to dump collective and pitch the aircraft into a vertical dive. The helicopter accelerated rapidly in its hair-raising descent but this kept the rotor blades spinning at a safe speed. The nose was then pitched up quite rapidly with the ground rushing up as the rotor blades spun up to maximum rpm, providing plenty of rotor speed to reduce the descent rate to zero for a gentle roll-on landing. As with the power-off practices from forward flight, use of the collective pitch control, other than to prevent the rotors from over-speeding, had to be left to the last moment to utilise the kinetic energy within the spinning rotor blades to make a controlled touch down. Good judgement was paramount.

Roland made it known to Air HQ just how important it was for pilots to experience and handle unexpected power failure. This was accepted and 7 Squadron instructors were cleared to cut power in flight. However, Air HQ ruled that this was only to be done at base where the resultant forced landing would be onto a runway. This ruling completely defeated Roland Coffegnot's insistence that pilot reaction could only be adequately tested if engine failure was induced when a pilot least expected it. When flying anywhere near the main runway with an instructor, pilots were always wide awake and expecting fuel flow to be cut.

Operation Griffin

IN MID 1968 BERYL AND I went on long-overdue leave. During our absence ZAPU made its third attempt to establish the safe route through Rhodesia that they so dearly wanted to create for their SAANC mates. The employment of large forces during Operations Nickel and Cauldron had failed dismally, but ZAPU's James Chikerema and SAANC's Oliver Tambo did not seem to grasp the reasons for these failures with high losses. This time they used a small group of twenty-nine men who crossed the Zambezi River on the night of 15 July.

Their crossing point between Chirundu and the Kariba Gorge aimed for a shorter route to the African populated areas of Vuti Purchase Land and Nyaodza Tribal Trust Land where they intended to establish firm bases. However, unbeknown to them, they had an SB plant in their midst. Glenn MaCaskill had launched his agent into Zambia in April 1968 and was surprised by his early return as a 'trained terrorist'. The agent had slipped away as soon as it got dark and made a beeline for the Police base at Chirundu to report the incursion.

The group's spoor was located at 08:30 on 16 July by trackers and Border Control troops. RLI troops were brought to immediate standby at Kariba and four helicopters with two Provosts bolstered FAF 2's regular contingent. Terrorist tracks were followed westwards to the opening of the Kariba Gorge then southward up the steep escarpment line before entering a level, south-flowing valley with moderately high hills bounding its flanks.

Ahead of the tracker group, Second Lieutenant Jerry Strong's callsign was established in an ambush for the night of 17–18 July. At 07:00 on 18th he broke ambush to conduct a cross-graining search. He came upon the terrorists' tracks and asked his OC, Major Rob Southey, for two additional sticks (then five men) including a tracker to be flown to him.

A narrow river running from the eastern high ground with very steep slopes was the place the terrorists had moved from the main valley to rest and shelter in amongst large boulders that packed the twisting ravine. Jerry's callsign moved along the north bank of the river line with a supporting callsign paralleling on the south bank. Two terrorist backpacks were then located giving warning that the terrorists were very close by. Twenty metres farther on lead scout Lance-Corporal Lahee on the north bank came under fire from about ten terrorists. This forced him and the whole of Jerry's callsign to retire a short distance and regroup in cover.

Jerry and Lahee then moved to higher ground and crawled forward onto a ledge to overlook the cave from which terrorist fire had come. They lobbed in all of their hand grenades, fired one 32Z rifle-grenade each and emptied their rifle magazines before they became pinned down from a different terrorist position. They could not withdraw.

Overhead, Norman Walsh and his gunner 'TJ' van den Berg stood by to give covering fire from their MAG but, because he was pinned down, Jerry found it impossible to give proper direction. The callsign on the south bank then made contact killing one terrorist but sustained one wounded casualty before becoming pinned down also. Reinforcements arrived on Jerry's side of the river allowing him to draw back under their covering fire. At this point Major Southey arrived and, together with Jerry, he moved callsigns downriver before crossing over to move up the south bank with the aim of relieving the pinned-down troops who were taking casualties every time they moved. This failed and the rescuers themselves became pinned down by heavy accurate fire from well-sited terrorist positions.

Up to this point the terrorist group was thought to be ZANU because ZANU had not shown up for a long time and the crossing into Rhodesia had been conducted in typical ZANU fashion. Besides, SB had not disclosed anything to ensure their agent and their methods remained secret. But now the aggressive resistance, good tactical siting and controlled accurate fire, made it obvious to the troops that they were in contact with ZAPU.

While refuelling, Norman Walsh discovered that his helicopter had sustained two 7.62mm strikes to fuselage and tail rotor and Peter Nicholls' had taken a single strike through the rear fuselage and fuel tank which, by design, had self-sealed. This was the first time aircraft had sustained hits, but at no stage had the aircrew seen a single terrorist.

Unable to give direction for helicopter supporting fire and realising that terrorists under boulders would be immune to vertical gunfire anyway, Jerry suggested to his OC that Provosts with Frantans might provide a solution. Time had flown by and it was already 15:00 with only two and a half hours of daylight remaining.

Tony Smit and Ken Law flew in from nearby FAF 2 with two Frantans each. With the troops so close to the terrorists, it was essential to drop the first Frantans short of their target. Release of each Frantan had to be made in a steep dive whilst turning hard starboard to avoid the southern face of the mountain. After release, still turning steeply, high 'G' and full power had to be applied to recover from the dive where the river exited into the open valley.

First Frantans fell well short against the mountain face. Tony and Ken returned to FAF 2 for more Frantans, which they managed to drop into the riverbed itself then progressed in two steps nearer to the pinned-down troops. Unbeknown to Tony and Ken, terrorists were taking casualties from their fiery strikes even before they reached their intended strike point.

By this time Major Southey and Jerry Strong, having sustained two wounded casualties, had pulled their callsign back using the Provosts attacks and smoke grenades to cover their withdrawal. But the callsign they had attempted to relieve remained pinned down, even after the last of sixteen Frantans had been expended. Because of this, Hunters and Vampires on airborne standby over the area could not be used before dark. Meanwhile more Frantans were flown to FAF 2 from New Sarum.

It was not until 19:30 that the callsign, which had been pinned down for over eight hours, managed to move out under cover of darkness with its casualties. RLI, PATU and South African Police callsigns set up ambush positions in the riverbed base and on the high ground as helicopters came in to lift out the RLI casualties. In doing this, Norman Walsh and Peter Nicholls faced great difficulty because of steep mountainsides and the blackness of the night in conditions of thick haze.

As soon as the landing light was switched on, it lit up the haze ahead making visual contact with ground impossible until dangerously low and close. Fortunately Norman noticed that, when flying to one side of Peter, he could see the ground quite clearly where Peter's light was aimed, whereas Peter himself was blinded by his own reflected light. Norman told Peter to switch off his landing light whilst he flew high at ninety degrees to Peter's flight path and illuminated the landing area.

Norman, blinded by his own white pool of illuminated haze whilst flying high enough to clear all high ground, could just make out Peter's bright red rotating beacon lights which helped him point his landing light onto the area ahead of Peter's flight line. Now Peter could see the ground clearly all the way and only needed to switch on his own landing light for the landing itself. This worked like a charm so, having collected casualties, Peter climbed and gave the same assistance to Norman. This virtually eliminated the dangers of approaching high ground at night. The same procedure was later used successfully in many night operations where Trojan aircraft, equipped with a hand-held searchlight accompanied single helicopters for casualty evacuations at night from difficult terrain.

No contact was made with terrorists during the night. Tony Smit and Ken Law dropped a few 600,000-candlepower flares before midnight to help troops search for movement but none was seen. At 06:10 next morning Tony and Ken placed down four more Frantans on the terrorist position that had been so troublesome the previous day. Then Jerry Strong led a sweep up the river. There was no resistance because the terrorist survivors had made good their escape over the high ground between ambush positions. Twelve dead terrorists were found, most burnt by Frantans.

Sergeant Major 'Bangstick' Turle in the meanwhile was leading a tracker-combat callsign on the trail of survivors whose tracks were found to be moving south over the high ground, then across the main Kariba road into flat ground east of Kariba Airfield. As the callsign was approaching a dry riverbed, the sergeant-major smelt the unmistakable stench of rotting flesh. One hundred metres farther on he came upon the terrorists and took out all ten ZAPU, without casualties to his callsign. Most of the dead terrorists had been burnt by Frantan, which accounted for the early warning stench.

Twenty-seven ZAPU had been killed and one captured. Another was thought to have escaped but in reality, though listed in capture documents as a member of the group, he was the SB plant.

Tracker dogs proven

FOLLOWING AIR HQ APPROVAL TO progress the radio tracker dog project, BSAP Dog Section Officer Ted Spencer and his dog Jill joined Peter Allen and me. From the outset Jill, a Doberman Pinscher–Bloodhound cross, worked well with Beau. But Beau refused to be outdone by the bitch that was a much faster tracker. He stubbornly insisted on working every inch of every trail himself.

The route the Op Griffin terrorists had followed from the Zambezi River up to where contact occurred offered us the most difficult testing ground for the dogs. In August the area was very hot and dry giving the worst possible condition for scent tracking. Accompanied by Wing Commander Porky MacLaughlin from Air HQ, the original trackers of Op Griffin commenced a moonlight retrace of the terrorists' route and timing from the point where tracks had originally been detected. By dawn they were moving along the valley on the high ground.

Keeping to the same timings of the original follow-up operation, the dogs were placed on tracks at 08:30 when the sun was high and ground conditions were already hot. Jill set off on the trail immediately but Beau had to cast back and forth across the trail, so poor was the scent. Jill never moved more than 100 metres before stopping and looking back to wait for Beau to catch up. This went on for a while until Jill ran into a herd of elephants giving her such a fright that she rushed back to Beau. Beau took no notice of Jill, now following him, and led her straight through the elephants which, in spite of the helicopter's presence overhead, all turned to watch the dogs pass by. Then a young bull with trunk high, and presumably trumpeting, gave chase for a short distance before breaking away. Beau had never seen an elephant before, so we were surprised and delighted by his apparent nonchalance as he passed through before Jill resumed the lead.

During the steep climb up the escarpment, it was very noticeable that the dogs were moving faster. Peter Allen attributed this to improved scent retention by higher grass and larger areas of shade. When they came out onto the open ground at the top of the escarpment Jill ran straight into a bull rhino, which immediately charged, sending her helter skelter back to Beau. Beau saw the big fellow coming and ran in a semicircle, which Jill and the Rhino followed.

Once the rhino broke off his chase we thought the game was over, particularly when we saw Beau plunge into a waterhole with Jill in tow. Both dogs submerged their bodies and enjoyed a long drink. We were considering landing to pick them up when Beau ran out of the water, shook himself vigorously, and started casting for scent. Again, Jill followed suit and, of greatest importance, the radio links were still working. They had to range more than 200 metres across the original line of movement before Beau picked up the trail and Jill, as always, moved off ahead of him. I picked up the steep riverline into which the terrorists had turned from the valley in which the dogs were still running strongly. Both dogs disappeared into thick riverine bush and we watched anxiously for them to reappear in the rocky river-line itself. Instead we spotted them coming out of the trees well beyond and continuing to run along the side of the open valley.

Again I wondered if we should recall the dogs, particularly as I was running low on fuel. But then they turned into the next gully running into the mountain. At this point both dogs went to ground and Beau gave his funny yelp. Just ahead of the dogs we saw Porky MacLaughlin and his group. The men who tracked the Griffin terrorists had taken more than twenty-four hours to cover the same ground that these two dogs had run in a little under one-and-a-half hours.

At that very moment there was no way I would have believed that the radio tracker dog system would never be used in operations. We had just seen it work in the worst possible conditions. Unfortunately however, Air HQ passed the entire

Patrol Officer Ted Spencer with Jill, PB, Warrant Officer Peter Allen with Beau.

project to the Police. Though some effort was put into continuing with the work already done, it failed because regular police dogs were expected to conduct routine urban dog patrol work with the specialist radio tracking as a sideline. Worse still was the fact that operationally inexperienced handlers managed the dogs and all training was done at Mabelreign, which was a long way from New Sarum.

Had I remained on helicopters things might have been different because I envisaged Air Force Dog Section preparing four dedicated dogs in conjunction with a handful of battle-experienced soldiers who would be trained to handle them in the field. All training would have been done at New Sarum where all important helicopter participation was at hand.

Operation Mansion

AS A CONSEQUENCE OF OP Griffin, ZAPU had failed for the third time to establish a safe route through Rhodesia. But they tried again in yet another attempt in mid-August 1968. The crossing was made way over to the west at the headwaters of Lake Kariba. Operation Mansion was established when the crossing was detected 500 metres from where the Gwai River flows into the Zambezi Gorge.

Terry Jones, with his helicopter gunner Senior Technician Willy Armitage, tried unsuccessfully to get at the terrorists who were cornered in a cave on a steep riverbank with RAR troops poised on the ridge above them. Then Mark McLean and Corporal Technician John Ness had a go at dislodging them. Although one terrorist was killed, Mark could not flush the terrorists out into view of the RAR troops, so he requested his supporting FASOC to call for heavy airstrikes.

Vampires flown by Keith Corrans, Wally Galloway, Graham Cronshaw and Prop Geldenhuys struck with rockets and cannon fire. A Canberra piloted by Peter Woolcock with John Digby delivered a noisy load of ninety-six fragmentation bombs. The airstrikes broke the terrorists' will and RAR troops inflicted some casualties before nightfall allowed survivors to escape back into Zambia.

ZAPU's operations had been receiving a great deal of press coverage outside of Rhodesia. The party's propaganda machine, ignoring dismal failures, claimed that its military wing had killed many Rhodesian troops with the downing of many more helicopters than we owned.

Operation Excess

ZANU HAD BEEN QUIET FOR AGES but then, spurred on by ZAPU's exaggerated claims and an urgent need to prove itself to the Organisation of African Unity, launched a large group across the Zambezi River at Mpata Gorge. Having failed repeatedly, ZANU had learned to avoid the long distances previously used to reach populated areas. In this case they aimed to get to the large sparsely populated Dande Tribal Trust Land, but without getting too close to the police station and Army base at Kanyemba.

A border patrol unit only detected the crossing eight days after it had occurred. This was the consequence of infrequent surveillance of the rough ground at Mpata Gorge and because, in winter, there was no water for many miles beyond the Zambezi River. Operation Excess commenced when Lieutenant Christopher John (Dumpy) Pearce of the RLI took over from the border control unit and commenced a follow-up southeastwards through rough, dry country. The whole region had plenty of trees but in the dry season they were leafless making the hot breezeless conditions extremely uncomfortable.

An RLI Tactical HQ commanded by Major Rob Southey was established on the site of a disused road camp on the main east–west Zambezi Valley road where it crossed the Angwa River bridge at Mato Pools. The main JOC that had been established at Karoi for Operation Cauldron was still in situ to oversee Op Excess. On 28 July 1968 I led a flight of four helicopters to support the RLI operation.

My first task was to resupply Dumpy Pearce with water and rations a little after midday. I located Dumpy near the source of the small bone-dry Ruponje River on the north side of a watershed ridge, where I shut down to have a chat. Dumpy's callsign was hot, sweaty and tired, but in good spirits. The men welcomed the cold water and ice I had brought them and rested whilst Dumpy and I talked. Dumpy estimated that they were seven days behind a group of approximately fifty terrorists. I asked him to point to the spot on the nearby ridge where he believed the tracks were heading. Having noted this, I got airborne and found I could actually land there.

It was obvious that aerial tracking this old trail in such dry grassless conditions was a non-starter but I had other ideas in mind. Looking over the ground ahead I could not help seeing a patch of bright-green trees about twelve kilometres away beyond a series of descending ridges. The walking distance was at lease twice the direct distance. The trees were off to the right of the direction the terrorists had been heading, but they gave the distinct impression of being sited on water. I was absolutely certain the terrorists must have been drawn to the spot having travelled so far without water. I called Dumpy and asked if I could fly his trackers forward to see if my guess was right, promising to have them back within fifteen minutes if I was wrong. Dumpy said it suited him but I must first get Rob Southey's blessings. For this I had to climb quite high to make contact with RLI Tac HQ. Rob Southey did not accept my suggestion, so I set heading for base.

About one minute later, I received a call to say it would be fine to return to Dumpy and lift his trackers forward, providing Dumpy was with them. I raced back to pick up Dumpy and two trackers. When we landed on smooth short green grass next to the copse of green trees, the trackers climbed out and immediately pointed to terrorists tracks on the very spot we had landed. They established that there was no surface water as I flew the rest of Dumpy's callsign forward to tracks now assessed to be five days' old.

Pressing my luck, I headed off low and slow over a vast expanse of leafless trees in the direction the trackers were moving and noted a single prominent and unusually high tree with distinctive smooth yellow bark. Although it was a long way ahead it was certainly on the line the trackers were moving. At this stage I was short of fuel and returned to base.

I went to Rob Southey to suggest moving the trackers forward again. Colonel John Hickman, the Officer Commanding the RLI, was visiting and I learned that it was he who had persuaded Rob Southey to let me try the first move. Though this had been successful and had brought the RLI two days closer to the terrorists, Rob seemed reluctant to move trackers to 'the tall tree'. One could hardly blame him, because it must have seemed improbable that the terrorists would have seen things the way I did. However, he changed his mind when Colonel Hickman said, "You have nothing to lose Rob!"

I returned to Dumpy, picked up his trackers and put them down close to the yellow tree. They were more surprised than I to find that a man had climbed the tree to scan the route ahead whilst the rest of the group had waited close by. Dumpy's men were brought forward onto tracks, now estimated to be thirty-six-hours old. Again I pressed my luck and, dealing only with Dumpy, moved trackers forward about six kilometres to where the trees gave way to open ground along the dry Mwanzamtanda River. Here the trackers had to cast 200 metres before locating tracks that were under twenty-four-hours old. I had just sufficient fuel to bring the whole callsign forward before returning to base feeling well pleased with myself. We had closed from seven days to one day in less than three hours. Had Colonel Hickman not been at the Tac HQ, this would certainly not have occurred and a new method of gaining ground might have been lost.

It was late afternoon and with my enthusiasm at a peak I searched forward. I dared not proceed at low level with terrorists so close and climbed to 1,500 feet. Almost immediately I saw dark-green trees ahead and sensed this was the actual position of the terrorists. Alan Aird had been with me the whole time and he also saw the water in the heavily treed tributary that flowed into the Mwanzamtanda. This otherwise dry rivulet ran northwards along the edge of a rocky outcrop, then looped southward around a moderately high rocky feature. In this bend lay surface water with the dark-green trees lining the banks. Alan agreed with me that the terrorists were under those big shady trees and said he was certain he had seen bundles of something or other under the northernmost trees.

Back at base it was agreed that Dumpy Pearce should continue his follow-up and that fresh troops would be lifted into the suspected terrorist base early next morning. I do not remember the reason for this, but I only carried Alan, his MAG and a full fuel tank when I flew ahead of the three helicopters carrying Jerry Strong and his troops. I passed over the suspect point where both Alan and I saw what we believed were shell-scrapes at the edge of the tree line. We did not change direction until the other helicopters had passed over the site to drop troops behind a small ridge just 100 metres away. The helicopters lifted immediately to return for more troops as Jerry led his men directly to the suspect site. As he entered the trees, he called, "Terrs left about one minute ago—in a hurry. There is abandoned equipment—no time to collect—moving east on tracks."

Poor Dumpy Pearce who had followed these terrorists so far was not at all happy that Jerry was right on the tail of the terrorists his callsign had been mentally prepared to contact in less than two hours. Major Southey refused to let Dumpy's force join Jerry's fresh troops, even though helicopters could have moved them forward in less than five minutes. Nevertheless this turned out to be a good decision.

Being under-strength, Jerry was moving cautiously in rough country. Soon enough the rest of his troops arrived and, though able to move faster for a while, patches of heavy bush in rough terrain well suited to ambush slowed Jerry down. His trackers reported following less than twenty men, which was way below the number Dumpy Pearce had given. In the meanwhile Dumpy had reached the terrorist base by the water where he found that a big force of about forty men had broken south. The only other tracks were those that Jerry was following.

Before Jerry's troops reached one particular spot, I asked for 37mm Sneb rockets to be fired into a patch of bush on the lip of a ravine through which Jerry and his men would be passing. To assist Flying Officer Chris Weinmann, who was flying a Provost, identify the correct position, I asked him to follow my helicopter's shadow until I called, "Now" to pinpoint his position of strike. So far as I know, this was the first time that one pilot guided another by using his aircraft's shadow; but it worked perfectly and Chris placed the strike exactly where I wanted it. When Jerry reached the point a few minutes later, he reported that the tracks went through the point of strike but the terrorists had passed there some time earlier.

By late afternoon Jerry's callsign had slowed to the extent

that they were over one hour behind the terrorists when tracks crossed the north–south road leading to Kanyemba. Because the terrorists were heading directly for Mozambique, diplomatic clearances were needed to enter that country in 'hot pursuit'. When it was too dark to track the troops settled for the night at the borderline. The road crossing had allowed trackers to get an accurate count of the number of men they were pursuing. This confirmed that, with only fifteen sets of prints, Dumpy was following the greater portion of the original group.

During the night authority was given to cross into Mozambique. At first light Jerry's men received water and Mozambican maps before continuing the follow-up into flat, dry mopani country where the temperature would rise to thirty-eight degrees by midday. No aircraft came near Jerry until he said he was close to contact. As I approached his area, a radio transmission from Jerry was so heavily overlaid by the sound of automatic gunfire that I could not hear what he was saying. That he was in contact was obvious.

Jerry had heard voices ahead and opened out his callsign for a sweep through moderately open bush towards the voices. The terrorists saw the troops emerging from the bush line on the other side of a dry riverbed and opened fire, wounding one RLI trooper. Jerry called on the terrorists to surrender, whereupon they responded with vile language and anti-white slogans before resuming fire that kept Jerry's troops pinned down for a short while.

The terrorist position was under trees on slightly higher ground on the other side of the dry riverbed. The RLI threw phosphorus grenades into the river line to give smoke cover to Jerry's left echelon as it rushed over the riverbed and positioned itself on the terrorists' right flank. With pressure on them from front and side, the terrorists' action abated and Jerry crossed the river under covering fire to sweep through the camp where he found seven dead terrorists and one wounded. This meant there were still seven others close by.

Alan Aird and I searched forward and saw two terrorists lying against the bank of a small gully with their weapons pointing towards the advancing troops. Alan opened fire, forcing them to run in a crouch along the gully in the direction of Jerry's flanking callsign. One fell then rose as Alan's fire struck the second man who went head over heels. He rose again just where the gully seemed to end next to a clump of trees. Here both injured men disappeared from view. A gully line beyond helped us understand that a tunnel existed were the roots of the trees bound surface soil to form a natural bridge. The two terrorists were obviously in hiding under this bridge.

Then from above we witnessed a very strange action when two soldiers, one wearing a bright green item of headgear, moved to where we had lost sight of the terrorists. These two men were bending over the bridge and gesticulating wildly before both dropped on their stomachs moments before a grenade detonated in the gully next to them. They rose and did what they had done before, again dropping facedown as

another explosion occurred. The act was repeated but, this time, the two wounded terrorists emerged and were taken prisoner.

Later we were to learn that Lance Corporal Lahee was the wearer of the green headgear, a tea cosy, which was the lucky charm he had used during Op Griffin to attract enemy fire. During the action in which he had been pinned down with Jerry Strong, he had lifted the tea cosy on a stick into terrorist view to confirm their continued presence and position. In so doing the cosy collected a number of holes. I knew the man had to be a bit crazy to be wearing such a bright article because it made finding him from the air so much easier than any other RLI soldier.

Lahee had watched the dust from our helicopter's gunfire, which drew him to the terrorists under the earth bridge. Here he shouted to them to surrender. They refused, so he threw a grenade into the tunnel. The terrorists were just around a bend in the tunnel that protected them from the two detonating grenades that they had thrown back out into the gully. Lahee told them the next grenade would detonate as it reached them and this is what had brought them out of hiding at the very moment another terrorist was seen and killed by other troops.

A little past the point where the gully entered the dry river, I spotted a terrorist as he ran under a tangle of roots overhanging the bank of the main river. Alan had not seen this, and the terrorist was no longer visible to me. With Alan holding the MAG steady, I manoeuvred the helicopter and told him when to pull the trigger. With a touch of rudder I brought strikes to the correct spot for Alan to identify. We then made three passes down the river putting in accurate strikes on the spot before running out of ammunition.

The terrorist had not fallen into view so Flying Officer Tudor Thomas and his gunner, Senior Technician Butch Phillips, put in a pass into the same spot were troops immediately found the bullet-riddled body of a terrorist lodged in tangled roots that had been exposed by erosion. This brought the tally to twelve with three remaining.

I landed to relieve Jerry's men of the three captured terrorists and flew off to hand them over to the Special Branch at Kanyemba. I can still picture the combination of arrogance and fear etched on their faces when they looked at Alan and his MAG machine-gun, but they dared not move because Alan had them covered with his FN rifle. Two of the terrorists had long deep furrow-like wounds to arms and legs that typified those received from steeply inclined helicopter gunfire. Though these looked pretty frightful at the time, medical attention at Kanyemba and later in Salisbury prison resulted in their full recovery.

An RLI callsign of five men under Fanie Coetzee had been put down ahead of Jerry's callsign to cross-grain along the Angwa River. With contact having been made, Tac HQ asked me to get Fanie's callsign over to Jerry to assist in the follow-up on the three missing individuals who had become separated from each other.

With the burly Alan Aird and 400 pounds of fuel I knew a lift of six men and equipment would be difficult. I had not seen Fanie before and groaned inwardly when I realised just how big and heavy he was as he lumbered across the soft river sand with his men. Lift-off necessitated the use of emergency power, but I was able to reduce this within the gearbox time limit once in forward flight. On return to the contact area my landing in a small hole between high trees with such a heavy load was difficult enough, but seeing a terrorist go to ground directly ahead of the aircraft made my hair stand on end because it was too late to abort the landing.

I shouted to Fanie, "Terrorist directly ahead," just before touch-down then I lifted smartly as the troops cleared. Fanie's attention was drawn to firing over to his left so he did not get to clearing the area I had indicated to him. Two days later an uninjured terrorist, captured by Mozambican villagers, was brought to Tac HQ. He recognised me immediately and told his interrogators that I was the pilot he aimed to kill if he thought we had seen him hiding in an antbear hole. The reason he recognised me was because, instead of wearing a helmet and mask, I wore earphones with a throat microphone. Thank goodness he did not fire. It would have spelled disaster for eight men and a helicopter.

The two remaining terrorists were killed in separate actions and the focus of Op Excess swung over to the larger terrorist group. Their tracks had not been found by either of two cross-graining callsigns patrolling the main dirt road on the line of Dumpy's follow-up. The reason for this became clear when Dumpy reached the road. The terrorists had applied effective anti-tracking procedures over long stretches, moving singly in a widespread line-abreast formation. When they reached the road they grouped and laid clothing, like stepping-stones across a river, which all the men followed, leaving no boot prints on the roadway.

Unexpectedly, locals well to the south in the Dande Tribal Trust Land reported the terrorists' presence. Following this, a series of contacts occurred but each firefight had ended before helicopters arrived. During the first and largest of these, Fanie Coetzee's leading scout and part of his callsign came under heavy fire from a high ridge towards which the trackers were moving. Fanie manoeuvred elements around the flank and from their rear gave the terrorists a serious walloping.

Shooting had just ended when I arrived and the troops were sweeping through the contact site. I landed and switched off close to big Fanie who nonchalantly handed me an RPD machine-gun, barrel forward. I took hold of it but dropped it immediately when the hot barrel burned the palm and fingers of my right hand. The weapon fell to the ground still smoking where some of my skin was stuck to it. For over a week flying, eating and every other activity involving the use of the right hand, was absolute agony.

As with most operations there occur amusing incidents that remain clear in ones memory. The first of my Op Excess memories involved a toilet. A concrete plinth set over a deep hole had once been the road-camp latrine. It was on the high bank of the Angwa River and now, with a 'thunder box' in place, served as the officers' loo. A hessian screen surrounded three sides of the toilet with the open end overlooking pools in the river below. In the heat of the valley this facility started to smell and its stench invaded the operations room tent and the officers dining table set under trees. I was present at the lunch table for the first time when Major Rob Southey asked Sergeant-Major 'Bangstick' Turle to attend to the problem.

The sergeant-major ordered two RLI troopies to get rid of the smell, fully expecting the youngsters to do the usual thing of pouring lime into the pit. But he had not spelled this out to them. Obviously the soldiers did not know the standard procedure because they set out to deal with their task in their own way. One poured a gallon of petrol down the hole and turned to his mate asking for matches. His mate did not have any and ran off to find some. By the time he returned, the heat had turned the petrol into concentrated vapour so, as a match was struck, the vapour ignited instantly setting off a powerful explosion that sent everyone in camp diving for cover believing the base was under attack.

Only when a shower of indescribable, stinking muck rained down, did someone shout, "Some silly bugger has blown the shithouse down!" The force of the explosion threw both young troopies down the bank, one having lost most of his hair to flame. They both recovered, but the concrete plinth and the thunderbox were totally destroyed.

The second incident involved Tudor Thomas who was still airborne one evening and became disoriented in the haze and blackness of the night. I got airborne immediately to orbit over our base with my landing light on to assist him. It took a long while before Tudor picked up my landing light because he was miles away. On the ground some troopies knew a helicopter was having difficulty in locating the base and, seeing me orbiting above, one asked another, "Why doesn't that stupid Blue Job just look down? There is plenty of light in this camp."

Concern for Tete Province

ZANU HAD FAILED AGAIN BY losing all but two of its men in Operation Excess. However the operation showed us that ZANU had at last come to realise that they must find the shortest route to the African population if they were to avoid being mauled again and again by Rhodesian forces. The Mozambican pedicle of Tete Province provided them the only viable option to achieving this and FRELIMO (the Front for the

Jacklin Trophy awarded to No 7 Squadron, 1968. Back row: Cpl Tech K. Smithdorff; Cpl Tech A.Aird; Snr Tech J.Norman; Snr Tech W.Armitage; Snr Tech M.Maughan; Cpl Tech J.Ness; Snr Tech J.Green; Snr Tech G.Carmichael; Cpl Tech B.Collocott; Jnr Tech B.Daykin; Snr Tech B.York. Front row: WO1 H.Marshall; Flt Lt P.Nicholls; Fg Off M.McLean; Flt Lt J.Barnes; Flt Lt M.Grier; Sqn Ldr N.Walsh (OC—holding trophy); Flt Lt PB; Flt Lt M.Hofmeyr; Flt Lt I.Harvey; Fg Off H.Slatter; Fg Off T.Jones; Chf Tech D.Theobald. Not present: Fg Off C.Dixon; Snr Tech M.Philips; Cpl Tech R Whyte.

Liberation of Mozambique) had already established its second front in this region. Rhodesian fears were that FRELIMO would eventually gain control of those areas where tribal clans overlapped the international borders of Mozambique and Rhodesia. To be in a position to take advantage of this, ZANU had to be accepted by FRELIMO who also depended on Zambia as its rear base for second front operations.

Rhodesians were most concerned about the Portuguese ability to contain FRELIMO in Tete. Should they fail, which we guessed they would, we would lose our two greatest military advantages. These were having the Zambezi River as a barrier along which to detect crossings and the wide stretches of difficult terrain between the river and the inhabited areas.

Portugal was already facing major financial and morale problems in her wars against communist-backed liberation movements operating in all three of her African territories. These were Portuguese Guinea, Angola and Mozambique where most men under arms were conscripts from metropolitan Portugal. They showed little interest in fighting for territories that neither interested nor concerned them, which gave us the distinct impression that their whole approach to service in Africa was to take as little risk as possible and get home in one piece. One could hardly blame them! Nevertheless we hoped that the Portuguese would play a leading role in preventing Russia from achieving her goal of establishing a communist bridge across central Africa from which to drive south. Angola constituted the most important target in Russia's plans but Rhodesians saw the Tete Province as the immediate threat.

Unlike the Portuguese, Rhodesian forces, though small in numbers, were fighting on home soil and would not shy away from taking risks. To protect her interests, South Africa was providing much-needed manpower along the strategically important Zambezi River, intent on beating Russian supported terrorism in depth. An extension of this strategic defence line was in the offing because, unbeknown to us at squadron level, plans were in their final stages for Rhodesians to participate with Portuguese forces in Tete.

This happened to be a quiet time when operations within Rhodesia had returned to routine border-control operations and 7 Squadron had been awarded the Jacklin Trophy. For my part I completed helicopter conversions for Randy du Rand and Barry Roberts and was involved in a Police ATOPS (anti-terrorist operations) exercise codenamed Mannix. Norman Walsh and I flew two of the three helicopters assigned to this large exercise conducted close to Umtali.

Casevac of gored ranger

EXERCISE MANNIX INVOLVED TWO GROUPS of police—the 'Rats' and the 'Terriers'. The Rats were small teams acting the part of terror gangs. Terriers, the good guys, were policemen whose job it was to eliminate the Rats. We were amazed that war games conducted in the mountainous eastern districts were almost as exciting as the real thing, but with no danger to ourselves.

Within the pine forests and thick bush of the area I

was having the usual problem of picking up men wearing camouflage. Remembering how easy it had been to find Lance-Corporal Lahee during Op Excess and the way we kept track of our radio tracker dogs, I asked for small red day-glo patches to be affixed to the top of Terrier caps. This worked very well for the helicopter and Police Reserve Air Wing crews and thereafter red and orange day-glo patches were used from time to time during offensive operations.

One evening my father visited me at Grand Reef, the airfield we used for Exercise Mannix. We were having a few drinks together at the end of the day when I was called to the Ops Room. Air HQ required me to fly to Buffalo Bend immediately to casevac a wounded game ranger to Chiredzi Hospital; an elephant had gored him.

Having had three beers, I approached Norman Walsh who had also been drinking. We agreed it would be much safer to fly together, one piloting whilst the other navigated. Big Alan Aird was our technician. Norman piloted the 370-kilometre leg to the distinctive loop on the Nuanetsi River, named Buffalo Bend in Gona re Zhou (Place of the Elephants) Reserve. Thanks to half-moon and clear-sky conditions I was able to direct Norman along the precise track. From a long way out we could see the huge bonfire at our landing place. When we landed the injured man's girlfriend and three game-rangers, all with loaded rifles, were watching out for the angry cow elephant that had gored the ranger. She was lurking about close by and trumpeted once just to make life interesting. I was most disappointed that my pilot training coursemate Ron Thompson, then the Senior Warden at Gona re Zhou, was not present because he was away from his base at the time.

I cannot recall the injured ranger's name but can still picture him lying on his back exactly where he had been downed. In the late afternoon he had been out on foot with his little dog and another ranger. They were watching elephants browsing when the dog became excited and started barking. This made one cow angry. She charged, knocked over the ranger and quick as a flash drove one long tusk through his pelvis then kneeled on his body to extract it. The other ranger managed to drive the cow off by firing a shot over her head. Once the cow was clear, he fired three shots in quick succession—the recognised SOS signal to anyone in earshot.

The injured ranger gave us instructions on how to manoeuvre him ever so slowly onto the helicopter stretcher because he was in too much pain to be handled in any other manner. When, however, we got him into the helicopter his six foot, seven inch-length was greater than the helicopter's width. There was no option but to subject him to excruciating pain by bending his legs to close the rear doors. We had just enough fuel to get to Chiredzi and the moon was about to disappear below the western horizon, so I elected to navigate again whilst Norman Walsh piloted the helicopter. We landed at Chiredzi Police Station with five minutes of fuel to spare. Having seen our casualty safely into a waiting ambulance we refuelled

for the dark leg back to Grand Reef. Since they could be of no assistance to me on the return flight, Norman and Alan accepted cold beers whilst I drank strong black coffee.

The flight to Grand Reef in pitch-blackness had to be made entirely on instruments using heading and time alone because there were no visible features to assist navigation along the route. I climbed high and was quite settled. Beside me I could see that Norman had fallen asleep as had Alan Aird who was sprawled out in his rearward-facing seat. We were about halfway home when, without warning, Norman grabbed the cyclic control and pulled it back sharply. I shouted and Norman let go, instantly realising he had responded to a bad dream. Although normal flight was regained immediately, I was unsettled by the incident and remained tense for the rest of the route, expecting Norman to react to another dream. Fortunately this did not happen.

When eventually I picked up the lights of Umtali and then Grand Reef it was almost 03:00. I was really tired and could not bring myself to do a simple straightforward descent onto the lights of the base. It took me an age to let down in a series of orbits over the unlit runway despite the fact that I knew we were well clear of the high mountains to the north of the airfield. Even in real emergency situations I had never suffered such uncertainty as on this particular descent. Norman Walsh was awake and, even though he must have been fully aware of my predicament, he did not say a word; such was the nature of my boss.

Having had less than two hours' sleep, I was awakened early for a deployment of Police Terriers at sunrise. Just as I was about to place them down in a vlei my technician John Ness shouted, "Lines, lines," but it was too late. The rotor blades severed the thin telephone wires whose posts, both left and right, where hidden by clumps of trees. Many farms were without telephone communications for the day and I received one hell of a ribbing from the Police Reservists in the Odzi Sports Club that evening.

Tripper operations

ON 7 DECEMBER 1968 WE learned that four helicopters would be deploying into Mozambique the following day. Great secrecy surrounded the Portuguese–Rhodesian inter-service co-operative deployment. This and other Tete operations to come were codenamed Operation Natal whereas, for internal purposes, our Air Force used the codename Tripper. The first of these was an experiment in inter-force co-operation and lasted for only ten days. Our task was to assist Portuguese to combat FRELIMO so as to render it incapable of providing ZANU or ZAPU safe passage to Rhodesia through Tete.

Not knowing what to expect we set off early next morning for a Portuguese Brigade HQ at a hamlet called Bene. Only Wing Commander Ken Edwards, the Air HQ representative and detachment commander, had received a briefing; such was the importance given to secrecy.

Tete had become the most important front for FRELIMO because their operations in far-off northeast Mozambique, though tying down most of the Portuguese military effort, had not attained the depth of penetration they sought. So, under guidance from their Chinese communist advisors, FRELIMO moved to strike at Mozambique's soft underbelly via Tete Province.

Malawi would have been a much better country from which to launch this offensive but Doctor Kamuzu Banda had no wish to involve his country in any conflict with the Portuguese Government, upon which he was heavily dependent. This meant that FRELIMO had to use the longer route through Zambia, which already hosted a number of liberation movements operating against Angola, Rhodesia and South Africa.

FRELIMO's Tete offensive might have started earlier had a proper accommodation been struck with Zambia. When eventually this was achieved, FRELIMO progressed to its first goal, the Zambezi River, easily and rapidly. It was all too clear that the Mozambican authorities did not view Tete in the same light as Rhodesians did. For the Portuguese there was little commercial value in that vast chunk of undeveloped territory other than at Cabora Bassa. Here in the deep gorge through which the Zambezi River flowed was the vital hydro-electric scheme that had already reached an advanced stage in its construction. Its purpose was to provide Mozambique's electrical power needs and earn much-needed foreign currency through the sale of excess power to South Africa.

Pathetically low force levels were deployed in a manner that confirmed the Portuguese were only really interested in keeping FRELIMO away from the tortuous terrain surrounding their Cabora Bassa project. In this deep gorge construction work on the dam wall and its associated electrical generating rooms was well advanced. Beyond this site and the main road leading to it, the Portuguese placed heavy reliance on *aldeamentos*. Guarded by local militiamen, these were enclosed and defended village forts housing tribesmen dragged in from miles around. The military objective was to deny FRELIMO access to the tribesmen and food in the manner Britain employed so successfully during the Malayan Campaign.

The civilian people who had been living a simple lifestyle for centuries were perplexed by the situation in which they found themselves. On the one hand the Portuguese said that the *aldeamentos* were there for their own protection. Protection from what they did not know because they had not yet learned to fear the politically motivated 'comrades' of FRELIMO. On the other hand FRELIMO told the tribesmen that they had come to "liberate the people" from the oppressive Portuguese who they must no longer obey. But the simple tribesmen could not understand 'liberation', never mind what they were being liberated from. The need to stay close to the spirits of their ancestors was their only wish.

The inevitable happened. As in most wars, these innocent people became involved in a tug-of-war between the Portuguese, insisting that they must be contained under armed surveillance, and FRELIMO insisting that they must be spread out in the countryside to be freely available to provide them with food, shelter and plenty of women for their comforts. Portuguese forces attacked those in the countryside. FRELIMO attacked the *aldeamentos*.

In these circumstances tribal unity was destroyed and families disintegrated. Those forced into the *aldeamentos* dared not venture out without armed protection, meagre as it was. Those who had chosen to remain in the areas of their ancestral spirits made every effort to avoid detection by either side but, inevitably, most were roped into FRELIMO's net.

We flew low-level directly from Salisbury to the Brigade HQ at Bene, northeast of Cabora Bassa. The dam wall had not yet interrupted the Zambezi River's flow so the river course still remained as it had been for centuries. Having watched Kariba being built in the late 1950s, we were somewhat disappointed by the small dimensions of Cabora Bassa's concrete wall spanning the deep but narrow gorge. The dam wall had reached about half its final height and the surrounds were badly scarred by heavy earth and concrete workings. A fenced minefield ran around the perimeter.

Butch Graydon with his MAG in foreground.

Beyond the dam site, ridges and ravines gave way to gentle rolling countryside that was covered in a mix of forested areas and grassy vleis. Everything was so beautiful after good rains and there was so little evidence of human habitation that it was hard to imagine a war was in progress in the untamed region. Set in this paradise we found the base at Bene looking neat and clean yet giving no hint of the dreadful pong that we were going to encounter as we landed on the only open area within the defence lines of the base.

The stench emanated from a communal toilet facility right next to the landing zone. It was so overpowering that we had to take a few deep breaths to help us acclimatise before getting on with the job of refuelling. The latrine arrangement was one single trench line of about forty-five metres in length over which a continuous wooden seat was set with at least thirty holes for users who were afforded no privacy. Many places were rendered unusable by mislaid faeces from those preferring to squat with their filthy boots astride holes rather than sit in the manner intended by the toilets' designer. I felt like returning to Salisbury right away.

Happily the smell did not affect the area of the messes, Ops Room and accommodation huts where waterborne toilets, though not great, worked after a fashion. The problem was that they were not hygienic. Our reluctance to use these toilets was handled in an unusual way. We ran daily 'toilet flights' to the top of a high domed-rock hill close to the base. Setting the helicopter down on the crest, we moved out in different directions to attend to our private needs. Our exposure against the skyline made a perfect target to any FRELIMO mortar team that might be so close to the Portuguese base, but the risk was considered worthwhile.

The whole purpose of our detachment was to establish if the Rhodesian Air Force and the Portuguese Army forces could operate effectively against FRELIMO to the mutual benefit of both countries. The first thing we needed was a briefing on current Tete operations.

The base commander, a short, fat, bright-eyed and rather arrogant brigadier, conducted the briefing. This was translated into good English by one of his junior staff officers. We could see from the outset that military intelligence on FRELIMO's dispositions and modus operandi was very scant and that Portuguese successes had been minimal. The capture of a single terrorist weapon following a major assault on a FRELIMO base just before our arrival was considered a 'successful operation'. The brigadier's boastful unveiling of a 'score board' astounded us because, in Rhodesian terms, it revealed pathetic returns if the costly military efforts we were hearing about were to be believed. As the briefing progressed we came to understand part of the reason for Portuguese failures.

There was no aggressive patrolling to search out FRELIMO groups and base camps. Most of the imprecise information upon which the military appeared to rely came from the *aldeamento* militiamen who seldom ventured beyond the fenced perimeter of their protected villages. Upon such dubious information military plans would be drawn up with detailed orders for vehicle convoys, the formations each unit would adopt when attacking and the exact timings for commencement and termination of each operation. A glance through operational orders for past events showed that conventional war methods were being employed against an elusive non-conventional enemy that was heavily schooled in the need to avoid armed confrontation in all circumstances, even when undertaking planned hit-and-run raids.

Because the brigadier sensed unspoken disapproval of his own operations, he invited the Rhodesians to illustrate to him and his staff something of the style of Rhodesian operations that he had heard were very successful. Following an impromptu briefing by Norman Walsh, who emphasised our use of aggressive ground patrols, we were briefed on a forthcoming operation we were to support.

My most vivid memory of that Portuguese operation was the length of time and effort needed to dig vehicles out of the mud along one of many poor tracks they used to get around the countryside.

In retrospect I realise that we must have appeared pretty arrogant, being so used to Rhodesian Army methods and having experienced nothing but high levels of success against our own enemies. Our contempt for the *aldeamento* system also sticks in my mind.

We could not accept

Toilet run. Squatting: Tudor Tomas, Tinker Smithdorff and PB. Standing: Bob St Quinton, Randy du Rand, Butch Graydon, Mark McLean and 'TJ' van den Berg.

Typical Tete road conditions.

that this system was right for Africa, possibly because our own black folk living in open villages were still providing us with intelligence on the presence of terrorists. At that time we could not visualise that, within seven years, our own situation would change so radically that we too would employ a similar system, albeit on a smaller scale.

We returned to Mozambique four times during 1969 and were always received with open arms and treated to the outstanding hospitality for which the Portuguese people in general are so well known. On my second detachment to Bene, the Portuguese were as pleasant as ever but the toilet problems had not changed one iota.

This detachment differed from the first in that we had with us three experienced RLI officers. The brigadier gave us another lengthy briefing following which he asked for a Rhodesian update briefing for the benefit of senior staff officers visiting his Brigade HQ. Norman Walsh and Captain Ron Reid-Daly made an impromptu presentation, again laying emphasis on the need for offensive patrols to seek out and destroy FRELIMO. This briefing was well received and resulted in an agreement that Portuguese soldiers would be placed under command of RLI officers to see how offensive patrolling might work in Tete Province.

After spending some time in the field, Ron Reid-Daly told us that there was nothing much wrong with the average Portuguese soldier's fighting spirit but he lacked fire discipline, creating unnecessary noise and expenditure of ammunition. To be led from the front by Rhodesian officers was good experience for the troops at Bene. Notwithstanding language difficulties they enjoyed a new sense of confidence that made them braver soldiers through having a commander visible up front giving the silent hand signals they understood. We learned that Portuguese officers born and bred in Mozambique were greatly favoured by the troops because they also led from the front. But because they were so few in number, most troops were led by metropolitan officers who commanded from any positions but right up front. This is borne out to some extent by the very high casualty levels amongst Rhodesian Army and Mozambican-born officers when compared, pro rata, to their Europe-born equivalents.

At every opportunity and with Norman Walsh's blessings, I pursued my interest in trying to rustle up FRELIMO targets through visual reconnaissance, which I conducted at low level. I would later discover that this was very dangerous and not an efficient way of searching large tracts of ground. Nevertheless the effort proved worthwhile and assisted in generating targets for joint actions. But so poor was the quality and so vague the physical details of river-lines and surface gradients of the maps issued to us that we concluded they must have been drawn by Vasco da Gama himself. This made low-level map-reading particularly difficult.

Operating independently out of radio range of any forces was really dangerous for my technician and me. We got ourselves into hot situations on some occasions when FRELIMO, rather than going to ground as they had been taught, chose to stand upright to fire at us. Fortunately their anti-aircraft fire was still poor though we suffered moments of terror when numerous men fired their automatic weapons at very close range as we twisted right and left passing over them at treetop level. Many hundreds of rounds were fired so we were lucky to sustain only two non-critical hits through the tail boom.

In consequence of these recce flights, we provided more intelligence to the Brigade HQ in a week than had been received in a year; or so it seemed. Two young Portuguese Air Force pilots who operated single-engined Dorniers from the small airstrip at Bene were interested in establishing what I was finding that they themselves had been unable to find. A comparison of maps immediately revealed that they had reported almost every location I had plotted. It was hardly surprising that they were deeply distressed by this because the very same Army officers who were happily responding to my reports had been fobbing them off, month in and month out. Nowhere on the Ops Room wall map or intelligence logs was any of the Portuguese Air Force information recorded. This was not only absolutely disgraceful from our point of view; it exposed one of the greatest flaws in Portuguese operations.

Rhodesians believed that inter-force co-operation was fundamental and of paramount importance. From time to time there were hiccups, but one force never totally ignored intelligence given by another. Because of this we found it difficult to understand how inter-force jealously or rivalry, call it what you may, within the Portuguese forces could be allowed to limit their operational effectiveness against FRELIMO. Through this spirit of non-co-operation we recognised that the threat posed to Rhodesia by FRELIMO was far more serious than we had first imagined.

As with two other RLI officers, Captain Ron Reid-Daly continued to lead a small force of Portuguese troops. Ron was a pretty tough customer with considerable experience, including combat service with the SAS in Malaya. Yet he continued to believe in the ordinary Portuguese fighting soldier and was only too happy to take on FRELIMO with these men, providing he used his own FN rifle and not the Portuguese issue 7.62mm Armalite rifle.

I located a base area early one morning from barely discernible smoke rising out of heavy riverine bush west of Bene. Ron was flown in with fifteen soldiers to check it out. Before he commenced a sweep through the area I warned Ron that this might be a civilian camp. Soon after the sweep commenced a Portuguese soldier opened fire on movement he had seen. Immediately all the Portuguese soldiers let fly causing Ron great difficulty in getting them to cease firing. He too had seen human movement just before the firing started but immediately realised these were from terrified women running for their lives. Fortunately the troops had been shooting blind and casualties were limited to a mother and her baby.

Back at base I saw that the baby had been shot through the flesh of one buttock and his mother had been grazed in her flank by the same round. Kindly medical attention was given to mother and child before they were taken to an *aldeamento* along with all the other women brought in from the bush camp. Like so many of their kind, they had been in hiding from both FRELIMO and the Portuguese forces. Hearing this, I felt really guilty for being responsible for bringing them into Portuguese custody.

Whilst the two casualties were still being attended, a Portuguese major asked who had initiated the fire. One soldier pointed to Ron Reid-Daly intimating that he had been the first to fire. Ron's fiery temper showed deep red in his taut face as he literally threw his rifle into the hands of the surprised major saying, "Judge this for yourself." The embarrassed major sniffed at Ron's FN rifle and realised that it had not been fired at all. Then, followed a severe blasting for indiscipline by all the soldiers, the unfortunate soldier who had pointed to Ron was taken off for twenty-one days' detention.

I was not involved with other deployments to Tete that year as I had new pilots to instruct. But during one of these a very unpleasant incident occurred when, following a particular action, helicopters were recovering troops and taking civilians back to the Army base. Flying Officer Hugh Slatter landed when only five soldiers and two young African women remained. The five Portuguese soldiers made a dash for the helicopter and boarded. Hugh shook his head and hand-signalled that the two women must be lifted out first; another helicopter would return to collect the soldiers.

A Portuguese sergeant returned negative gestures then, before Hugh or his technician realised what was happening, stepped out of the helicopter shot both women dead where they stood and casually returned to his seat. Hugh's horror and rage was such that he was simultaneously crying, screaming and drawing his pistol to shoot the sergeant. Seeing the danger, Hugh's technician intervened and persuaded him to let the matter be handled at base. Hugh reluctantly agreed but, upon landing, he tendered his 'immediate resignation' to Air HQ by signal. There was a general revolt by the Rhodesians aircrews causing considerable embarrassment to the Brigade HQ staff. The Portuguese sergeant was arrested and charged with murder whilst communications went back and forth between the Mozambican and Rhodesian authorities. Though the Rhodesians were persuaded to stay on in Tete, Hugh refused point-blank to do so, preferring to face court martial rather than operate with the "murdering Portuguese forces". He was flown back to Salisbury where considerable effort was needed to persuade him to withdraw his resignation.

Our experiences in Mozambique concerned us deeply because everyone realised that military failure in that country would have serious consequences for Rhodesia's security. We also felt deeply for the Mozambican people, black and white, who knew their country's future was being mishandled by their metropolitan government 10,000 kilometres away.

Judging by the results that were jointly achieved during our detachments to Tete, a continuous presence of Rhodesian forces operating with Portuguese forces would have made all the difference in curbing FRELIMO and denying ZANU and ZAPU use of the Tete Province. In fact, if we had been granted continuous access along the Zambezi River's southern bank within Tete province this would have met our strategic needs. It would have allowed us to extend our border-control operations eastwards to capitalise on the successes we had achieved along this same river at home. Unfortunately, politics disallowed this critical advantage and history records the consequences.

Tripper operations continued on and off and Peter Briscoe had this to say to author Beryl Salt about one attachment to Portuguese forces at Chicoa in late1970:

We formed a detachment based on Chicoa on the south bank of the Zambezi just west of the Cabora Bassa Gorge. Chicoa was a hellhole. We anticipated a lengthy stay and we had learnt to take our own field kitchen and cooks. It was the rainy season and the afternoons were punctuated with the usual thunderstorms. Cleanliness was a problem so we rigged up showers. These were serviced by a tank of water that was filled from the waters of the Zambezi. However, the water was chocolate brown and we ended up dirtier after the shower than before. So we found the answer—wait for a rainstorm, strip naked, bring out the soap and shampoo and use Mother Nature. Except for our feet and ankles we were clean. The only person who enjoyed shower time more than we did, was the postmistress who watched from a distance.

The thing we envied most about the Portuguese Air Force stationed at Chicoa was that their Alouette helicopter had a 20mm cannon. Compared with our 7.62 machine-gun this was a real killing machine. It was patently apparent that they had little or no idea how to operate this weapon or even service it and this was graphically demonstrated one morning when the gunner's replacement arrived. The new incumbent had never seen a weapon like this before and was given a quick tutorial. The tutor, demonstrating how to load the gun, pulled back the moving parts and released the breechblock. He had, however, forgotten to clear the weapon. It picked up a 20mm round that went off with a fearful bang, travelled across the open ground towards the Portuguese camp, entered a tent and hit the cook who was taking his post-breakfast siesta. It removed a large part of his skull and he was casevaced to Tete by chopper. That evening the commander came over to tell us that the cook was dead. Seeing the looks of dismay on our faces, he immediately qualified his remark by saying, "Oh, don't worry, he was a 'sheet' cook anyway!" We were stunned by this callous disregard for human life, but it was typical of the overall attitude.

As there seemed to be little action at one stage, we threatened to pack up camp and return to Rhodesia, which was bad news for the Portuguese Army colonel. We had just been to a scene where there had been a report of a Fred (FRELIMO) camp but it was a 'lemon'. The Portuguese had to return by vehicle. No sooner had we landed back at Chicoa than the Portuguese Army colonel came running to our camp, in itself an unusual sight. Panting and puffing he approached Wing Commander Ozzie Penton, and, scarcely able to contain himself, he blurted out what was to become the most famous words ever uttered at Chicoa. "Colonel Penton, good news, good news, we have been ambushed!" Ozzie's face was a picture. Recovering, he looked at the Colonel and said, "Well Colonel, if that is good news, what the hell is the bad news?" We deployed the troops but rain had washed the tracks away.

One morning Captain Neves, their OC, gave the whole company a pep-talk, telling them that convoys were going to be sent out on the three roads that led out of Chicoa to locate mines. This was a good plan—except for one small drawback—the intention was to discover the mines by hitting them. The plan also required volunteers to drive the vehicles. As these vehicles were not mine-protected, the volunteers were, in effect, going to their deaths. The troops got into a huddle and a group of volunteers stepped forward to loud applause from their comrades. They boarded the vehicles and drove off. Within the hour we were called on to pick up the casualties and drop trackers to search for spoor but, even in the case of freshly laid mines, the rains soon washed any evidence away. The young people lost their lives needlessly but this did not seem to bother the officers. After a few days the exercise was called off—there were no more vehicles. There was one concession, however. The drivers of the Bedford trucks were allowed to remove the bonnets because if they hit a land mine the bonnets would flip back and crush the driver!

Then we were off again on our 'magical mystery tour', on this occasion to the picturesque resort of Tembue, an Army camp encircled by a few mud huts. We were billeted in a corrugated-iron shed, which had a hessian partition across the middle to separate the officers from the other ranks. A short walk found us at the officers' mess, next to which was an open kitchen in which the chef was preparing our evening meal, surrounded by a host of flies. A severely undernourished cow, which should have been put out of its misery months ago, was tethered nearby. On the second day, we returned to camp to find the cow missing. We decided not to risk it, so we dined on corned beef and 'dog' biscuits washed down with copious amounts of cerveja (beer). The following morning the cow reappeared, so we needn't have worried, but the threat was ever-present that she would one day go missing for good.

Animal incidents

FOR THE MOST PART RHODESIAN troops were pretty bored with border-control routines though the abundance of wild life often helped break the monotony. The Zambezi Valley teamed with wild game in the early 1960s before they became disrupted by terrorist and security force activities, which forced some to

move to quieter regions; many elephants crossed the Zambezi River for the tranquillity of Zambia.

On a number of occasions we saw soldiers swimming in deep water close to sandy beaches along the Zambezi River. From our helicopter my technicians and I could see the semicircle of large crocodiles lying submerged in close proximity to the naked men. Every radioed warning was ignored because experience had shown the troops that, if a group of people remained close together, crocodiles kept their distance. If however anyone separated from the group, or was alone, crocodiles would attack. A number of men were lost to crocodiles in this way, including some members of SAP operating in the Victoria Falls area.

Situations of confrontation between soldiers and big game occasionally induced friction between National Parks and the military, particularly when charging animals were gunned down. There were also situations in which the Army shot for the pot and to produce biltong (dried meat) in quantities exceeding Parks' approval. But the presence of game had its lighter side.

A high-ranking aged policeman flew into Mana Pools during a joint-force inspection tour of border-control units. He was a keen photographer and left the helicopter immediately on arrival to take photographs of a large lone bull elephant he had spotted from the air just before landing. This was 'Twinkle Toes' who was well known to the locals, but not to this policeman.

Some months earlier Twinkle Toes had been darted by National Parks rangers to record his vital statistics and to mark him with a large white painted number for ease of tracing his movements. Before the recovery drug was administered, the rangers had a bit of fun painting the big jumbo's toes in a variety of bright colours; hence his nickname.

When the visiting team was ready to fly on to their next port of call they could not find the aged policeman. A quick search around found Twinkle Toes circling the base of a large, straight-trunked tree. He had taken exception to the clicking of the camera and had charged the policeman who was now perched out of reach amongst the high branches. The jumbo was chased off but no amount of persuasion could get the policeman to slide down the huge, straight and smooth tree trunk. Use of the helicopter's hoist was discounted because of the density of the tree's foliage. How he managed to climb the tree the aged policeman could not explain; how he eventually came down I do not remember.

At Mana Pools there was a treetop lodge whose owner spent the six coolest months of the year running a game-viewing business and the rest of the year at his home in England. I landed at the treetop lodge to conduct one of multiple location tests on an SSB radio unit that had been specially developed for deployment by helicopter. It so happened that this coincided with the impending departure of the owner of the lodge who was packing up for his return to Britain. Since he had so much curry in his fridge he asked my technician and me to take lunch with him on the high balcony that overlooked the Zambezi River.

Having set up the SSB aerials and tested the set with satisfactory calls to Air HQ, we left the equipment in situ and went off for a leisurely lunch because we had two whole hours to waste before the next radio test. We had finished eating and were chatting when I asked my tech to check on the aircraft, which was out of sight to us. Immediately he saw the helicopter he called saying, "Just take a look at this!" Surrounding the helicopter was a herd of about fifty jumbos, huge to tiny, all sniffing and feeling the helicopter and laid-out equipment with their trunks. There was nothing we could do because forcing the big fellows to move away might have caused damage. Seeing one large trunk wrapped around the flimsy plastic hydraulic fluid reservoirs of the main rotor blade dampers worried me. When the elephants moved off we went down to inspect for damage. None was found though there were snot marks covering everything and our slimy helmets and masks stank strongly of jumbo.

Mick Grier had just landed troops in the Zambezi Valley when, out of the corner of his eye, he detected movement. The next moment a large angry black rhino bull burst out of the bush charging directly at the helicopter. Mick, who had a good sense of humour, told me how, "With one graceful fluid flowing movement, I applied full collective and watched the beast pass inches under the aircraft." Luckily the rhino did not notice the two soldiers he had barely missed and, with horns and tail held high, followed Mick who drew him away to a safe distance from the men on the ground.

An ambush was hastily laid by an RLI callsign on the extended line of terrorist tracks that were being followed by another RLI callsign. After a long uncomfortable night the ambushers were looking forward to daylight when they all became aware of noiseless movements bang in the middle of their 'killing ground'. They waited tensely for their officer to spring the ambush. The officer was fully aware of the movement but was waiting for it to reach a point directly in front of him when the movement ceased and everything went still.

A very light breeze was blowing from the ambush position towards the killing ground. Had this not been so, the troops would have been aware of the unmistakable, pungent smell of the pride of lions that lay facing them. Only when there was sufficient light did the soldiers find themselves staring straight into the eyes of a line of big cats that faced them with curiosity wrinkled on their big faces. After what seemed a very long time the officer fired a single shot into the air. The lions moved as one with deep-throated growls of protest as they turned and disappeared with mighty leaps into the safety of their habitat.

The Army base at Kariba was set on the edge of Kariba Heights giving it a superb west-facing view of Lake Kariba whose closest shore lay 1,400 feet below at the base of the mountain. I was talking with Army friends on the verandah of the Officers' Mess and enjoying the beauty of a sunset when I received a mighty blow between my legs that laid me flat on the ground and writhing in agony. I had no sooner been downed than a wet grunting snout pushed at my ear and neck. This was young 'Oink' the warthog who had introduced himself with that mighty upward thrust into my crutch. Only Archie Wilson's handshake compared with the agony of this encounter.

Oink had been found abandoned by Border Control troops who took him into their care and brought him to Kariba Heights as a baby. Oink wandered around the camp like a dog and was very spoilt. His in-built habit of thrusting upward with his snout was well known to the inhabitants who knew better than to stand with legs apart when he was around. Many unwary visitors received the same welcome as myself, which amused the Army no end. When, however, Oink's tusks started to grow he became too dangerous to have around and was handed into the care of a Karoi farmer.

Oink being given a drink of beer by Air Force Radio Technician, Ray Hooper.

The Kariba Heights base had a variety of animals over time, two of which were confirmed alcoholics. A dog and a baboon visited the pubs every evening and wandered around begging for beer. The young soldiers poured portions of their drinks into bowls from which these two animals drank. It did not take too much to make either the dog or the baboon drunk yet they continued to be plied with beer until they disappeared into the night to sleep it off. Badly hungover next morning, these animals behaved differently but their plight was all too obvious. The dog slept in the darkest places indoors whilst the baboon spent much of the morning hunched up in the shade of a tree with his hands over his eyes emitting occasional grunts.

By midday they were fine and in the evening they returned to the pub.

Fish may not necessarily rate as animals, but I found one fishing incident amusing. It involved an NCO of RLI who was a dedicated and capable fisherman. He invited another RLI colleague who had never fished before to accompany him in a small boat to do some fishing on Lake Kariba. This novice experienced all the frustrations of 'bird's nest' tangles and hooking himself whilst attempting to cast his lure. Then, more by accident than skill, he hooked a small Tiger fish. The experienced fisherman warned him to be careful in boating his fish because of its razor-sharp teeth, but in his excitement the novice lost his top dentures, which flip-flopped down through the clear water until lost from sight in the dark depths. With first success having been achieved, the experienced fisherman let his friend continue as he prepared to fish for vundu. When he landed a medium-sized vundu, he hit on the idea of pulling his friend's leg. He stuck the vundu a lethal blow to the head and placed his own dentures in the vundu's large mouth. "Hey look, Charlie, this vundu has your false teeth." His friend's eyes lit up as he took the dentures saying, "Gee that's great." But then he looked at them again, and said, "No these aren't mine!" and threw them over his shoulder. Flip-flop, down they went to join his own dentures in the watery depths.

Death of Don Annandale

SOUTH AFRICAN POLICE HELICOPTERS HAD been operating in Rhodesia ever since they first appeared during Operation Nickel. With further SAANC incursions giving rise to Ops Cauldron and Griffin, their numbers were increased to six SAP Alouettes, all of which were flown by South African Air Force pilots. Peter Briscoe had been one of these until, in January 1969, he became the first SAAF pilot to join our Air Force on direct entry. More were to follow his lead in later months. I ran Peter through the entire range of helicopter flying exercises to ensure that he was totally au fait with Rhodesian Air Force methods and standards. Since he was experienced on helicopters, this was an easy and pleasant task.

Along with SAP helicopters there were a few Cessna 185 aircraft (named Kiewiets—an African bird belonging to the Ground plover species) that undertook light communication work. SAAF pilots, some of whom were very junior, also piloted these aircraft. One of these young pilots was a menace because he was way too sure of himself. He delighted in beating up various locations, always coming down too low for his level of experience. Within his own service Lieutenant van Heerden was known as 'Odd Job'—a nickname that suited him well.

The Makuti Hotel was sited on a hill with a steep drop away from the edge of the swimming pool. I was standing there in the late afternoon having a beer with Lieutenant Fanie Coetzee when we saw a low-flying Cessna coming straight towards us across the low ground. This was Odd Job who left his pull-up to clear the hill so late that his aircraft's tail wheel touched a small tree, barely four metres from Fannie, as he zoomed past in a steep climb. The matter was immediately reported to the Officer Commanding FAF 2 who had received similar complaints before mine. But the admonitions given him by the SAAF Air Liaison Officer, on this and other occasions, seemed to go straight over his head.

Don Annandale.

Some time passed when Odd Job, then operating out of Thornhill, was tasked to fly the Station Armament Officer to Kutanga Range. As well as being the S.Arm.O, Flight Lieutenant Don Annandale was responsible for administering Kutanga Range, whose staff he visited regularly. When he had completed his work and was ready to return to Thornhill, Don learned that Odd Job had told the range staff he would be showing them a slow roll before heading for Thornhill.

Don refused to board the Cessna saying he would use road transport to get home. Odd Job assured Don that he had only been pulling the rangers' legs and that he had no intention of rolling his aircraft. Relieved by this, Don climbed aboard.

Once the aircraft was airborne, Odd Job climbed for height and dived for a fast, low-level run past the master quadrant hut. This was standard practice and Don did not worry about it. But when the aircraft was climbing away from the pass, Odd Job commenced a slow roll. He reached the inverted position all right but then scooped into a steep dive in the second half of the roll. The aircraft was too low and struck the ground in a high-nose attitude with wings level. Odd Job died instantly.

Don was thrown through the windscreen over the propeller and flew through the air surrounded by burning fuel that followed him to where he came to rest. By the time the three black crew of the fire Jeep reached him, Don's rich red hair and his clothing had been burned away and his skin was hanging in sheets from his blackened, bleeding body. Amazingly Don was on his feet and got into the front seat of the Jeep unassisted. He urged the shaken driver, "Get me to hospital—I'm dying."

The driver set off for Que Que, which was forty minutes away. He drove as fast as the Jeep would go but fifteen minutes out from Que Que the vehicle failed to negotiate a road bend, left the tarmac paving and went into a broadside before flipping over as the wheels struck soft sand. Once again Don went flying and crashed down in soft sand and rolled to a halt with sand and dust embedded in his suppurating flesh. The three black firemen were unhurt.

A farmer driving from Que Que came upon this awful scene and immediately turned around to take Don to hospital. On his admission it was clear to attending doctors that there was no hope of his survival because Don had third degree burns to over 90% of his badly battered body. He survived a couple of agonising days during which time he bravely briefed his lovely wife Pat on exactly what she must do when he was gone. Don's grieving family and the Air Force were badly shaken by the loss of this superb officer through the harebrained actions of a stupid pilot.

The consequence of Odd Job's appalling stupidity.

Recce training and Willie de Beer

GROUP CAPTAIN DICKY BRADSHAW RETURNED from a liaison visit to Portuguese forces operating against communist terrorist factions in Angola. Whilst there he was given a briefing on the visual reconnaissance methods the Portuguese Air Force had developed for slow fixed-wing aircraft operating at 1,500 feet above ground. Dicky was taken on a recce flight to see for himself and was very impressed by all he saw and learned. Upon his return to Salisbury he lectured a number of pilots in the matter of visual reconnaissance. But only in me did he find a pilot who was genuinely interested in all he had to say because I had already experienced some recce successes, albeit conducted at low level in helicopters.

Because of this, Dicky Bradshaw tasked me to join No 4 Squadron on an exercise that Squadron Leader Peter Cooke was conducting in Wankie Game Park. My task was to introduce the fixed-wing pilots to visual recce. Though this was a pleasant enough task it really was a matter of the blind leading the blind

because I had not yet acquired any experience in fixed-wing recce. Using my Alouette as a perfect platform from which to observe the ground, I was able to show 4 Squadron's pilots how to correctly employ sunlight to follow freshly laid trails from the air. But it was impossible to simulate operational conditions such as I had encountered in Tete, so my part in 4 Squadron's training exercise was really a waste of rations. Nevertheless it was good to spend time with Peter Cooke and his crews who were flying the newly acquired Trojan aircraft. I shall say more about this aircraft shortly.

Peter Cooke, seated centre, behind the mounted Secretary bird which was 4 Squadron's badge emblem.

I also met up with Willie de Beer who I had not seen since the buffalo hunt that ended in the death of the lone terrorist during Operation Nickel. Willie had a young lion that followed him wherever he went. This playful animal took a liking to my helicopter. Leaping in and out at every opportunity, he chewed any loose item he could find. This did no good to my flying helmet or my Air Force cap, which the brute tore to shreds.

The 4 Squadron technicians put the cub onto the flat rear fuselage of a Trojan with a view to taking a few photographs for the Squadron Diary. The little guy immediately ran up the fuselage, along the starboard wing and flopped down at the wing tip. A Lion beer bottle was placed between the cub's paws for a snap shot. When developed it was submitted to Castle Breweries in a failed attempt to swell squadron funds from an envisaged Lion Beer advertisement.

The ever-playful cub became over-excited one evening

Posed on the rear fuselage of a Trojan.

Willie's lion took a liking to my helicopter.

and sank its teeth and claws deep into Willie de Beer's back and shoulder. It was amazing to see how Willie managed to keep still whilst drawing the lion's attention to a fly switch he flicked around. When the cub let go, Willie removed his shirt to inspect and clean up the wounds. I noticed that the puncture marks were very deep and black in colour.

Not too long after this Willie had two hairy encounters with full-grown lions. The first involved a lioness that wandered into his thatched home in the Wankie National Park and inadvertently cornered his frightened wife in the bedroom. A neighbouring ranger responded to her screams for help but was killed by the panicking lioness before she broke clear just as Willie arrived. He was knocked down and slightly injured by the escaping animal.

The next encounter occurred when Willie had to shoot a large lioness that was killing villagers' cattle in the Tjolotjo Tribal Trust Lands. His first shot only wounded the lioness, which immediately attacked Willie and sent his gun-bearer

running for safety. Willie had the presence of mind to ram his left arm way down the lion's throat but he was being savagely clawed all over his body while his left arm was being mauled by the cat's huge teeth. It was impossible for Willie to use his rifle as he frantically called for his gun-bearer to come back and help him. After a while the trembling man arrived. Willie, holding the gun-barrel to the lioness's head, instructed his shaking gun-bearer to manoeuvre the rifle into the right position before telling him to pull the trigger. His scars bore testimony to this awful experience, which he was lucky to survive.

Trojans

THE TROJAN AIRCRAFT THAT 4 Squadron operated was nothing like the Trojan aircraft originally ordered. During October 1964, AVM Bentley initiated inquiries through the Ministry of Rhodesian Affairs in Washington in his attempt to find a suitable training aircraft to replace our ageing Provosts. He made it known that such replacement machines should, ideally, have a much better ground-strike capacity than the Provost.

The most suitable machines available at the time were American T28 Trojan trainers. There were a fair number available with 800hp engines and life spans ranging downwards from three years to zero life. It so happened, however, that a number of handpicked T28s were being completely stripped down and rebuilt to create T28D models powered by 1475hp motors. Their mainplanes were also stressed for high loads and incorporated six, instead of the original two, hardpoints on which to carry weapons. At the time, each T28D was available at $125,000 per unit. Though this was more than Air Force intended to spend, eighteen of these aircraft suited AVM Bentley's needs perfectly. So, in a letter to the RAF Chief of Staff, Air Chief Marshal Sir Charles Elsworthy GCB, CBE, DSO, MVO, DFC, AFC, our Air Force Commander wrote, *The US State Department has replied to the effect that there were many difficult considerations affecting the export of commodities of this kind to Africa, and that it would greatly ease these difficulties if the British Government could say they had no objection to the deal.* The Royal Rhodesian Air Force need was duly relayed to the British Government which had no objection to the acquisition by Rhodesia of 'training aircraft'. Nevertheless the US State Department refused to let a deal go through.

Precisely what occurred thereafter is not altogether clear to me other than that Rhotair (Pvt) Ltd, of Salisbury got in on the act by using their strong association with Français D'exportation de Matèriel Aéronautique (OFEMA). The

Wing Commander Harold Marsh.

T28 Trojan.

Crates used to smuggle the Trojans into Rhodesia.

French had no difficulties with American attitudes and offered to upgrade T28s, from either Algeria or Iran, to French Air Force standards closely equating to the American T28D.

The first that I knew of these huge single-engined aircraft having been sent to Rhodesia occurred some time after the Americans had spiked the French deal. A senior officer on Air Staff told me about the T28 deal and why it had gone wrong. He said that when the ship carrying these aircraft and their spares to Cape Town was in sight of Table Mountain, the ship's master received orders to turn about and return his cargo to France.

At the time it was considered that this disastrous failure to secure ideal machines was the consequence of some loose-mouthed bragger's words reaching top officials in the US State Department. Because the T28 Trojan aircraft rebuilt under licence in France, the USA had used its power to force France to observe UN sanctions and recover the machines to French soil.

Since nobody at squadron level knew anything about the huge T28 Trojans, there was no disappointment when the small Aeromacchi/Lockheed 260 aircraft arrived in crates for secret assembly at New Sarum.

Yet in this deal the supplier had duped Air HQ. Instead of receiving 450hp aircraft, as ordered, we received 260hp machines whose airframes made it impossible to upgrade them with 450hp motors.

Despite this, the name Trojan was given to these piddling little aircraft because of the paperwork previously completed for the big machines. At squadron level it was thought, erroneously, that the name derived from the 'Trojan Horse' type crates used to smuggle the machines into Rhodesia.

It was not until the year 2000 that I learn from historian Richard Wood of documents he had located in UK from our Director of Legal Services Wing Commander Harold Marsh's office telling of the impending arrival of the Trojans. By then, however, it was too late for the shipment to be intercepted and impounded by Britain.

What other secrets Harold Marsh passed on to the Brits, or how many others like him were acting against Rhodesian interests I cannot say, but it helps explain why we lost the T28 Trojans and why there were so many more problems of 'leaked' secrets yet to come.

Roll cloud incident

AFTER THE 4 SQUADRON RECCE exercise my technician Butch Phillips and I had to return to New Sarum via Thornhill. Heavy storms were forecast for the flight that commenced after lunch. About halfway to Thornhill we encountered large storms that I was able to avoid until we were passing one huge cumulonimbus on our left and noticed the rapid development of a strong roll cloud to our right. Turning back I found the roll cloud was worse in the direction from which we had just come so I turned to resume our course to Thornhill.

Ian Smith with Group Captain Dicky Bradshaw and the technical team that assembled the Trojans.

It was not possible to break away left or right from the serious condition developing so unbelievably fast around and ahead of us. Very quickly, heavy rain was falling out of the base of the cumulonimbus and sweeping outwards to remove the ground below from view. For a short while we remained in smooth air in a huge tunnel such as surfers enjoy when riding under the curl of a breaking sea wave. But this tunnel was dark and ominous.

The smooth ride suddenly changed when the aircraft entered turbulence and started to rise in super-strong uplift. Collective pitch was dumped reducing power to zero but the ascent continued. As the aircraft was about to enter cloud, the ascent turned to a descent which maximum power failed to check. Full power only helped reduce the descent rate to something in the order of 3,000 feet per minute in turbulence. I knew that this powerful down current would not drive us into the ground but I feared entering the heavy sweeping rain we were approaching. Converting to flight instruments, we entered the blinding noisy torrent and almost immediately were lifted by another invisible force for a powerless climb through the centre of the swirling tunnel. The end of this passageway of cloud and rain came into view just as the climb reversed into another descent that, again, full power could not counter until we broke out into clear smooth air. Having recovered our senses, we landed to inspect the aircraft for stress damage.

None was found.

Bad weather and violent wind conditions did not only concern pilots. I witnessed a strange incident that was caused by a passing whirlwind. Flight Lieutenant Boet Swart, the

senior PJI (Parachute Jumping Instructor) in charge of the Air Force Parachute Training School, had just landed on the normal training drop zone next to runway 14. He was drawing in his parachute when a whirlwind inflated it and lifted him into flight.

On the opposite side of the runway, next to the security fence where I was standing on the helicopters concrete pad, OC Flying Wing Ozzie Penton was sitting astride his service motorcycle watching the PJIs do their mandatory monthly parachute descent. He saw Boet land then lift upwards and drift rapidly in his direction. Boet returned to earth but was dragged roughly across the ground as Ozzie desperately tried to kick-start his motorbike to get the heck out of Boet's way—but Oz was too late! The parachute canopy knocked him half over before Boet crashed into the bike, whereupon a jumble of motorbike, OC Flying and senior PJI went sliding for some distance amidst bellowed curses until the whirlwind let go of the parachute!

A roll cloud developing along the advancing front of a cumulonimbus storm.

Engine failure

HAROLD GRIFFITHS WAS POSTED TO helicopters in February 1969. I had instructed him on BFS in 1963 and flew with him again during his Flying Instructor's course on 2 Squadron. Of all the pilots I instructed on helicopters, I enjoyed teaching Griff most. In and out of working hours we became close friends and our families got together regularly. At the swimming parties Beryl and I held at our Hatfield home and those in the garden of his own home, Griff was always happiest braaing (barbecuing) and handing around 'snackers' to all and sundry whilst he sipped away at an ice-cold beer. I have never met anyone who enjoyed food to the extent Griff did; yet he retained a relatively trim figure throughout his service life.

During his operational conversion phase, we were flying in the farming area north of Salisbury when I surprised Griff by cutting the fuel flow to test his reaction to engine failure. I had done this with everyone on 7 Squadron ever since Roland Coffegnot of Sud Aviation told me it was the only way to confirm that pilots reacted correctly to this potentially deadly situation.

Griff acted as he should and was autorotating towards the landing point of his choice. I was satisfied and prepared to advance the fuel-flow lever to bring the engine back to its governed speed of 33,500 rpm for a powered over-shoot. As I looked down at the rpm indicator I was astonished to see that it was reading way down near zero meaning that the engine had flamed out instead of maintaining idling rpm.

I immediately took control from Griff and transmitted a Mayday call to Salisbury Approach whilst turning for a gentle up-slope landing on a fallow field that was covered by tall dry grass. A strong flare cushioned the aircraft's high rate of descent before collective pitch was applied for a slow roll-on landing. We had rolled no more than two metres when an unseen contour ridge stoved in the nose-wheel causing damage to its mountings. Our technician, Willie Jevois, only realised that we had made a genuine forced landing when the rotors stopped turning with no noise coming from the engine.

Whilst waiting for the squadron technical team to come in by helicopter, I considered the implications of having tested Griff, and many pilots before him, in a manner contrary to the Air Staff Instructions (ASI) that disallowed engine-off testing of students anywhere but at New Sarum. Although I had been in trouble so many times, particularly during my tour on helicopters, I had always stuck with the truth. But this situation had me in a quandary because, although it was obvious that a technical fault had caused the idling fuel-flow valve to close down the engine, I had knowingly tested Griff in a manner contrary to the ASI that I had signed.

There was another matter too. I had recently been told, on the quiet, that I was about to be promoted to Squadron Leader, a situation I did not want to jeopardise. Wrongly I know, I asked Griff not to say anything about my having cut fuel flow but simply to tell the inevitable Board of Inquiry that the engine had failed in flight.

When my time came to give evidence I said the engine quit in flight—which it had—but I said nothing about having deliberately reduced fuel-flow to idling rpm. Had the right question been asked, I would have been forced to admit my guilt. Fortunately a technical inquiry had already established that a faulty electrical micro switch, which cut off the idling fuel flow, could just as easily have cut fuel flow in powered flight. A minor modification was introduced to prevent this happening in future and the matter was laid to rest.

Joint Planning Staff

I LOOKED FORWARD TO BECOMING A staff officer, which I knew would be quite different to any administrative post on any air base. Until now I had considered everyone working in, or for, Air HQ was flying on 'cloud 9'.

Following the retirement of Air Vice-Marshal Ted Jacklin, the post of Commander of the Royal Rhodesian Air Force became limited to a four-year term. AVM Jacklin was followed by AVM Raf Bentley smartest dressed officer I ever encountered in any force.

AVM Raf Bentley was followed by AVM Harold Hawkins, an Australian by birth.

AVM Archie Wilson became our fourth commander following the retirement of AVM Harold Hawkins in April 1969.

Just before he became the commander, I received official notification of my promotion and posting to the Joint Planning Staff (JPS). Keith Corrans gained his majority at the same time and our independent interviews with the new Commander took place on the day of my move to JPS.

Keith Corrans and I were very conscious of having been

AVM Raf Bentley (top left), AVM Harold Hawkins (top right), AVM Archie Wilson (bottom left), Keith Corrans.

promoted over many senior Flight Lieutenants, most of whom we held in high regard.

In my interview this was the first matter that AVM Wilson raised by telling me my promotion was purely on merit and that I must not be embarrassed or concerned about superseding men who had been my senior. He told me a number of flattering things that had led to this early promotion before telling me he also knew more about the naughty side of me than I would have wanted him to know.

First he told me of Beryl's nightly visits when he had made me Orderly Officer over Christmas and New Year back in 1957—a story I have already covered. My flights under the Chirundu and Victoria Falls bridges had not passed unnoticed nor the 'looping' of the Victoria Falls Bridge in a helicopter. The latter arose from a silly bet with the local Police. All I did was fly under the bridge, rise up, reverse over the top of the bridge then descend to pass back under it, all in a manner that described a complete vertical circle. The AVM knew all about my family's ride in a helicopter at Kariba in 1967, including the circumstances and names of the NCOs that had brought it about. He knew I had mastered a technique of catching guinea fowl with a helicopter and that other pilots had followed my example. The AVM covered other misdemeanours, including the unauthorised project works, but it was clear to me that his whole purpose was to let me know that he received more information about the goings-on at squadron level than any of us realised.

The Joint Planning Staff, sited in Milton Building close to Air HQ, was under the chairmanship of Group Captain Mick McLaren, who was my first flying instructor. His was a two-year posting that alternated between Army and Air Force. Mick's promotion to Group Captain had brought him level with his archrival, Group Captain Frank Mussell.

Some years earlier, when Frank Mussell was promoted to Squadron Leader in command of No 6 (Canberra) Squadron, Mick McLaren was still a flight lieutenant. AVM Wilson had changed this and was later responsible for Mick's meteoric rise to succeed him as the Air Force's fifth Commander.

As Chairman of JPS, Group Captain Mick McLaren's responsibility was to provide secretarial and joint planning services to the Operations Co-ordinating Committee (OCC) and to conduct studies and produce papers on matters required by the OCC. His permanent staff consisted of six officers, two each from Army, Air Force and Police plus a typist and an Army Warrant Officer as Secret Registry clerk.

The OCC was made up of the Commanders of the Air Force and Army, the Commissioner of Police and the Head of CIO (Central Intelligence Organisation). Mick produced the minutes for all meetings and received instructions for JPS tasks. His staff operated as three teams of two and met regularly under his chairmanship to receive OCC instructions as well as discuss every paper produced. I worked with Lieutenant-Colonel John Shaw. Wing Commander Harry Coleman worked with a Police

superintendent and a Police chief superintendent worked with Major John Cole. Anne Webb, who I nicknamed 'Machine-gun Annie' because of the incredible speed at which she typed, was typist for the whole staff. Warrant Officer Shaun Stringer ran the Secret Registry.

Initially, I felt awkward with John Shaw; not that he seemed

Frank Mussell (standing), Flight Lieutenant Mick McLaren (nearest seated).

John Shaw.

The Operations Co-ordinating Committee of 1969. From left: Air Vice-Marshal Archie Wilson, Mr Ken Flower (CIO), Group Captain Mick McLaren, Major-General Keith Coster, Commissioner of Police, Jimmy Spink.

to be aware of this. He was a graduate of the British Army Staff College, had an excellent command of the English language and indulged in crossword puzzles at every opportunity. I learned that he had been a heavy drinker with a very rude and abusive manner but, having dropped the habit, he had become a much nicer person. Because John Shaw did not talk very much and would not join us for a drink in the small JPS bar after working hours, I did not get to know him too well. However, he was great at delegating all work to me so that he could concentrate on the most difficult of crossword puzzles, which he imported from Britain. I profited from this and learned a great deal from him whenever he went through the drafts I had prepared.

Operations within the country were low key throughout my time at JPS. From a selfish point of view this pleased me because I was not missing out on any excitement and anyway I enjoyed most of what I was doing. One task that proved difficult was briefing Ian Smith. JPS faced onto the Prime Minister's Offices from which Ian Smith appeared on frequent but irregular visits for personal briefings on current operations. No matter how much the staff discussed the matter, we never once anticipated the difficult questions he asked at the end of his briefing and he seldom seemed convinced by the answers he was given.

The only bad incident I recall in this period was when the rotors of an Alouette beheaded RLI Trooper A.J. Johnston. He was the son of Air Force Flight Sergeant Les Johnston and was doing his National Service, which applied to all Rhodesia's young white males. This horrible accident resulted in the helicopter's destruction when it rolled onto its side as the rotors distorted and smashed the airframe. Fortunately, no one else was seriously hurt. The pilot had been unable to place all three wheels on the ground of a narrow riverbed whose bank sloped upwards on his right side. Only the right rear wheel had been placed on a rock whilst the soldiers disembarked. Trooper Johnston went out on the right side but ran up the slope instead of remaining where he was until the helicopter lifted. Great effort had been put into helicopter emplaning and deplaning drills for all Army and Police personnel to guard against such accidents, but not every circumstance could be foreseen.

Unrelated to this incident were some in which small dogs, troubled by the high-pitched noise of helicopters, ran yapping and snapping at the tail rotor that was the source of intense irritation to their ears. At least two that I can remember were chopped to pieces when they leapt up to snap at blades spinning at 2,001 rpm.

Paris Air Show

I HAD ONLY BEEN WITH JPS for about six weeks when summoned to AVM Wilson's office. He wanted to know if I held a British passport. I did not; so he asked if I would be prepared to apply for one since he knew I qualified on the grounds of parentage. I told him that there was no difficulty from my side. However, being a staunch Rhodesian who had developed an aversion to most matters British, the AVM apologised for asking me

to do this but said it was necessary because he needed me to accompany him on a visit to the Paris Air Show. In particular he wanted me to fly the Sud Aviation Puma helicopter to assess its suitability for Rhodesian operations.

Most of my time in Paris was spent with Ken Edwards because we were the only two members of the team of eight who were booked into a middle-class hotel. It suited both of us to be freed from the nightly dinners and high-level meetings with industrialists and French Government officials.

For three days we roamed around the Paris Air Show viewing large numbers of aircraft and visiting all the display stands to gawk at equipment we had only read about. I was alone and admiring a large model of the proposed Anglo–French Alpha fighter when a man of my height came next to me and asked what I thought of the design. I knew immediately that face and voice were familiar but only realised it was Britain's Prince Philip in the middle of answering his question. A little earlier in the day we had watched the British and French supersonic airliners, Concorde, pass each other in their historic first meeting. Prince Philip had come to the air show in the British machine.

On our second day in Paris, AVM Wilson told me to go to the Yugoslav pavilion to collect every bit of available information on the Galeb jet trainer and its fighter version, the Jastreb. He said, however, that I must not let it be known that I was a Rhodesian. Although our French hosts knew exactly who we were it was upsetting to be regarded as illegal undesirables by all the other nations present. To present myself at the Yugoslav pavilion and pose as someone else was quite beyond me. I had received no training whatsoever in this line nor had I time to think it over. Nevertheless, I was under orders and did what I thought best.

My uncle, Wing Commander Bill Smith, was our Air Liaison Officer in Pretoria, South Africa at the time. I decided to use his name and address as my cover. When I introduced myself to the only man in the Yugoslav pavilion, he asked me for my business card. I apologised saying I had inadvertently left my cards in another jacket in my hotel room. He was hesitating over my request for specifications, prices, delivery, and so on when another man walked in. This was obviously the senior man who reached out to shake my hand as the first man hesitated in introducing me, so I helped out by saying, "Peter Petter-Bowyer," then, "Damn it, I'm sorry," and walked out.

Back in the Sud Aviation pavilion I was feeling pretty bad about my blunder when an AVM from the Pakistani Air Force walked over and introduced himself. His skin colour struck me as being too white for a Pakistani but he was such an open person that I used my correct name and let him know that I was a 'rebel' from Rhodesia. He was fascinated and, having told me he had no hang-ups about Rhodesia, ordered coffee so that we could have a chat. I told the AVM how difficult it was to try to act at being someone else and how relieved I was by his attitude towards me. This led me to telling him of my failure with the Yugoslavs. In a flash he called over a Pakistani squadron leader and asked me to brief him on my needs.

The AVM and I talked a great deal whilst awaiting the return of the squadron leader. He wanted to know all about Rhodesia and told me how much Ian Smith was admired in his country. When the squadron leader returned he was laden with everything the Yugoslavs could provide and said how excited they had been over 'Pakistani Air Force interest in their aircraft'. AVM Wilson received the huge pile of documents in a manner that showed he never doubted my ability to acquire them, and I chose to leave it that way—until now!

The purpose of my being in Paris was to fly and assess the Sud Aviation Puma. This was conducted on a freezing cold day with the chief test pilot, Monsieur Moullard. None of us possessed the clothing needed for this unseasonal weather and I for one appeared somewhat overweight with jacket stressed over vests and a thick jersey.

Monsieur Moullard had to curb my handling of the fairly large machine when I attempted to fly it like its baby sister, the Alouette III. Once I became used to the larger cyclic and collective controls I was handling flight in a more circumspect manner and found the Puma was easy to fly and exactly what Rhodesia needed. It was obvious that, being a large machine it could not land in tight LZs, such as those suited to Alouettes, nor could it be put down too close to an enemy position. However, its soldier-carrying capacity equalled that of four Alouettes, which more than compensated for these limitations.

Unfortunately we never did acquire Pumas because, unlike the Alouette that had been produced for civilian use, Puma was specifically designed and designated for military purposes. The UN mandatory sanctions imposed against Rhodesia made the sale of such equipment to Rhodesia impossible—even for the French.

Participating in the Puma test flight were from left to right: Gp Capt John Mussell, Gp Capt Alec Thomson, Wg Cdr Charlie Goodwin, Air Cdr Jimmy Pringle, Mr Trollope (Sec Defence), AVM Archie Wilson, Monsieur Moullard, PB, Wg Cdr Ken Edwards and Henry Ford (Rhotair).

Board of Inquiry

ON 23 JULY 1969 I was summoned to Air HQ where I was instructed to head a Board of Inquiry into an accident that had occurred earlier in the day. This involved an accidental Frantan ignition in dispersals at Thornhill. Senior armourer Ron Dyer and I flew to Thornhill where we met the third member of the B of I, Justin Varkevisser. Varky had made a preliminary investigation into the occurrence and was able to give us background to what actually happened.

Cyril White and Prop Geldenhuys had returned from Kutanga Range with a Frantan hang-up, after all efforts to release the unit in the air had failed. Because the Frantan remained in position during the landing, the aircraft was taxiied into dispersals for a routine manual release. The Station Armaments Officer, Flying Officer Bob Breakwell, was on the flight line to meet the aircraft. With him were armourer Corporals Steve Stead and Ian Fleming. As soon as the Provost parked, but before the engine closed down, the armourers went under the port wing. Having removed the arming wire and ensured that the ground-safety pin was placed in the tail fuse, they prepared to remove the Frantan from the carrier.

Instead of using a stretcher-like carrier to bear the weight of the Frantan before Bob rotated the manual release mechanism, Steve and Ian put their arms under it. This had been done many times before but they obviously did not have a good enough hold because upon release the Frantan tail dropped to the ground. Immediately the fuse fired, thereby bursting the nose casing and spraying burning gel over Bob Breakwell. Because the weapon was static the main body remained intact and retained more than 90% of the napalm gel. Nevertheless some spilled and burnt Steve and Ian as they backed off.

Steve and Ian were extremely lucky to get away with scorched faces and hands. They were also able to shed their smouldering cotton overalls, which had given protection to their bodies. Bob Breakwell was not so fortunate. He ended up with third degree burns to most of his body. Although Bob had copped a heap of burning gel it was from his burning uniform that he received the majority of body damage. Not only did the man-made fibres of his summer-dress uniform melt into his skin, his nylon socks did the same. But for his cotton vest and underpants, which prevented molten fabric from directly contacting skin in critical areas, Bob would not have survived. Nevertheless he was in deep trouble.

Cyril and Prop were still in the cockpit when the Frantan ignited but, apart from suffering a severe fright and intense radiation heat, they were able to avoid the flame by exiting along the starboard wing. The Provost was burned beyond repair and stood forlornly over blackened concrete with blobs of molten aluminium outlining its position.

Bits and pieces of the Frantan fuse were handed over to us with the safety pin still in place. But an important component was missing. This was a soft metal dome that retained the 50mm steel ball that played a vital part in firing the fuse, irrespective of the attitude in which a Frantan impacted ground. The component was eventually located in grass a considerable distance from where it had been propelled by the igniter compound. The moment I had this in my hand I saw the deep indentation that clearly showed the Frantan had rolled slightly before striking tail down against the concrete. But this did not explain why the fuse had fired with a safety pin in position.

The burned Provost.

In my room that night I studied the offending pistol and fuse components comparing them with new ones. Though the details are lost to me now, I recall taking a long time to discover why the fuse had fired. In so doing I established that this could not have occurred had the Frantan not rolled to the precise angle it did. Next morning I demonstrated these findings to Ron and Varky and both were satisfied with what they saw. For the next four days we took evidence and statements from a string of witnesses and experts, including the Rhodesian manufacture of our Frantans.

Ron Dyer and I returned to Salisbury to interview our last witnesses who were Bob, Ian and Steve in hospital. It surprised us to find that all three were in the Lady Chancellor Nursing Home, the place where I was born. For some technical reason, plastic surgeon Mr Owen-Smith preferred to keep his patients in this maternity home.

As a WWII pilot, Mr Owen-Smith had been severely burned in an aircraft incident. His experiences in various hospitals made him determined to become involved with improving management of severely burned people and to undertake the cosmetic repair work that usually followed. I believe that, thanks to his wife's hard work and financial support, he went through university in between many hospital confinements for progressive facial rebuild. He became world-renowned for his ability in his field and we all knew our Air Force fellows were in the best hands possible.

Ron Dyer and I were shaken when we first saw Bob Breakwell. His head was twice its normal size, completely ball-shaped and black. His eyes moved slightly behind burned slits and he could barely speak. His wife Joan was at his side where she remained all the time Bob was in intensive care. But for Joan and his cotton underwear, Bob would not have made it through the long and painful recovery process that followed.

Nextdoor were Ian and Steve, each with heavily bandaged hands, held high in slings. Their facial burns appeared like severe sunburn that made smiling painful but did not limit their ability to speak. Beside them were copious quantities of Castle beer, which they were required to drink through long pipes. They had orders to drink as much as they could manage.

Being told to drink beer for medical purposes was no problem to either of them but the consequence of doing so was the need to urinate frequently. Neither man could help himself and for some reason both had been refused drain lines, so they had no option but to call on the nursing staff to help them as the need arose. For this help they were prepared to wait, often in agony, for one or other of two coloured nurses to show up. They were too embarrassed to call on the white sisters who stood to attention, remained silent and stared into space whereas the coloured nurses talked and laughed all the time.

When we finally had all our facts assembled, I dictated the board's findings and recommendations for Ron to record in his notoriously neat, easy-to-read, handwriting. Three thick files, the hand-written original plus two typed copies, containing supporting photographs and diagrams were submitted to Air HQ. About a month later I received a personal letter from Air Commodore John Deall saying the Commander had directed him to convey HQs appreciation to the Chairman and members of the B of I for an investigation thoroughly well done. So far as I know this had not occurred before, nor had such an inquiry been passed to the Prime Minister and cabinet to demonstrate how the Air Force conducted its inquiries.

Alcora

GOOD POLITICAL AND INTER-SERVICE relationships between South Africa, Mozambique and Rhodesia were being strengthened. The intention was to assess resources and develop plans for mutual support in the face of the mounting communist threat to southern Africa. Angola was obviously Russia's key objective but exploitation of FRELIMO, SAANC, ZAPU, ZANU and other lesser African nationalist parties operating out of safe bases in Zambia and Tanzania were being encouraged through ever-increasing Russian and Chinese assistance by way of arms, advisors and instructors.

Joint military planning between the three countries commenced under the general codename 'Alcora'. Several committees were established for airfields, mapping, radio communications, vehicle mine-proofing and so on. I was a member of the Alcora Mapping Committee. It was during the setting-up phase of Alcora that we received a large contingent of Portuguese political figures accompanied by senior Army and Air Force officers in what was called Exercise Cauliflower. Included in their itinerary was a large-scale demonstration in the farming area near Salisbury to show our operational techniques.

A wide valley allowed good viewing of a 'terrorist group' moving into the area and basing up on a small bush-covered hill in the centre of the valley. This was followed by cross-graining troops that detected 'the incursion' before a hunter-tracker group followed-up leading to a vertical envelopment by heli-borne troops.

Under the shade of msasa trees on a brilliant clear day, the colourfully dressed spectators sat in comfortable chairs on high ground overlooking the demonstration area. Behind the visitors, Army caterers were putting finishing touches to a lavish luncheon in a huge marquee complete with a bar that served every conceivable drink. Brightly coloured mobile toilets were dotted around giving a carnival appearance in this park-like setting. The whole spectacle appeared more like a royal garden party than one intended to deal with the serious business of bush-warfare tactics. There was a great deal of noise and smoke in the final stages of the demonstration and the smell of burnt cordite coming to the spectators on a light breeze generated a strong sense of realism.

At the end of their three-day visit, our Portuguese guests said they had enjoyed a wonderful time and had learned a great deal from us. For this they were thankful and invited the Air Force and Army to send delegates to visit their operational area in the northeast of Mozambique. The offer was eagerly accepted.

It was at this time that Mr Clifford Dupont, until now the Officer Administering the Government, became the Rhodesian President. In 1969 the Rhodesian electorate had gone to the polls in a referendum to accept or reject a new constitution and to establish if Rhodesia should adopt republican status. The Republic of Rhodesia and the Presidential Office came into effect of 2 March 1970. This effectively severed our ties with Britain, or so we hoped.

The prefix 'Royal' was dropped. Along with national and other forces, the Rhodesian Air Force raised its new flag. Air Force rank badges bore the 'Lion with tusk' emblem in place of the crown. Aircraft roundels incorporating the same 'Lion with tusk' insignia replaced the three vertical assegai heads that dated back to 1953.

'Lion with tusk' emblem.

Visit to Cabo del Gado

IN MAY 1970 PETER COOKE and I were selected to visit Portuguese Air Force operational establishments and report on our findings. We flew by Viscount to Beira where we spent a night in the Air Force Officers' Mess. Next morning we boarded a PAF Nord Atlas and flew to Nampula, capital of Cabo del Gado Province.

Here we booked into a mediocre hotel, which was the finest in town. Food and bar services were fair but the plumbing was something else. Peter's bathroom and mine were back-to-back drawing off the same supply lines. Peter started pouring his bath before me so no water flowed when I turned on my taps. Once Peter's bath was full, the taps in my bathroom flowed but the hot water had been exhausted. We were in no hurry, so I decided to order a Manica beer and wait for the water to heat up.

After a while I went to investigate a noise coming from my bathroom. Peter had pulled the plug to empty his bath water which bubbled up into my bath through the drain plug, bringing with it lumps of gooey muck. When his bath and mine reached the same level, both baths emptied very slowly. Eventually I had my bath and the incident amused Peter and me rather than annoying us. But we were both put out by boxes placed next to the toilet bowl into which used toilet paper was to be placed to avoid blocking the drainpipes. This would have been fine had soiled paper from many previous users been removed before we moved in.

The next morning we met Captain Joao Brito who was tasked to fly us around the operational areas in a brand-new Alouette III. We became friends with this good-looking young officer who spoke excellent English and accompanied us throughout our visit. Sadly we learned of his death two years later when he was killed in action in Portuguese Guinea.

Our first place of call had nothing to do with operations. Typically the Portuguese wanted us to enjoy our stay, so we were flown to Lumbo on the coast and driven by staff car down a long causeway linking the mainland to incredible Ilha de Moçambique.

The mainland of Ilha de Moçambique.

Peter Cooke talking with the garrison.

Most of the black women had white mud smeared over their faces to prevent them from becoming 'too black' in the hot sun by day and to make their faces smooth and beautiful at night. With its crystal-clear water, coral reefs, palm trees and pure-white beaches this island should have been a big draw for tourists. Because of the war, however, Peter, Joao and I were the only visitors. Here we booked into a quaint, clean hotel before exploring Vasco da Gama's old fort and other exquisite historic places.

Next day we flew up the unspoiled and breathtakingly beautiful coastline to Porto Amelia. The air base there was set on a long, high promontory with the Indian Ocean on its eastern side and the deep-blue water of Porto Amelia's natural harbour on the western side. Just beyond the runway's northern end lay the narrow entrance to the world's largest natural deep-water harbour. The setting was quite magnificent and stimulating.

We were billeted in tents within the large Army base sited close to the runway and visited the docks and a factory that produced most of Mozambique's famous *castanha de caju* (cashew nuts). The clarity of seawater in the harbour was amazing. The entire keel, propeller and anchor chain of a Portuguese naval frigate lying at anchor more than 200 metres from the docks, though compressed by light refraction, were clearly visible.

The Army garrison commander, a Mozambican officer, told us a great deal about FRELIMO's operations in the Cabo del Gado region and why these differed so much from the situations we knew in Tete. It was because FRELIMO forces in this region were primarily from the warlike Makonde tribe.

The Makonde were of the same Nguni line as the Zulus down in South Africa and our N'debele in Rhodesia. However, during setting up of the international line between Portuguese Mozambique and German Tanganyika in the nineteenth century, no account was taken (as in almost every country during the scramble for Africa) of the Makonde people who became divided by a borderline with no fence. The Makonde were not affected until black rulers in Tanzania and white rulers in Mozambique interfered with their freedom of movement and right to tribal unity.

Just like their southern cousins these Nguni held all other tribes in contempt. The Makonde were only concerned in fighting the Portuguese to re-establish freedom of movement within the region they had always controlled. The border had no more meaning to them than in times before armed men of the FRELIMO movement drew Portuguese forces into their ancestral grounds.

Linking up with FRELIMO had not been for the good of Mozambique in general, but it suited the Makonde to receive free military training and arms of war to expel the Portuguese military. Any hope FRELIMO's hierarchy had for the warlike Makonde to push south beyond their own homelands was wishful thinking. Not only were Makonde interests limited to regaining control of their own ground, they had no wish to have other tribes within FRELIMO using their territory as a transit area. It was largely for these reasons that FRELIMO had been forced to open a second front. Malawi was the preferred country from which to launch this new front but Doctor Hastings Banda's refusal forced FRELIMO into using Zambia and the Tete Province.

Our flight to Mueda was at high altitude to avoid FRELIMO's 12.7mm and 14.5mm anti-aircraft guns that made a low-level approach to the high ground on which Mueda stood too dangerous. Very little habitation existed between Porto Amelia and Mueda and the lack of game-trails suggested that all large game had been shot out. Otherwise the countryside was lovely. A widely dispersed Army establishment with the Air Force base and runway lying just to the south surrounded the small trading post of Mueda. Mueda was linked by a gravel road to the coastal port Moçimboa da Praia in the east. From miles out we picked up the line of this road because the bush had been cleared on both sides to a depth of 1,000 metres.

Joao remained at high level until directly over the runway where he made a spiralling autorotative descent to a gate leading into the air base. The high rectangular earthen wall surrounding the air base gave protection against FRELIMO rocket and gun assaults. Other than covered bunkers for personnel, no overhead protection existed for mortar attacks, which occurred frequently. Pits with 81mm mortars at permanent readiness were sited close to the Officers' Mess.

The entire base contingent was on hand to greet their first Rhodesian visitors and it was clear from the outset that we were going to enjoy typical Portuguese hospitality. Whereas everyone, including cooks and bottle washers, wanted to be photographed with us, only the fourteen pilots on base at the time were permitted to do so.

We were shown to the officers' quarters. These incorporated two dormitories with heavy-tiered steel beds and simple lockers. Loos, showers and hand basins were in between the dormitories in a central ablution block.

Standing: Joao Brito, Base Commander (3rd from left), PB and Peter Cooke. The short pilot in dark overalls standing next to Peter flew the twin Dornier on hairy reconnaissance missions.

I wanted to wash my hands but the basins were so filthy that I started to scrub one clean. When one of the officers noticed this he summoned an airman to do the job. From then on this basin remained spotless in a line of otherwise filthy ones and, in Portuguese, was marked 'Visitors Only'.

The toilets were just as I had expected—bloody awful. Apart from the seats and bowls being filthy, the boxes that were provided for used toilet paper were full to overflowing. Peter and I nicknamed them 'skid boxes'. To avoid using the loos, I attempted to go off into the bush beyond the earthen wall but was disallowed from going through the security gate because, apparently, FRELIMO snipers often operated close by.

Other than the ablutions, the base was clean, the food was fantastic and the Portuguese were as friendly as ever. Having Peter and me around was great for those wanting to practise their English. This was both heavy going and amusing. One officer complained of his sleep being regularly interrupted by a colleague who suffered 'bad night horses'.

On our second night at Mueda my sleep was interrupted at around midnight by the sound of heavy explosions. Artillery shells then howled low overhead from the Army camp and exploded in an area just beyond the end of the runway as FRELIMO mortar bombs exploded in our base. I leapt out of bed so fast that I cut open my forehead on the steel bar of the bunk above me. I was first in the crude mortar bunker with Peter Cooke right behind me. The Portuguese officers were obviously used to the noise of artillery and incoming mortar bombs because they stopped to light cigarettes in the lighted passageway leading to the dark bunker then moved slowly down the steps into cover and safety.

No serious damage was caused in this short exchange and I

was the only casualty on base. However, we had seen the burnt remains of two Harvards, one twin-Dornier, an Alouette III helicopter and a store showing that FRELIMO attacks had been successful in the past. At Mueda it was very obvious that the Portuguese Army's war was separate from the Portuguese Air Force war. Not one Army officer was seen at the air base during our stay and we only got to visit the Army side because Peter and I requested to be taken there.

Mortar-damaged Portuguese fuel bunker.

We were called to an operational briefing following lunch on our first day. I cannot speak for Peter Cooke, but I was in an alcoholic haze following a welcoming lunch that included too much Manica beer, wine and *aguadente*. The black-on-white map on the Ops Room wall looked as if it had been produced in the previous century because it was so basic with limited contour information and river-lines appeared only to approximate their true paths. Photographs taken the previous day by a Dornier recce pilot of a camp assigned as target for the following morning were handed out to six pilots. Shadows of trees and the angle at which the photographs had been taken made me realise that all had been taken during one close range low-level orbit.

A red arrow on the map pointed to the target. This was about fifty kilometres northwest of Mueda on the eastern bank of a prominent river. Destruction of the makeshift shelters (bashas) that covered a relatively small area under trees was to be by napalm. We learned that take-off was for "06:00 as usual, weather permitting". Peter and I were told which pilots we were to accompany to observe the action.

The fact that 06:00 was the standard time for first sorties shook us because all FRELIMO camps must surely be abandoned by then as a matter of routine, particularly following low-level photo-recce sorties. As it happened, low thick radiation fog delayed take-off to around 08.30. Whilst we waited, breakfast was served on a verandah next to our billets. It consisted of a bowl of light-coloured soup in which a fried egg floated. A Portuguese bread roll (*pao*) and a lump of butter came on a side plate. Ignoring how others tackled this unusual meal, I put the fried egg into my buttered roll, consumed the soup then ate the delicious egg roll.

The rear cockpits of the Harvards in which Peter and I flew were almost totally stripped of their instruments. An inspection of other rear cockpits revealed a similar situation, the instruments having been removed to replace unserviceable ones in front cockpits. The Portuguese pilots nicknamed their Mk52 Harvards 'F110' because they climbed, cruised and descended at 110 knots. Immediately my pilot was airborne in the third position he turned steeply to port and, following the lead aircraft, orbited the airfield and Army base until over 2,000 feet above ground. This was to avoid flying near the lip of the high ground where FRELIMO's anti-aircraft guns were sited. The guns were considered to be too dangerous to be taken out by the Air Force and the Army passed them off as an air problem. Unbelievable!

I had not been in a Harvard before and enjoyed flying with the hood rolled back because it made photography easy. As we were approaching the target there was excited babble between the pilots with much screeching in earphones due to overlaid transmissions. This was so different from the limited crisp procedures of my own force. The aircraft were positioned in long line astern with canopies closed when a steep dive was made well short of the target for low-level deliveries of two napalm bombs per aircraft.

Looking along one side of the cockpit past pilot and aircraft's nose, I saw the first napalm tanks ignite in trees. About half a kilometre ahead the lead pilot was already in a climbing turn starboard to look over his shoulder to pass correction to the next in line. Both napalm bombs from the second aircraft landed with a splash and sent lines of flaming fuel along the surface of the river on which they landed.

I watched closely as we dropped our tanks and saw bashas in the area where they ignited. It was only possible to get an idea of the camp size when we pitched up in a climbing turn to watch following strikes land in the target area. Out of twelve bombs released only the latter eight were on target. We made one orbit climbing for height and noted that about one third of the bashas were burning, adding white smoke to the columns of black smoke from napalm gel that was still burning in patches along lines of fading red flame. No person or anti-aircraft fire was seen.

Back at base a steep spiral descent over the Army camp placed us on short finals for the runway. The aircraft turned off about two-thirds of the way down the runway's length directly into camp through the rolled-back security gate, which closed behind the sixth aircraft.

At 10:00 we declined the offer of whisky. At 10:30 the offer was repeated and again declined. At 11:00 we accepted but asked for Manica beer instead. By lunch at 13:00 I was feeling on top of the world and this was heightened by wine for each of three courses, the main one being piri piri prawns.

One of the Venturas taxiing out for the attack we witnessed.

Photo by Peter Cooke of PB in back seat of Harvard after the attack.

The recce Dornier with 37mm Sneb rocket pods.

Lunch ended with *aguadente*. It was only then that Peter and I learned that we were to accompany a recce pilot on a post-strike assessment flight.

We flew in a Dornier piloted by a short stocky officer with a permanent smile on his round merry unshaven face. Peter sat next to him but I had to stand and brace myself using the front seats as anchors because there was no seat in the rear. My legs had to be set wide apart either side of a crude sprung-loaded door through which target markers and other small items were dropped. It ran along the centre of the rear fuselage floor and required very little pressure to open. Should I step on it or fall down, I would immediately fall free of the aircraft. I did not like this one bit but could not see any real problem so long as I retained my braced stance; but I did not know what lay ahead.

Three PV1 Venturas (twin-engined bombers) came into our

view as we approached the target. They were flying long line astern at about 6,000 feet and we were at 2,000 feet. We saw them enter into a steep dive and release six 500-pound bombs from around 3,000 feet. All the bombs exploded in an area of large trees, creating visible shock-waves that radiated outwards from the bright orange flash of each explosion. The resultant bangs that reached us in the noisy Dornier were dull; like the thud of footballs bouncing on concrete.

As the third Ventura pulled out of his dive our bonny pilot bunted into a dive that had me hanging on for dear life. He levelled out with high 'G' that almost collapsed my legs. The pilot then flew below the overhang of high trees either side of a long curved passage through a forest, firing pairs of 37mm Sneb rockets as he made a casual visual inspection right and left into forest where the bombs had exploded.

My eyes were wide open with fear of striking the overhanging branches or being hit by shrapnel from the 37mm Sneb rockets exploding just ahead of us. I saw nothing else in that first pass. Two more 'dicing with death' low passes were made through the same passage terrifying me no less than the first but at least I saw something of what our pilot was interested in. It looked pretty dark under the forest of huge trees that flashed by and many bashas were evident along the entire length of our run. It surprised me that not one was burning and no soul was seen.

We accompanied the Harvards on further attacks but declined offers to ride with the crazy Dornier pilot again. Nevertheless we were interested to know why such a dangerous method of checking out strikes was necessary. The answer was simple; the Army had no interest in assisting the Air Force to establish the effectiveness of its airstrikes. Unbelievable!

The most interesting aspect of our visit to the Army base was the huge vehicle park, half of which was a graveyard for many destroyed vehicles. Serviceable vehicles, mainly Berliot and Unimogs, were adorned with a variety of emblems. One Berliot had affixed to its front grill the longest pair of ox horns I have ever seen. Its driver was a coloured man who spoke good English and was happy to tell us about 'Hell's Run', the route from Mueda to the coast.

It took a whole day for each resupply convoy to reach Moçimboa da Praia. The following day was used to load and the third day to return to Mueda. Receiving double pay to compensate for the danger they faced on every trip were volunteer drivers who made the round trip on a regular basis. Officers were required to remove their rank tabs so as not to draw FRELIMO sniper attention to themselves. The aggressiveness of the Makonde operating against the Portuguese convoys had been enhanced by devious techniques taught them by the Chinese instructors in Tanzania. We were given two examples.

A Portuguese Army boot, filled to overflowing with chicken blood, had been placed in the centre of the road with a trail of blood leading off beyond the verge. The lead vehicle stopped to investigate. The investigating soldier then hurried down the line of vehicles to show the boot to the convoy officer who wore no rank insignia. BANG! The sniper had waited for the officer to be identified then took him out with one shot.

A particularly nasty incident involved a horrible trap the Chinese had dreamed up. The lead vehicle in an unusually large convoy was brought to a halt by a command-detonated mine. Typically the convoy bunched up as all following vehicles came to a halt. All the soldiers and drivers had debussed to take up defensive positions when a ripple of small explosions ran down the edge of the road along the entire length of the convoy. These small charges released millions of angry bees from the plastic bags in which they had been held captive. Not one person escaped multiple bee stings that resulted in the death of a huge proportion of the men due to their distance from medical facilities. We were told that the 'bee ambush' was responsible for Mozambique's greatest number of casualties from a single incident.

Separate written reports submitted by Peter and me on our return to Rhodesia were surprisingly similar to those submitted by six Rhodesian Army officers who also visited Mueda. In particular the information we had gleaned emphasised the seriousness of the threat posed to Rhodesia from FRELIMO's second front in the Tete Province.

Back in JPS I asked John Shaw one day if I could submit a paper I had written on my personal opinion of what should be done about the Mozambique situation. He read the draft and burst into laughter saying, "This will get the OCC pretty excited." Nevertheless, he agreed that he and I should present it to Mick McLaren. Mick did not read far before he asked angrily what right had we to say the Portuguese would collapse, and who the hell were we to suggest that Rhodesia and South Africa should take over friendly Mozambique's territory south of the Zambezi. The paper found its way into the shredder but I retained a copy for many years beyond the time the Portuguese did finally collapse. We were given a not-too-unkind telling-off and asked never again to waste time on work not tasked by OCC. John Shaw took the telling-off with a fixed expression on his face and never let on that I had written the paper.

Medical hitch

I BECAME CONCERNED ABOUT A NASTY-LOOKING black growth on the mid-upper thigh of my right leg. If subjected to sunlight when swimming it would subside and turn red but it became bigger and blacker in no time at all. I was sent by the Air Force doctor to see a specialist who would not even allow me time to go home for pyjamas and toothbrush but committed me to hospital immediately. The specialist surgeon told me the growth appeared to him to be a malignant melanoma that had to be removed without delay. He explained that he would have to remove the entire upper muscle from knee to hip together with the glands in my groin. "Don't worry, you should learn to walk again within nine months." I was horrified, believing this spelled an end to my flying career.

When readied for theatre and very drowsy from the pre-op drugs, a very brash individual accompanied by two nurses came to my bedside. He demanded to see my decorations. In my dopey state I said, "I don't wear decorations on pyjamas," whereupon Doctor Gregg, a radiologist, pulled back the bed sheet and pointed to my leg. He inspected the growth from every angle and reaching for a marker pen said, "If you do have a problem here I do not want to have to deal with a large wound." He then drew a line around the spot in the shape of an eye, saying this was the limit of the muscle section that would be removed down to bone level. He departed saying, "Do not be concerned, you will fly again."

In a small passage outside the operating theatre I had been waiting for ages on a wheeled trolley when a matron passed by and slapped a file on my chest. More time went by so I decided to see what my file said. I was amazed to find that I was Mrs Somebody-or-other and that I was about to have a hysterectomy. I called a passing nurse and, showing her the file, offered to prove I was not a woman.

When I was coming around from the anaesthetic, I felt my leg and groin and was delighted to find a relatively small dressing where Dr Gregg had done his artwork. For the next three days I walked without pain or limp going up and down the passageways visiting people, three of whom I knew. Squadron Leader Rob Gaunt was in for cartilage removal, Reverend Frank Mussell, father of Frank and John, was in for cancer treatment and Flight Lieutenant Paddy Rice was suffering the indignities and pain that accompany a piles operation.

It was only when the dressing was removed that I realised I had a really deep hole in my leg that had been filled with some special gunk. When I got up to walk it hurt like hell and no matter how I tried I could not help limping. Laboratory tests proved the growth to be benign—an enormous relief.

I had not been out of hospital long when Beryl and I attended a 'Roman Night' at the New Sarum Officers' Mess. It was one of those lovely parties that went through the night, ending with a superb pre-dawn breakfast in the dining hall. At the end of this Christine Nicholls, just out of hospital with leg in plaster, Rob Gaunt with leg in plaster and myself heavily bandaged were all lifted onto the table to give the gathering reasons for sporting apparel 'unbecoming to our Roman dress'. Rob Gaunt had started speaking when fire hoses were turned on us. The whole place was awash with everyone slipping around before the culprits were overpowered and the hoses switched off. With Roman togas and flimsy dresses soaked through, everyone ended up in the swimming pool where we were treated to some unusual diving exhibitions.

Dawn was breaking when we heard the pounding of hooves and saw Phil Schooling galloping through the trees with cloak flying as in a Roman movie. When we all repaired to the bar, Phil brought his horse to the counter. The floor was slippery from wet bodies which caused the horse to slip, panic, fall and vacate its bowels before being led to a safer environment. I ended up at the doctor's rooms to have the hole in my wound mended because its over-stressed stitches had failed. But, all in all it had been a great party.

Aircraft accidents 1970–1971

MY ROUTINES IN JPS WERE interrupted from time to time to retain currency on helicopters and conducted Final Handling Tests on pilots trained by Hugh Slatter and Harold Griffiths. Norman Walsh handed over No 7 Squadron to Squadron Leader Gordon Nettleton in early 1970 but his command terminated in a freak accident on 1 July 1970.

Lieutenant Mike Hill (left) and Squadron Leader Gordon Nettleton (right).

Gordon had been 'under the hood' on instrument flying practice with Flight Lieutenant Mike Hill as his safety pilot. At the end of the flight a radar talk-down onto the grass runway 14 was completed and, so far as could be judged, control must have already passed from Gordon to Mike. At this point observers saw the helicopter pitch up and roll sharply to starboard. The roll and pitch continued in a tight descending path that ended when the aircraft impacted belly down on the main road verge against the airfield security fence. Both these fine men died instantly.

Assisted by French experts from Sud Aviation, the Board of Inquiry realised that mechanical failure of the cyclic controls system would have resulted in a roll to port so only pilot action could have been responsible for the starboard roll. This being so, there could only be one conclusion; Mike was suffering from 'flicker vertigo' before he took control.

Flicker vertigo in helicopters is an unusual condition caused by rotor blade shadows that are seldom noticed. Put very simply, flicker vertigo is to do with synchronised frequencies in which the frequency of shadows perceived by the eyes, consciously or subconsciously, divide perfectly into the brain's functioning frequency to produce a whole number. This upsets normal brain function causing mesmerism and haphazard muscular movements as in an epileptic fit. Such a condition is known on roadways where the shadows of trees interrupts direct sunlight during early morning and late afternoon. Motorists can go off a roadway when impaired by flicker vertigo.

On 28 October 1970, Flying Officer Al Bruce was on a pairs formation exercise when his Hunter started venting fuel. He turned for Bulawayo Airport but his engine flamed-out short of the runway leaving him with no option but to eject. Al suffered bad bruising of the spine but otherwise he was fine. For the Air Force, however, the loss of our first Hunter FB9 was a major blow, reducing the fleet to eleven aircraft.

Keith Corrans and I were at Voortrekkerhoogte (previously Roberts Heights) in Pretoria for most of 1971, undergoing the South African Air Force Staff Course. In the latter stages of this eleven-month course we were shaken by news of the deaths of Flight Lieutenant Alex Roughead and Air Lieutenant Robertson.

On 16 November 1971, a formation stream take-off of Canberras from Salisbury turned out right to climb through cloud. Alex's aircraft did not appear when the other Canberras broke out above cloud. Following a short air search, wreckage of his aircraft was located and an inspection of it showed that Frame 21, which connects the airframe to the main spar of the mainplanes, had failed, resulting in loss of the starboard wing.

Prior to this terrible accident, hairline cracks in Frame 21 of all B2 Canberras had been a cause for major concern and they were monitored regularly. The RAF was aware of this problem caused by work hardening of the aluminium castings. This had been overcome by improved material and design for later Canberras, but Rhodesia was stuck with the MkB2 model.

Almost daily, Master Technician Brian Goodwin was seen on the flight-line with black material wrapped around his head to protect him from the ultrasonic emissions of his non-destructive, crack-detecting equipment that tested Frame 21 sections. Whenever a crack was located there was need to carefully 'blend out' the offending area to stress-relieve affected sections. Why Alex's aircraft suffered catastrophic failure of the Frame 21, having only just been declared free of cracks, was the subject of much conjecture but it was eventually concluded that Alex must have inadvertently exceeded the airframe's 'G' limit in turbulence.

Canberra pilots and navigators were already recording time spent in every condition of every flight and a 'fatigue factor' was being applied to each of these conditions. I do not recall the fatigue-factoring figures but they ranged upward from something like 1.5 for normal cruise at 250 knots in turbulent conditions to 30 for the speed range 330–350 knots. After applying the appropriate factor to the time spent in each flight condition, the 'factored flight time' was deducted from the number of airframe hours remaining. This substantially reduced our Canberras' life spans even though Frame 21 cracks were occurring at progressively reducing frequency, thanks to successful stress-relieving procedures.

Exercise Blackjack

BY NOW THE AIR FORCE Volunteer force had increased considerably with VR Squadrons having been established at Bulawayo, Gwelo, Salisbury and Umtali—more were to follow. All VR personnel had undergone considerable field training in operations management, air movements, security and so on. Air HQ was pleased with progress and the fact that so many regular pilots and airmen had been freed to concentrate on their primary roles. But there was need to test the whole service in a countrywide exercise codenamed 'Blackjack'.

A long-range navigation exercise went badly wrong for the crew of a Canberra flying in the northwest sector. Due to

Alex holding the Jacklin Trophy awarded to 4 Squadron in 1965. To his left are Bruce Smith and Prop Geldenhuys. Behind him are Henry Elliott, Tony Smit, PB and Ian Harvey.

weather and unreliable NDB aids, the crew became uncertain of their position and were forced to eject when their fuel ran out. A very uncomfortable night was spent on the ground where the widely separated pilot and navigator experienced the terror caused by lions roaring within yards of their locations.

The exercise was a great success in so far as proving the VR. On the flying side it had also been a success save for the loss of the Canberra and the exercise finalé. This finalé included a series of airstrikes on the Army Weapons Range at Inkomo. Almost every weapon-carrying aircraft was involved, all approaching from different directions to conduct independent squadron attacks on targets assigned by grid reference only. Mistakenly, Air HQ invited top brass from Army HQ and Police General Headquarters to witness these strikes. The position selected as an ideal observation platform for the ground party was the wall of a small dam that would obviously be one of the reference points some pilots would need to confirm their targets. It so happened, however, that there were other dams of similar size close by.

The Hunter and Canberra strikes went off fine. 4 Squadron was next in line but had the big brass diving for cover when the formation erred by attacking a point very close by. The strike leader had selected the correct point relative to the dam wall—but this was the wrong dam!

All the spectators were up on their feet laughing nervously and dusting themselves down when they were forced to dive for cover again as Vampires unleashed rockets close by. Never again would Air HQ dream of exposing other services to exercises intended to test the force. There were many red faces that day but, when the crunch came, Air HQ would have every reason to be proud of all squadrons' performances.

Staff College

IN LATE JANUARY 1971 KEITH Corrans and I were sent to South Africa to attend the South African Air Force Staff College (SAAFCOL) course. Prior to Rhodesia's Unilateral Declaration of Independence, our officers, accompanied by wives and children, underwent Staff College training at RAF Bracknell in Britain. RAF staff courses were designed to run for twelve months with compulsory time-off every weekend for family affairs and rest.

Although the subject matter of the South African course was taken directly from the RAF, a different approach had been adopted. The American technique of pressurising officers was applied by compressing the British course into ten and a half months. This meant having to work seven days a week with only two free days during the entire course; consequently heart attacks amongst older officers undergoing SAAFCOL were not uncommon. Because the South African course was less than twelve months, Rhodesian wives and families were not permitted to accompany husbands, so Sue Corrans, Beryl and the children had to stay home.

For me it was a gruelling experience, particularly as I had been given only three months' notice to learn Afrikaans having only learned French at school. Keith had studied Afrikaans at Churchill High School so he was better prepared than me. Although we had been led to believe that half of all lectures and presentations would be in Afrikaans and half in English, it turned out to be 73% in Afrikaans. This placed me at a distinct disadvantage, particularly when advanced Afrikaans was being spoken so quickly that I could not even pick up the trend of what was being said. Fortunately, Keith and I were allowed to write appreciations and papers in English.

Because we worked all day every day and late into the night, Keith and I decided to take in a movie every Saturday to get a short break from never-ending studies and tasks. Only once did I go out for a night on the town and this turned out to be a costly error. A notoriously naughty SAAF pilot and an equally mischievous SA Army major invited me to accompany them for dinner at a posh restaurant. At this dinner I drank too much and was introduced to the art of eating carnations and other flowers that decorated our table. Following a good meal and having had more whisky than I was used to, I helped these crazy fellows swallow every one of about twenty goldfish swimming in one of the restaurant's beautiful fish tanks. Not caring that our shirtsleeves were soaking wet right up to our armpits, we scooped out the highly prized Chinese Fantails whenever nobody was looking. These we swallowed head first and washed them down with a slug of whisky.

The sensation of a panicking fish swimming down one's gullet before thrashing around for a short while in the stomach is not one I would have chosen. On that night, however, I had no difficulty in meeting the unspoken challenge. Next morning things caught up with us when the restaurant owner pitched up at the college demanding replacement of his prized fish.

The Afrikaans language was a major problem for me even though I could usually follow the gist of lectures. But there were occasions when I became lost the moment professors and other high-speaking lecturers got past the greeting 'Goeie môre here'. Following such lectures I was surprised to find that my South African colleagues had experienced great difficulties in understanding new words and phrases of the still-expanding Afrikaans language. It was during one such presentation when I noticed that Major Blackie Swart dealt with his boredom in a very strange way.

Blackie was a very tall, slim, balding man who sat in front and to one side of me. With his right hand he took hold of his right eyelashes and, pulling gently, stretched the eyelid forward. When his eyelid sprang back, Blackie brought his fingers to his lips and made small sweeping motions. If he felt a lash tickle his lip he placed it on a matchbox lying next to his pipe on the broad wooden arm of his chair. This he repeated until no more loose lashes came away, whereupon he changed hands to subject his left eye to the same treatment. Next he turned attention to hairs in both ear-holes and the pile of hairs on his matchbox became visible to me. Then came the hairs in his nostrils. These were subjected to fiercer treatment as hand and head jerked in opposite directions. Wiping of eyes to remove consequential tears followed every successful extraction.

When our lecture programme showed that one particular professor was returning, I asked my colleagues if they had noticed what Blackie did when he was bored. None had but all eyes were on him as he went through his strange ritual. None of us dared look at another whilst the lecture was in progress for fear of breaking into uncontrolled laughter.

PB receiving Staff College graduation certificate from a very tall South African Air Force Commander, Lt–Gen Vestér.

Sue Corrans and Beryl flew to South Africa to be with us for our end-of-course party. All men were dressed in full mess kit and wives wore long evening dresses. Beryl, dressed in a lovely sari, drew disparaging stares from the older women but my SAAF coursemates and their young wives thought she looked wonderful. Before the party ended Major Paul Nesser had somehow persuaded Beryl to bid the senior officers' wives 'good night' in Afrikaans. His strange sense of humour was typical for his breed and I had suffered from this on a few occasions. But I was not aware of what had gone on until I noticed the horrified expressions on the faces of the ladies as they passed Beryl. I shot across and asked her what she was saying.

"Leave me alone. I am saying 'good night' in Afrikaans."

"Yes Beryl, but what is it that you are actually saying?"

"I am saying 'harn kark', which is Afrikaans for 'good night'."

"Damn it Beryl, not only are you pronouncing the words incorrectly, the words '*gaan kak*' mean 'go shit yourself'."

It was an enormous relief to get back to Rhodesia and have time to spend with my family.

Debbie and Paul were equally pleased to be home on their six-week Christmas break from boarding school.

Following the successful completion of my staff course, I had naturally expected to be posted into a staff position in Air HQ. So it was something of a surprise to learn that I was to take command of No 4 Squadron at Thornhill.

Deaths of Munton-Jackson and Garden

I WAS STILL ON LEAVE WHEN, on 17 January 1972, Air Lieutenant Guy Munton-Jackson and Flight Sergeant Peter Garden were killed in a very unfortunate and totally unnecessary helicopter accident. From the time Alouettes first arrived in Rhodesia, warnings given by Sud Aviation never to fly these aircraft at night had been ignored. None of our high-ranking officers had flown helicopters themselves and they did not seriously accept that momentary loss of control could lead to airframe failure in flight. For ten years our helicopters had been flown at night with only minor accidents occurring during landings, so the Sud Aviation warnings had continued to be ignored until these men lost their lives.

Two helicopters were tasked to fly from New Sarum to Thornhill to be available from first light to assist police against mobs that had started rioting in the Gwelo townships late that afternoon. It was known that the rioting would resume early next morning.

Storms and heavy cloud in the vicinity of Gwelo forced both helicopters to enter cloud in turbulent conditions. On instruments and with no way around the storm clouds, both pilots asked for a radar-controlled approach into Thornhill. The first helicopter arrived safely; the second disappeared off the radar screen. Guy Munton-Jackson had almost certainly got into difficulties and over-controlled on cyclic causing the main rotor blades to pitch back severely enough to sever the tail boom.

The Board of Inquiry into this accident was conducted by experienced helicopter pilots who recommended that, henceforth, helicopters should only be flown at night in clear weather conditions with a distinctly visible horizon. Air HQ accepted the recommendation and issued the appropriate Air Staff Instruction.

Chapter

7

No 4 Squadron

MY POSTING TO 4 SQUADRON was a huge disappointment because I had hoped one day to be given the helicopter squadron. There was another reason for my disappointment—No 4 Squadron was considered to be 'a penal squadron'. The reason for this unfortunate reputation was obvious. The squadron operated the least inviting aircraft—Trojans and Provosts. Upon completion of OCU training, the best PTC pilots went to jet and transport squadrons and the balance were posted to 4 Squadron. For any young pilot coming off jets, the step down to piston aircraft was bad enough but, mistakenly, it appeared to them that their flying capabilities were in question because 4 Squadron's flight commanders were senior instructors.

When I reported to Air Staff for briefing, DG Ops, Group Captain Dicky Bradshaw, congratulated me before passing me on to D Ops, Wing Commander Sandy Mutch, for a detailed briefing. I could not see the point in being congratulated for what I perceived to be a low-grade posting until Sandy's briefing helped me see my situation in a better light.

Officers returning from Staff College had always been posted to Air HQ, but an increasing security threat required that 4 Squadron's pilots become highly proficient in visual reconnaissance work. No serious preparation had been made to meet this need because there was nobody able to instruct pilots in the art. Since I was the only man in the force who had shown any interest in visual recce, and had a few successes to prove it, the Air Staff concluded that there was no alternative but to give me the squadron. Sandy Mutch also gave me the sop that I had been a particularly successful 'A' Flight commander on 7 Squadron and 4 Squadron was deeply in need of good leadership.

This was somewhat flattering, but I had serious doubts about being the right man for the job. There were two reasons for this.

Firstly, my entire bush-fighting experience was on helicopters, which seemed to me to be so much more worthwhile and exciting than the fixed-wing activities I had observed in the field. Secondly, Flight Lieutenant Gordon Wright was the current 'A' Flight commander on 4 Squadron.

Flight Lieutenant Gordon Wright.

Peter Cooke with Air Commodore Archie Wilson discussing newly acquired 37mm Sneb rocket system.

Gordon and I had been students together on No 10 SSU. Unlike me he was a natural sportsman who always struck me as possessing a stubborn and difficult nature. But then Gordon had reservations about working under me because, not knowing how often I had broken the rules, he mistakenly believed that I was a man who worked 'strictly by the book'. He was man enough to let me know his concerns, making it easier for me to express how I viewed my new job and how I was counting on his support. Happily our fears were misplaced because, from the start, we clicked.

Top Row: WO 1 'Spike' Owens (Sqn WO) Flt Lt
Gordon Wright ('A' Flt Cdr) Sqn Ldr Peter Petter-
Bowyer (Sqn Cdr) Flt Lt Rob Tasker ('B' Flt Cdr).
Standing: Sgt Cox R, Sgt Sinclair D, Sgt McCormick
H, Sgt Britton J, A/S/L V Culpan, A/S/L A W.
Wild, A/S/L SM Caldwell, Air Lt John Carhart,
A/S/L Mike Litson, A/S/L Tony Oakley, A/S/L
Dave Rowe, Flt Sgt Bruce K, Sgt Jelliman N, Sgt
Smit C. Squatting: Sgt Forrester N, Sgt Menhenick
C, Sgt Mare N, SAC Bartlett A, SAC Jenkins D,
Cpl Tubbs P, SAC Keightley B, SAC Louw P, SAC
Singleton R, SAC Wilkinson B, SAC Parker M,
Sgt Charles R, LAC Besant P, Cpl Badenhorst B,
LAC Steyn M, LAC van der Merwe J. Sitting: Sam,
Philip, Karata, Ayton. Inserts: Sgt Jarvie H, Flt Lt
Bruce Collocott, Air Lt John Blythe-Wood.

During my first days with 4 Squadron I felt distinctly uncomfortable. Having been away from Thornhill for a long while, I had lost touch with junior officers and technicians and knew only a handful of my men. To me there seemed to be a depressed atmosphere, one totally lacking in spirit. This surprised me because, notwithstanding the 'penal squadron' tag, Squadron Leader Peter Cooke followed by Squadron Leader Peter McLurg had both led what I understood to be a cheerful unit. However, so far as I can remember the next in the line was Flight Lieutenant Peter Knobel, as acting OC, who lost all of 4 Squadron's experienced pilots on various postings. Flight Lieutenant Gordon Wright, again in an acting OC position, followed Peter. Together with Rob Tasker and Bruce Collocott, Gordon had found himself in a particularly difficult position with a bunch of puppy pilots with no experience whatsoever.

The building in which the squadron was housed was set way back from the flight lines. This was unacceptable to me because the squadron building that had been vacated when the Canberras moved to Salisbury had been taken over by Station Equipment Section. My first priority was to have the situation reversed and within four weeks we were on the flight line in our freshly painted building. This in itself lifted spirits.

During my first month with 4 Squadron I was in need of a haircut and visited Mac the barber in Gwelo. Mac only knew one cut, which left me almost bald. Reaction to this was "Oh boy, we are in for a tough time with this boss!" It was certainly not the image I sought and I wondered how I might weld the personnel into a spirited group of men determined to make 4 Squadron great. Beryl gave me the lead on how to do this.

I instructed all squadron members, including wives and children, to gather for an open-air spit braai at a quiet spot at White Waters just twenty kilometres from Thornhill. When Beryl and I arrived there at around 10:00, we found a team of four technicians basting a whole impala carcass on a spit over deep coals. These guys had been working since first light and

were already pretty plastered, pouring as much beer over the roasting carcass as down their throats.

About eighty people gathered under lovely trees with colourful chairs, umbrellas, shade tents and tables laden to bursting with food all beautifully set out. Children clambered over the domed granite hill against which we were gathered and everyone got to know everyone else. Beryl insisted on being called by her first name and not Mrs Petter-Bowyer, which endeared her to everyone. I acquired the name 'Boss PB' which I much preferred to being called 'sir'. Thereafter the prefix 'Boss' was applied to a number of officers who were popular with junior pilots and technicians.

The roasted impala, superbly tasteful and tender, was wholly consumed but the rest of the food spread proved to be more than ravenous youngsters could manage. Beer and wine flowed freely and everyone enjoyed the best open-air party I can remember. When the squadron's personnel reported for duty at 06:30 on Monday, I knew I was leading a totally changed team of men. There was sparkle in their faces, spring in their step and the mischievous spirit that continued beyond my three years with 4 Squadron had been unearthed.

My good friend Flight Lieutenant Rob Tasker with whom I had served as an instructor on 2 Squadron, was 'B' Flight Commander. He ran me through Provost re-familiarisation flights. Having lost the stomach for fuel vapour, spinning and aerobatics I felt really ill after the first two flights.

Gordon Wright conducted my conversion to the Trojan. This was an aircraft that was easy to handle in flight but one that tested one's abilities when it came to engine handling and limit flying. The engine was too low-powered for the Trojan's bulky airframe and thick high-lift wings, which severely limited payload. Increasing and reducing power was not a simple matter of opening and closing throttle control. With every change of power or engine rpm the fuel mixture had to be adjusted to prevent power loss. This meant that any change in engine setting necessitated rapid movements between throttle, pitch and mixture control, which took some time to master. I found no joy in flying the Trojan, preferring to fly a Provost at every opportunity. Gordon, however, enjoyed instructing on the Trojan because, of all our aircraft, it was the most challenging one to handle proficiently.

Provost.

My first solo in a Trojan ended with a forced landing on the Gliding Club strip at Moffat Airfield because of partial engine failure with insufficient power to reach Thornhill safely. At first I thought the problem was engine mismanagement on my part, but it turned out to be a fuel feed problem.

The Trojan was a very noisy machine because its propeller tip speed was supersonic in the higher rpm range. Take-off performance at Rhodesia's high altitudes was marginal and in flight the aircraft was slow. Because of these characteristics the Trojan attracted unkind clichés such as—having constant power with variable noise—noise generated by five pistons clapping for the one doing all the work—reliance on the curvature of the earth to get airborne—the only aircraft that received bird strikes from the rear.

The latter saying came to mind one day during operations when I was conducting visual reconnaissance. I was making a gentle turn to port when a Bateleur eagle overtook me on the inside of the turn just a couple of metres off the wing tip. Through the open window I shouted. "Bloody show off! I hope your eyes are watering."

Because of the Trojan's power limitations and the need to operate in and out of short runways, Gordon placed great emphasis on preparing pilots for short-field operations. We flew long low-level flights, hopping from one airfield to another, sometimes stopping over for a break in Bulawayo where three or more Trojans crews met for lunch in Gordon's favourite Chinese restaurant. This was considered a real treat and emphasised just how much I missed flying versatile helicopters with frequent luncheon stops at farms and hotels or simple picnic breaks in beautiful surroundings.

Whereas we usually made a low-level inspection-run of every remote runway before each roller landing, Gordon told me not to worry about this procedure when we were approaching the airstrip at Guyu. On very short finals we both realised that the grass was far too long for a safe landing but, because it took so long to power up, the aircraft came to ground as full power was achieved. Fortunately we had not lost too much speed, but drag on wheels and airframe threatened to overcome the thrust of the propeller that was slicing through thick grass. We were fortunate to lift off with absolutely no runway remaining. Whereas Gordon was very annoyed with himself, the experience was important to me. When added to all of Gordon's work it fully prepared me for many strange and often frightening flights to come.

Learning recce

As soon as I was proficient on the Trojan, all my attention turned to learning visual reconnaissance in a fixed-wing aircraft. I had little idea of how to go about this but persuaded myself that, since man is a creature of habit, his routine movements must give a picture of his activities. I felt that if I fully understood the pathways of ordinary tribesmen who had no need to obscure their movements or presence, it should be possible to detect those made by men in hiding. I already knew something about aerial tracking and how to find terrorist and civilian camps in Mozambique, but all of that had been done at low level.

Flying at 1,500 feet above ground, because it was considered to be high enough for safety from enemy ground fire, I spent hour after hour studying every pathway and disturbed area over hundreds of square miles of tribal territory. I watched people moving along pathways, found where women bathed and laundered clothing along rivers and even watched people move into cover near their homes to attend to their toilet needs. Slowly I picked up similarities that helped me understand what I was seeing and how to use the sun to illuminate very faint pathways. Herds of cattle in the tribal areas were usually too large for the ground that supported them, resulting in hundreds of cattle paths which ran in parallel lines. Though clearly visible, they were not as well defined as human paths and had many distinctive shallow-angled linking lines—something like railway yards.

Of specific interest to me were small short paths close to huts that followed erratic courses into tree cover. At the end of each pathway there were barely discernible patches of bare ground that I had already established were toilet points. But it was noticeable that one group of paths had four bare patches at their ends whereas others had only three. I guessed that the former were women's toilet paths and the latter were those made by adult men. At most villages there were also patches of haphazard trail lines that crossed over each other in a jumble. I concluded that these were the loo paths of children.

When I thought I had a fair understanding and was reading ground well enough, I made a specific study of one small group of huts that were close to a road and not too far from Thornhill. I attempted to determine the exact numbers of men and women living there and identify the purpose of every pathway leading from these huts. Having decided that there were three adult men and five women, I motored to the village to check this and other aspects of my assessment.

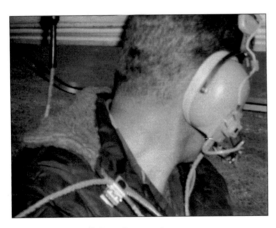

Hours spent studying the terrain.

When I reached the place, I drove off the road and stopped just short of the village. In a loud voice I called "Kokoko" which is the polite way of calling for attention to be invited in. Kokoko represents the sound of knocking on a door. The old man who emerged from one of the huts turned out to be the local *sabuku* (keeper of Government record books). As is customary, we talked about the weather, cattle and crops before coming to the purpose of my visit. I asked the old man if he had seen an aircraft circling above his kraal earlier in the day. He said he had. When I told him I was flying that aircraft he told me I was not telling him the truth because he could see that I was much too big to fit into that tiny *ndege*. Fortunately there was a vehicle parked at another kraal about two kilometres away. I told him that though the vehicle looked small it was farther away than I had been above him. Since he knew he could fit into that vehicle he was able to accept that the aircraft must have been big enough for me.

He asked what I had been doing flying over his kraal, so I

told him and said I had come to seek his help to confirm my assessment of his family's routines. The pathways the family used to go to the river, the location of the women's bathing place and that used by the men were correct. We walked along the paths to confirm all of this. Communication lines to drinking water, to maize fields, to the local store and the community school were all spot on. I was pleased and asked if we could turn to the toilet areas used by his family. Immediately he said this was not for men to discuss; his wife would have to help me with such delicate matters.

The *mbuya* (grandmother) came to us full of smiles. Her husband told her all about how this white man could fit into the small *ndege* they had seen flying above. He pointed to the parked car way off to prove his statement. He told of our walk along the paths, telling his wife how I had said what each path was used for even before we followed it. Exclamations emitted from the old lady with every statement her husband made. He then told her that she must help me with a matter I would explain before hurrying off to the safety of his hut.

The *mbuya* was amazed by what I wanted to know and even more so when I pointed to specific areas saying I judged these to be toilet area for five women, four men and a number of children. She wasted no time and led me down the path used by one of her daughters. At the end of its short run, I saw fresh evidence of a recent visit at one patch, one was clean and two showed that previous wastes were all but cleared by busy ants. With the old lady's help, I learned why there were four positions.

Bowel movements for the average black person occurred at least twice a day because of their high-bulk maize diet. Two squat points used today would be cleaned by ants within twenty-four hours so only four points were needed. I asked her about the matter of urinating. She said this always occurred at the same time as the bowel movements. In-between needs were met on the previous day's patches to "help the ants finish their cleaning-up act". Having said this, the *mbuya* gave a very graphic demonstration of how women, standing with legs set wide apart, pulled their pants to one side then let their fluid flow. Screeching with laughter, she said how much easier this was for men.

I was taken down three more toilet paths used by two other daughters and a daughter-in-law. However, there was absolutely no question of going down the path she used. So I had been right; five women. The men's lines, three of them, were checked out. Sure enough there were only three cleared patches for which the old lady had a simple explanation. Because the men were often away from the village during the day, three points sufficed and all in-between urinating occurred along the path, not at the squat points. The children's toilet area was just as it had appeared from the air—a shambles requiring close attention to every step one made.

Now I had a fair idea of the basics but needed to know more about patterns that developed when humans occupied ground temporarily. Army bush camps, farm workers felling trees for tobacco barn boilers and grass cutters reaping thatching grass were some of the activities that helped build a picture of fresh human disturbances in open grassed and bush areas. Remembering how pigs had confused me during Op Cauldron there was need to find a way of distinguishing between game and human pathways. Wild pigs move about in an erratic manner often doubling back and crossing over their own tracks. Sharp kinks in their path lines were easily recognised and they seldom used a pathway twice.

Fresh elephant feeding paths and human transit lines through grassed areas gave me some difficulty until I passed the shadow of the aircraft along them. In doing this I noticed that human paths, and those made by wild pigs, left a continuous chevron pattern pointing in the direction of movement. Elephants on the other hand created a series of half-moon patches with undisturbed grass in between these patches. The explanation was simple. Humans hardly lift their feet when walking and draw grass blades forward, then bruise and flatten the stems under foot. In green grass a single human leaves a faint but detectable trail. When others follow in single file, the visible intensity magnifies rapidly until it stabilises when six or more men have passed along the same line.

On similar ground, elephants tended to move about individually in random patterns. They only follow each other in single file when the matriarch cow leads the herd from one area to another, in which case jumbos prefer their established pathways.

Rhino were seldom seen in numbers exceeding three. Their trails through green grass were indistinguishable from elephants but I could not see them presenting any difficulty to recce pilots. I found that the only barely discernible difference between established elephant pathways and those of humans was that those of elephants, over flat ground, exhibited smoother and longer curves than those made by humans. The width of elephant paths is greater than that of humans but this is impossible to judge from height.

On hillsides, human paths followed the most direct route, often ascending steeply, whereas elephants and all other game follow shallow inclines with sharp turn-abouts like hairpin bends on a mountain roadway. In flattish country it was obvious that humans used elephant routes wherever these coincided with their direction of travel. In fact it was for this reason that ZAPU and SAANC had used elephant paths before they were detected at the start of Op Cauldron.

These issues added together made it clear that, in remote areas populated by elephants, detection of terrorists would only be possible from the air wherever they set up bases. In such cases I expected that radiating toilet paths would be a give-away and since a base had to be close to water the areas to be recced should be relatively small, particularly in the dry season.

Buffalo herds created patterns identical to domestic cattle and most antelope used buffalo or elephant paths when commuting to water. Otherwise they left no visible trail whatsoever. Apart from elephants, rhino and to a lesser extent hippopotamus, I concluded that game paths should not mislead pilots searching for terrorists.

After two months I was ready to start teaching pilots and technicians but I realised that such training as I could give would have little impact unless it involved working over terrorist affected areas. It was obvious to me that what I had been doing would be far too boring for most men and their enthusiasm would soon wane. So, at the beginning of May, I approached Air HQ for permission to conduct recce training inside the Tete Province of Mozambique. This was eventually cleared with the Portuguese authorities with the proviso that all flights remained south of the Zambezi River and west of the Dague River.

This was a much smaller area than I had hoped for but it encompassed one sector that I believed ZANLA was likely to use in the future. For the time being I felt it would be a good training ground because FRELIMO was known to be operating in the block.

Aloe Festival

BEFORE CLEARANCE WAS GIVEN TO train in Mozambique, the squadron paid its annual visit to Umtali on 4 May 1972. The town in which I had schooled had adopted No 4 Squadron and always invited the unit to visit for the weekend of its annual Aloe Festival. Our direct involvement was limited to cocktails with the mayor and city councillors, providing a formation flypast over a colourful parade of floats along Main Street and

Umtali, surrounded by mountains. The town centre is behind the photographer who faces up Main Street.

to crowning the Aloe Queen at the Aloe Ball; the highlight of the festival. Otherwise we were guests of the Town Council who treated us like royalty. 4 Squadron spirits were high and a particularly naughty element had developed amongst the technicians. At the centre were Sergeants Henry Jarvie, John Britton and Phil Tubbs whose every move needed to be closely monitored.

Wives and girlfriends accompanied most officers but the technicians elected to go stag. The unmarried technicians pooled money for a 'Grimmy prize' to be awarded to the one who dated the 'grottiest-looking grimmy' for the Aloe Ball. This idea of 'grimmies' was one adopted from RLI troopers. At the end of a party, the man who had brought along the grottiest (least attractive) grimmy (grotty female) received the Grimmy prize. John Britton decided he could win this prize if he dated Henry Jarvie in drag.

Dressed in a badly fitting three-quarter-length floral dress, lipstick almost to his nostrils and wearing way too much eye shadow and rouge, Henry completed his attire with thick brown stockings and heavy boots. He certainly was the ugliest-looking partner whose actions and antics had everyone in fits. But he and John Britton were discounted from the Grimmy contest because Henry was judged to be grottier than grotty.

As the fanfare heralded the Aloe Queen's entry into the huge ballroom, slim Henry and big John moved ahead of her approach-line to the throne. Henry pirouetted neatly revealing hairy legs above knee-length stockings; his right index finger in John's raised left hand. John moved in smooth steps with feet splayed in exaggerated ballet fashion, straight-backed, right arm bent with hand on hip. They continued down the length of the aisle before Henry leapt into the air with arms spread and head back to land horizontally in John's outstretched arms.

Most people found this impromptu ballet display unbelievable and very amusing, but not so the organisers who were badly put out as it had drawn attention away from the Aloe Queen's grand entrance. Soon enough the Aloe Queen was seated on her throne and, by the time I had crowned her, all was forgiven and everyone enjoyed a grand evening.

Grimmy prize winners.

ZANU and ZAPU activities

THE WARS BEING FOUGHT IN the Portuguese territories, like Rhodesia and South Africa, were to prevent liberation movements, inspired and supported by communists, from taking control by force. We all knew that the Soviets planned to form a bridge of states across Africa from which to drive for their ultimate prize, South Africa. Should they succeed the Soviets, and possibly the recently involved Chinese, would have access to the vast mineral wealth of southern Africa and control of the strategically important sea route around the Cape of Good Hope.

As in other African countries, the emergence of Rhodesian liberation movements was made possible by white politicians' actions and laws that placed many constraints on the black people. Contrary to the glowing history lessons given to my generation of Rhodesia's pioneers, our black folk were presented the contrary view that their territory had been taken by political intrigue and force of arms before laws were introduced to ensure their subservience. Whereas the N'debele and Shona people attempted to reverse this situation during the Matabeleland and Shona rebellions of 1896 and 1897 they failed in the face of superior weaponry and white rule was established.

Nevertheless the country developed rapidly to the mutual benefit of all Rhodesia's citizens. An impressive infrastructure was already in place when the African National Council (ANC) was established in 1934 with the intention of gaining black political inclusion in government. This should have worked to everyone's advantage, judging by later constitutions drawn up by Rhodesians. These all made unimpeded progress to majority rule a clear objective. However the new world force, communism, had been created following the Bolshevik Revolution. This new order, the Union of Soviet Socialist Republics, considered white governments in Africa to be a major stumbling block to its stated intention of gaining total domination of the entire world.

The communists turned full attention to acquiring control of the mineral and oil reserves of Africa and the Middle East that, combined with those of the USSR, was key to gaining the economic subservience of Europe, the Americas and the Far East. This was approached on two fronts. One worked southward from the USSR and the second was to develop a 'bridge across Central Africa' from which to launch southward to the Cape of Good Hope. The objectives of the second front were to be achieved by a 'divide and rule' philosophy which was to undermine the white governments created by Portugal, Britain and Belgium and promote black nationalist forces to oust them.

The Soviets were fully aware of black inexperience in managing any country they may acquire but counted on this inexperience to bring about situations in which they would move in later and take control without a shot being fired. By using a combination of approaches that enhanced African desire for power, the Soviets exaggerated existing grievances that blacks had against whites and cleverly engineered many new ones. Whether existing or created, the Soviets knew they could get the black folk to take up arms and fight 'wars of liberation' intended for the ultimate benefit of the USSR.

Thirty years after the formation of the ANC by Aaron Jacha, and following the formation, amalgamation and fragmentation of a number of black parties, the first act of communist-inspired terrorism occurred when the 'Crocodile Gang' of the Zimbabwe African National Union (ZANU) murdered Petrus Oberholzer.

White Rhodesians in general held the black folk in high regard, hoping in time to elevate their status, lifestyle and opportunities as the infrastructure expanded and the economy strengthened. But to achieve this meant retaining government in responsible hands. We realised how important it was to deny black power-seekers opportunity to destroy our beautiful country in the manner we could see occurring in newly independent African states to our north. History has proven that we were fully justified in attempting to do this. But instead of lessening burdensome laws on the black folk, more were added, making it increasingly easier for nationalist parties to associate with communist ideals and the communist states themselves. This suited communist planning perfectly. Yet for most Rhodesians talk of communist objectives was not taken seriously. Before we came to properly understand the reality of the threat, we had tended to think our government a bit paranoid in 'seeing communists under every bush'. When reality eventually caught up with the likes of myself, we were not to know that Russian communism would eventually flounder but we knew for certain that any black nationalist government would destroy the economy and infrastructure of the country.

Nowhere in Africa was more done to elevate the black people within the limits of Rhodesia's financial resources. At the time there were twenty blacks to every white, placing too great a burden on the drivers of the economy, the whites, who nevertheless wanted to provide good schooling and services to everyone. The great majority of black people were subsistence farmers living as they had for centuries. In less than eighty years their numbers had blossomed from around 400,000 to over six million due to white medicines and the curtailment of tribal wars. The population explosion was way larger than the rate at which schools could be provided and this angered many young blacks who neither accepted nor understood the realities of the situation. Attempts to elevate the economy to improve schooling and create new jobs for black people involved bringing in more skilled white immigrants to the country. But sanctions and mandatory military service for all white male adults had reduced immigration to a trickle by 1972.

ZAPU and ZANU both claimed to have the majority following of black Rhodesians yet both organisations resorted to destroying the very infrastructures intended for the good of the people they claimed to lead. Schools were burned down and cattle dips were either destroyed or the tribesmen were instructed not to observe Rhodesian Government efforts designed to protect their primary measure of wealth, cattle, from deadly tickborne diseases. Contouring of agricultural land to prevent soil erosion also received negative attention.

Bored and unemployed youths were excited into destructive activities that turned youths against their parents and parents against their children. This resulted in the banning of ZAPU and ZANU with many leaders being imprisoned or escaping into political exile. Despite their early efforts ZAPU and ZANU exiles, having turned to arms, became deeply frustrated when they realised both urban and rural folks preferred the benevolence of their white government to fighting for a vote that could not be eaten, sold or screwed.

Inside the country the majority of black people were content, showing no desire to leave home for military training in foreign lands before returning to fight a war they neither wanted nor understood. Consequently ZANU and ZAPU resorted to press-ganging Rhodesian youths who had gone to Zambia for higher education. Many black expatriates returned to Rhodesia, allowing our intelligence services to draw up detailed lists of those outside the country. Special Branch also took opportunity to send trained agents to Zambia, posing as students, to be press-ganged into ZAPU and ZANU ranks.

Josiah Tongogara of ZANU was a prime mover in bringing about the changes that led him to become overall commander of the military arm of ZANU (this was ZANLA—Zimbabwe African National Liberation Army). He headed the fourth ZANU intake at Itubi Training Camp in Tanzania where he showed his determination to improve training and redirect ZANU's military efforts towards something more worthwhile than had been achieved by party politicians. He realised from the outset that prospects for joint action with ZAPU were dim. ZANU was essentially a Shona organisation and was trained by Chinese communists, whereas ZAPU were N'debele-led and Russian-trained.

Joshua Nkomo was the leader of ZAPU and was generally, but mistakenly, hailed by the leaders of Africa to be father of the Zimbabwean (Rhodesian) nation. In consequence, President of Zambia, Doctor Kenneth Kaunda, being related to Nkomo by marriage, favoured ZAPU and paid little attention to its rival ZANU. Initially FRELIMO also favoured ZAPU to keep in Kaunda's good books in a quest for unrestricted use of Zambia as a rear base. This is why FRELIMO repeatedly offered ZAPU free passage through Tete to reach the Rhodesian population, believing implicitly that Joshua Nkomo was the true leader of all Rhodesia's black people. But ZAPU kept stalling on this offer.

ZANU's Tongogara faced enormous problems that any

lesser leader would not have overcome. He knew that only through improved performance in Rhodesia could ZANU gain the support of African leaders and receive financial assistance from the OAU's liberation funds. However, having led his organisation into improved preparedness for military operations, he faced difficulties in transiting men and materials through hostile Zambia. This was overcome with FRELIMO's secret and somewhat reluctant connivance to allow ZANU men and equipment, dressed and assigned in FRELIMO's name, to transit Zambia.

Even as late as 1970 ZANU was still committed to the 'no win' routes across the Zambezi River where Rhodesian forces blocked all hopes of turning in an improved performance. Tongogara realised that ZANU's salvation lay with FRELIMO for unimpeded access via the Tete Province, which FRELIMO now controlled, to the black population that straddled the Rhodesia/Mozambican border.

A meeting between FRELIMO and ZANU eventually took place in mid-1970 when FRELIMO agreed to assist ZANU. This was because FRELIMO had finally realised that ZAPU was not going to accept the long-standing offer of assistance. Despite Nkomo's claims, FRELIMO had made contact with the Shona people inside Rhodesia and learned that ZAPU had absolutely no support outside of N'debele territory. Also established was that ZANU enjoyed much wider support in Rhodesia. Yet of greater importance to FRELIMO was ZANU's obvious and urgent desire to prosecute a war of liberation in the manner FRELIMO supported, understood and practised—the Chinese communist way. Nevertheless co-operation started on a small scale.

Tongogara sent four of his senior men to report to FRELIMO's Jose Moyane, Commander of the Tete Front. They were integrated into FRELIMO's ranks for the purpose of gaining first-hand knowledge of FRELIMO's war against the Portuguese, their control of local tribesmen, their handling of recruits, caching of arms and so on. The lessons learned were passed back to Tongogara who sent increasing numbers of his men to learn from FRELIMO.

A few men within ZANU's ranks had received Russian training before crossing over from ZAPU to ZANU. This caused differences in opinions between the advocates of Russian and Maoist philosophies. In a nutshell the Russians believed in direct confrontation for a quick result whereas the Chinese approach accepted that a long period was needed to adequately prepare the ground for widespread insurrection and protracted armed action. Whereas the Russians relied on arms, the Chinese relied on people.

FRELIMO settled the matter by insisting that only the Maoist approach would work. ZANU were given directions on how they had to prepare their firm support base amongst the people for recruits, security, intelligence and the subsistence needed to support large numbers of fighters on a continuous basis over a protracted period.

In the meanwhile many ZANU men were being prepared for combat at Mgagao in Tanzania. This new training base had replaced Itubi in 1971. It was in this year too that our doubts about Portuguese forces' ability to contain FRELIMO were confirmed when Rhodesian forces came into contact with FRELIMO forces along our border during an operation codenamed 'Lobster'. By early 1972 ZANU was ready to make its first reconnaissance probes into Rhodesia, FRELIMO having secured the ground right up to the border and having also concluded preliminary arrangements with some tribal chiefs inside Rhodesia.

Special Branch detective Section Officer Peter Stanton, who I would come to know quite well, had warned of ZANLA's imminent arrival in the northeastern sector of Rhodesia. First indications from sources inside Zambia showed that ZANLA would be probing on a wide front. Then civilians coming over our border seeking refuge from FRELIMO domination told Peter that ZANLA reconnaissance units were based near the border east of Mukumbura. In late March they named one location as Matimbe base. This was confirmed when the SAS (Special Air Service) mounted an operation that resulted in a number of kills. All the bodies were dressed in FRELIMO uniforms but documents confirmed most were ZANLA men.

Documents captured at Matimbe base revealed two important things. One was that indoctrination of headmen within Rhodesia had already succeeded in obtaining willing recruits to swell ZANLA's numbers, thus eliminating any further need to press-gang for recruits in Zambia. The other confirmed that ZANLA intended to infiltrate on a wide front to spread Rhodesian forces and interrupt the smooth running of the economy by forcing an increase in the call-up of Territorial Army soldiers.

External recce training

4 SQUADRON'S RECCE TRAINING AREA WAS limited to ground west of where the SAS had contacted ZANLA at Matimbe Base. I had a fair idea of what we would be looking for in Mozambique but felt apprehensive about teaching my men whilst learning the ropes myself. Although I was only expected to teach pilots recce, I decided that the technicians should participate to involve them directly and to see how they took to the task. To make things manageable, separate periods of ten days were allocated to each of two halves of the squadron.

Following introductory flights to study tribal patterns near Gwelo, I took the first half of the squadron to Kariba to compare animal paths with those of humans. We then moved to Gutsa Airfield sited on the west bank of the Musengezi River at the base of the Zambezi escarpment and forty-six kilometres south of the Mozambican border.

Air Force Volunteer Reservists under Flight Lieutenant Geoff Fenn, who had his faithful old servant 'Sixpence' in tow, had already prepared Gutsa base for us. In addition to the tented accommodation, Geoff had set up an operations tent with radio and telecommunication facilities. The camp lay under tall mopani trees between the runway and an established Army base. At the time D Coy RAR under command of Major Bruce Hulley was there.

It was the start of winter so the weather was pleasant and relatively cool. This was important because, in the very hot conditions of the valley during summer, it would not have been possible for the Trojan aircraft to take off with full fuel and four men. As it was we had to turn right when airborne to avoid the high banks on the eastern side of the Musengezi River and climb along the course of the river until high enough to turn for Mozambique.

Gutsa base camp.

On our first night at Gutsa I noticed abnormal drum-beating activity both close and far off downriver. I asked Bruce Hulley what this was all about. He said that in all his previous stints at Gutsa no such drum-beating occurred other than during customary beer-drinking parties every Saturday night. Yet during this spell there had been many drums beating every single night. The abnormal activity worried him and he had made this known to Army HQ.

One night the drums stopped their perpetual throbbing because, at the request of the local tribal chief, Bruce had undertaken to shoot a troublesome crocodile. The beast had lived in a large pool on the Musengezi River for as long as the chief could remember and it had been responsible for killing a number of people. Recently the dreaded reptile had dragged a young girl screaming into the river. She was never seen again.

I accompanied Bruce and two of his men to the large boomerang-shaped pool in which the crocodile lived. We were all armed with FN rifles and Bruce had a powerful headlamp plus four hand-grenades. The intense beam of light tracked back and forth over the water and along the reeds of the far bank searching for crocodile eyes that reflect light like bright

stars. There was no sign of the brute so Bruce lobbed two widely separated grenades into the water. As the grenades went in, I slipped on the steep slope of the high bank overlooking the pool and very nearly went over the sheer drop into the water just as the dull thuds from the grenades mushroomed in the water. My slide was checked in time to see the huge crocodile's eyes light up in the beam of torchlight midway between the turbulent patches of water. We all fired together hitting the croc several times. When spray from the hail of bullets settled there was no sign of the brute, which was never seen again. Next night the drums were beating again.

4 Squadron needed to make detailed reconnaissance of almost 3,000-square nautical miles of territory. This was divided into five overlapping sectors and each crew was allocated to a sector that was changed every day to allow everyone to work every inch of the entire area twice. I flew with all crews in turn and from the sixth day roamed the entire area in my own aircraft checking on previous day reports and picking up on any information that had been missed.

Within the first four days the Ops Room map had every path, village and field plotted. The fields were marked accurately to show size and shape for future comparison. Villages were marked in two colours. One colour showed occupied villages with the number of huts in active use whilst the other colour recorded the position and size of abandoned villages.

Once the primary and obvious information had been acquired, we commenced a search for hidden habitations. This resulted in the location of a handful of hidden camps complete with bashas, which were judged to be for civilians in hiding. They were difficult to see from our operating height, which I had set at 2,000 feet above ground. All crews had been briefed that, under no circumstance, were they to descend below this height. In the event that a crew located something that needed a second opinion, they were either to call me over or ask another crew operating close by to do so.

During the morning of the seventh day, with three days still remaining before the second half of the squadron was due to arrive, John Blythe-Wood and David Rowe disobeyed my instruction. These two young officers and their two technicians located a place in a line of thick riverine bush where faint human paths (they proved to be toilet paths) suggested that there was a camp hidden under the trees. Rather than bother me, they decided to make a low pass to get a close look under the tree canopies.

I was about forty-five nautical miles away when John Blythe-Wood called to say that he was returning to base. His transmission was distorted and unusually weak but I gathered a fire had been put out, the turbo-charger had failed, level flight was being maintained and he would reach base safely. I was not concerned because John's voice, though faint, was calm. Some time passed before I heard him call finals at Gutsa; so I put the matter out of my mind and continued my work.

It was only when I returned to base that I learned that these

Dave Rowe (left) and John Blythe-Wood (right) with Roger Watt.

youngsters had been shot up as they made their fast run past the hidden camp. They had all spotted the bashas under the trees before seeing men firing at them from close range. One tracer round entered the aircraft and set fire to clothing and equipment, filling the cabin with smoke before the technicians extinguished the flames. The turbo-charger had been put out of action and only excess speed had allowed John to gain sufficient height to stagger home on limited power. Two tyres were burst though they did not know this until they touched down on landing.

Other holes in the aircraft proved that at least one machine-gunner understood how to aim-off on a moving target. Dave Rowe had a hot expended round fall into his lap but otherwise all four crewmembers escaped injury by inches. Air HQ over-reacted to the incident by ordering termination of our training with instruction for me to report to Air HQ immediately.

At Air HQ I stood up for the pilots and told my seniors that I could see no advantage whatsoever in subjecting two young officers to a court martial for disobeying my instructions. I felt that they had displayed the same curiosity as any one of the Air Staff members might have done in the same circumstances. A court martial would serve no greater purpose than the harsh lesson of the incident itself and it would certainly be bad for morale throughout the squadrons. The Air Staff agreed but nine long weeks passed before approval was given to proceed with training because there had also been some questioning of my decision to include the squadron's technicians in recce training. So again I had to go over the importance of upholding morale and a need to explore their recce potential

When I returned to Gutsa with the second half of the squadron, drums still pounding away every night and on my very first recce flight I was astounded by the changes that had occurred during our short absence. For the first five days I flew with each crew as before. All information was plotted

onto plastic sheeting laid over our original map to highlight what had changed, and where. Of particular interest to me was the emergence of four routes that started miles apart on the Zambezi River and converged in stages to a common point a few hundred yards north of the border on the west bank of the Musengezi River. Parts of these routes had been plotted during the first recce training period but the clarity and continuity of the pathways showed unmistakably that they were now carrying heavier traffic. My crews were picking up more small camps with bashas this time round, mostly tribesmen in hiding, because the dry winter conditions had substantially reduced bush cover.

Technicians at Gutsa. The high ground is a low section of the Zambezi escarpment range which in winter is dry and bare of leaf.

Having flown with every crew, my interest turned southwards into Rhodesia where I was able to follow the single route out of Mozambique southward along the Musengezi River. The route alternated from one side of the river to the other and passed Gutsa Airfield on the opposite side of the river before climbing steeply up the escarpment to where St Albert's Mission lay a short distance behind the lip of the high ground. I was totally convinced that ZANLA terrorists were active right there.

Bruce Hulley was still at Gutsa though his company was about to be replaced. We had long discussions on my findings and Bruce said his RAR troops had noticed increased traffic on the pathway along the river but it all seemed to be from barefooted tribesmen. Nevertheless Bruce said that his troops knew something was amiss because the locals were not behaving in the co-operative and friendly manner of the past.

Since his area of responsibilities lay on the valley floor, Bruce would not release troops to go up to St Albert's Mission to check out that area. He said, however, that his own observations had been passed to Army HQ and that Special Branch, who had also found things greatly changed, had made this known to their own HQ.

On completion of our training I went to Air HQ to make a presentation of 4 Squadron's findings. Although all the information signalled daily was plotted on the Ops Room map, it failed to convey what I was able to give verbally with emphasis and expansion on details. In particular I stressed the fact that terrorists were active in the St Albert's Mission area of the Kandeya Tribal Trust Land (TTL) posing an immediate and serious threat to the Centenary farmers bordering on that area.

AVM Archie Wilson took the matter up at a meeting of the OCC and suggested that the Army Commander should get troops into the suspect area to check it out. However, because neither the Army Commander nor the Head of CIO knew of any reports from their own men, the matter was held over for the Prime Minister's forthcoming National Defence Council Meeting.

At this meeting the results of 4 Squadron's reconnaissance findings were presented, with stress given to my belief that terrorists had been active in the St Albert's Mission for some time. The Army, Police and CIO agreed that the area should be checked without delay. But the Prime Minister wanted to know why the Department of Internal Affairs (INTAF), which was responsible for all matters in the TTLs, had not reported this matter. In answer, he received assurances from Secretary of INTAF, Don Yardley, that no such activity could possibly occur without INTAF's knowledge and a guarantee was given that not one single terrorist was anywhere near the Centenary farming area.

I was again summoned to Air HQ where I was told what had transpired and was given a serious telling-off for, "reading into the ground situations that simply do not exist" and for, "causing unnecessary alarm and despondency." But then on 21 December ZANLA's future commander, Solomon Mujuru (also Mutizwa and pseudo-named Rex Nhongo), led an attack on Altena Farm from his base camp close to St Albert's Mission. When it was known that he and his ZANLA followers had been there indoctrinating the locals since May, no word was said about 4 Squadron having given ample warning of their presence five months earlier. By that time there was nothing to be gained in saying, "We told you so!" But it was bloody maddening!

I was in Air HQ a couple of weeks after the Altena Farm attack and was leaving the building when Air Commodore John Moss saw me and invited me into his office. Throughout my service time I had limited contact with him. Of medium build, good-looking and very popular with everyone, this silver-haired officer was well known for his even temper and softly spoken manner. All Air Force officers knew that John Moss was a raconteur of note, possessing that amazing ability to tell stories and jokes for many hours without pause. It was not that he enjoyed his own voice but simply that he could hold the attention of willing listeners and entertain without apparent effort.

John Moss obviously knew I had given accurate warning of ZANU's routes and location and that all had been ignored. He did not exactly apologise but asked that I commend my squadron for a good performance and assure the men of better support in the future.

Preparing for bush ops

BACK AT THORNHILL I SET about improving 4 Squadron's operational techniques and equipment. One idea I had, though unrelated to counter-insurgency warfare, was to assist Police identify ringleaders during mob riots. Rioting in Gwelo's townships had continued throughout the day after the death of Guy Munton-Jackson and his technician when their helicopter broke up at night in bad weather when positioning to support the Gwelo Police. 4 Squadron pilots told me how they had been able to see the ringleaders quite clearly from the air, but these fomenters of trouble were always farthest from Police forces, stirring up trouble from behind the rioters. Once rioting ceased the police were unable to identify the ringleaders.

I decided to produce a tank to carry liquid dye that could be dumped on riot leaders to make their identity known long after rioting ceased. I sought help from Thornhill's medical staff and selected Brilliant green because it was reputed to be harmless and very difficult to wash off skin and clothing. So far as I remember, Brilliant green was a water-soluble dye used to track bloodflow through the human body.

Once the tank I designed was working satisfactorily, I looked for opportunity to test the system on a live target to confirm delivery technique and the longevity of the dye. The Brilliant green crystals, being water soluble, turned the water in the tank to a dark blue–green colour with no mixing problems. So I placed the mixed liquid in a forty-four-gallon drum suitably elevated to fill the tank quickly when it was secured to the floor next to the rear door of a Trojan.

I was returning from a routine flight when I noticed a gang of prisoners working on a taxiway close to the threshold of grass runway 13. Gwelo Prison Services provided Thornhill with a limited labour service and had a small prison at Thornhill for the minor-offence prisoners who were about to become my target. The dump tank was fitted to a Trojan, chop chop, and charged with the liquid dye. I then got airborne on the pretext of needing low-level circuit practice. Once airborne I manoeuvred to pass over the prisoners in what would appear to the Air Traffic Controllers to be a low tight turn onto the runway. As the men came almost abreast of me on the outside of the turn the dye was dumped. Control Tower immediately called to say a shower of green liquid had been seen to fall from my aircraft. I acknowledged this by saying the fluid had been dumped deliberately and that I was returning to the squadron.

I got into my car and drove over to the prison gang. Every prisoner was covered in green on one side of his body and all had copper-gold hair. Unfortunately the two uniformed prison guards, whom I had thought safe, were also green from cap to boots. I cheered them all up with two large bottles of Coke and set off to visit the Prison Superintendent in Gwelo to let him know what had happened. I told him exactly what I was trying to achieve and offered to pay for the cleaning or replacement of uniforms. He said there was no need for that because he was delighted that in future it would be possible to mark riot leaders. He agreed to let me know how long it took to remove dye from the uniforms of both guards and prisoners. I told the Superintendent that I was more interested in the length of time the dye remained visible on skin and hair. Ten days later I received the answers. Seven launderings for uniforms, three days to restore hair colour and four hours for skin. I was pleased with the results but no riotous situation ever developed to put the system to the use for which it was intended.

Next I produced a simple, cheap projectile to simulate the clumsy flight of Frantans and teargas so that we could make low-cost simulated attacks outside approved weapons ranges. This was a 100mm Kaylite foam tube filled with sand and white powder with flat discs taped on each end. The armourers called them BUBS, which simply stood for Break-up bombs.

It was already clear that there was going to be a need for 4 Squadron to undertake accurate marking of targets for jet-strikes. 37mm Sneb rockets provided the best option to cater for adequate standoff range, accuracy and reasonable cost. However, we needed to introduce highly visible smoke into these small rockets to clearly show their points of impact. To achieve this, the armourers produced aluminium extension-tubes filled with white phosphorus. These were screw-threaded to fit between the rocket motors and their high-explosive heads. It was pleasing to find that the accuracy of these extended rockets was better than standard ones and that the increased weight only required a small sight adjustment to cater for increased gravity drop.

Delivery of 37mm Sneb rockets from Provosts was well tried but an attack profile had to be developed for the Trojan. John Blythe-Wood and I flew together to develop a profile that would allow a steep delivery from 2,000 feet without over-stressing the airframe during recovery from the dive. I discounted medium dive angles because it would mean having to pass too low over hostile targets.

It took only one flight to find a suitable profile. Keeping the target visible just to the left of the flight line, we ran up until the target was almost at right angles to the aircraft. At this point the nose was pitched up to around forty degrees, followed by a full aileron port roll through 180 degrees, assisted with plenty of rudder.

John Blythe-Wood.

This allowed the nose to pitch down into a sixty-degree dive commencing at low speed. Minor corrections brought the collemateur sight onto the target and immediately a pair of Sneb rockets was fired. Quite unlike the powerful whooosh of 60-pound rockets, Snebs went away with a sharp crack. Accuracy was excellent and recovery from the dive was gentle. Having tested this method of marking targets a few times, John taught the profile to all the squadron's pilots.

To give very close armed-support to the Army in bush-warfare conditions, we needed to develop slick, uncomplicated procedures that soldiers under stress could use to bring a pilot's attention to the precise position of any target he was required to strike.

FAC (Forward Air Controller) training for Army officers learning how to direct heavy jet-strikes in conditions of conventional warfare had done wonders in bringing the Air Force and Army close together. We now had the opportunity to build on this by introducing different techniques required in bush warfare. For this GAC (Ground to Air Control) was introduced.

For GAC we needed to have a thorough understanding of each other's situations and difficulties. When flight trials started, Army officers flew in the strike aircraft (Provosts and Trojans) to experience and appreciate air perspectives and pilots joined Army on the ground for the same purpose. At Kutanga Range aircraft could land after each GAC run. This facilitated quick debriefing, re-planning and switching of personnel. Procedures and techniques were modified and improved until GAC procedures were considered ready for operations.

On the ground the commander of an Army callsign would have a good idea of an enemy force's disposition and where one or more air strikes needed to be placed. Generally he would also know the air weapon best suited considering the enemy's situation and how close his troops would be to the strike. Guns and Frantans could be used as close as thirty metres but bombs and rockets needed more than 100 metres separation to cater for potential errors and shrapnel effect. A pilot had to know with certainty the disposition of the entire callsign calling for support—we called this the FLOT (Front Line Own Troops). He also needed to know the nature of support required to be certain of selecting the correct weapon switches, the direction of attack, enemy distance from FLOT, and the precise position he had to strike. FLOT was seldom a straight line so only the extremities of troops nearest the enemy were marked. This could be done in a number of ways. The simplest of these was an unfolded map placed upside down on the ground but this usually delayed the air strike because a pilot might not see the small white markers in heavy bush conditions until he was directly above the callsign.

The preferred method of marking was by smoke grenades, yellow and white were best, which could be used as soon as the callsign could clearly see or hear the approaching aircraft. Too often in operations, heavy ground fire made this difficult so an initial indication of a callsign's position might need a single highly visible white phosphorus grenade. It was then up to the pilot to call for FLOT markers when he was close enough for his attack.

FLOT markers provided a pilot the reference line for his attack direction. As soon as he had FLOT he would position to attack along that line. At 'perch' (start of attack dive) the pilot would call "Mark target", whereupon the ground commander fired a red flare which he attempted to place in the centre of the intended strike point.

By the time the flare reached ground the attacking aircraft was usually established in its attack-dive. The callsign commander would then give quick corrections. He would either call "On target", if the flare had landed where he intended or give corrections ADD or DROP, LEFT or RIGHT with appropriate distances. Typically this might be, "To my marker, Drop 20—left 10". Add and Drop, Left and Right corrections all related to the aircraft attack-line. This meant that the GAC soldier on the ground had to adopt the pilot's perspective to bring about the corrections he wanted.

We perfected procedures and ran many successful courses for all RLI, RAR and Territorial Army platoon commanders and senior NCOs. Inter-service and personal relationships that developed between the bush squadrons (ourselves and helicopters) and the Army's fighting soldiers proved to be of immense importance in operations.

When our GAC procedures were eventually used in hot operations, marking FLOT became impossible during high-stress running firefights, but pilots were able to adapt by attacking at ninety degrees to a single marker flare and responding to the usual corrections.

4 Squadron was doing well, morale was high and training had become interesting. We flew many first-light and last-light GAC strikes and also made first-run attacks on targets marked by airborne FAC using 37mm Sneb rockets. Realising it may be necessary to call in a number of aircraft from different locations to link up for combined first-light strikes, we ran exercises in which three or four aircraft met before dawn at a prearranged position well away from target.

Meeting in the dark required height separation initially and cautious manoeuvring to come into formation on the navigation lights of the assigned strike leader. There was something magical about those early morning flights when the progressive brightening of the sky revealed the black shapes of Provosts, or Trojans, flying together in loose formation.

First light for callsigns on the ground occurred as much as twenty minutes before pilots' visual contact with ground was good enough to safely make diving attacks. Only by flying with us did Army officers appreciate our problem. In consequence, any ground force needing close air support at dawn always had to endure an agonisingly long wait beyond 'soldiers' first light' for 'pilots' first light'.

To reduce training costs, live strikes were made using one machine-gun or just a pair of 37mm Sneb rockets. The low-cost Kaylite sand-and-powder BUBS were always used in place of Frantans.

Jungle Lane

THERE WAS NEED FOR ALL squadron personnel to be reasonably well prepared for self-defence if downed amongst the enemy and to be able to assist in the defence of airfields. Every pilot and technician underwent weapons training on rifle ranges and all had to be proficient with both rifle and pistol.

Whereas the Army always received maximum Air Force assistance in preparing for FAC, GAC and helicopter-trooping, the same could not be said of the Army when we sought professional assistance to prepare aircrew in ground-fighting techniques. Fortunately we had one or two ex-Army men ourselves, so 4 Squadron was given the necessary training by Warrant Officer Barney Barnes. One Army exercise he put us through was known as the 'Jungle Lane'.

Jungle Lane was designed to develop snap reaction and accurate shooting whilst under high physical and mental stress. Preparation for this involved setting up a number of hidden pop-up 'hostile' targets along a difficult twisting bush course known only to the man who prepared it and conducted the training runs.

Barney Barnes took one pilot or technician at a time with FN rifle and three magazines of live ammunition to run the course. He followed close behind bellowing instructions on which way to move or firing his FN to signify when to dive for cover. Man-sized targets, standing, crouching or lying, popped up when Barney pulled on hidden strings. The man running Jungle Lane had to fire two shots from the hip immediately a target appeared but without losing forward momentum. Targets could appear as far back as forty-five degrees, which meant having to cast around for them but still avoiding obstructions along the way.

I hated Jungle Lane with a passion. Barney Barnes, on the other hand, revelled in my breathless agony. Being a smoker did little to help me run in deep sand along a dry river-course with Barney's live rounds sending spurts of sand and rock splinters flying left and right about me. The steepest banks were the points he selected to change from riverine to bush and vice versa whilst he trotted gently along level high ground.

Having passed the first five targets and diving for cover I felt my legs would carry me no further. My mouth tasted of blood and my lungs were close to bursting. Twice I received a verbal blast for not counting how many rounds I had fired when I was about to move on without changing magazines. When fifteen or so targets had gone by Barney declared the run completed. We then backtracked the course to count hits on the targets. It took me the entire route back to recover my breath but I was always pleased to have seen every target and equalled the results of the best of my men. Nevertheless, those Jungle Lane runs made me decide that, if I was downed, I would go into cover and let the bloody enemy do the running.

Jungle Lane and all other ground-combat training had me wondering what attracted men to a career in infantry. I knew they had to be barmy to enjoy filth, sweat, breathlessness, leopard-crawling and diving for cover at full running speed with heavy kit and weapon impeding a gentle touch-down. I never came to any conclusion on the issue but found it interesting that soldiers wondered what madness made a pilot operate in full view of the enemy with no place to hide.

'October Revolution'

THE PRESIDENT OF THE OFFICERS' Mess Committee at Thornhill, Squadron Leader Ralph Parry, was the station's Senior Technical Officer. It was unusual to have a non-flying PMC, but there he was sitting at the centre position of the top table for a dining-in night in October.

Bad habits imported from RAF Aden dining-in nights broke loose on this particular occasion when Rich Brand set off a very loud cracker that filled the room with strong-smelling smoke. The PMC rose to his feet and called for order, whereupon another cracker went off. Infuriated by this, Ralph Parry returned to his feet and in an uncertain manner threatened to expel the culprit if the incident was repeated. Following a much bigger bang with more dense smoke, the perplexed PMC rose to his feet yet again and ordered the culprit to leave the room. Since he did not know who the culprit was, he became even more perplexed when twelve of us rose as one and departed from the dining-room.

When we were outside laughing our heads off at the way our gentle PMC had handled misbehaviour, Tol Janeke invited everyone to his home to continue the evening there. Where all the beer came from remains a mystery but I remember Tol attiring everyone with his wife's prized lampshades as headdress over mess kit. A very merry party ensued.

Some of the wives, including Tol's wife June, pitched up from a gathering they had been to and went behind the neighbour's hedge to watch their rowdy men partying in the house. The position they chose to lie in the shadows was not a good one. Cyril White, coming out of the light into darkness,

failed to see the girls on the other side of the section of hedge into which he relieved his bladder. Mildly splattered, the girls backed off but managed to suppress their mirth until Cyril let loose a very loud fart.

Many parties were held in many places, most to be forgotten. But this night, nicknamed the 'October Revolution', was an impromptu affair that remains clear in my memory.

Operation Sable

IN SPITE OF ALL THE assurances given by the Department of Internal Affairs (which we nicknamed Infernal Affairs) it was obvious that they had no clue of what was actually happening in the remote places of northeast Rhodesia. The intimate contact that existed back in the days of horse and bicycle patrols, when every tribal kraal, big and small, was visited regularly, had been progressively lost with the advent of motor vehicles. The same might be said of the Police but for their 'ground coverage' men and agents who continued to make Peter Stanton and his colleagues our best source of 'people intelligence'.

From information gleaned after the SAS attack on Matimbe base, it was clear that ZANLA had reached the Rhodesian population earlier than expected. This brought about increased military activity in the northeast, including RLI and RAR deployments along the border inside Rhodesia with SAS working inside Mozambique.

4 Squadron positioned a Trojan and four Provosts to support RLI and SAS sited at a small remote airfield called Nyamasoto

Nyamasoto airstrip.

and were joined there by four of 7 Squadron's helicopters. The RLI and RAR were cross-graining along the border to try and pick up terrorist transit points whilst the SAS conducted over-border reconnaissance. A Joint Operations Centre, JOC Sable, was established at Nyamasoto Airfield for SAS and RLI ops whilst RAR operated out of Mtoko.

The Nyamasoto airstrip was little more than an opening in the bush with no buildings or amenities besides tents and flysheets. Lieutenant Colonel Peter Rich, ex British SAS and previous OC of 'C' Squadron (Rhodesian) SAS, was then CO of the RLI and based with his soldiers at Nyamasoto.

Immediately 4 Squadron arrived, I suggested that I should go over border to build up an intelligence picture of the ground. Initial reaction from Peter Rich was negative. He felt that I would upset ZANLA and make the Army's task more difficult. However this officer with a fast penetrating wit eventually gave in to my nagging and agreed to "give this new-fangled air recce a try". Within an hour on my first flight, I picked up a temporary base in a small break in a line of low hills, fairly close to a main path. Initially I was concerned this might be a path network created by wild pigs either side of heavily treed and broken rock cover. However, a strong link to the main pathway did not fit with anything but men, so I called for troops to be brought in by helicopters. Peter Rich sounded distinctly sceptical but he agreed to respond.

Although I was quite certain that this was a base without structures, I had no way of knowing if it was occupied. Nevertheless I did not wish to give any terrorist the impression of being too interested in the spot so continued to orbit getting progressively farther away. When four helicopters checked in with me, I cut across country to pick them up to ensure we arrived at the base at the same time. Immediately we got there the helicopters landed all their troops in long grass south of the base. I watched the troops shake out into an echelon formation then move directly towards the gap in the hill line.

I was greatly relieved when contact was made with terrorists who had gone to ground inside the base area. From Nyamasoto, Peter Rich called, "Bloody marvellous, I owe you a beer." Had he taken my information more seriously, the advice to split the troop deployment either side of the gap would have disallowed escape of most of the terrorists who broke northward. Final results were fair with seven killed, two escaped wounded and three captured out of a group of twenty-four ZANLA. This was one of a number of groups that had come from Zambia through Tete carrying supplies, now hidden in Rhodesia. We had caught these terrorists on their way back to Zambia in what was no more than a regular resting spot on water along their route to and from Rhodesia. Personal equipment that had been abandoned by terrorists was booby-trapped with phosphorus grenades, accounting for another terrorist two weeks after this action.

Back at Nyamasoto, Peter Rich apologised for not having taken me seriously because he did not believe it was possible to locate terrorists from the air. I told him there was no need for any apology because my squadron was still on a pretty steep learning curve.

I do not know if it was our three captures or an SB agent within ZANLA that led Peter Stanton to ZANLA's bush 'post box'; a lone hollow tree inside Rhodesia in which instructions were lodged for ZANLA's group commanders. Not only was Peter able to record the latest instructions found in the 'post box', these led him to a huge arms cache, which included landmines, on the side of a prominent hill not far from the post box. Here Peter unearthed weapons in such numbers that he was astounded so much communist equipment could have come into the country unreported by the locals and undetected by police 'ground coverage'. Obviously, indoctrination of the local people was already well advanced!

My plan to continue putting together all available visual recce information along the border was temporarily interrupted by a call to assist the SAS. Callsign 21 reported being pinned down inside Mozambique by enemy fire coming from a high ridge overlooking their flat exposed position. There was no way the callsign could advance or retreat from where individuals lay in the best cover available. I raced to the Provost and flew directly to the given map reference. This particular Provost was different from the others in that it had a trial-fit of four .303 Browning machine-guns, two in each wing, instead of the standard pair. The four guns had received limited testing so this call gave opportunity to see how they would fare on their first live target. It happened also to be my first-ever live attack in a light fixed-wing aircraft.

The target description was so well structured that I knew where to lay down fire whilst still some distance out. I told callsign 21 that I would commence firing at long range and asked him to give me corrections on fall of shot that he should pick up easily from dust and tracer rounds. As soon as I started firing I received his call, "On target". So I laced the appropriate section of the ridge-line, then stood off to await developments.

The terrorists, who were almost certainly FRELIMO and obviously shaken by the noise of 1,000 rounds cracking around them, ceased firing at callsign 21 to flee from the area—though I saw nothing of them. A sweep up and over the ridge succeeded in locating the terrorist firing positions but apart from expended communist 7.62mm cartridges and many .303 bullet holes in the trees nothing was found. The SAS continued on their intelligence gathering patrol and I returned to Nyamasoto.

Visual reconnaissance across the border was made difficult by the paths of many refugees, some into small hidden camps and others into Rhodesia. Quite why they were running from FRELIMO was difficult to understand initially. Then, following up on an SAS report, I picked up the trail of a very large herd of cattle that had obviously been stolen from the Mozambican tribesmen. They had been driven away to the north by FRELIMO but I broke off my search having tracked the herd for more than forty kilometres from our border.

I also noticed that most Mozambican villages had been abandoned and that no crops had been planted. All this confirmed that FRELIMO had been in control of Tete, all the way up to our border, for some considerable time. It also meant that we would have to fight both FRELIMO and ZANLA to prevent terrorism from taking root in Rhodesia.

Although every consideration and effort was given to preventing civilians becoming involved in any armed conflict, it was inevitable that unexpected incidents did occur. One such occasion gave rise to a situation that was described to me by one of the helicopter pilots. Although I was not involved in any way, I think it is a story well worth repeating in the style of its telling.

Nicholas and the old man

RLI PURSUED A MIXED GROUP of FRELIMO and ZANLA in a running action from the Rhodesian border deep into Mozambique. Most Mozambican civilians dispersed and ran from the fighting in the general direction of Rhodesia. Then during this day, one RLI callsign of four soldiers came upon a very old, partially blind man standing by himself under a large tree. He was in a state of fear and confusion. The soldiers did what they could to calm the old fellow with drink and food but it took time to understand that his distress centred on the loss of his personal donkey. It transpired that the donkey's name was Nicholas and that he was no ordinary donkey; he was blue-grey in colour. The old man relied on Nicholas to carry him about and he had been trained to answer to his name. Nicholas was also trained to make mounting easy for the old man.

The soldiers called for helicopter assistance but were told that all the helicopters were too busy—one would come over when there was opportunity. The hours moved on and, though the white soldiers with their new-found charge tried to be patient, they called many times to make sure the Air Force had not forgotten its promise. When eventually a helicopter could be spared, the pilot was surprised to be asked to search for a blue-grey donkey.

Helicopters are extremely expensive to run and, in operations involving the movement of troops, fuel endurance is limited. Nevertheless the RLI soldiers' story touched the pilot's heart so he started a search. He managed to find a handful of donkeys, which he herded together before driving them towards the far-off tree under which the old man waited with his RLI friends. When the donkeys were close enough, the pilot broke away for Rhodesia to refuel.

The RLI soldiers were tickled pink when one donkey responded to the old man's frail call, "Nicholas, Nicholas". Sure enough the donkey that came to them was blue-grey, not like those other common brownie-grey jobs. He trotted straight to the old man whose eyes streamed with happy tears. But this was not the end of the story for the Air Force. The RLI troopies were not going to leave the old man and Nicholas behind because all of his kinsfolk had disappeared; so they called for helicopter uplift of themselves, the old man and Nicholas.

When a helicopter pilot said he could take the old man but that there was no possibility of getting Nicholas inside the helicopter, the RLI soldiers already had the answer to that problem. They had ripped apart their webbing and had fashioned a harness to lift Nicholas back to Rhodesia by way of the cargo sling, which was fitted to every helicopter.

By this time the helicopter pilots, who had just about completed the uplift of RLI troops back to Rhodesia, were getting a bit fed up with the persistence of the troopies. Being closest to the border, they were assigned for the last lift but their persistence and 7 Squadron's flexible attitude soon had the callsign and old man airborne with one braying donkey hanging under the helicopter.

The flight had to be made at slow speed so as not to spin the donkey or drown him in the airflow. At the RLI's bush base, Nicholas came into contact with the ground gently, the pilot pressed his cargo release button and Nicholas waited patiently for his harness to be removed. Within five minutes he was nibbling fresh green grass. The old man had his own tent, complete with the most comfortable bed he had ever known. He was given a hot shower and fresh clothing to replace his rags.

The old man and Nicholas were tended day and night by the troopies who had found him. When these soldiers went on patrol they handed their wards into the care of other soldiers. For two weeks Nicholas and the old man were comfortable and both gained weight. Then, out of the blue, there was the sharp crack of a rifle shot in the camp. The small contingent of soldiers and helicopter crews in base rushed to investigate and were horrified to find Nicholas lying dead from a bullet through his brain. A vehicle was racing away westward and the INTAF man, who came to shoot Nicholas for being 'illegally imported into the country without veterinary inspection and compulsory quarantine', was lucky to get away with his life. Had the RLI soldiers who gave chase in a lumbering Army truck caught up with this guy, there can be no doubt that they would have killed him, so great was their anger.

The helicopter pilot who told me this sad story was the one who intercepted the INTAF man, possibly a District Officer acting on instructions from the District Commissioner, and flew him to safety. This he did to protect RLI soldiers from committing murder, certainly not out of pity for the detestable INTAF man. An attempt to console the old man and find a replacement blue-grey donkey failed when, just a few days later, he died broken-hearted. Internal Affairs' reputation, already poor amongst operational soldiers and airmen, worsened.

For me, this story highlighted the very best and worst of the human spirit but it also raises another issue that you, the reader, can judge for yourself. I recorded what you have just read in about 1985. Now in 2001, following publication of Beryl Salt's book—*A Pride of Eagles*—I read Ian Harvey's account of an airlift of hundreds of civilians from Macombe in Mozambique to higher ground near the Musengezi Mission in Rhodesia. This move of people was at the request of the Portuguese to save them from the rising waters of the Cabora Bassa dam. This is part of what Ian told Beryl Salt:

As the final day progressed, with time running out, I was able to pile more and more people into my Alouette III as fuel burned off. My last load, with fuel down to 110 pounds, was a total of twenty-nine passengers (surely a world record), with my tech Finn Cunningham sitting outside on the running board with his feet on the port wheel.

This load included an old man with a crude type of skateboard. The RAR CSM approached me saying that the old man was a cripple who had trained a donkey called Reggie to pull him around the village and into the fields. It was his most treasured possession. In the fading light, I agreed to do one more lift. We set off with a cargo net and sure enough, there in the field standing alone was Reggie, a riempie halter around his neck. We loaded him into the net without any fuss and with the donkey dangling under the chopper we delivered him to his owner who was beside himself with joy at having been reunited with his companion.

The District Commissioner, who was probably under orders, had specified that no livestock would be permitted. He summarily shot Reggie. The RAR were so incensed that they had to be restrained from evening the score.

I prefer the first story and like the name Nicholas better than Reggie, but I am left wondering if Ian Harvey's account is the correct one or if there were two old men with special donkeys. Seems unlikely!

Beit Bridge rail link

THE SERIOUS DEVELOPMENTS IN THE northeast confirmed our worst fears that the Portuguese would not contain FRELIMO. It also brought into question just how long our roads, railways and oil pipelines linking us to the port at Beira would remain secure. Similar concerns were developing for the future security of Rhodesia's other rail lines to the coast. These ran to Lourenço Marques, the capital of Mozambique,

and to South Africa via Botswana. Botswana showed no sign of outright hostility to Rhodesia, but it was clear that Seretse Khama's black government could be forced by African governments to turn the screws on us.

Ian Smith knew that only a direct rail link with South Africa via Beit Bridge would overcome future political crises; to which end planning for a new line from Rutenga to the Limpopo, to link into the South African rail system at Messina, was stepped up. This 147-kilometre line was eventually built in just three months instead of twelve months as originally planned.

Commencement of Operation Hurricane

BY DECEMBER 1972, REX NHONGO'S ZANLA group had been in the St Albert's Mission area for over seven months, politicising the locals, taking out recruits for training and building up war supplies. His group was based exactly where 4 Squadron had reported its presence in late July. Undisturbed, Rex Nhongo (his *chimurenga* pseudonym) and his men had lived in relative luxury, sometimes in caves, enjoying all the free food, beer and women, provided for 'the boys in the bush' by willing locals.

By now Rex was ready for offensive operations that he planned to launch between Christmas and New Year when he guessed many servicemen would be on leave. ZANLA groups to his east were supposed to open their offensive at the same time. But news from the eastern groups was bad, so Rex decided to strike immediately with a view to drawing Rhodesian forces away from stressed comrades.

On the night of 21 December he attacked the farmstead at Altena Farm, which was to the west of his base area. Though this attack occurred earlier than intended, it fitted with Rex's fundamental plans. A list of farmers who were unpopular with their labourers had been drawn up as primary targets. Popular farmers were also identified so that they might be left alone, at least for the time being.

His plan was to attack Marc de Borchgrave's Altena Farm then stand off to see how the security forces would react. There was no special planning for the attack itself. During the approach to the homestead, the telephone line was cut and a landmine was laid in the roadway. A close-in recce of the house was made before Nhongo and his men stood back and emptied two magazines apiece from their AK-47 assault rifles through windows and doors. The group then ran off into the night, whereupon Rex found himself separated and alone.

In the de Borchgrave home the children were sobbing with fear and Marc was perplexed by his family's isolation with no telephone or any other means to alert police and neighbours. His one little girl of seven was hurt but fortunately not too seriously. Fearing there might be another attack or that an ambush had been laid for his vehicle, Marc waited with his family for some time before setting off across country on foot to get help. The possibility of a landmine in the roadway had not crossed his mind.

Seeing military activity developing around him at first light Rex Nhongo, having first hidden his outer set of clothing, weapon and other paraphernalia, commandeered a bicycle from a youth. He was stopped by police and questioned. He claimed he had neither seen any armed men nor heard any firing. Presenting his *situpa* (identification document) that gave his name as Solomon Mutuswa, he was allowed to go on his way.

Many, many terrorists were to escape capture in this manner. From the earliest days of Op Hurricane, which was established the morning after Altena Farm was attacked, terrorists wore more than one set of clothing for two basic reasons. Firstly, an armed guerrilla is better off without telltale rucksacks to carry changes of clothing and, secondly, identity of dress could be switched by exchanging inner with outer clothing or simply removing and hiding the outer clothing. Pseudonyms were discarded for real names and authentic *situpas* were presented.

The de Borchgrave family moved in with friends whilst Altena Farm was thoroughly checked over. They were unlucky enough still to be at Whistlefield Farm when another of Rex Nhongo's groups attacked it two nights later. Rex told me eight years later that this attack had also been made to study security-force reactions.

On this occasion, Marc de Borchgrave and another of his daughters were injured, but again not too seriously. Unfortunately, however, Corporal N. Moore of the RLI died when the Army vehicle in which he was travelling to Whistlefield Farm detonated a landmine on the approach road to the farmstead. This occurred in spite of the fact that, during the follow-up at Altena Farm, the landmine planted by Rex Nhongo had been found and lifted.

At this time the SAS had been withdrawn from operations over the border in Mozambique to assist JOC Hurricane, which based itself at the Centenary Airfield. Rex Nhongo's plans to draw forces from the east had worked, just as he hoped.

SAS trackers accompanying the RLI on the Whistlefield call-out were lucky because they had climbed off the truck to commence a search for tracks just before the vehicle hit the landmine. These same trackers, now angered by the mine incident, picked up the trail of the terrorist group and started after them. They tracked all day until darkness fell. Unknown to them, they slept very close to where the terrorists had stopped to rest. They only found this out when they came upon ZANLA's campfire soon after tracking recommenced at dawn.

Major Brian Robinson, who had recently taken command of the SAS, was at Centenary. He decided to deploy another SAS

callsign by helicopter as a cut-off force ahead of the tracker group. The position he chose was spot-on and resulted in the death of three terrorists and the capture of two others in the first military contact of Op Hurricane. The RLI were especially pleased by this success against the group that had laid the mine that killed one of their men and injured others.

Countering landmines

EVEN BEFORE THE COMMENCEMENT OF Op Hurricane, landmines had become a serious menace, playing havoc with vehicles and causing serious injuries and loss of life. On 27 April 1971 Lance Corporal Moorcroft and Trooper Meyer were killed in a single mining incident. Two months prior to Op Hurricane, Sergeant Hill died in another landmine detonation.

Efforts to counter the threat were redoubled and many satisfactory though crude solutions were found. First efforts revolved around correct sandbagging of floors and filling tyres with measured quantities of water. Within eighteen months hideous-looking vehicles started making their appearance and, insofar as military vehicles were concerned, landmines ceased to be the dangerous weapon of early times. Rhodesia and South Africa worked together to become world leaders in counter-mine warfare. This was achieved with specially designed mine-deflecting modules affixed to standard truck and Land Rover chassis.

Loss of life and injuries to military and paramilitary personnel was almost completely eliminated and most vehicles that struck landmines could be returned to service at relatively low cost. When death or injury did occur, it was usually through failure of passengers to observe correct seating and securing procedures. Hapless civilians were not so fortunate; hundreds were killed or severely maimed when unprotected buses and cars detonated mines that had been laid without concern for civilian traffic.

There was always a worry that airfields would be mined because there was no way of protecting aircraft from catastrophe if one detonated a mine. Why the terrorists did not capitalise on this one cannot say, yet I only recall two landmines laid for aircraft. One was planted in the aircraft parking area of a remote airfield but was detected and lifted. The other occurred on 19 February 1979 when Byrne Gardener, an Internal Affairs pilot, died when his aircraft activated a land mine on the Mrewa Airfield.

Because landmines planted by well-trained individuals are impossible to detect visually, many electronic devices were developed as substitutes to the slow and laborious ground prodding method. One electronic system was borne by a vehicle known as the 'Pookie' (nickname for a Night ape). Its purpose was to act as lead vehicle to detect mines ahead of vehicles travelling in convoys.

The Pookie was a light vehicle based on the Volkswagen Beetle chassis, riding on four very wide, low-pressure tyres. It was fitted with a single-seat mine-proof module for the driver who monitored signals coming to him from a wide mine-sensing unit mounted crosswise to the module base. This vehicle, which looked as if it had come from outer space, could pass over a mine without detonating it. But because the detector response rate was slow, and the need to stop quickly to prevent following vehicles reaching a detected mine, Pookies could only travel at about 40 kph (25 mph). These vehicles came into Rhodesia's bush war in small numbers and only served to give convoy protection along the highest-risk routes. In consequence, most convoys continued as before.

One such convoy was travelling along a typical TTL dirt road with gunners standing in their vehicle cabs manning machine-guns mounted on a ring affixed to a hole in the cab roof. From their elevated position they had a good vantage point from which to search for threats on roadway and surrounding bush. They passed a couple of young children who, as the lead vehicle went past, stuck their fingers in their ears and distorted their faces in obvious expectation of a big bang. The lead gunner slammed the top of the cab with his hand to signal the driver to brake hard. It only took a minute of prodding to find the landmine lying just two metres from the front right wheel. The kids had disappeared, probably disappointed, but they had given the best mine warning any soldier could hope for.

Centenary days

WHEN JOC HURRICANE WAS ESTABLISHED, I sent Rob Tasker with three pilots, four technicians, two Provosts and two Trojans to join four helicopters at Centenary Airfield. This airfield, initially with grass runway, became FAF 3 under command of Squadron Leader Peter Cooke who did such a fine job that he remained there for many months.

When operations in the northeast spread eastwards from Centenary, JOC Hurricane, the senior controlling body, moved to Bindura and the regional Sub-JOCs adopted the name of the place at which they were based. This gave rise to Sub-JOCs Centenary, Mount Darwin and Mtoko. The associated Air Force bases were FAFs 3, 4 and 5 respectively.

Back at Thornhill I had lost Gordon Wright on posting to Hunters. Rob Tasker became 'A' flight Commander and Bruce

Collocott 'B' Flight Commander. Since Rob and I were the only instructors on 4 Squadron and Rob had done little time on ops, I decided that I should remain at base to complete Greg Todd's conversion and handle general squadron matters. In particular, I needed to run Bruce Collocott through his new management responsibilities.

Peter Cooke (centre) with President Clifford Dupont and Air Marshal Mick McLaren. Loading a .303 ammunition belt to the starboard wing gun of a Provost are Sergeants 'Flamo' Flemming and Chris Nienham.

This photograph is of FAF 5 at Mtoko.

Flight Commanders Bruce Collocott, Rob Tasker and Gordon Wright.

For a while activities in the northeast were limited to follow-up operations on increasing numbers of farm attacks, sightings and reports, but physical contacts with elusive terrorists were limited. Having secured the support of the locals, ZANLA groups were operating so much more effectively than in previous times and for very little effort they were able to tie down hundreds of security force men. 7 Squadron's helicopters were busy all the time whilst 4 Squadron provided some top cover, made a few airstrikes and conducted casualty evacuation to rear base hospitals.

Territorial Army and Police protection teams were allocated

to farmsteads whilst private companies made a financial killing setting up an inter-farm and Police radio-communication network (Agri-Alert) and erecting security barriers with flood-lights around farmsteads. The farm workers' compounds were not protected in the same way because it was realised that to do so would bring terrorist retribution on workers' families living in the TTLs.

Because of the demand for trackers and follow-up forces, the SAS continued to be used as infantry, which was a terrible waste of their potential. Brian Robinson pressed for his squadron to return to the role for which it was intended and trained. This was to operate in depth inside Mozambique to counter ZANLA's freedom of movement through Tete Province. He did not have long to wait, though the SAS return to Tete came in an unexpected way.

On 8 January 1973, three white surveyors and two black assistants were ambushed in their vehicle near the Mavuradona Pass on the road to Mukumbura. Robert Bland and Dennis Sanderson were killed. They were the first whites to die at the hands of terrorists since the Viljoens were murdered at Nevada Farm in May 1966. Gerald Hawksworth and two black assistants were abducted and marched off towards Mozambique.

Under pressure from the Rhodesian Government, Portuguese approval was given for the SAS to move back into Tete, ostensibly to free Hawksworth and his two black companions. Their operations were initially limited to areas south of the Zambezi River but, having got a foot in the door, the SAS were to continue operating in Mozambique for many months to come. They failed to find the abductees who had already crossed the Zambezi because the SAS were belatedly cleared for the search.

ZANLA's direct entries from Zambia into Rhodesia had ceased long before Op Hurricane started, so it came as a shock when Ian Smith closed the border with Zambia on 9 January. He blamed Zambia for allowing ZANLA and ZIPRA free access across the Zambezi to attack white farmers and to abduct civilians. South Africa and Mozambique had received no warning of this unilateral action that threatened their lucrative trade with Zambia. Despite the ideological differences that existed between South Africa and Zambia, Prime Minister Vorster and President Kaunda favoured dialogue with free trade in southern Africa and a situation of détente developed between their two countries. South Africa was incensed by the situation, which if allowed to continue, would mean the loss of over 300 million rands in valued annual exports.

Ian Smith had been under pressure from South Africa for some days when he received assurance from a Zambian envoy that no terrorists would be allowed to cross the Zambian/Rhodesian border. This gave him the excuse needed to reverse an obvious political error and the border was declared open on 3 February. Kaunda however refused to reopen it. The economic effects of this emotional decision on South Africa, Mozambique and Rhodesia were enormous; for Zambia they were disastrous. By throwing his toys out of his cot, Kaunda denied his country access to four major seaports in South Africa and Mozambique. He was therefore limited to Dar es Salaam and Luanda, the latter involving enormous distance via unreliable Zaire and war-torn Angola. Neither of these routes was efficient and the implications of Zambia's self-imposed vulnerability introduced new factors into Rhodesian counter-terrorist thinking.

A week after Kaunda decided to keep the border closed, I was tasked to make a study of the Zambezi River from Kanyemba to Kariba, concentrating mainly on the Zambian bank. This three-day recce task was a welcome break from instruction but, apart from updating maps, nothing suspicious was located. By this time, most callsigns along the river were South African Police units who exhibited the same habits I had seen five years earlier when I was still flying helicopters. They swam naked in the Zambezi River and continued to ignore the crocodiles around them.

Deaths of Smart and Smithdorff

HAVING COMPLETED THE BORDER recce I reported to Air HQ. Whilst I was there on 21 February, Flight Lieutenant John Smart and his technician, Tinker Smithdorff, were reported overdue on a flight from Rushinga to a location to the northwest. Why Wing Commander Sandy Mutch was required to oversee a search for the missing helicopter I cannot say, but I was tasked to fly him to Rushinga and remain there to assist him.

I hardly knew John Smart who had recently joined us from the RAF. On the other hand, Tinker was well known to me. Brother to Mark Smithdorff, Tinker was quiet by nature and very popular with all who knew him. He was also an excellent technician and a good rugby player.

Whilst Sandy gathered in aircraft and tasked them for what was expected to be an easy search, I was finding out what had been happening in that area. From the Special Branch and Police I learned that a group of terrorists had

Tinker Smithdorff.

been reported moving northward along the Ruya River two days previously. I asked if John Smart knew about this group, to which I received an affirmative reply; so I went to Sandy Mutch and suggested he should include the Ruya River in his search plan. He would have nothing to do with this because the Ruya did not fit in with his now finalised search plan.

I explained to Sandy that I felt certain that John had done what I would have done in his situation. I would have diverted from the direct track to run up the Ruya at low level in the hopes of catching the terrorist group in the open. There had been no urgency for John to reach his destination so a deviation of some forty kilometres would not have concerned him. Sandy still took no notice and two whole days of intensive but fruitless searching passed.

The wreckage of John's helicopter was then located by accident. Hugh Chisnall of the Police Reserve Air Wing was on a routine flight along the border when he noticed strong sun reflections flashing off items in heavy bush in the Ruya riverbed. He knew an air search was being conducted for a missing helicopter and guessed that the flashes he had seen might have been from wreckage of that machine. His report was investigated by one of the search helicopters whose pilot immediately confirmed the reflections had been from the scattered wreckage of John's helicopter.

Troops were flown in to secure the area before an Air Force team arrived to conduct a detailed investigation. The findings were that the helicopter had struck a tall, dead tree that John had obviously not seen (a known hazard when low-flying). Whether the impact incapacitated John or the helicopter was not clear, but some 100 metres had been traversed before the helicopter reached high bush and broke up in a long crash path. John and Tinker had been killed instantly and there was no evidence to suggest any enemy involvement.

Offensive recces

ALTHOUGH I HAD BEEN IN and out of Centenary to change over crews and receive updates on what was happening in the Op Hurricane area, I did not deploy to Centenary until March. Back at base Rob Tasker was busy with Trojan conversions and operational orientation for a new crop of youngsters fresh off PTC. These were Peter Simmonds, Chris Dickinson, Ken Newman, Cocky Benecke, Mark Aitchison and Willie Wilson.

There were limited calls on 4 Squadron in this period, so I decided to get back into Tete to see what was happening in the same area 4 Squadron had used for recce training eight months

earlier. Mike Litson flew with me and we were both astounded by the changes.

SAS teams had been operating in this same region since January and had scored small successes against ZANLA. However, the area was simply too large for the limited number of foot-bound SAS callsigns to fully reconnoitre, monitor and ambush an expanding network of routes to Rhodesia.

Although in three days I could provide the basic intelligence the SAS would take more than a month of hard work to glean, Brian Robinson was dead against my continued presence over any area in which his men were operating. Since I held the SAS in high regard, I honoured Brian's wishes, but I have to say that I never did agree with his thinking.

We knew ZANLA was making inroads into the populated areas. When a question arose as to how far their influence extended, I offered a simple way of finding out. I got most of my squadron crews and aircraft, from Thornhill and elsewhere, to meet at New Sarum. After my briefing we flew ten aircraft low-level along parallel lines set five miles apart heading due north from a start line that ran eastwards from Salisbury. We flew due north to another line running due east from Centenary to where the Mazoe River exited Rhodesia. Along this line, all aircraft headed east for fifty miles and repeated the parallel pattern heading south.

Each aircraft had a crew of two whose task it was to study the local peoples' reaction to the presence of their aircraft. My observation over years had been that all the black folk, men, women and children, living normal lives instinctively waved at low-flying aircraft, even when they were caught stark naked. However, whenever there had been any political tension, such as occurred during the banning of ZAPU in the 1960s, nobody would look up at an aircraft, let alone wave at it.

The crews were asked to plot the point at which peoples' responses to the aircraft changed from open friendliness to indifference. In this way we found that the terrorists were active in northern Chiweshe TTL south of Centenary, throughout that part of the Kandeya TTL lying north of the Ruya River, the northern half of Chimanda TTL and the whole of Masoso TTL. The Ngarwe and Mkota TTLs in the east appeared to be free of ZANLA influence.

In the manner we had come to expect, Internal Affairs paid no attention to our information but Special Branch men like Peter Stanton and Winston Hart took it seriously. These two men had already learned what pilots could pick up from the air using God-given Mk1 eyeballs.

Blonde-haired, softly spoken Winston Hart, like Peter Stanton, was a top-rate intelligence officer. Both of these men became key figures in future SAS and Air Force planning. As early as 1970 they were already well known but were seldom seen because they were forever on the move, and always in a hurry. Winston was particularly lucky to have been blessed with the lives of a proverbial cat but unlucky in another sense to be involved in two landmine explosions in the space of a few days at the beginning of Op Hurricane. In these incidents he was fortunate to get away with temporary deafness and severe bruising because proper mine-proofed vehicles did not exist then.

Non-offensive casualties

AN UNFORTUNATE FACT OF LIFE is that lives are lost or seriously affected by accidents. In the normal run of things they seldom draw public attention because accidents are simply regarded as risks of living. This changes the moment they involve men in uniform. In Rhodesia routine accidents continued but new situations introduced new hazards. The greatest of these came from killing devices such as rifles and explosives as well as increased vehicular movement of men.

So far as I remember, we lost more uniformed men to accidental gunshot wounds than to offensive actions. These incidents were recorded as 'accidental discharges', abbreviated to 'AD' in the daily Sitreps (Situation Reports) sent to OCC from the JOCs. Reports of deaths and injuries by ADs became so commonplace in Sitreps that the horror of these was usually lost to those who read them. But one thing was clear, ADs hardly ever occurred amongst highly trained and disciplined units. Road accidents also made too high a claim on our uniformed men and one such incident involved my cousin, Brian Ade.

Brian was the son of my Uncle Eric Smith who had died in Italy when his Spitfire struck high-tension cables. Eric's wife, Eileen, remarried some years later and changed the surname of Eric's son Brian and daughter June to that of her husband, Cliff Ade. Nevertheless, Brian and June Ade were still my first cousins and were special to me.

Brian was in charge of a number of TF (Territorial Force) soldiers being transported to Mukumbura on the Mozambican border in one of a convoy of Bedford trucks. The road to Mukumbura descended from the highveld into the Zambezi Valley floor via a steep, winding pass down the Mavuradona mountain range. During its descent, the vehicle on which Brian was travelling suffered total brake failure. Brian immediately realised that the steep gradient and sharp corners spelt disaster, so he ordered everyone to jump off the moving vehicle. Whereas most did so, a few men froze. Brian manhandled some over the side of the truck and was so engaged when the vehicle rolled on a sharp corner. Brian was flipped out and flew through the air in a near-vertical descent onto rocks. Unfortunately he landed on a wedge shaped rock that broke his back, confining him for life to a wheelchair.

Not content to be just another paraplegic number, Brian

coached hockey and learned to drive a car with tailor-made accelerator and brake hand-controls. He often used to go off into the bush to photograph wildlife. Using his photographs, Brian eked out a living as a painter of wildlife. On one occasion he had left the road and was taking photographs of a baobab tree when he found himself surrounded by armed terrorists. Not wishing to let the CTs know he was incapable of normal movement, Brian quietly countered threats by launching into a lecture on the finer points of the giant baobab. Quite why they enjoyed Brian's talk I do not know, but they moved on and let him be.

The Peter Simmonds incident

ALTHOUGH THERE HAD BEEN MANY occasions in which enemy fire had been directed at aircraft, there had been no serious damage or injuries. On 4 July 1973 this changed for Air Lieutenant Peter Simmonds. He was piloting a Provost on a sortie giving support to an RAR tracker-combat team inside Mozambique. Along for the ride was his technician Mike Guy.

Army Lieutenant Mike Wilson had followed a group of terrorists across the border into Mozambique but the depth of his penetration was such that he had moved beyond the coverage given by his maps. Although there was need to know Mike's location, his major back at base in Mukumbura had been reluctant to use air, as this would arouse the terrorists to the follow-up operation. After four days however, Peter Simmonds was asked to find the RAR callsign and drop a supply of maps and radio batteries to him. Neither Mike Wilson nor Pete Simmonds were to know that the callsign was within 100 metres of the terrorists as Peter descended for a slow low pass over the ground force. As he and Mike Guy threw out the stores, there were two loud bangs that Pete thought had come from his engine. He immediately applied full power and was relieved that the engine responded normally.

It was only as Pete gained height and closed the canopy that Mike Guy pointed to Peter's legs. Considering a bullet had shattered his left femur and gouged a hole in his right leg, it is surprising that Peter had not felt the strike and that there was no pain whatsoever. Realising he was bleeding heavily and might lose consciousness, Pete asked Mike Guy to handle the aircraft whilst he stuck his fingers into the holes in his left leg to stem the blood flow for the twenty-minute flight to Mukumbura.

Unlike most aircraft, the Provost's rudders pedals had leather toe straps that, together with hand-operated wheel brakes, were a godsend to Peter in this predicament. His left leg was quite useless to him but his right leg could still push to apply right rudder and pull on the toe strap to apply left rudder. Having thought things through before landing, Peter was able to put the aircraft down safely before executing a deliberate ground loop with full braking when the aircraft had slowed to a safe speed.

The agony he was to endure over the next six months first came to him as he was extracted from the Provost cockpit. The pain that comes with a shattered femur and a useless dangling leg moving in uncontrolled directions is impossible to describe and one never to be forgotten by Pete Simmonds. It was a pitch-black night with no horizon but Peter Woolcock flew Pete Simmons to Centenary in an Alouette. Alf Wild then took him on to New Sarum in a Trojan and the Station Sick Quarters ambulance completed this 'impossibly painful' casevac to Andrew Fleming Hospital.

Flight Sergeant Benji

THE GRASS STRIP AT CENTENARY had become very worn and dusty from high-volume traffic when it was decided to lay down a tarmac runway, so all personnel and aircraft moved to an airstrip on Eureka Farm, just a short distance away. The tented camp at Eureka suffered terribly from dust stirred up by every helicopter and fixed-wing movement. Whenever the wind blew from the flight lines to the camp, it brought dust that penetrated bedding, clothing, radios and kitchen; not that this dampened the spirits of the men.

An over-supply of camp toilet seats, nicknamed 'thunder boxes', provided an answer to the shortage of seats for a pub the technician constructed from scrounged materials. Elevated to barstool height, they gave the option of hollow or solid seating at the bar counter of 'The Thunderbox Inn'.

One of the Eureka Farm dogs, a scruffy terrier named Benji, took to the Air Force in a big way. Benji was returned to his owner many times but he simply ran back to the camp. He was always in evidence lying on anything that was elevated, such as the sandbag walls around the camp. When the Centenary Airfield tarmac runway was completed and the Air Force returned to comfortable accommodation, Benji followed. The farmer felt there was no point in returning Benji to the farm every day and was happy to pass the scruffy little mutt into Air Force care.

Benji stayed with Air Force for years. In October 1973 he was inducted into the force with the rank of corporal. Later he was posted to FAF 4 at Mount Darwin. Having risen to the rank of

flight sergeant Benji disgraced himself by peeing on the Camp Commandant's cap and was demoted back to sergeant. When he regained his rank for outstanding service and devotion to duty, Benji was posted to FAF 7 (Buffalo Range) in mid-1978 where he continued service to the end of the war. When FAF 7 closed at the cessation of hostilities, Benji was taken by car to New Sarum but, probably sensing the changing times, he died before reaching his new home.

Flight Sergeant Benji.

Another Aloe Festival

AT THE END OF JUNE 1973, No 4 Squadron was given clearance to withdraw most aircraft and crews from operations to participate in Umtali's annual Aloe Festival. It was wonderful to have the majority of our squadron together for the first time in eighteen months and to sense the spirit and esprit de corps that existed throughout the ranks. The technicians were an incredible bunch of men whose wide-ranging characters and talents too often manifested themselves in impish acts.

The officers and wives stayed at the Wise Owl Motel whilst the technicians all booked into the Flamboyant Hotel. This was not a case of rank separation but was the consequence of insufficient accommodation for everyone at either location.

At a civic function on the first night, I presented the mayor with a 4 Squadron plaque that, between deployments, I had personally crafted for the Umtali City Council.

Just after sunrise on the day of the flypast and Aloe Ball, I received a visitation from the Police who reported that a whole bunch of my technicians had been seen running down Main Street totally naked save for Air Force caps, black socks and shoes. Few people were around at the time and none of the surprised onlookers had lodged a complaint. The Police had gone directly to the hotel only to find every tech 'fast asleep'. Of course everyone who was questioned knew nothing about a mass streak and since no complaints had been received, no charges were laid; but the Police felt I should know of the incident to avoid trouble in the future.

PB presenting the mayor with a personally crafted 4 Squadron plaque.

Having been warned to behave themselves at the Aloe Ball, all squadron members were on their best behaviour. I crowned the Aloe Queen, everyone enjoyed a great meal and good music had brought most people onto the dance floor when Henry Jarvie started an impromptu act that stopped everyone in their tracks. I knew Henry would be the instigator of something unusual because of his naughty nature, but I had no need to worry about him being crude or destructive.

The band was playing 'Hey Girl' when Henry climbed onto the stage with a pint of beer in his hand. He placed the beer on a stool at one end of the stage and, moving his lanky body to the rhythm of the music, proceeded across stage sliding off his jacket, which he then twirled above his head on one finger. At stage end he placed the jacket neatly on the floor and, mincing to the music, returned slowly to his beer. He took a great swig, turned about and repeating the first act, this time removing his wristwatch, again twirling it over his head before placing it on the jacket. The band clicked with Henry from the outset and just kept repeating the very catchy theme of 'Hey Girl'. All eyes remained on Henry as he made pass after pass, never once using the same style of dance and always removing one item of clothing. It took two passes just to remove cuff links. Ripples of laughter passed through the crowd who loved Henry's facial expressions and lanky body movement, everyone wondering just how far he would go. I knew he would not push the limits.

Following the removal of his shirt with Superman poses to show off scrawny muscles, Henry was left with slacks and socks. The removal of the second sock gave Henry opportunity to demonstrate his sleight of hand by giving the distinct impression of filling the sock with beer and straining it into his mouth as he crossed the stage to lift his clothing and disappear as women yelled, "Encore! Encore! You haven't finished yet!"

The next day, Sunday, the squadron was invited to join the mayor and senior town counsellors for tea at Leopard Rock Hotel in the Vumba mountains. Beryl and I, together with other officers and wives, were having tea with the mayor and mayoress on the hotel lawn when Henry Jarvie appeared at the top of the hotel stairway high above us. He was resplendent in full chef's regalia, high cap and all.

On the open palm of his left hand he held a silver salver with a serving towel perfectly draped over his forearm. Down the steps he came, stiff as a board, looking straight ahead with a fixed expression. He came directly to our table and placed the salver in front of me, bowed and turned towards hotel guests seated under umbrellas. As he moved away we spotted the full beer glass held behind his back.

Chef Jarvie.

The silver tray contained a note and a sandwich. The note read, "Boss PB is in need of nourishment". The sandwich consisted of two tomato toppings between very dry crusts of butter-less bread.

Facial expressions of hotel guests to whom Henry moved showed he was up to no good. Initially they thought he was the hotel's senior chef. At one table Henry warned that there would be a slight delay in serving lunch because all meat stocks had "gone off slightly due to refrigeration failure but a good soaking in vinegar will solve this problem". To others he told of stale bread rolls that only needed a good soaking and re-baking to make them good and fresh. One group learned that the speciality of the day, crayfish, was giving the entire kitchen staff a major headache following their escape from the refrigerator. They had run off into flowerbeds and the fishpond but all would be rounded up soon, and lunch should be served on time.

I intercepted Henry on his return to the stairway. I thanked him for the sandwich and instructed him to eat it on my behalf. Not saying a word, he took the silver tray, bowed and climbed the stairs, beer still behind back. When he reached the balcony he placed the tray and his beer on the serving towel spread neatly on the balcony wall.

With much ceremony he broke the sandwich in two and

summoned John Britton to assist him. Looking straight-faced at the distant Himalaya mountain range, he commenced eating. Next to him John Britton attempted to follow Henry's act but, as with others who tried to emulate our squadron clown, John failed; he was just too big and clumsy next to his slim nimble friend.

As he ate, Henry's cheeks started to fill like a monkey's pouches. When he had the entire sandwich in his mouth with cheeks fully extended, he commenced a violent choking and sneezing act. Each time he sneezed, with right forefinger held horizontally under his nose, a small stream of bread pieces flew vertically downwards from his mouth giving the distinct impression of muck flying from his nose, which he then wiped on his sleeve in long exaggerated strokes. Few comedians could bring an audience to such fits of laughter as Henry Jarvie. The hotel guests, now realising he was no hotel chef, enjoyed the act even more than we did.

Opportunity was taken to fly the squadron from Umtali to Centenary to link up with crews who had missed out on the Aloe Festival. The purpose of gathering the whole squadron was to have a squadron photograph taken, as this might not be possible for ages to come.

Himalaya mountains viewed from Leopard Rock.

In line with the propeller boss of the Trojan is Bruce Collocott. Moving left are Rob Tasker, PB, Warrant Officer Spike Owens and Chief Tec Mick Fulton. Pilots are to the right of those named and technicians to the left.

Early FAC to jets

MY FIRST CALL FOR STRIKES by Hunters occurred inside Rhodesia, though much work had been done before I gained sufficient confidence to do this. Air recce inside Rhodesia was much more difficult than in Mozambique. Within the country the locals had no reason to hide from ZANLA and any stresses that existed within the population could not be detected from height; all path systems appeared quite normal.

Because terrorists were known to move position continuously and reside at night in different kraals in ones and twos, their presence within the TTLs was impossible to detect. It was only within the boundaries of white-owned farms that terrorists based up in the bush, but never for more than two nights at a time.

For years the African nationalists had complained that white farmers had the best land and the African folk had been allocated those regions with poor soil. From the air one could see that there was no truth in this allegation. The Centenary farmlands bordering the Kandeya TTL typified most boundaries between organised commercial farmland and the subsistence farming areas inhabited by tribesmen.

Except for patches of bush on hills and rocky ground, Kandeya was substantially overgrazed and all maize fields were so over-utilised that the TTL exhibited a near desert-like appearance. Across the cattle fence that separated the TTL from adjoining white-owned farms, lush bush and grass cover contrasted as chalk with cheese, even though soil types were identical. Crop rotation and the use of fertilisers made white farmlands look rich and neat. This was why fresh pathways inside these areas stood out strongly. Although I was finding temporary bases in the farming areas, which were all confirmed by co-operative ground forces, I was gaining nothing more than an idea of what a temporary base looked like. I visited a couple of these places with ground forces to see for myself.

It perplexed me to learn from Special Branch who had interrogated captured terrorists that bases I judged to be for twenty terrorists were in fact for only ten. I could not reconcile this until Special Branch established that there had also been ten women in residence to provide female comforts to 'their boys in the bush'. The lesson was clear—divide estimates by two.

I approached JOC Hurricane with the problem of not being able find terrorists in the TTL and requested that wide-ranging surprise visits be made on villages at all times of the night. The purpose of this was to see if we could force the terrorists away from the villages and make them base up in the bush. I guessed that, if they did this, each terrorist group would tend to site itself in a position with easy access to more than one village so that the daily feeding load could be spread whilst also giving them all-round early warning of any security force activities. I also guessed that female feeding parties would create telltale paths leading from villages to bases that, together with the inevitable paths within the bases, should make detection an easy matter. This ploy worked almost immediately. I picked up a well-defined campsite in the Kandeya TTL south east of St Albert's Mission with fresh squiggly paths running to it from four different villages.

Established paths change direction frequently but exhibit a smoother flow than fresh paths that route around the smallest of obstructions. With the passage of time and season, the sharp kinks that characterise fresh paths progressively smooth out because man, being a creature of habit, will shortcut any sharp bend once he knows the route.

Having located this camp, which I estimated to be for thirty people, meaning fifteen active terrorists, I considered how it might be tackled with a handful of troops flown in by the only two helicopters available at the time. Looking back on the lessons learned on Op Sable it was obvious that most, if not all, terrorists would escape. A large ground force closing in on the camp might have worked but it meant gathering troops from far and wide with no certainty that the terrorists would be in residence when the force closed in. I opted instead for an airstrike that would shock the locals who were providing succour and, hopefully, account for a few terrorists.

My style of reconnaissance involved continuous elliptical orbits that moved along a general line. Orbiting was essential because paths that could not be seen when viewing down sun stood out clearly when looking up-sun. At the end of one line of orbits, I would shift position by one orbit width and commence orbiting along a parallel line in the reverse direction. This was repeated until a whole block of territory, usually over 800 square kilometres, had been covered in a five-hour sortie. The sun angle played an important role in visual reconnaissance and 10:00 to 15:00 was the ideal time-block.

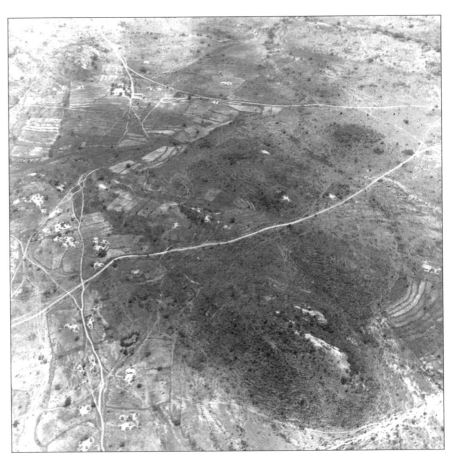

This photo is not of the target in question but it shows the nature of terrain in the Kandeya TTL where hill features disallow cropping thus protecting some natural bush cover.

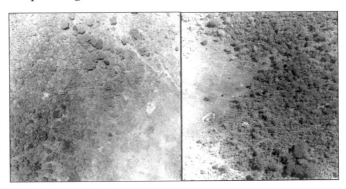

Down-sun blur versus up-sun clarity (same orbit).

I was running the first line when I located the camp. The orbits were continued along the search line so as not to give anyone any indication of my having seen the base. I called Peter Cooke in the Ops Room at FAF 3 and we discussed the matter before jointly agreeing to set up a jet-strike for 16:00 when, we guessed, the terrorists would be in base awaiting their meal.

By the time I landed, Peter had submitted an Air Request for a strike by Hunters and this had been accepted by Air HQ. The Air Task sent to No 1 Squadron was copied to FAF 3 to allow us opportunity to ensure that the Hunter pilots had received the correct details.

Using a Provost, I marked the target with smoke rockets at precisely 4 o'clock and pulled up into a steep climbing turn to watch the lead Hunter's 30mm cannon strike running right through the centre of the target. Three following Hunters, responding to my directions, patterned their 68mm Marta rocket strikes perfectly. As the Hunters cleared, I moved back over the target and saw many civilians running helter-skelter from the nearest village.

Helicopters dropped off troops who found the fresh base well laced by cannon and rocket shrapnel. Unfortunately there had been no terrorists in residence at the time. Later we established that the terrorists had been with civilians at a beer-drink in the very village from which I had seen so many people running. I had been mistaken in thinking these were all innocent civvies, thereby losing the chance of diverting the helicopters and troops onto a good opportunity target.

This, my first attempt at directing jets by airborne FAC, had worked better for the jet pilots than any one of many GAC strikes made over-border in support of SAS operations. The secret to success in first-run strikes under FAC control lay in four basic factors. These were, good timing, minimal radio chatter, excellent visual markers at target centre and control by a pilot who knew the precise location and extremities of the target and had witnessed the placement of each aircraft's strike.

Air Staff was not put off by the absence of terrorists; rather it commented that this strike had proven that airborne FAC could provide consistent precision and allow jets to strike closer to troops and civilians than had previously been considered possible.

The face of terrorism

HAVING ESTABLISHED THEMSELVES WITH THE locals, ZANLA realised they had, at last, entered into a decisive phase which they named the 'New Chimurenga' war. The first Chimurenga had been the Mashona Rebellion of 1896. During that rebellion, the BSA Company executed the leading *zvikiro* (spirit medium), Nehanda, whose spirit lived on in successive living female persons. The current incumbent, who relayed messages from the all-important spirit of the first Chimurenga war, was Mbuya Nehanda. She advocated war as the only way of wresting power from the white government.

Mbuya (grandmother) Nehanda was a frail old woman but her guidance was considered of paramount importance to

ZANU and its military wing ZANLA. To ensure her safety and to allow her total freedom to communicate with the original Nehanda, she was carried by stretcher all the way through Tete to a camp known as Chifombo on the Zambian border. From this place she gave ZANLA commanders the encouragement they needed when proceeding southbound for Rhodesia. The old *zvikiro* also blessed all arms of war that were paraded past her private hut.

By mid-1973 terrorism was spreading southward at an alarming rate and the names of three particular ZANLA regional leaders were on everyone's lips. They were James Bond, Mao and Rex Nhongo. We were particularly keen to eliminate James Bond and Mao who were responsible for horrifying acts of brutality designed to put fear in the hearts of black people. They were eventually killed in 1974, whereas Rex Nhongo left Rhodesia and survived to become ZANLA's commander at the end of the war.

Gone were the days when tracker-combat groups could relentlessly follow and destroy terrorist groups before they reached the black population. Gone too were the days when locals reported the presence of terrorists. At first some tribesmen did not understand the terrorists' determination to fight for 'freedom' and 'the vote'. So far as they were concerned, it seemed an awful waste of time and life to fight for something they could not eat, drink, smoke or poke. But when promised that they would inherit European farms, equipment and cattle, ZANLA's objectives made a great deal more sense. Political indoctrination was not the whole reason for tribesmen failing to report the presence of terrorists; it was more to do with having become more afraid of ZANLA than the forces of government; and with good reason.

For anyone suspected of being a 'sell-out' (informer) to the SF, terrorist retribution was swift and cruel. Too often this gave rise to misinformation by opportunists who, having a grudge against another and knowing terrorists never bothered to check out any accusation, deliberately and wrongfully reported them as 'sell-outs'. However, even wrongful killing of this nature fitted well enough with ZANLA's campaign of terror.

Atrocities committed against the people, their livestock and possessions were widely reported in the media with graphic photographs of destruction, murder and maiming. Whereas the international community chose to ignore these horrors, the mindless slaughter of innocents angered urban blacks and the entire white community.

I saw the poor woman whose husband was killed in her presence before the gang leader cut off his ears, nose and fingers. The wife was then forced to cook and devour the grizzly items. No pity was shown when she retched and vomited; she was beaten until she retained even that which she had thrown up.

Another woman was flown in for medical attention. Her entire top lip had been cut away from back molars via her nose with electrician's side-cutters.

The naked body of a young woman was found staked to

the ground, arms and legs outstretched on ropes that were pegged into the ground. A blood-covered maize cob remained imbedded in her vagina as well as a thick burning pole that had been driven into her rectum to cause her an indescribably painful death in a very lonely place.

In the presence of his family and other petrified tribesmen, this wrongfully accused youngster was murdered. After his death his body was repeatedly bayoneted (note no blood), to drive home ZANLA's message.

A woman whose top lip had been cut off by terrorists.

In many cases the use of burning poles driven into women's vaginas and men's rectums was done in the presence of villagers who witnessed such horrifying murder that they dared not report the atrocities for fear of becoming victims themselves. Whole herds of cattle were slaughtered with automatic gunfire or were hamstrung, necessitating their destruction by government agencies.

The term 'terrorist' was entirely justified for cowardly leaders of ZANLA gangs who wantonly brutalised hundreds of hapless civilians; yet the international community called them 'guerrillas'. These bullies, though intent on murdering white farmers, lacked the courage to achieve the levels sought by their ZANU politicos. Night attacks on white farmers mounted but the casualties and damage caused was so much lower than might have occurred if undertaken by men of courage. ZANLA could intimidate their black brethren but not the white folk. There were many instances of a farmer and his wife fighting off the most determined of terrorist forces, usually in excess of fifteen men, because the terrorists could not match their sheer guts and determination. Yet a mere handful of terrorists could have hundreds of tribesmen cowering from the simplest of verbal threats.

In the course of moving around their farms and out on the country roads, farmers and their families needed to be prepared and armed to face the ever-present threat of landmines and ambush. Incredibly, very few farmers abandoned their farms because of these dangers. The vast majority stubbornly refused to be intimidated, as ZANLA had been assured they would. Most children attended boarding schools and were brought home to the farms for their holidays. Every effort was made to keep farming life as normal as possible and many incredible stories can be told of the community that bore the brunt of the war against whites.

One Centenary farmer received a hand-written note from the leader of a particular terrorist gang asking him not to allow his daughters to ride their horses on an adjacent farm where their safety could not be guaranteed. So long as they rode on their own farm they would be safe. It seems the farmer in question was popular with his workers whereas the farmer on the adjacent farm was not.

Amongst Christians there were stories of divine intervention. One of these emanated from a captured terrorist who explained why his especially large group abandoned their planned attack of a farmstead. He said the attack was aborted when, upon arrival at the farmstead, many armed men dressed in illuminated white clothes and riding white horses surrounded the place; yet not one horseman had been present that night.

ZANLA recruitment

TERRORIST NUMBERS INSIDE THE COUNTRY during 1973 were insufficient to spread the SF as thinly as ZANLA had hoped. ZANLA losses, particularly to its leadership, were having a greater detrimental effect than we realised. Recruits sent to Tanzania for training would only be available in late 1974, but ZANLA could not wait that long. The short-term solution was to train recruits internally.

Diverting for a moment—our verbal, written and radio terminology changed in this period to identify individuals. These were:

CT—Communist Terrorist
EFA—European Female Adult
LTT—Locally Trained Terrorist
AFJ—African Female Juvenile
AMA—African Male Adult
EFJ—European Female Juvenile
EMA—European Male Adult
AMJ—African Male Juvenile
EMJ—European Male Juvenile
AFA—African Female Adult

Willing and unwilling recruits, mainly young males, were inducted for immediate training inside the country. Given old SKS and PPSH weapons, these young men and teenagers were taught rudimentary skills preparatory to armed combat. In most cases no more than two rounds were expended in training to conserve ammunition and limit the risk of exposure by the sound of gunfire. Inevitably these LTTs gained their shooting experience in combat, providing they survived the first contact with our troops; many did not!

The real value of LTTs to the regular elements of ZANLA was their local knowledge and their ability to move amongst the people. They could also expose themselves openly amongst the RSF when unarmed to gather intelligence and provide early-warning services. But the LTTs themselves gave ZANLA leaders many headaches since most became nasty little thugs who committed murder and rape, causing a great deal of tribal chaos. Many other youths, impressed by LTT thuggery, fashioned replicas of CT weapons from wood to terrorise adults, thereby creating a general breakdown in family unity and discipline.

Along with the training of LTTs, ZANLA commenced forced recruitment of youths, male and female, for external training. This came to the country's open attention on America's Independence Day when, during the early evening of 4 July 1973, seventeen heavily armed CTs stormed into the usually peaceful St Albert's Mission, causing fear and panic as they rounded up over 270 people. They stated that they were taking the secondary-level children, together with a number of adult teachers and mission staff, for military training outside the country.

Harassing and hurrying their frightened abductees, the CTs used force to accelerate the collection of food, clothing and blankets for the long walk through Mozambique to Zambia. From there they were to be transported to the Tanzanian training camps. Father Clemence Freymer bravely insisted he must go along to be with the children. He was the only white member of the group that set off that dark night for the steep descent down the escarpment. The missionaries, fearing landmines and ambush, set off on foot to raise the alarm at the nearest white farm. This could not be done by telephone because the lines had been cut and the mission had opted not to be on the Agri-Alert radio network.

At Centenary I was awakened at 02:00. It was normal practice to have two Provosts on immediate standby loaded with eight 4-inch para-illuminating flares to respond to CT attacks on farmsteads, so two of us scrambled to light up the route along which the CTs were taking the abductees.

My intimate knowledge of the route from St Albert's Mission to the base of the escarpment near Gutsa paid off. On the basis of the time that had elapsed, approximately seven hours, it seemed that a slow-moving party should be close to the valley floor. Though the night was black, there was sufficient starlight for the people on the ground to grope their way down the steep pathway.

Commencing a run from the mission, my first 600,000-candlepower illuminating flare was released on heading and time. Below my aircraft the flare, descending slowly on its parachute, created a pool of white light that reflected strongly off the haze. This made visual contact with ground impossible. After about five minutes' flare burnout, which was preceded

by bits of burning pyrotechnic compound falling free from the flare, signalling the second aircraft to drop his first flare. By standing off to one side and flying lower than the flare, I could see ground sufficiently to see the escarpment base and positively identify a well-defined ridge down which I knew the pathway ran. For forty continuous minutes we kept this area illuminated.

Later we learned that the flares had been directly above the CTs and their abductees. Initial reaction had caused sufficient panic and confusion for a number of children and one teacher to make good their escape and return to the mission. However, aided by the flares, the CTs regained control of those remaining and, knowing SF follow-up would come at first light, they split into two groups. In retrospect we realised that we should have ceased illuminating ground after ten minutes, in which case more abductees might have escaped under cover of darkness.

Upon reaching the valley floor, ten CTs took the adults off in one direction and seven CTs took the children along their normal infiltration route running alongside the Musengezi River. An RLI follow-up resulted in contact with the latter group. However, the troops were faced with a dilemma when the CTs used the abductees as human shields and opened fire from behind them. To mask a bit of fancy soldiering aimed at wresting advantage from the CTs via their left flank, half of the troops returned heavy fire deliberately aiming high above the terrified youngsters.

The children realised what was happening when the flanking troops opened fire and most managed to escape by running straight for the RLI troops. One mortally wounded CT was screaming loudly which added to the general confusion of gunfire and movement that persisted until the six CTs had made good their escape, but without any abductees. Had the RLI not been forced to avoid hitting any child, those six CTs would not have survived.

At this point the troops and Father Clemence Freymer gathered the children together and calmed them preparatory to their helicopter flight back to the mission. But valuable time had been lost before RLI learned of the second group with the adults.

All day I searched well ahead of a slow-moving tracker group but apart from seeing fragments of an ill-defined trail in the dry conditions, I could not spot a soul. This was frustrating and, at the time, I had no way of knowing that I had been instrumental in helping another thirty-three abductees escape. Those that returned to the mission said my aircraft had been directly above them on a number of occasions during the day. Whenever the aircraft came close, everyone was ordered to take cover and remain dead still. The lucky ones had remained in cover when the CTs ordered resumption of the march. The escapees told of terrible beatings for those who were discovered in their hiding places. Thanks to relentless pressure on the CT abductors, three of their numbers were killed and all of their abductees were eventually saved. In spite of failing on this particular occasion, ZANLA continued recruiting by force.

Pseudo-terrorist beginnings

AS EARLY AS THE LATE 1960s the Army Commander, Major-General Keith Coster, had given his support to ideas generated by Assistant Commissioner 'Oppie' Oppenheim of the BSAP. This was to develop pseudo-terrorist teams (not to be confused with SB plants into terrorist organisations). Selected Army, Police and SB personnel involved themselves in extensive trials but the exercise was shelved following incorrect assumptions and because their anti-terrorist plans did not suit the times. By 1973, however, changes in CT modus operandi suited pseudo-terrorist operations perfectly.

The only good to have come out of the early pseudo-terrorist trials was the development of the Tracker-Combat team concept. The first commander of the Territorial Army's Tracker-Combat School was Lieutenant Alan Savory, a politician, noted ecologist and master in bushcraft. Later his school was expanded to train regular Army personnel including the SAS and RAR, hence their availability as early as Op Nickel. African game-trackers were still being used extensively by the RLI during Op Cauldron.

Arising from his experiences in Malaya, Colonel John Hickman favoured pseudo-terrorist operations but his ideas differed from existing plans to draw all pseudo operators from SF personnel. John believed in 'turning' captured terrorists and inducting them into service under direction of regular personnel trained in pseudo ops. At that time, however, it was considered that all captured terrorists should be hanged, or at least receive life sentences. Any thought of integrating them with the regular Army was rejected out of hand. So John Hickman had to wait until he became the Brigadier Commanding JOC Hurricane before he could implement his own theory; and this turned out to be very successful.

John had the reputation of possessing the finest military brain in the Rhodesian Army and his flexibility and tactical thinking adapted quickly to every change in enemy strategy and tactics. I had witnessed his flexible approach during Op Excess when he persuaded Major Rob Southey to let me try my hand at moving Dumpy Pearce forward on an old trail.

Realising the time was right to put his pseudo ops theories into practice, the brigadier set up a secret 'safe house' from which his first small pseudo team prepared to emulate ZANLA gangs. The intention was to pose as ZANLA to gain the necessary intelligence that would facilitate destruction of whole ZANLA groups by regular forces. First to be co-opted were two SAS master trackers who also spoke Shona fluently. They were Sergeants André Rabie and 'Stretch' Franklin. From the RLI the brigadier brought in Sergeant Peter Clementshaw

and from RAR he selected three African soldiers. To this group was added a captured ZANLA terrorist who had been 'turned'.

By nature the African people of Rhodesia were gentle folk until subjected to the lies, false promises and other propaganda output of power-seeking individuals, who themselves had been duped by communists. The term 'turned' simply meant that an individual terrorist had been returned back to his original state and would willingly serve the Rhodesian cause.

Prior to deploying as pseudo CTs, the group was briefed in detail by Peter Stanton on the all-important 'does and don'ts' in their contacts with the African population. ZANLA, acting on the advice of their Chinese instructors, had adopted procedures by which the locals could recognise authentic ZANLA personnel or spot aliens purporting to be ZANLA 'comrades'. In early times ZANLA told the people what their men would eat and what would be left uneaten to prove their authenticity. Peter Stanton made sure he was always up to date with the latest feeding details by making this his first priority when interrogating captured terrorists. Other SB interrogators did likewise, though they were unaware of the reasons Peter kept pressing for such apparently mundane information.

Right from the start the locals were easily misled by the white pseudo operators who came to them in the black of night with blackened faces and arms. But it was worrying to be welcomed with open arms with not a word of their presence ever passing to the authorities.

Sadly, André Rabie was accidentally killed when the RLI, responding to André's call to action, misidentified him as a terrorist. On close inspection of the body the RLI were greatly distressed when they realised that they had killed a white man and even more so when they recognised André. Somehow André had passed an incorrect grid reference that led to the tragedy. Nevertheless sufficient success and experience had been gained to satisfy Brigadier Hickman that there was need to expand pseudo operations.

By October 1973 ground intelligence had virtually dried up; most available information was of an historic nature and of little use for military planning. The need to extend pseudo operations to generate up-to-the-minute information on the actual location of terrorist groups had been left rather too late and this brought the Army Commander directly into the picture. Major-General Peter Walls recalled Major Ron Reid-Daly from his leave pending retirement from the Army. The General invited Ron to remain in service to form and command a new regiment that would prepare for and conduct pseudo operations. The unit was to be named 'Selous Scouts'.

The nature of the new regiment's task was camouflaged by making it appear to be a specialised tracking establishment. For ages very few people knew of the Selous Scouts' real purpose. This was to develop and control many teams of pseudo-terrorist operators whose job it was to infiltrate ZANLA and ZIPRA with a view to eliminating terrorist groups and breaking up their organised structures. Ron Reid-Daly succeeded in creating his regiment in spite of untold obstacles that were placed in his way. His problems were almost entirely due to the fact that the Army HQ officers from whom he sought co-operation were totally in the dark on Ron's 'real' task.

When eventually he moved his ever-growing Selous Scouts' operational forces to their newly built battalion headquarters at Inkomo, Ron named it 'André Rabie Barracks' in memory of a fine soldier who had been the first of many pseudo operators to die in action.

Night-strike trials

ARMY HQ, RESPONDING TO CALLS from officers in the field, asked the Air Force to look into the possibilities of providing ground forces fire support at night by helicopters and Provosts. Air HQ expressed reservations but tasked me to conduct night trials for GAC strikes with guns and rockets. Using Provost 3605, the only aircraft fitted with four .303 machine-guns, I flew the trial, accompanied by Major Mike Shute of the School of Infantry.

Bright ground flares were used by an Army GAC callsign to mark FLOT. A level pass was made to see if the ground was visible. It seemed fine so I decided to try a live attack with a very early pullout. At the commencement of the dive from 1,500 feet I could see the ground around the flares, but as soon as I opened fire, tracer rounds streaming from both wings towards ground burned so brightly that only the ground flares remained visible. I pulled out at what I judged to be more than 500 feet above ground. However, the Kutanga Range Safety Officer gave me a low warning saying that I had cleared the ground by no more than a few feet.

On the second attack I was certain that I had pulled out much earlier than the first time only to be told that I had been so low that my navigation lights had disappeared from view in a shallow depression beyond the FLOT flares. I thought the RSO was having me on until the Army officer conducting the GAC confirmed how close we had come to death. There was no question of continuing this dangerous trial so I headed for base, much to Mike Shute's relief. My report to Air HQ advised against any night attack involving a dive profile as this would certainly result in disaster. Nevertheless, Army pushed for further trials, this time using Canberras in level flight.

Army field officers suggested that two or more machine-guns firing tracer rounds from different directions at the centre of a target should give a bomb-aimer a perfect aiming point. Again there was scepticism but the concept had to be tried. I was involved again, this time to assess the visible effects of

marking with tracer before committing a Canberra to the test. Flying at height I watched two guns firing with a convergence angle of little more than fifteen degrees. The crossover point was clear-cut and would be easy for the Canberra bomb-aimer to see. However, a Canberra's bombing run is very long when measured against the time machine-guns could provide continuous fire. There was a need, therefore, for many very short bursts to be fired simultaneously to ensure Canberra line-up, and a long burst for final aiming. So we put this to the test.

Repeatedly the Canberra ran in, but the gunners on the ground could not synchronise their firing during run-up, and both ran out of ammunition at the critical moment on each of a number of runs. It was obvious that, since this system could not be made to work in clinical conditions at Kutanga Range, there was no point in expecting better results in the field. In time to come an altogether better solution was found, as will be revealed later.

Pre-selection of Air Force commanders

FLIGHT LIEUTENANT MICK MCLAREN HAD been my first flying instructor in 1957 and I had served under him in 1969–1970 when he was Chairman of the Joint Planning Staff in the rank of group captain. His meteoric rise brought him to be the Commander of the Rhodesian Air Force in 1973 in the rank air marshal.

There were no doubts in the minds of most officers that Mick was the right man for the job because he had proved himself in every way. However, the discontent of one or two superseded senior officers reached political ears. For reasons I do not know, the politicians decreed that no such accelerated promotion should occur in the future and that Air HQ must pre-select officers to be groomed for the top Air Force post.

Frank Mussell was the obvious man to succeed Mick McLaren when he retired in 1977. For the term commencing 1981, Keith Corrans and Tol Janeke were earmarked as running mates and were immediately promoted to wing commander. This politically induced situation proved to be a bad move because it had forced Air HQ to pre-judge individual standings eight years ahead of time, and this had the effect of limiting the prospects of many officers who might have aspired to positions that now seemed blocked. Keith and Tol were both fine men but we could not understand how either one of them could have been selected ahead of Norman Walsh. Anyway, this early selection failed because Keith and Tol both took early retirement and Norman became Commander in 1981 in circumstances that couldn't have been foreseen in 1973.

Night ops difficulties

MY EXPERIENCE ON HELICOPTERS HAD highlighted the dangers of flying on dark nights. This was largely due to the helicopter's inherent instability, but following Guy Munton-Jackson's death, helicopter pilots were forbidden to fly unless there was a clearly defined horizon. For slow fixed-wing pilots who continued to operate at night in all conditions, save for low cloud and storms at destination airfields, dark nights presented very real difficulties.

Most readers will have flown many hours in airliners and may wonder what is so difficult about flying at night. Many scheduled departures and arrivals occur at night in marginal weather conditions, so where are the problems? Well, it is all a matter of instrumentation, flying aids, navigational aids and a second pilot to monitor and assist his captain at every stage of flight. These are all routinely available in all airliners that operate in and out of fully equipped airports having qualified air-traffic and radar controllers.

Although we were equipped with standard flight instrumentation, it was necessary to physically control an aircraft every second it was airborne. There were no such luxuries as autopilot, a second pilot, aids to pinpoint one's position or to guide one in for a safe landing. The airfields into which we operated had no let-down aids of any description. Very often, when cloud cover necessitated flying above minimum safe altitude to clear all high ground, our best assistance came from men on the ground saying something like, "We can hear you to our northeast."

Once guided to approximately overhead it was a matter of entering into a gentle descending turn hoping to break cloud close to the airfield before reaching minimum safety height. Over flat sections of the Zambezi Valley this was not too bad, but in mountainous terrain immense tensions built up in one's mind and body before breaking out below cloud and seeing one's destination.

With no aids to assist navigation and let-down in remote areas I, like most pilots, often wondered how I could have let myself in for such a hazardous occupation. On these occasions I longed for the safety of jet flying which always brought one back to a major airfield with all aids, including radar. But, being stuck with the problem, one had to work at remaining calm and reminding oneself that Air Force training had been geared to cater for these frightening situations.

Even when the destination airfield, other than Air Force FAFs, had been located, danger existed because pilots were forced to rely on soldiers, policemen and civilians to mark the runway. I will say more about this subject later.

Flying Provosts was always less trying that flying Trojans in identical situations. The Provost felt sturdy, it had ample power to cater for the unexpected and responded well to throttle and flight controls. Wearing a parachute also gave some comfort if everything went pear-shaped. On the other hand, the Trojan could be a real bitch, particularly when laden and there was no alternative but to stay with the beast, no matter what happened.

Trojan characteristics

THANKS TO SUPERB TECHNICIANS AND the excellent training given to its pilots, the Trojan did a marvellous job despite its limitations. All the same, this aircraft's unusual characteristics often took one by surprise by day as well as night.

I was returning from one recce sortie in Mozambique low on fuel when I encountered a solid line of cumulonimbus running the length of the escarpment. There was no way around the storm line, which was putting on a spectacular display of near-continuous lightning strikes. My destination was Centenary and it was already too dark to go into Mukumbura or Musengezi, so I selected a section between two huge cumulonimbus columns that appeared to offer the safest passage through the storm line.

With lights set to maximum brightness and having transferred attention to instruments, the cloud was entered with stopwatch running at an indicated height of 6,500 feet above sea level. Instantly smooth, straight and level flight changed as unseen forces within the storm cloud took hold of the Trojan and lifted it as if it was feather-light. Inside the aircraft the sensations, sounds and instrument indications were terrifying.

With all my strength I worked to keep wings level, paying scant attention to the varying pitch attitude as the airspeed indicator fluctuated rapidly between stalling speed and somewhere beyond VNE. The Vertical Speed Indicator was against its upper stop and the whole airframe shuddered and shook so violently that I thought it might break up. One minute and ten seconds after entering cloud, which felt like an eternity, the aircraft was spewed out of the storm into clear, calm air at 11,500 feet above sea level. Stretched out ahead was a fairyland of security lights burning brightly from Centenary's farmsteads.

5,000 feet gained in such a short time was one thing; unstoppable descents towards the ground with full power applied was quite another. There were times when it seemed such descents must end in disaster. On one particular occasion I was flying along a narrow valley in the Shamva area with the high ground right and left a little below the level of flight. The aircraft started to descend rapidly under the influence of a strong crosswind flow so I applied full power and was in a normal climbing attitude, but the aircraft continued descending into the valley.

I was not concerned about going all the way to ground because it was obvious that wind flow must level off before this occurred. My concern was for the ridge at the end of the blind valley that was too narrow to allow turn-about. The aircraft levelled out at about fifty feet as expected and remained there until lifted upwards so fast that it had risen above the high ground well before valley's end.

The Trojan's response to local windflow and thermal activity could have it descending like a streamlined brick or climbing like a homesick angel. For me the Trojan's sensitivity to air currents was especially annoying when I first started visual recce. It took some time to get used to trimming the aircraft and allowing it to float up and down without fighting to hold a fixed height. Somehow the downs seemed to equal the ups as the aircraft yow-yowed about the intended recce height.

SAS ops in Tete

UP UNTIL AUGUST 1973, SAS operations in Tete had not achieved what Brian Robinson had hoped for. Patrols succeeded in locating groups of ZANLA moving through the area but infantry reaction to SAS hot intelligence had been agonisingly slow and poor for a variety of reasons. The greatest of these was the pitifully small lift-capacity of only two helicopters operating from the co-located SAS and RAR Tactical HQs on the border at Musengezi Mission. Other helicopters were always tied up elsewhere on internal operations.

Parachute deployment of the infantry by Dakotas was an obvious solution but at the time there were no paratroopers besides the SAS. This was because the Air Force had only sufficient parachutes for the SAS and the Air Force Parachute Training School was short of PJIs (Parachute Jump Instructors). So, although planning and provisioning was underway to make all regular soldiers paratroopers, we were stuck with what was available.

When the SAS located CT groups, the two Alouettes had to make a number of round trips to position sufficient troops ahead of the assessed line of CT movement. This in itself involved a lot of time. But a greater limitation came from the noise of helicopters that carried for miles in the flat Zambezi Valley. CTs, having travelled through the silence of bush for many days, could hear helicopters flying as much as thirty

kilometres away, which accounted for major deviations in their headings that invariably bypassed the awaiting troops.

The SAS had been entirely successful in their classical role of finding the enemy for the infantry. However, repeated failures by the RAR to capitalise on the good work of his men made Brian Robinson reconsider the SAS role. He concluded that SAS callsigns must continue in their classical role but take on the ZANLA groups themselves.

In essence, Brian advocated a 'seek-and-find then shoot-and-scoot' style of operation. To be effective in mobile reconnaissance as well as in static surveillance necessitated the use of small patrols. This meant that, when they came upon large groups that had previously been passed on to the RAR, they would not be able to engage the enemy in typical infantry fashion. Relying entirely on surprise, they would have to act rapidly to inflict maximum casualties and get the hell away as fast as possible. Such hit-and-run operations would obviously be dangerous and immediate air support had to be discounted. Nevertheless, Brian pushed for this new approach because he had supreme confidence in his men. They had all been painstakingly selected from the best volunteers and were trained to the highest degree possible. But he also realised that, if there was to be any hope of turning the ZANLA tide, it was essential that the SAS should operate in depth north of the Zambezi River with regular infantry covering the ground south of the river. For this he had to have at least two helicopters and two Provosts permanently available on immediate readiness at his Tac HQ.

For this new role, there were three essential changes to be made. Firstly, an SAS Tactical HQ would have to base permanently inside Mozambique next to a runway that could support Provosts and laden Dakotas. Secondly, patrols would have to operate in groups of only four men (known as a stick); a limitation imposed by the lift capacity of an Alouette III carrying a machine-gun and gunner. Finally, SAS sticks would have to operate six weeks in the field with only ten days' leave between deployments.

In September 1973 Brian got his way and an SAS Tac HQ was established next to a scruffy little airstrip at Macombe. Macombe was a Portuguese *aldeamento* on the south bank of the Zambezi River lying midway between the north-flowing rivers Angwa and Musengezi. Two Provosts and two Alouettes positioned forward from Musengezi Mission to Macombe on a daytime-only basis, as SAS could not guarantee their safety at night.

From the outset the SAS was entirely successful in this new style of operation but the RAR deployment to Macombe was withheld for months. So any advantages given by the natural Zambezi River obstacle and the disruptive effects of the SAS operations to its north were largely lost. Nevertheless SAS disruption of ZANLA's supply lines greatly assisted in relieving internal stresses.

I visited Brian at Macombe when he first moved there and

passed him all the information I had gained from my recce work north of the Zambezi. Again I suggested to him that I should continue visual recce to continuously update the information and provide him with a daytime radio link to his troops. Brian would not entertain the idea. He continued to insist that, except in emergency, the SAS areas of operation should be free of any air activity. Contrary to Brian Robinson's thinking, mine was that aircraft on visual reconnaissance should be a permanent feature over the entire Tete region, both within and beyond the SAS areas of operations. I contended that it was essential to provide the SAS with fresh intelligence upon which to plan, thereby saving lengthy ground recces to find the best sites to monitor, ambush or attack.

Over months to come I would build up information on civilian locations, routes and terrorist camps covering large areas beyond those in which the SAS were active. When SAS operations switched to areas I had covered, as much as six weeks previously, Brian reported that my information, though correct, was out of date. Not surprisingly the men on the ground ignored much of the air recce intelligence that had been so painstakingly put together. But one thing they helped clarify was that I had been accurate in my assessment of terrorist bases, as opposed to civilian camps. What had helped me distinguish between these sites, which looked much the same from height, were female toilet paths leading out of civilian locations.

I was so frustrated by Brian Robinson's attitude that I opted for air-controlled strikes on fresh terrorist bases. The Air Force never expected the successes that could be achieved by a pure SAS ground attack or those involving air strikes in conjunction with the SAS. Nevertheless, we knew that FAC strikes would demoralise and disrupt FRELIMO and ZANLA in areas unattended by SAS. In too many respects our Air Force had been forced to act independently in like manner to the Portuguese, which we had criticised so strongly—but there were advantages to be gained. I continued recces north of the Zambezi, always keeping well clear of the SAS and taking time before calling for jet-strikes. Once these got under way we developed procedures that required close understanding and co-operation. It took a few calls before FAC-controlled airstrikes became a well-honed routine.

As mentioned earlier, jet-strikes in direct support of earlier SAS operations had been very hit-and-miss affairs that improved little over time. For the men on the ground, particularly in flat terrain, there were considerable difficulties in judging the exact point of a jet-strike because bush and rough ground usually intervened between the GAC location and target. This meant that corrections had to be assessed from the sound of exploding weapons or from dust rising above the bush some seconds after each strike. FAC did not suffer these difficulties.

The cost of live strikes on terrorist bases was naturally much greater than on routine weapons training, but routine training was conducted on a range that every pilot and navigator knew intimately. Unlike calls to live targets, routine training required no hurried navigation planning or the split-second timing involved in co-ordinating fast jets with a slow-flying FAC aircraft.

Perfect timing for maximum surprise followed by slick and accurate placement of weapons were all essential ingredients considering the speed at which terrorists could run clear of their bases. The value gained by jet crews scrambling to meet FAC in remote areas for strikes on never-before-seen targets was immense, and it prepared us well for the future.

With every target's grid reference I also gave an IP (Initial Point) and the exact time of my marker strike. The jets planned to fly directly to the IP—a clearly identifiable feature out of sight and hearing range of the target itself. Formation leaders worked out the heading and precise flight time from the IP to target so as to strike no more than three seconds behind my target markers. I too would have an IP point from which to move in orbits towards the target.

Canberras could not strike anything like as quickly as the fighter-bombers because the bomb-aimer required time to pass heading corrections to his pilot which necessitated quite a large stand-off distance at the moment of mark, so they were never used alone for FAC work against fleeting targets. In addition to the long run in, the flight time of bombs exceeded 10 seconds and shrapnel settling time limited following Canberras to long intervals between individual strikes. Consequently Hunters or Vampires usually preceded Canberras. Strikes initiated by Canberras with fighter-bombers following became commonplace in later years when the bombers made their attacks in formation. However, most early FAC work was with Hunters only—usually four of them.

When the lead pilot checked in about five minutes before reaching the IP, we would synchronise watches and confirm individual running times from IPs to target. I would be told what weapons were being carried and the sequence in which they were to be delivered. This gave opportunity to suggest how the weapons should be distributed on the line of attack, relative to my target markers.

Formation leaders normally planned to arrive at IP with as much as three minutes to spare. This was useful as it allowed me to make a slow approach onto my own IP in a series of orbits that the enemy on the ground recognised as my normal flight pattern. Even when out of sight, the sound of a piston aircraft indicates whether it is flying on a straight line or orbiting. In orbit the sound varies from highest frequency when approaching to lowest frequency when departing. For reasons of surprise, I needed to ensure that this continued right up to the moment that I turned in to fire my markers.

For Hunters covering ground at the rate of seven nautical miles per minute, or Vampires and Canberras at five nm per minute, changes in wind velocity seldom affected their timing by more than parts of a second. However, the same conditions could make an enormous difference to the slow Trojan, which is why my own IP was always relatively close to target.

Because it was important to mark bang on time I planned my final orbit line to be farthest from the jet attack line. In this way I was able to make adjustments in response to the strike leader's calls. If I was running late I could turn in early, and if running early, turn in late. There were other important reasons to be on the side opposite to the jet attack direction.

The Trojan noise covered that of the approaching jets and its presence drew terrorist attention away from the direction of their approach. In earlier times I was seldom aware of enemy fire though I knew it was happening because of the odd hole in my aircraft; but any ground fire directed at me provided additional noise cover and a perfect distraction.

The camouflage paint on all of our aircraft was incredibly effective. This made it very difficult, even impossible, for high-flying jets to spot the FAC aircraft before reaching target. A variety of visual aids were tried. These included flashing strobe lights but only one worked reasonably well. This was a huge white 'T' painted on the top surface of the Trojan's fuselage and wings. To make the 'T' clearly visible to the leading jet was another reason for marking towards the jets.

Visibility markings.

The Squadron Commander of Hunters in the period 1973–4 was Rob Gaunt. Flying FAC for him was quite an experience. Unlike other leaders, Rob favoured a procedure that worked well for him. He descended from the IP to run in at low level about one minute out from target. In this way he always picked up my aircraft flying at 2,000 feet before he pulled up to his 'perch' point, keeping me visual all the way.

As I pulled up to roll over into the dive, Rob had his nose pointing towards the target, finger on trigger. Just by watching my dive, Rob placed his gunsight pipper at the point he expected to see the marker rockets. On three occasions I recall seeing Rob's 30mm cannon shells exploding bang on target just before my phosphorus rockets reached ground. The white markers looked puny in the centre of the large area covered by his 30mm cannon shell flashes that rippled through target at forty rounds per second. This was very spectacular but I always

tensed my buttocks expecting Rob to collide with me. There was really no danger at all; his Hunter always flashed through well below me.

There was seldom need to call corrections to succeeding pilots, usually three of them, who placed their strikes to cover the target area without overlaps. When all was over, the jets returned to base and I continued recce, seldom to know what results had been achieved. Occasionally I saw individuals running during my marker attack, then nothing until the last Hunter had run through target. There were always bashas burning furiously with much black smoke and dust drifting on the wind before any human movement was observed. On occasions secondary explosions removed any doubts I might have experienced when no persons were seen.

I continued to deeply regret not being able to work in the SAS areas of operations. Had this been allowed, no airstrike would have been made without SAS verification of ZANLA or FRELIMO presence. Following an airstrike the SAS would have been able to capitalise on enemy confusion and the Air Force would have known what results had been achieved. Many months were to pass before SAS moved in immediately after every air action. In the meanwhile, the SAS created havoc on the ground using no more than twenty-four men in six sticks of four men each. It took FRELIMO some time to realise what was happening and then they themselves started employing large forces to search for the elusive SAS; a kind of terrorist war in reverse!

A pathfinder group making a free-fall parachute descent at last light from a Dakota flying high-level over unpopulated territory usually preceded deployment of the main SAS force. The four-man pathfinder group would then search for a suitable site to receive twenty men who would be flown in the following night.

At their selected DZ (drop zone) the pathfinders provided pilots with the QFE (altimeter setting for zero height at the DZ) and guided the Dakota captain by VHF radio directly towards the DZ. Flying at 500 to 800 feet above ground, the pilot was told when to switch on 'red light' (standby) and when to switch on 'green light' (go); whereupon twenty men would launch themselves into the black. The reason for such low-level drops was to minimise the possibility of paratroopers drifting beyond the DZ. With the advent of anti-collision aids for aircraft known as strobe lights, their highly visible flashes provided perfect beacons for pilots to home on. To screen a strobe light's potent flashes, SAS set them up in such a way as to make them visible only to the para-Dakota.

By daybreak all parachutes and stores had been cached and, following a final briefing, all six sticks split up into four-man patrols and dispersed to their allocated areas. During the following six weeks the sticks operated independently, except when a target required them to rendezvous to strike in strength. Otherwise regrouping occurred at fortnightly intervals to receive night deliveries of rations and munitions from a Dakota that would, again, be controlled from the ground.

Back at Macombe, the Provosts and Alouettes remained on immediate standby. Calls for support always involved a long wait for the SAS men working a long way from Macombe. Brian Robinson often accompanied Provost pilots, not only to talk to his men directly but because he was crazy about flying. Helicopters were often called for casualty evacuation or 'hot

SAS training on low-level static-line delivery. Note the various stages of parachute canopy development.

extraction'. Provosts usually accompanied these helicopters and were also called upon to provide close fire support to any callsign being harassed by large FRELIMO forces. Considering the vastness of the territory and the minimal effects of Provost machine-gun and 37mm Sneb rocket strikes, there was little more that one or a pair of Provost pilots could do other than provide distraction and interfering fire to give the SAS a chance to break contact.

Hot extraction by helicopters necessitated great courage by the helicopter crews who almost always came under enemy fire before, during and after snatching breathless soldiers away to safety. With little or no time to find suitable LZs, and under stress from enemy attention, many helicopters suffered minor damage to rotor blades as they sliced their way into extra-tight landing spots before struggling upward with the extra weight of troops.

Hoisting gear was seldom fitted to helicopters on operations because of the weight penalty they imposed. In any case the cable took ages to reach ground and was slow in lifting one or two men at a time; an absolute no-no for hot extraction! So an alternative device was employed. Where landing was not possible, a fixed length tethered cable with a crude bar arrangement at its end was thrown over the side to lift a maximum of four soldiers out of hot spots. Once well clear of the enemy, the soldiers were put down where the helicopter could either land to bring them inside or leave them to continue their work. But use of the hot extraction cable was a last resort. When a helicopter is hovering close to the ground, it is flying 'in ground effect' which means that the cushion of air caused by backpressure from the ground assists in producing lift. In this condition the power required to remain airborne is a great deal less at any given weight than when the helicopter is hovering high 'out of ground effect' at the same weight.

When the hot extraction device was used to lift only two soldiers, power demand was usually close to maximum. With four soldiers clinging to the hot bar the power demand was always above gearbox maximum allowance, causing rapid overheating of the main rotor gearbox. Because of this, a pilot lifting more than two soldiers needed to get into forward flight as quickly as possible to bring down the load on gears. In so doing, soldiers were sometimes dragged through bushes and trees during lift-off from the ground. Landing them was easier because the pilot could choose his ground away from enemy attention.

Seldom were SAS sticks returned to base. They were simply moved away from the immediate danger area and re-deposited to continue their offensive work. The admiration aircrew had for these amazing SAS men was beyond expression and, despite the dangers involved, every effort was made to ensure their safety. The SAS had reciprocal opinion of the Blues

At the end of six weeks the sticks moved to their original cache point for helicopter uplift of parachutes and men. Extra helicopters were usually made available from internal operations for these pre-planned extractions. For the men on the ground there was no sound in the world so pleasing as that of helicopters flying in to take them home. For the helicopter crews this particular task was a bittersweet one.

Just consider picking up men who had been operating in the bush for six weeks in conditions alternating between blinding heat and ice-cold rain, yet wearing the same sweaty grime-caked and torn clothes day in and day out. With blackened and bearded faces to hide their whiteness, they had had no chance to bath or wash their clothing. On the other hand the helicopter crews, fresh and clean from daily showers, comfortable beds and good food, could never be fully prepared for the appalling stench that invaded their helicopters. But SAS smiles, exaggerated by the whiteness of teeth and eyeballs, made their job very special.

On arrival at Macombe the weary men were treated to long-awaited baths or showers, shaves and the joy of fresh clothing. Only when clean and comfortable did they turn to ice-cold beer and a good fresh meal. Following a full debriefing the men were flown back to Rhodesia for their short ten-day R&R (rest and retraining—also known as rest and recuperation) break. Whilst this was happening, other SAS callsigns were deploying for their long stint in hostile territory.

On Christmas day 1973, I cut short a visual recce flight to go into Macombe to collect the Army Commander, General Peter Walls. He had parachuted in during daylight hours to be with the deployed SAS callsigns who had congregated to celebrate Christmas miles from any FRELIMO area. Descending with him were parachutes delivering hampers of hot turkey, ham and all the trimmings.

After two hours with the men, the general was taken by helicopter to Macombe where I picked him up for a flight to Centenary for further visits with his troops. Along the way I took the opportunity of showing General Walls a major base that had been established by ZANLA inside Rhodesia. ZANLA called it 'Central base'.

First internal recce success

GROUND FORCES CAME UPON CENTRAL base during a follow-up on CT tracks. This base was on the Zambezi Valley floor many miles from the nearest village. When I saw it I was horrified that I had been working in Mozambique in the belief that I could not be too useful in Rhodesia. But Central base, though quite different to any base in Mozambique, was so blatantly obvious that I decided to get back to internal recce.

Having covered the remote regions on the Zambezi Valley

floor without finding anything like another Central base, I returned to the difficult terrain in the populated areas on the high ground. After two days of fruitless work, I found a small base near Mount Darwin and judged it to be occupied. The base itself was in a line of thick bush running north to south along a ridge. A river ran east to west past the north end of the base and open ground lay on both the east and west sides. I gained the impression that CTs would only break south through the best bush cover available.

I landed at FAF 4 where arrangements were made to borrow two helicopters from FAF 3 to add to the two helicopters based there and the RLI put together twenty troops. When all were assembled, I briefed everyone before getting airborne to mark the target with a salvo of thirty-six rockets. When I pulled out of my attack, the helicopters swept around the target dropping their RLI sticks as planned. From there on, four groups of troops, who I could see clearly, moved forward ever so slowly, fearing to bump into each other. I attempted to direct them but the officer on the ground was reluctant to accept advice and directions from above. Only when they were close up against the base did the CTs open fire.

As soon as the CTs started running I saw them clearly and could not understand why I had not seen them before. However, every time an individual stopped moving he was lost to my view, even though I knew precisely where he had stopped. The action was short, resulting in six CTs dead and one captured wounded. Nine got away through the cover in the south, just as I had expected. It was a frustrating experience to see those CTs slipping away when I was unable to strike and had no 4 Squadron aircraft or helicopter airborne to kill or block them.

Up until this action helicopters had seldom gathered to place meaningful numbers of troops around CT groups. I cannot say for certain that this marked the beginning of what was to become Fire Force, but I do know that it influenced the Army to have an officer airborne for similar set-piece actions that followed.

Having experienced this minor success inside the country, it was time to teach internal recce to my pilots. This was a difficult task considering I myself was still struggling to develop the art of finding CTs in TTLs. Mike Litson was the first pilot to fly with me because he had shown keen interest in the role. Together we had a few more successes. Unfortunately I did not get any further with other squadron pilots for a while because Police General HQ brought pressure to bear on Air HQ to teach visual recce to the Police Reserve Air Wing.

Training PRAW

WING COMMANDER OZZIE PENTON HAD become deeply involved in managing the Air Force Volunteer Reserve squadrons and, through this, had been roped in by PGHQ to act as an air liaison officer for their PRAW. It was he who had been persuaded by PGHQ to have PRAW trained in visual recce as a matter of urgency, so Ozzie sought my co-operation.

The Police Air Wing pilots and observers were very keen to become as active as possible against CTs; a welcome break from dull communication flights as glorified taxi drivers. Of greater importance was the fact that most PRAW were farmers who longed to settle scores with those CT groups that had been attacking farms in their areas.

Unlike most of the young pilots on my squadron, these reservists were very attentive, never seeming to be bored during detailed lectures and long training flights. But, despite their keenness, it soon became clear to me that few would master the art of scanning large tracts of ground and become proficient at separating normal from abnormal signs in the vast networks of paths created by men and beasts.

Bill Ludgater and his observer, Wally Barton, spent enormous effort and time making long reconnaissance flights in Bill's Cessna 180. Unfortunately, their efforts amounted to very little. The problem was that Bill had far too many places checked out by ground forces that soon lost interest in chasing 'lemons'. ('Lemon' was a term used to indicate the non-presence of CTs; a sour experience.)

Hamie Dax and his observer Sarel Haasbroek were at the other end of the scale. Right from the beginning it was obvious to me that they would do well. The aircraft they operated was far from ideal because its low forward-set wing design made it a very poor reconnaissance aircraft. In time, and in spite of this limitation, these two were so successful that they gained an excellent reputation with Air Force and RLI following a number of good contacts they initiated within the Centenary and Mount Darwin regions.

In the meanwhile the number of armed contacts with ZANLA groups was rising. In one of these, Air Lieutenant Dave Rowe had a lucky escape thanks to cool thinking between himself and his technician, Sergeant Carl de Beer. Dave's right arm and right leg were instantly incapacitated by enemy fire during an approach to land troops. Transferring his left hand to the cyclic control column Dave was able to hold direction but he needed Carl to manage the collective control lever. Once full control was established with the aircraft level at cruising speed, Carl turned up the friction knob to hold the collective lever in position so that he could safely leave it and attend to

Dave's wounds. Having repositioned the troops that were still on board. Carl worked from an awkward angle behind Dave's seat to stem the flow of blood. On arrival at base Dave and Carl co-ordinated their control movements for a roll-on landing that, to the relief of the troops, was a safe one.

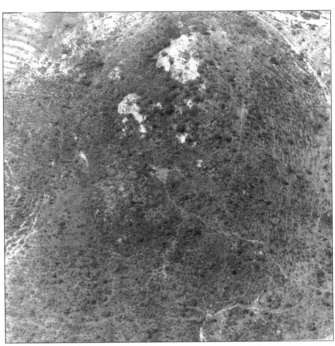

Note the profusion of pathways in this photograph. Sweeping around the hill from top to right are typical cattle tramlines. Others are normal human routing paths. The squiggly pathway centre bottom leading to the regular path rising from right to centre was the telltale indication leading to the terrorist base amongst large trees within the rocky outcrops at photo centre.

Strela missiles

RUSSIAN ANTI-AIRCRAFT MISSILES (NATO codename Grail but better known as Strela) were known to be in FRELIMO's possession so, late in 1973, I made a request to Air HQ to take steps to protect our aircraft from these 'heat seeking' weapons. It was only a matter of time before one of my squadron's aircraft would be shot down and I was acutely aware that I was the most likely candidate because I was exposed to FRELIMO forces for many hours on end, flying at heights perfectly suited to Strela.

Apart from myself, I worried about my Provost pilots acting

in support of the SAS in FRELIMO-dominated territory, particularly when they conducted strikes on the enemy. The helicopters, though vulnerable at height, always flew just above the trees to give them best protection against all types of enemy fire except when hovering, landing or lifting off.

Months passed but no action was forthcoming from Air HQ or the technical boffins at CSIR (Council for Scientific and Industrial Research) in South Africa. During a visit to Air HQ I raised the matter again and was told that counter-missile work could not be undertaken, as this had not been catered for in the Air Force budget. Instead I was instructed to include Strela protection in 4 Squadron's 1975 bids. Being really upset by this standard response, I expressed the view that we would have to lose aircraft and crews to Strela before any action was taken. Unhappily I was proven right.

Crop-spraying in Tete

IN JANUARY 1974 I NOTICED that maize crops, which had not been grown in Tete south of the Zambezi for the past two years, were flourishing. This meant ZANLA would be able to feed off the local people who were obviously returning to areas from which they had fled in 1972. Most of these people, then living in small hidden camps, appeared to have come out of the Portuguese *aldeamento* at Macombe. However, the benefit that would derive to ZANLA from the availability of maize meal was unacceptable and a decision was made to destroy the crops and force the civilians to return to the *aldeamento*.

A Cordon Sanitaire was still being constructed along the northeastern borderline where thousands of anti-personnel mines were laid between two electrified fences. Between and either side of these fences, a chemical defoliant had been sprayed to destroy vegetation. The defoliant had worked well on bush but its effectiveness against crops was not known. Nevertheless it was decided to use the same stuff because ample stocks were immediately available.

Only one civilian crop-sprayer pilot was prepared to take on the job in hostile Tete. I cannot recall the name of the well-built pilot I briefed at Mount Hampden Airport. He calculated the amount of fluid he required and this was positioned at the RAR Tac HQ at Musengezi Mission. I provided top cover and guided the pilot from field to field. Once he saw each field, or complex of fields, he did his own planning and meticulously covered the awkwardly shaped crops whilst I looked on from above.

On return to Musengezi after his fourth flight to recharge his tanks, he experienced difficulty in keeping his twin-Comanche on the runway. A bullet strike to the aircraft had punctured a main wheel tyre but little other damage had occurred. As soon as a replacement wheel from Salisbury was fitted the pilot got airborne again and we completed the job on 19 January 1974. Fortunately the rain held off long enough for the spray to be absorbed by the maize plants and in five days browning of the crops confirmed that the spray had worked.

Chris Weinmann joins 4 Squadron

BECAUSE I SPENT MOST OF my time in the operational areas, I placed great reliance on Rob Tasker and Bruce Collocott to manage the squadron at Thornhill. However, we started experiencing some discipline difficulties amongst a handful of young pilots because Rob and Bruce, though excellent officers, were too gentle in nature to handle them. Another problem I had was that 4 Squadron had no qualified PAI to ensure pilot proficiency in weapons delivery at a time when we most needed this. Until this time we had been reliant on John Blythe-Wood and myself, both unqualified substitutes.

Air HQ approval was given to my request for Chris Weinmann to replace Bruce Collocott. Flight Lieutenant Chris Weinmann seemed to be the ideal man for our needs because he was a qualified PAI who struck me as being a no-nonsense disciplinarian. Rob Tasker, being the only instructor beside myself, remained essential.

Chris had flown Trojans when they first arrived in Rhodesia but was then flying Hunters In November 1973 he was posted to 4 Squadron and Bruce went to 3 (Transport) Squadron.

Chris Weinmann.

Whereas Bruce was openly delighted with his posting Chris secretly hated having to leave the glory of Hunters to step down to slow piston-driven machines. Typically, he put his personal desires aside and settled to his new responsibilities with the determination I had expected from him. As soon as Rob re-familiarised him on Trojans and Provosts, Chris got stuck into improving weapons proficiency amongst all pilots, myself included. Thanks to him, disciplinary difficulties that had existed at junior pilot level ceased.

Night casevacs

4 SQUADRON PILOTS WERE FACED WITH major problems operating Trojans into remote airstrips at night in response to calls for casevac or urgent re-supply. This was because no facilities existed to clearly demarcate runway boundaries for take-off and landing.

On grass runways at main and established Forward Airfields, gooseneck flares were placed on the 100-metre markers along one side of the runway. Two flares at start and end of the runway, on the side opposite to the flare line, defined where runway centre-line lay. This assisted pilots to clearly identify the runway and to judge their landing approach angle and hold-off height for touch down.

A gooseneck flare was something like a squat domestic watering can with carrying handle. A thick wick in the spout was exposed for about four inches outside the spout with the other end lying in raw paraffin inside the can. The wick fitted tightly in the spout to ensure that flame at the lighted end did not transfer to paraffin in the can.

In remote areas there were no cumbersome gooseneck flares, so a crude system of marking the airstrip was used. Invariably there were Army or Police vehicles at the strips into which 4 Squadron aircraft were called, so we used these as runway markers. Two vehicles were placed on the runway centre line, one at each end of the runway. With head and taillights on, the vehicles faced the direction the ground forces wished a pilot to land. On his approach for landing, a pilot saw the rear lights of both vehicles and the headlights of the first vehicle, when bright enough, helped him judge the round out for landing.

Though this method was successfully employed it required great skill in judgement and I considered it too dangerous to continue. What was needed was something along the lines of the gooseneck flares to mark an entire runway; so I produced small one-time disposable mini-flares for all ground forces to carry as standard equipment.

I acquired empty half-pint paint tins with metal bungs and screw caps. Each tin was filled with paraffin and a round wick was inserted into the paraffin through a hole in the metal bung. The screw cap trapped the outside of the wick and sealed in the paraffin until removed for use. Night-landing trials with these mini-flares were successful and eliminated any need for vehicles that were, themselves, hazardous obstructions on any runway.

Boxes containing twelve filled, sealed and ready-to-use mini-flares and a box of sealed matches were issued to Army and Police with simple instructions on how to lay them out on a 1,000-metre runway. For the most part their introduction into the field made night landings at remote airfields simpler and safer. However, there were two incidents that raised serious questions about some ground forces' understanding of air operations and their ability to interpret the simplest of instructions. The first was when I was called out late one night to casevac an SAP man from Sipolilo to Salisbury. We were told that the man had suffered a heart attack and was in such a bad state that he had to be taken to Salisbury urgently.

When I arrived over Sipolilo, the runway flare line was so short it appeared as if I was flying at 30,000 feet, when in fact I was only 1,500 feet above ground. The callsign on the ground had great difficulty speaking understandable English and I could not understand his fast-spoken Afrikaans. Eventually I was able to understand that all the flares had been incorrectly laid between two 100-metre markers instead of one flare on each of the ten 100-metre markers along one side of the runway. After a while the flares were relayed correctly and I made a normal landing. But when I taxiied to waiting vehicles, I was greeted with the sight of the 'heart attack' victim walking briskly and unaided to the aircraft.

The second incident ended in tragedy near the end of my tour with 4 Squadron. During the night of 17 December 1974, Brian Murdoch was called to uplift two Army casualties from Mushumbi Pools airstrip in the Zambezi Valley. The callsign concerned were either unaware of the mini-flares they were carrying as standard equipment or were too lazy to find them. Whatever the case, they used vehicles to mark the runway.

Brian landed on the wet muddy strip, then turned around and taxiied back to the vehicle over which he had passed on landing. The vehicle that had been at the far end of the runway had, for some reason, been right next to the Trojan during the loading of the casevac. When Brian was ready to take off, this vehicle repositioned but, through ignorance, the driver did not go all the way to the end of the runway. He stopped some 300 metres short of the runway's end next to a large puddle of water "to make sure the pilot missed it."

In the wet conditions that prevailed, a Trojan needed the full length of Mushumbi Pools runway but Brian had no way of knowing the ignorant driver had shortened this. It can only be guessed that Brian was forced to heave the aircraft into the air too early by yanking down full flap; but he did not achieve sufficient height to prevent his nose wheel from striking the vehicle. The low-powered engine was hard-pressed to propel the bulky Trojan at the best of times, but full flap and impact with the vehicle placed Brian, flying on instruments, in a no-win situation. The aircraft was observed to change course to the right before crashing into a riverbed where Brian, Corporal Parker and Lance-Corporal Povey died instantly. Had the callsign used the mini-flares, which we later established they had, this wasteful tragedy would not have occurred.

Improving tactics

TEN MONTHS PRIOR TO HIS DEATH, I had instructed Brian Murdoch along with Chris Weinmann on internal and external recce. From this time on I progressively worked through all the squadron pilots, which was both necessary and frustrating. It became clear that only one in fifteen pilots had any hope of succeeding in visual recce work because it required stamina and patience for lengthy flights and, above all, an earnest desire to locate CTs. Too many pilots were quite happy to sit back at base waiting in comfort for calls to action. Such calls came in response to CT actions from RSF men in observation posts on hilltops, from recce pilots and more and more from Selous Scouts pseudo operators, though at the time these were being attributed to normal ops because few people knew of Selous Scouts' secret penetration into terrorist networks. However, this changed when deployments of pseudo groups was made by helicopters because this brought helicopter crews into direct contact with the pseudo terrorists and exposed their ops areas. To retain the highest degree of secrecy possible, Selous Scouts 'forts' were built at Air Force FAFs. From the high security walls of forts, the pseudos were driven in closed vehicles to the end of a runway or a suitable secure area close by for helicopter uplift to their operational area drop-off points.

It was during recce training with Chris and Brian that we located a 'live CT camp', which led to a successful follow-up operation. This was on 15 February when the three of us split up to strike with three fixed-wing aircraft ahead of helicopters bringing in RLI ground troops.

Every air action involving expenditure of weapons necessitated the submission to Air HQ of an Air Strike Report. ASRs tended to be very matter-of-fact in style so they failed to convey any sense of excitement and fear, nor tell of the hard sweat and toil of troops on the ground.

The ASR raised for this specific operation is used to illustrate the composition and handwritten contents of ASRs. Excluded from this and all other ASRs in this book are the accompanying technical details and weapon expenditure schedules. The exact words recorded in manuscript by officers in the field and up the chain of command in Air HQ, are reproduced without regard to grammatical errors.

PILOTS REPORT
1. As a result of 4 Squadron's visual recce training a number of terrorist bases and suspected bases were located. A terrorist base a US 468605 appeared to be occupied at 151415B. Lt Col Southey and Flt Lt Bennie were briefed on the situation at 1500 at which time it was decided that immediate action should be taken.

2. Five helicopters were on hand as well as the recce Trojan that was armed. Two Provosts were called for and flown by pilots Weinmann and Murdoch who were familiar with the target lay out.
3. The Trojan was flown by OC 4 Squadron at 2000' agl and 200 yds ahead of the two Provosts. The five helicopters with assault and stop troops followed immediately behind the Provosts. Take off and lift off occurred as planned at 151615B.
4. All weapons were placed on target points selected at the pre strike briefing.
5. Due to a shortage of ground troops, ground to the north of the river which formed the northern barrier to terr escape was covered by OC 4 Sqn and east of the camp was patrolled by Air Lt Law and Air Lt Thorne.
6. Air strike must have severely disrupted the terrorists because the assault troops made contact 4 minutes after strike. At this time it is known that 8 ters were killed and equipment has fallen into troops' hands.
7. Reason for success of this exercise was undoubtedly Lt Col Southey's faith in air recce and his willingness to strike without delay. Army/ Air force co-operation could not have been better.

(Signed) Squadron Leader P.J.H. Petter-Bowyer

Comments by OPS CDR., OCFW, Sqn Cdr
1. a. Trojan 3234 was holed by one bullet. Whether this was during the recce phase or during the attack is not known.
*   b. The success of this operation goes to prove that recce can be extremely valuable and thought should be given to the greater use of this role in our present situation; the advantage being that up-to-date information can be gained and if the reaction to this intelligence is swift, results will be achieved.*
*   c. If the use of air recce (visual) is increased with the view to using this type of quick reaction tactic, ground forces will have to be made available, on a prompt force basis, at either Centenary or Mt. Darwin or both. If this was done, the type of attacks planned for 19th, 20th Feb 74 could have been handled in a similar way using jet effort as the air strike medium. Therefore, the attack would have been on the date the targets were located instead of a week later.*

(Signed) Squadron Leader H.G. Griffiths

2. (1) No requirement for GAC or FLOT.
*   (2) I fully agree with the comments 1 b. above but our ability to meet this requirement is not possible at the present time on a continuous basis. No 4 Squadron has a major problem in training recce pilots and no sooner do they build up to a good standard when postings intervene and thus back to square one. As Ops Cmdr I would dearly love to have a good recce pilot of the calibre of Sqn Ldr Petter-Bowyer on permanent attachment at FAF 3 but the way I see it at the present time it is not possible, but we must work to this aim. The proof lies in the fact that during the period in which Sqn Ldr Petter-Bowyer was training Weinmann and Murdoch, the info gained led to this Air Strike plus 4 other major ter strikes, 3 of which were on occupied camps.*

3) Para 1 c. refers. Ground troops within Rhodesia are available for prompt force type actions and this is how the follow up to this strike was made possible. In respect of the strikes carried out on 21, 22 and 23 and 24, these were all in Mozambique and required regrouping of ground forces. It is appreciated that it has been agreed that jet ops need not be followed up by immediate ground ops but in this respect it was agreed to do so in order to gather intelligence. In three out of four cases intelligence was gained to the benefit of the over-all operation. The delay in mounting attacks does not appear to affect the results.

(4) In respect of this strike it can be considered a first class example of joint planning and what we hope for daily. However, this situation does not present itself often. The base camp was in fact just a resting place and Sqn Ldr Petter-Bowyer is to be congratulated on his powers of observation. The more I have to do with this man the more I am convinced that he has an inborn ability so far as visual recce is concerned which is unequalled in the Force. Added to which is his never failing enthusiasm and strong belief in the concept.

(5) Results of subsequent follow up Ops accounted for 8 terr and one AFJ killed. Sitreps 46/74 Para Alpha Two (2) and 47/74 Alpha Two (1) refer..

(Signed) Wing Commander P.D. Cooke

Comments by SO OPS
Sqn Ldr Petter-Bowyer has undoubtedly created an awareness in the force that visual recce pays dividends and this is being actively pursued.
We have been concentrating, possibly too much, on recce outside our borders. JOC commanders must make more use of recce, based on the intelligence picture, in their area of Ops. They have been advised.
A strike well executed. Good initiative displayed. Well done strike team.

(Signed) Wing Commander W.H. Smith

Comments by DG OPS
The planning, concept and conduct of this operation gives great satisfaction. We pressed the possibilities of this type of operation for some time and I trust the successes recently achieved has proved the point. Jointry at its best. Our increased allocation of effort should ensure that the essence can be reaped as often as opportunities present themselves. The increased effort should also allow for greater air recce coverage.

(Signed) Air Commodore D.A. Bradshaw

Comments by C of S
a. Good effort on P-Bowyer's part, specifically, and a good show by forces involved.
b. Without a doubt, we must make increasing use of air recce.
(Signed) Air Vice Marshal F.W.Mussell
Comments by Commander

Noted and I concur with all the remarks. With the increased deployment we must press for exploitation of every possible opportunity. We have accepted increased flying effort so let us make full use of air recce. Good show all round.

(Signed) Air Marshal M.J. McLaren

Although this was a very small action compared to those to come, important issues were raised in the Air Strike Report. Firstly Harold Griffiths, supported by Peter Cooke, had added weight to calls by others and myself for a force that Griff refers to as 'Prompt Force'. This, together with the Air HQ decision to put more aircraft in the field, led to the establishment of Fire Force shortly thereafter when the Army made RLI Commandos permanently available to an increasing number of deployed helicopters.

The delayed attacks that Harold Griffiths and Peter Cooke referred to were bases in Mozambique found by Mike Litson. Unfortunately this pilot was lost to 4 Squadron on posting to helicopters just when he was becoming a useful recce pilot. Brian Murdoch was not really cut out for the job, leaving Chris Weinmann and myself as the only functioning recce pilots who could seldom be spared for ops at the same time; so the greater use of recce expounded by everybody was fine in theory but impossible to implement. Hamie Dax was the only other recce pilot we could rely on but, being a busy farmer, his services were somewhat curtailed.

Selous Scouts

AT ABOUT THIS TIME I met Major Ron Reid-Daly at JOC Hurricane HQ in Bindura. He was on his way to visit his top secret Selous Scouts 'safe house' base and invited me to accompany him. I knew very little about Ron's operation, still believing he was running a specialist tracker school.

We drove along a dirt road running along a rising valley south of Bindura. As we bumped along the old mine road Ron told me his work was very much an undercover operation which would rely heavily on Air Force support; hence his preparedness to expose me to what was going on at the temporary base we were visiting. The road led us to a previously abandoned mine house on a ridge way off the beaten track. Two marquee tents provided soldiers' accommodation and an array of radio aerials rose from the ops room inside the old house.

Ron parked his car under the shade of a huge tree at the rear of the house where he was met by the scruffiest, most heavily bearded men I had ever seen off cinema screen. They seemed so out of place in the presence of their immaculately dressed CO. One of the men came over to me and greeted me in a manner that suggested he knew me well. Ron was amused by my puzzled look and helped me out by saying, "You remember Basil Moss don't you?" Basil had lived only seven houses away from mine in the Married Quarters at Thornhill but I had not seen him for many months. It needed a closer look before I recognised the face behind the beard.

Flight Lieutenant Basil Moss, a fluent Shona linguist, had become bored with commanding the Thornhill's General Service Unit. The GSU, mostly black servicemen commanded by white officers, provided airfield security services at Thornhill and New Sarum. Basil, a strong fit man of about forty years, needed something more challenging when there was so much action out in the countryside, but he could find no way of getting to the 'sharp end'. Then an advertisement for Shona linguists led him to Special Branch HQ and thence to the pseudo operators, André Rabie and Stretch Franklin. The unfortunate loss of André had occurred about three months earlier.

Ron walked around the temporary Selous Scouts base with Stretch Franklin, Basil Moss and me in tow. Black men lay about in the marquee tents dressed in scruffy garb with filthy-looking hair. They each listened to portable radios that were all tuned to different channels and blasted out at maximum volume. Waving his hand across these men, Ron asked me if I could differentiate between the RAR soldiers and 'turned terrorists'. I could not for they all looked the same. Nevertheless, I was astounded having never heard the term 'turned terrorist' before.

From the very beginning the Selous Scouts recognised the importance of having 'turned ters' within their pseudo groups. In so doing it was easier to gain the confidence of tribesmen who had known particular CTs before their capture. However, to gain maximum advantage, the period between capturing a genuine CT and having him in the field as a Selous Scout had to be very short—a week was considered too long. The Scouts found 'turning' CTs very easy. There was no need to bash heads or use threatening tactics. By nature black Rhodesians were gentle people until subjected to political misdirection as occurred with ZANLA cadre. By comparing the teachings of political commissars with reality and having being made aware that their lives were being risked for greedy politicians rather than for the people, captured CT opinions changed. Being cared for by the Scouts, rather than being shot out of hand as had been taught, made the transition from enemy to friend quick and easy.

The atmosphere, one of excitement, was very infectious. So closely had the successes of early pseudos operations been kept secret that it was wonderful to be taken into confidence and brought up to speed on what had happened and what was being planned. There was no doubt in my mind that Selous Scouts would soon be pre-empting action rather than us continuing to respond to terrorist activities or having to rely on visual recce and OP sightings. Tribesmen were the keys to CT successes, so they had also to become the key to countering them.

Expanded pseudo operations had come at a critical time considering the rate at which ZANLA's influence was spreading south and eastwards with ever-increasing numbers of CTs and LTTs. We were gaining in our successes but not sufficiently to contain, let alone reduce, ZANLA numbers.

The American military contended that in Viet Nam it was essential to have ten fighting soldiers to counter every insurgent in the field. For us this was a joke. We felt that a ratio of five to one would be adequate but this would soon be impossible considering Rhodesia's financial and manpower constraints. At the height of our bush war a two-to-one ratio existed within the country whereas, outside of Rhodesia, we were always greatly outnumbered and 30:1 odds against us was not unusual.

The Army's attempts to increase force levels by forming a second RAR battalion was disallowed by right-wing politicians who refused to accept black soldiers in numbers exceeding those of white regular and territorial soldiers combined. Any idea of using armed militiamen to protect tribesmen was also discounted for the same reason. So we were stuck with existing regular force levels and placed heavy reliance on the Territorial Army for effective levels in the field. Inevitably this placed formidable burdens on commerce and industry. However, manpower alone could not provide the successes we needed in a spreading bush war against an elusive enemy fighting for personal gains carelessly promised them by uncaring, greedy politicians; but these were promises in which they truly believed. Intelligence had to be the key to getting to grips with ZANLA. Reliance on historical facts gleaned from captured CTs had to be replaced by up-to-the-minute intelligence that could only be acquired by Selous Scouts pseudo operators. That intelligence was not long in coming.

By April 1974 Selous Scouts were coming to grips with ZANLA groups but too many of their successes were wasted because so many follow-up operations were mishandled; usually the consequence of inappropriate force levels to contain CT groups that bomb-shelled outwards to escape through large gaps between thinly spread troops.

It was only in June that helicopters became regularly grouped in sufficient numbers with the RLI Commandos who soon learned how to conduct the 'vertical envelopment' (surrounding) operations that capitalised on Selous Scout calls. As already mentioned, the combined reaction force became known as a Fire Force. This subject is covered later.

Cordon Sanitaire

DURING 1973 A VERY EXPENSIVE undertaking codenamed 'Operation Overload' was put into effect in the Chiweshe Tribal Trust Land. This was to place over 60,000 tribesmen in Protected Villages. The PVs system equated to the Portuguese *aldeamentos* that we had considered such a joke in earlier times. However thinking had changed, because Chiweshe TTL was perfectly situated as a base area from which to launch attacks against white farmers. This was because the TTL happened to be long, narrow and totally surrounded by the European farming areas of Centenary, Mt Darwin, Bindura, Glendale and Umvukwes. Tribesmen were placed in the fortified villages where they were protected and fed with the intention of denying terrorists access to food and people comforts. At the same time, an even more expensive undertaking was ongoing along the northeastern border.

In an endeavour to stem incursions across the border, a cordon sanitaire was built. It comprised a narrow minefield bounded by a double fence-line. Starting at Mukumbura, this arrangement extended eastwards along the borderline for about 400 kilometres. The cordon sanitaire concept, copied from Israel, was not only enormously expensive it was a complete 'waste of rations'. The non-operational people who had promoted it as an effective defensive barrier were deeply criticised, and with good reason.

Every soldier knew that no military obstacle is worth a damn unless its entire length can be covered by effective fire. Some 3,000 men in 1,500 towers would have been needed to meet the need but, because this was impossible, electronic warning devices were used to compensate for the lack of manpower. But these warning systems were seldom successful because wild animals and the elements triggered too many alarm signals. When genuine CT-induced alarms were received, mostly at night, they invariably came from positions that were too far for forces to reach before the CTs had moved away into the safety of the bush.

CTs soon found a way through the Cordon Sanitaire. They simple dug a trench under the first fence then crawled along a line taken by a lead man who probed and lifted anti-personnel mines as he moved cautiously forward. A second trench under the next fence got everyone safely through the barrier. No electronic warnings occurred when this was done so a whole group of CTs could easily transit the Cordon Sanitaire before first light and be far away by the time a daylight patrol detected the breach. Many groups crossed the Cordon Sanitaire in this way both coming in and going out. No trench was used twice for fear of Rhodesian booby traps. Some crossings failed and

one of these sticks in my mind.

A CT had his leg blown off just below the knee by an anti-personnel mine during an attempted crossing from Mozambique into Rhodesia. His companions, ignoring his pleas for help, high-tailed back into Mozambique leaving the stricken man to his fate. The fellow lay in the minefield all night and was only found by a routine patrol at about 10 o'clock next morning. A helicopter was called for, but it was impossible in the meanwhile for the Territorial soldiers to enter the minefield to administer first aid.

In spite of enormous blood loss, severe shock and a long cold lonely night, the CT was still conscious and able to communicate with the soldiers whilst awaiting rescue. There was then considerable danger for the Air Force technician who was lowered to the injured man by hoist, but he was placed in the small crater made by the mine that had blown the CT's leg away. Without moving his feet the technician secured the CT, then both were lifted into the safety of the helicopter cabin and flown straight to the Selous Scouts 'fort' at Mtoko.

In the small hospital within the fort, the attending doctor put the CT on blood and saline drips then attended to the stump of his shattered leg. He expressed amazement that the CT had survived so long but had no doubt he would regain strength quickly. I was at Mtoko at the time and was taken into the fort to see this CT during his first evening in hospital. He was propped up in bed with blood and saline lines to both arms. His colour was a pasty grey, his face was drawn and his eyes half-closed.

I saw him again the following evening and could not believe this was the same man. Although still on drips he was sitting up in bed shirtless because the weather was hot. The man's shiny black skin enhanced his muscular upper body. The grey was gone and his face was full of smiles. Few, if any, white men could have survived such an ordeal, let alone recovered so rapidly.

The CT had already been 'turned' in this short time but, because of ZANLA's propaganda, he had some doubts for his safety in Selous Scouts hands. So he offered to take the Scouts to the base in Mozambique from which he and his group had come. When asked how he would do this he said he was fit enough to hop all the way.

Odds and sods

IN SOME AVIATION MAGAZINE I read of someone using a fixed-wing aircraft to rescue a man from the ground whilst airborne. I was intrigued by the technique described and attempted to do it myself. The idea was to let out a long length of rope from the rear cabin (about 500 feet of rope), with a suitable dead weight at its end, then turn steeply towards the rope's end in the manner of a dog chasing its own tail. By holding the turn, the majority of the rope was supposed to descend with its end section hanging vertically downwards. With correct handling of turn and height it was reported that the weighted end of the rope could be positioned over any selected spot. This allowed a man on the ground to take hold of a slip harness, fit it under his shoulders, remove the weight and await uplift.

Once the man was secure in the harness, the pilot simply had to increase power, still in the turn, to lift him clear of the ground before rolling out into straight and level flight. Thereafter the man at the end of the rope could be placed back on the ground in another location in similar manner to his uplift. Alternatively, he could be hauled up into the aircraft.

My trial might have succeeded had the Trojan been able to sustain a very tight turn but this proved impossible because of that aircraft's power limitation, so the experiment was dropped.

In one of the Hunters hangars at Thornhill a tractor used for towing aircraft to and from the flight lines refused to start one very cold morning. One of the technicians decided he had the solution. He placed a 'little bit' of Avpin in the carburettor to get the engine running. When subjected to pressure, Avpin combusted spontaneously giving off the high volumes of gas that powered the Hunter's Avpin starter-motor turbines. But Avpin was certainly not suited to containment because its gas generating potential was awesome. It took just one turn of the tractor's starter motor for the 'little bit' of Avpin to blow the tractor engine's head clean off the engine block and through the high roof of the hangar.

In the self-same hangar another hole was made in the roof, but in this incident the circumstances where far from amusing. Armourer Mike Ongers was standing on the Hunter ejector seat he was servicing when the ejector cartridge fired. The seat itself went through the roof but Mike impacted the roof and was thrown back through overhead lights before dropping onto the concrete floor of the hangar. His injuries committed him to a wheelchair for life.

On 4 Squadron the technicians were getting very upset with my Squadron Warrant Officer, Spike Owens. They complained that their WO was nicking their costly tools thereby forcing them to take special precaution whenever Spike was around.

Spike Owens had come to Rhodesia from the RAF many years before and was well known for his huge collection of vehicle parts and home appliances which he claimed he had bought at bargain prices with the intention of re-selling them for profit. His collection included every tool imaginable. Where he got all these things from I cannot say but Spike was always able to produce spare parts and items that were hard to find.

I was very fond of Spike. He was always bright and helpful and I was especially thankful for his resourcefulness when it came to keeping our aircraft flying. Any suggestion that he might have 'inadvertently' picked up so and so's tools was met with vehement denial. I could not pin him down but remained pretty sceptical. Nevertheless the unfortunate nickname given him by Henry Jarvie stuck. 'WOBOTOC' stood for Warrant Officer Bill Owens Thieving Old C....

FAC errors and successes

CHRIS WEINMANN COMMENCED VISUAL RECCE in Mozambique on his own on 16 February 1974. Two days later he called for jet action on a large camp he had found just north of the River Daque fairly close to the Rhodesian border. This base had definitely not existed ten days earlier when Chris, Brian and I had been together on recce training. He chose to fly to Salisbury to brief Canberra and Hunter crews for a strike that for some reason or other did not involve FAC marking. Bill Buckle provided photographs taken for mapping purposes during the dry conditions of winter and, on these, Chris marked the extremities of the area to be struck from the target picture he had in his mind. The target of approximately 700 metres in length and 600 metres wide appeared to be a combined FRELIMO and ZANLA base.

An attack plan was formulated in which four Canberras, flown by Squadron Leader Randy Du Rand, Ian Donaldson, Mike Delport and Prop Geldenhuys would employ 'lead-bomb technique' to deliver two loads of nine 500-pound bombs and two loads of ninety-six 28-pound fragmentation bombs. The Canberras would be followed by four Hunters, flown by Don Northcroft, Ginger Baldwin, Rick Culpan and Jim Stagman firing 30mm cannon on the periphery of the target with re-strikes to fill in any obvious gaps that appeared within the Canberra bomb patterns.

Lead-bomb technique involved the lead bomber passing to his No 2 an aiming correction if his first bomb was not spot-on its intended strike point. I strongly opposed this method of bombing live terrorist camps because the delay between each stick of bombs gave terrorists way too much time to run clear of target. Lead-bomb technique was only suited to fixed targets such as ammunition dumps, fuel storage farms and buildings.

Nevertheless the bombs on this attack exploded on their planned positions despite the cloud base being lower than expected. This had forced navigators Doug Pasea, Bernie Vaughan, Bill Stevens and Bill Airey to make last-minute setting corrections to bombsights late in the attack run. The Hunters patterned as planned.

According to Randy du Rand's Air Strike Report, he struck

at 1259:50B with last Hunter clearing at 1303B. This meant it had taken three minutes and ten seconds to place down all weapons, which was at least two and a half minutes too long. If Hunters had led this attack, the four Canberras could have been much closer to each other and the re-strike by Hunters could have finalised the attack in less than forty-five seconds.

To add to this unsatisfactory situation, Chris realised too late that the target was displaced 200 metres north-eastward of the position he had marked on the photographs. This meant that only two-thirds of the strike was inside the actual base. The reason for Chris's error lay in the considerable difference between the dark-green bush lines, as they appeared to him in the month of February, and the leafless trees and bush line as it appeared on photographs taken in winter. FAC marking would have eliminated the error and Chris was wiser for his mistakes.

Three days later I also made a mistake by agreeing to fly with Hugh Slatter in a Vampire T11 to mark a target for Hunters and Canberras. Aerial photos of a camp I reported had been taken from a Canberra flying at 40,000 feet the day before but it was agreed that the target lay in such flat, featureless ground that the jets would have no chance of locating it on an unmarked first-run attack. Air HQ was always keen to try new approaches in operations and had decided that I should lead the attack in a jet instead of my puddle-jumping Trojan. Having not flown in a jet aircraft for over ten years, the speed at which ground was being covered and the height at which we flew compressed the terrain I knew so well from 2,000 feet into unfamiliar perspective.

In the long dive to the target, Hugh adjusted his aiming according to my instructions and pressed the firing button for a salvo of four 60-pound squash-head rockets, but they failed to fire! Only then did I realise we had aimed at the far end of the terrorist base and not at its centre, so I transmitted an immediate correction "Drop 500". Fortunately Rob Gaunt, having assessed where the failed rockets would have landed, picked up the correction and fired. Hugh was pulling up steeply and turning out right to allow me to look over my shoulder to see Rob's strike to pass further correction to Rich Culpan, Chris Dixon and Ginger Baldwin.

I had completely forgotten how to handle 6G, which locked my head awkwardly forcing me to roll my eyes hard up and right to spot the strike just before experiencing 'grey out'. Fortunately the lead 30mm cannon strike was just where it needed to be but I could not lift my hand to the radio transmitter button on the throttle to say this. Hugh had to relay my G-stressed and awkwardly spoken words, "On target".

Following this experience, thought was given to converting recce pilots onto Hunters so that future strikes need not involve FAC and would ensure that recce pilots could switch between 'puddle-jumpers' and jets without the problems I had just encountered. For Chris Weinmann this would have been a simple matter because he had recently come from Hunters. I was really keen to fly these lovely aircraft but, very reluctantly, came to the conclusion that the advantages to be gained were outweighed by the cost of training and the time it would take to position at Thornhill or New Sarum for each airstrike.

The Air Staff had been under directive from Air Marshal Mick McLaren to try every tactic possible to improve airstrike versatility and accuracy. To this end, and unknown to me, photographic reconnaissance (PR) had been flown on Mozambican targets that Chris and I had reported but not committed to airstrike.

Repeated PR had been conducted to watch for obvious changes on those targets best suited to first-run jet-strikes. Then Flight Lieutenant Bill Buckle and his Photo Reconnaissance Interpreter (PRI) team at New Sarum selected a target set in heavy bush on the east bank of a dry river where a distinctive bend with visible water made identification certain. I was called to New Sarum to look at the photographs. The PRIs were happy when I agreed the camp was much larger than when I found it two months earlier. Bill briefed the jet crews at 9 o'clock on the morning of 23 February, just two days after the attack I had led with Hugh Slatter. It went in at 1228B and worked out exactly as planned.

During March I led two successful ops against terrorists inside Rhodesia. Externally I picked up a small base near Mukumbura in which fifteen head of cattle were penned at its centre. Being so close to the border, it was decided to attack this base with Hunters at first light the following day and follow up immediately with RLI heli-borne troops. The plan was for helicopters and myself to fly from Centenary to Mukumbura where the troops would be waiting for first light lift-off.

At Centenary I was doing my pre-flight inspection with the aid of a torch when I found a yellow bone-dome hanging from the pitot-head under the port wing of my Trojan. It belonged to Flight Sergeant Ray Cox who was one of the technicians on the flight line at the time. I called him over and asked him to remove his bone-dome, then continued with my inspection.

The helicopters were lifting off as I taxiied out to the runway. Late in my take-off run I found I had to apply a great deal of right rudder to counter a strong yawing force to the left. By this time it was too late to abort take-off. Once airborne I saw the helicopter lights winking away ahead of me and continued my climb, still with heavy pressure on the right rudder to maintain balanced flight. I told the lead helicopter pilot I was experiencing some difficulty but said I would establish the cause when we reached Mukumbura.

We crossed over the escarpment as the first rays of dawn lit up the horizon on our right side. By this time my left foot was over my right foot to help maintain pressure on the right rudder pedal. I turned to look at the rotating beacons of the helicopters flying below and to my left when, with horror, I saw somebody hanging upside-down on my left wing wearing a bone-dome with its visor closed. It took a moment or two to realise there was no actual body involved; it was Ray Cox's yellow helmet hanging on the pitot head by its chinstrap.

Foolishly I told the lead helicopter pilot the cause of my flight control problem. I could have saved myself the ribbing that came my way had I simply kept quiet and pulled ahead to land and remove the bone-dome at Mukumbura before the helicopter boys arrived.

When I marked for the Hunters, I was happy to see that the cattle-pen was empty. Helicopters were on the ground within thirty-five seconds of the lead strike and the troops were already moving in during re-strike. Unfortunately the CTs must have heard the helicopters before the noise cover of the Trojan became effective because fresh tracks of running terrorists were located going south–east towards another base I had located but discounted.

Cattle tracks heading north were aerial-tracked for no more than three kilometres were I found fifty-five head of cattle. These were rounded up by the troops and driven back into Rhodesia because, having been stolen from those few unfortunate Mozambican locals who still lived in the area, they constituted an immediate source of CT food.

Fear of landing in enemy territory

FROM THE SAS TAC HQ at Macombe, 4 Squadron pilots continued to be scrambled to assist troops deep inside hostile territory. This Air Strike Report by Chris Dickinson on 8 March 1974 gives an idea of the sort of work the youngsters were doing.

While doing Telstar for RAR c/s 42, I was tasked to go overhead c/s B13 SAS and help them out. Difficulty was experienced in getting to their location i.e. UT 368920 because of low cloud but once in the area I was able to maintain 1500 ft AGL. c/s B13 were manning an OP and they directed me to attack a small valley at UT 364914 from where they had been fired upon. I did two strikes from north to south using front gun and SNEB. They then asked me to attack an area around a mealie field some 200 yards to the west of my first attack. This was done using SNEB. They then indicated a suspected ter camp at UT 358905 adjacent to a mealie field. I did one attack from south east to north west using front gun and SNEB. They then indicated a further suspect area at UT 353888 which was to the east of two mealie fields. I did a north to south attack using SNEB. At this stage it was at last light and I proceeded back to Macombe as the Musengezi airstrip was unserviceable and I did not have sufficient fuel to get to Centenary. The weapons were on target and it was later learnt that my rockets had destroyed part of a camp complex although everything had been concealed in thick bush.

STOP PRESS. When the c/s was recovered from the area it was confirmed that three people had been killed and buried at the point UT 364914 where the strike had gone in on the camp complex.

There was always concern for single-engined aircraft operating alone deep inside Mozambique, as in this case. Anti-aircraft action or engine failure might force a pilot down; a situation that was fraught with peril. If a pilot survived the landing, whether hurt or unhurt, his chances of survival were very low unless he was close enough for anyone to pick up his radio distress call. However much of the time was spent beyond 'friendly forces' radio range.

Personally I was petrified by the work I did over Mozambique and worried that others might notice this. As I write, a quarter of a century later, it is easy for me to admit to this failing. At the time however, I was annoyed by my inability to overcome the tight knot in my stomach and having to relying on four stiff whiskies after dinner to help me get some sleep. If I was on internal work, I always enjoyed a good breakfast that set me up for the day's work; but before recces over Mozambique I could not face a meal knowing that I would be operating for over five hours beyond radio range of any Rhodesian.

Everyone knew that if I ran into trouble this would not be known until too late and that a search and rescue attempt would defer to the following day. So, to assist searchers, I carried a small emergency radio beacon which, when switched on, transmitted a continuous low-powered coded distress signal. This device also had a voice and receiving facility that was limited to a very short duration before its battery was drained.

I think it was Captain Mick Graham of SAS who flew one Mozambican sortie with me. He enjoyed the experience because it allowed him to see for himself what he had read in my recce report signals. But the main purpose of his flight was to assess the feasibility of an SAS soldier accompanying me on future missions to keep me out of trouble if I went down. My hopes were dashed when Mick said that, having seen the ground we had covered, this was simply not on. A single, super-fit, SAS soldier might evade hostile forces on his own, but not if he had to take care of me as well.

An alternative solution was offered. It involved eight recently trained RLI paratroopers loitering at height in a Dakota close to the area over which I was operating. The experiment failed within the first two hours when Squadron Leader Peter Barnett told me all the paratroopers in the back of his aircraft were so airsick that they would be of no help if I needed them. I thanked Peter for trying and told him to take the men back to base. There was no alternative; I had to work alone. In the meanwhile Air HQ was looking into equipping 4 Squadron aircraft with HF/SSB to provide long-range communications with Air HQ and FAF Operations Rooms.

I always briefed the FAF 3 commander (mostly Peter Cooke) on my intended outward and inward routes with details of the area to be covered, but those horrid butterflies in my stomach only slowed down when I was strapped into my seat with the engine running. Flight over Rhodesian soil felt quite normal until I reached the border. At this point the engine always appeared to be running roughly. Once across the Zambezi River the engine seemed to be running so roughly that I feared it might break from its mountings. This phantom situation continued until I reached the area over which I was to operate. As soon as I started searching the ground all fear vanished and I no longer worried about the engine purring away at low-cruising power.

Unlike American and Canadian aircraft designers, those of British, French and Italian aircraft did not cater for pilots' bladder needs. As early as 1939, Canadian and American designers provided aircrew with what was crudely known as 'the pee tube'. This consisted of an extendible funnel on the forward edge of a pilot's seat that connected to a tube leading to a low-pressure point on the underside of the airframe. Considering the restraints of harness, parachute straps and flying overalls, it was awkward to get one's twin to the funnel, but at least it catered for minor misdirection and there was ample suction to take the urine away. Our Trojans did not have this luxury, so I had learned to manage seven-hour recce flights. But there was one day when things did not work out too well.

In spite of the normal pre-flight precaution of 'emptying the tank', on this particularly cold day I was in need of a pee even before I crossed the Zambezi still flying outbound. Two hours later with much ground yet to cover, I could not hold out any longer. There was no bottle or similar receptacle in the aircraft and, though I thought about it, opening the door in flight was fraught with peril. However, next to me on the right hand seat was my bone-dome (pilot's crash helmet). There was no option but to use it. The weather was particularly turbulent when I undid my seat straps, opened my fly and raised my body against the rudder pedals to get things into position. Head-support webs within the bone-dome compounded the problem of turbulence and fully stretched legs. As soon as I let go, the high-pressure stream struck the nearest web, spraying urine all over my legs and onto the instrument panel. I managed to change direction, but in no time the shallow basin of the bone-dome was close to over-flowing. Forced stemming of the steam was essential but at least my discomfort had been reduced. The next problem was how to get rid of urine in the bone-dome. To allow it to spill inside the cockpit was simply not on because urine is highly corrosive to aircraft surfaces.

My window was always open during recce, so I decided to hold the bone-dome firmly and spill the urine into the outside airflow. As I did this, my arm was almost ripped off as the slipstream sucked the bone-dome through the window. The disturbed airflow blew back most of the bone-dome's contents into my face, wetting half of my torso and the whole instrument panel. I managed to hold on to the bone-dome but the rest of that long flight was miserably cold and uncomfortable.

Chifombo Base

GOING AHEAD IN TIME, I was operating deeper than before and close to the Zambian/Tete border averaging about 3,000 feet above ground. Cloud build-up was making coverage difficult and I could only read ground where the sun was shining. I had just started picking up the signs of considerable human activity in the heavily treed region and was plotting this on my map when a loud crack on my right side made me look up at the starboard wing. I was astounded to see hundreds of green and red tracer rounds flying upward at differing angles but all appearing to emanate from the aircraft itself. I had seen tracer many times before but never so densely as the 12.7mm, 14.5mm and, possible, 23mm guns whizzing past. I immediately entered a vertical dive.

Looking down towards the ground I saw what appeared to be a lesser number of tracer rounds coming my way but, when I looked towards the sky again, they were just as thick as before. Another crack sounded behind me by which time I was weaving left and right in a high-speed descent towards a huge terrorist base that spread outwards in every direction I turned. When I levelled off at tree-tops, the Trojan, still taking hits, slowed down horribly and there were hundreds of people firing small arms so close that I knew I was about to die.

Twice I passed across open patches and saw big guns flashing. For what seemed like a really long time I was locked in a terrible slow-motion nightmare as I passed over row upon row of small and large thatched buildings under tall trees, all the time under fire. Unlike all I had read about people facing death, my whole life did not flash before me as I looked at point after point ahead believing I would surely die there. The ground tearing past me registered in my brain as the aircraft took hits in a mixture of sharp cracks and dull thuds.

Suddenly I was clear. It felt as if I had dived into cool water from burning-hot flames. Bullet holes in the airframe and windscreens were generating a strong whistling sound but the motor sounded fine.

I had been looking for the big FRELIMO-cum-ZANLA base known as Chifombo but had not expected such a hot reception when I found it. Still breathless I held a straight course for some time before coming to my senses inside Zambia. It took a little while longer to pull myself together and register that the flight control instruments had all been rendered useless. Having turned southwest, as judged by the sun's position, it took more time to gather courage to commence a climb for height. Only when established in the climb did I realise that I was bleeding from many places, making my overalls and face cold and sticky, but there was absolutely no pain. The fuel gauge for both left and right tanks worked fine and I could see no fuel leakage, nor could I smell fuel vapour. Every minute or so I flicked from one tank to the other to check for fuel loss and after ten minutes knew I would get back to safety, providing the engine kept going. I set power by ear and knew from engine response that the turbo-charger was working; but there was no way of knowing if engine oil was being lost, so I followed a route as far removed from human habitation as possible. I had considered going into Macombe to get first-aid from the SAS but then decided to press on to Centenary when I realised that, although there was a lot of blood about, the wounds to my face, chest, arms and legs were no more than shallow penetrations from bits of metal and broken glass.

During an earlier recce deep inside Mozambique I had been feeling distinctly lonely and afraid when suddenly I became acutely aware that I was not alone at all. This was an experience I find impossible to put into words because the sudden knowledge of the presence of God is awesome, powerful and exciting all at the same time. Now, having survived passage over Chifombo Base and heading for home, the immediate presence of God overwhelmed me again. The feeling I experienced this time was different but just as impossible to explain by words alone.

It was in this amazing state of comfort that I looked down at the ground as I climbed through about 5,000 feet and realised that I was seeing pathways with the clarity needed for over-border recce. I should have known this before but, being a typical creature of habit, I had stuck to the level I first thought was right. From that day onward I never flew recce in Mozambican territory below 5,000 feet.

At about 8,000 feet radio contact was established with the Army relay station on the high Mavuradona mountain inside Rhodesia. I told the operator that I had sustained damage but expected to make it back to Centenary safely. I could see my left main tyre and knew it was fine but I was prepared for difficulties if the nose or right tyres had been punctured. Fortunately there was no problem on landing and I taxied into dispersals to find Peter Cooke and a couple of TF soldiers waiting for me with a stretcher. I recall FAF 3 being almost deserted because Mount Darwin and Mtoko had become the operational focal points.

I had set off on this flight from Bindura where I received a briefing from an SB officer who wanted more details on Chifombo. My reason for recovering into Centenary was that I knew there were spare beds there. But I cannot say why Peter Cooke was also there because he had left FAF 3 when operational activity moved east with Centenary passing into the care of a VR Camp Commandant. He may have been helping out as a (retread) helicopter pilot because I do not recall seeing another pilot for the only helicopter parked next to my Trojan. Anyway there were certainly no 4 Squadron personnel or aircraft around.

Initially I declined to lie on the stretcher but the sharp fragments in my legs made walking so painful that I was forced to accept the lift to an Army medical tent. Having the bits and pieces removed without any anaesthetic by a very young TF medic was an unpleasant experience made easier by slugging neat whisky. I was very sore, stiff and covered in bloody dressings when Flamo Flemming, and I think Jungle Forrester, came to me in the medical tent with a request. "Boss PB, please come with us to your Trojan. We want you to explain something to us." With the foreign bodies removed and being somewhat anaesthetised by whisky I was able to limp along with them.

Using long 'spear grass' that grew along the airfield fence line, these two technicians had lined up all the bullet entry and exit holes. There were 123 strikes of which four were from heavy-calibre rounds that had failed to explode (guns too close to target), yet not one had struck the fuel tanks or any other vital part. This in itself was a miracle but Flamo wanted me to explain why I was not dead considering one bullet's path appeared to have gone through my left flank.

One length of spear grass ran from the port side of rear cabin through the backrest of my seat and into the instrument panel. Not bothering to prove to myself that the bullet line was correct I foolishly choked up and simply pointed heavenward. When I regained composure I was able to tell of my terror over Chifombo and how God's powerful presence had overwhelmed me.

This incident persuaded me to turn back to Christianity. I had abandoned the Anglicans at age twenty, swearing never to return to a church that laid emphasis on the pomp and ceremony I had experienced as an altar server. Now, some eighteen years later, I decided to find a church that practised biblical Christianity. This led Beryl and me to the Methodists in Waterfalls, simply because Beryl preferred we go to the pastor she had watched on TV. He was Reverend Gary Strong who, in his youth, had been a rough and tough 'Main Street Cowboy' biker.

New offensive trials

OUR ASSOCIATION WITH THE SOUTH African Air Force strengthened over time and much of the increased helicopter effort in 1974 had come from the SAAF in the form of machines and aircrews. This was as much for SAAF's benefit to gain 'on the job' experience as it was for Rhodesia. It was for this reason too that Captain Kapp was sent to fly recce with me to assess the value of sending other pilots at a future date. Captain Kapp must have turned in a good report because SAAF sent four young pilots for recce training in 1975.

Whilst I was instructing Captain Kapp, Chris Weinmann and Brian Murdoch continued to find CT camps inside the country and had initiated air and ground operations on them; but not once were terrorists in residence, all camps having been freshly vacated. The CTs had obviously become wise to the fact that the Trojans they saw flying in their area of operations were the same ones that brought trouble to their camps. This forced us to rethink tactics.

I decided to try flying offensive low-level battle formations with four armed Provosts to see if we could catch CT groups in the open. By setting propeller speed to 2200 rpm, the Provost was very quiet and sufficient boost could be employed to ensure adequate flying speed for the undulating terrain in northeast Rhodesia. Flying this configuration, it was possible to come to within less than 500 metres of people on the ground before they heard the aircraft.

Our flights were flown along random routes since we had no way of knowing where terrorists might be. Numerous bases discovered during recce were over-flown too, yet none of these flights produced any result. On one particular sortie I picked up a man on the horizon carrying what appeared to be a weapon over his shoulder. He was so close that it was too late to select guns and the man was not yet aware of my presence, so I manoeuvred to kill him with the left undercarriage. At the last moment he heard me, and as he turned, I realised that his 'weapon' was a simple *badza* (hoe). Only he and his laundry woman knew what a fright he received as I passed inches above him.

Beginning of Black Month

BACK IN MOZAMBIQUE AGAIN, I picked up two new bases and returned to New Sarum to give briefings for two jet-strikes. It was decided to use a Vampire in which Hugh Slatter and I would mark one base at 1100B for the usual four Hunters and two Canberras. After that strike, I was to fly a Trojan from New Sarum directly to the second base for a routine FAC controlled strike at 1500B.

This time Hugh let me handle the Vampire until the attack dive was established and then took control to fire four 60-pound rockets. I had no orientation problems this time and Hugh placed the rockets exactly where they were needed. The rest of the aircraft struck as planned.

Following a short debrief back at New Sarum, I took off in my Trojan and headed for the SAS Tac HQ at Macombe then continued on for thirty kilometres northward to commence the southward orbits that would place me over the target. This base lay twelve kilometres north of the Zambezi River. I had just located a brand-new base in hills to the north of the target we

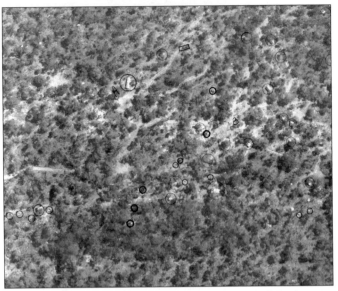

A small, typical and easy-to-see FRELIMO-cum-ZANLA staging base. The markings on the photograph are by JSPIS. The vehicle track on the left proved FRELIMO's presence but was unusual for buses far from primary roads.

were about to attack when the Hunters checked in. I put this base aside for the moment and continued towards the assigned target.

This particular attack marked the beginning of what became known to Air Force as 'Black Month'. Flight Lieutenant Don Donaldson constructed this Canberra Air Strike Report:

PLANNING. This sortie was planned as an FAC directed Hunter/ Canberra air strike on a terrorist base in Mozambique (TT 856799). Marking was carried out by Sqn Ldr Petter-Bowyer (A4) in Trojan using white smoke SNEB. The main strike component to be four Hunters (Red Section) leading two Canberras (Green Section).

BRIEFING. Main target briefing was given by Sqn Ldr Petter-Bowyer at New Sarum at 0800 on Thursday 4th April. OC 1 Sqn and both Canberra crews attended the briefing. Photography (OP JUNCTION) supplied by JSPIS. A combined attack pattern using SOPs was agreed between RED and GREEN Sections.

TACTICS. RED to operate out of Thornhill using 18lb RP and 30mm front gun. GREEN to operate from New Sarum using 96 x 28lb FRAGMENTATION. Sections to meet at IP Delta (UT 115619). Bombing height 1200 ft AGL. Control on Channel 3. After mark the Hunters to put in RP attacks on central area, the Canberras following with minimum time delay on single run releasing full weapon load. Hunters to re-attack after Canberras clear.

SORTIE. GREEN Section airborne at 1420 aiming for IP 1452. Contact made with IAK and IZP on route. Red and GREEN joined as planned at the IP and RED leader made contact with marker aircraft A4 who began positioning for his attack. The combined

formation with Canberras on the starboard of the Hunters left IP at 1456. A4 marked on time and called "on target". I positioned Green Section for a final attack heading of 240 deg. M turning left as the Hunters pulled up into Perch position. GREEN 2 was briefed to be about 1000 yds behind me. The bomb run was normal and the target identified by white marker smoke and Hunter RP strikes. Bombs were seen to leave and the strike detonations heard clearly. I continued straight ahead as planned. A4 then called to say that GREEN 2 had exploded over the target. This was confirmed by RED LEADER. No parachutes were seen and it was obvious that both crewmen had died in the initial explosion which was reported to have been a large fireball. I searched the area after the Hunters had completed their re-attack. Several areas of burning wreckage were visible. YELLOW section then began trooping into the area and I returned to base after establishing that there were no survivors.
REMARKS. The SOP HUNTERS/CANBERRAS worked well and with a minimum of fuss. Briefing was adequate but although we had the benefit of a very full description of the target by A4, I am certain we could not have identified the target without the very good marking we had.

(Signed) Flight Lieutenant I.H. Donaldson

It will be helpful to clarify a few abbreviations in the sequence Don used them:

OP JUNCTION was the codename for the photographic coverage of Mozambique to upgrade poor-quality Portuguese mapping.
JSPIS—Joint Services Photographic Interpretation Services.
SOP—Standard Operating Procedures.
1AK and 1ZP as written, ONE ALPHA KILO and ONE ZULU PAPA as spoken, were the callsigns of JOC Hurricane at Bindura and FAF 3 at Centenary.
YELLOW section was the callsign of helicopters based at the SAS Tac HQ, Macombe.
GREEN 2—Canberra flown by Air Sub-Lieutenant Keith Goddard with Air Sub-Lieutenant Bill Airey as navigator.
RED Leader was Rob Gaunt, leading Hunters flown by Don Northcroft, Danny Svoboda and Paddy Bate.

The 1 Squadron's (unsigned) report, probably by Rob himself, followed by Wing Commander Tol Janeke's remarks as OC Flying Wing Thornhill, are typically low-key.

1. The sortie to the IP was SOP. At IP 'Delta', Green Section was located and after join up, Red and Green Sections left the IP for the target area on a heading 313 deg M. The FAC aircraft Alpha 4, was sighted and target marking and identification was carried out.
2. The first aircraft on target were four Hunters firing 18-pound 3-inch RP's, the second aircraft on target were two Canberras dropping frag bombs.
3. On the downwind leg of Red Section's next attack, Red leader observed a large ball of fire falling towards the target area and was informed by Alpha 4 that it was the number two Canberra that had exploded in mid air. The scattered wreckage of the aircraft landed 500 yards to the north of the target.
4. The third and fourth attacks were carried out by four Hunters with 30mm. After the last attack Red Section joined up and on climbing away, Red lead gave an in-flight report to One Alpha Kilo giving details of the attack and the Canberra. Red Section recovered to Thornhill and the remaining Canberra to Salisbury.

(Unsigned)

Comments by OCFW
1. This strike was well co-ordinated with No 5 Squadron and the FAC aircraft. The only incident that marred an otherwise good strike was the fatal Canberra accident.
2. Weather at Thornhill on recovery was poor with low cloud and intermittent drizzle. It was apparent on speaking to the crews after the sortie that the loss of the Canberra had had a marked effect on them. It is to the credit of the junior pilots on this flight that the recovery in bad weather was well handled.

(Signed) Wing Commander F.D. Janeke

My perspective of this airstrike was quite different considering I watched each aircraft as it attacked. Rob Gaunt's rockets were exploding on target before my marker rockets were down. As usual I tensed up until I saw the Hunter pass under me. Once the fourth Hunter passed through target I looked up to watch Don Donaldson's bombs appear out of the bomb bay at the very moment I expected to see them. The bombs ran the full 950-metre length of the target before I saw a number of men running in many directions within the base. I looked up for the second Canberra, hoping its bombs would reach target quickly.

Keith Goddard was too far behind and still turning onto his attack line. With my own motion this gave the impression that the Canberra was skidding sideways against the beautiful backdrop of bluish purple hills. When on line, the Canberra made a couple of sharp corrections in response to the bomb-aimer's instructions. At the very moment I expected to see the bombs falling, there they were but, as they reached about one-fuselage depth below the aircraft, the graceful Canberra disappeared in an orange fireball of enormous dimension. I knew immediately that a bomb had detonated prematurely setting off the full bomb load. Moments later the loud bang and pressure wave came to me through the open window of my Trojan.

Rob Gaunt asked, "What the hell was that?" I told him Green 2 had exploded. Rob then asked if it had been Strela to which I answered, "I saw no trail. I think it was a premature detonation setting off the whole bloody frag load."

In a fraction of a second the fireball had increased in size and changed to a mixture of deep-red flame billowing out of dense black smoke with a tongue of orange flame spewing out of its centre and curving downwards. This was the flaming forward section of the fuselage that tumbled slowly leaving a trail of white smoke and unburnt fuel along its long path to ground. Both engines passed the fuselage throwing up showers of soil and red dust as they impacted. By then the fireball had given way to dense black tumbling smoke from which sections of wings, tail and other wreckage left many trails of light grey and white smoke as they descended at varying velocities. Like falling leaves the wings and large bits of wreckage wafted down slowly.

By the time the last piece of wreckage reached ground the smoke ball had become brownish grey which reduced in density as the wind took it westwards past numerous columns of smoke rising from the sparsely-treed ground, some 500 metres to the north of the target.

Rob Gaunt had not missed a beat and ran the four Hunters through the target a second time as if nothing had happened. I was only vaguely aware of these strikes low on my left side because my attention was fixed on the awful drama I have described. When the Hunters cleared I switched over to the SAS radio frequency and moved over to the crash site where I noticed Don Donaldson's Canberra orbiting above me.

The SAS on the ground at Macombe, just fifteen kilometres away, had heard the explosion clearly. Four helicopters were heading for the target, at last to check out air strike effectiveness. However they witnessed the disaster and headed directly for the Canberra's nose section. In moments confirmation was given that both crewmen were dead and that their bodies were intact. Having heard this, I returned to the airstrike frequency and gave Don Donaldson the bad news.

Flight Lieutenant Al Bruce in the meanwhile was airborne out of Macombe and met me over the crash site preparatory to an attack on the small base I had located just before the jet strike. We made our strikes and were well clear of target when the SAS troops at the Canberra crash site reported hearing a large explosion from the position we had just struck.

I landed at Macombe to collect the bodies of the Canberra crew and flew them back to New Sarum. On arrival there, well after dark, I was feeling very depressed by events and for having to carry the bodies of two fine young men, whose deaths I had witnessed.

In spite of the fact that I was extremely tired and had not had anything to eat or drink all day, members of the Board of Inquiry into the Canberra incident insisted on taking my evidence right away. This was because they planned to fly to the crash site first thing next morning. By the time my statement had been recorded and answers given to many questions, I was too clapped-out to fly back to Centenary and stayed over at New Sarum.

Operation Marble

NEXT MORNING I WAS ABOUT to return to the operational area when called to the secrephone (telephone that scrambles and unscrambles voice conversation). Group Captain Dicky Bradshaw instructed me to return to Thornhill, as I was required to proceed on a top-secret mission next day, 6 April. His signal to Thornhill would fill me in on the details.

In his Flying Wing HQ office at Thornhill Wing Commander Tol Janeke handed me two signals to read whilst he and Rob Gaunt chatted. The first was an Operational Order for Operation Marble. It required a small team of recce pilots to position at the Portuguese Brigade HQ at Estima Air Base close to the hydroelectric construction site of Cabora Bassa.

The task was to locate FRELIMO targets for a Portuguese assault force. Rob Gaunt was to be the Ops Commander of a temporary FAF at Estima Air Base with all necessary equipment and communications. I was to lead a team of four recce pilots to provide targets for offensive operations by Portuguese heli-borne troops and helicopter gunships.

The second signal advised that presidential confirmation had been received for me to receive an award that made me a Member of the Legion of Merit (Operational). The congratulations I received from Tol and others went straight over my head because I was already too preoccupied with my fear of the forthcoming recce flights. These would be over areas in which I knew FRELIMO forces possessed many Strela missiles.

Some weeks later, MLM investiture by President Dupont.

A chat with Prime Minister Ian Smith after the ceremony.

Tol told me to take the day off to be with Beryl and the children who I had not seen for some time. Rob Tasker and Chris Weinmann were both at base and they agreed that there was nothing requiring my immediate attention; so I briefed them to prepare three Trojans for Kevin Peinke, Mark Knight and me to fly to Estima. Kevin and Mark were the only pilots available who had shown any interest in recce, and Mozambican ground was fairly easy to read anyway. Chris Weinmann, using the fourth Trojan, was to operate out of Centenary to cover territory in the southwestern sector of the area I planned to cover.

Chris had a fair idea of the ground he would be covering but I gave him warning to be especially careful of a particular mountainous place from which heavy fire had been directed at me every time I had been there. In particular I made it clear that I would cover those areas in which Strela was known to exist and asked him not to operate above a particular line of latitude, which I marked on his maps.

At home I told Beryl I was only there for one night to change over an aircraft. She was disappointed but asked me several times what was troubling me. I assured her all was well and that I should be home within ten days; but she seemed to know otherwise. It puzzled me that she could see through my attempt to appear happy and relaxed.

On the way to Estima I popped into FAF 3 to brief Peter Cooke on the Portuguese need for recce assistance and what was required of 4 Squadron. Chris would be operating from FAF 3 so we made plans for copy of his signalled recce results to HQ to be relayed to me at Estima. We also decided on the VHF 'natter' frequency Chris and I would use for direct communication between each other whilst airborne, because we would be beyond the range of all other stations.

I continued with Kevin Peinke and Mark Knight to Estima where Rob Gaunt was already set up. He introduced the elderly, good-looking and immaculately dressed Brigade Commander who made it clear to all of us that he was a cavalryman, which in his view placed him amongst the ultra-elite.

Following a short planning session with the Army and Air Force officers of the assault force, we were invited to the open-sided thatched bar of the Officers' Club for refreshments and lunch. It was there that the brigadier offered me a bottle of any drink I chose for every live FRELIMO base my youngsters and I could offer his troops. It seemed to me that he did not believe we were all we had been cracked up to be by his superiors in Lourenço Marques. The brigadier said my choice of the cognac Antiqua was a good one.

After lunch Kevin and Mark helped sort out our maps before accompanying me on a familiarisation flight to get a first feel for the area of Operation Marble. We spent a lot of time over the Cabora Bassa Dam site and westward along the northern bank of the Zambezi River whose shoreline was changing as the water backed up slowly from the new dam wall. Kevin was to operate in the area next to Chris and south of the same line of latitude I had marked on Chris Weinmann's maps. Mark was to fly with me for a day or two on extended recce training.

On 7 April, we were routing north through the area assigned for Mark when we happened upon a large FRELIMO base. I had no doubts that it was occupied and called for the assault force to meet us at one of the river junctions we had selected for RV purposes. The brigadier could not believe we had found a target so soon after take off on our first mission.

Because of language difficulties the plan was to lead the assault force Pumas and Alouette gunships from the selected RV directly to target. The Trojan task was to provide noise cover to the approaching helicopters and mark the target with thirty-six Sneb rockets. Thereafter control would pass to the two gunships, both armed with 20mm side-firing cannons. When the gunships ran out of ammunition they would pass control to the ground force commander.

Having continued northwestward to get beyond sight and sound range of the FRELIMO base, I followed a long circuitous route to get back south to the RV point where we waited for the airborne force. Mark and I were green with envy when we saw it approaching us. In this single lift the four Pumas were carrying more troops than could be carried by all the helicopters in Rhodesia. As for the two 20mm gunships, we simply did not have any then.

As agreed, the helicopters held a loose formation to my left so that I could watch them all the way. I marked target with a raking salvo of rockets and pulled up to see how the Portuguese handled themselves. Coming around in long line astern for a left-hand orbit around the base, the two gunships went into action immediately because there were FRELIMO people running in all directions. The time was about 10:15.

All four Pumas dropped their troops south of the target but so close together I could not believe it. They then lifted, turned about in the hover and disappeared the way they had come. The gunships were busy but made no attempt to stop FRELIMO breaking northward.

Never before had I seen so many armed terrorists. Down at about 1,500 feet, flying a little higher than the gunships, I could see everyone was armed, some with RPG rocket launchers. I was so sorry that I had expended my rockets because there were tight groups which remained stationary to fire at the two gunships whenever they came close and then moved on. The gunships concentrated on buildings that caught fire immediately. Their crews had either not seen the concentrations of terrorists I could see so clearly or had chosen to ignore them. At the end of their second orbit all ammunition had been expended so they rolled out and disappeared in the direction the Pumas had gone.

I watched at least six large groups of FRELIMO move away in good order. They were paying no attention to my aircraft so far as I could see. Over one kilometre to the south of the FRELIMO groups, the assault troops were still being shaken out into an extended sweep line before commencing a painfully slow advance towards the base. At least fifteen minutes had elapsed from the time they were dropped to the time the troops reached the southern edge of the base. By then every FRELIMO group had melted away into the bush farthest from the troops. I left the area in disgust because this, the target of my dreams, had been totally wasted.

Instead of continuing on with our recce, we flew back to Estima to reload rocket pods and tell Rob Gaunt of the frustrating balls-up Mark and I had witnessed. Then, whilst positioning to continue our recce, we found that the Pumas were already back at the FRELIMO base, uplifting assault troops and captured equipment. It was not yet 12:00. All structures in the camp were burning; so that was that! No follow up on tracks as might be expected. Just packing up and going home!

The clear blue cloudless sky conditions and the presence of Strela made me move up to 6,000 feet above ground. Moving on from the smoke-covered base, we picked up strong trails leading northwestward. The route given by a number of converging and diverging pathways was a cakewalk and we found four more large bases along the line, all of which were in use. Tucked away in the densest cover either side of the tracks were many small camps linked to fields of maize, rapoko and cassava; obviously civilians were giving FRELIMO succour and hiding from the Portuguese.

With no protection against the heat-seeking sensors of Strela missiles, and flying in perfect conditions for these weapons, I watched for them every second. If I spotted one coming up, my plan was to cut power and roll upside down to screen off the hot exhaust stubs. At the time I did not know that the paint over the entire surface of my Trojan could be 'seen' by these weapons and that my plan was utterly worthless.

Having worked for some time I had become quite relaxed when, out of the corner of my eye, I picked up a near vertical zigzag line of faint greyish white smoke. It ran through a position we had passed in orbit about thirty seconds earlier. Immediately I thought of Strela and looked up the line of barely discernible smoke to see if there was evidence of an airburst where Strela should self-destruct at around 13,000 feet. I could see nothing and soon lost the smoke trail altogether. When in later times I actually saw Strela missiles in flight, I realised that the trail I had seen here was definitely from a Strela that had been fired at us. The operator almost certainly fired when the aircraft was passing too close to the sun, which attracted the missile's sensor to itself. This may very well have been the first Strela to be launched against a Rhodesian Air Force aircraft. Unfortunately it was not to be the last.

At half-hourly intervals Chris, Kevin and I exchanged information on how each of us was doing. By the end of our first day we had accumulated nine major bases between the three of us but made no call on the assault force because there was need to debrief on the first operation and make plans to improve tactics.

Back at Estima we found an elated brigadier who ceremoniously handed me a bottle of Antiqua. I was completely disarmed by all the Portuguese officers' congratulations to 4 Squadron for setting up such a 'magnificent operation'. They were tickled pink by the tally of sixteen FRELIMO dead and the largest haul of captured FRELIMO equipment in Tete to date. This included four 14.5mm anti-aircraft guns.

The assault commander said my Trojan had been under intense fire from the time the gunships left until I cleared back to base. He expounded on the bravery Mark and I had shown and how this had impressed and endeared us to his troops. We neither let on that we had been unaware of the fire nor that the Trojan had taken no hits.

With spirits so high, the brigadier and his assault force officers were confounded by the criticisms levelled against them by Rob Gaunt and me. We noticed, however, that the six Portuguese Air Force gunship and Puma pilots took kindly to our observations and that they were very keen to respond to suggested tactical improvements.

We had too many targets lined up for the assault force so it was decided to let the main line of bases settle down for a couple of days. Lesser targets were to be used to test and modify tactics during the next three days with only one being attended to each day. These were small enough for groups to be placed in stop positions on three sides to cover CTs escaping from the fourth group as it swept through target.

All three bases turned out to be FRELIMO regional bases supporting small numbers of men, most of which were away from base at the time of the assaults. The results in FRELIMO killed and captured were disappointing to the Rhodesian contingent but the brigadier and all of his staff were delighted, particularly with the quantities of weapons and landmines captured. All structures that had not been ignited by Sneb rockets or gunship fire were set alight by the troops. The brigadier acknowledged that he owed me three bottles of Antiqua.

Thursday 11 April was the day chosen to take on the main line of bases which, on the Ops Room map, were numbered from the first base we struck as (1) and ascending up the communication line to base (5).

Rob Gaunt and I were keen to take the assault force onto Base (5) then put in airstrikes on the other bases (2, 3 and 4) in that sequence. After their move through Base (5), the assault troops were to set up numerous ambushes both north and south. The southern ambushes were for FRELIMO moving up from the bases attacked by aircraft; the northern ambushes were to cater for FRELIMO coming down on normal resupply or to investigate air and ground activities of the previous day.

Unfortunately the Portuguese would not accept the plan or the idea of leaving forces in the field overnight (something to do with fresh bread). Instead, the assault force was to take on base (2) with Rhodesian Air Force jet-strikes on bases (3 and 5). The Portuguese Air Force would strike Base (4) with Fiat jet fighter-bombers; to which end English-speaking PAF officer Major Vizlha would fly with me to communicate with the Fiat pilots of Scorpion Formation.

I led the assault force to Base (2) for a strike at 09:00. This time two Pumas placed troops about 100 metres apart at one end of the base and two Pumas landed troops east and west to cater for lateral breakout. The northern end of the base was to be contained by the gunships. This time marking was by two rockets only to retain plenty for the forthcoming FAC marking runs for jet strikes. I had contemplated bringing in Kevin and Mark to take on opportunity targets with their Sneb rockets before proceeding to their recce areas but dropped the idea to avoid any confusion that might arise through language difficulties, I regretted the decision immediately because FRELIMO, seeming to believe the Pumas had surrounded them with troops, milled about in the opening several seconds presenting many good and concentrated Sneb targets.

Again the two gunships, which were active at the northern end of the camp, did not see the bigger target opportunities in the base centre. I had not seen 20mm cannon fire from helicopters before Op Marble and was impressed with the visual effects of the exploding shells. However, considering the low kill-rate that had been achieved in the four previous bases, I moved above one gunship and watched it fire at dispersed individuals. In spite of the large flashes that were really close to running FRELIMO, the shells seemed to have little effect on them. Some FRELIMO tumbled but got up and ran on, probably slightly wounded and certainly shaken.

Then two running men went down when a couple of shells exploded halfway up the wall of a pole and dagga building they were passing. They dropped immediately and lay dead where they had fallen. Seeing this, Major Vizlha and I agreed that the shells landing on soft ground were exploding below surface causing them to lose shrapnel effect. (When we acquired 20mm cannons for our own helicopters later in the month, the neutralising effect of soft ground became well known. Because of this, many of our gunners became expert at using rocks and trees to gain airbursts for maximum lethal effect.)

At midday I marked Base (3) sited in a mountainous area. It was not the crisp operation I had hoped to show Major Vizlha because of localised low cloud at 1,500 feet agl and a fifteen-second error in my understanding of Rick Culpan's intended strike time.

Part of the Air Strike Report submitted by 5 Squadron reads:

From the IP to the final turn onto the target it became evident that the jet formation was too close to the marker aircraft. Speed was reduced to 200 kts. In spite of this the jets arrived too early and turned on to heading 225 deg M. This resulted in all the aircraft being in line astern formation with the marker aircraft leading. (Note: This must have been short-lived because:-) The target was marked and appeared at 90 deg to the formation 2000 yards away. The Hunters turned in and released their weapons on a heading 120 deg M. This was too close for the Canberras to bomb and they were forced to follow the Hunters for a restrike on the planned heading of 210 deg M.

Rob Gaunt had passed command of 1 Squadron to Rich Brand but for some reason he did not lead this attack. For a short while the timings of lead Hunter strike on FAC mark were not as crisp as I had become used to. In spite of this, all strikes were on target with the exception of one 500-pound bomb that must have hung up temporarily. It exploded directly below our Trojan giving Major Vizlha and me quite a shake up.

Digressing for a moment—The Board of Inquiry into the loss of the Canberra just seven days prior to this attack

Unrelated to the Op Marble airstrikes, Canberras and Hunters climbing in formation.

had concluded that an arming cap vane from one 28-pound bomb had managed to reach deep into the nose casing of a following bomb. In doing so it activated the pistol's reversible diaphragm causing the detonation that set off the whole bomb load. (A reversible diaphragm was used to achieve an airburst just above ground level when backpressure from the ground caused the pressure-sensitive diaphragm to reverse and fire the cap that detonated the bomb.) The Rhodesian-designed and manufactured 28lb fragmentation bomb system was withdrawn from service leaving 250-pound, 500-pound and 1000-pound bombs as the only weapons available for Canberra strikes, hence the use of 500-pound bombs on this strike.

Major Vizlha was amazed to see each one of our jets passing through target and asked me if the pilots knew there were Strela missiles in the area. I responded by saying we were all acutely aware of this before he told me how fearful he was to be flying with me. He said the Portuguese Air Force dared not operate above 100 feet and below 15,000 feet because of the missile threat between these heights.

We could not stick around to watch for movement in the Base where some buildings were burning furiously because Scorpion formation checked in way too early just as the Hunters and Canberras cleared target. This forced us to move on to Base (4) earlier than planned.

It was pleasing to hear the Portuguese transmissions between Scorpion leader and Major Vizlha. I understood nothing of what was being said until I was told that three Fiats were holding at 30,000 feet over the cloud-free target, each carrying four 250-pound bombs and awaiting my markers. This distressed me because I was still ten minutes away and I knew that FRELIMO would certainly hear and see the jets. Nevertheless, there was nothing I could do but run straight to target, pitch up and roll over into the dive to fire the marker rockets. Major Vizlha gave a running commentary on our progress and reported the mark.

The Fiat pilots were obviously super-sensitive to Strela. They turned into their attack dives about five seconds apart from 30,000 feet and probably released their bombs at around 15,000 feet. We did not see the jets at any stage.

I was beginning to doubt that the markers had been seen because nothing happened for ages. Holding well away from the base, I had completed half an orbit before the first cluster of four 250-pound bombs landed in the base. A long pause followed, then the second cluster struck, again inside the target. In the same way we had heard the first two strikes, the third 'krrrump' of bombs sounded much louder but we had not seen them explode. It took another quarter of the turn before we spotted the dust cloud of the strike behind us about 800 metres short of the target.

The combined area covered by the two sets of tightly grouped bombs within the target was substantially smaller than that obtained by a single Hunter using Matra rockets. This strike had been a complete waste of time and we saw no movement whatsoever in or near the base. Major Vizlha agreed that the Fiats had given the game away long before the marker rockets were fired.

Though embarrassed by the strike of his own force, Vizlha was very impressed by the swiftness of the final FAC-controlled strike by Hunters and Canberras against Base (5) and remarked on our radio disciplines, which involved only a few short verbal exchanges.

Base 5's anti-aircraft guns were sited well outside the perimeter of the target and they put up so much fire at us that I broke away and returned to base. In this case the anti-aircraft gun tracer rounds coming our way had been made highly visible because the whole area of the target was in the shadow of high-level cloud. Major Vizlha's high-pitch Portuguese outburst did nothing to dampen my own fear.

Next day the assault force was used to check out the effects of the air strikes on the three bases. Considerable quantities of FRELIMO equipment were recovered out of each of the bases though this would have been greater had the force been used straight after the strikes. Anti-aircraft shell casings littered a number of gun positions but all guns had been taken away during the night.

In Base (3), eight FRELIMO bodies were found burnt in or next to thatched structures with evidence of the burial of others. No bodies were found in Base (4). Something in the order of twenty FRELIMO dead were in Base (5) where many fresh field-dressing packets showed that a number of wounded had been taken to safety.

On 13 April the assault force was put in on a base, I think by Kevin Peinke. I continued with my own recce directly to the north of Chris Weinmann's area with our Director of Operations, Wing Commander Porky MacLaughlin, who was visiting the Air Detachment at Estima. He had insisted on accompanying me on a flight during which we conducted FAC for another combined jet strike before we led Clive Ward flying a Trojan and Chris Dickinson flying a Provost onto a smaller base.

My recall of these strikes is vague, but the Air Strike Reports indicate that the thatching of buildings in the base struck by jets was so green that the troops had difficulty in setting them alight. In spite of this, the base had been deserted before the strike went in, indicating that FRELIMO had become jittery. So it was decided to switch all attention to a new area.

On 14 April I moved east of the areas we had disturbed. At midday Chris Weinmann and I checked in for a routine exchange of information. Chris said he was onto something big in the very area I had warned him to treat with caution. I was doing well myself and told him so. At 12:30 I checked in with Chris again but received no reply.

Every five minutes thereafter I called Chris, but still no reply. I wondered if he had returned to Centenary, or maybe the small Portuguese base at Nova Mague just south of the Zambezi River. Maybe he was trying to arrange for attacks on whatever he had found. But I could not understand why he would have done this without letting me know. By 14:30 I had become very concerned but was unable to talk to Rob Gaunt because Estima was out of radio range and a relayed discussion was not possible as Kevin and Mark had already returned to base.

When I reached Estima at around 15:30, Rob Gaunt sent a signal to Air HQ requesting Ops to establish if Chris had returned to Centenary. The Portuguese were asked to check with Nova Mague but, unfortunately, that small base was only contactable on routine radio schedule at 17:00. In the meanwhile, Rob Gaunt had accepted a challenge from the brigadier and his adjutant to a shooting competition with Rob and me.

On our first shoot from 100 metres Rob and I, using FN rifles, had fired off ten rounds each before the brigadier and his adjutant, using Armalite rifles, had fired their second shots. We beat them hands down. The brigadier was not at all impressed by the 'reckless rate of fire' we had displayed and emphasised how one needed to fire, settle, aim and squeeeeze the trigger. We said we should try this at 200 metres. But, again, Rob and I cleared our magazines before our challengers had fired second shots. We were already standing up as the brigadier fired his third shot and Rob whispered to me, "I put my tenth round into the brigadier's target. Lets see how he reacts to being called a cheat." We never did find out because, during our walk to inspect targets, we were all summonsed urgently to the Ops Room. Chris Weinmann had not landed at Centenary or any other Rhodesian base and Nova Mague reported that no aircraft had been seen or heard all day.

Search for Chris

I PREPARED IMMEDIATELY TO COMMENCE SEARCHING for Chris who I knew must be in serious trouble. Rob Gaunt advised Air HQ of my intention but received an order that I was not, under any circumstances, to fly until cleared to do so. This clearance was only given one and a half hours after sunset following continuous niggling to let us off the leash. I intended to fly alone but Mark Knight persuaded me that I needed a second pair of eyes to watch my blind side for any distress signal that Chris may use if his emergency beacon was not working.

It was a very black night and the vague line of the Zambezi River was just sufficient to get us to a point south of where Chris had reported "something big". Although we were flying around 10,000 feet above the ground, it still makes me shudder

to recall how, for Chris's sake, we deliberately flew with our rotating beacons flashing brightly. This provided any Strela operator with the most perfect aiming point for a missile that would easily detect our exhaust heat against the cold black sky. Were we brave or stupid? It is impossible to say because our safety seemed less important than the safety of our colleague on the ground.

Mark and I had agreed that lights had to be used just in case Chris was running, breathless and unable to hear the aircraft. For three hours we ran an expanding square search but heard no emergency signal and saw absolutely nothing save one group of small fires burning inside a Portuguese *aldeamento*. We felt totally helpless and were overwhelmed by a deep sense of foreboding by the time we returned to Estima after midnight. Rob told us that our three Trojans and crews were required to position at Nova Mague next morning to participate in a search for Chris. He also let me know that he had received a signal revealing that one of my junior technicians, Senior Aircraftsman Rob Durrett, had been flying with Chris.

Rob left all of our ground equipment at Estima, at least for the time being, so that we could continue with Op Marble when this became possible. He returned to Thornhill by Dakota once my three aircraft were airborne for Nova Mague.

At Nova Mague, the Operations Officer (I cannot recall who it was) and a team of Volunteer Reserve men were setting up communications in a tiny building next to the grass airstrip whilst others unloaded tents and supplies from a Dakota. Four helicopters, two Trojans and two Provosts released by FAFs 3 and 4 arrived just behind us. More aircraft arrived later from New Sarum and Thornhill.

Inside the small communications room was a large, beautifully carved wooden casket containing the body of a Portuguese soldier. It had been there for many months awaiting shipment to Portugal. The casket lay elevated on boxes at a height that made it an ideal working platform for 4 and 7 Squadron's flight authorisation and aircraft F700 technical log books. Each time a pilot or technician came to attend to these he would say something along the lines, "Excuse me Alfredo" and on completion, "Thanks Alfredo".

Based on what I knew, and supported by Peter Cooke's knowledge of Chris Weinmann's intended recce area on the day he went missing, a search involving every squadron had been planned by the Air Staff. The area stretching northwards from the Zambezi River had been broken into defined blocks, each to be searched by its assigned squadron. Operating in pairs, Hunters, Canberras, Vampires, Dakotas, Provosts, Trojans and Alouettes were involved. A commando of the RLI was on hand to protect Nova Mague and to give ground assistance as soon as either the missing aircrew or the Trojan was found.

Since we had an uneven number of Trojans, I paired up with Al Bruce who was flying a SAAF Cessna 185. Three of these aircraft had recently been delivered on long-term loan to 4 Squadron. We had planned for Chris and me to do

4 Squadron were now operating three aircraft types. Bottom to top: Provost, Trojan, Cessna.

conversions onto this aircraft because it afforded much better visual freedom for recce than the Trojan. However Op Marble interrupted our plans and Al, having done his conversion, came to lend a hand.

We passed a formation of four helicopters going in the opposite direction along the southern boundary of our search area. Their decision to use four aircraft for maximum security was a wise move made possible by their ability to hold open formation in the rough terrain allocated to 7 Squadron. At 10:00 Red Section, a pair of Hunters flown by Ricky Culpan and Vic Wightman, was flying wide line-abreast at 500 feet past a high feature on their right side when a Strela missile was fired. Part of Vic Wightman's ASR read:

The missile had already passed No 2 when the report was made and a break starboard called. Leader then positioned and carried out a guns attack on the top of the hill, marked clearly by the smoke of the missile. This was approx. 30 secs after the missile had been fired. No 2 reversed his turn to position for a rocket attack on the hill. Leader repositioned for rockets and further gun attacks covering the hill and its surrounds. The section then climbed to height and reported the incident and position to Nova Mague before setting course for New Sarum.

Had that missile been fired at a slower aircraft the result would have been fatal. So, at 17:00 on the same day I led a strike by four Hunters on a base twelve kilometres to the southeast of were the Strela had been fired. Ricky Culpan and Vic Wightman were striking for the second time on this day led by Rob Gaunt with Don Northcroft flying No 4. The strike was made with a view to dissuading FRELIMO from firing at any searching aircraft.

It was getting dark when I decided it was my duty as OC 4 Squadron to get back to see Ellie Weinmann at Thornhill and Rob Durrett's parents in Bulawayo. Although I was certain in my mind that both airmen were dead, I used the long night flight to conjure up suitable words of encouragement for the families. Eventually I came to the conclusion that no such words existed and that I would have to play things by ear when the time came. At Thornhill Ellie Weinmann, already receiving encouragement and support from Beryl and other squadron wives, had no doubts that Chris was alive and that he would be found soon. I was relieved by this and went home to bed totally exhausted.

Next morning I left early to meet Rob Durrett's family. I told them that, although we had not given up hope, things did not look good. They were obviously distressed but were grateful that I had taken the time to pay them a personal visit and had not tried to hide realities. I returned to Thornhill and by midday had completed a hurried conversion onto a SAAF Cessna 185 with Captain van der Linde who, after forty-five minutes in the circuit, declared me safe to fly the aircraft. This aircraft was fitted with an SSB radio for long-range communication, which is the reason I needed it in a hurry for improved communications during the search and for Op Marble when it resumed.

En route back to Nova Mague I received an unusual instruction on the SSB radio from Wing Commander Porky MacLaughlin in Air HQ. He asked me to search the Mucanha River line. This river was on the north side of the Zambezi into which it flowed but was outside and to the west of the search area. Porky explained that the Rhodesian Broadcasting Corporation had reported that a Rhodesian Air Force aircraft was missing in the operational area but no mention had been made of Mozambique. Yet two female clairvoyants had voluntarily and individually phoned Air HQ to say they knew where the aircraft could be found and that both airmen were alive. The aircraft was reported to be right next to the Mucanha River itself and not too far from the Zambezi River.

Porky said it was so uncanny that these ladies, acting independently, had identified Mozambique and that both had pointed to the same river. This information could not be ignored, particularly as both women had previously assisted the Police in finding missing persons whose bodies had been located where the Police were told to search.

The Cessna I was flying had an unpainted silver surface making it an even better target for Strela than the camouflaged Trojan. Because of this I elected to search the river-line at low level and take my chances with smallarms fire. I could find nothing even though every tree, bush, nook and cranny had been inspected up and downriver until it became too dark to continue. I saw people on the ground three times but only once did I see a pair of men firing at my unarmed aircraft.

It was completely dark when I reached Nova Mague for my first solo landing in the tail-dragger Cessna 185. This was not the easiest of aircraft to land because of its narrow, undamped, leaf-spring undercarriage; so I was apprehensive about landing without a flare path. The dull lights within the camp helped me assess the position of the threshold and I used my instruments to assess the runway direction. On short finals I switched on the landing lights just in time to see a large tree directly ahead. I lifted over this and a little further on put the aircraft down so smoothly it surprised me.

Two days of intensive searching had yielded nothing and for the next three days the intensity of the search was maintained with as many as sixteen aircraft actually airborne at once. At no time during daylight were there less than six aircraft searching.

Under pressure from the Portuguese to resume Op Marble, Air HQ instructed me to reposition at Estima on 20 April. I was airborne out of Nova Mague flying my Cessna 185 with Chris Dickinson following in a Trojan. At 09:00 I was climbing at low power to allow Chris to hold formation when I heard Greg Todd calling urgently, "Willy where are you? Willy this is Greg. I cannot see you. Willy are you all right?" These calls were to Willy Wilson who had been flying No 2 to Greg.

I called Greg by his correct callsign and asked him what was going on. "Boss PB, I cannot see Willy. I have lost him." For Greg Todd to call me Boss PB and refer to himself as Greg was reason enough to know he was already a frightened man. "Where are you now Greg?" I asked. He told me where, then said, "I can see black smoke along the route we were flying". Moments later he said, "There's a ball of white smoke rising from there, I'm sure Willy's rockets have exploded." The position Greg was reporting was smack in the centre of the area I had warned Chris Weinmann to be especially wary of and where he had said he was onto something big. Immediately I instructed Greg to move south and take cover behind a high feature whilst I moved over to him. As I flew there I requested Nova Mague to recall the helicopters and prepare to move troops. The smoke rising from Willy's crash site was faint but obvious. I could see where Greg and Willy had passed over the south-to-north spur of a high dogleg ridge-line that turned ninety degrees westward into higher ground. I had come to know this particular feature well during earlier recces. From the south leg the pilots had descended to flatter terrain where the smoke was rising.

In the dogleg bend of the ridge there ran a number of steep ravines that merged into a small river with surface water. FRELIMO had favoured this river for its bases, particularly in the dry season, so I called for jets. Greg and Chris linked up and held south whilst I climbed to 15,000 feet before moving up to the river and ridge-line. Immediately I saw the huge base that Chris Weinmann had obviously found under heavy cover astride the river at the base of the dogleg.

This was the sixth day of the search, which meant that Trojans and Provosts must have traversed this spot at least six times, yet no pilot had spotted the base. Presumably this was because of the density of trees and the fact that they were either

climbing or descending the very steep ridge when they passed over it. From my lofty height it was easier to see the telltale sections of pathways and two particular paths leading steeply to worn patches on two small ledges between ravines high above the base; perfect anti-aircraft sites.

A pair of Hunters flown by Don Northcroft and Paddy Bates checked in with me before the helicopters reached the area. Bearing in mind that A4 (Alpha 4) was my callsign and K4 was Chris Dickinson's, this is what Don Northcroft recorded in his Air Strike Report:

1. We were ordered by SDO New Sarum to go direct to the search area and were provided a grid reference. RPs were not carried, as a recce task was expected.
2. En route Air Det Mague advised that A4 would be directing our attacks.
3. A4 advised that he had no weapons but that K4 would mark for him. We were to attack a ter. camp in the vicinity of the crashed Trojan so that helicopters and troops could land in the area.
4. Some difficulty was experienced in locating K4 so A4 gave a heading to steer from a prominent feature. K4 was then sighted and he marked soon after.
5. Red section was redirected from the mark to a ravine 1200 yards east. It is thought that only the 5th and 3rd attacks were the strikes on target as there were several ravines in the area which made redirection and recognition very difficult.
6. Red section cleared for New Sarum after expending all 30mm.

This had been an unusually scruffy strike because Chris marked too far southwest of target. Nevertheless with Chris Dickinson and Greg Todd holding top cover, the helicopters put the troops down at the crash site without incident.

Willy Wilson and his accompanying technician, Flight Sergeant Roger Andrews, were found dead. The troops said Willy had crawled some distance from the aircraft before he was killed when one pod of rockets detonated. They also reported that a Strela missile had exploded smack bang on the engine exhaust. There was no doubt that this had been a Strela strike and that Chris Weinmann's aircraft would be found somewhere fairly close by.

Any thought of continuing to Estima for Op Marble was dropped. Instead I returned to Nova Mague where a group of men stood silent around the bodies that had just been brought in from the crash site. Each one of those 7 Squadron's crews present had served on 4 Squadron and they felt just as keenly for these downed men as the men still serving on my squadron. I addressed them but cannot recall what I said, other than that Chris Weinmann and Rob Durrett had obviously suffered the same fate and would be found by the troops within hours. More troops were flown in and the air search was terminated in favour of an RLI ground search. I returned to Thornhill to see Roger Andrew's widow, Muriel, then continued on to Victoria Falls to see Willy Wilson's folks.

The next day troops found the engineless Trojan hanging by its tail in a large tree on the south side of the base Chris had discovered. The engine had been blown from its mountings by a Strela missile that had obviously entered next to the exhaust pipe and exploded between firewall and engine. The engine and its propeller were never found. The firewall was no more than a few inches above the ground and both doors lay open against the ground. Shallow graves next to each open door contained the maggot-infested bodies of the airmen.

Six men dead and three aircraft lost in sixteen days ended a very sad period for the Air Force. What made it all so much worse was the unexpected revolutionary change of government in Portugal following a left-wing military coup on 25 April. All in all April 1974 had been a very 'black month' for Rhodesia. Op Marble, due to resume on 26 April, seemed to have been a total waste of time and had cost us four dead plus the loss of two valuable Trojans. Its resumption was called off which, on a lighter note, cost me eleven bottles of Antiqua, unclaimed from the brigadier.

For ages I found difficulty in coming to terms with the fact that Chris and Willy had been taken out by Strela and that I, having spent so much more time over Mozambique and having deliberately operated the areas I considered most dangerous, was still alive. There were no simple answers; it was just a matter of getting on with the job in the knowledge that the war was about to intensify and that many dangers still lay ahead.

Chris Weinmann had been a great water-polo player and always wore around his neck a water-polo medallion inscribed with his name. In 1980, whilst serving as the Rhodesian Security Forces Ceasefire Commissioner, I was introduced to a FRELIMO officer at Nyamasoto. Not only was he wearing Chris's medallion, he wanted to let everyone around know that he was the man who had fired both the Strela missiles that had downed our two Trojans. He said that he had been celebrating his first Strela success and was too drunk to fire at the aircraft he had seen flying overhead that night. How it came to be I cannot say, but he knew I was the pilot of that aircraft. Strangely enough I was not at all put out by his boastfulness. Times had changed too much to make the matter seem important.

Hunter commanders

THE OFFICER WHO BLEW UP a lavatory bowl, Mike Saunders made an excellent squadron commander because of his natural abilities and a very naughty nature. When making his last flight as OC of Hunters, he showed his displeasure at being replaced by Norman Walsh in the manner expected of him. He made a low-level supersonic pass over the airfield that resulted in cracked windows in a number of buildings.

Norman Walsh though outwardly quiet, was probably the naughtiest of all 1 Squadron commanders but he took his job very seriously and became a main player in Air Force affairs, as will be seen later in this book.

Rob Gaunt had been an excellent leader and I remember him best for his incredible anticipation and precision in FAC-led strikes. Rich Brand followed Rob in 1974 and Vic Wightman replaced Rich in mid-1978. As with all our squadron commanders, they were vastly different characters in all respects, but they were all great pilots.

Mike Saunders (top left), Norman Walsh (top right), Rob Gaunt (bottom left) and Rich Brand (below).

Rob Gaunt spent some time in Air HQ before leaving the force to enter into politics. Mentally gifted, he followed in the footsteps of his father, John Gaunt, who had been an outspoken politician in Federal times and again as a minister in the first Rhodesian Front Government. Rob was still a member of the Rhodesian Front party after

Robert Mugabe's ZANU party came to power, by which time he had put on a great deal of weight. Rob had the unusual knack of criticising black ZANU politicians without really upsetting them. On one occasion, when ZANU was giving ZAPU's immensely fat Joshua Nkomo a particularly hard time, Rob leapt to his feet and looking directly at Nkomo said, "Honourable Minister, you have no need to concern yourself with what you are hearing because I can assure you and all the honourable members present that you and I carry a lot of weight in this House!"

Rich Brand was the grandson of the famous Sir Quintin Brand who, together with Pierre van Reyneveld, made history in March 1920 by flying the Vickers Vimy bomber 'Silver Queen' from Britain to Cape Town. Rich was a quiet man, something of a loner that, in Air Force circles, made him appear to be at odds with most pilots. He spent much of his spare time building and flying radio-controlled model aerobatic aircraft. His talents here and his ability to deliver weapons with great accuracy were well known to all—but nobody ever recognised the huge potential that lay dormant within the man.

He left the Air Force in 1980 and moved to the USA where he was associated with an American tycoon who had an interest in building and flying model aircraft. Amongst other things, this tycoon owned a large hotel and casino in Las Vegas. When one day he asked Rich what he had in mind for his own future, Rich said, "I want to start at the bottom of your Las Vegas enterprise and work my way up until I head it." Without further ado Rich was given the broom and mop brigade. He progressed rapidly through every position rising through management of the gambling halls, the hotel and finally becoming Managing Director of the entire Circus Circus enterprise. He endeared himself to every member of the enormous staff who he greeted personally by first name. Rich Brand, the quiet person in Rhodesian Air Force days, turned out to be a much-revered multi-millionaire in a niche none of us would have believed possible.

Vic Wightman was an eccentric who would not allow his family to use salt in any food. He had three hates. These were Americans, dogs and insurance agents. His worst fear was to be visited by an American insurance agent with a dog. Vic was

Vic Wightman with Ginger Baldwin behind.

an excellent squadron commander and strike pilot whose name comes up often in this book. When Vic left the force he ended up flying a Lear Jet out of Nelspruit in South Africa on cloud-seeding and other weather-related work. He started his day there by walking barefoot from home to work over a forested hill to enjoy the bush and the local wildlife. He remained without shoes when flying his executive jet and sometimes astounded his bosses in Johannesburg by emerging barefoot from his aircraft to attend company meetings. In addition to one already covered, some of Vic's experiences will be revealed later.

Army claims air kills

4 SQUADRON PROVOSTS WERE BECOMING MORE and more involved with internal strikes whether operating in conjunction with helicopters, being called to assist ground forces or acting against targets located during visual recce by other 4 Squadron pilots.

All 4 Squadron pilots were great operators but one junior pilot was already emerging as a star performer. Almost every action involving Air Sub-Lieutenant 'Cocky' Benecke with the callsign Juliet 4 turned to success. This had much to do with his amazing eyesight, as will be seen.

Brian Murdoch (E4), Cocky Benecke (J4) and Kevin Peinke (R4), all flying Provost, were involved in an action inside Rhodesia on 18 April when others of 4 Squadron were still tied up with the air search in Mozambique. Selous Scouts operator Mick Hardy and his pseudo terrorist group had initiated this widespread running action.

Mick had been successful in locating three bases that one particularly large ZANLA group used in random rotation. Mick's problem was that he could not tell which of the bases was occupied at any given time. His Officer Commanding, Ron Reid-Daly, went to JOC Hurricane at Bindura to arrange for the grouping of all available helicopters and troops to move in behind simultaneous air strikes on all three bases. Unfortunately there was some confusion and the terrorists survived.

Undaunted, Mick picked up the trail and established two alternative bases for which a first-light attack by RAR was planned. Due to scepticism following the abortive attack of the previous day, the local RAR commander approached his task in an uncaring manner, causing Mick Hardy to realise that his target of about thirty CTs would be lost if he did not take the initiative. He did this by dealing directly with the Air Force.

Following the action that accounted for eight CTs killed and four captured the RAR, who came to the party late, proudly claimed all to their own credit. This was an ongoing difficulty for the Air Force; not that it should have mattered who achieved the successes. But apart from niggling the airmen, problems caused by ground forces claiming most Air Force successes, a consequence of inter-company rivalries, could prejudice annual allocation of funds to Air Force by the Government Treasury. Fortunately a more balanced situation developed as time went on but the reader can judge who did what in this particular action. The Air Strike Report is difficult to follow without an accompanying sketch, but it gives a fair idea of the widely spread actions involved. As with most hurriedly written ASRs, little attention was given to grammar.

Juliet 4 and Yellow section consisting of 4 helicopters were scrambled to just north of Banji acting on information received from c/s 91 that 14 terrs were heading in a north westerly direction from their location. This group was not seen and whilst orbiting overhead 4 terrs were seen to run into a thicket north east of 91's location. J4 then directed two choppers onto either side of a stream that they had gone into, to act as stop groups and the one helicopter came under fire. J4 put in a strike using front gun and Sneb with no results. J4 remained in the area and saw one terr running east along the river just south of Bobgarande School. He carried out a front gun attack and was hit in the process. J4 was then informed of 4 terrs running in the fields to the south of the river and was directed to them. A strike was carried out by J4 and one terr with an RPD fell. E4 arrived at this time and carried out an attack on the subsequent three. All 3 fell, 1 then got up and started running again. E4 carried out another attack on him and he fell again. E4 then directed ground forces onto their position. The last terr to fall opened fire on the ground forces and he was shot by them. The other two who were shot by E4 were found dead by ground forces. J4 returned (from rearming) and directed ground forces to the body with the RPD; he too was dead. E4 then departed to rearm. J4 then directed troops to the area just south of Bobgarande School where he had come under fire. An air strike was carried out by J4 and the subsequent sweep revealed 1 dead terr. J4 returned to rearm and R4 took over. More firing had started from the same area, which was a thick reed area on a riverbank. J4 then rejoined R4 and led a further strike that resulted in 1 dead and 4 surrendering, all of whom were wounded. J4 returned to rearm. R4 did a further 2 strikes; as a result 2 more dead terrs were found.

Gungwa mountain

FOLLOWING A BREAK AT THORNHILL I returned to ops earlier than planned on 4 May. This was in response to a call from JOC Hurricane at Bindura. SB had received reports of a large ZANLA base just across the border in the vicinity of a high feature known as Gungwa mountain, upon whose summit was one of the border beacons. I was asked to pinpoint the base.

Flying a Cessna, I searched outwards from the mountain but failed to find any base. Only one place remotely resembled the type of temporary camp found inside Rhodesia. This lay in dense jesse bush at the base of Gungwa mountain itself. Because it was not possible to remain overhead for a detailed look, I had to fly all over the place before returning for a second and then a third look. I was not convinced that this was a base but I could not reject it either because too many cattle paths ran in parallel lines within and outside the jesse bush. If in fact it was the site of a CT base, I decided it was for no more than ten CTs residing on a temporary basis.

At Bindura I reported that there were no CT camps near Gungwa and that only the large patch of jesse bush offered the remotest possibility for a mere handful of CTs. I thought no more about the matter believing an OP (observation post) callsign would move in to monitor the site. However, a couple of days later I received instructions to fly to New Sarum and report to OC Flying Wing. On arrival, Wing Commander Bill Jelley told me that I was to fly lead Vampire on 6 May for the biggest air strike to date on the Gungwa mountain base. This was to be followed by every available helicopter making a vertical envelopment with RLI troops. I protested and made it quite clear that I felt that Air Force was being drawn into a huge 'lemon'. My objections were noted, but SB interrogations of captured CTs had satisfied JOC Hurricane that the jesse bush lying at the base of Gungwa mountain fitted with the intelligence. The strike would go ahead as planned. It was then that I came to realise that the whole fiasco was going to be recorded on film. In fact I saw myself on national television giving the air briefing for the very air strike I had tried to prevent.

I flew in the lead Vampire piloted by Justin Varkevisser. We marked with a full load of 20mm cannon and two 50-gallon Frantans and were followed in rapid succession by two Vampires, six Hunters and three Canberras. Four Provosts came from behind the mountain just ahead of about twelve helicopters. The whole operation went like clockwork on a patch of bush that was devoid of any ZANLA presence.

As expected, I was used as the scapegoat for the wastage of air weapons. Because of this I refused, with Air HQ support, to be involved in a similar situation in late 1974.

Countering Strela missiles

AS I HAD PREDICTED, WE needed to lose aircraft to Strela missiles before the Treasury hurriedly provided funds for the research and modifications needed to protect helicopters and piston-driven aircraft. Flight Lieutenant Archie Ramsbottom was appointed the technical officer for the project. I became involved with him immediately on an ad hoc advisory basis and together we paid a visit to CSIR in Pretoria for discussions on Strela missiles and the steps to be taken to render them harmless.

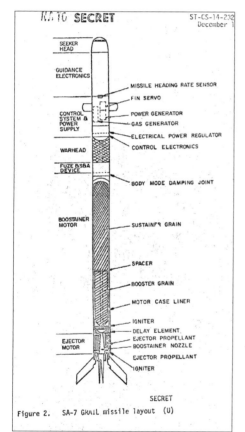

These were the first schematic drawings from CSIR. Strela missile (left), missile launcher (below).

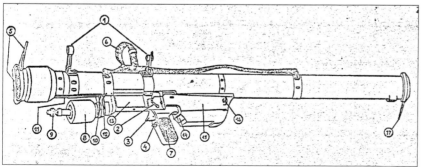

A sensor that could 'see' objects radiating infrared energy in the 2-micron wave band controlled Strela flight. Highest intensity emissions were from the relatively small exposed sections of exhaust pipes and hot engine parts. However, the cumulative value of infrared radiating from an entire standard airframe, although apparently cold, presented a good target. Strela would initially home on the entire heat signature of an aircraft and only seek out the hottest spot late in its flight; hence the strikes on the exhausts of the two Trojans.

Exhausted gas plumes did not present any problem but it was quite obvious that hot exhaust stubs and any exposed sections of engines had to be shielded. This needed some clever design and engineering work, which our technicians managed quite easily. Surface paint was the bigger problem. We established that colour was not the main criteria in selecting a paint mix that exhibited low radiation properties in the 2-micron wave band. In fact, and surprisingly, it was easier to achieve this with white paint than in the camouflage colours we intended to retain.

Archie worked long hours with paint manufacturers and the Paint Shop at New Sarum to develop the ideal paint mixes for our camouflage colours. What they eventually produced virtually eliminated radiation of infrared energy in the critical wavelength sector, even when the surface was hot.

The dedication and enthusiasm of Air Force technicians and paint manufacturers made Archie's job easier and the results were impressive. Provosts and Trojans looked the same as before except for strange-looking fibreglass fairings shaped like half cups that screened exhaust stubs that had been turned to face upwards. Simple screens were also used to disallow Strela from 'seeing' hot components through the cooling-gills under the engines.

Dakota exhausts required a different solution. This involved extending the exhaust pipes all the way to the trailing edge of the mainplanes where the pipes turned upwards to exhaust gases vertically. A wide tunnel-like fairing through which air flowed to keep the outer surface of the tunnel cool surrounded each long exhaust line. At the trailing edge of the mainplane, the tunnel fairing rounded upwards to screen the hot upturned outlet of the exhaust pipes.

Counter-Strela modifications for Alouettes and Cessna 185 aircraft were created by SAAF in conjunction with CSIR. The Cessna modifications were much the same as those developed for the Trojan. Alouette helicopters presented bigger problems because the entire engine and exhaust pipe were exposed. As with fixed-wing aircraft, it was necessary to modify the jet pipe to exhaust upwards and the entire engine was shrouded in a bath-like shield. This shield was without a top to allow access for engine servicing in the field. Because of this, the engine and jet pipe could be seen from the ground when a helicopter banked steeply.

Pre-mod (top)—engine fully exposed, Post Strela mod (above)—engine screened.

All anti-Strela modifications were very successful and many Strela missiles were wasted against our slow aircraft.

Jets, however, could not be protected to the same degree. There was no easy fix to the exposed ends of jet pipes. All that could be done was to paint the airframes with the new paint to minimise total radiation, thereby limiting Strela's ability to acquire target until a jet aircraft had passed its operator's position.

When all the Strela protection work was completed, Archie and I paid a visit to Air Rhodesia's top managers to suggest to them that their Viscount airliners should be protected along the lines of our Dakotas. The reason for our visit arose from tests we had conducted with a Strela missile that had been acquired by Air Force to evaluate our counter-missile work.

The missile's firing mechanisms were neutralised and a battery pack replaced the regular pyrotechnic generator. As a mobile test bed, this modified missile worked very well. Our tests confirmed that our light aircraft and Dakota modifications were satisfactory, and that the missile could not easily 'see' Canberras and Hunters until after they passed abeam. During these tests we noted that, whereas a Viscount produced a stronger signature from its four exhausts than either a Hunter or a Canberra, its entire airframe and large under-wing exhaust pipes made the aircraft highly visible, irrespective of range and direction of travel.

We were told that Air Rhodesia's engineers and upper management were fully aware of what had been done to protect Dakotas and they agreed that a similar style of engineering could be employed to shroud Viscount exhaust pipes. The matter of repainting the Viscounts presented no special problem. However, despite a very cordial meeting, both Archie and I sensed that there was no real interest because Air Rhodesia's managers seemed unable to accept that Strela would ever be a threat to civilian airliners.

Army Sub-JOC commanders

ON 4 JUNE 1974, LIEUTENANT-COLONEL Dave Parker, the Army Commander at JOC Darwin, asked me to take him along on a recce flight. He had been impressed with air recce successes and wanted to gain first-hand knowledge of how we searched for CT camps and what ground patterns attracted a pilot's attention. His open-mindedness and desire to learn from direct experience was very refreshing. Throughout our flight his questions and observations made it plain that he was very switched-on. Having shown Dave a few bases I had found previously we were fortunate to find a new one that appeared to be in use. Surprisingly he saw the base more easily than many of the pilots I had trained and his excitement was infectious.

Three helicopters brought in twelve RLI troops. Dave could see immediately that they were going to be too thin on the ground to have any chance of boxing in the area around a camp site that offered the CTs a number of escape routes in good cover.

Three-ship Fireforce.

I directed the lead helicopter to position 150 metres to one side of the CT base by calling "Camp centre 150 to your right... NOW." Troops were put down simultaneously on three sides of the camp before the lead helicopter climbed to 1,000 feet to direct the troops towards the camp. The other two put in dummy drops in gaps between the troops in an attempt to make CTs uncertain of which way to break. They then returned to Mount Darwin for more troops.

Contact was made before Dave and I saw two groups of four CTs breaking at high speed through a huge gap between the soldiers. Being unarmed I could do nothing about this, and the orbiting helicopter was already engaging CTs inside the camp. We had to be content with two CTs killed and one captured wounded with no less than eight CTs seen to escape. This experience certainly highlighted for Dave Parker the reason why Air Force had been asking to concentrate helicopters with permanent reaction troops, not simply to reduce the size of gaps, but to improve soldiers' efficiency under the direction of their own airborne commanders. Greater levels of immediate intelligence flowing from Selous Scouts made the availability of this type of reaction group all the more important.

There had been a few successes when helicopters and troops were brought together with an Army commander directing his troops from a helicopter. For the most part, however, helicopters had been penny-packeted to meet far too many unprofitable calls. This had been at high cost considering the unacceptably low returns for effort expended.

It so happened that two Alouette gunships were used for the first time on this very day, though neither one was available for our small action. Earlier in the day, Flight Lieutenant Rob McGregor and Sergeant Henry Jarvie had flown top cover to trooping helicopters. When the trooper helicopters had left the scene, a well-known wounded CT leader, who was hiding in a hut with other wounded CTs, pinned down the ground forces. This gave Rob and Henry opportunity to employ their 20mm side-firing cannon, which resulted in the death of all the CTs. During the late afternoon Flight Lieutenant John Annan and Sergeant Morris fired their cannon in another action but with no confirmed results.

The arrival of gunships, improving Selous Scouts effectiveness and Dave Parker's influence in the field made it possible, at last, to introduce the permanent reaction force the Air Force had been advocating for some time. The Air Force had not been alone in seeking this concentration of forces because a number of RLI commando commanders had been pressing for the same thing. To my own knowledge these included RLI Captains Jerry Strong, Pat Armstrong and Dumpy Pearce.

As with the Portuguese assault force at Estima, this involved grouping troops, trooper helicopters, helicopter gunships and armed fixed-wing aircraft. We could not possibly match the lift capacity of the Portuguese but we had the advantage of having very aggressive RLI soldiers and could provide their commanders a seat in a gunship from which to observe and direct them. The continuous presence of a gunship overhead each action also facilitated immediate supporting fire to ground troops or to engage targets moving beyond their reach.

Within a few days this reaction force, soon to be called Fireforce, was put into effect and the results achieved over the following six months were astounding. Dave Parker had much to do with bringing the first permanent combined force into being at Mount Darwin.

Dave was a truly superb individual who was held in high regard by all who knew him. He was blessed with many talents that included flexibility of mind and a desire to actively seek and receive the opinions of others without regard to their rank. He absorbed everything he heard before reaching decisions that were reduced to clear-cut plans and instructions. He also had the rare ability to admit to occasional error, never offering excuses for his own mistakes. It was no wonder that the RLI troops nicknamed Dave Parker 'The King'.

Five weeks after my flight with Dave Parker I flew with Lieutenant-Colonel Bert Barnard, an RAR officer. Bert was the Army commander at JOC Centenary, the post he had held from the outset of Op Hurricane. Along with most Army and Air Force officers I found Bert Barnard to be the exact opposite of Dave Parker. He was pompous, highly self-opinionated and intolerant of opinions emanating from any rank below his own.

My Flying Logbook shows that he accompanied me on a visual recce sortie that lasted for only one hour and twenty-five minutes. Bert became bored and asked to return to Centenary on the pretext of matters requiring his urgent attention; a marked contrast to Dave Parker's flight of over six hours, following which he had expressed disbelief at having been airborne so long.

Fireforce might have come into effect much sooner, admittedly without gunships, had Bert Barnard listened to Air Force and RLI opinion. However, none of us had yet realised that we should have pressed for penny-packeting of helicopters to bring him, inevitably, to the opposite view of needing to concentrate forces.

Fireforce and Scouts

ON COMPLETION OF TRIALS AND training for the new 20mm helicopter cannons, helicopters and RLI commandos teamed up to form two assault forces, initially comprising one 20mm gunship and four trooper helicopters, each carrying four soldiers. Mount Darwin and Centenary had one force each.

To distinguish between gunships, Rhodesian troopers and SAAF troopers, abbreviations were introduced. Influenced by a popular British Police TV series then showing in Salisbury and entitled 'Zed Cars', the helicopters became:

K-Car (Kay)—gunship (killer)-cum-command post
G-Car (Gee)—trooping and general purpose—Rhodesian
Z-Car (Zed)—trooping and general purpose—SAAF

The first action out of Mount Darwin occurred on 21 June 1974. John Annan, flying the gunship with Sergeant Garry Whittal as his gunner, led four trooper helicopters and a Provost. Two G-Cars were crewed by Squadron Leader Eddie Wilkinson (OC 7 Squadron) with Sergeant Pete McCabe and Flight Lieutenant Ken Law with Flight Sergeant Farrell. Two Z-Cars were crewed by Captain du Plessis with Sergeant Hulatt, and Lieutenant Anderson with Sergeant Veldman. Air Lieutenant Steve Baldwin flew the Provost.

The ASR is typically brief. It reads:

1. K-Car led four troopers in an assault on a position where an observation post reported seeing 6 terrorists being fed. Troopships landed assault force in vicinity of kraal to southeast of terrorist position. K-Car engaged terrorists in a passing attack pattern to cover the landing.
2. Position of terrorists was exactly as given, but approximately 20 terrorists were seen. K-Car engaged terrorists as they split up and ran. Then assisted by a Provost and the troopships, the terrorists were engaged for approximately 20 minutes until all had "gone to ground". The aircraft continued to orbit the area in order to limit terrorist movement while ground forces moved into the contact area.
3. Approximately 15 ters seen to fall during strikes, but several of these were seen to move again afterwards.

4. Return fire was heard on many occasions but the aircraft were only hit twice. (Provost one round, Zed car 3 rounds)
5. Good surprise was achieved due to an approach route screened by hills and the Provost providing some screening of the helicopter noise during the approach.

John said, "Return fire was heard on many occasions …" Bearing in mind the high level of noise inside a helicopter and the marked reduction in surrounding noises when wearing padded earphones under a 'bone-dome', the sound level of sharp supersonic cracks from rounds passing close to a helicopter was substantially diminished. In fact passing machine-gun rounds sounded something like a swarm of bees striking the windscreen of a fast moving motorcar. So when helicopter crew heard this, they knew rounds were passing either through their craft or very close to it.

Wing Commander Roy Morris was OC FAF 4 at the time. His comments were:

The reaction with all available effort was quick and efficient. Full credit must go to all aircrew involved with this most successful operation which lasted for 4 hours. The participation of the two South Africans, Capt du Plessis and Lt Anderson is worthy of special mention. Their enthusiasm and high standard of professionalism was most commendable. The general co-ordination of all parties involved (Support Gp - RLI, 4 Sqn and helicopters of 7 Sqn) was first class. Of a group of approx. 35, some 25 were accounted for. A first class show highlighting the effectiveness of helicopter firepower. This action accounted for 20 CTs dead and 5 wounded. Most of the dead and all of the wounded had been accounted for by the 20mm gunship, which was operated by Garry Whittal. He had only just arrived at Mount Darwin on crew changeover having never fired the 20mm cannon before. His squadron had planned for him to do this on arrival at Mount Darwin. However, the Fireforce call came too early so his first experience with the weapon was made in anger. He did well!

In his ASR a couple of days later, Flight Lieutenant George Wrigley, flying K-Car, with Sergeant Pete McCabe as his gunner, made this observation:

The group was engaged and ters were seen to fall but rise and run again. It was frustrating to watch groups of 5 - 6 with rounds burst amongst them. Many managed to recover enough to clear from the contact area before the troops had swept through. It is felt, however, that 70 - 80% suffered hits of some degree.

As I had witnessed in Mozambique, the 20mm rounds were bursting below surface where the full effect of shrapnel was lost. Whereas this troubled the Air Force, the Selous Scouts were very pleased because the number of CTs captured wounded helped swell their 'tame ter' ranks. The Selous Scouts had learned very early on how easy it was to denude CTs of politically induced hullabaloo and bring them back to being themselves again.

Although most shrapnel was lost into the ground, a limited number of low-grade bits of 20mm shell casing burst steeply upward. Any CT close enough to a below surface burst was usually subjected to minor wounding of legs, buttocks and groin. Occasionally large pieces of casing caused death or serious injury. Gunners soon learned that a direct hit on a CT, effectively an airburst, was disastrous for him and others in his proximity, but this was difficult to achieve with the slow-firing cannon. Good gunners, of which there were many, learned to aim for hard surfaces such as rock and large trees to induce lethal effect and often withheld fire until CTs moved close to such surfaces.

Initially, every fifth 20mm round in the 20mm ammunition

K-Car during a turn-around servicing. Note that the rear cabin had only a kneeling cushion to give the gunner maximum freedom of movement. Army commander's seat is just visible in front corner of cabin. Observers on the ground or in the air could easily identify K-Car by the highly visible long 20mm gun barrel. Terrorists were especially aware of K-Car position during contacts.

belt was a tracer round which proved to be unnecessary for air-to-ground firing. The highly visible flash from each exploding round was more than sufficient for sighting corrections, so tracer rounds were removed.

Tol Janeke had just taken over the post of OC FAF 4 when Selous Scouts initiated an action that ran smoother than any previous Scouts call. On 28 September Air Lieutenant Roger Watt, flying K-Car with Flight Sergeant Norman Farrell, led two G-Cars and three Z-Cars to a CT base whose location had not been precisely identified. Roger's ASR gives references to his accompanying sketch of the action. Since the sketch is not reproduced here, the references appear as blanks in this otherwise verbatim report:

1. I was the pilot of the K-Car detailed to lead an assault on a suspect terrorist base camp at approx. US504754 as indicated by Selous Scouts. The helicopter formation approached the area from the East preceded by a Trojan at about 1,500 feet AGL to act as a noise decoy, and a Provost followed behind in support.

2. On arrival in the area the Scouts told me that the camp was on the southern bank of the river, but they weren't sure exactly where. I got into an orbit in the centre of the area and asked Yellow 2 to orbit to the East and Yellow 6 to the West, while the rest of the formation just did a wide orbit of the area.

3. After a visual search of the area for about 5 minutes, the Army Commander and I decided to deplane the troops to search out the odd suspicious area. The sticks were dropped off at .... and were instructed to move to ....

4. I then sent Yellow 2,3 & 4 back to Mt. Darwin to take part in another planned assault, while Yellow 5 & 6 and I remained in the area. After a further 5-8 minutes nothing had occurred so I sent Yellow 5 & 6 to Dotito to refuel.

5. At this stage my tech saw birds fly out of a thickly wooded ravine, but I decided not to fire into the area, as we could not see anything and were therefore uncertain whether the birds had been scared off or not, and also that stick No 2 was soon going to search the area anyway.

6. After a further 5 minutes I was orbiting Stick 4 when stick 2 called "Contact". I immediately flew to the area and found out that the stick leader had a slight leg wound, and that he had killed 2 terrs.

7. As we got to the contact area I saw a group of 5 terrs running along the southern bank in an easterly direction. We opened fire on them and immediately killed one at .... The other four ran into a small river and started running south, but we killed all four at .... We then saw two terrs running along the river in an easterly direction and killed both of them.

8. During this engagement I had recalled Yellow 5 & 6 from Dotito and they had uplifted sticks 4 and 6 and flown them in to reinforce stick 2. Yellow 5 had been recalled from Darwin with a doctor to tend to the wounded (2 terrs died before he arrived) and to take care of the casevac (Lt. Bax).

9. I then directed the callsigns onto the bodies and we found that Stick 2 had killed 3 ters at .... and Stick 3 had killed 2. I then returned to base.

As OC FAF 4, Tol Janeke had this to say:

a. This was a first class operation in every respect. The co-operation between air and ground was good and at no time was there any confusion. The movement and deployment of troops was handled by Maj. Lambert from the 'K' car. This personal contact with his sticks paid dividends.

b. The entire group of terrorists was accounted for in this contact. This would probably have not been the case if the 'K' Car had not been available. It would certainly be a great loss to the operational effectiveness of the <u>fire force</u> if we should run out of ammunition.

c. Pre-briefing of the Trojan to act as noise cover was also successful. The callsign which had reported the presence commented that he had not heard the helicopters until they were within 1000 metres of the area. This tactic will be used when possible but it will no doubt soon become known to the terrorists.

d. The 'K' Car on occasions fired within 50 metres of our troops but discussion with these troops indicated that they considered it safe under the circumstances. The 'K' Car, having deployed the sticks was fully aware of their positions on the ground at all times.

The term 'Fireforce' (my underlining above) was used for the first time in this ASR and Major Lambert was the first 'official' airborne Army Fireforce commander. However, as previously stated, control of ground troops by Army commanders flying in helicopters had been used previously. Tol Janeke referred to a shortage of 20mm ammunition for our gunships. This problem applied to many other critical commodities and the reasons for this will become clear later. What is not made clear was the decision to move back-up troops and fuel forward to Dotito (a small village) by road at the same time that the main force flew out of Mount Darwin. This became fairly standard procedure for many Fireforce operations that followed to reduce reaction time.

In all actions the K-Car orbited to the left because the 20mm cannon, whose long barrel protruded out into the airflow, was mounted on the port side. The gunner needed maximum traverse of his cannon, which was difficult in the confines of the cabin. This would have made an airborne Army commander's presence intolerable if he had occupied a standard forward-facing seat. To resolve this difficulty, his seat was reversed and secured in the front left-hand corner of the cabin. Although this meant having to face backwards, Army Fire Force commanders had an unrestricted view of the ground that concerned them and most mastered with ease the problem of 'flying backwards'.

Whereas a pilot's view was totally unrestricted in a right-hand turn, this was not the case in the offensive left-hand orbit. The presence of the Army officer, the instrument console, the cabin floor and the gunner, particularly when he was firing, restricted a K-Car pilot's visual freedom. Nevertheless, by having control of the aircraft flight path and bank angle, K-Car pilots managed very well indeed.

Détente

ACROSS THE ZAMBEZI RIVER TO our north, Zambia continued to be openly hostile to Rhodesia. The Portuguese were already

passing control of Mozambique to the unprepared leadership of their former enemy who would soon give ZANLA open access to Rhodesia's entire eastern flank. To the west Botswana was showing increasing signs of willingness to allow ZIPRA access to our entire western flank and, to our south the Government of South Africa seemed to be pressurising Ian Smith by deliberately interfering with the free flow of vital imports. So, all around us the signs were ominous as 1974 drew to its close.

Within Rhodesia the score in CTs killed and captured was mounting rapidly, though there was absolutely no room for complacency and, as already stated, our war supplies were often too low for comfort. It was only a matter of weeks before Mozambique's ports would be lost to Rhodesia and, being a landlocked country, this left us totally dependent on South African for all our imports and exports. This new situation brought with it very unpleasant changes in South Africa's political posture, not that the South African Defence Forces or the general public of South African ever wavered in their support to Rhodesia.

Following the collapse of the Portuguese, détente became the tool by which Prime Minister Vorster and a limited number of his party faithful intended to gain favour with Black Africa's political leaders. Détente was the route by which Vorster hoped to reduce African antagonism toward his party's apartheid policies. Furthermore, he seemed to have written off the Zambezi River as a natural defence line against communism now that half of its previously useful length was lost. The long-standing relationship between South Africa and Rhodesia, one of unquestioning friendship and co-operation, was changing to one in which Rhodesia had become the vital pawn in Vorster's détente game.

This situation forces me to run a little ahead in time, because détente would surpass every political danger Rhodesia had ever faced in its fight to retain responsible government. For the likes of me, first signs of serious trouble came in early August 1975 with the sudden withdrawal of the majority of South African Police units. This suggested to us that Vorster was being outmanoeuvred by black governments, yet his obsession with détente continued. If senior military commanders understood what was going on, it was not being passed down the line to operators in the field. The loss of the SAP impacted badly on our own overstretched forces and I guess it must have angered those SA Policemen who served in Rhodesia. Nevertheless there was for us no alternative but to keep our noses to the grindstone.

From the outset men of the South African Police forces that were sent to Rhodesia were totally untrained in bush warfare and this never really improved because South Africa's move to assist us was heavily motivated by self-interest. Men trained for riot control and other policing duties in South Africa were sent to Rhodesia to gain on-the-job training in counter-insurgency operations. As soon as they became proficient, they were substituted by a new batch of men. Nevertheless, their numbers had been of great assistance and they were sorely missed. The removal of the SAP through acquiescence of politically manipulated Police commanders was one thing, but the South African armed services' reaction to political pressure seems to have been very different.

Even before the withdrawal of the SAP, SAAF had increased helicopter and crew levels in a scheme known as Operation Polo. The substantial improvement in helicopter numbers was to help offset the loss of over 2,000 South African Police, but again, it suited South Africa to have its aircrews gain 'on-the-job' operational experience. No criticism is intended because this was a sensible line to follow and Rhodesians were only too pleased to build on strong bonds that already existed with the SAAF.

Initially an Air Force major headed the Op Polo crews but he made a bit of a mess of things when he forced rank to flying K-Car lead before gaining any Fireforce experience. This caused such a nonsense with the Army that, thereafter, only captains and lieutenants remained to fly Z-Cars until, at a later time, the Op Polo crews on detachment wore Rhodesian Air Force uniforms and ranks.

A SAAF liaison officer was permanently attached to Air HQ. A number of wing commanders (SAAF rank—commandant) and squadron leaders (SAAF rank—major) occupied this post over the years and all of them proved to be excellent men who handled the few problems that arose quickly, quietly and efficiently. All the South Africans enjoyed their participation in operations and found the Rhodesian military living standards, at base and in the field, to be better than those back home. They also enjoyed their attachments to our Air Force for another reason. When in Rhodesia the officers and men received a handsome daily allowance whilst their regular pay accumulated to sizeable sums for collection on return to home bases.

Authentication of pseudo groups

ON 24 AUGUST 1974 I LED an attack on a camp that appeared to be occupied. Although the camp appeared fresh, and was unmistakably CT in pattern and location, it was unusual in that sun reflections blinked off tins and other items of litter. I had not seen this before. The Fireforce troops I called upon reported that the camp had been vacated that morning and that the litter was from Rhodesian ration pack items left lying about by Selous Scouts. Ron Reid-Daly hotly denied that the position had been a Scouts base and made the point that his men were never issued with ratpacks (Rhodesian Army

ration packs). Certainly I had not ever seen litter in Selous Scouts pseudo bases, and I saw many of them. From my own observations, litter was associated with Police and TF callsigns operating from high points on ground surveillance work. However, though no one owned up to being responsible for the litter in this camp, much fuss was made of the matter and littering ceased to be a problem.

Although the Selous Scouts were doing extremely well they sometimes ran into difficulties when tribesmen appeared so uncertain of their identity that they became reluctant to co-operate with the pseudo teams. In order to gain the locals' confidence, which was of paramount importance, Ron occasionally arranged a Fireforce action on the bases his men were using. This was potentially dangerous because, for security reasons, it was necessary to conduct genuine Fireforce actions in which only two officers in the K-Car knew that the men on the ground were Selous Scouts and not CTs.

To ensure that the locals were totally impressed, the pseudo ZANLA group needed to pull out of its camp position only seconds ahead of leading air strikes, and certainly before the arrival overhead of the K-Car. The pseudo ZANLA men, using cover off to one side of their 'abandoned camp', would impress the locals by sending up heavy fire, aimed well behind passing aircraft, though tracer rounds were not used by the pseudos and the airborne Army commander deliberately kept his troops well clear of the pseudo CT position. This was a dangerous game and there were some close shaves.

ZIPRA plans upset

SPECIAL BRANCH IN BULAWAYO HAD managed to break into ZIPRA's network of agents in Matabeleland, thereby discovering the location of many pits that had been prepared to receive large quantities of war matériel from Zambia. ZIPRA was clearly intent on getting internal operations moving to counter all the glory that was going ZANLA's way. Quite unrelated to this was the discovery through Canberra photographic reconnaissance over Zambia, of a large hole in a remote place north of the Zambezi River between Victoria Falls and the headwaters of Lake Kariba.

In the latter half of 1974 the SAS enjoyed a change from Tete ops by moving into Zambia to investigate ZIPRA's activities in a large region south of the main road from Livingstone to Lusaka. Amongst other things, their reconnaissance revealed that ZIPRA cadres were involved with intensive manual work at the site of the hole the Air Force had found. The sounds of sawing and hammering led the SAS to the firm conclusion that a major underground arms store was in the making. The

Air Force was asked to monitor the site regularly and report on progress. The resultant photographs showed conclusively that the SAS had been correct in their assessment. Now it was a matter of waiting the right moment for ZIPRA to complete the construction of this huge underground bunker and fill it with war matériel. Equally important was to strike before the onset of the rains when ZIPRA was most likely to commence moving equipment forward to the prepared sites in Rhodesia.

In early October over forty SAS men moved in after aerial photographs showed that many vehicles had been to the cache site, which by then was totally covered over. They killed all the sentries in a set-piece dawn action involving assault and stop groups. Having secured the site the cache was inspected. Those who had a chance to enter the massive store were shaken by the quantities and variety of war matériel that far exceeded their wildest expectations, but the volume was so great that only half an inventory count had been completed when carefully laid demolition charges were ready to wreck ZIPRA's planning.

No thanks to the restraints of détente, it was impossible to consider recovery to Rhodesia of anything from this monstrous find. For the SAS it was painful to destroy so much brand-new equipment, all of which would have been so useful in their own hands.

The big bang that followed set ZIPRA back for something in the order of a year. It was to be the first in a series of seemingly endless setbacks for ZIPRA.

7 Squadron gains at 4 Squadron's expense

THROUGHOUT 1974 MY SQUADRON HAD been losing experienced pilots and technicians on posting to helicopters. Pilot replacements coming directly off PTC courses placed a continuous load on 4 Squadron both at Thornhill and in the field. In consequence Rob Tasker at base and myself in the field were both tied to instruction throughout the latter half of the year.

Due to the nature of helicopter operations 7 Squadron's morale had always been good. However with the on-take of operationally experienced pilots and technicians there came an infusion of the naughty spirit that had developed on 4 Squadron. The antics of two of the technicians, Henry Jarvie and Phil Tubbs, though generally conducted in a spirit of good fun, forced OC 7 Squadron to rule against both men ever being attached to the same FAF together. Stories about these two, as well as those of others, would not pass censorship.

One antic Henry Jarvie was often asked to perform was his Sumo wrestler's act. His scrawny build, exaggerated poses and noisy grunts with underpants stretched upward to the limit was

Sumo Jarvie.

Helicopter technicians had to be proficient at both ends of hoisting operations. Pilots also had to do this to ensure their proficiency in responding to the hoist operator's directions on positioning and height over points not visible to them.

guaranteed to make the most spiritless observer laugh.

Henry's sense of occasion on 7 Squadron was just as it had been on my squadron. This was demonstrated when he was being instructed in hoisting. Pilots and technicians were taught how to lower or raise men in and out of places where helicopters could not land. Whilst operating the hoist a technician had to give a running commentary to the pilot who could not see the cable position. This was one component of hoist training. Another involved being lowered on the cable and learning how to effect the recovery of injured persons.

Henry had heard that any new pilot or technician undergoing hoist training was likely to be dunked in Prince Edward Dam whilst he was suspended helpless at the end of the hoist cable. Having made certain that Fynn Cunningham would be training him, Henry changed into the man's uniform jacket, slacks, shirt, tie, socks and shoes. Over these clothes he wore his regular flying overalls and pulled its zipper right up to his chin.

When the time came to make his first descent, he was lowered onto a very high rock near the edge of Prince Edward Dam. From this rock he was lifted upwards and, as expected, flown through the air until over the water. The pilot, Roger Watt, then came to a hover and descended until Henry disappeared under water. Fynn Cunningham, operating the hoist, did not see Henry slip out of his harness below the surface of murky water and got one heck of a fright when the helicopter lifted to reveal an empty harness. Roger Watt also became agitated when Henry failed to reappear. Unbeknown to pilot and technician, Henry was swimming underwater heading for the shore. Suddenly he popped up some distance away at the edge of the dam. Stomping around to ensure that the shoes he was wearing filled with sticky black mud, Henry waved for uplift. When back inside the cabin, Henry put on his flying helmet and grinned broadly at Fynn who wanted to know why Henry was looking so smug. "I am wearing your uniform, that's why!"

Fynn did not believe Henry and forgot about the matter until he went to his locker at work's end. His clothing was so wet and his shoes and socks so mud-filled and sodden that he was forced to return home in working overalls and shoes with his wet uniform and service shoes wrapped in muttoncloth.

Ceasefire

ALTHOUGH I WAS IN THE field for most of the time, I could not participate directly in the excitement of increasingly successful operations as 1974 closed. I found it difficult to be content with listening in on Fireforce actions whilst continuing with my losing battle to produce replacement recce pilots. Because of this, news of my posting to Air HQ brought prospects of a much-welcomed break and opportunity to spend time with my family.

My hackles were raised on my first day in Air HQ when an officer one rank senior to me foolishly but officially questioned my handling of men. He accused me of being the only squadron commander ever to have completed three years in command without making or hearing a single charge against any one of his squadron's personnel. I responded by saying I was proud of the fact that my flight commanders, squadron warrant officer and senior technicians had handled the men in a manner that produced results but avoided having ever to resort to punitive measures. I reminded him of the fact that Chris Weinmann might still be alive had I not asked for him to ensure

Cyril White.

the maintenance of discipline, whereupon I became somewhat aggressive and asked to be appraised of my squadron's failure to meet any of its obligations in the field and at base. This officer, who over time had proven to be a lone antagonist toward me, admitted that there had been no failure whatsoever and immediately changed direction by saying he was not criticising me but merely 'making an observation'. He had never seen flying service in bush operations—enough said!

From my own very selfish point of view, relinquishing command of 4 Squadron occurred at an ideal moment because a ceasefire came into effect on 11 December 1974. Following three years in command with only one three-week break, it felt great to hand over 4 Squadron to Squadron Leader Cyril White and return to our own home in Salisbury.

South Africa's Prime Minister Vorster and Zambia's President Kaunda, in another of their détente initiatives, had orchestrated the ceasefire.

The nationalists, Joshua Nkomo of ZAPU and Robert Mugabe of ZANU, had been released from detention to attend talks in Lusaka that helped bring about this farce and our forces were under orders not to interfere with any CT group exiting the country.

The ceasefire could not have come at a worse time for Rhodesia. For the first time terrorist numbers within the country were diminishing rapidly, primarily through Selous Scouts-generated Fireforce successes, and their areas of influence had shrunk in spite of the continued inflow of those CTs who managed to bypass the SAS in Tete. Security Force morale was high whereas almost every CT group had been broken up, forcing union of surviving elements under diminishing direction and reduced qualities in leadership. Externally ZANLA was in disarray. Yet here we were being ordered to let the enemy off the hook! Many ZANLA groups made the best of the opportunity to get back to Mozambique to regroup and rethink strategy whilst taking with them hundreds of youngsters to be trained in Tanzania and Mozambique.

For servicemen who had fought so hard, this situation was scandalous!

There was no honest explanation forthcoming from our leadership to reduce our frustrations from knowing that the ceasefire would surely fail and that ZANLA was being given sorely needed opportunity to reorganise and prepare for operations along the entire length of Mozambique's border, now entirely in FRELIMO's control.

Yet here we were under orders to sit back as very unwilling members of a 'Mushroom Club' that kept us in the dark and fed us shit! Despite the silence we could see that what was happening was so madly wrong that our government was surely being blackmailed. There was simply no other explanation!

We were not to know, officially that is, that Rhodesia was being used as a pawn by Prime Minister Vorster to appease Kaunda, Nyerere and the rest of Africa to gain favour and divert attention away from South Africa's apartheid problems.

Nor were we supposed to know that subtle pressure was being applied on Ian Smith's government through the deliberate slowing down or withholding of vital supplies moving up from South Africa. It was known to us, however, that Rhodesia had often been dangerously low on fuel and munitions due to 'South African Railways bottlenecks'. We had become somewhat accustomed to the 'free world' governments knocking us but to think that South Africa might be doing the same seemed incomprehensible! I remember wondering in my anger why we did not make a direct approach to the Kremlin to circumvent so-called friends and make a short-cut deal that would allow us to get on with our normal lives. I know this makes no sense but to still believe so strongly in British standards and be treated in such shoddy manner by the 'free world" including, possibly, South Africa, made my mind tip.

Dakotas dropped thousands of leaflets on the night of 11 December declaring the ceasefire. The leaflets offered amnesty and freedom to terrorists who handed themselves over to any Rhodesian authority. The entire operational area then went quiet for ten days before an offensive CT action occurred on 20 December.

The Mount Darwin Firforce deployed and a Z-Car pilot, Lieutenant Francis, was wounded before he had a chance to land the RLI stick he had on board. In a very calm manner he advised the K-Car pilot, Roger Watt, that he had been shot and was putting down south of the terrorists' location. Only when he was on the ground, and under CT fire, did he let Roger know that his knee was shattered. His technician, Sergeant Knouwds, lifted him out of the helicopter into cover whilst the RLI stick moved out into all-round defence and directed the K-Car onto the spot where the CT fire was coming from. The K-Car cannon then suppressed CT fire, resulting in the safe recovery of the Z-Car and the capture of one wounded CT.

Then on 23 December a South African Police callsign met with tragedy after its OC received a written invitation to meet one of ZANLA's senior commanders, Herbert Shungu, to discuss surrender terms. Seeing opportunity to shake Rhodesia and South Africa and wishing to shatter the ceasefire, Shungu selected a hiding place on the south bank of the Mazoe River not far from an SAP camp that was also sited south of the river. His message to the SAP commander stated that he was ready to discuss surrender terms as set out in the leaflets. His selection of SAP was deliberate.

On a bridge spanning a remote section of the Mazoe River, the SAP stopped their Land Rover on the south side when they saw a handful of apparently unarmed 'friendly terrorists' waving and approaching them from the northern end of the high-level concrete bridge. Totally off guard, four unarmed South African policemen debussed and strode forward to meet the CTs in the middle of the bridge. They had not taken many paces towards the men they expected to meet in peace when machine-guns opened up from the hidden force behind them.

The four white policemen died but one black soldier survived.

He was an N'debele member of RAR who had been allocated to the SAP as an interpreter. He did not trust the Shona and had held back slightly, walking against the railing of the bridge. Though wounded in the initial burst of fire, he managed to dive into the water far below the road deck. A long wait in the crocodile-infested water worried him because of his bleeding, but his instinctive actions had saved his life. The terrorists had hurried away from the murder scene without waiting to ensure that everyone was dead. When the survivor eventually got back to his base, he told the story of what had happened.

The sight of their slaughtered companions and the theft of arms, ammunition and grenades from the empty Land Rover angered the SAP and sent ripples of resentment throughout South Africa. So much for the Vorster's ceasefire that had been forced on Rhodesia! So much too for the instruction to leave CTs alone! For us the ceasefire was over. Nevertheless everything went quiet again.

Firelighters

WHENEVER I VISITED CSIR in Pretoria, I called in on engineers Dr John de Villiers and Vernon Joynt because they were great men and always had something new and interesting to show me. In 1974 they introduced me to small delayed-action flame generators. Each unit came in the form of a 100mm-square sealed plastic packet containing potassium permanganate powder. To activate the powder, a small quantity of glycol, deliberately dyed red, was injected by hypodermic syringe into the packet. The liquid migrated rapidly through the white powder turning it pink. For about forty seconds nothing changed until the packet swelled rapidly, then burst into flame and burned fiercely for about eight seconds.

I asked Vernon if 1,000 of these packets and an appropriate quantity of dyed glycol could be prepared and sent to me in Salisbury. He agreed and a large cardboard box duly arrived at Air Movements addressed to me. My interest in these little flame generators was to establish if it was possible to burn large tracts of Mozambican grass and bushveld in the hope of destroying minor crops, thatching grass and the overhead cover upon which FRELIMO and the CTs depended.

One night during the 1975 dry season I flew a ten-kilometre radius route around the Mozambican side of Mukumbura to initiate a burn-line that was expected to run inwards to Mukumbura and outwards as far as the fire would go.

The rear door of my Cessna 185 had been removed and two technicians sat facing each other behind me with the box of plastic bags between them. As fast as they could, they injected fluid into the bags and tossed them out into the black. By the time we completed our circular run, all 1,000 packets had made their long drop to ground and had set off the line of fires that clearly marked our passage. Initially it looked as if our objective would be realised, but when I flew over the area the next day, long fingers of burnt grass stretched outward through countryside that was 90% unscathed.

Although this did not work for us in savannah country, it is interesting to note that Canadian fire-fighting helicopters use a similar method to initiate back-burning lines when combating large forest fires. For this, the powder is encased in ping-pong balls that are automatically injected with glycol as they pass rapidly through a very fancy automatic dispenser.

Quiet times

MY AIR STAFF POST AS Ops 1 suited me nicely and it was wonderful to go home every evening and have weekends off. The workload was low with very little associated stress at a time when operations in the field were virtually at a standstill. However, we had no doubt that the war would resume and we used the break to prepare for this.

Ian Smith had been given a Beech Baron twin-engined, propeller-driven executive aircraft, I think by a lady in America who greatly admired our Prime Minister's stand against communism. The PM passed the aircraft to the Air Force for its own use providing it was always made available to him to fly on regular visits to his farm 'Gwenora' near Selukwe.

Having been a fighter pilot himself, Ian Smith always flew his aircraft and favoured Flight Lieutenants Bob d'Hotmann or Ivan Holshausen to fly with him. On two occasions I flew passenger in the back of the aircraft sitting next to the PM's friendly wife who talked a great deal. Janet never once entered into a non-political discussion and asked many searching

Ian Smith at the controls.

questions to test my opinions on Rhodesia's political affairs. I do not believe she found me wanting.

In addition to Ian Smith's Baron, the squadron acquired four Islander light-transport aircraft that came into the Air Force inventory in an unexpected way. First one, then another, then two more Islanders arrived unannounced at Salisbury Airport carrying Portuguese families evicted from Mozambique in FRELIMO's erroneous drive to rid the country of whites. The owners of these aircraft, like all those being evicted from their homes and businesses, had lost all they possessed, so they brought their machines secretly to Rhodesia to sell for money to start new lives.

The Islander was ideal for light communication work and came at a good price. A fair amount of hard work was needed to bring them up to Air Force standards and to regularise equipment and fittings before entry into regular service. Later more Islanders were added to the fleet.

Islander.

What the Air Force really needed at the time was a replacement aircraft for 4 Squadron's ageing Provosts and the underpowered Trojans. I was tasked to make an assessment of light civilian aircraft that, if modified for weapons delivery, would meet our needs. We really wanted an aircraft specifically designed for our type of war but, though there were plenty on the international market, none could be sold to Rhodesia because of the UN mandatory sanctions. This gave us no option but to identify a standard 'civilian' aircraft that we could buy, preferably from France, for operational upgrade. The French, more interested in commerce than in UN restrictions, had been good to us. In spite of sanctions, France had helped to increase our helicopter fleet from eight Alouettes to more than double that number, even with losses taken into account. How this was done and how we acquired 20mm cannons and other matériel was not for me to know.

The most suitable of the fixed-wing aircraft available inside the country appeared to me to be the American-designed twin, in-line, push-pull Cessna 337 with retractable undercarriage. Of importance was the fact that this aircraft was built under licence in France. The owner of the only available 337 and Wing Commander Bill Smith handled the machine whilst I looked on from the back seat. I was satisfied that the aircraft possessed the power, lift capacity and speed we needed and, like the Cessna 185, it was well suited to recce.

Orders were immediately placed with the Reims factory in France, then manufacturing Cessna 337s under licence from USA. My greatest pleasure in the initial exercise came from an instruction to decide what aids and comforts must be incorporated into these brand-new machines. Having done this, my list was strongly criticised by some Air HQ officers, mainly technical, who could not justify the added expense of aids and comforts we had been doing without for so long. Not one of the critics had any idea of the difficulties, dangers and discomforts our pilots endured in the field, so it was pleasing that the Air Force Commander, Air Marshal Mick McLaren, ruled in favour of operational pilots.

Although most CTs had exited the country, a few groups remained, some leaderless. Many of these were LTTs who had grouped together, fearing to venture into Mozambique because, for them, it was unknown ground. Measuring the activity level from Air Strike Reports, only four occurred in January (the same number as occurred on the day before the ceasefire) and only one produced any result. This was an over-border Fireforce action initiated by a Selous Scouts recce team, which accounted for seven CTs killed. From the beginning of February to 24 July only seventeen ASRs were recorded, most inside Mozambique with minimal returns.

On 14 June 1975 I was appointed OC FAF 5 at Mtoko because the regular OC, John Digby, was going on overseas leave. In the absence of any offensive action, my time was spent improving the campsite and finishing off building the pub John Digby had started. Gordon Wright, who was OC FAF 1 at the time, assisted by finding a good N'debele thatcher. This man did a great job of thatching the pub roof despite his continuous complaints about the 'poor quality of Shona grass'.

The 'Chopper Arms' was a great success for deployed Air Force personnel and became a happy watering hole for Army, Selous Scouts, Police and surrounding farmers. It was officially opened on three separate occasions.

When I had run out of things to do around the camp, I became agitated by the lack of action and spent much of my spare time on air recce. I submitted this report to Air HQ:

1. I was OC FAF 5 during the period 14 June to 26 July 1975. Prior to this period I had visited Mtoko and learnt that all flying, other than casevac, relay changes and courier flights, had been in response to terrorist activities. No intelligence had been forthcoming to allow aggressive planning to be made and only one terrorist had been killed in the Mtoko area in a chance encounter during 1975. Selous Scouts were not providing any up-to-date intelligence at that stage.

2. In response to my request, A/D Ops and SO Ops agreed that I could use 4 Squadron's Cessnas for reconnaissance at FAF 5, as the squadron was not using these aircraft. The object of wanting to recce was essentially to try to provide intelligence that would allow pre-emptive rather than reactive planning against any of the few terrorist gangs remaining in the Hurricane area.

3. It was also agreed that 4 Squadron would provide selected pilots for recce training whilst I was at FAF 5. These were to be Sqn Ldr White, Flt Lt Bennie and Air Sub-Lt Boulter. Sqn Ldr White did not deploy to FAF 5 and Air Sub-Lt Boulter was killed (in a flying accident at Thornhill) just before he was due to undertake recce training. Flt Lt Bennie's training was cut short after the first flight due to Operation Newton. However, he managed to fit in two days of training some days later. Flt Lt Bennie also arranged for Flt Lt Graaf and Air Lt Benecke to undertake short periods of recce training but all three pilots require further instruction.

4. I was current on Trojans and was given a refamil on Cessna by Flt Lt Bennie. During the first four weeks of recce in the Mtoko area I located in excess of 200 ter bases and feeding places. However, the dry conditions made ageing of these points very difficult. Therefore it was only in the last two weeks that I was providing up-to-date information when bases found had not been plotted previously. One of these was considered suitable for air strike in conjunction with the Fireforce, as it was miles from any Army callsign. OC Air Det Hurricane confirmed by signal that I could mark the target with smoke rockets as my weapons categories had lapsed. The Fireforce action was routine but unsuccessful and the base, though in current use, had been vacated by LTTs just prior to FF arrival. They seem to have developed a taste for orgies with the local girls. ASR 04/75 refers.

5. There can be no doubt that 4 Squadron will be in need of good recce pilots when ZANLA returns and cannot afford to await the event. However, I must request that serious thought be given to keeping the few pilots who show any interest and ability in recce on 4 Squadron. Not one of the useful recce pilots I taught 1972–4 remains on 4 Squadron and I am disheartened by the negative attitudes of the pilots I have instructed.

Clever intelligence work by the Selous Scouts Intelligence Officer deduced that ZANLA's remaining leaders would be meeting in the vicinity of a particular contact man's village during the latter part of June. A force of regular troops cordoned off a large area around this village in northern Kandeya Tribal Trust Land. Unfortunately there were too few soldiers to box in the terrorists who gathered, as predicted. Out of about thirty terrorists only six were killed and one was captured. So far as I recall, this was one of the reasons many survivors chose to leave for Mozambique. Those who remained had their minds changed six weeks later.

Upon his return from leave, John Digby resumed command of FAF 5 and I remained there with him to continue teaching recce to 4 Squadron pilots and PRAW crews. It was a difficult and extremely boring task because there were very few CTs around, particularly after a flurry of successful actions involving Cocky Benecke. This will be covered shortly.

Brown Jobs versus Blue Jobs

As in the years before and in those to come, the Annual Army versus Air Force rugby match was a great occasion. Being a much larger force, the Army should have beaten the Air Force every time but, for the most part, the Air Force thrashed the Army. The rivalry that built up was good-spirited and the commanders of both forces always sat together to rib each other throughout each match.

In 1975 the big contest was held in Salisbury on the main rugby field in the BSAP sports grounds. With five minutes to go before kick-off, four Hunters flew over in perfect formation. As they did so, automatic gunfire, simulating anti-aircraft action, opened up from behind tall gum trees to the left of the main stands. The noise frightened a number of crows from the trees and, as they flew past the grandstands, the Air Force pointed at them shouting, "Army flypast!—Army flypast!" Next moment an Army wrecker vehicle appeared in the grounds carrying the twisted remains of 'the destroyed aircraft'. But the outcome of the rugby contest was less of a joke for the Brown Jobs because the Blue Jobs beat them—again!

Doctored radios and ammunition

For a number of months Provosts and Trojans had been taking off at sunrise in search of VHF signals from portable radios that had been passed on to some CT groups. Doctored radios, known a 'road-runners', came into existence because CTs were known to be listening in to Rhodesian broadcasts and Mozambican stations, particularly during early morning.

Special Branch produced a number of road-runners which, when switched on, emitted a VHF signal on one of our least-used air channels. Trials showed that the low-powered signal could be detected from as far as ten kilometres and, using Becker Homers, it was possible for a pilot to identify the position of each doctored radio with reasonable accuracy. The radios were given to individuals who knew how to get them into CT hands or were prominently displayed on outlying store shelves, madly overpriced, knowing the locals could not afford them and that CTs would steal them.

This system of detecting CTs might have worked from the beginning had each VHF transmitter been programmed to remain on for a few minutes after a radio was switched off. As it happened, pilots homed in on signals that cut off before they reached the radios' locations. The sound of any aircraft obviously caused CTs to switch off the radios to allow them to listen and watch for the high-flying planes. This weakness was rectified later.

Doctoring of CT ammunition produced positive results. When standard Russian and Chinese equipment was located in CT arms caches, the standard ammunition was substituted with 'doctored' ammunition. Cordite propellant in standard rifle rounds burns at a relatively slow rate to drive a bullet down a rifled barrel at progressively increasing speed without risk to the weapon handler. When, however, cordite was substituted with any one of a number of plastic explosives in a 'doctored' round, instant over-pressure in the combustion chamber shattered it into a shower of lethal shrapnel that killed the weapon-handler and others near him.

In the case of 'doctored' mortar bombs, they exploded immediately on launch, and hand-grenade delay fuses were exchanged for instantaneous ones that made them function immediately the firing handle was released. Though these foul devices produced excellent results the practice of doctoring ammunition ceased when every item of captured equipment was needed for SAS and Selous Scouts operations.

Cocky Benecke

Along with many other 4 Squadron pilots, Cocky Benecke had flown recce with me before. Like most, he had shown little interest and became thoroughly bored within an hour. On 11 August I flew with him on further training at the request of his OC, Cyril White.

There had been no complaints when he had flown with me in July but, just before we got airborne on this particular day, Cocky said, "Sir, I am not cut out for recce. This is a job for old men with patience, like you." I was not yet forty and took exception to being referred to as an old man by this cocky young pilot. He received a bit of a blasting for the 'old men' bit, but much more for using age as the reason for his disinterest in recce.

"Cocky, I know you enjoy action and that you have done

well whenever you have been called. So tell me, are you happy to keep on sitting around just waiting for someone else to call you to action? Are you too special to act on your squadron's motto 'Seek and Find' or are you going to get off your arse, find gooks and lead others to action?"

I cannot remember his response, but I do know that he was wide-awake two hours later when I pointed out another of many old CT bases I had been showing him. This one was on the western side of the Nyadiri River valley. "The base is in use, sir", he said. "There are gooks down there. I can see their kit under the trees."

My reaction was one of disbelief but, as we continued on along our search line, Cocky insisted he had seen plenty of kit. I knew how often he had seen motionless CTs when no other pilot or gunner could see them, but again I asked, "Cocky, are you absolutely certain there are ters in that base?" "No question about it, sir. I am absolutely certain."

I called FAF 5 to have the Fireforce brought to readiness and asked for two Provosts to be armed with eight fragmentation bombs each. Cocky was champing at the bit and pressing me to go straight back to base, so I had to make him understand that in these circumstances it was essential to keep orbiting along our recce line so as not to give the CTs any clue that they had been spotted. At a safe distance we headed east for a while before racing south to Mtoko.

Having briefed the Fireforce, Cocky and I got airborne again, each flying an armed Provost. Flying 4,000 feet above the helicopters, we weaved left and right to remain behind them. Five minutes out from target with Cocky following 200 metres behind me, we put our propellers to maximum rpm to maximise noise effect and overtook the helicopters that were flying very low on their northward course in the Nyadiri River valley.

When abeam the target, I rolled the aircraft over and entered into a steep-dive attack to release my bombs into the base. Cocky did likewise and followed me in a wide orbit to watch the Fireforce helicopters deploy their troops. They came into contact very quickly and the entire group of fifteen CTs died in this combined ground and air action.

Cocky's attitude to recce had been instantly reversed. He wanted to be released right away to work on his own. I would have nothing of this until we had covered a few more aspects of recce he needed to know. These were met the next day before we found another CT base. My immediate assessment of the small base was that it was fresh and occupied by six to eight CTs, even though I had seen no persons or equipment to reinforce the assessment. Again Cocky said he could see kit and at least three men wearing dark-blue clothing inside the base. For many months CTs had favoured blue denim slacks and tops, which made any man wearing dark-blue clothing a suspect.

Fireforce was called and we continued along our orbit line, which was in the direction from which the helicopters would

be coming. We picked up the five helicopters flying line astern at treetop level with K-Car leading. This time we tagged along to give a verbal talk onto target. "Yellow, go five degrees left—that looks good—base approximately five kays ahead." A little later I called, "Base is on the south slope of the ridge ahead of you. Stand by—pull up now—base ninety degrees left, 200 yards—NOW." From there K-Car took control.

Cocky again said, "Gooks visual in the base. They are lying still in the shadows." I could not see any myself but relayed Cocky's information to Yellow 1. The K-Car pilot was busy instructing the other helicopter pilots on where to place down their troops, but his gunner concentrated his attention on the base area. He could see the base clearly enough but could not pick up any sign of kit or men under the trees.

Even though K-Car was at 1,000 feet above the base and we were at 2,000 feet, neither the pilot nor his gunner could spot the individuals Cocky insisted were lying prone in shadows against the bases of trees. It was only when firing started and the CTs moved that the K-Car crew and I saw what Cocky had been reporting all the time. Five of the terrorists were killed and one wounded CT was captured. Later we learned that one CT had managed to escape. Cocky's recce training was complete, so I arranged for a Cessna to be delivered from Thornhill for him to commence his own recce work out of FAF 4 at Mount Darwin.

The next morning I was airborne again to inspect the surrounds of the many collective villages (CVs) that had sprung up in the operational areas. CVs were very different from protected villages because the PVs, as initially installed in the Chiweshe TTL, were far too costly to build, man and provision on a large scale. Before Selous Scouts became effective, the concept of CVs had been under instigation by JOC Mtoko from early 1974 because of a serious decline in field intelligence and the need to reduce the CT threat to tribesmen in small isolated family kraals. A CV (collective or consolidated village) was simply an amalgamation of many small villages into one large village. A curfew from 18:00 to 07:00 was imposed on the tribesmen who knew they would be shot if seen outside the CV between these times.

At about 11 o'clock I changed frequency to the Mount Darwin Fireforce channel. The force had been inactive for ages but I could hear that it was in action following a call by none other than Cocky Benecke. I listened in for two hours during which time Cocky repeatedly directed the K-Car onto small groups and individuals. His voice never once showed the frustrations he was experiencing flying an unarmed Cessna.

Cocky had flown all his previous engagements in Provosts or Trojans, which allowed him to strike at those targets which he was trying, usually unsuccessfully, to draw to the K-Car's attention. Although Cocky was cool, the K-Car pilot's frustration was obvious. "I am looking at the corner of the bloody field but cannot see anyone there." Cool as a cucumber Cocky said, "Try a short burst thirty metres right of the western edge and ten metres up from the south." A short burst and the

K-Car crew had the CT up and running before dropping him.

Later in the day I heard the Fireforce back in action. On his first day on recce Cocky was responsible for actions that depleted ZANLA's few remaining CTs within the country by seventeen killed or captured. These actions seem to have been the final straw that forced most surviving CTs in the country to exit to Mozambique. ZANLA, however, had arranged for at least one group to remain in their Nehanda sector in a caretaker role and had sent an execution group to the Chaminuka sector with a list of 'sell-outs' to be eliminated.

I found Benecke's successes astounding and confusing. I had brought forces to contact with many CT groups and had gained a fair reputation for the successes achieved. Ground troops gave me a variety of nicknames, including 'Hawkeye' and 'Grid Square Charlie'. Yet for every success my record showed that I had been responsible for three 'lemons'. It was difficult to figure out why Cocky's unusual sight was giving him 100% success and even Hamie Dax was doing better than me by scoring two successes to one failure.

Cocky and Hamie Dax (both sitting). This photograph was taken at a PRAW recce training camp. PB with arms around the lady caterers.

At Station Sick Quarters New Sarum, I asked to have my eyes tested and the results compared with Cocky Benecke's test results. I was assured that we enjoyed equally good eyesight. I knew that colour-blind people had been used during WWII to detect German camouflaged gun emplacements and tank formations that normal-sighted people could not see. In the eyes of colour-blind individuals, military camouflage has no effect. But Cocky could not have passed his flying medical examinations if he had been colour blind so I could only guess

that his colour perception was different from mine, even though he named colours just the same way as the rest of us did. I went to an optician and an oculist to arrange for a variety of tinted and polarised lenses with which to experiment; but none of these helped me see the dark items I had personally placed in the shadow of trees.

Throughout the war Cocky continued to display his uncanny talent. However, it was not only his eyesight that made Cocky a truly exceptional operational pilot. He was aggressive and brave in all that he did, yet never did he become big-headed or arrogant. His happy nature and huge smile endeared him to all.

I questioned every doctor and eye specialist I encountered to try and find out what it was about Cocky's eyesight that made him one in a million. Doctor Knight eventually gave me the answer in late 1979. He had established that Cocky's colour perception was slightly defective in the green-brown range. This was why, for Cocky, deep and mottled shadows did not blend out anything that lay in them.

Not all of Cocky's recce finds were successful in later times and he was responsible for a few Fireforce 'lemons' which made the likes of me feel better about the 'lemons' we had generated. For the most part, helicopter crews and Army elements of the Fireforce had come to accept that recce pilots would lead at least two 'lemons' for every success; but not so with Cocky. His reputation reversed their expectations.

Earlier criticisms against me for involving Fireforce in 'lemons' reached me indirectly. Possibly due to my seniority, minor niggling had occurred behind my back. It is an unfortunate fact that operational pilots take for granted another pilot's successes and only remember his errors. So ribbing of young recce pilots by helicopter pilots of the Fireforces may have caused them to miss out on good targets for fear of generating 'lemons'. What interested me was that no helicopter pilot who had flown recce himself was a critic. It was only those who had come from the jet squadrons and considered their leisure time too precious to waste. Cocky was ribbed for his failures but his record was such that he simply brushed off any criticism with a cutting retort. Nevertheless, I was very sensitive to remarks made by a small prima donna element that did no more than was absolutely necessary at base and in the field. To commit these remarks to paper, even in jest, sent my blood pressure soaring as it did other Air Staff officers. Flight Lieutenant Danny Svoboda's ASR of 30 March 1977 is a case in point. In spite of the successful contact that resulted from Cocky Benecke's recce information, Danny initiated his report with these words:

1. On a bright Wednesday afternoon with nothing to do the Fireforce decided to check out two possible terr camps found by Air Lieutenant Benecke in his Lemon-Car.
2. The first camp at US966236 proved fruitless. The Fireforce then proceeded to the second camp at VS013192.
3. On arrival at this camp the target was marked by 24 Sneb rockets

from Benecke. Terrs broke out of the camp heading north etc. etc.

The Director of Operations at Air HQ, Group Captain Norman Walsh, expressed his displeasure over Danny's report in strong terms, particularly as Fireforce pilots seldom criticised the higher proportion of 'lemons' generated by Selous Scouts and other callsigns.

Last air actions of 1975

THE CT CARETAKER GROUP AND the assassination group were contacted on 9 and 10 September. The first was when an Army callsign on patrol in a remote area below the escarpment made contact with the Nehanda caretaker group. The Mount Darwin Fireforce led by John Blythe-Wood deployed with three Z-Cars and Cocky Benecke flying a Provost. Working ahead of trackers, Cocky picked up the CTs and the action that followed resulted in the total elimination of this group, with seven CTs dead and five captured wounded.

The Mtoko Fireforce had moved to a temporary base at Mutawatawa on the edge of high ground. For what reason I was visiting Harold Griffiths and his men at Mutawatawa I cannot recall, but the sheer beauty of the surrounding hills and the long valley down which the Zvirungudzi River flowed to the Nyadiri River remains firmly embedded in my memory. I knew the area well from recce, but its beauty could only be appreciated when flying low-level in a helicopter or being on the ground in the tented base.

Griff had recently taken command of 7 Squadron and it was from this base that his Fireforce was scrambled at sunrise on 10 September along with a second Fireforce operating from another temporary bush base, Pfungwe. They were responding to a police patrol that had bumped into the CTs assassin group in their temporary base on the slopes of a heavily wooded hill known as Chipinda.

SAAF Major van Rooyen and all other SAAF members of Op Polo had reverted to Rhodesian Air Force ranks and wore Rhodesian uniforms. So now as Squadron Leader van Rooyen he commanded the Pfungwe Fireforce leading two Z-Cars flown by Flight Lieutenant Kruger and Air Sub-Lieutenant Milbank plus two G-Cars flown by Flight Lieutenant Bill Sykes and Air Lieutenant Jo Syslo.

Air Lieutenant Syslo was new to our Air Force, having come in on 'direct entry' from the USAAF. He had served in Vietnam, flying as a helicopter pilot in a casualty evacuation unit. This dark-haired man of small build had more ribbons on his chest than the most highly decorated Rhodesian serviceman. He claimed that more ribbons were still to be added to those he wore at a time when most of our pilots wore one measly General Service ribbon. This was a source of much amusement and, for some, outright annoyance.

Griff met up with the Pfungwe Fireforce that carried Major Hammond, the airborne ground-force commander. Having deployed the troops, Griff put down with his force at a small Police base known as Alpha Base and awaited developments. When the Pfungwe K-Car ran out of fuel, Griff filled in for him until he himself needed to refuel, and passed Major Hammond back to the other K-Car.

In this way the ground forces enjoyed almost unbroken attention from their airborne commander. The results of this contact were disappointing. One killed, two captured wounded and five known to have escaped, wounded. But this was the last time ZANLA CTs were seen or contacted in 1975. Thereafter minor contacts occurred with LTTs only.

Loss of top army officers

ARMY CHIEF OF STAFF MAJOR-General John Shaw and Officer Commanding RLI Colonel Dave Parker with Army Captains David Lamb and Ian Robertson visited a number of military bases that had recently been established in the eastern districts in preparation for the imminent return of ZANLA. On completion of inspections in Umtali their next port of call was Melsetter.

On 23 December, Op Polo pilot Air Lieutenant Johannes van Rensburg flying a Z-Car lifted off from Umtali for a straightforward flight to Melsetter. His technician was Sergeant Pieter van Rensburg. In keeping with practice, even in quiet times, the helicopter flew at low level as a precaution against Strela and smallarms fire. The route over the high ground of the Vumba mountains was followed by a steep descent into the low ground of the Burma Valley. The helicopter was following a descending river-line with high ridges left and right, when it flew into a rusty old hawser cable that ran across the flight path. The helicopter broke up and crashed, killing everyone but the pilot whose injuries resulted in the amputation of one leg.

The long-forgotten cable was anchored on the high right-hand ridge and descended to a disused track on the opposite side of the river. Its purpose had been to pass logs from the high inaccessible forest down to a track used by tractor-drawn trailers. The cable was not displayed on any map and no 7 Squadron pilot had ever seen or reported its presence. The young SAAF pilot could not be blamed in any way for this accident as he would not have seen the rusted cable that blended perfectly with the background until it was too late to take avoiding action.

News of this horrific accident shook the entire country because it robbed Rhodesia of its next Army Commander and its finest field commander. I am one of many who believe that, had John Shaw and Dave Parker lived, the Rhodesian war would have followed a better course.

Lull before the storm

FOLLOWING FAILURE OF THE ZAMBIAN–SOUTH African détente-induced ceasefire there could be no doubt that ZANLA would be returning in greater strength. The general feeling was that they were still in disarray but détente had given them the golden opportunity to prepare for a big push. This would commence when the rainy season provided plenty of surface water for the long trek through Mozambique with maximum bush cover inside Rhodesia. It was the best time to strike externally but, because of Vorster's détente and his threat of cutting supplies from South Africa, this had been ruled out.

With Mozambique under complete FRELIMO control, it was obvious that Rhodesia's entire eastern flank would be exposed for ZANLA, though we believed that in the initial stages this would be limited to the border section north of the eastern border mountain ranges. This is why most troops were deployed along the border north of the Inyanga mountain range where daily cross-graining patrols watched for ZANLA's return to areas already known to them.

The squadrons used the break in operations to catch up on training new pilots and brush up flying standards. The PJIs of Air Force Parachute Training School began training RLI paratroopers after which they would commence training RAR.

In spite of their heavy schedules, the PJIs managed to give interested pilots a short course for a parachute descent into water. Until now, Air HQ had followed the RAF lead in not allowing pilots to participate in any parachuting activities. The thought was that a pilot who enjoyed parachuting might abandon his aircraft at the first sign of trouble, rather than attempt to bring it home. In Rhodesia it was obvious that pilots were so dedicated to the safety of their machines that it was perfectly safe to let them enjoy one parachute descent. Many pilots, including me, leapt at the opportunity.

To limit the risk of unnecessary injuries, our drop was into Lake McIlwaine, west of Salisbury. Following a compressed training course and dressed in flying overalls and tennis shoes, twenty of us piled into a Dakota for a nice long 3,000-foot descent.

I expected that we would all experience fear before the drop

but this only seemed to affect Wing Commander Sandy Mutch who sat scowling at the floor until it was time for him to 'stand in the door' as first to exit. I was next in line.

All of our preparatory instruction made the leap into space fantastic but I was mildly surprised when pitched into a horizontal posture as the parachute deployed with noticeable creaking of the harness at shoulder level; then everything became dead-quiet. As instructed, I looked up to check the canopy and noticed that it appeared much smaller that I had expected. All was well, so it was just a matter of pulling the seat strap under my buttocks to get into a sitting position and then, with left hand holding the right-hand lift web above my head, I undid the harness buckle and pulled the securing straps away from my front. Having done this, the right hand crossed over to hold the left lift strap above my head, and I was set to enjoy the ride down, with Sandy Mutch ahead and below me.

Lake McIlwaine's water was pea-green with algae due to abnormally high levels of nutrients that had come downriver from Salisbury. On the green surface were two powerboats waiting to collect us. From one of these there came the clear voice of Flight Lieutenant Boet Swart, OC Parachute Training School, who was bellowing at Sandy Mutch to undo his harness. Sandy stubbornly refused to comply.

One seemed to be suspended in a static position for ages until, suddenly, perspectives changed rapidly as the water rushed up. Seeing this, it was just a matter of straightening one's legs to slip off the seat strap and remain hanging on the lift webs. As my feet touched water I let go of the lift webs. The water was surprisingly warm with zero visibility as I swam under the canopy and came to the surface to find outstretched hands reaching from the recovery boat. Once on board I saw that my parachute had already been recovered.

As the other recovery boat passed us to collect following

Standing: John Blythe-Wood, PB, Peter Knobel, Boet Swart, Sandy Mutch, Keith Corrans, Derek de Kok, Pete Woolcock and Brian Murdoch. Kneeling: Frank Hales, Bill Maitland, Ian Harvey, Lofty Hughes, unknown. Sitting: Tol Janeke, Ed Potterton, unknown, unknown

parachutists, Boet Swart's angry words carried across the water. He was blasting Sandy Mutch for not having observed safety regulation by remaining in the harness that was still firmly strapped to him when he was pulled into the boat. I found this an amusing end to a superb experience.

Although a member of Air Staff, I had been deployed from June right through to the end of September to teach many pilots visual recce; there being no one else to do the job. When eventually I returned to Salisbury, hoping to commence work on a few projects I had lined up, I learned that four South African pilots were on their way to Rhodesia for recce training.

Jan Mienie, Francois du Toit, Eugene Coetzer and Don Jordaan were by far the most willing pilots I had flown with. This made teaching them, even in the most trying dry conditions with no terrorists around, a much easier task than expected.

These four men could not get over the living conditions at FAF 5, Mtoko. They considered this to be a place of luxury and found the food equal to the best of home cooking. They were right I suppose, because we tended to take for granted the efforts of Squadron Leader Murray Hofmeyr and other members of Air HQ staff. They went to great lengths to provide the best possible accommodation and comforts, including swimming pools, from the meagre funds allocated for each forward air base.

Swimming pool at FAF 5 with Chopper Arms beyond.

Regular caterers from the various messes at New Sarum and Thornhill did two-week stints in the field where they did wonders with the regular run of fresh rations for their kitchens. The squadron technicians always praised the quantity and quality of food served by preceding caterers to ensure that the current staff would compete for higher accolades.

Jan, Francois, Eugene and Don flew with me in pairs for three sorties each before launching off on their own to cover ground allocated to them. Every fourth day one of them flew

with me so that I could check out the places they had marked on their maps. By Christmas they had covered the entire operational area from Mount Darwin eastward to the border and had pinpointed every old CT base and feeding-point previously recorded in the dry season.

The rains had set in and the bush was thickening when I took the opportunity to take my four South African charges to Salisbury for a grand Christmas luncheon with my extended family. The next day we returned to Mtoko believing that ZANLA's return was imminent.

At about this time Shell & BP installed underground fuel tanks for Avtur and Avgas at FAF 5. Amazingly the engineer responsible for the work was a very good-looking woman, Di Edmunds. In the evening she was beautifully dressed and trimmed, every bit a lady. By day she was something else. In overalls and wielding a heavy pipe wrench with the ease of a tough rigger, she drove her team of four black men relentlessly to keep up with the high rate at which she worked. In doing this, she employed the foulest language I have ever heard. This not only amazed the men at FAF 5; it caused them to keep well clear of her in daylight hours.

Détente and SB

FOUR MONTHS EARLIER, ON 25 AUGUST 1975, a much-publicised South African and Zambian détente-generated meeting between the Rhodesian Government, ZAPU and ZANU took place in a South African Railways carriage on the Victoria Falls Bridge midway between Rhodesia and Zambia. The meeting was another détente failure despite the assurances given Ian Smith by Prime Minister Vorster and President Kaunda that ZAPU and ZANU were ready and willing to meet formally with the Rhodesian Government leaders. To facilitate this meeting, leading men of ZAPU and ZANU had been released, on parole, from Rhodesian prisons; another huge political error forced on Rhodesia by Vorster.

The object of the meeting had been to give the parties opportunity to express, publicly and without preconditions, their genuine desire to negotiate for an acceptable settlement. This was to be followed by the disengagement of forces and talks between the parties on Rhodesian soil.

As expected from past bitter experience, preconditions were raised in the very first statement that was made on behalf of ZANU and ZAPU by Bishop Abel Muzorewa. At the luncheon recess, ZANU and ZAPU delegates cleaned out the vast liquor holdings of the South African Railways bar before making a drunken departure back to Zambia. They were totally incapable of returning for the afternoon session. Later a message from Zambia indicated that neither ZAPU nor ZANU had any intention of honouring their agreements with Kaunda and Vorster. So that was the end of Vorster's 'guaranteed' détente initiative.

At the time it was clear that ZAPU had one undisputed leader, Joshua Nkomo, who continued to be wrongly viewed by Kaunda as the leader of all Rhodesia's African people. Within ZANU there was turmoil with three people claiming to be its leader. They were Bishop Abel Muzorewa, the Reverend Ndabaningi Sithole and Robert Mugabe. Not only was there confusion in political ranks; there existed huge rifts in the ZANLA ranks between members of the Karanga, Manyika and Chizezuru factions. Such is the nature of African politics.

A Special Branch agent in Zambia had used a custom-made bomb to assassinate ZANLA's operations chief, Herbert Chitepo, to engineer more confusion. Chitepo's VW Beetle activated the bomb's electrical firing mechanism when he reversed out of the driveway of his rented home in Lusaka. The assassination had been rigged in a manner that fingered members of ZANLA's DARE (military high command) and led to the arrest and imprisonment of Josiah Tongogara and other senior military personnel; leaving ZANLA headless.

It was all very well to be content with a high attrition rate amongst ZANLA's numbers inside the country, but as I have said, most Rhodesian officers realised that the best place to fight the enemy was beyond one's borders. With reducing numbers of ZANLA personnel inside Rhodesia and troubles in ZANLA's command structures, it was the perfect time to strike hard and in depth to stem the inward flow of replacements. However, as has been stated already, South Africa made overt action impossible.

Frustrating political constraints on the military desire to take the war into hostile Mozambique and Zambia continued to be, so far as we could see, the consequence of Vorster's obsession with his détente initiatives. Ian Smith's book *The Great Betrayal* released over twenty years later confirms these suspicions.

However, because of the nature of its operations Special Branch had never been constrained in the same way as the military, and SB was determined to make the best of this unique situation. They had no intention of sitting back and waiting for increased troubles with intensified bloodshed when détente initiatives for the December 1974 ceasefire were seen to be against Rhodesia's interests. The SB knew that this and future détente initiatives would fail; so they aimed to capitalise on ZANLA's confused situation by intensifying it. Inside Mozambique, no great distance from Mukumbura, SB and Army intelligence officers managed to set up meetings with Thomas Nhari. He was a ZANLA field commander and member of the DARE. Meetings with Nhari and his lieutenants occurred on three or four occasions between September and November 1974. This was a period when ZANLA was already pretty punch-drunk from our mounting successes inside the

country and from the SAS's continued attacks along their 'safe routes' in Mozambique.

Thomas Nhari, like Rex Nhongo, had been a Russian-trained member of ZAPU before defecting to ZANU in 1971. For the SB and Army officers, posing as white left-wing agitators, it was easy to persuade Nhari that ZANLA was failing inside Rhodesia because they were following Chinese philosophies and using light weapons when what they really needed were heavy weapons, as advocated by the Russians.

The enormous casualties suffered by ZANLA seemed to give credibility to the lie and Nhari and his followers were fired by these thoughts. They accepted as truth many accusations that pointed to the fact that all ZANLA's weaknesses lay squarely with ZANU politicians and senior DARE members. These people lived lives of luxury in Lusaka, never caring a damn for the lives of armed ZANLA comrades who suffered immense dangers and hardships in blind support of selfish 'fat cats'. Nhari was persuaded that he could secure power to himself and his followers and then come to an accommodation with the Rhodesian Government.

The SB selection of Nhari was no mistake. He happened to be a highly respected leader who treated his men well and protected them from the bully elements amongst ZANLA's field commanders. Once convinced he should take action against his seniors in Lusaka, it took little time for him to gather together a suitable force for a task he liked to believe was entirely of his own making. The SB did not expect Nhari to succeed; in fact they hoped he would fail.

Nhari's rebel force first secured ZANLA's main base in Mozambique. This was at FRELIMO's HQ base, Chifombo. Any resistance to his leadership was handled by burying his detractors alive. Nhari then set out for Lusaka to overpower the ZANU hierarchy and ZANLA's ruling committee, the DARE. Fighting broke out in the streets of Kamwala in Lusaka as the Nhari rebel force tried to gain control. Tongogara's wife and a number of ZANU and DARE officials were kidnapped. As had been hoped, Nhari botched the job and, together with many of his followers, died for his efforts; but not before bringing about serious repercussions within the high command and drawing down on ZANU the displeasure of the Lusaka Government.

The 'Nhari Rebellion', as it became known, caused serious disruption in ZANLA ranks and it took the remaining elements of the DARE some time to regain control and neutralise all of Nhari's followers. The SB was well pleased with Nhari's achievements and even misled Lusaka with trumped-up intelligence reports to capitalise on the rebellion and further undermine Zambian relationships with ZANU.

CTs prepare to resume war

THE PRESIDENTS OF THE FRONTLINE States had been misled by ZAPU and ZANU into believing there could be no accommodation with the Rhodesian Government, so they pressurised ZAPU and ZANU into establishing a unified political front. Presidents Kaunda and Nyerere also insisted that ZIPRA and ZANLA must go back to war as one unified force.

A few ZANLA commanders, and particularly Josiah Tongogara who was still in prison, saw the sense of unification. They had seen that, following Angola's independence, the split interests of four guerrilla forces was already developing into a civil war that was certain to last for years; and they did not want to see this happen in 'free Zimbabwe'. ZAPU and its military wing ZIPRA were still intact and enjoyed total support from the Zambian Government. For ZANU things were not so rosy, particularly with Tongogara and his DARE still ensconced in a Zambian prison. Sithole had been rejected as the political figurehead in favour of Mugabe, but for the time being Mugabe was out of reach.

Robert Gabriel Mugabe was fifty-one years of age when he and Edgar Tekere broke parole in March 1975. Then, acting on instructions from the ZANU Central Committee in Lusaka, Chief Tangwena smuggled them across the border into Mozambique. Mugabe was one of the few academics in ZANU and for some years had been recognised as a revolutionary activist whose thoughts and ideals were deeply rooted in Marxist teaching.

Mugabe's task in Mozambique was to regroup ZANLA's forces, receive large numbers of school children pouring into Mozambique for training and resume the war with all haste. Though he and Tekere commenced work immediately, they were limited by FRELIMO who, not realising these men were high-ranking officials acting under mandate from ZANU's executive, took them away from the ZANLA camps and confined them to the coastal town of Quelimane. Whilst there, Mugabe was appointed President of ZANU by the DARE members still in prison in Zambia and this was confirmed by ZANU forces in Mgagao in Tanzania. But it was not until early 1976 that Mugabe's appointment to the leadership of ZANU became known to FRELIMO, after which he was free to exercise his authority in Mozambique. By that time the war had already resumed under the leadership of Rex Nhongo.

Mugabe's leadership of ZANU, and therefore of ZANLA, would not have occurred but for his release from detention to satisfy the Vorster–Kaunda détente initiatives. Even so, he might never have gained ascendancy had tribal rivalries and personal ambitions not plagued the nationalist cause with continuous unrest. In 1975, for instance, there existed a number of organisations. These were the ANC, ZAPU, ZANU and FROLIZI. The ANC was supposed to be the umbrella organisation under which the three independent opposition formations were expected to unify. But, as with any unification attempts in Africa, the ANC failed to overcome never-ending jostling for personal power.

ZAPU, for its part, attempted to capitalise on its politically stronger position to gain the upper hand by insisting that the unified force sought by the Frontline presidents must fall under ZAPU's control. Mozambique's Samora Machel saw through this and concluded that military leaders must control fighting men. He ruled in favour of ZANLA and, on 12 November 1975 in Maputo (previously Lourenço Marques), forced ZIPRA into signing an agreement for the formation of a new Zimbabwe Liberation Army (ZIPA) under overall control of ZANLA's Rex Nhongo.

ZIPA was supposed to launch its offensive before Christmas Day 1975. Three sectors of Rhodesia's long eastern border were to be penetrated simultaneously by ZIPA with the aim of spreading Rhodesian forces as thinly as possible. The northernmost push was to be through ZANLA's Takawira sector towards the old battlegrounds of the Chaminuka and Nehanda sectors. The central push was to be along the mountainous border region centred on Umtali, and the third through the flat lands of Mozambique's Gaza Province in the south.

ZAPU reneged on its agreement by sending only 100 men to the ZIPA force instead of the thousands promised. When eventually they entered into Rhodesia, the ZAPU elements promptly deserted their 'ZANLA brothers', dumped their weapons and uniforms, and made their way to Matabeleland and thence through to Botswana back to Zambia. So much for the unified force! ZIPA never got off the ground. The SAS had severely blunted ZIPRA's plans but ZANLA was refreshed and, although its political organisation was in a shambles, many armed men were ready to move into the country.

At about this time I read an article in the American *Time* magazine reporting an incident in one of the American cities. This had absolutely nothing to do with Rhodesia but it struck me how much the reported incident illustrated the situation that was about to befall us.

The report told of a woman who was refuelling her own motorcar. Having placed the fuel nozzle into her vehicle's filler neck, she set it to run and went to check the engine's oil level. Whilst she was doing this, the nozzle dislodged from the filler neck and fell to the floor still spewing fuel. Somehow the fuel ignited, making it impossible to get to the nozzle or the pump-stand. The car caught alight and burning fuel poured into a shallow water drain along the main road. Many people, including the owner of the petrol station, panicked and rushed in with fire extinguishers from adjacent stores but theirs was a no-win situation. The fire continued to worsen until a sensible old man arrived on the scene. He immediately asked for directions to the station's electrical control box. He went quietly to the box and switched off the electrical mains switch. This stopped the flow of fuel and the fire burned itself out quickly.

The analogy of this story with Rhodesia is that the continuously flowing fuel represented the terrorists. The panicking people fighting the burning fuel represented the Rhodesian Government and our security forces. The sensible old man represented senior military officers who sought to turn off the switch by striking every external structure involved in supporting the flow of trained CTs. But access to the switch was barred by South Africa.

Return of ZANLA

IN EARLY JANUARY 1976, THE northern penetrations commenced. Plans for simultaneous crossings on the other two fronts were stymied for a short while by logistical shortcomings and because FRELIMO was experiencing difficulties with dissident elements within its own forces close to the Rhodesian border. These dissidents may well have been those responsible for firing at every Rhodesian vehicle or aircraft moving near the border over previous months.

ZANLA's first entry occurred just north of the Mudzi River and was detected by a routine border patrol just after dawn. I was at Mtoko with my four South African recce students when news of the resumption of war reached us at the breakfast table.

The elevation of the sun is vitally important for visual recce work. Because of this, most recce flights were conducted between 10 o'clock and 3 o'clock. However, aerial tracking could be done for at least two hours either side of these times. Since I was committed to a recce task inside Mozambique, not too far from the entry point, I tasked Francois du Toit to precede me and try his hand at aerial-tracking the CTs who were reported to have split into three groups of about fifteen men each.

When I got airborne, Francois had already been flying ahead of trackers for about an hour. I listened in on the operations frequency but only heard general natter between the ground callsigns and supporting helicopters. I had been working inside Mozambique for some time when I heard Francois 'sunmistakable Afrikaans-accented voice calling for troops to be lifted forward to a patch of thick bush where he had lost one trail he had followed for some distance from the

border. He did not sound too confident but his request was met without question. The action that followed accounted for some CTs killed and the capture of large quantities of equipment abandoned as survivors scattered. With his ability in aerial tracking now proven, Francois went after the trails of the other two groups and brought troops into contact with both of them.

Sitting at height over rough terrain in Mozambique, I was following the action in Rhodesia with interest and a sense of pride in the young South African I had trained. I had become so engrossed in what I was listening to that I did not immediately understand the meaning of dense white smoke that suddenly blossomed on the ground 5,000 feet below me.

The smoke densified slightly and appeared to be drifting quite rapidly when I noticed a shadow line racing down-sun from the smoke. I clicked to the fact that this was the trail of a missile coming my way. It would not have helped one bit but I instinctively closed the throttle and switched off both magnetos and watched the smoke line streaking upwards. I did not see the Strela missile itself but watched its swirling white plume pass about 200 metres behind the aircraft. Thanks to the anti-Strela modifications to the Cessna, the missile had failed to 'see' the aircraft. The operator must have tracked the aircraft until he received a false 'lock-on signal' from the sun. Nevertheless I was happy to signal Air HQ with the good news that we had outright proof of the effectiveness of our anti-Strela modifications.

Shortly thereafter the four South African pilots returned to their home bases. However, Jan Mienie and Francois du Toit had enjoyed their time with the Rhodesian Air Force so much that both of them resigned from the SAAF and joined us later in the year.

Lynx ferry

IT WAS AT THIS TIME that final preparations were being made to take delivery of the new twin-engined (push-pull) Cessna 337 aircraft from Reims in France.

If the story about a Trojan T28D shipment being turned around within sight of Cape Town is correct, it is hardly surprising that the option to sea-freight the Cessnas had been discarded. But it is more likely that an existing problem influenced Air HQ to opt to fly the machines directly from France to Rhodesia. A batch of SAIA-Marchetti SF 260C training aircraft, which were to replace the Provost as a basic trainer, had been shipped from Europe months earlier but all trace of them had been lost. Although the first batch of seventeen (to become known as Genets) eventually pitched up, there was great concern for their safety when the Cessna 337 aircraft were ready for collection.

To ferry the Cessnas such a long distance was a dangerous undertaking at a time when a Rhodesian might be arrested on sight in many countries, and more so in the black African countries through which the aircraft would have to transit. To reduce the risks, considerable trouble was taken to disguise the ownership and destination of the aircraft. French-speaking Malagasy was chosen as the ultimate destination for two separate flights; the first down the western side of Africa and the second down the east.

The Government of Malagasy knew nothing of this plan nor did they know about the fictitious Malagasy Fisheries Surveillance Company whose fancy crest was emblazoned on variously coloured and brightly painted Cessnas. The false company's name was Sociedad Estudios y Pescas Maritimas, registered in Spain. All documentation, flight planning and correspondence was in French and, where appropriate, gave the impression that the original paperwork had been sent ahead to the Malagasy-based company. Considering Rhodesia's considerable successes in sanctions-busting, it would not surprise me to learn that there were agents of the bogus company actually sitting in Tananarive to handle mail and queries.

Two ferry flights following widely separated routes was considered essential, as more than ten aircraft flying one route could draw attention; eighteen aircraft would certainly look too much like squadron strength to any knowledgeable observer. Separate timings of the two flights was another issue. To minimise risk, it was necessary to keep the number of stops along each route to the barest minimum. This necessitated the use of specially designed long-range fuel tanks that occupied the entire volume of cabin space behind the pilots' seats. Direct injection into the engines of oil for the long flights was also necessary. However, the fuel tanks were so expensive that only ten were made to cater for both ferry flights. After the first ferry, tanks were to be flown to France as quickly as possible by a Rhodesian-owned sanctions-busting airline to get the second ferry completed before hostile intelligence services picked up on what was happening.

Considerable care was taken in the selection of nine Rhodesian Air Force pilots. Seven would be used on the first ferry, but only two on the second ferry. This was to avoid having recent entries in their false passports evidencing passage down the west coast of Africa, which might raise unwanted questions along the east coast route.

The plan was for each participating Rhodesian pilot to be accompanied by a French pilot. The Frenchmen had to do all the talking at the various refuelling stops as 'proof that the ferry was a purely French affair'. The explanation for the presence of English-speaking pilots with southern African accents was to be that they were commercial pilots who had been hired to

ensure safe passage through tropical weather conditions with which the French pilots were unfamiliar. I was one of the pilots selected to go to France for a quick conversion onto the Cessna 337 before the first ferry commenced. But then at short notice I was withdrawn because a SAAF delegation that was about to visit us specifically requested my presence in Salisbury. In consequence I did not attend the pilots' briefing by the Commander and DG Ops who made it clear that, if things went wrong, the Rhodesian Government could not guarantee the safety of individuals.

The pilots who went to France for the first ferry were Wing Commander Rob Gaunt (in charge), Eddie Wilkinson, John Barnes, Dave Thorne, Vic Wightman and John Bennie. Wing Commander Keith Corrans and Mike Gedye were there too, preparing for their participation as the only two Rhodesian pilots on the second ferry.

My disappointment at this turn in events switched to outright annoyance when the South African visit was delayed to a time beyond the period of the ferry. However, probably in compensation, I was instructed to accompany Wing Commander Len Pink on a mission to Ruacana in South West Africa. The purpose of this mission was to monitor the first ferry during the times the aircraft were airborne all the way from Reims in France to Ruacana.

The ferry refuelling stops were Palma (Balearic Islands), Agadir (Morocco), Dakar (Senegal), Cotonou (Benin), Port Gentil (an island just off the coast of Gabon) and Ruacana. At the Ruacana airfield we were accommodated in tents with a resident South African Army company. The Rhodesian team assisted Chuck Dent to erect an HF radio aerial that he had personally designed for this mission. To Len Pink and me the aerial looked like a large, flimsy, horizontally inclined turntable washing line that wobbled in the breeze high above the radio tent. We said nothing but both of us wondered if the aerial would work at all, never mind receive and transmit signals between far-off France and Ruacana.

Bob d'Hotmann (hat), technician John Potts, Chuck Dent (glasses) PB (right) Len Pink (kneeling, left) and telegraphist 'Tweaks', Fawns.

Having prepared everything for the first leg of the ferry, which was on the night of 14/15 January 1976, we made a curiosity flight to the coast that particular afternoon. This was not a requirement but it would familiarise us with the ground over which the ferry flight would route when it turned eastwards from the Atlantic to head for Ruacana. Bob d'Hotmann, who had flown us to Ruacana in a Dakota, flew us over territory that was completely unknown to any of us.

The terrain around Ruacana was familiar savannah country with large expanses of treed areas and narrow open grasslands running along the river-lines. As we progressed westward this gave way to very broken dry rocky terrain and a range known as the Zebra mountains. Any artist painting this incredible spectacle might not be believed because the sharply defined black and white stripes that cover the mountains looked so much like zebra markings that it was hard for any of us to accept that they were natural.

Beyond this, scrub-covered slopes met the brilliant white sands of the coastal desert in a defined line with no transition from one to the other. High, sharp-peaked dunes running in lines roughly parallel with the coast curved their way beyond sight. Next, the deep-blue Atlantic added yet another dimension to changes of scenery that had us spellbound.

As if this was not enough, ahead of us was spread an enormous fleet of Russian fishing vessels with three large 'factory ships' festooned with eavesdropping radio aerials and receiver dishes. We counted over sixty vessels spread either side of the extended borderline between SWA and Angola. Our excited report-back to the South Africans was met with a very casual "Thanks buddy, we know all about the Ruskies. Maritime surveillance has been watching them for over two weeks. Their interest seems to be with the fighting in Angola."

Our doubts about the effectiveness of Chuck Dent's aerial increased when we had heard nothing from the aircraft following an Air HQ signal that let us know two flights of four aircraft were airborne and heading for Palma. Rhodesians, each with a French co-pilot, flew six aircraft. Two experienced French airline pilots flew two aircraft but only one of these had a second pilot. This was due to my having been withdrawn too late to find a suitable replacement.

At around 10 o'clock on the night of 14th Chuck's optimism had already turned to serious doubt when Squadron Leader Eddie Wilkinson's voice came through faint but clear. He said, "I have been receiving you strength five all the way. Landing in ten minutes. Second flight thirty minutes behind. Will call airborne 09:00 Zulu. Cheers for now. Out."

The first and final legs of this ferry were conducted at night for security reasons. Brightly coloured aircraft in formations might attract attention over France, but over Rhodesia they would undoubtedly cause unwanted excitement. The four intermediate legs were flown in daylight.

The legs from Palma to Agadir, Dakar and Cotonou were uneventful and we had communication with the aircraft all the way. However, out at sea on the leg to Port Gentil both formations encountered frontal weather conditions with visibility so poor that visual contact between the aircraft was often lost. It was in these conditions that Dave Thorne experienced falling rpm on his rear engine and was forced to close it down.

In a twin-engined aircraft it takes both fans turning to keep pilots cool over land, never mind flying way out over the ocean in heavy storms. So, with only one fan thrusting above a vast expanse of storm-tossed ocean, Dave and his French co-pilot were in a real sweat. There were still three hours to reach destination at normal cruise speed but, with his reduced speed on one engine, Dave had to make a decision on whether to hold heading or divert to a closer destination. In the event Dave elected to turn left for Libreville and take his chances if he was forced to land there; providing he reached the coast in the first place.

Dave, my coursemate back in 1957, had left the Air Force in the mid-60s to join the Australian airline Qantas. He had enjoyed flying in the comfort of Boeing 707 airliners but, for family reasons, had returned to Rhodesia and the Air Force. Flogging across the Atlantic on one engine in bad weather must

Lynx formation.

Lynx line-up.

have made him long for those safer times flying four-engined airliners. As it happened, Dave and his wide-eyed Frenchman made it to the coast at Libreville then turned south staying over the sea within gliding distance of the steamy coastline until they reached Port Gentil safely. The reason for the engine problem was detected and easily rectified. The next morning the aircraft took to the air heading south for Ruacana.

The arrival of the Cessnas left me with a lasting impression of how ugly the aircraft appeared in flight and how noisy the machines sounded as they streamed past before landing. On the ground they looked much neater as they taxiied quietly to line up in a single row. Three colour schemes had been used and all were very bright and cheerful. The elaborate crests of the fictitious fisheries surveillance company were eye-catching—intentionally so!

The crews were clearly delighted to be on friendly ground following four whole days of long flights with periods of tension between. Cameras were uncovered and a babble of French and English voices dominated as crews instructed each other on how they were required to pose. Whilst this was going on, storm clouds were towering in a continuous line to the east with much lightning and grumbling thunder.

Keith Corrans, held back for the second ferry, arrived at Ruacana to take the place of the one missing French pilot and following a happy evening, the crews were able to lie in next morning. However, one French airline pilot who was to fly the only aircraft with a French crew decided he needed to get back to France in a hurry and insisted on being taken to the nearest international airport. According to other French pilots, this fellow had become afraid of African weather conditions following the Cotonou-to-Port Gentil flight. When on arrival he saw the line of storm clouds building near Ruacana and learned of ITCZ conditions prevailing over Rhodesia, he was very jittery and became determined to get off the last leg. Air HQ instructed a very annoyed Bob d'Hotmann to fly the

The shirtless man and the short-arse one seen talking to John Barnes, Eddie Wilkinson and Rob Gaunt were two of the nine French pilots.

Frenchman the long distance to Windhoek and I was instructed to take that Frenchman's place. Immediately I signalled Air HQ to make certain that DG Ops knew that I had not flown a Cessna 337 before and that my instrument and night ratings had expired 18 months ago. In his reply DG Ops said he was aware of these issues but was relying on my experience and the French co-pilot's assistance to get the aircraft safely home.

Our brief was to enter Rhodesian air space after dark, but all eight participating French pilots were very eager to see the Victoria Falls. By staggering take-off it was decided that only two aircraft would be seen at any one time over the Falls and that nobody on the ground would know whether they were Zambian or Rhodesian sight-seeing flights.

We were happy to comply in any event because with bad weather forecast over western SWA and much of Rhodesia, and with difficult featureless terrain to navigate along the Caprivi Strip, it would be good to have a precise start-point before nightfall. During the flight we were not permitted to contact any Air Traffic Control centre other than Salisbury. Thornhill was available for diversion, but only in dire emergency. The specified natter frequency allocated for the ferry was to be the only one we could use until Salisbury's control boundary was reached.

I invited my French pilot, Monsieur José, to take the left-hand (captain's) seat. He declined, saying I was the one who knew how to handle the weather he could see building up across our path. He said he knew how to manage the fuel and oil transfer systems and this was best handled from the right-hand seat. M José's English was only marginally better than my all-but-forgotten schoolboy French, so we relied on single words and hand signals. Pointing his finger at switches and instruments M José guided me through pre-start checks and engines start-up. His double thumbs-up signified all was well. We taxiied out sixth in the line of eight aircraft and lined up on the runway to watch number five labouring into flight and heading for the cloudbanks we ourselves would soon encounter.

The aircraft was loaded beyond design maximum weight so acceleration was slow and there was not much runway left when she lifted off with an uncomfortably high-nose attitude; but she soon accelerated to climbing speed. Response to rudder and elevator control movements was familiar but I found that the control yoke, which was narrower than any I had used before, made aileron handling heavy.

Transfer to instruments was made before entering cloud with instrument lighting set to maximum. Turbulence was mild in the climb to 11,500 feet where we levelled off. For some time I could not understand why we had not accelerated to the cruising speed I was expecting and it took a while before I realised that I had not raised the wing flaps after take-off. M José had not spotted this at all. With flaps up the speed stepped up nicely.

Not long after settling in the cruise, the rear-engine rpm started to hunt and I could not settle it down. M José's response to my query was the typically continental one of screwing the face and raising both hands and shoulders. John Barnes, flying eighth in line, told me to do something or other, I cannot remember what, and the problem cleared. From then on both engines purred in perfect synchronisation for the rest of the flight.

Halfway to Victoria Falls we cleared the cloud that, though dense and dark in patches, had been relatively smooth and had given me no difficulty. I searched all around but could not see any of the other aircraft. From there on it was a matter of working out our exact location from the limited information printed on the 1:1,000,000-scale maps. M José shook his head when I confidently pointed to our position on the map. To him everything on the ground looked flat with all vleis (wetlands along river-lines) running almost parallel to our course.

Fifty kilometres before reaching the Victoria Falls we could already pick out the vertical pillar of spray from the falls illuminated by the setting sun. Once over the Falls, M José was amazed by the sight of this great wonder and took many photographs as we made one wide orbit. I have no idea how well the photographs turned out because the sun had just set below the horizon.

Even before we reached the Falls I heard the seventh and eighth aircraft broadcast that they were leaving Victoria Falls on course for Salisbury. Only then did I realise that both of them had passed me in the cloud, because of my flap selection error.

The Rhodesian weather forecast received before take-off warned of the ITCZ storm-line we could see running

eastwards from Wankie. I had no desire to fly the direct route to Salisbury in such rough weather. Instead I chose to fly to Sinoia in clear skies, and then turn southwards for the shortest possible run through bad weather to Salisbury.

M José and I flew just south of the Zambezi Gorge to the headwaters of Kariba Lake, which was barely visible before it became totally dark. Flying conditions were smooth with absolutely nothing to see below us. M José pointed to the sky and my schoolboy French recognised sufficient words to understand that he had never seen so many stars in his life. The conditions were perfect and I had to agree that the brilliance and multiplicity of the stars was awesome.

Whilst we were enjoying our smooth ride and admiring God's heavenly firmament, we listened to transmissions between the other pilots who were having a very rough ride down the ITCZ storm-line that we could see continuously illuminated by rippling lightning flashes way off to our right. Why the other pilots had not taken our 'soft option' route I cannot say, but I know that flying Trojans had taught me a thing or two about avoiding bad weather whenever possible.

All the other aircraft had landed by the time we eventually entered the bad weather about ten minutes' flying time from Salisbury. We passed over the city in cloud and rain that was illuminated all around us as we descended towards the airport. Salisbury Airport controllers had no idea of the aircraft types arriving that night because one of our Air Force ATC officers, I think it was John Digby, sat with them to assist with what he had said was 'the recovery of 4 Squadron aircraft returning from an operation in the Wankie area'. Approach Control expressed some concern because no one had heard from my aircraft until the last of the others had landed.

My French companion had been completely lost without the ILS-VOR assistance he relied on wherever he flew in Europe. On the other hand, I had never used such aids before. Under his guidance I learned how to interpret the instrumentation that brought us in for a bad weather landing which was so smooth it surprised me. After such a good let-down and smooth landing, M José made it clear that he was sure I had lied to him about never having used ILS-VOR or flown a Cessna 337 before.

When we taxiied into dispersals at Air Movements Section, there was not a single Cessna 337 to

Eastern half (Zambian side) of Victoria Falls with part of the Main Falls (left) and famous road–rail bridge bottom left.

be seen. M José and I climbed out of our machine into soaking rain and ran for the Air Movements Section. As I entered the building I looked back and saw our aircraft being towed away to a top-security hangar where the other aircraft already stood dripping water onto the concrete floor.

Inside Air Movements Section, Air Marshal McLaren and his senior staff officers were celebrating with the other crews. Eight Cessna 337s were home. Ten to go!

For the second ferry, Chuck Dent's special HF aerial was erected at New Sarum to provide communications for Wing Commander Keith Corrans and Squadron Leader Mike Gedye.

Mike Gedye, Eddie Wilkinson, Len Pink and Keith Corrans, photographed at Ruacana.

This is Keith's account of the second ferry:

The second ferry comprised 10 aircraft (2 sections of 5 aircraft led by Mike Gedye and me, the only Rhodesian pilots on this route). To minimise the risk of compromise Mike and I had been "kept back" as even the most simple en-route immigration official might have wondered, from our passports (false as they were) why we had been in West Africa, heading south, only 10 days or so before we were in their area heading the same way. The second, but shorter, route down through central Africa was, as a result, largely rejected to ensure additional distance between East and West Coast 'tom toms'. In retrospect the ploy worked and we routed across North Africa and down the East coast departing Europe on 27 January 1976. The first leg to Las Palmas (3 hrs 40) was a 'swan' although we left departure point a little hurriedly ahead of an oncoming snowstorm. Leg 2 (6 hrs 30) was east across the Med and the foot of Italy (intercepted by a section of Italian Air Force F104s) and on to Ikaklion in Crete after an unplanned 1-hour dogleg to avoid a weapons range on the west coast of the island.

The next legs were to be the longest and potentially most dodgy. We departed Ikaklion before dawn on leg 3, penetrated Egyptian airspace west of Alexandria, routed up the Nile to Aswan and were provisionally flight planned to land at Port Sudan, assessed to be potentially the highest-risk location. Fortuitously, by cruise climbing to Flight Levels around 120 we were able to pick up a favourable tail-wind and, by "rationing" 6 ½ hrs oxygen to cover an extended flight time, managed to stretch the leg for eventual landing at Djibouti in Afas Isas (formerly Somalia in the late 1950s). It would seem that the in-flight destination change (plus perhaps the number of aircraft in the 2 section 'gaggle') generated "agitated" RT. transmissions from Ethiopian Military ATC (all totally and studiously ignored) who seemed to be attempting to drum up aircraft to intercept us. As the leg had been intentionally planned for Saturday, and it was late afternoon, they did not really have time to get their act together and we departed the area hastily, descending to low level on the Red Sea Coast somewhere near Massawa Island. After a 10 hrs leg we eventually arrived at Djibouti after dark in the "Mother" of all thunderstorms, and had a most magnificent meal at a local Shebeen in the town square (probably camel steaks) with copious quantities of Stella Artois and French wine, before kipping in primitive conditions—on bare mattresses—in a local down-town Djibouti/Somali "hotel".

Leg 4 was to Mombassa, the next high-risk point. After a flight of 6 hrs 30 east and across the Somali Desert to the coast (Indian Ocean) and then south, at a comfortable altitude down that attractive coastline, we landed (in old stomping grounds) and were surprised by most efficient and courteous arrival procedures. Overnight accommodation was at a superb coastal/tourist hotel; we did however have to wait until almost midnight for the resident German/Scandinavian tourists to vacate the rooms and catch their flights north before we could take occupation! And then we found that the water supplies to the hotel had been on the blink for about 2 weeks and there was no hot or cold running water and the toilet had to be flushed by bucket using water stored in the bath! The breakfast next morning on the verandah did however partially offset the hassle and the lack of sleep.

The next leg started in superb weather; the scenery down the coast was fantastic. The colour of the water on the coral at Pemba and Zanzibar Islands has to be seen to be believed; shades of Bazaruto and Paradise Island, Mozambique. And then one of the French crews, who had consistently failed to maintain any semblance of formation discipline—dropping out of formation to low-fly down the "mile-long" beaches, declared an emergency/instrument panel fire and made a precautionary landing at a disued airfield a little north of Mtwara on the south-eastern border of Tanzania. Sods Law! The ant bears had got there before them and the landing path was pitted with holes! Exit one Cessna prop, nose wheel and wingtip! After 2 or 3 circuits of the scene it was obvious that there was little or nothing "we" could do to assist and the 2 French crew had to be left to their own devices (with ferry tanks there was no room in any aircraft to rescue them).

Although the Frenchmen were stranded they were unhurt, so Keith wished them well and promised to send help as soon as possible. The welcoming party in Salisbury was somewhat dampened. Even with seventeen Cessnas safely home and tucked away out of sight, there was deep concern for the one lying damaged in hostile territory. Fortunately, Keith Corrans knew its precise location and had the necessary details of the damage sustained.

Local tribesmen took the two Frenchmen into their care until FRELIMO officials arrived from northern Mozambique and, fortunately, no Tanzanian officials showed up. The Frenchmen did a first-class con job using language difficulties to maximum effect. This was matched by the senior French pilot in Salisbury who telephoned Maputo direct from Salisbury to ask for FRELIMO's permission to mount a recovery operation for the 'French-owned' aircraft. He explained that the downed aircraft had been flying to Malagasy when it suffered engine problems. This had forced the crew to land on an airstrip on Tanzanian soil very close to Mozambique rather than risk the long over-water leg to Malagasy. FRELIMO's authorities were assured that this was a purely civil aviation matter in which Rhodesian civil aviation authorities had agreed to give full technical assistance to the French.

FRELIMO, still new in government, took the Frenchman at his word and made no attempt to contact the Governments of Tanzania or Malagasy to verify a request emanating from 'hostile Rhodesia'. Approval was given for the use of a Rhodesian-registered aircraft to fly Rhodesian personnel in to effect necessary repairs for a one-time flight. They agreed also that the Cessna 337 would need to be flown to Beira for fuel and then on to Salisbury for final repair work before undertaking the long flight to Malagasy.

Group Captain Charles Paxton had been earmarked to become the Commander of the Rhodesian Air Force but he opted for early retirement instead and was then flying for a civilian charter firm. His current employment and Air Force background made Charles the ideal person to conduct the recovery operation. This had to be done rapidly for fear that FRELIMO might establish the true ownership of the damaged aircraft. It meant getting to site immediately, performing the barest minimum of repair work and departing with minimum delay. In the meanwhile the French crew and FRELIMO had arranged for the holes in the runway to be filled in by the locals. The plan worked well. The rear engine was replaced, the nose wheel was jacked up and bolted into place, the front propeller was replaced and engine checks were conducted. A large box of goodies for FRELIMO and the locals ensured full co-operation without interference. Both aircraft then departed for Beira.

Since the Cessna had to fly with undercarriage down, the flight to Salisbury via Beira was a long one. Charles Paxton escorted the Frenchmen all the way for a night arrival at Salisbury. The Cessna was wheeled off to the security hangar and a third celebration marked the conclusion of the second ferry with all eighteen aircraft safe on Rhodesian soil.

With one aircraft requiring major repairs and five others awaiting camouflage paint, the Air Force defiantly rolled out twelve camouflaged Cessna 337s into the open for the whole world to see. It felt and looked great, and the new war-machine became known as the LYNX!

All that remained to be done was to modify the aircraft for their armed role. Work on this started the day after the first flight arrived. Mainplanes had been especially stressed during manufacture to cater for increased 'G' loads. Under-wing pylon mountings were installed at New Sarum to allow for the carriage of SNEB rocket pods, bombs, Frantans, flares and teargas. Within a week all 4 Squadron's pilots had been converted onto type. Fitment of machine-guns had been considered but this was held over for the moment. It is a great credit to all participating technicians and pilots that these aircraft did a marvellous job for the Rhodesian war effort. The Lynx came at the right time and its selection had been a good one.

Charles Paxton.

The first record of a Lynx accompanying Fireforce was on 7 March 1976, though Flight Lieutenant Ed Potterton did not use weapons on that occasion. Fitment of guns came later.

Fireforces back in action

ZIPRA, HAVING BEEN DEALT A few severe blows by SAS inside Zambia in late 1974, and again during 1975, did not seem to be ready to rush into any major offensive actions simply to keep up with ZANLA. Nevertheless its existence necessitated ongoing patrolling in the west. All of ZANLA's effort was concentrated in the east.

Following their return in January 1976, ZANLA groups moved with great caution into their original sectors Nehanda, Chaminuka and Takawira taking pains not to draw attention to themselves before they were re-established amongst the locals. By early February the game was on once more. ZANLA's intention to launch on all three fronts had been delayed as previously mentioned, but their presence just across the mountain border near the Mozambican town of Espungabera brought the newly formed Chipinga Fireforce, led by Mike Litson, into its first action on 7 February. Two months later, penetrations in the southernmost sector meant the RSF was tied up along the entire Mozambican border.

Back in the Op Hurricane area, Wing Commander Tol Janeke had anticipated that his Fireforce might be called to action in the rough terrain of the Zambezi escarpment some thirty kilometres northwest of Mount Darwin. So on 6 February, with the concurrence of his Army counterpart, he moved the whole Fireforce to Stacey's Farm to cut down reaction time.

To help follow the ASR below, the helicopter pilots were Flight Lieutenant Rob McGregor flying K-Car; Yellow 1, 2 and 3 were, respectively, Air Lieutenant Jo Syslo, Air Sub-Lieutenant Venter (Op Polo) and Flight Lieutenant George Sole.

Tol Janeke (left) and Rob McGregor (right).

Air Lieutenant Norman (Bambam) Maasdorp, N4, flew the Provost. The Police Reserve Air Wing pilot, Copper 08, was Hamie Dax whom I have already identified as the most successful of the PRAW recce pilots. The abbreviation PATU stands for Police Anti-Terrorist Unit and c/s is the abbreviation for callsign.

Rob McGregor's illustration, cut from a 1:50,000-scale map is reproduced to assist the reader in following his ASR. It reads:

On Fri. 6 FEB 76 at approximately 1030B Fire Force Mt. Darwin was tasked to position at Stacey's Farm in support of a PATU stick c/s BX who was on tracks of approximately 10 terrorists at TS 983757 (A on map). After positioning at the farm, PRAW aircraft c/s Copper 08 got airborne to establish communications with BX and attempt to track the terrorists from the air. At the same time N4 was airborne in a Provost in order to provide armed support if required. After making contact with BX, Copper 08 was able to track the terrorists to position C where a very distinctive path was picked up and followed down the mountain to the valley floor. At the bottom a hut was seen at position B and movement was observed in the vicinity of the hut.

It was then decided to put two sticks with trackers in at position B to attempt to pick up tracks. This was done and at the same time K-Car got airborne to give cover. The trackers were unable to locate any tracks of any significance at position B. Copper 08 and N4 then talked K-Car back up the line to position C. It was noted that the

tracks were very distinctive from position C to D but then tended to break up so it was decided to bring in 2 more sticks (c/s 23/25) with trackers and to drop them on tracks at D. They were to track down towards the hut where the initial sticks were left to act as stop groups. At this stage K-Car and Yellow formation returned to Stacey's Farm and left N4 as top cover.

Tracks were followed to point E where it was decided to leapfrog c/s 25, 23A and the trackers to catch up time. This was done by Yellow 3 to point F. About fifteen minutes later at 1545B c/s 25 called contact. Fireforce immediately proceeded to the scene from Staceys. On arrival in the contact area c/s 25 reported he was being mortared and that the line of flight of the terrorists was down the river-line towards position B. He estimated he had contacted a group of 20 terrorists (8 were killed in the initial contact). K-Car then saw 3 terrorists at position H and engaged them. They ran into thick bush on the river-line where further terrorists were seen and engaged. At this time the K-Car came under heavy fire from the ground. K-Car then called on N4 in the Provost to carry out a strike into the area of the K-Car attack to attempt to flush the terrorists out. N4 carried out 2 attacks with Sneb and Frantans and strikes were observed to be in the area of the target. (5 dead terrorists were later found in the area of K-Car and Provost air strikes.)

During this time c/s 25 had followed up and killed a further 2 terrorists in the riverbed. Very little movement could be seen from the air and K-Car instructed Yellow 1 to carry out dummy drops to the east and west of the river line to attempt to keep the terrorists in the river line and force then towards the stop groups at position

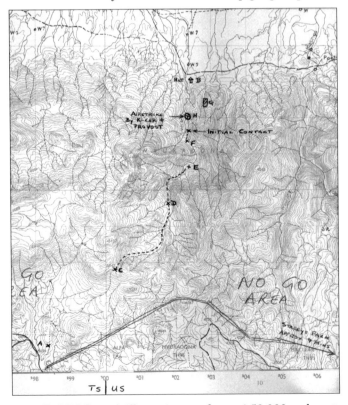

Rob McGregor's illustration, cut from a 1:50,000-scale map.

B. Shortly after this c/s 23 in the stop group reported contacting one terrorist who was killed. c/s 23 also reported movement in the area of position G which appeared to be terrorists attempting to break over the ridge line. Yellow 1 was then instructed to fire into the thick bush in that area to attempt to flush out anyone who may be there. The following day it was reported that Yellow 1 came under fire but at the time he had heard nothing and the ground forces had not reported anything.

The light was now fading fast and follow-up and mopping-up operations continued until last light with no further contact with terrorists.

Wing Commander Janeke's report reads:

a. This is a splendid example of success resulting from first class co-operation between air and ground forces. The entire operation lasted over a period of eight hours. At no time was there any unnecessary confusion or delay. A total of 17 out of a probable 22 ters were accounted for.

b. The decision to move the Fireforce with air support to Stacey's Farm was a wise one as it reduced reaction and ferry time to less than ten minutes.

c. Flt Lt McGregor, together with Air Lt Maasdorp, contributed towards the professional control of operations. De-brief of the crews also highlighted the excellent work done by 2nd Lt Nigel Theron of 2 Commando RLI, whose personal leadership and courage led to more than half of the kills. Any Army recommendation for an award to this officer would be strongly supported.

Squadron Leader Harold Griffiths as OC of the helicopter squadron wrote:

I agree with FAF Cdr's comments re the splendid effort of all forces concerned in this highly successful operation. It is very pleasing to see that such methods as aerial tracking, leapfrogging, positioning of forward stops and dummy drops were used and obviously contributing to the overall successes. A well-written report which is easy to follow.

Griff's remarks about the employment of techniques used in the past but now almost forgotten are valid. However, in this case, the follow-up on terrorists moving through very rugged unpopulated terrain lent itself to the re-employment of methods used in the days before CTs lived and operated amongst the population.

Tol Janeke was a taskmaster who demanded the best of the men under his command. He was not too popular and some individuals were even frightened of him. One such individual was Flying Officer George Sole who, though a bit of a dandy, was a very nice guy.

When one day the Fireforce callout siren sounded at FAF 4, George rushed to his helicopter, which was already occupied by the soldiers he was to carry into action. Relating to what was to follow, George said, "As I moved onto the step to get into my seat, I let off a friendly fart but shat myself instead!"

George apologised to his gunner and the troops and ran off for a shower and a change of clothing. Tol, seeing one helicopter still on the ground after the others had flown off, enquired loudly, "What the hell is going on?" The gunner said, "The pilot has gone back for a shower and clothing change because he had a bit of an accident." Tol went through the roof and ran off to find George Sole. George received a telling-off that left him in no doubt that Tol had no sympathy for his situation. "A Fireforce call out takes priority over all things. I don't care if you are uncomfortable and that everyone will be subjected to your foul stench. You fly the mission and only clean up when it is over!"

A couple of days later George rushed out when the Fireforce siren sounded. In his hurry he tripped over a tent peg and fractured his ankle. Though in absolute agony, he dared not complain and flew the long Fireforce action before seeking medical attention.

The first airstrike by a Lynx was made on 25 March. It so happened that Air Lieutenant Bill (Starry) Stevens was on his first-ever operational deployment and this was his first operational strike. He did well when the K-Car, flown by Flight Lieutenant Dick Paxton, ran out of ammunition due to a runaway 20mm cannon. Sergeant Brian Warren handled his cannon's misbehaviour coolly and still had CTs visual. Bill Stevens, having watched the K-Car's strikes, knew the exact location of the CTs and though he could not actually see them was able to kill the lot with Sneb rockets.

On 27 March Selous Scouts controller callsign 69B was visual with CTs two kilometres south of his elevated position within the Mtoko Tribal Trust Land. He called for the Mount Darwin Fireforce, then operating out of Mudzi. Air Lieutenant Childs was flying the K-Car with Major Mike Ainslie of A Company 1RAR as the airborne Army commander, and Sergeant du Preez, as his gunner. Childs and du Preez were both Op Polo men. Air Lieutenant Mike Borlace, with Flight Sergeant Mike Upton as his MAG gunner, led three G-Cars of Amber formation.

Amber lead (Borlace) spotted the terrorists immediately upon arrival over the point the Scouts had given and Mike Upton opened fire. Childs had turned the K-Car away at that moment in an attempt to re-establish communications with c/s 69B. For some time Mike Borlace could not interrupt the K-Car radio transmissions to let Childs and Ainslie know he had the CTs visual. When he did, the K-Car moved to him, picked up the scattering CTs, and opened fire with the 20mm cannon. Heavy fire was being directed at both aircraft as they pursued visual targets.

It was in the second orbit when rounds narrowly missed the K-Car gunner, mortally wounding Major Ainslie and hitting the pilot's left leg. Air Lieutenant Childs calmly broadcast his situation and instructed Amber 2 to follow him. He landed some way off next to an already deployed stop group to transfer the unconscious major to Amber 2 for casevac to Mtoko. Whilst this was being done Borlace took hits that knocked out the hydraulic servo-system, which operates the cyclic and collective controls.

Mike Borlace, now on very heavy manual control and still carrying troops, refused to disengage the CTs until the K-Car returned. He was still orbiting over the CTs with Mike Upton firing burst upon burst when the gearbox warning light came on. Then, to add to their problems, the machine-gun ceased firing because a CT round had severed the ammunition belt. Undaunted, Mike Upton took an MAG from one of the Army soldiers and continued firing free-hand at visual CTs. Borlace said Mike Upton's fire continued to be very accurate.

Though wounded, Air Lieutenant Childs returned to resume command of air and ground forces, allowing Mike Borlace to break contact and make a forced landing next to the stop group at whose location Major Ainslie had been transferred. Together with the stop group and the stick that had been on board, the two airmen armed with their personal weapons, took up positions that strengthened the original stop group and provided protection for the downed chopper. The troops that had been in Mike's helicopter were immensely relieved to be on terra firma. Though used to being at the receiving end of enemy fire, these soldiers had been absolutely terrified by the ground fire whilst totally exposed in the air with nowhere to hide.

FAF commanders such as Tol Janeke and Peter Cooke always highlighted jobs well done by aircrew personnel. In Contact Reports submitted to Army HQ, Army field commanders often praised their own men and the aircrews who supported them. But Air Force officers were generally less forthcoming. So it was good to see the following signal to Air HQ from John Digby who was OC FAF 5 at Mtoko:

1. For atten D Ops.
2. This signal supplements the Air Strike Report submitted by Air Lt Childs on the contact that occurred in this area on 27 March 1976.
3. Very shortly after the commencement of the contact Maj. Ainslie the Fireforce Commander was seriously wounded and died almost immediately and Air Lt Childs received minor wound near his left knee. Air Lt Childs arranged for the Major's casevac and then took control of the air and ground forces involved in the contact. He continued this control for approximately one hour until his ammunition was finished and he had to leave the area to refuel and re-arm. FAF 5 and FAF 4 were able to listen in on his transmissions throughout this period.
4. Air Lt Childs' control of the air and ground forces was outstanding and equal to or better than any within the operational experience of the OCs of FAF 4 and FAF 5. He maintained a clear picture of the situation at all times, showed remarkable qualities of personal control and leadership, and very aggressively progressed the contact until he had to leave to refuel and re-arm. On handing over he gave a very clear and complete briefing to the relieving K-Car.
5. After receiving medical attention, refuelling and re-arming, he returned and resumed his duties with Lt Col Heppenstall as Fireforce Commander. By this time no contacts were in progress and he assisted the Fireforce Commander by advising on the position of ambushes.
6. It is recommended that consideration be given to the award of an appropriate honour to Air Lt Childs in the near future.

ZANLA's ability to hit our aircraft had improved significantly, indicating that, again no thanks to the Vorster imposed ceasefire, a great deal of effort had been given to anti-aircraft training prior to the CTs return to Rhodesia. Almost all engagements hereafter resulted in hits on aircraft, sometimes killing or injuring aircrew and soldiers. The centrally mounted fuel tanks of the Alouettes presented a relatively large surface area and over time they suffered many hits. Fortunately Avtur fuel does not ignite easily and a self-sealing compound wrapped around the tanks prevented fuel loss.

Seven days after his forced landing, Mike Borlace took hits once more. Flying Amber lead, again with Mike Upton, Borlace was asked to put down his troops. As he approached to land, his aircraft took strikes. He received a hit on his right hand, limiting him to the use of index finger and thumb. A hit on his left inner-thigh was superficial but another bullet went through the arm of one of the soldiers on board. Mike pulled away, saw five terrorists and immediately engaged them. Only when K-Car came across, taking on three surviving CTs, did Borlace drop off his stick, less the one that was bleeding badly from his wound. He returned to Mtoko and was out of action for the rest of that day.

Air Lieutenant Troup and his gunner Sergeant Knouwds, both Op Polo men, had proven themselves to be an excellent K-Car crew on a number of occasions. They led Fireforce to a contact with a group of CTs just 3,000 metres to the southeast of the position at which Major Ainslie had been mortally wounded two weeks earlier.

During this typical Fireforce action in which one helicopter had already taken hits, Flight Lieutenant Russell Broadbent, a medical doctor who had joined us from the RNZAF, was flying his third operation on Lynx when he was called upon to make strikes. Acting on GAC directions from an Army callsign of the Fireforce he fired Sneb rockets, which was fine. The callsign then required another position to be attacked, this time with Frantan. Russell took hits during this delivery causing him to include the following paragraph in his ASR:

It seems to me that the Frantan Profile attack on the Lynx is suicidal as there is no covering fire, making the Lynx a sitting duck. I recommend that a combined SNEB/FRANTAN attack be made SOP until guns are fitted to this aircraft. I also think that priority *should be given to some form of protection for the pilots.*

Before the arrival of the Lynx, only Provosts had made Frantan deliveries and few hits were received because .303 Browning machine-guns were fired all the way down the delivery run to the point of Frantan release. This is the 'covering fire' Russell Broadbent referred to. His suggestion that Frantan attacks should include Sneb rocket fire during the delivery run was fair enough but it presented a very real danger. Sneb rockets sent a shower of shrapnel into the air through which the Lynx would have to transit after a low-level Frantan release; too dangerous to contemplate. There was only one solution and that was to fit machine-guns to the Lynx. The operational pilots had not forced this matter on Air HQ. Design work had been on the go for some time with two options in mind. The first was to produce wing-mounted gun-pods because the mainplane structures disallowed internally mounted wing-guns. The second option was to mount two .303 Brownings above the cabin roof.

The first option was thrown out because of unacceptable weight and aerodynamic drag penalties whereas the drag generated by light fairings over guns mounted above the cabin was negligible. One Lynx was taken off-line for prototype fitment and firing trials. The prototype fit was subjected to many tests and alterations before Squadron Leader Dag Jones, who was then OC 4 Squadron, finally accepted it. Thereafter all metal components, fibreglass fairings and wiring looms were made ready before Lynx were pulled off-line for modification.

This photograph shows the twin .303 gun-mountings above Air Lieutenant Kidson when he was presented the dubious Boo Boo Shield for mis-selection of armament switches. The 4 Squadron shield was presented each month to the pilot who made the biggest cock-up during that month.

Patchen explorer

FOR A LONG TIME I had been interested in building a tandem-seat aircraft specifically designed for visual reconnaissance. I considered that an ideal recce aircraft had to be very quiet and almost impossible to see when flying at 5,000 feet against a clear-sky background.

Matt black was the best colour and a shielded up-turned muffled exhaust system for a motor driving a slow-revving paddle propeller would be very quiet at cruise power. Of greatest importance was the need for all-round visual freedom of ground. This meant having large, sliding side-panels reaching to floor level.

It was impossible to gain any support to build the machine I had designed in detail. It was based on proven glider technology with wooden frames under fibreglass cladding. The Air Staff considered this was beyond Rhodesia's capability and, anyway, financial constraints ruled against such a project. I was not totally ignored however and was sent to South Africa's CSIR to explore possibilities.

The South Africans showed considerable interest in my design and their interest was not limited to military reconnaissance. The concept seemed ideal for police surveillance work as well. I was shown a gyrocopter that had been built with the express intention of testing CSIR's developmental work in carbon-fibre rotor blades. The gyrocopter had an ideal cabin with good visual freedom and, if fitted with a paddle-bladed propeller and muffled exhausts, it seemed to be the answer to my dreams. However, this machine was not ready for flight-testing because the prototype rotor blades were not yet completed. Because the gyrocopter would not be ready for many months, I was invited to look through *Jane's Book of Aircraft* to see if there was any machine in it that might fit the bill.

I went right through the book and pointed out a Canadian experimental aircraft called Patchen Explorer. I thought nothing more of this until the one and only Patchen Explorer was purchased by South Africa. SAAF Captains Dean and Rawston flew this machine, bearing South African registration ZG-UGF, to Rhodesia for me to assess. Being a slow aircraft, it took them five hours to fly from Pretoria to Salisbury. They then continued on to Centenary to meet up with me.

My first trial flight was made with Captain Dean. It was immediately obvious that the side-by-side seating arrangement was not ideal but, otherwise, the visual freedom was really good. The real problem with the Patchen Explorer, apart from being very noisy, was the amount of physical effort required to handle it. After two hours I was quite exhausted and happy to get back on the ground.

The next day I flew with Captain Rawston and asked him to do the handling whilst I concentrated on the visual aspects. From this I concluded that, with servo-assisted controls and modifications to quieten the power unit, the Patchen Explorer had real possibilities.

We landed at Everton Farm for lunch with Hamie Dax and his wife Petal. Hamie continued to be very successful with his recce work in spite of the severe visual restrictions imposed on him by his low-wing Comanche; hence my reason for dropping in to show him the Patchen Explorer.

After its return to Pretoria I heard no more until I learned that it now resides in the SAAF Museum at Swartkops, Pretoria.

War spreads and hots up

BY APRIL 1976, FIVE FIREFORCES were permanently deployed. Two of these continued to operate out of Mount Darwin and Mtoko, as before. Two had been established in the new Op Thrasher area, operating from Grand Reef (FAF 8) near Umtali and Chipinga (FAF 6) near the southern end of the eastern mountain range. The fifth force was based at Buffalo Range (FAF 7) serving newly established Op Repulse in the southeast. Some time later, FAF 9 was established at Rutenga when another Fireforce came into being. Whereas the Hurricane and Repulse forces comprised a K-Car and four G-Cars each, Thrasher had been allocated two K-Cars but only four troopers for use as OC Air Detachment Thrasher deemed fit. Consequently the Grand Reef and Chipinga Fireforces were two troopers below strength, except on those occasions when the two forces came together.

Wing Commander Roy Morris commanded Air Detachment Thrasher initially and was relieved by Squadron Leader Cyril White, after he relinquished command of 4 Squadron to Squadron Leader Dag Jones. Wing Commander Rob Gaunt had been the first commander of Air Detachment Repulse but was replaced by Wing Commander Tol Janeke in August. Tol's proven successes during his time at Mount Darwin were needed in what was considered to be the most critical of all the operational areas. This was because Rhodesia's road and rail lifelines to South Africa, running through the Op Repulse area, were known to be ZANLA's top priority targets.

Op Hurricane Fireforces were being employed on a daily basis, whereas within the Thrasher and Repulse areas the forces were used less frequently in the first half of 1976. This was partly due to the terrain and more so because the CT groups were still trying to establish themselves amongst the local population.

Consequently, almost all of the early contacts in Thrasher and Repulse occurred along the border with Mozambique and, initially, succeeded in severely hampering ZANLA planning.

At that time ZIPRA's long-term intentions were not known. It was clear, however, that it was preparing a large conventional army and only committing small irregular units into the Op Tangent and Splinter areas to keep the Frontline States happy. It was presumed that ZIPRA's long-term objectives were to let ZANLA take a beating whilst wearing down the RSF. It would then launch massive effort against Rhodesia, and probably more so against ZANLA. Whatever ZIPRA's true intentions, Rhodesia would have been stretched beyond limit had ZIPRA come over in strength at the same time as ZANLA, because ZANLA alone was tying up most of our air and ground effort. No 7 Squadron faced many difficulties in providing helicopters and crews to the Hurricane, Thrasher and Repulse areas. There were also others needed to support lower-intensity operations against ZIPRA in the Op Splinter (Kariba Lake), Op Tangent (western border and western Zambezi River) plus Op Grapple (Midlands area).

Harold Griffiths commanded a squadron that was four times larger than a standard squadron. Although it was an Air HQ task to decide on the actual allocation of helicopters, Griff, his flight commanders and squadron warrant officer had to continuously juggle aircraft and crews to meet these allocations whilst also being committed to increased levels in major and minor servicing schedules and the repairing of battle damaged aircraft. At the same time they had to train new crews and maintain standards amongst the operational pilots and technicians who moved in and out daily. The very nature of operational flying invariably involved harsh handling which made it necessary to re-hone pilot and technician skills every time they returned to base.

Seldom did a day go by when 7 Squadron did not have to re-plan for unexpected issues such as wounded aircrew and aircraft damage. There was always a need for some immediate remedial action to be taken. For Griff and his senior men there was such high stress at base that they looked forward to their own field deployments that, though loaded with periods of extreme tension and danger, afforded them some degree of respite.

The jet and transport squadrons were regular-sized units and their personnel for the most part were base-bound, so they did not suffer the high stresses of the bush squadrons. Like 7 Squadron, 4 Squadron's crews spent most of their time in the operational areas but their problems were of a different nature. 4 Squadron's greatest difficulty was the never-ending loss of experienced pilots and technicians to meet increasing needs for helicopter crews. With each crop of brand-new pilots off training, 4 Squadron had virtually no chance of providing adequate guidance to youngsters by seasoned operators. In fact, 4 Squadron was sometimes so short of aircrew that retired officers, unkindly referred to as 'retread pilots', were re-called to duty to make up numbers in the field. The retired officers I remember operating Lynx included Group Captain Charles Paxton, Wing Commander John Mussell, Squadron Leader Mike Saunders, Flight Lieutenant Dickie Dives and even Squadron Leader Ted Brent was borrowed from 5 Squadron for a while. Flight Lieutenant Don Northcroft (Sword of Honour student of No 19 PTC) who was a bright gentle-natured man had returned to farming was another of the retread pilots until a gang of CTs gunned him down whilst he was inspecting his lands.

It was at about this time that the members of my training course, 10 SSU, came together for a re-union party. Unfortunately Gordon and Faith Wright chose not to attend, whereas Ian and Helena Ferguson took the trouble to leave their farming business and drive seven hours to be with us. It was a very happy occasion in spite of all the troubles that surrounded us.

Ian and Helena Ferguson, Dave and Val Thorne, Ian and Priscilla Law, Keith and Sue Corrans, Murray and Muriel Hofmeyr, Bill and Maureen Galloway, John and Jill Barnes and Peter and Beryl PB.

SO Plans

IN MARCH 1976, I WAS promoted to the rank of wing commander in the Air Staff post of Staff Officer Planning. Air Marshal Mick McLaren as Commander of the Air Force altered the terms of reference for this post to allow me to assume responsibility for all Air Force projects and to commence the weapons development work I had been pressing for over the years.

So Plans was the only post in the Air Force that allowed the incumbent officer direct access to the Commander without the approval of DG Ops and the Chief of Air Staff. Though this was very useful, I never once used the privilege without first advising Air Vice-Marshal Frank Mussell or Air Commodore Chris Dams about the project details I needed to discuss with the Commander. I will discuss the project work shortly because it was delayed a while.

In June I was pulled away from my post to assist 4 Squadron, yet again, with recce training. I was very put out by this as I had spent more than fourteen months in the field during my eighteen months as Ops I in Air Staff. Fortunately Cocky Benecke was made available to cut down on training time and advantage was taken of my presence at Mount Darwin to allow OC FAF 4 to take some well-earned leave.

Recce pilots training June 1976: From left: (First individual—see note below), OC 4 Sqn Dag Jones leaning on prop boss, PB, Francois du Toit (downed by FRELIMO—Allouette), 'Starry' Stevens (downed by FRELIMO—Lynx), Cocky Benecke, Flt Cdr 4 Sqn John Bennie. The first individual in this photo confuses me. It looks like Brian Murdoch, but he was killed in December 1974. Note— Lynx not yet fitted with guns and mortar net over revetments (to be discussed later).

This period of training was for the new OC 4 Squadron and some of his pilots. It was also my first experience in teaching from the rear seat so that I could see ground on Dag Jones's side of the aircraft. During our second sortie on 11 June 1976 we were aerial-tracking a strong trail that led us to a brand-new CT camp. We immediately called for a depleted Fireforce of K-Car plus two G-Cars. Being passenger caused me to see the action from a new perspective that turned out to be very useful for reasons still clear in my mind.

Firstly, I had not seen a fresh base for a long time. Secondly I could see that, as in many actions past, there were insufficient troops immediately available to Kip Donald, the RLI Fireforce commander. I knew there were plenty of troops available at Mount Darwin and that a Dakota, then available on the ground at FAF 4, could have brought them across at the same time that the helicopters arrived; but none of these troops was para-trained.

The third point of importance came from my direct observation of Frantan effects at the moment of ignition. All of my many Frantan attacks had been from Provosts whose wings disallowed observation of weapon effects at the moment of impact. Now I saw one Frantan spew flaming gel at forty-five degrees to flight line thereby missing two CT's I saw so clearly. The second Frantan did a similar action but actually killed one CT that I had not seen at all. I realise immediately that steel construction and the container's impact orientation were the reasons for haphazard distribution of flame. I vowed to myself that I would do something about producing highly frangible units that were both stable and aimable.

The CTs had chosen a site in thick but narrow riverine bush with open grasslands all around, except at one end where a sparsely wooded ridge met up with the bush. In the dry season, the CTs would only have had the ridge as an escape route but, because of late rains in 1976, the grass was still high and green and severely impeded the forward-visibility to the soldiers on the ground. With too few troops, Kipper Donald forced the pace of his troops, resulting in the wounding of one of his men in the first contact before the responsible CT was dispatched.

In this action, as with so many others, it was obvious that there was need for more troops to be immediately available in the vital period. With limited helicopter availability, this could only be achieved if Fireforces included paratroopers in an accompanying Dakota. In this particular contact, Kipper Donald could have used paratroopers the moment the CTs' presence had been confirmed. This would have prevented six CTs crawling away through the long grass. When I took the idea of a para-trooping Dakota with each Fireforce to Air HQ, Group Captain Norman Walsh told me that, having been approached with the same idea by Army HQ, he was actively attending to the matter. In fact the RLI had already commenced paratrooper training. This was good news indeed.

Alouettes trooping.

Operation Sand

IN A TOP-SECRET EXCHANGE (Operation Sand), Rhodesian Air Force instructors, technicians and students were attached to the South African Air Force. This was necessary because our ageing Vampires could not keep up with the production of new pilots. Flying training on Impala jets was conducted at Langebaan Air Base and later in Durban. This was a quid pro quo exchange for our training needs and for operational experience needed by SAAF helicopter crews. At the time we also manned one entire SAAF Mirage lll squadron in another top-secret arrangement.

Flt Lt Ricky Culpan.

Although I was aware of this and had met some of the personnel during my many visits to CSIR in Pretoria, it is surprising how little I knew about the reasons and objectives involved. They might even have been preparing for the on-take of Mirages by our own Air Force but no questions were asked and no information was given. 'Top Secret' meant exactly what it implied and to this day I do not know the answers. But, from one senior SAAF officer I later learned something that really intrigued me. Unfortunately the Rhodesian jet pilot involved in this story died in an air accident before I could verify what I now record.

It was Flight Lieutenant Ricky Culpan who was very disappointed by Mirage III air-to-air gunnery results. Ricky was not content to accept that such a sophisticated aircraft could be equipped with an air-to-air aiming system that gave excellent pilots very poor results. To cut a long story short, I understand that he came to the conclusion that an essential component of information was missing and had to be introduced into the software of the gunsight's computer system. This was the precise angle between the gun-line and the airflow that, in the case of this delta-wing fighter, varied more than in conventional fighter designs. The actual airflow angle had to be provided by an externally mounted vane.

How Ricky got through the 'red-tape' at SAAF HQ I do not know, but permission appears to have been given to fit this sensor vane on a Mirage III airframe and link it to the sighting computer. An acquaintance of Ricky's, who I was told was a fundi in computer software, upgraded the gunsight's computer programme by integrating the sensor vane's input. This resulted in a manyfold improvement in air-to-air gunnery results.

By recording this story I hope one day to receive confirmation of it because it places my one-time neighbour in Thornhill Married Quarters, Ricky Culpan, on a higher level of imagination and determination than I thought he possessed.

Diverse personalities and different situations

BY MID–1976 ALL THE FIREFORCES were engaged daily in a variety of actions against ZANLA. Some actions were very successful and others drew blanks. There were so many individuals involved, and the actions so widespread and diverse in nature, that it is impossible to give a chronological sequence of events or provide a concise picture of the happenings in each area. By this time ZANLA had extended operations from the northeast all the way down the eastern side of Rhodesia to the South African border.

I have taken a very small sample of events during 1976 in each area and have focused on three individuals having different ranks and operational functions. One was a commander on the ground, one flew helicopters and one flew Lynx.

My selected individuals are Tol Janeke, Mike Borlace and Cocky Benecke. The first two individuals might not have been first choice for many but almost every Rhodesian serviceman would have selected Cocky.

All helicopter aircrew were top-line operators; too many to mention personally. However, one pilot's name kept coming to the fore and would remain there for some time. Many of the helicopter technician-gunners loved to fly with him whilst others considered him too bloody dangerous. Nevertheless, Flight Lieutenant Mike Borlace, who has already featured in other actions described in this book, recorded his seventh ASR as K-Car pilot in the Op Thrasher area at the beginning of June. His gunner was Sergeant Henry Jarvie, a clown when occasion permitted, who was deadly serious in his duties.

Due to the decision to have two Fireforces, one at Grand Reef and the other at Chipinga, Mike had only two troopers carrying eight soldiers, plus a supporting Lynx. He was called upon to take on a group of CTs reported to be resting by a small stream. The soldiers were inexperienced in Fireforce operations and did not have their own officer airborne; not that this mattered because K-Car pilots had so often proven that their abilities were equal to the best of RLI commanders.

Air Lieutenant Chris Dickinson (M8 Black Lead) had Sergeant Phil Tubbs as his gunner. Air Lieutenant Atkinson (V8 Black 2) and his gunner Sergeant Griffen, were both Op

Polo men. Air Sub-Lieutenant Ray Bolton (M4) flew the Lynx. In his ASR Mike used # in lieu of the usual c/s and # Sparrow 1 was a tracker callsign.

Mike's ASR reads:

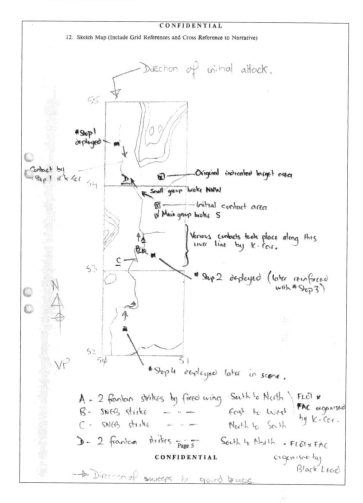

As there was no airborne army commander, Black section & Stops 1 & 2 were briefed by K-Car pilot on the basis of the information received from the informant. It appeared from a study of the map that there were two likely escape routes from the indicated area; accordingly it was decided to run in low-level along the Mupudzi River and into the target area from the NNW, Black 2 being briefed to deploy # Stop 1 in the areas VP504545 and Black Lead in the area VP507533 with no further direction from K-Car.

We ran in as briefed with K-Car two minutes ahead of Black section pulling up to orbit the target area at 1508B. On our second orbit we observed in the area VP508537 a group estimated as 20 terrorists, armed and dressed in a semi-uniform garb generally blue or black trousers & a green top shirt.

Sgt Jarvie was visual with the target(s) & was briefed to fire at targets of his own choosing. Very accurate fire was brought to bear and the ters were seen to start moving around at high speed in great confusion.

The group broke into two parts, the majority breaking along the river line to the south & a smaller group along the river line to the NNW.

I instructed Black section to engage the northern group & continued engaging the main group with K-Car. Sgt. Jarvie was bringing very accurate fire to bear & several characters were being knocked down.

Stop 2 were warned that business was coming their way & when they were visual with the ters were able to bring fire to bear that caused the ters to go to ground. As things were stabilising I sent Black 2 for reinforcing sticks & Black Lead for ammunition. Conversation with # Stop 2 resulted in them marking a target for K-Car. A further series of brief but final contacts ensued.

Stop 2 were reinforced with # Stop 3 & # Stop 4 were deployed in the area VP 504525. # Stop 1 was instructed to start sweeping south towards the original contact area. They soon encountered ters who were trying to ease their way northwards & a brief contact ensued before K-Car became visual with the ters & engaged them which resulted in a couple more characters falling down.

At this stage K-Car was out of ammunition, but M4, previously requested, was running into the area.

Before moving # Stops 2,3 & 4, I wanted a couple of areas softened & directed M4 in a series of strikes, using Frantan in two South to North attacks onto a bush area in the river line at VP506534, a Sneb rocket attack East to West into bush area in the river line at VP505533 and a Sneb rocket attack North to south into bush area in the river line at VP505532.

Airborne control was handed over to Black Lead whilst K-Car departed to refuel & rearm.

At 1710B, before K-Car returned, Black 2 was directed to recover bodies adjacent to # Stop 1's position at VP505539 and was shot at by ters who were also adjacent, resulting in a gunshot wound to the gunner & extensive damage to the aircraft which exited the area to our refuelling point nearby from where it will be recovered by road. As Black Lead had the picture of the scene airborne control of M4 was left to him to direct two Frantan strikes delivered south to North on the area VP 505539 before K-Car resumed airborne control. Before the strikes were delivered, # Stop 1 had been removed to a safe position & FLOT indicated to M4 by orange smoke.

As conditions were now becoming fairly dark M4 was dispatched home, a quick ammunition supply for the ground troops was arranged, # Stops 1,2,3, & 4 were joined up in the area VP 506538 & told to arrange ambush positions, & # Sparrow 1 were deployed in the original contact area & told to ambush there for the night. Sweeping operations will commence at first light tomorrow.

Please note that trying to operate a 'fire force' of two troopers is probably going to cause severe casualties to security forces before long.

Thirteen CTs were killed in this action, two of which were accounted for by the ground troops. Had there been more soldiers available to Borlace in the opening minutes the CTs would have fared even worse than they did. Notice that Mike

This photo of Mike Borlace was taken at his investiture for the Silver Cross of Rhodesia, awarded him for bravery in a number of actions.

said CTs were wearing "a green top shirt". Under that would have been more shirts to facilitate change of visual appearance and identification.

A week later, Mike Borlace, flying K-Car with Henry Jarvie, ran into heavy fire. This occurred in an action that was so close to the Mozambican border that at times the Fireforce, and a pair of Hunters which came to assist, had fire brought to bear on them by FRELIMO forces firing from a store across the border.

Part of Mike's ASR reads, *We came under substantial automatic small arms fire which unfortunately smashed the sight glass of the 20mm cannon. K-Car pilot was visual with the ters who were running towards thick bush to the East. Without sighting information it was difficult for the gunner to bring the gun to bear, but several accurate bursts were delivered and one ter was seen to drop and stay down.*

Wing Commander Roy Morris, as OC Air Detachment Thrasher, revealed what Mike did not record in his pilot's report. Part of Roy's report reads, *Flt Lt Borlace's performance is to be commended. Although wounded in the left leg above the knee, at the very beginning of this action, he continued in the K-Car and directed Lynx and Hunter strikes with a great deal of efficiency. His dedication to duty is unquestionably praiseworthy. It took OC Air Det. Thrasher to finally go to RUDA and extricate Flt. Lt. Borlace from the damaged K-Car and organised Air Lt. Dickinson to take command.*

Eighteen months had elapsed since I left 4 Squadron; yet only Cocky Benecke remained when Dag Jones took over command from Cyril White. Although he clearly deserved a posting to helicopters, as had occurred with all of his PTC colleagues, Cocky had been left on 4 Squadron because his unique talents were best suited to fixed-wing operations. Funnily enough

Cocky was pleased with this. Because of the relatively low cost of flying light strike aircraft, Cocky felt he could pursue his talent and his desire for action just as far as his passion drove him. Again I say, "What a change in attitude from those days when I struggled to get him interested in recce."

The number of Fireforce successes directly attributable to 4 Squadron recce pilots, especially Cocky Benecke, was astounding. In spite of its limited strength in machines and operationally seasoned men, 4 Squadron was the most cost-effective military unit in Rhodesia. This statement in no way detracts from the undeniable potency of our squadrons, the SAS, Selous Scouts, RLI or any other unit. It simply conveys the undeniable fact that a small complement of pilots, ably supported by an equally small group of dedicated technicians, induced and participated effectively in more actions, pro rata, than any other Rhodesian unit.

Cocky displayed his talents, courage and aggressiveness for the umpteenth time in a lone action in the Op Repulse area. This occurred just after Tol Janeke was posted there. On 2 August 1976, Cocky was sent to provide top cover to c/s 143 of H Coy 1RR, a Territorial Army tracker unit, that was following blood-spoor from a contact with CTs earlier in the day.

Having established the position of the trackers and the direction in which the CTs were heading, Cocky commenced a recce forward of the troops over flat, featureless terrain. He soon found a group of people sitting under shade at the edge of a bushy patch that was set well away from local villages. It is unlikely that any other pilot would have seen them.

He was asking the trackers what colour clothing the CTs had been wearing when he came under fire and saw two CTs break from the group. Cocky attacked immediately and took them both out with rockets. Fire continued so he turned and attacked the main group that was breaking up. Having expended all rockets, Cocky still had one CT in sight.

Part of Cocky's ASR reads, *Owing to having no troops or aircraft to assist me, and my rockets were finished, I was not prepared to put my aircraft in a dangerous situation by attacking a lone ter who fired 4 standard magazines and one of tracer at me.*

Cocky was wise not to attack with Frantans as his aircraft was not fitted with machine-guns to give him covering fire, and there was no way of knowing if more CTs were still around. The fact that he could see, from height, precisely how many magazines of ammunition had been expended was yet another example of this man's intriguing talent.

I am convinced he was wounded and would not get too far. Had I had front guns to protect me, I would have been prepared to attack with Frantans.

Apart from four CTs killed, five females, hidden in the bush too close to the CTs, also died when Cocky made his second rocket attack. The loss of civilian lives in these circumstances, though deeply regretted, was inevitable when CTs failed to send women away before initiating offensive action. Happily, there were many other occasions where women saved themselves by moving into the open so that soldiers and airmen could identify them by dress. But even in these situations care had to be taken to ensure that they were not being used by CTs as human shields.

Continuing with Cocky for the moment. He was in the Hurricane area with me during my short stay at FAF 4. Whilst I was instructing Dag Jones, Cocky was also teaching recce to Bill Stevens. Day after day he had been leading successful Fireforce actions, one of which occurred so close to FAF 4 that it caused me, as acting OC FAF 4, to comment:

a. Excellent work by Benecke who was still wide-awake to the need to cover ground, even with wheels down on approach for landing. He was returning from an instructional sortie in recce for Air Lt. Stevens.

b. Of group strength 28–30 ters reported by Benecke only 3 were seen and contacted resulting in one killed and one captured wounded by K-Car fire. Though this was a disappointing score the close proximity of the action to FAF 4 assisted greatly in occupying the attention of the Prime Minister who was visiting JOC with the OCC.

K-Car pilots recorded most ASRs covering actions in which Cocky was involved. His own ASRs were therefore those in which Fireforce was not involved. His thirtieth ASR reports the situations arising from actions of 17 August 1976 when he was tasked to provide top cover to an Army tracker callsign of 2 Independent Company that was following fresh tracks of a large group of CTs that had broken through the Cordon Sanitaire minefield. Cocky's own callsign was H4 and Mike Delport, who was flying with him, was G4. His ASR reads:

H4 had been tasked to assist c/s 71G who was on tracks of approximately 50. G4 was in the aircraft with me as I intended to demonstrate aerial tracking to him. As we were approaching the callsign, I thought I had heard shots going past the aircraft. I turned around and G4 said he saw two figures running in a NE direction. Tracer was observed passing very close to the aircraft and c/s 71G confirmed that he could hear heavy firing. We then observed large explosions on the ground. There also appeared to be several flak bursts exploding underneath the aircraft. We were at approximately 1,500 feet AGL and the bursts were about 500 feet below us. I called for Fireforce and passed on a sitrep about the explosions and apparent flak bursts.

I then saw a ter running south down a path away from the explosions. I commenced a rocket attack on this ter. Heavy ground fire was experienced on numerous occasions but more so during this attack.

I then saw about 15 ters moving through some trees and commenced an attack. The rockets were on target and as I commenced a pull out I heard a loud bang and felt a strike on my left thigh.

I informed G4 who immediately took control of the aircraft whilst I inspected my thigh for damage.

We discovered that we had no aileron control and were in a severe yaw and rolling. G4 righted the aircraft with the use of rudders and we commenced a slow climb.

I then jettisoned the Frantans and the rocket carriers and carried out a quick inspection of the aircraft for damage.
The ailerons were both observed to be stuck in the upright position. G4 commenced a slow yawed turn towards Salisbury whilst settling elevator trim and power settings.
We informed Darwin of our predicament and intentions. A strong smell of fuel was experienced and we opened the DV panel and fed both motors from the starboard tank. At this stage we had full left trim and a fair amount of rudder to remain wings level. G4 had control of the aircraft so I left him to continue the flight.
As we approached Salisbury I noticed a large amount of fuel on the floor and discovered the fuel leak to be right next to where I was sitting. I extracted the fire extinguisher and moved into the back seat so as to be able to direct the fire extinguisher onto the fuel in case of fire and rearranged loose articles in the rear of the cabin.
A perfect landing, under the circumstances, was carried out by G4 and the motors were closed down immediately after touch down together with mags and all electrics. We abandoned the aircraft as the fire-fighting crew arrived on the scene.

Cocky was lucky to have only been badly bruised by a chuck of airframe debris from a heavy-calibre bullet strike, and Mike Delport did a great job in getting the aircraft back to Salisbury.

Because of the long distance involved, Fireforce arrived a long time after Cocky and Mike had cleared target. Two trooper helicopters took hits that resulted in the death of Corporal Titlestad and continuous fire from a heavy machine-gun relentlessly followed the K-Car flown by Flight Lieutenant Terence Murphy (ex-British Marines helicopter pilot) but without scoring any hits. Due to fading light and some confusion caused by many widely spread enemy firing positions with troops in between, K-Car was reluctant to bring down any air attacks and the airborne commander, OC Support Commando RLI, had no choice but to issue orders for night ambushes.

Although there were no proven kills, this operation happened to be very successful because the CTs lost everything but their personal weapons. The group of about fifty had come in with a large re-supply of equipment which included an STM heavy machine-gun, a type 56 recoilless rifle, RPG launchers with many rockets, TM46 landmines and piles of 7.62mm ammunition; all of which was added to Rhodesia's growing supply of captured equipment.

The reason for the ground explosions and apparent flak bursts that Cocky reported was explained by the discovery and capture of 'air ambush' (CT term) equipment. The CT group had come into Rhodesia with their new 'air ambush' weapon system that they had confidently rigged to protect their re-supply equipment against air attack. It consisted of many TNT charges planted in small holes in the ground with a stick grenade placed above each charge with its firing pin tethered to a ground peg. The TNT and stick grenade combinations were set in clusters, each cluster being linked by Cordtex to be fired simultaneously. Upon firing each cluster of TNT (the ground explosions Cocky reported) the stick grenades were propelled vertically to withdraw firing pins and detonated four seconds later at around 1,000 feet above ground (the suspected flak).

Having lost all of their 'air ambush' equipment during their very first day in the country, the CTs must have lost confidence in the system because I cannot recall another incident of this type inside Rhodesia. Occasionally they were employed in Mozambique. Long before this incident, I had read of an anti-aircraft system, which Mao Tse Tung developed and named 'ground cannon'. Later I will discuss my own tests of this crazy, crude and effective system.

Down in the southeast, on 27 August, a Grey's Scouts callsign on horseback was following tracks of a large group heading straight for the Mozambican border. Tol Janeke called upon the Chiredzi Fireforce to join up with his Repulse Fireforce and placed the joint force close to the area of anticipated action.

Tol amalgamated forces whenever he judged it necessary, which is why in my opinion he was a particularly successful field commander. Every officer had been taught the 'Ten Principles of War'; one of which is the all-important need for concentration of forces. Few heeded this in the great spread of activities where too few aircraft were called upon to meet too many needs. Tol not only practised this principle, he ensured that the concentrated force was correctly placed for immediate use.

In this particular case, two K-Cars, six G-Cars and two Lynx moved to c/s 24B, who reported that he was two hours behind the CTs. Flight Lieutenant Ginger Baldwin, flying lead K-Car, was surprised by the speed at which c/s 24B was covering ground on horseback. He knew the Fireforce troops could not possibly keep up with them and, since there was no fuel close at hand, decided to land the helicopters and await developments. The two Lynx loitered over the helicopters and maintained communications with 24B.

The horses were watered at a pan where c/s 24B reported twenty-nine CTs had been at water's edge about one hour earlier. Noting how far this pan was from a game fence that lay beyond, Ginger decided to deploy two stop groups to the fence on the line of movement. This had only just been done when 24B called contact. The Fireforce was over the CTs shortly afterwards and learned that one of 24B's men had been killed during the engagement.

Ginger described the ground over which most of the aircraft took on groups of bomb-shelling CTs as "... so flat and vegetation so uniform that it was impossible to pinpoint a specific point."

Tol's comments on the ASR were:

(1) The FAF 9 Lynx, K-Car and G-cars were positioned with the FAF 7 Fireforce when the follow-up started. This resulted in a

combined effort of 2 Lynx, 2 K-Cars and 6 G-Cars being brought to bear when contact was made.

(2) The final count was 40 killed and 13 wounded captured, 8 with weapons. Intelligence has confirmed that 10 ters were escorting 97 recruits to Mozambique for a week of training before returning to Rhodesia with weapons. This contact will no doubt discourage recruits from willingly joining the ters.

(3) It would have been almost impossible to tell who was a terrorist and who a recruit once contact had been made, particularly as the MIU rifleman was killed in the initial engagement.

From our point of view, any man who would be returning to the country trained and armed within a few days, was a CT already.

Chapter

8

Project Alpha

FOR MANY YEARS I HAD questioned the effectiveness of conventional bombs and rockets. Earliest doubts about the efficiency of cylindrical-shaped bombs and warheads were confirmed when I studied their effects at the conclusion of the big Air Force Weapons Display at Kutanga Range twelve years earlier, back in 1964.

Senior officers had laughed off these concerns because they had used the weapons during WWII and had nothing but praise for their efficiency. In fact one very senior WWII officer asked, "What gives a young puppy like you the right to question proven weapons?"

Whilst agreeing that they were well suited to many of the situations for which they had been designed, I was unable to convince my seniors that these same weapons were totally unsuited to counter-insurgency bush warfare. During my FAC work with jets, I watched many strikes but these only reinforced my lack of faith in both imported and homemade bombs.

For over eighteen months Canberras had been limited to using 250-pound, 500-pound and 1,000-pound bombs, none of which was effective and they all involved unacceptably high expenditure of valuable foreign currency. Everything pointed to a need for a drastic change to provide Canberras a safe and effective anti-personnel strike capability.

Although work had continued in an ongoing effort to sort out the 28-pound fragmentation bomb problem that led to the destruction of a Canberra, this weapon system could only be employed with any degree of accuracy inside the Strela missile and anti-aircraft gun envelopes. This in itself was unacceptable, but the thin line of widely spread, puny detonations running through any target was also unacceptable. What we needed was an anti-personnel weapons system that would give a Canberra clout to match its load carrying potential. For safety reasons

alone, such a system had to allow Canberras to fly over the most hostile of targets below 500 feet at speeds exceeding 280 knots. If this attack profile could be achieved, it would render Strela harmless and would also substantially reduce threats from manually operated guns.

I was certain we needed a system based on large numbers of small bomblets that could be induced to spread laterally in a wide carpet over an effective strike length of at least 800 metres. Each bomblet would have to retard very rapidly to be well behind the aircraft at the moment of detonation. And, of paramount importance, each detonation had to occur above ground to ensure that shrapnel reached an enemy hiding in ground recesses and trenches.

Having read about the USAAF's use of solid steel ball bearings to flatten sizeable sections of jungle in Vietnam, I became interested in the idea of producing spherical bomblets. High-speed, low-level deliveries of enormous quantities of three-inch steel balls released from Phantom jets had been used to clear thick jungle vegetation. What really caught my eye in the USAAF article was the fact that balls spread themselves laterally during their short flight to ground.

One foundry in Salisbury and another in Bulawayo produced thousands of round balls for me. Because I was in a hurry and needed to keep costs down, the lead balls they manufactured were crudely made. The bag and string system I employed to release clusters of two-inch and three-inch lead balls from a Canberra, flying at 300 knots at 500 feet, was just as crude. No wonder the Canberra crews were not at all impressed with 'PB playing high-speed marbles' but I needed, and got, answers from the drop tests. Firstly, it was clear that turbulence from leading balls forced those following in their wake to move sideways. Instead of striking ground in a straight thin line, a random scattering of both two-inch and three-inch lead balls occurred along the attack-line; some as far as forty metres either side of centre. Secondly, the balls left long grooves in the Kutanga Range sandveld but every one of them lifted back into flight and thirdly, the balls retained lethal velocity way beyond first contact with ground.

Squadron Leader Ken Gibson.

I was encouraged by these results and was considering where to go from there when providence took a hand. Senior Staff Officer Air Armaments, Squadron Leader Ron Dyer, was my right-hand man in all air weapons projects. Immediately after our crude tests he brought his predecessor, retired Squadron Leader Ken Gibson, to see me in my office Ken was then working for the engineering firm that manufactured our locally designed bombs and Frantans. Because he knew something of what Ron Dyer and I were doing, Ken had come to Air HQ to give us wonderful news.

An engineer who had recently joined the company was studying the 28-pound fragmentation bomb problems with the managing director of the company who had designed the system in the first place. The specific problem they were studying concerned safety of nose fuses which, though designed to activate bombs just above ground level, had been responsible for the premature detonation that killed two officers and destroyed a Canberra.

Ken told us that when the new engineer learned of the importance of airburst, he said it might be easier and safer to produce round bombs that would find ground level for themselves. The ground impact would initiate a delay fuse as the bomb bounced back into flight to detonation at a chosen height, just as we had been considering. Ken Gibson could not have brought better news and I set off immediately with Ron to visit the company.

For convenience the managing director of the company, whom I had know for some years, will be referred to as Denzil and the man with the new ideas, Bev. We were introduced to Bev whom I took to immediately. We had a long discussion during which he said the bouncing-bomb idea was no more than that—just an idea. I told him why I favoured this approach and why I had been testing spheres to facilitate low, safe and accurate delivery with maximum lateral distribution. Since Bev had no experience with bombs or bombing and did not know any of the inherent dangers involved, he needed to learn about the operational requirements for the Canberra, as I saw them. I told him of my experiences and the reasons I wanted to move away from conventional bombs.

Explanation was given as to why cylindrical bombs suffered too many weaknesses in bush warfare situations. The primary weakness of cylindrical bombs and warheads is that, when they burst, shrapnel is driven out at ninety degrees to their longitudinal axis. To be wholly efficient against enemy personnel, a cylindrical bomb needs to be about six feet above ground and vertically oriented at the moment of detonation, but even when dropping bombs from very high levels the vertical attitude cannot be achieved and accuracy is poor.

If the same detonation occurs when the bomb is horizontal, it is at its least efficient angle because only a narrow band of shrapnel strikes ground at ninety degrees to the bomb's longitudinal axis. The remaining 95% of the ground around the bomb is unaffected; yet paradoxically this is the situation that occurs when bombs are dropped at low level to ensure high accuracy.

Being streamlined, bombs descend directly under the delivering aircraft until they have fallen some 2,000 feet clear. Thereafter drag and the progressive nose-down pitch cause

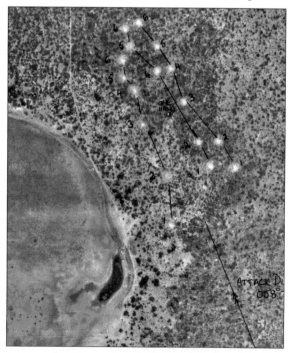

This photograph shows a total of seventeen 500-pound bombs dropped by three Canberras. Note the huge gaps of 'safe ground' between the strikes.

bombs to slowly trail behind the bomber. But a safe separation height can never be less than 2,000 feet to avoid damage, and even destruction, from large weapons detonating directly below the delivering aircraft.

In our case this meant that, for accuracy to be assured, the Canberras would have to pass over target in perfect range of missiles and guns. The alternative was to bomb from great height and accept both loss of accuracy and the fact that cloud could limit windows of opportunity for strikes. Neither of these situations was acceptable. Another unacceptable issue, no matter the bombing height, was that large gaps in a string of bombs left too much ground uncovered.

An inherent problem with conventional bomb design is the need for tail cones and stabiliser fins that are costly and occupy potentially useful space in a bomb bay. Spherical bombs are quite different. They do not poses wasteful appendages, nor do they suffer orientation problems. A spherical bomb bursting above ground will consistently deliver shrapnel through 360 degrees in all directions but always lose half into the air.

Delivered in clusters, spherical bomblets moving through air at high speed create high-turbulence wakes that induces lateral movement to following bomblets. Moreover, high drag on every bomblet causes rapid deceleration from the moment of release. Another important advantage is the natural tendency of round bombs striking the ground at shallow angles to skip back into flight, making airburst possible. Admiral Nelson used this principle to good effect against enemy ships by skipping round cannon shell off water to improve the chance of gaining waterline damage.

Having understood these explanations, Denzil and Bev were eager to assist us develop a spherical cluster-bomb system for Canberras because it was agreed that such a system was within the technical competence and capacity of the company. Denzil kindly undertook the initial research work at his company's expense and I opened a project file marked 'Project Alpha'. Projects that followed were Projects Bravo, Charlie, Delta, etc.

Bev considered it necessary to use a central spherical bomb-core fashioned from 8mm steel plate to house the explosive charge and a multi-directional delay-fuse. This fuse would initiate a pyrotechnic delay-train and without regard to the orientation of a bomblet when it struck ground. The central core was to be encased within a larger 3mm steel sphere with many super-rubber balls tightly packed between the inner and outer casing.

The purpose of super-rubber balls was to allow the inner core to compress them on impact with ground, thereby creating a latent energy source that would enhance a round bomblet's natural tendency to bounce into flight. At the time we did not see that the rubber interface would be giving bomblets vitally important secondary characteristics. One was an inherent ability to absorb sharp shock loads on the fuse if a bomblet was inadvertently dropped onto concrete during handling and loading.

A variety of tests were conducted to prove prototype bomblets' ability to recover off ground even when dropped vertically from a helicopter at great height. When we were certain we had a worthwhile project on our hands, I went to the Air Force Commander's office late one afternoon with an eight-inch bomblet in my hands.

Having explained the design, I held the ball at waist height and asked Air Marshal McLaren to watch how the bomb recovered into the air after impacting the ground, whereupon I released the ball onto his office carpet. His reaction to the metallic clang was not what I expected and I do not think he even noticed the bounce. "Get that confounded object out of this office. You have six weeks in which to produce your system for full load strikes by four Canberras." I was astounded by such a quick decision and said, "Sir, there is no money budgeted to meet your instruction!"

Mick McLaren was known for his ability to come to quick decisions. His reply was typical. "You concern yourself with technical matters and I will take care of the money. I am counting on you for success. You have six weeks to do the job, so get cracking!"

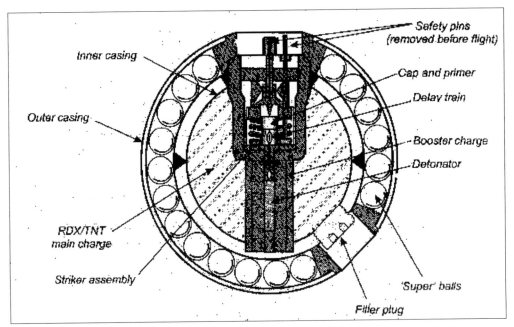

Schematic diagram of the Alpha bomb.

Air Marshal McLaren was the first Air Force Commander not to have serviced in WWll, so he had a flexible attitude towards weapons in general. He had studied every ASR and had called for detailed post-operational studies of Canberra bombing effects following a number of strikes in a variety of bush conditions. I was not involved in any of these studies but had read every report. None that he received gave the Commander any reason to be satisfied with cylindrical bomb efficiency. Without him actually admitting it, he agreed with what I had been saying for many months and obviously liked the spherical bomblet concept as the means by which to make his Canberra fleet effective. I suspect that Group Captain Norman Walsh may have had a hand in influencing the Commander's opinion on the need for a cluster-bomb system.

I made a telephone call to Denzil and told him we had 'green light' on the Alpha Project and that Ron and I would be around to see him immediately. Denzil and Bev were waiting for us in the company boardroom together with the company's accountant and a third engineer. Our excitement was somewhat tempered by the realisation that a project of this nature, if undertaken in the USA, would require many millions of dollars, involve many engineers and would take no less than five years to complete.

With only six weeks to finalise research and development and produce four complete carriage and release systems along with hundreds of bomblets, it was obvious we had to make final but correct decisions right away. Denzil did some preliminary calculations that made it clear that cutting of metal had to start next day. In turn this meant we had to finalise the specific dimensions of both inner and outer casings at this very meeting so that preparation for half-sphere presses could be initiated that night.

Canberra bomb-bay drawings were spread out on the boardroom table to confirm preliminary designs generated during our earlier work. I had to specify the number of bomblets in a single load so that Denzil and Bev could calculate final bomblet dimensions. For convenience we had already started referring to the bomblets as Alpha bombs (Project Alpha) and I gave the operational requirement as 400 Alpha bombs to be released from eight independent containers, which we named 'hoppers'.

The engineers quickly sketched profiles of four units comprising two hoppers each to establish the internal volume of each hopper. Having done this, they established that the external diameter of each Alpha bomb would be 155mm. From this the size of the rubber balls and inner bomb core were also determined.

The very next day preparations were in hand to press the metal blanks into half spheres. By Day Three the welding of half-spheres for inner cores and outer casings was already under way. The first hundred outer casings were taken off-line and filled with concrete for initial proving trials.

At New Sarum Warrant Officer John Cubbitt had his Drawing Office staff busy finalising the hoppers design and within two days Station Workshops were fabricating prototypes for preliminary drop trials of the concrete-filled Alpha bomblets. The concrete units approximated very closely to the calculated final weight of explosive ones.

At my insistence flight trials commenced with the fitment of a camera into a Canberra bomb bay to record the release characteristics of the old 28-pound bombs from the 'bomb box' unit. The bombs we used were practice units that had the same shape and ballistic characteristics as live ones. Two full-load tests of ninety-six bombs each were made. In addition to the bomb-bay camera, each drop trial was filmed from a formating Vampire.

What we saw was very disturbing. Bombs exiting the bomb box into the very high turbulent airflow, particularly at the rear of the bomb bay, gyrated, tumbled and jostled with each other. Some bombs were even blown back into their compartments before emerging again to join other wildly twirling and twisting bombs. Why film recordings such as these had not been made and studied previously, I cannot say; but it made us realise that the Board of inquiry into the Canberra disaster had not come up with the correct reason for the premature detonation that destroyed the Canberra.

First drop tests of the Alpha bombs were recorded in the same way and we were delighted to see how cleanly they dropped away and how rapidly they spread out and trailed back from the aircraft. Because the concrete Alphas suffered little damage on impact, we were able to gather them up for repeat drop trials, including releases at low level. All low-level runs were filmed from the bomb bay, by a chase Vampire and from the ground. The results were very encouraging. Impact with the ground was occurring well behind the aircraft, lateral spread was better than expected and every unit skipped back into flight.

Bev had designed and produced a small number of multi-directional fuses for first non-explosive trials. Our first live trial only involved five Alphas fitted with delay fuses amongst concrete units. No explosive was included to allow post-strike inspection of each fuse. Two of these fired instantly on impact with the ground, two functioned correctly and one failed to fire. Inspection of the latter showed that the initiating cap had fired but the delay link failed to transfer to the detonator cap. In the case of the two instantaneous bursts, initiating caps' flame had flashed past the delay links directly to the detonator caps.

Modifications and rectification followed rapidly and we were soon testing whole clusters of Alphas charged with explosive. During this time we established that the Alpha bomblets exhibited two unexpected but highly desirable characteristics due to the rubber balls interface. The first was discovered when one bomblet had been deliberately detonated in the midst of a pyramid of unexploded bomblets (UXBs). It failed to cause a sympathetic detonation of any of the other bomblets as occurs with other explosive units—our problem was to find the widely scattered survivors for independent destruction. The second peculiarity was that we were finding hundreds of thin 20mm-round shrapnel pieces that propelled like spinning saws and sliced their way into the hardest of trees. Formed by the 147 rubber balls that pressed out discs from the outer casing they spun like crazy saws aligned with their direction of flight.

By the seventh week, one week behind schedule, the engineers were totally exhausted from their intense work schedule and many sleepless nights. However, we were ready to demonstrate to the Air Staff a full-scale Alpha strike on a 1,200 x 200-metre target that had been prepared by the Range Warden, 'Kutanga Mac'. Hundreds of cardboard and steel targets were set above ground and in trenches throughout the length and breadth of the target.

OC 5 Squadron, Randy du Rand, had not been too interested in our work at the start of Project Alpha, probably the consequence of my early tests with lead balls. However, once the project started to show positive results, nobody could have given greater support and assistance to the project team than Randy.

The Commander and his senior staff officers flew to Kutanga Range to witness the demonstration and see for themselves if the Alpha system was ready for 'the real thing'. The project team had witnessed many trials but this was to be the first full-scale drop. We had reduced the original 400 Alphas per Canberra load down to 300 to facilitate easy loading and because we had come to realise that the reduced load covered a greater strike length than the original 800 metres we had set for ourselves. The 25% cost savings was not the reason for the reduction, but it was a huge bonus.

There was great anticipation and mounting excitement as Squadron Leader Randy du Rand opened his bomb doors late on his run-in at 400 feet at a speed of 300 knots. None of the Air Staff expected such a spectacle of dust and multiple airburst flashes as 300 bomblets did their thing. That the Alphas were bursting at perfect height well behind the Canberra was obvious to all before the sound of the explosions reached the observation point. This came as a thrilling continuous thundering of overlapping explosions.

The Commander was quite overcome by what he witnessed and showed it by shouting, "Bloody marvellous. Absolutely bloody marvellous!" Everyone present congratulated everyone else before we all set off to walk the full length of the prepared target area.

First inspection made it clear that the Alpha bomb system was just what we needed. When the visitors left, the project team commenced the detailed study that showed that the effective coverage of 300 Alphas was 1,100 metres in length by 120 metres in width. We had achieved more than we planned for! Fourteen unexploded bombs (UXBs) were defused for inspection in our ongoing attempts to reach 100% efficiency but, with 5% bomblet failures, the system already rated slightly

better than the USA and UK guidelines for acceptable UXB rates in any cluster-bomb system.

The important thing was that the Alpha system was cleared for operations and the Canberra had been given the anti-personnel punch it deserved. Training of crews had been done but it was considered necessary to prepare for formation attacks, initially by three Canberras. This involved flying a very flat echelon with the aircraft spaced 100 metres apart. In this way a strike length of better than 1,000 metres and a width exceeding 300 metres could be assured. The reason for the very shallow echelon was to make certain that formating aircraft did not fall back into the curtain of shrapnel rising from the exploding bombs dropped by adjacent aircraft.

This photo shows the first half of 300 Alpha bombs dropped at a demonstration in South Africa. Note the distance of explosions behind the Canberra. The second aircraft is a long way off on photo-chase.

Pyrotechnics and boosted rockets

TARGET MARKING BY FIXED-WING aircraft using phosphorus rockets had been on going and all Army units carried smoke grenades and flares to mark FLOT and enemy positions. However, helicopters lacked the ability to put down markers from which to give other aircraft and ground troops direction. Rocket launchers were considered but discounted on the basis of weight and the fact that they would hinder rapid emplaning and deplaning of troops. Normal smoke grenades were unsuitable because they disintegrated when dropped from height.

I read all ASRs and, having noted pilot requests for a long-duration, pyrotechnic marker device, I took this on as a project to run concurrently with the Alpha Project. Besides, there was another pyrotechnic project already in hand for a RAMS requirement.

Air Force technicians at New Sarum had recently developed a ground marker system for night bombing by Canberras. The system, known as RAMS (Radio Activated Marker Service), involved two ground flares, one of which was ignited by a radio receiver in response to a coded signal from an attacking aircraft. The other flare was manually ignited by troops on the ground. The purpose of RAMS was to give ground troops the ability to call for precision bombing of CT targets at night. This involved placing one flare as an inner marker within 300-500 metres of a live target. Having placed the inner (radio activated) marker, a bearing was taken from it to the centre of the target. The second (manually activated) flare was then sited as an outer marker on a reciprocal bearing that might be as much as 1,000 metres from the target.

To prepare for a RAMS attack, a Canberra crew needed a fairly accurate grid reference of the target itself, the magnetic bearing from outer flare to inner flare and the distance from inner flare to target. For this type of attack, bomb-aimers (Canberra navigators) used a method known as 'off-set aiming'. It involved calculating the difference between the normal direct aiming angle at the planned bombing height and the steeper angle given by the inner flare position. The bombsight was then depressed to the calculated 'off-set' angle. There was nothing to prevent a reciprocal attack-line being used, in which case the sighting angle would be shallow, but it was more comfortable to over-fly the outer marker before bomb release.

When approaching target on the assigned attack heading, the pilot instructed the Army callsign to activate the outer flare for initial line-up. Thereafter the coded radio signal from the aircraft ignited the inner flare on the ground. Final adjustment to flight path was made to ensure correct alignment of the aircraft with the flares and bombs which were released the moment the bombsight crossbar reached the inner marker. 5 Squadron had practised and perfected the offset bombing system, all of which had been done at fairly high level.

Randy du Rand was happy enough with the existing RAMS system but felt it necessary to improve on the intensity of the flares for low-level night attacks. He was looking ahead, having visualised the need to use the proven offset bombing method for low-level delivery of Alpha bombs. Randy's initiative was surprising on two counts. Firstly, the Alpha system had not yet been proven when he asked for brighter flares and, secondly, the new flares only became available in the nick of time for Randy's first night attack with Alphas.

Bev introduced me to an eccentric American pyromaniac who revelled in flames, smoke and big bangs. He was an extremely difficult man to give direction to because he kept going off at a tangent to any subject being discussed. Nevertheless, he was a real boffin when it came to producing prototype smoke generators and immensely bright flares.

Bev made the steel containers into which the American loaded his concoctions. When we were satisfied with results we asked for repeat samples, but none gave identical results because the crazy fool kept changing ingredients without ever recording them. To pin him down was impossible and he refused point-blank to allow Bev to assist him so that Bev could establish precisely what chemicals were being used, and in what quantities. Much messing around occurred before it was realised that the man, already receiving good money for his work, sought to make a fortune from his secrets; so he was dropped, but not before Bev had established the primary chemical ingredients he had used.

It took some time for Bev to perfect a very robust smoke generator for helicopters to use as a ground-marker device. These manually activated generators were dropped over the side of helicopters from as high as 1,500 feet above ground, which subjected them to immense impact forces. It was essential to ensure each unit could survive high-speed collision with solid rock and still generate three minutes' worth of dense white smoke. Many failures occurred and it took many weeks before reliable smoke markers became available.

A modification to the pyrotechnic composition for existing RAMS flares achieved the intensity of flame Randy sought. Here again much trial and error was involved along the way and without Bev's incredible effort and technical expertise we would not have been ready for the first low-level night attack on Madula Pan. This attack will be discussed shortly.

One simple project Ron Dyer and I took on was to rectify the poor returns Lynx pilots were getting from their 37mm Sneb rockets. All we had to do was ask our engineering colleagues to manufacture in steel the same extension tubes used for phosphorus marker rockets. These tubes were then filled with RDX–TNT.

Tests showed the heavier 37mm (boosted) rockets were noticeably slower in flight than the lighter smoke markers, but they were just as stable. More importantly the shrapnel effect of boosted 37mm SNEB showed a ten-fold improvement over standard ones. Thousands of 37mm extension pieces were produced and filled at Thornhill over the next three years.

CS pellets

MOST FIREFORCE ACTIONS OCCURRED ON hills, in forested areas and riverine vegetation because this is where CTs enjoyed best cover. Most of the hills (*kopjes*) possessed huge granite boulders and vast granite surfaces. When CTs managed to get into good cover between or under granite boulders they became a dangerous menace and were almost impossible to flush out.

Cannon fire and Frantans were seldom effective and too many soldiers were killed or wounded when attempting to kill or dislodge them. On two occasions I recall dogs attempting to flush men from hiding but they were killed.

I considered many possibilities in trying to find a way to incapacitate or force CTs into the open and even looked into firing rockets or dropping containers filled with anaesthetising fluid, but none of these ideas was practical. Then I came upon information about talc pellets impregnated with CS (teargas). I cannot recall where I read about this but remember the effects CS pellets exhibited on trials.

Teargas grenades employ a pyrotechnic cake from which CS is released when the charge burns. The resultant gas is hot and initially visible but its spread tends to be upward and the resultant gas cloud is wholly subject to wind drift. Irritation effects are short-lived and affect some people more than others. Dogs can tolerate CS gas because they do not possess the irritable sweat glands of human skin. CS pellets act differently in that they release invisible gas over a long period of time. The unheated heavier-than-air gas spreads out at ground level and migrates into every nook and cranny. Above all its presence makes it quite impossible for any human to remain where pellets are present.

I discussed the matter with John de Villiers and Vernon Joynt of CSIR and asked if they could produce CS pellets. They liked the concept and thought it possible providing they could establish a suitable talc powder binder to form pellets. I left the problem with them and returned to Rhodesia to design and manufacture an appropriate dispenser that would disperse the pellets over large areas. The dispensers worked well but unfortunately the CS pellets never materialised because CSIR had more urgent matters to attend to.

Hispano cannons for Scouts

THE SELOUS SCOUTS HAD EXTENDED their roles beyond pseudo operations within and outside the country. During May and June 1976 they conducted vehicle-borne operations across the border into Mozambique. On one excursion, they went into the Gaza Province in an attempt to stem the tide of ZANLA forces that were using the road and rail from Maputo to Malvernia. Air support for this operation was limited to one Alouette for casualty evacuation and one Lynx flying at great height to act as a radio relay between the 'flying column' inside Mozambique and the Scouts' forward HQ inside Rhodesia.

For over a year Selous Scouts' over-border operations had been conducted with the clear understanding that no air support would be given, even if the units ran into life-threatening situations. This restriction applied equally to operations in Botswana and Zambia. Even after the new President of Mozambique, Samora Machel, closed the border with Rhodesia on 3 March 1976 and vowed to provide full support to ZANLA, the 'no air support' ruling remained. Machel's statements were, in effect, a declaration of war, but this made no difference. Political restraints on the external use of air support were almost certainly intended to keep international pressure off Prime Minister Vorster; otherwise we might have experienced further disruptions in our supplies from RSA.

This situation was no less frustrating for the men on the ground than it was for the Air Force. We knew that Scouts had suffered the loss of Sergeant-Major Jannie Nel, killed at Mapai on 26 June 1976. In the same action, Lieutenants Dale Collett and Tim Bax were seriously wounded. Tim recovered after many months, but Dale's bullet wound confined him to a wheelchair for life. Although I did not know the exact details, the lack of air support and possible limitation in ground firepower led me to make a telephone call to Ron Reid-Daly.

Some time in April 1976, I had approached Major Brian Robinson at his SAS HQ to ask him if he was interested in 16 of our 20mm Hispano cannons that had been removed from four time-expired Vampires. Considering the great weight of these guns and the nature of SAS operations, Brian could see no use for them at the time, but he did not close the door on the offer. My approach to Ron Reid-Daly met with a totally different response because he was in urgent need of improved firepower for his mobile columns operating in Mozambique.

Within an hour of the call I met with Captain Rob Warraker and a small group of Selous Scouts territorial engineers at New Sarum. With Air Force armourers and myself, the Scouts engineers lay under a Vampire to be shown how the cannons were mounted on swinging arms that allowed them to rock backwards under recoil, and forwards from the press of sturdy rear-mounted springs. This rocking action was used to retain a powerful spring in the BFM (belt-feed mechanism) that was fitted next to the cannon. The BFM was the essential component that pulled the heavy ammunition belt from the ammunition-bay and fed rounds into the gun's breach.

Air Force had considered mounting the cannons in purpose-made swivel platforms for vehicles assigned to airfield defence, so we had a good idea of what technical work needed doing. The Scouts engineers picked up the ideas immediately and Rob Warraker, fearing we may change our minds, hastily left with the four cannon and 20,000 rounds of ammunition he signed for. In no time at all the Scouts completed the mountings and finalised range testing. Three vehicles were fitted with these cannons for a forthcoming external operation against a large base in Mozambique where ZANLA groups were assembled, armed and briefed before being launched into the Thrasher area.

Captured CTs repeatedly referred to 'Pungwe Base', which they said was sited on the banks of the Pungwe River, but photo-reconnaissance along this large east-flowing river failed to find anything. Then, quite by chance, Squadron Leader Randy du Rand was returning from an unrelated Canberra task when he happened to fly directly over Pungwe Base. His navigator spotted the large camp through an opening in the cloud and rolled the cameras just before cloud obscured the ground again.

When the JSPIS interpreters at New Sarum viewed the photographs of this large base, they were astounded to see hundreds of people gathered in a box formation around a flagpole in the centre of a large parade ground. What excited them was the fact that the flagpole itself stood at the centre of an outline of Rhodesia that was fashioned from whitewashed rocks. The word ZIMBABWE, also laid out in painted rocks, clearly identified the base as belonging to ZANLA.

First photograph of Nyadzonya. Note the number of people mustered on the open ground. JSPIS head-count was over 800 on parade with at least another 200 visible amongst the buildings. The river on the right is the Nyadzonya River.

Ron Reid-Daly was delighted with the Air Force find that gave final proof of the large number of ZANLA in residence. The location of this base was not on the Pungwe River as reported but was on one of its south-flowing tributaries, the Nhazonia River, also known as Nyadzonya. With the position of the Pungwe Base established, the Canberra squadron flew repeated photographic sorties to monitor developments. These showed that base occupancy was increasing daily. Captured CTs continued to indicate that this was ZANLA's primary base and their hand sketches confirmed the base layout, including the whitewashed outline of Rhodesia surrounding the word ZIMBABWE, also structure from whitewashed rocks.

After much detailed planning for another 'flying column' assault, a Scouts force was authorised to attack the Nyadzonya

base. But again, direct air support was disallowed. The attack was a huge success and something in excess of 2,000 armed ZANLA, plus a few FRELIMO, were killed, wounded or drowned in the Nyadzonya River. The barrage of light and heavy automatic gunfire, including high-explosive rounds from two Hispano cannons, had been devastating. (The third vehicle fitted with a Hispano cannon met with misfortune just before the raid was launched.)

Only when the column was under attack from FRELIMO very close to the border during exfiltration, was air assistance authorised. A pair of Hunters flown by Flight Lieutenant Abrams and Air Sub-Lieutenant Lowrie neutralised troublesome FRELIMO mortar and gun-emplacements in failing light. A helicopter collected the most serious of four wounded men and a Lynx, flown by Air Lieutenant Ray Bolton assisted the column by choosing the best route for it to bundu-bash its way to safety inside Rhodesia.

A Canberra photo-recce sortie was run over Nyadzonya after the attack. The resulting photographs revealed hundreds of bodies strewn across the parade ground, between the many burnt-out buildings, and in the adjacent bush. As our politicians had feared, but expected, the international press reported the action as a slaughter of innocent refugees—ZANLA having registered Nyadzonya and all its other bases as refugee centres.

For years Rhodesia had suffered bad international press at the hands of unscrupulous sensation-seeking reporters and photographers. Even before ZANLA became effective, British reporters deliberately produced misleading articles that were supported by concocted photographs. For instance, one reporter and his photographer threw coins and sweets into rubbish bins to induce children they had gathered together into frenzied scrambling for prizes in what the children believed was a lovely game. Photographs appearing in overseas newspapers showed 'starving children scrambling for food on the streets of Salisbury'.

For years the residents of Salisbury had been used to the sight of many black office workers taking a lunchtime nap on the lawns of Cecil Square, a small park in central Salisbury. Overseas photographers recorded this common sight. Next day photographs appeared in UK papers under the banner headline 'Slaughter of innocents by the Smith regime'.

Mixed events

1976 HAD BEEN A YEAR OF mixed events. Robert Mugabe had been installed as President of ZANU. South Africa was under increased pressure from the West following a civil uprising in Soweto. Dr Henry Kissinger, the US Secretary of State, visited South Africa as the somewhat reluctant conveyer of a joint American and British proposal for a suicidal change in political direction by Rhodesia. By highlighting western concern over the Soweto tragedy and manipulating South Africa's power over Rhodesia, the 'Kissinger Proposals' were forced on our country by both Kissinger and Vorster. One component of these proposals was for the Rhodesian Government to participate in negotiations with ZANU and ZAPU in what was to become the Geneva Conference. Both ZANU and ZAPU had been pressurised into accepting the 'Kissinger Proposals' by the Frontline States though they disliked the conditions as much as the Rhodesian Government. Anyway the Geneva Conference, chaired by Britain's lacklustre Ivor Richard, ended in total failure.

During the year the Air Force lost men and machines in offensive actions and accidents. Without exception they were superb individuals whose loss emphasised the sheer wastefulness of war and the high cost in lives from accidents associated with war.

On 16 February, Squadron Leader Rusty Routledge was killed when a young SAAF pilot attempted to overshoot his overloaded Cessna 185, following a botched approach for landing at Perrem Airfield near Umtali. The aircraft stalled at low level and all three souls on board died when it ploughed into the ground.

On 10 June, following a FRELIMO cross-border attack on Zona Tea Estate inside Rhodesia, a Hunter flown by Flight Lieutenant Tudor Thomas received a fluke bullet strike during a rocket attack on offending forces at Espungabera in Mozambique. The bullet severed a hydraulic line resulting in the loss of all hydraulic fluid. In fading light Tudor returned to Thornhill where the OC Flying Wing, Wing Commander Keith Corrans, ordered him to abandon his aircraft. This was because Keith did not want Tudor to attempt a very fast, flapless landing at night with his flight controls in manual mode and too many other associated problems. Main undercarriage legs were drooped but not locked whereas the nose wheel was down and locked. In addition the air brake was half-extended and full left aileron was needed to hold wings level at 210 knots. Undoubtedly the slightest error would have been fatal.

Tudor positioned wide downwind for runway 13, trimmed fully nose-down and ejected. As intended, the Hunter crashed in open farmlands and Tudor escaped with little more than a bruised back. The loss of this Hunter was devastating because it reduced our Hunter strength to ten aircraft.

On 13 June 1976, a Z-Car gunner (name forgotten) was killed whilst firing at CTs in a Fireforce action. Then on 18 July, air-gunner Sergeant J.P. Graham was killed in the same way in the Inyanga area. Six weeks later, on 1 September, air-gunner Sergeant Belsted was killed in yet another Fireforce action in a helicopter flown by Flight Lieutenant Ian Harvey.

Flight Lieutenant 'Starry' Stevens died the very next day when he flew into an air ambush deliberately prepared by FRELIMO forces acting in support of their ZANLA colleagues. A group of CTs made their presence purposely known to induce a hot-pursuit operation into Mozambique. Their path ran along the base of a 1,200-foot-high west-to-east ridge along which FRELIMO had set up a number of heavy-calibre anti-aircraft guns to take on aircraft they knew would come. Starry's Lynx stood no chance as it passed close to and level with the guns.

On 11 August, as a direct result of the Selous Scouts attack on Nyadzonya, FRELIMO retaliated by mounting a mortar attack on the city of Umtali. Superficial damage was caused to buildings in the eastern suburbs of Greenside and Darlington. Fortunately, not a single casualty was reported and very little structural damage occurred.

On 21 October, Flight Lieutenant Roy Hulley was flying a Vampire FB9 on a routine gunnery sortie at Kutanga Range. He had completed a pass on his target and was running low-level on the downwind leg to position for another attack when his aircraft suddenly dived into the ground, narrowly missing the tented base of a small Army training camp. It was assumed that Roy might have been reaching for something he had dropped on the cockpit floor because there was no other explanation for this sad occurrence. It seems more likely, however, that seat-locking on the height adjusting mechanism disengaged in turbulence dropping the seat so low as to place Roy's eyes below the cockpit combing. This technical difficulty became well known before the FB9s were withdrawn from service.

Larger groups of CTs were crossing the border when, on 15 November, a Fireforce action in the Honde Valley resulted in one CT group being cornered on a long, heavily forested hill. At the end of a long day of fighting, thirty-one CT bodies were counted. This was the largest number of kills in a single internal action to date. Regrettably, three weeks later this action brought about a CT reprisal with the murder of twenty-seven workers on nearby Katiyo Tea Estate.

Although brutal murders by CTs were commonplace, this one was unusual and difficult to understand, because the victims were Mozambican migrant workers. FRELIMO had made it clear to ZANLA that Mozambican people were royal game, never to be touched, no matter where they were. Yet the CT gang visited this workers' compound after sunset and went about their business in their usual way.

They rounded everyone up and, whilst getting high on *dagga* (marijuana), they demanded and consumed all the food and beer the villagers possessed. The headman was then tied up and forced to kneel in the sight of all his followers. Death only followed after the helpless old man had been forced to eat his own ears and nose which, despite his screams for mercy, had been brutally hacked from his head. His lips were then cut off before the fatal thrust of a bayonet released him from his agony. Not content, the CTs grabbed a baby from its mother and ordered another woman to batter the child to death with a stick. The horrified mother saw this all happening before she was raped by every CT and then bayoneted to death. Only then did indiscriminate firing kill another twenty-four innocent souls together with all their prized cattle.

On a lighter note, I received visitations from a few Americans during the year. One of these was an arms dealer. He was a neat, dapper, dark-haired fellow whose good looks and quiet manner gave no hint of his sadistic nature. He hoped to interest me in a new type of bullet that he could supply for any calibre ammunition of my choosing. The 8mm rounds he showed me looked and felt quite normal. However, the projectile consisted of a light outer casing within which were tiny tightly packed steel slivers. The American told me that upon impact with anything, the casing yielded and released the slivers in a high-energy, fan-like shower. A single strike anywhere on a human body created such trauma that death was virtually guaranteed. The man told of this awful killing device with such passion and enjoyed the gory supporting photographs so much, that he had my blood boiling. I kicked him out of my office saying we had no interest in such dastardly devices. However, when he was gone, I wondered why I had been so put out by the man and this style of killing when I myself was so tied up in developing and producing a whole range of very unpleasant killing devices.

Another American who visited me must have done the Dale Carnegie course that teaches one to remember names by association. Knowing I was called PB, he obviously linked my name to fuel because, when he spotted me at the end of a long corridor a year later, he shouted at the top of his voice, "Hi there Shell."

Roofless protection pens.

At about this time I met a very different type of American. Bob Cleaves came to my office with Ian Player, brother of the world-famous golfer Gary Player. Bob Cleaves's purpose in regularly visiting South Africa and Rhodesia lay with his wildlife interests. However, Ian Player, a noted wildlife man

from Natal, had brought Bob to Air HQ at Bob's request. Bob was both very pro-Rhodesia and fiercely anti-communist so, with his good connections in the USA, he wondered if there was anything that he could do to help us. I asked him for samples of three things. Gyro-stabilised binoculars for visual recce, intensified-light night-vision binoculars for night recce and bulletproof vests for aircrew protection. All of these were delivered when Bob came back again six months later.

A strange incident occurred on 17 December 1977 when CTs mounted an attack on FAF 8 and the Army base that was also sited on Grand Reef Airfield. A long time prior to this, a project proposal by armourers at Thornhill was brought to me. This was to arrest enemy mortar bombs in heavy diamond-mesh fencing stretched above the roofless protection pens in which our aircraft parked at forward airfields. I was very sceptical initially, but the armourers proved their theory by successfully arresting a number of captured 82mm mortar bombs, none of which detonated. In consequence all forward airfields had the appropriate heavy netting stretched out high above aircraft pens.

When I heard that mortar bombs had been used against Grand Reef, I flew down immediately without waiting for details. On arrival I spoke to Flight Lieutenant Rob McGregor who was FAF Commander and was disappointed to learn from him that none of the bombs had come down over the aircraft pens. Nevertheless, it was interesting to see how the CT group, which had been specially trained and briefed for this job, had botched it.

The group, consisting of about forty men armed with AK-47 assault rifles, RPD machine-guns, RPG rocket-launchers and another six men with a single 82mm mortar tube, approached Grand Reef under cover of darkness. All the CTs carried mortar bombs, which were dropped off with the mortar crew who set up about forty metres behind the left flank of the main line. In this line the men set up next to a cattle fence that ran parallel to the runway. Just 150 metres from their position, across the runway, lay the Army camp with the Air force camp adjoining its right side.

All guns opened up together, sending a hail of bullets towards both bases. Rob McGregor told of the incredible noise and brilliant display of red and green tracer bullets, most of which went over the camp. The CTs may have been over-excited or blinded by their own tracers because, considering the weight of fire, amazingly few rounds hit their intended targets, though a few RPG 2 rockets detonated on sandbag protection walls.

In the meanwhile the CT mortar crew, launching bombs as fast as they could, were oblivious to the incredible cock-up they were making, simply because they had been too lazy to bring along the heavy but all-important base-plate for their mortar tube. The first mortar bomb landed in the Army camp, killing an unfortunate soldier, Signaller Obert Zvechibwe, whose body was found lying under his bed. With the launching of this bomb the mortar tube, without a base-plate to distribute the heavy shock-load, bedded into the ground. With each successive firing, the tube bedded deeper and deeper causing the tube angle to progressively steepen. The consequence of this was that the second bomb fell short of the Army camp and every bomb thereafter moved further from target and ever closer to the line of CTs still firing their guns along the fence line. When the angle of the tube was close to vertical, bombs fell amongst the CT gunners, killing two and seriously wounding others. Panic set in because the men believed the mortar bombs were coming from the Army camp. The attack broke off and the CTs ran for their lives, leaving their wounded to crawl away unaided.

Vic Cook

ON 20 DECEMBER 1976, THERE WAS a lucky escape due to brave and aggressive actions by Flight Lieutenant Vic Cook. Vic was a quiet character who was often ribbed by his colleagues for appearing to be a bit dozy. An example of this occurred when he was in his second-floor bedroom at his parents' home. He was awakened after midnight by the sound of someone creeping up the staircase. Arming himself with a baseball bat, Vic waited for the intruder to come through the door then laid a genuine thief low with a mighty blow to the throat. He then called the police. When asked how he knew this was not one of his parents coming to his room, Vic said he had not considered that possibility.

In the Op Repulse area, Vic was flying a G-Car with Corporal Finch Bellringer and an army medical orderly en route to casevac black civilians who had been injured by CTs near Malapati. He was some way short of the Army callsign to which he was going when he came under intensive smallarms fire that severed his tail-rotor drive shaft. This is a situation that every helicopter pilot dreads. During the short period of the forced-landing, the helicopter continued taking hits. Vic was struck in the foot, though he did not know this at the time, and his technician was rendered semi-conscious by two rounds that struck his 'bulletproof' vest.

Vic did very well to retain some semblance of control as the aircraft drove sideways through trees. He spotted terrorists "as many as a rugby team" with five directly ahead; all were firing at him. He aimed for the group of five and came to an abrupt halt amongst them, but this was smack-bang in the centre of the other CTs. With the force of impact, Vic's head was thrown forward onto the cyclic control column. Though stunned and hurt, he was able to pull out his MPK sub-machine-gun from

under his seat only to discover it had been rendered useless by a bullet strike. Surprisingly, though the battered rotor blades were stationary, the engine was still running when Vic jumped out of the aircraft. He wrestled a terrorist, injured by the crashing helicopter, for his AK-47 and shot him dead.

Still under fire, Vic opened up on the CTs forcing them to run for cover before assisting the shaken but uninjured medical orderly to pull the incapacitated technician out of the aircraft and into cover. Once he was certain that his tech and the medic were safe, he went back to the dead CT, firing as he went, to collect all the CT's ammunition. He then attempted to move from cover to cover firing at CT movements, but he found that he kept tripping and falling. Only then did he notice the large bullet gash in his foot, so Vic assumed a good position on a small rise from which he succeeded in holding the CTs off until help arrived forty-five minutes later. Vic received the Silver Cross of Rhodesia for his determination to protect his tech and the medic in very adverse conditions when he himself was hurt and under near-continuous fire.

After Vic left the force he worked for the South African Electricity Supply Commission. In the mid-1990s he was involved in a fatal accident when laying new power-line cables. Vic's task was to pull lead lines over the high electric pylons which heavy ground winches then used to draw the heavy cables into position. Precisely what went wrong I do not know other than the ground anchor point of one lead line broke loose and recoiled towards the helicopter where it became entangled in the tail-rotor causing the crash that killed Vic Cook.

SAS externals

FOR SOME TIME DURING THE second half of 1976, the Special Air Service squadron was employed in the Repulse area and participated in a number of Fireforce actions. Although there was urgent need for experienced soldiers in the south at the time, use of the SAS inside the country was an incredible waste of their specialist skills.

Nevertheless, on 22 September, the first use of a Dakota in support of Fireforce was made possible because all the SAS were para-trained. The ground action was controlled from a K-Car by Major Brian Robinson who, because of his eighteen paratroopers, had more than double the number of troops that would normally have been available to a four-G-Car Fireforce.

In another SAS Fireforce action on 10 October, Brian Robinson was flying with Flight Lieutenant Ken Law in a K-Car. They were fortunate to have Cocky Benecke supporting in a Lynx. Cocky found a group of CTs hiding under bush 1,500 metres away from where troops had been deployed. This initiated actions with other CT groups scattered about in the same vicinity. The Dakota flying in support of Fireforce was called upon to drop its load of twenty SAS paratroopers, which was a task made easy because the K-Car was able to mark the drop-line with the first of our newly developed smoke markers. Happily Cocky Benecke was the first pilot to be armed with boosted 37mm rockets that gave spectacular returns. Between himself in his Lynx and Sergeant Merber firing the K-Car's cannon, they accounted for fourteen CTs.

Whilst they were still in the Repulse area, the SAS were used for a pre-planned attack on a ZANLA staging camp known as Mavue Base, which was just over the border inside Mozambique and a little south of the wide slow-flowing Sabi River. Again Brian Robinson was in K-Car, this time with Mike Borlace who was leading another K-Car, and five helicopter troopers.

The OC SAS seemed to be present in a number of Air Force 'firsts'. This time it was the first live Alpha bomb attack by three Canberras. The operation did not go too well for many reasons, the greater of which was that the Canberras missed their assigned targets because the Hunters responsible for marking for the bombers had misidentified the base centres. Mike Borlace in his ASR said that, *this had been a great pity because, having seen an Alpha bomb attack for the first time, the CTs, who were in both bases in great numbers, would have suffered high casualties had the strikes been on target.*

Three Dakotas dropping SAS troops west, south and east of the target from 500 feet were all observed to have airburst explosions around them. In their descent to ground, the paratroopers experienced plenty of ground fire and airbursts. Because there were ground explosions preceding the airbursts, it was assumed that ZANLA had employed their TNT and stick grenade 'air ambush' system.

Brave and accurate boosted rocket and Frantan attacks by Air Lieutenants Clive Ward and Mike Delport flying Lynx took care of troublesome anti-aircraft fire. The SAS conducted a sweep through the target but apart from capturing large quantities of equipment that had not been destroyed during Hunter re-strikes; they found only thirty-two CTs dead. From an SAS point of view, this was less than they were used to achieving in Tete with a handful of four-man callsigns.

Shortly after this action, increased infiltrations down the old Tete routes into the Hurricane area forced the SAS back to the style of operations that suited them best. They returned to the Tete Province of Mozambique south of the Zambezi to take on both FRELIMO and ZANLA. Air involvement in support of SAS operations remained low-key until 1977.

SAS hit-and-run tactics had been developed to such a degree that the small four-man offensive units had, themselves, become the elusive terrorists within Mozambique. They had learned how to keep out of trouble whilst meting out hell and destruction in no small measure. Apart from the odd casevac, helicopters only flew in to recover four-man patrols to Rhodesia. Dakotas were used in HALO (High Altitude Low Opening) deployment of two or more sticks from high altitude necessitating the use of oxygen until the free-fallers actually left the aircraft. HALO deployments were usually made just after sunset, and on the whole seemed to go unnoticed. Dakotas were also used occasionally at night to resupply the ground units.

The SAS were so successful that ZANLA and FRELIMO were forced to abandon forward bases and move right back to the FRELIMO main base town, Tete. Undeterred by the fact that the enemy had moved so far from the Rhodesian border, the SAS worked on the fact that ZANLA would have to cover the increased distances to the Rhodesian border by vehicle, and this offered new possibilities.

To circumvent the problem of working too far to the north of the border and too close to Tete town, the SAS decided to turn things around by using the newly formed Lake Cabora Bassa as a safe haven. Canoes were to become their means of transport, thereby turning the direction of attack southwards. Villages that used to be on the banks of the Zambezi River had disappeared under water and most of the population had moved miles away. No one was living in the ground beyond the lake's southern shoreline but ZANLA and FRELIMO were committed to using the few roadways that ran through remote countryside some distance farther south.

Only three four-man callsigns were used and they played merry havoc against an enemy that could not understand where their problems were coming from. Whereas the men in the canoes, nicknamed 'Cockleshell Heroes', gained most of their ammunition resupply from captured equipment and had plenty of water when not too far from the lake during their offensive forays. On the lake they needed regular resupply, which came in by Dakota at night.

I managed to tag along on one of these midnight flights. Together with spares, some canoe components and ration packs to be para-dropped were hampers of fresh hot food and other perishable delicacies prepared at SAS's Kabrit Barracks just before we climbed aboard the Dakota. For me, this was a great change from project work and I had not been airborne at night since the Lynx ferry twelve months earlier.

Flight Lieutenant Bob d'Hotmann was the skipper with Flight Lieutenant Bruce Collocott as his second 'dicky. I was standing between and behind the pilots watching proceedings with interest whilst squeezed against an SAS officer who I think might have been Scotty McCormack. Initially Bob could not raise the callsign whose position was on a tiny island fairly close to the southern shoreline almost due north of Nova Mague. The night was clear and very black. Even though the lake was vaguely illuminated by starlight it was insufficient to pick out any island, even from our height of only 500 feet.

Then we spotted a flashing strobe light that stood out so

clearly from the air it seemed impossible that the SAS position would not be compromised. Scotty said it was OK because the strobe would be so positioned that nobody on the shoreline would see it. We had turned towards the strobe when the callsign came up loud and clear. Because the aircraft was heading directly for the strobe, all that needed to be said from the ground controller was "Red light on.... Green light on". The pannier was launched into the night; and that was that! The callsign confirmed that he had received resupply, thanked Bob and bid him farewell.

The descent to the lake had been a long one at low power. Bob had been at pains to ease on the power very gently as he approached his run-in height so that nobody on the ground would detect any change in engine note that might give away the SAS position. Having completed the drop, Bob held heading and height for at least ten kilometres and even then he powered up very slowly, allowing the Dak to drift gently upwards, again to avoid drawing attention. We were miles past the Cockleshell Heroes before turning for Salisbury.

Canberras join Fireforce

SEVEN DAYS AFTER FIRST USE of Alpha bombs in Mozambique, Randy du Rand and his navigator, Flight Lieutenant Terry Bennett, got airborne from Buffalo Range in support of the Repulse Fireforce. This came about because Randy was keen to gain operational experience with the new weapon system and I needed plenty of feedback on bomblets' performance. The idea of deploying a Canberra to Repulse was greeted with enthusiasm by Tol Janeke because it had become abundantly clear that, as expected, ZANLA's main thrust was coming through the Gaza Province of Mozambique.

Under guidance from a K-Car, a cluster of fifty Alpha bombs was delivered and all landed in the base from which eight CTs had moved immediately upon hearing the approaching K-Car. Squadron Leader Graham Cronshaw in the K-Car and the Army callsign who had called for Fireforce reported being thoroughly shaken by the sight and sound of the Alpha strike, even though it was only one sixth of a full load.

The Army callsign swept through the CT base and confirmed shrapnel had saturated it. Although the bombs had killed no CTs, who were a short distance away, the effect of the strike so unnerved the eight members of this group that they surrendered without a shot being fired. Randy remained the heavy arm of Fireforce for a while and was able to prove the Canberra's ability to bring quick and accurate strikes to bear wherever they were needed, because K-Cars could place down

reference markers with their new smoke grenades. Having satisfied himself, Randy rotated each of his squadron crews to Op Repulse to gain experience.

During November a ZANLA base in Mozambique close to the border was positively identified by Canberra photo-recce. An operation similar the one at Mavue was planned but, due to good features around the target, three Canberras led the strike for maximum surprise. They made the attack from 500 feet at a release speed of 300 knots. The strike went in just before the arrival of the heli-borne and para force and all the bombs landed on target as planned. Instead of arriving over a subdued enemy however, the helicopters faced a hornet's nest of alert and angry ZANLA firing many small arms and heavy AA guns.

Following some brave action to silence the AA guns, particularly by Mike Borlace, troops eventually overran the base and found the reason for the Canberra's failure to provide any subduing effect. All but two of the Alpha bombs had broken through a crust of sand and buried in thick wet clay before exploding harmlessly below the surface. The whole target area was covered with black bomblet craters. Two bomblets that struck trees caused the airbursts that accounted for only the three ZANLA killed in the airstrike.

There was deep consternation at Air HQ and within my project team. We had not foreseen this problem, which was entirely my own fault. I knew how similar ground conditions in the Zambezi Valley had presented the Army with serious vehicle movement difficulties. Following heavy rains, such as had occurred in the area of this target, the softened sand crust above damp clay yielded without warning. When this occurred, vehicles sank to their axles and other vehicles attempting to pull out a stricken one usually ended up in the same mess.

Although I should have foreseen the problem earlier, I was certain that the correct combination of delivery height and speed would prevent further failures, no matter the nature of surface. So we immediately set about finding a test location close to Salisbury where sufficient clay, hard ground and water existed in close proximity to each other. The place we selected was a small dam at Inkomo Range. We used concrete Alpha bomblets, knowing that live ones would perform better.

Randy du Rand and Terry Bennett flew the same attack profile they used on the failed attack and dropped a cluster of fifty concrete Alpha bombs. They were bang on target and those that struck dry ground recovered into flight normally. All the bomblets that landed on water and most that landed on sand-covered clay disappeared below the surface. Those few that struck sand over clay yet found their way up to the surface were coated with a thick layer of gluey black muck.

The next delivery was made from 400 feet at a ground release speed of 300 knots, giving marginally improved results. Delivery height was then stepped down to 300 feet, again at 300 knots. Most of the bomblets bounced back into flight from mud and water, though some of the units that landed in mud were so thickly coated that their recovery was way too low and sluggish. Three runs were then made at 300 feet at 350 knots. All bombs bounced into flight though the ones from clay did not rise as high as from water and normal ground.

From then on 300 feet was the preferred attack height at an attack speed of 350 knots, which still provided adequate separation between detonating bomblets and the aircraft. However, the increased attack speed presented a major problem in terms of airframe fatigue factoring. Fortunately the Canberra could accelerate from 280 knots to 350 knots very rapidly, which minimised the time spent at attack speed. Nevertheless the high fatigue factor applied for this speed converted three minutes to something in the order of one hour of expended airframe life.

Inevitably with so many bomblets being dropped, there were some unexploded units (UXBs). A total failure rate of around 3% was either caused by technical problems or by bomblets passing through vegetation that progressively decelerated them to such an extent that they failed to realise the 100G-impact force needed to activate pistols. All bomblets were painted red to simplify UXB collection and soldiers had been advised that they were perfectly safe to handle and transport. So it was with some alarm that they learned of a UXB that had killed two African children and wounded another.

I immediately went to the scene of the tragedy and noticed that the bomblet in question had exploded on a solid flat section of granite with large boulders around it. Near the point of explosion, I saw red paint marks at different places on the flat rock and came to the conclusion that the children had been throwing the bomblet from the boulders above.

The surviving little boy in hospital confirmed this. He was lucky because, being fearful of his friends' attempts to break the 'ball' open, he had watched from a distance as the others climbed small boulders to throw the bomblet onto the flat rock. His friends could not crack the unit open so they went up onto the highest rock. The bomblet pistol received the necessary G load and bang went their lives.

Yellow Submarine

SELOUS SCOUTS WERE COMMITTED TO using noisy vehicles and experienced a variety of difficulties in their attempts to render the rail line from Maputo to the border town of Malvernia inoperable. Then, whilst they were working on this difficult task, they noticed that a yellow Alouette III came up the rail line from Maputo and turned northwards along the Cabora Bassa power-line. Radio intercepts on FRELIMO's

radio network soon established that this was a regular run for a Maputo-based engineer to inspect a section of the power-lines running from Cabora Bassa to South Africa. Intercepted messages also showed that all FRELIMO posts were told not to shoot at the yellow Alouette. Ron Reid-Daly approached Norman Walsh to see if Air HQ would consider painting one of our own Alouettes canary yellow so that rail and train destruction parties and recce teams could fly unchallenged directly to their selected targets. Norman sorted this out without delay and John Blythe-Wood flew the aircraft, nicknamed 'Yellow Submarine', from its secret covers at New Sarum for a night flight to the Selous Scouts forward HQ. The rail wreckers enjoyed a trouble-free period until FRELIMO finally tumbled to what was happening.

Schulie

CAPTAIN CHRIS SCHULENBURG, KNOWN AS Schulie, served with the RLI and SAS until he returned to his native South Africa when his contract with the Army expired. He was later invited by Ron Reid-Daly to re-join the Rhodesian forces for service with the Selous Scouts to exploit his special talent in ground reconnaissance conducted in the manner Schulie considered essential.

Arising from his specialist recce work with the SAS, Schulie had been awarded the Silver Cross of Rhodesia for valour—but he could not buckle down to SAS four-man recce principles. Schulie wanted to conduct recce on his own, believing this to be safer and more efficient. Ron Reid-Daly was more amenable to this view than the SAS; though Ron insisted that one man, of Schulie's own choosing, must always accompany him. Somewhat reluctantly Schulie agreed and conducted a number of successful two-man recce patrols. Initially he used a white soldier as his partner until he came to the conclusion that a black soldier was a more sensible option. The reconnaissance forays worked well enough and neither man suffered undue stress until things went badly wrong early in November 1976.

Two recce teams were tasked to provide early warning of FRELIMO and CT movements for a Selous Scouts vehicle-borne force. At an appropriate time these teams were to harass FRELIMO—a diversionary tactic. One team worked north of the Scouts force while Schulie and his partner worked to the south. Schulie and his black companion (Steven was the name I heard the helicopter crews use) had descended into Mozambique by HALO entry. They were in position when the vehicle-borne force was moving in to attack the ZANLA staging base at Jorge do Limpopo on the Maputo rail line to Rhodesia. When he judged the time was right, Schulie deliberately made his presence known to FRELIMO but, in so doing, he attracted much greater reaction than he expected. Using Claymore and other anti-personnel devices, Schulie inflicted serious casualties on his pursuers who became so angry that they re-doubled their efforts and force levels in a determined attempt to take out the troublesome Rhodesians running through the bush ahead of them.

Schulie and Steven became separated during their running retreat under fire. Thanks to superb strength and fitness, Schulie managed to evade the large force that had no difficulty following his tracks in the soft dry sand of the region. By nightfall FRELIMO slowed to a crawl but no radio contact could be made with Schulie and Steven so Selous Scouts approached Air HQ for assistance. Late at night Schulie was barely able to give his position to the high-flying Canberra sent to find him because his radio batteries were almost flat. It was only then that Selous Scouts learned that Steven, who did not have a radio, was missing.

I heard the story of Schulie's hot extraction from the helicopter crew who rescued him. Although I cannot remember who they were, their story remains clear in my memory.

The pick-up at first light occurred when the FRELIMO follow-up force was dangerously close to the open pan where Schulie said he would be waiting. Heavy fire was directed at the helicopter during entry and exit from the pick-up point. Once clear the pilot flew low over bush heading for the railway line. On reaching it he flew just far enough away to keep the railway in sight. Schulie was not too happy about this but the pilot refused to move away, which turned out to be very fortunate. Some distance on a man on the line was seen to be jumping up and down waving a white object over his head. When close enough, Schulie realised this was Steven. He was many miles from where Schulie had last seen him, yet there he was waving his map madly.

The pilot said that Schulie was so overcome with relief and joy that he leapt out of the aircraft before touch-down and ran up to Steven to give him a powerful hug that lifted the lighter-built man clean off his feet. Once inside the helicopter, Schulie unceremoniously commandeered the aircrew water bottle and poured it down his companion's parched throat. Thereafter the two Scouts looked at each other laughing and occasionally patting each other in expressions of immeasurable friendship and relief. This was the same team that was called upon to mark a major ZANLA target for an Alpha bomb night attack by a formation of Canberras.

Madula Pan

RADIO INTERCEPTS GAVE WARNING OF a large group of ZANLA CTs in transit to Rhodesia. It was established that they would be at Madula Pan on the night of 11/12 January 1977. This pan lay close to and south of the main Maputo rail

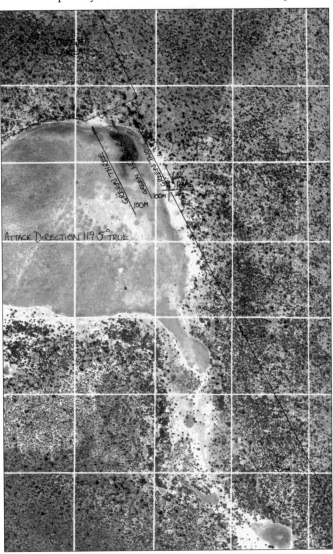

The dark patch at the top right-hand end of the pan was the only water for miles around, hence the ZANLA base position extending on the lines marked for the attack by Green leader and his two wingmen. The Inner Marker Rams was sited at the base of the tree at the top end of the white sand bank marked +. The outer marker was under the middle tree of the cluster of five largish trees to the right of the end of the pan's phallic-like projection.

line and air reconnaissance photos confirmed the location as having been used by previous groups. It was no more than a transit point without shelters of any kind but it covered a large expanse of bush at the southeastern edge of the almost dry Madula Pan.

The size of the Madula Pan target required a formation attack by three Canberras to cover the entire rest-up area. Randy du Rand was keen to conduct the attack at night to ensure maximum surprise at a time when all CTs could be expected to be in their base. So Schulie and Captain Rob Warraker met with 5 Squadron, Norman Walsh and me to discuss and plan the strike. Schulie's role was twofold; to confirm ZANLA was resident in the expected position and to position RAMS and outer marker flares for the Canberra strike.

A large tree on the southern edge of the pan was selected for the RAMS inner flare. This looked like a good site in terms of distance from target and bush cover to shield the bright light when the flare ignited shortly before strike. Selecting a position for the outer flare, which Schulie would ignite manually, was no easy matter. The density of bush and trees on a back-bearing from the inner marker was fairly even, which would make identification of a specific position very difficult. Eventually a particular group of trees was chosen which Schulie felt he should be able to find in the forecast weather condition of half-moon and a clear sky.

A first-light follow-up attack was to be made at 05:00 by an RLI Fireforce with paratroopers. This meant the airstrike needed to be made as late as possible. But since it was known that CTs tended to rise at 04:00 and disperse for fear of dawn attacks, 04:00 was the time chosen to strike. A delay of one hour between airstrike and ground follow-up was not ideal but it was considered acceptable. An extra Canberra with a full Alpha load, two pairs of Hunters and two Lynx were to be on airborne standby to assist Fireforce.

Because there was time to do so, it was decided that a realistic rehearsal should be conducted at 04:00 on 6 January in similar terrain inside Rhodesia. This was to familiarise Schulie with the handling and positioning the flares and to allow Randy to practise the low-level formation attack. Following their flight from New Sarum to the NDB at Chiredzi, the Canberra formation planned to descend to its IP at 2,000 feet above ground. From the IP, the formation would accelerate to 350 knots during a second descent to their attack height where Randy would be at 300 feet above ground with his two wingmen stepped up 100 and 200 feet above him and spaced 100 metres to his left and right. Schulie, acting alone, made a HALO descent during the evening before the practice strike into an area that was known to contain CTs near the selected target. He laid the flares and the Canberras strike went in as planned.

Rob Warraker flew with me to Boli airstrip in a Cessna 185 where we were collected by the G-Car that took us the short distance to meet up with Schulie and twenty RLI paratroopers

who had been dropped at 05:00. Just before landing at Boli, Rob and I had seen the Dakota that had dropped the RLI paratroopers passing us on its way back to Buffalo Range.

We inspected the Alpha strike from the air and on the ground and saw that all bomblets had landed on target. Schulie was satisfied with his side of the exercise but said that, although he had received Randy loud and clear on his radio when the Canberra formation was approaching at high altitude, there had been difficulty in hearing Randy's instruction to light the outer flare during the low-level run toward the target. We decided that this would not be a problem for Madula Pan because the fourth Canberra could act as a radio relay back-up between Randy and Schulie. This extra Canberra could also light the inner marker RAMS if Randy was unable to do so.

From the practice site, Schulie accompanied Rob and me for the short helicopter ride back to my Cessna at Boli. Both Rob and Schulie were huge men and Schulie also had his parachute and heavy Bergen. My aircraft was carrying a high fuel load because we had planned to fly directly to New Sarum for a debriefing with 5 Squadron. But even the nippy little Cessna struggled to make take-off speed with so much weight on board and I had a few anxious moments skimming very low over trees with the speed failing to build up in the very hot conditions that prevailed. A gentle fall of ground helped us slip off the 'drag step' and we were soon climbing comfortably on course for Salisbury.

When I checked in with FAF 7 to say we were climbing out, I was asked if I had heard or seen the Dakota, then three hours overdue. We diverted to Buffalo Range immediately to participate in the air search that was being mounted. I had just reached the airfield when we were told that a survivor had just reached a working party in the sugar-cane fields and reported that the Dakota had crashed on the banks of a large river; presumably the Lundi.

I dropped Rob and Schulie off at the Selous Scouts Fort at Buffalo Range and turned back immediately to search the

Lundi crash.

Lundi River. It did not take long to find the Dakota on the south bank. The aircraft was broken in two with the cockpit smashed to bits and its rear fuselage lying under a large tree.

On recall from his civilian job for 'retread' duties, Squadron Leader Peter Barnett, the previous OC of 3 Squadron, had been second 'dickey' to Flight Lieutenant Dave Mallet who had joined our Air Force from the RAF. According to survivors, Peter had objected when Dave descended to fly low-level just above the surface of the Lundi. Whatever the verbal exchanges, heavy electrical power-lines running across the river from unseen pylons amongst trees on both high banks, sliced through the cockpit windscreen and decapitated both pilots.

Two bulkheads immediately behind the pilots' seats arrested the cables. This saved the life of the flight engineer who was standing behind the pilots. The aircraft decelerated down to stalling speed before the power-lines on the starboard side sheared, causing the aircraft to be dragged left by the binding cable into trees above the riverbank. Fortunately there was no fire, but Army Corporal A. Bradley was killed in the ensuing crash. Four men survived with relatively minor injuries due to the fact that the aircraft had cleared the riverbank itself and had been subject to sufficient bush-drag to soften deceleration.

Peter (right) is seen here with 3 Squadron Commanders, Mike Gedye (left), George Alexander and Bill Smith. In the middle is AVM Harold Hawkins who had just presented the squadron's Colours to George Alexander—the current OC.

Madula Pan attack

ON THE NIGHT OF 10 JANUARY, Schulie and Steven did a HALO descent well to the south of Madula Pan and made their initial approach to target before dawn. They lay in hiding for the day then, under cover of darkness before moonrise, made a final approach for Steven to crawl right up to the edge of the base to ensure that ZANLA was in residence. Having listened to many noisy conversations, all spoken in Shona, Steven moved back to Schulie who passed the word back to Scouts HQ.

Schulie positioned the RAMS flare without difficulty. Around about 03:00 he was close to calling for a postponement of the strike because he could not find the selected clump of trees for the second flare. With little time to spare he eventually identified the spot and set up.

Flying his Canberra at about 30,000 feet, Flight Lieutenant Ian Donaldson with the callsign Green 4, made

Captain Chris Schulenburg, as he was best known, in his recce gear.

radio contact with Schulie at 03:45 and received confirmation that all systems were 'go'. Flying with Don were his navigator, Dave Hawkes, and Captain Rob Warraker the Selous Scouts operations co-ordinator. Ian had taken off from Buffalo Range where he was currently part of the local Fireforce. Green Leader with Green 2 and 3 had taken off from New Sarum and were flying 20,000 feet lower than Ian.

Randy du Rand was leading with Mike Ronnie, No 2 was Al Bruce with Doug Pasea and No 3 was Ted Brent with Jim Russell. Randy's ASR reads:

FLOT DETAILS: Two Selous Scouts more than 2,000 metres away.
CONTROL ARRANGEMENTS: c/s 55 on channel 21.
WEATHER: Wisps of stratus at about 1,500 feet AGL. Half moon fairly high in the sky giving good visibility.
NARRATIVE:
1. Four Canberras each carrying 300 x Mk 2 FRAGS (Alpha bombs) were briefed for this strike. The first three were to run in on

a first run attack at low-level using marker flares correctly placed on the ground to indicate target and direction of attack. The attack was planned for night time using low level offset bombing technique. The fourth aircraft was positioned at high level to ensure communications with the ground force and act as top cover for the helicopter assault due to occur at first light. This aircraft was based at Buffalo Range.

2. Route to the Target. The route chosen was via Fort Victoria and Chiredzi NDBs and then to the Nuanetsi/Mozambique border which was the initial point (IP) for the bomb run. The aircraft took off at 15-second intervals and routed at Flight levels 100, 105 and 110 to top of descent near Mabalauta. A gradual descent was made to 2,000 feet AGL to the IP maintaining a ground speed of 300 knots.

3. Run from IP to Target. The IP was overflown at 2,000 feet AGL and six minutes from the target the ground party was warned to light the flare in one minute's time. At five minutes from target the ground party was instructed to light the manually operated flare and 15 seconds later the fuse was reported burning. The aircraft descended to 1,000 Feet AGL. At two minutes out the manual flare ignited and was observed by all three aircraft. Speed was increased to 350 knots ground speed and all descended to their bombing heights of 300, 400 and 500 feet respectively. As the lead aircraft was about to pass the first flare the second flare (RAMS) was initiated. Final heading corrections were made and all the bombs dropped in the target area. This was reported by c/s 55 and later proven by photography. No sign of any activity was seen by any of the aircraft.

4. Recovery. The three aircraft recovered to base at FL 250. After landing it was discovered that Green Leader and Green 3 had 50 hang-ups each.

5. Green 4. Green 4 was heard relaying messages from high altitude during the run-up to target and subsequently as Green 1, 2 and 3 returned to base. He was last heard still at high altitude awaiting the helicopter assault.

The significance of Randy's last paragraph will become apparent shortly.

Schulie and Steven had heard the deep rumble from the open bomb bays then saw the aircraft brightly illuminated by the outer flare as they flashed over their position. Even at two kilometres from the ZANLA base, the roar that came to Schulie and Steven from multiple Alpha bomb explosions impressed the two Scouts enormously.

Whilst they waited for the flare to stop burning, Schulie heard the Canberras climbing and turning for Salisbury. Then the sound of human screaming and shouting came across the quiet bush from the ZANLA camp. Schulie had to recover both flares for burial well away from Madula Pan. As he did this, he realised that ZANLA had taken a pounding because of the troubled noises that continued to reach him. He was well out of the way by the time the helicopters arrived with the assault force.

From what they had heard from the high-flying Canberra the lead K-Car crew, carrying assault force commander Captain

Richard Pomford, expected to oversee a simple mopping-up operation. Instead they were met by anti-aircraft fire of such intensity that they had to back off and call for the Hunters to strike. At the same time, Ian Donaldson, who was about to turn back to Buffalo Range in the reserve Canberra, was asked to give assistance.

Ian made a high-rate descent and, for a reason that will never be known for certain, broke through low stratus cloud directly over Malvernia. It must have had something to do with canopy misting following the dive from the freezing conditions at high altitude into warm air with both engine throttles closed. This, coupled with a glaring sunrise ahead of the aircraft flight line, might have been the reason Don did not see the railway line which, had he done so, he would undoubtedly have avoided.

Rhodesian forces based at Vila Salazar just across the border from Malvernia witnessed extremely heavy anti-aircraft fire with masses of tracer being directed at the Canberra before it rolled sharply and dived into the ground from where a huge fireball was seen to rise. Ian Donaldson, Dave Hawkes and Rob Warraker died instantly.

The FRELIMO force at Malvernia had obviously been aware of the air attack at Madula Pan and was fully alerted when Ian inadvertently passed over them in perfect range for every one of many heavy and light guns. Some airbursts were seen which suggests RPG rockets may also have been launched at the aircraft.

Back at Madula Pan, fire from the ground continued to be so intense that the helicopters and Dakota retained their troops, hoping for the Canberra and Hunters to make a difference. They did not know of the Canberra's fate at the time. However, Selous Scouts Major Bert Sachse, flying as an observer in a Lynx, had watched a number of Hunter strikes before he realised what had gone wrong. His assessment was later confirmed by radio intercepts on FRELIMO's command channels.

A large FRELIMO mobile force happened to have spent the night very close to Madula Pan on the road running next to the railway line. These troops were mounting their vehicles to continue their journey when they heard the bomb strike go in on Madula Pan. The whole force turned to investigate and give assistance to their ZANLA comrades who they knew were based at Madula Pan. They arrived before first light to find ZANLA had suffered many casualties and were in a state of panic and disarray. In addition to aiding the wounded, FRELIMO prepared defences for the assault they knew would come with the dawn.

In the face of this unexpected opposition by a force that was obviously much larger than his own, Richard Pomford called off the assault to avoid unnecessary casualties and Randy returned with three Canberras to deliver eighteen 500-pound bombs onto the target for good measure. He would have much preferred to deliver that load onto Malvernia in response to the downing of one of his Canberras; but airstrikes on any Mozambican town were taboo.

First radio intercepts reported that ZANLA had suffered six dead and seventy wounded during the night attack. These figures were later updated by FRELIMO with final figures being ten dead and 102 wounded from a force of 120 CTs at Madula Pan. The majority of wounded were described as 'amputees', having lost limbs.

Five months after this, the RLI parachuted into Madula Pan in support of Selous Scouts who were mauling ZANLA and FRELIMO forces close by. It was interesting to learn from them that, though there were no ZANLA in residence at the time, the whole camp area was littered with many human skulls and bones. Presumably these were mainly from FRELIMO men caught in the Hunter and Canberra attacks.

The Air Force reaction to first casualty reports on the Madula strike was one of great disappointment, particularly by Randy du Rand. We had become so preoccupied with kills that wounding was almost totally discounted in assessing airstrike effectiveness. Randy even advocated reverting to the conventional bombs that we knew did little more than cost us dearly in precious foreign currency.

I was very distressed by all of this until Group Captain Norman Walsh told Air Marshal McLaren that he believed the Alpha bombs had done a much better job than anyone realised. His opinion was later fully supported by the Army and Special Branch who expressed a different viewpoint from that initially expounded by many Air Force officers. Selous Scouts were the first to expand on this view in writing. Ron

During Federation days, the Rhodesian and Portuguese Governments exchanged names for two establishments that lay side by side across the common border. The Mozambican town in this picture was named after Lord Malvern (one time Prime Minister of the Federation) and the small village inside Rhodesia (out of sight on left side of the clearly visible borderline) was named after the Portuguese Head of State, General Salazar.
Note the large empty railway yards that had previously handled heavy traffic moving to and from Lourenço Marques from Rhodesia, Northern Rhodesia and Nyasaland

Reid-Daly's contention was that the Alpha bombs had done a much better job by inflicting 90% living casualties with 10% kills than would have been the case if the figures were reversed. Air Staff opinion changed but Randy remained sceptical.

The Scouts recognised that dead CTs were either abandoned or buried and forgotten whereas the living wounded presented an unwanted burden by tying up other forces and vehicles in long-range evacuation to rear hospitals. Along the way other CTs and FRELIMO would see these casualties returning from the border, creating a negative impact on morale. Mozambique's medical facilities had become totally overstretched and CTs with missing limbs and tall war stories had to be cared for. This all created a dilemma for ZANLA who kept war invalids in separate camps away from other cadres.

The Air Force Commander made it clear that he was delighted with the first Madula Pan strike because it was our best single result to date. It had cost a fraction of the follow-up air weapons costs with no foreign currency implications. However his greatest concern at that time was to recover the bodies and bomblets from the downed Canberra, providing this could be done without further loss of life.

For three days the Army made a number of attempts to get to the crash site but vastly superior FRELIMO forces, hell-bent on protecting a prize that lay so tantalisingly close to our border, repelled these attempts.

Then radio intercepts revealed that the bodies had been found, large quantities of 'ball bombs' had been collected and, together with Canberra wreckage, all was being loaded on vehicles for transfer to Maputo. In consequence, recovery attempts were called off.

When we were still developing Alpha bombs, Bev and I decided to stamp the fuses with Chinese hieroglyphics that translated to 'Made in North Korea'. Whatever the FRELIMO Government made of this when they studied bomblets, later piled next to aircraft wreckage, is not known but national radio and media coverage gave out that the bomblets had been manufactured in the 'Racist Republic of South Africa' and that the aircraft had been 'a gift to the enemy from the British Colonialist Government'.

Going back to the Alpha Project again—we had produced bomblets that would not detonate sympathetically if one happened to be set off by, say, an enemy bullet. Only a 100G shock could activate a pistol. Both characteristics gave protection against enemy fire and inadvertent mishandling of bomblets. In the case of Ian Donaldson's crash, the Canberra fuselage had absorbed so much of the shock loading on impact that not a single bomblet had detonated; which is why all 300 ended up in Maputo.

New Frantans

MY PROJECT TEAM HAD SUCCEEDED in its most pressing task of providing the Canberras with an effective anti-personnel strike capability. By January 1977 we were already engaged in a number of new projects. These ran concurrently, imposing a huge load on Denzil and Bev who were still heavily involved in the production of Alpha bombs, officially designated Mk2 Fragmentation bombs. In spite of this they had been more than willing to take on new developmental work. Projects Bravo and Delta (pyrotechnics and 37mm Sneb boosters) had been finalised. Next priorities, Projects Echo and Foxtrot, were for new Frantans and high-pressure bombs.

To provide the Lynx with an effective Frantan, we chose to move away from conventional napalm bomb designs. All those in use in the western world were simply metal tanks, most with small fins designed to pitch the unit nose-down at the moment of release to ensure positive separation from the aircraft. Otherwise, none possessed flight stabiliser fins.

After release, the tanks behaved in haphazard ways causing them to follow unpredictable trajectories. Tumbling, flying sideways, oscillating and corkscrewing were characteristics that set napalm aside from aimable bombs and made accurate delivery difficult. For instance, if two tanks were released together, with one pitching nose-down and another nose-up, they could land so far apart that one might fall short of target whilst the other passed over.

When Americans took on a target they dropped four or more napalm bombs from each of a number of aircraft to saturate large areas with flame and intense heat. Absolute accuracy and high costs did not bother them whereas we needed units that would follow a repeatable trajectory to make each unit aimable, accurate and highly effective. This meant we had to produce an aerodynamically shaped unit with low drag characteristics for carriage, but incorporating efficient stabiliser fins to ensure longitudinal stability for clean release and alignment in free flight.

Metal containers were no good, as we had witnessed on hundreds of occasions. Burster charges coupled with unpredictable case rupture resulted in equally unpredictable distribution of burning napgel. Too often large quantities of the gel remained inside partially burst tanks or sticky blobs of unburned gel lay all over the ground and stuck to vegetation. This was no good at all! I decided we needed tanks that would shatter like glass on impact to free their entire gel contents in a huge fan-like spray of tiny droplets with inter-linking volatile gas. I had learned that the Hunter disposable long-range tanks were constructed from fibres with phenolic resin and that they

shattered on impact. We followed this line and produced casings moulded from woven glass fibre and chopped asbestos set in a phenolic resin binder.

Prototype sixteen-gallon units were made and fitted with Alpha bomb fuses (suitably modified to function at low-impact levels) imbedded in the large pocket of flash-compound that ignited the napgel. From Day One the new Frantans were a great success and, with small modifications, were cleared for operational use on Lynx and Provosts.

Hunters used imported spun-aluminium fifty-gallon

Frantans but these suffered all the limitations we sought to overcome. So I arranged comparative trials between our low-cost sixteen-gallon Frantan and the very costly imported fifty-gallon units. The results were astounding. The Hunter pilots were able to deliver the local unit with great accuracy. In itself this was pleasing, but even more satisfying was the fact that the local unit, though only possessing one third of the napgel contents of a fifty-gallon unit, provided consistent coverage of ground that equalled the best of the imported variety. Foreign currency saving was another bonus.

Golf Project

IN PROJECT FOXTROT WE ATTEMPTED to produce fuel-air explosive (FAE) bombs, which American military journalists described as having 'near-nuclear' effect. One military article was supported by dramatic photographic records of the total destruction of an old US naval destroyer from just one of these FAE bombs. However, destruction of ships was not America's real interest in FAE. The weapon had been developed to clear large pathways through enemy minefields by detonating hidden mines with excessive over-pressure of ground.

Ethylene oxide was the medium we employed. There were two reasons for the choice of this liquid gas. Firstly, it explodes with as little as 2% of air inclusion and as much as 95% of air inclusion, whereas most other gases will only detonate within a very narrow gas to air ratio. The second advantage of ethylene oxide is that, when ignited, it produces gas volumes many times greater than any high-speed explosive, such as TNT.

Each American FAE bomb was dropped at relatively low level and descended to ground on a parachute. A ground-sensing device perforated a pressure disc to release the bomb's pressurised liquid contents at about twenty feet above ground and simultaneously fired flares upwards. The upward and downward flight time of the flares allowed the ethylene oxide gas skirt to widen to around twenty-five metres in radius before the first of the flares contacted the gas skirt setting off a vicious explosion. Lethal over-pressure from a mere five gallons of ethylene oxide dispersed and detonated in this way extended way beyond the edge of the gas skirt.

Very often the precise positions of CTs firing from dense bush were not known and we had no single weapon that could produce lethal effect over relatively large areas to cater for such situations. FAE seemed to offer a perfect solution to this on-going problem.

Considerable time, effort and cost went into Project Echo during which we succeeded in making huge expensive fireballs before, eventually, achieving two terrific detonations. The first of these broke many windowpanes in the Kutanga Range domestic area that was over 500 metres from the blast. What interested us about successful detonations were the sound effects they produced and the fact that they totally stripped vegetation, including substantial trees, up to forty-five metres radius from blast centre. The ground around was pulverised and powdered to a depth of several inches. The sound of each detonation was not a sharp bang, as from TNT, but a loud deep-noted 'crruuump' from an explosion, followed immediately by the 'cruump' of an implosion.

Ethylene oxide is a very dangerous substance to store and with Rhodesia being under UN sanctions it was also very expensive and difficult to source. Considering these issues, and realising that weapons that descend on parachutes would be difficult to deliver accurately, even in the lightest of wind conditions, we decided to drop the FAE project. Nevertheless, I was still determined to produce high-pressure bombs. Denzil was just as determined and acquired information on the gas-generating properties of every known explosive and combustible liquid compound. His hope was to identify a readily available safe-to-handle explosive that would exhibit similar characteristics to ethylene oxide. When he recommended ANFO we all studied the data before agreeing it exhibited suitable gas-producing properties. This was a pleasing discovery because we could produce ANFO very cheaply and easily.

Project Golf was initiated by making a direct comparison between an imported 500-pound TNT-filled medium-capacity bomb and an ANFO-filled 6mm steel casing having equal mass. Both units were mounted vertically on three-foot stands pointing nose down for command detonation from a safe distance. The imported bomb was detonated first. It went off with the usual bright flash, black smoke and a very loud bang with plenty of dust drifting away on the wind. The ANFO bomb was nothing like as impressive to the eye or ear. The explosive flash was nowhere near as bright as the TNT bomb and pasty-grey smoke mingled with dust was drifting off before a deep 'crrrrump' was followed immediately by a second 'crrump'.

Inspection of the sites showed clearly that we had a winner in ANFO. Loud bangs, such as thunder from lightning, are the product of huge energy releases to atmosphere. In the case of bombs filled with high flame-rate explosives, bright flashes and loud bangs of surface bursts are products of wasted energy following the disintegration of steel casings. When used against buildings, bunkers and other targets where detonation occurs within confined structures, the same energy is highly destructive, but not so in the unconfined conditions of open bush.

In the case of ANFO, the steel containers swell in size, as do the high-explosive containers; but ANFO, having a much slower flame-rate, continues its heaving detonation well beyond case disintegration. An ANFO mix, when confined in a steel container and given a hefty thump by an initiator charge such as Pentolite, ignites spontaneously to generate enormous amounts of high-pressure gas in a heaving EXplosion which forces air outwards from the generated gas bubble. The gas cools immediately, creating a void into which the air flows at supersonic speed, causing an IMplosion.

Digressing for a moment, the implosion following an atomic bomb blast causes more damage to structure than the initial explosion. In the case of ANFO, explosion and implosion are equally damaging—a double dose of no good.

The production of ANFO, a commonly used mining explosive, simply involves the thorough mixing of a small quantity of diesel fuel into prilled ammonium nitrate fertiliser. In the beginning we did this with a shovel in a wheelbarrow. Later we progressed to a simple motor-driven concrete mixer for large-quantity production.

ANFO offered a special advantage. From the start we realised that it would not be necessary to use special ammunition dumps for the safe storage of ANFO bombs. Unlike standard high-explosive units that had to be filled in specialised conditions, ANFO bombs could be stacked in the open and only filled when they were needed.

Digressing again and returning to the Mao Tse Tung 'ground cannon' mentioned in conjunction with the CT 'air ambush' system, I decided to test this 'cannon' using ANFO as the explosive. A one-metre round hole was dug to a depth of one metre. At the base we placed a 20kg charge of ANFO then filled the hole with rocks.

The project team was over 1,000 metres away when the 'ground cannon' went off with a dull thunderclap. Whilst the rocks remained close together, their rapid passage up to around 1,000 feet above ground was obvious. Thereafter we could see nothing of individual rocks that soared on to greater heights. We watched the ground ahead for ages waiting for the rocks to land but neither saw nor heard anything. I was heading for my vehicle when a peculiar sound, which I can only describe as something like static electricity, developed all around. Everyone dived under vehicles in time to avoid the rocks that came crashing down.

Used in multiples around airfields, this crude device would have been devastating to enemy paratroopers and ground-attack fighters. Fortunately however, there was never a need to employ Mao Tse Tung's crude but effective 'ground cannon'.

Further static 500-pound ANFO trials were conducted before making a direct comparison between an imported 1000-pound bomb and an ANFO unit of equivalent mass. For

Kutanga Mac places the final rocks watched by, Bev, with head down and Ron Dyer second from right.

Inspection the hole from the small charge of ground cannon trial. PB 2nd from left, Bev 5th with hand over eyes and Kutanga Mac in dark shirt 9th, view the large hole made by the small ANFO charge of our 'ground cannon' test.

Waiting for the explosion and ensuing rockfall.

this we acquired specially bred white guinea-pigs with black ears. They were placed in wire-mesh cages, set in deep holes (to protect them from shrapnel) next to which pressure pots and pressure discs were laid in a line at five-metre intervals from fifteen metres outwards to fifty metres from point of detonation.

The imported bomb explosion had no noticeable effect on the pressure pots and pressure discs beyond fifteen metres. In the fifteen minutes it took us to get to the test site, every guinea-pig, including the two at fifteen and twenty metres, had recovered from the big bang and were munching away at the feed in their cages.

Following detonation of the ANFO unit, we rushed back to the little creatures with a forensic pathologist in tow. I had persuaded this medical specialist to assist us in our ANFO tests by examining the bodies of snakes and frogs we found on the surface following every single ANFO detonation. All these cold-blooded creatures, though dead, appeared perfectly normal until dissected. Over-pressure had destroyed their lungs and other vital organs without any damage to outer skin. The frogs, which lived more than one foot below surface, were always found on top of the powdered earth, lying belly up.

At the 1000-pound ANFO detonation site we found every guinea-pig hunched up, motionless and covered in thick fine dust. Those at fifteen, twenty and twenty-five metres from blast had perished through overpressure. Those at thirty and thirty-five meters had perforated eardrums; the remainder recovered quickly enough but would not eat for more than ten hours. The pressure pots within twenty-five meters suffered distortion with permanent set and satisfactory over-pressure readings extended out to thirty-five metres.

The guinea-pigs that survived the ANFO blast were kept in a large pen separate from those that had been subjected to the imported bomb blast and Kutanga Mac looked after these little fellows better than any private home could. For reasons we never established, the guinea-pigs in the ANFO pen grew larger than the others and became enormously fat. The two deaf animals were the happiest, fattest and hungriest. All were eventually found good homes.

Our first ANFO bombs weighed 450kg, which was equivalent to the imported 1000-pound bombs. Canberras and Hunters released these in a series of tests. Although the tests themselves were successful, we were not at all happy with the loss of energy evidenced by large craters in the ground where they detonated.

Operational considerations clearly identified Hunters as the main user of high-pressure bombs, so we turned all attention to fighter/bomber style steep-dive (sixty-degree) profile attacks. To maximise blast effect each bomb was fitted with a one-metre-long proboscis to ensure airburst. To minimise energy losses downward and upward, and to maximise ground over-pressure, simultaneous initiation of Pentolite booster charges at the front and rear of the ANFO charge resulted in a very satisfactory 'squeeze' effect. In doing this, each bomb flattened

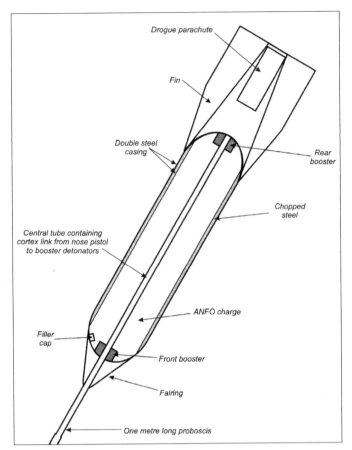

Golf bomb.

everything around the point of contact and no energy was lost to punching out ground craters. The entire tailpiece was usually found at the centre of detonation proving that almost no energy was going skyward.

During early tests each pair of bombs landed close together; so we decided to improve the ninety-metre diameter bush-clearing effect by retarding one bomb to force it to fall short of the unretarded one. Spring-loaded metal paddles were used initially but these were clumsy and inefficient. They were discarded as soon as we learned how to absorb the high shock loading involved in deploying our own designed and manufactured drogue chutes. The drogue chutes worked well and forced the retarded bomb to fall about thirty-five metres short of the streamlined unit. From then on a pair of ANFO bombs gave a bush flattening-pattern ninety metres wide by 135 metres in the line of attack.

450kg Golf bombs were cleared for operational use in March 1977. Testing continued for some time thereafter, resulting in the ANFO bombs being upgraded with double steel cylinders sandwiching thousands of pieces of chopped 10mm steel rod to give lethal shrapnel effect beyond the over-pressure boundaries. Although officially termed 450kg HP bombs, the project title stuck and everyone knew them as 'Golf bombs'.

Cavalry Fireforce

IN MARCH 1977, OZZIE PENTON asked for my temporary release from project work to conduct recce training camps for all PRAW crews. To make this manageable and to minimise disruption to my own work, I arranged for four separate five-day camps to be run in March, April, May and June. I chose Marandellas Airfield for the first recce camp and had Cocky Benecke, Francois du Toit and Norman Maasdorp along to assist me. Francois had resigned from the South African Air Force to join our force and was keen to get back to air recce work.

John Blythe-Wood, as lead K-Car pilot operating out of Mtoko, had been having a run of first-class successes in which he had twice called for Canberra Alpha bomb strikes. My wish was to find a target for John's Fireforce in the hope that he might use Canberras again because I had not personally witnessed an Alpha bomb strike from the air.

On 22 March I found a plum target and counted thirty-eight CTs moving out of a their well-defined base camp. Unfortunately the Mtoko Fireforce was not available, so the Grand Reef Fireforce, led by Mike Litson, responded instead. An agonising fifty-five minutes elapsed before the Fireforce came into view. I put Mike onto the campsite first for orientation purposes and, considering the long delay, it was fortunate that my guess at where the CTs might be found turned out to be correct. In the action that followed, sixteen CTs were killed, one was captured unhurt and seventeen escaped, most having been peppered with 20mm shrapnel from the K-Car.

Although I read all the Air Strike Reports in Air HQ it was not the same as seeing for myself the existing problems of having too few Fireforces. They had to cover many thousands of square miles in which ever-growing numbers of CT groups were operating. I wondered if employing a new approach might offset the shortage of Fireforces and allow air recce finds to be less dependent on their availability.

Lieutenant-Colonel Tony Stevens, commander of the horse-borne troops of the Grey's Scouts, listened to my ideas of using his Grey's Scouts as an alternative to the heli-borne Fireforce. He leapt at the opportunity and we made plans to give it a try the next day in the St Swithins Tribal Trust Land. This was to have a force of twenty horsemen moving along a pre-determined line at a gentle walk whilst I conducted air recce five kilometres on either side of their line.

I found the force immediately I arrived at the appointed RV and the sharp accent of the Grey's Scouts major made me realise he was Australian. He confirmed the line he would ride and I confirmed the procedure I would adopt. Not ten minutes passed before I found a base under trees on high ground, commanding an excellent view of surrounding grasslands in which were some bare maize fields, very few trees and three small villages.

My 1:50,000-scale map showed a shallow depression running west to east 500 metres to the north of the base but this was not obvious from my recce height. I had no knowledge of horse-borne tactics for approaching targets unseen. Having given him the relevant grid references, I asked the major's opinion on the cover the depression would afford him. He assured me he could get to a position 500 metres north of the base without being seen and said he would call me across two minutes before his arrival there. At the time I was about five kilometres away, having maintained a routine orbit line, but I could see the horses clearly even when they passed through tree cover. The speed at which the horses covered the ground was very impressive.

PRAW recce training camp, at Marandellas Airfield. Names that appear in this book are: Standing: Ray Haakonsen 7th from left, PB between catering ladies, Hugh Chisnall (bald next to blonde lady—he was the pilot who found John Smart's missing helicopter). Squatting: Phil Haigh and Francois du Toit (left), Sarel Haasbroek (2nd from right). Sitting: Cocky Benecke (centre) Hamie Dax (right).

When the force turned right to move directly towards the base, ten pairs of horsemen surged forward, galloping at different speeds to place them in a wide crescent before the centre horsemen came to a halt and dismounted. In no time there were ten pairs of men surrounding the base site. The nearest troops to the base were about 150 metres away. No more than ten minutes had passed from finding the base to having it surrounded by men who had dismounted to commence a cautious approach towards the base.

Disappointingly, the base was empty, having been vacated about two hours earlier. Nevertheless it was clear to me that this silent force would have achieved complete surprise and total encirclement. Had there been serious opposition, a status quo could have been maintained for as long as it took for a regular Fireforce to reach them.

Unfortunately, the success of the trial ended abruptly. I had continued searching for another target when I saw smoke rising from two villages close to the base. I could not raise the major on radio so flew back to see what was going on and was horrified to find all huts of the third village in the process of being torched. My presence overhead brought the major back to his radio set and we entered into a very heated exchange. The major maintained that the locals needed to be punished for feeding the CTs. I objected and insisted that these same locals, who really had no alternative but to feed CTs, would more willingly support ZANLA following this senseless action.

I terminated the trial even before a whole hour had passed because I needed to discuss Grey's Scouts' procedures and attitudes with Tony Stevens. He was very apologetic about his Australian major's actions and assured me that appropriate action would be taken. Nevertheless, Tony was delighted to learn that, in my opinion, Grey's Scouts could be employed in a Fireforce role in support of air recce and Selous Scouts. Regrettably I never found another opportunity to pursue the matter personally and the concept was lost.

Testing American equipment

BOB CLEAVES RETURNED FROM USA with the equipment I had requested for field trials. The gyro-stabilised binoculars were mind boggling on the ground. Superb magnification and a rock-steady image, no matter how much one trembled, made them a perfect aid for game-viewing. In the air, however, the binoculars were only useful to inspect selected points during a gentle orbit. The moment one tried to keep an eye on a point whilst in forward flight, even at 4,000 feet above ground, the rate of scan induced precession of the gyro beyond its limits and toppled the spinning mirror.

This was a great pity because from 4,000 feet one could clearly distinguish between an FN rifle and an AK-47. The only airman who showed any interest in the unit was Sergeant Pete McCabe who was also the only man I knew who used standard binoculars in flight. How Pete managed to see anything through binoculars when flying in helicopters that vibrated so much I do not know; but he was as successful with them as he was firing his machine-gun or cannon.

Having been designed for security surveillance, the night-vision unit worked wonderfully on the ground. In flight, there were too many problems in trying to match what one could see through the bright night-vision unit with one's dimly lit map. Only regular pathways through open ground could be seen but all hills and bush lacked any perception in depth.

The US bulletproof vests were better than the few we had previously acquired from some other source although one of these had saved Vic Cook's technician. The American vests were subjected to destructive testing from our own FN rifles and a variety of communist rifles and machine-guns firing 7.62 mm ammunition. Though the vests gave no protection against armour-piercing rounds they were considered both suitable and essential for Fireforce aircrew and airborne Army commanders. Thanks to Bob and his US contacts, our order for these life-saving items was met and became standard operational wear for aircrew and airborne Army commanders. Many men owed their lives to these vests.

I was keen to develop better ceramic platelets to produce our own protective vests and to use as protective cladding on helicopter engines. Doctor Patrick Grubb of the University of Rhodesia took up my challenge and succeeded in producing ceramic platelets that gave full protection against armour-piecing rounds fired from 100 metres. He was still negotiating with a manufacturer to produce them on a large scale when our war came to an end. For his efforts Pat Grubb was given clearance to use the technology for his own benefit but, so far as I know, this was another successful Rhodesian development that faded to nothing.

COMPOS established

FROM THE MID 1960S UNTIL MARCH 1977, overall control of operations vested with the Operations Co-ordinating Committee whose secretarial arm was the Joint Planning Staff. The OCC still comprised the Commanders of Army and Air Force, the Commissioner of Police, and the Director of Central Intelligence Organisation. The Chairman of JPS acted as secretary and he was responsible for the execution of all joint service decisions and directives emanating from OCC, whereas individual heads handled single service matters. Because service in the top posts of the Army and Air Force was limited to four years and the Police to five years, only Ken Flower of CIO served continuously on the OCC.

Under OCC were the Provincial Joint Operations Centres, JOC Hurricane (Bindura), JOC Thrasher (Umtali), JOC Repulse (Fort Victoria), JOC Tangent (Bulawayo) JOC Grapple (Gwelo) and JOC Splinter (Binga). At each JOC the Provincial Head of Internal Affairs was a permanent member. Other government departments, such as road and telecommunications, could be co-opted on an ad hoc basis. Below each JOC there were two or more Sub-JOCs. For instance, under command of JOC Hurricane were Sub-JOCs Sipolilo, Centenary, Mount Darwin and Mtoko.

At no level was there a recognised supremo. Chairing of JOC meetings was done in rotation between the Army, Air force and Police. This style of command and control expected "Reasonable men to act responsibly in co-operation with one another". So long as we were experiencing total successes against ZIPRA and ZANLA in the years prior to 1974, the system worked remarkably well. However, by late 1976 it had become clear to everyone that ZANLA was gaining ascendancy and that Rhodesia's resources were being stretched to the limits. It was also clear that, whereas ZANLA was working to a specific strategy, JOCs and sub JOCs were doing their own thing in the absence of clearly defined political and military strategies upon which to formulate plans and tactics.

Considerable enterprise was shown at every level in all services; but these unco-ordinated initiatives were not all good for the country. In the absence of a supreme commander with a staff of top line planners to give executive direction, it was not surprising that strong initiatives by men and units, all driven by frustration and the will to win, too often achieved negative results.

From my viewpoint, the most obvious of these was the negative mindset of many Army and Police officers towards the Selous Scouts, even though the Scouts were directly responsible for the majority of our internal counter-insurgency successes. Much of this arose from a lack of understanding of pseudo operations, and more so because Selous Scouts had to fight red tape and prejudice for everything they needed in terms of men and equipment. Ron Reid-Daly's fiery character and deep-seated secretive manner did little to help this situation.

It appeared to me that only the RLI, Air Force and Special Branch gave the Selous Scouts support and credit for the incredible work they were doing. Like others, I was often niggled by Selous Scouts 'freezing' areas in which pseudo teams were working when I myself had planned to operate over those same areas. But the reason for disallowing any security forces into the 'frozen areas' was so obviously intended to avoid misidentification and unnecessary casualties that one learned to live with the situation. Besides, I repeat, most of our successes were coming from the 'frozen areas'.

I believe the real reason for the Air Force's positive attitude was that, almost from the start, helicopter crews deployed and recovered pseudo operators to and from their screened-off 'forts', so they got to know the Scouts operators personally and were involved in most of their pseudo successes. Apart from this, the Air Force was totally unaffected by Selous Scouts manpower and equipment needs.

A major problem in not having a national military strategy was the periodic misuse of the SAS due to differences in opinions on how the specialist unit should be employed. When made available to JOC Hurricane, the SAS were correctly used to disrupt ZANLA's external communication routes. When detached to JOC Repulse, they were often used incorrectly on internal Fireforce tasks.

Another weakness in not having an executive command was that a general lack of co-ordination and co-operation went counter to ensuring the optimum utilisation of resources. Provincial JOCs hung jealously to whatever was theirs, often showing a marked reluctance to assist in matters outside of their boundaries—even though ZANLA's operational zones overlapped our provincial boundaries.

The consequence of all this, and ZANLA's ever-increasing numbers, was that an air of depression set in and many Rhodesians were emigrating in what was unkindly referred to as 'the chicken run'. Almost every able-bodied white male was involved in military call-up and everyone could see that the political assurance that Rhodesia would win through was no more than a smoke screen. The Rhodesian press and radio boasted high successes against ZANLA, but studiously avoided telling the civilian population that, for every ZANLA killed or captured two or more replacements flowed in. There was clearly a need to turn things around and indications that such action was about to be taken came when Ian Smith was seen moving around the op areas more than usual.

Pilot John Annan with Prime Minister Ian Smith and the Air Force Commander Air Marshal Mick McLaren about to take his seat. Army Commander General Peter Walls is on the other side of the aircraft. The aerials on the front of the aircraft were for the Becker Homer device that made locating callsigns so much easier.

The move came in March 1977 when a major change in command structure was implemented in an attempt to emulate the direction Britain had taken in handling a similar situation in Malaya during the early 1950s. The British Government appointed General Gerald Templar as Supreme Commander over every arm of government with instructions to reverse ever-mounting Chinese communist successes in their bid to take control of Malaya. As Malaya's Supremo General Templar's successes had been spectacular so now, almost too late in the day, Rhodesia aimed to follow suit.

Lieutenant-General Peter Walls was appointed Rhodesia's Supremo and his new HQ, known as Combined Operations Headquarters (COMOPS), was established in Milton Buildings next to the Prime Minister's offices. This same building housed Air Force HQ and the Treasury.

Throughout the military, there was a general air of expectancy and hope because most officers were familiar with the Malayan success story. Rhodesia's 'C' Squadron SAS had been formed to serve in Malaya and was used as an extension of 'A' and 'B' Squadrons of the British Special Air Service. In that war, the Rhodesian unit had borne the title 'C' Squadron Malayan Scouts and had been commanded by General Peter Walls, then a major.

When General Templar took control of Malayan affairs, he first planned his strategy to counter communist forces that had been giving the authorities a severe mauling. From the start he knew that arms alone could not win the war. He realised that success depended on every governmental and private organisation acting in perfect unison with well-honed, balanced and unified military forces all acting in harmony to gain the confidence and total support of the Malayan people. Neither petty jealousies between or within any structures nor any weakness in leadership could be tolerated. The enemy had to be denied access to the civil population along with the destruction of his hitherto safe-havens deep inside the jungles. But above all, the 'hearts and minds of the Malayan people' was recognised as the key to defeating the communists.

To achieve his political and military aims General Templar needed, and was given, enormous power to act unilaterally. He started by firing the Commissioner of Police and followed through by dismissing many high, and middle-ranking civil and military officers. Ignoring career planning for individuals, he promoted go-getters and soon gained the willing co-operation of the armed forces and the civil authorities. Everyone knew General Templar's overall plan and how they, individually, fitted into it. The rest is history.

General Templar's plans worked because he had the power to remould all organisations and dovetail their efforts to support and implement his clearly defined strategy. He did not involve himself in tactics or the nitty-gritty, day-to-day activities, but watched the overall situation closely to ensure that timely corrective actions were taken where and when necessary.

COMOPS had been established for the right reasons, but

General Walls was not afforded the powers General Templar had enjoyed. Without these I believe he was stymied. Within a couple of weeks of its formation, it became clear that COMOPS was not going to bring about what we were expecting. Our hopes of receiving clearly defined military direction were dashed because General Templar's single most important need to 'win the hearts and minds of the (African) people' found no place as the firm foundation upon which to build a total strategy. This vital issue was simply ignored. Furthermore there was no effort made to eliminate weakness in leadership at any level.

The real strength of the Rhodesian Army at the time lay in its battle-experienced colonels, lieutenant-colonels and majors, but they stayed in their positions whilst officers of questionable character and performance remained in harness. The same applied to the Police and many government ministries. I believe that, being the smallest of the three armed forces, Air Force leadership was sound at all levels.

General Walls (left) and Group Captain Norman Walsh (right), four years later after taking on his most difficult posting as Commander of the Air Force of Zimbabwe.

In effect COMOPS had merely replaced OCC, but with more people attending lengthier meetings of what became known as the National JOC (NATJOC). The selection of COMOPS staff officers was left to individual HQs and this resulted in General Walls failing to receive the powerful planning staff he needed.

The Air Force approached the formation of COMOPS seriously by posting in Group Captain Norman Walsh, a battle-experienced pilot with outstanding qualities in leadership and bags of common sense.

The same could not be said of Army HQ's approach to COMOPS needs. Army's initial allocation of officers was astounding considering it possessed many top-line leaders so essential to Rhodesia's all-important strategy-formulating body. Instead, it sent officers who were unsuited to appointments demanding clear thinking with proven records of operational proficiency and excellence in both personality and leadership.

COMOPS should never have given space to any prima donna.

All too soon it became clear that the new command was not going to serve its intended purpose but would make Rhodesia's already difficult situation even worse. Instead of formulating strategy, COMOPS involved itself in the day-to-day running of operations, occasionally even instructing JOCs where to move small units. Proven Principles of War were ignored. In fact the only useful function I remember COMOPS performing at that time was ordering reluctant JOCs to pass over their Fireforces to adjacent JOCs when such a need arose.

Why General Walls allowed his pompous Director General of Operations, Brigadier Bert Barnard, to bypass Army HQ and issue directives directly to formations under Army command I cannot say. A well-balanced and unassuming officer would have passed these to Army HQ to action, thereby avoiding the unnecessary antagonism that developed very rapidly between the Army and COMOPS. So far as I was concerned, Army HQ was partly to blame for having sent the wrong man to COMOPS but General Walls more so for accepting him.

Sadly COMOPS assumed outright operational control of the SAS and Selous Scouts, leaving Army HQ to attend to their administrative needs only. In consequence, a deep rift developed between Lieutenant-General Walls and Major-General John Hickman with devastating consequences to most aspects of Army's operational efficiency. It resulted in pathetic 'them and us' attitudes at a time we so desperately needed absolute unity.

The Police and Air Force were not affected in this way, but the all-important strategic plan we awaited was not forthcoming. I met Norman Walsh on a number of occasions and learned of his deep frustrations in this regard because the Army component of COMOPS, being greater than Air Force and Police combined, seemed unable to see the wood for the trees, and would not listen to reasoned argument. Even the Officer Commanding SAS, Major Brian Robinson, and OC Selous Scouts, Lieutenant-Colonel Ron Reid-Daly, told me, unreservedly, that the only senior officer in COMOPS with both feet on the ground and possessing any idea of what needed to be done was the 'blue job', Group Captain Walsh

In his attempt to coerce COMOPS into action Norman recommended the employment of the SAS, Selous Scouts, elements of the RLI and Air Force in the systematic destruction of all the external routes, specifically bridges, serving ZANLA and ZIPRA communication needs. This he considered essential to slow down the unimpeded flow of men and materials into Rhodesia. The secondary effect of such action would most likely force the governments of Mozambique and Zambia to cease hosting our enemies.

The need to destroy the communications infrastructures of both Mozambique and Zambia was old hat, having been recognised as an urgent matter ever since the collapse of the Portuguese. However, the Rhodesian 'political ruling' (in reality a South African imposition possibly exaggerated by CIO) against the destruction of any economic targets had always discounted such actions until, following total failure of the détente-inspired ceasefire back in August 1976, the Selous Scouts and SAS were eventually cleared to immobilise rail and road routes in Gaza Province.

Norman Walsh knew only too well that to raise the issue of destroying bridges on such a large scale would create a political storm but, from a military standpoint, the issues had to be pressed. In fact, Norman was not so sure that the 'politically sensitive issues' blocking the military originated from politicians; he guessed they were more likely imposed on NATJOC by Ken Flower of CIO. However, before presenting his plans for consideration by the NATJOC Norman, working with the OC SAS, needed to select all key targets to formulate a detailed campaign to be conducted in two phases; first the destruction of Mozambican and Zambian infrastructure and secondly all CT concentrations in those two countries.

The destruction of Mozambique's communications infrastructure would involve ten days of intensive flying to deploy and recover specialist demolition teams and their protection elements. For this, all helicopters and Dakotas would have to be withdrawn from internal operations. The month of July offered the best weather conditions for this tightly programmed campaign. At the end of the Mozambique phase, all helicopters would have to undergo major servicing over a period of three days before launching a six-day campaign against Zambia. This meant just nineteen days of intensive effort—start to finish.

As he anticipated, the Phase One plan failed to get past COMOPS. Had Brigadier Barnard been included in the planning, and presented it as 'his own idea', it might have made a difference. (This is my own biased opinion based on personal experience.) Nevertheless Norman's plans were shelved and were only resurrected in 1979 when it was too late to materially influence Rhodesian fortunes.

Apart from a reluctance to wage war on neighbours, which would surely increase tensions between the West and South Africa, it was feared that Zambia, seeing what was happening in Mozambique, might call for the physical support by surrogate forces (most likely Cubans) in anticipation of action against herself. Once invited, such forces would almost certainly remain in Zambia!

The second phase of Norman's operational plan, also external, was to become Rhodesia's first priority if the destruction of communications was denied. This was to attack ZANLA and ZIPRA concentrations in their external bases. Undeterred by the rejection of his primary plan, Norman turned attention to our enemies' major external havens. In the meanwhile, the SAS and Selous Scouts continued attacking small bases close to Rhodesia.

Internally operations continued apace though a certain amount of continuation training in the field remained essential. On 4 May 1977, Air Lieutenant Bob Griffiths was tasked to carry out GAC training for local army units at the Clydesdale Battle Camp near Umtali. Along for a joyride, was Lance-Corporal Compton Brown. On completion of the training run, Rob was returning to Grand Reef at low level. Due to inexperience, he flew up the centre of a rising valley, failing to observe the golden rule of hugging the valley's edge to give him the widest possible turn-back option, if needed. Too late he realised that he was not going to make the crest and tried to turn back. With too little space to complete a safe turnabout, he flew into rising ground. His survival in the ensuing fiery crash was a miracle and he was lucky not to have been brain-damaged, but his face was permanently fire-scarred. His young passenger died instantly.

Two weeks later, on 18 May, there was death in the air of a very different kind. Roger Watt was flying a G-Car with his tech, Rob Nelson. With them they had four game-ranger trackers who were required to assist an RAR callsign that had been in contact with a group of ZIPRA CTs near Gokwe. Roger dropped only two of the trackers with RAR because one had seen something whilst they were coming in to land. He got airborne again with the two trackers and was climbing out when all hell broke loose beneath him as he reached 1,200 feet. Smoke filled the cabin and with it there were flames. Roger immediately cut fuel-flow and commenced an autorotative forced landing but flames, coming from petrol spilling out of the aircraft's damaged portable-refueller, intensified and burned through the cabin rear wall by the left rear cargo bay, then swirled around throughout the entire cabin. (Portable petrol-driven refuellers had replaced the pressure refuelling units many months earlier.)

Somehow the two rangers got out onto the starboard step and were clinging on outside the cabin where they were protected from the flames by the pilot's door. Throughout the descent raw flames continuously licked Roger but he managed to pull off a well-judged slow landing. The rangers were fine and Roger was quite badly burnt but his unfortunate tech, Rob Nelson who had been engulfed in flames, died after leaping from the aircraft whilst it was still 300 feet up.

External operations March–June 1977

SAS 'COCKLESHELL HEROES' CONFUSED FRELIMO and ZANLA completely, and had forced them to abandon large areas of Tete. ZANLA was still based way back in Tete town, but had diverted routes eastwards and made an error in routing forces through a disused Tanzanian Army base close to FRELIMO's Chioco town.

The Chioco base was destroyed and most of its ZANLA inhabitants were killed in an SAS assault during March. But then FRELIMO made the mistake of accepting ZANLA into Chioco town itself and that once-pretty little Portuguese administrative village was totally destroyed two months later. Air Force involvement in both of these SAS operations was limited to deployments and recoveries, although a Lynx carrying Brian Robinson had been used to cover a casevac and a pair of Hunters was used for one strike.

It was during this period that Brian Robinson's love of flying was sorely tested. On the night of 15 March 1977, Air Sub-Lieutenant John Kidson was tasked to fly OC SAS on a sortie over Mozambique so that Brian could communicate directly with his SAS callsigns engaged in these external operations. The inexperienced young pilot got airborne from FAF 5 but failed to climb at a steeper inclination than the ground that rose from the runway's end towards Mtoko village. Fortunately the softer parts of many treetops dragged the aircraft speed down to a relatively safe speed for the eventual crunch with terra firma. The aircraft caught fire and was completely destroyed but Brian Robinson and John Kidson escaped unhurt. In spite of this experience, Brian's passion for flying never diminished.

In the Repulse area Fireforce was involved in an action in which the suspected presence of FRELIMO forces was confirmed when twenty ZANLA and FRELIMO died in an action inside Rhodesia. This prompted Selous Scouts to launch Operation Aztec, another 'flying column' foray into Gaza Province. On 29 May 1977, Scouts attacked ZANLA and FRELIMO at Jorge do Limpopo and Mapai. Although FRELIMO were getting stronger, they still had no answers to Scouts' techniques, firepower and aggression. Mapai Airfield was secured and declared serviceable before the town itself was taken on.

Most of the vehicles and many of the heavy guns in the Selous Scouts column had been captured during earlier operations in Gaza Province. Rather than destroy good equipment to prevent its use by the enemy, the Scouts preferred to recover whatever they could to bolster their increasing needs. During this operation they captured a number of vehicles and huge quantities of arms and ammunition. So they called for a Dakota on 30 May to fly in a team of Scouts mechanics to make necessary repairs so that their acquired vehicles could carry home all the captured equipment. Later in the day, the Dakota returned with demolition teams to assist in the destruction of structures in Mapai.

By late afternoon the demolition teams were running low on explosives and the defending troops needed more mortar bombs to hold off troublesome ZANLA and FRELIMO forces that were firing at them from beyond the town's outskirts. The Dakota landed for the third time that day, but this was shortly before sunset. Instead of offloading and taking off immediately, the aircraft was held up when the skipper agreed to a Scouts request to wait a while to load more captured equipment. In

Flight Lieutenant Bruce Collocott.

this case aircrew willingness to assist the Army turned out to be a very bad mistake because two hours elapsed between landing and the Dakota commencing its take-off run.

Enemy forces using the cover of darkness had been given plenty of time to establish themselves close to the centre of the runway. The hail of bullets and RPG rockets that followed the Dakota, just as it lifted off, gave it no hope of survival. Flight Lieutenant Bruce Collocott in the co-pilot's seat died instantly, the starboard engine was knocked out and leaking fuel ignited.

Skipper Jerry Lynch had no option but to close down the port engine and land straight ahead. He did an amazing job to bring the crippled aircraft to a controlled halt, allowing survivors to escape from the aircraft. His attempts to get Bruce out of his seat nearly cost Jerry his life before being forced to abandon the attempt due to the blazing inferno around him. Bruce Collocott, with his ever-ready wit was a great loss to the Air Force. So too was the loss of the very first Dakota ever owned by the Southern Rhodesian Air Force. By instruction of Prime Minister Jan Smuts, South Africa had sold it to Rhodesia in 1947 at a ridiculously low price.

Flechettes

THE FRENCH PRODUCED AN ANTI-PERSONNEL warhead for 68mm Sneb rockets that incorporated thousands of tiny darts known as 'flechettes'. When the rockets were fired they flew for just under one second before explosive charges burst warhead casings to release the flechettes into very high-speed free flight. A salvo of flechette-carrying Snebs resulted in a dense cloud of lethal darts covering a large area of ground.

For reasons I never understood, flechette rockets were forbidden by international law because the darts, upon impact with a human body, had the habit of tumbling and making nasty exit wounds. Yet ordinary rifle bullets, which caused more damage and were just as lethal, were considered acceptable. This has never made sense to me.

From as early as 1964 I had been interested in the possibility of using clusters of free-flying darts as a lethal weapon system. This had nothing to do with very lightweight rocket-borne flechettes that relied on very high velocity to make them lethal. I was thinking of large quantities of heavy darts flying in dense formation to produce an instant effect on the ground that could only be achieved by hundreds of machine-guns firing simultaneously.

At the time I was preparing Kutanga Range for the weapons demonstration in 1964, I loaded two teargas carriers with as many six-inch nails as they would accommodate. Flying a Provost, I delivered these from low level at 240 knots. The test was unofficial and was only known to the Kutanga Range staff. The standard flat head of the nails did not give all the nails stability, but those that struck nose-first embedded quite deeply into the trunks of hardwood trees. The test was sufficient to show that the use of six-inch nail shafts incorporating flight stabilisers would be lethal if delivered fast enough. In 1976 I was in a position to extend my explorations officially.

I arranged for an unserviceable Vampire long-range fuel tank to be modified to incorporate a downward opening trapdoor that was activated by the bomb-release button on the control column. Station Workshop at Thornhill produced 2,000 darts from six-inch nails whose flat heads had been removed and substituted by three small in-line fins.

A single-drop trial at 350 knots proved the accuracy, density and lethality of the darts. So, as soon as the Golf bomb project allowed, I turned attention to the matter and a file marked Project Hotel was opened. The project's aim was to produce many thousands of 'six-inch flechettes' for carriage by faster-flying Hunters in large releasable under-wing dispensers.

My visit to the Bulawayo factory that manufactured six-inch nails resulted in an emphatic "technically impossible" response when I asked for nails with no heads, but then an equally emphatic "Yes we can produce them", when I explained their purpose. My next visit was to a plastic-moulding company in Salisbury that produced the moulds for the plastic fin design that I had sketched in the MD's personal diary. The fins were pressure-moulded from recycled plastic and force-fitted over the blunt ends of the six-inch shafts to turn them into flechettes.

Bev designed and produced a purpose-made flechette dispenser that looked just like a streamlined bomb. It incorporated four radiused panels that, together, formed the main cylindrical body enclosing and bearing the heavy charge of 4,500 flechettes. Each of the four panels was secured at its front end to an explosive nose cone and was hinged at its rear into the forward ring of the flight stabiliser cone.

Upon release from its carrier a loaded dispenser dropped free for half a second before the nose cone's explosive charge fired. This released the front anchors of the four panels that rotated outwards and rearward in the air-stream to release 4,500 flechettes into free flight. 50% of the load was packed facing backwards to ensure maximum content but this

This flechette failed to go right through the ultra-hard mopani branch having suffered excessive retardation—but even the slowest of these projectiles was lethal.

This Hunter DFGA 9 armament layout excludes air-to-air missiles and Rhodesian-made Frantans. Back line from left: 130-pound (white) Practice bomb (local), 1000-pound GP Bomb (imported), 50-gallon Frantan (imported), 450kg Golf bomb (local), 4 x 30mm Aden cannon gun-pack. Middle line: 250-pound GP bomb (imported), 68mm Matra rocket pod, Flechette Dispenser (local), Foreground: 30mm cannon shells and 68mm Matra rockets.

enhanced lateral distribution at the expense of inconsequential retardation.

Tests conducted from Hunters, off a standard front-gun attack proved that the new weapon was accurate and highly effective. Released in pairs at speeds in excess of 450 knots resulted in an immensely dense cloud of 9,000 flechettes flying a shallow trajectory, which made survival of exposed people impossible within in the 900-metre-long by seventy-metre-wide strike area.

To give some idea of a flechette strike from a single Hunter—it would require no less than four hundred and fifty .303 Browning machine-guns firing in unison to match the projectile density in the single second it took for all flechettes, first to last, to reach ground.

The flechette-dispensing system was cheap; it did not involve foreign currency expenditure and, unlike exploding

weapons, was totally safe to the delivering aircraft. The system was demonstrated to Air Staff and immediately cleared for operational use, though the question of how our very large stable flechettes might be affected by the international ruling against small flechettes was never resolved. Because there was some doubt, we restricted their employment to strikes inside the country.

Having proved the flechette system for Hunters, I wondered if they could be useful for Canberra night-strikes. Being a silent weapon, I imagined what psychological effects they might have on CT morale if the silent death darts swarmed into ZANLA's external bases when the CTs were up and about during the night when they felt safest. Using a long delay to cater for the free flight time, we tested one flechette dispenser dropped by a Canberra flying 20,000 feet above target. We needed to know the distribution pattern created by such a drop and a water target was best suited for the purpose.

We chose Sebakwe Dam where a bright orange floating target was anchored 200 metres from the shoreline on which my party of observers and photographers was positioned. Ted Brent and his bomb-aimer, Doug Pasea, released the unit and confirmed, "bomb falling". On the ground we focused on the floating target and were aware of the Canberra passing over our position, but nothing happened out on the water for another few seconds. We had just started to comment on the possibility of aiming error when a sound like leaking, high-pressure air surrounded us just before 4,500 darts ruffled the water surface right up to our position. Had we placed the target any closer our ground party would undoubtedly have suffered casualties. The potential for flechette strikes at night was proven to be a possibility but we never used it offensively, because of the international ruling.

'Know your enemy'

SOME TIME AROUND MID-1977 I learned that a Mr Tony Dalton of the 'Shepherd Group' was looking for me. I had no clue who Dalton was or what his business was about. When Tony found me at Mtoko he introduced himself and asked if I was willing to let him pick my brain on a subject that concerned him deeply.

He told me that the Shepherd Group, including himself, comprised of three top-level commercial salesmen. Ian Shepherd had set up the small team to consider what should be done to rectify a transparent failing in Rhodesia's handling of tribesmen who were being subjected to intense ZANLA propaganda with no obvious Rhodesian counter-action. I was immediately interested because this was a 'hearts and minds' issue that I thought should have been COMOPS' highest priority.

Tony outlined the Shepherd Group's thinking and asked for my comments. I cannot recall details, but remember offering a number of opinions that Tony considered important. I found him to be a thoroughly likeable man who understood the fundamental differences between ZANLA and RSF handling of the local people far better than the politicians, Internal Affairs or the military. In a nutshell, ZANLA expended 95% of its efforts on politicising the people and 5% against the Rhodesian establishment. The RSF, on the other hand, was forced to expend 95% of its effort in response to ZANLA activity with a mere 5% given to badly misdirected psychological action.

Whereas the Shepherd Group eventually broke up because of the lack of interest shown by the authorities, Tony felt so strongly about the need to lead and direct psychological operations that he gave up his successful civilian job to join the regular Army. For his efforts he received little more than lip service from COMOPS who, I say again, should have been leading the action in the first place.

One issue that really troubled Tony Dalton and me was how little we knew about our enemies. Though CIO and SB knew much, Rhodesian secrecy phobias blocked important information from flowing through to the fighting men. So, with Ron Reid-Daly's active support and participation, Tony arranged a presentation entitled 'Know your enemy'. Surprisingly few high-ranking officers took the trouble to attend this presentation, which was held in the RLI hall.

Those of us who were there were treated to an eye-opening intelligence briefing on ZANLA and ZIPRA command and field structures and were exposed to first-hand experiences given by two ex-CTs serving with Selous Scouts. One was a recently captured ZANLA detachment commander who told us simple things we should have known, but didn't. The other was from ZIPRA. As with so many other issues that begged attention, Tony's theories and plans were initially ignored then rushed into ineffective action when it was too late to gain any worthwhile benefits.

Salisbury recce

IN AUGUST 1977, ZANLA LAUNCHED an ineffective long-range mortar attack against New Sarum Air Base. It was so badly conducted that the nearest bomb fell more than 500 metres short of the base. Nevertheless, this was the closest action to Salisbury city and confirmed suspicions that CTs had moved into the Chimanda Tribal Trust Land on the northern side of the capital. The question arose as to whether or not CTs were based in the Seki Reserve south of New Sarum or at any location within or around Salisbury itself.

I was asked to have a look around and was surprised to find many locations that looked similar to CT bases. There were also many other places that attracted my attention and all were plotted and passed to the SB and Salisbury Police who systematically checked them out. Instead of finding terrorists, the Police made numerous arrests because I had put them onto places where illegal activities were taking place. These included stolen vehicle strip-down joints, temporary hiding-places for stolen goods and illicit liquor-producing stills.

First employment of flechettes

ON 26 OCTOBER 1977, JOHN BLYTHE-WOOD, who had been posted to Hunters, together with 'Spook' Geraty responded to an Army callsign who reported a large female feeding-party attending CTs in a section of riverine bush between two hill features. The target description fitted the grid-reference given and first strikes went in. But then the ground callsign told the pilots they had struck the wrong point. By the time John realised that the ground callsign had misread his map and switched his attack across to the correct target, a parallel river between two hills 700 metres away, the birds had flown.

Two days later, a Selous Scouts' observation team on a high feature spotted this group again. The Scouts radioed that they could see 150 CTs moving northwest along the Pesu River, ten kilometres from the South African border. The Repulse Fireforce manned by the SAS responded. The K-Car, piloted by Ken Newman with OC SAS, Brian Robinson as airborne commander, called for Hunter airstrike. John Blythe-Wood and his wingman Air Lieutenant Lowrie were scrambled with Lowrie's aircraft carrying a pair of flechette dispensers.

Ken Newman's ASR is given in his rather unusual style. It reads:

The call-out was initiated by c/s 72B (chl 22). The sequence of events was as follows:
1. FF (1 K-Car + 4 Gs + E4) airborne from Malapati arrange for c/s A5 (Canberra) to bomb grid reference passed by c/s 72A and 72B at 30:10:02B. FF to arrive overhead at 10:03B. A5 does not identify target and does not bomb.
2. K-Car overhead area 'A' sees ters and opens fire. Pink Section (G-Cars) told to drop sticks to surround area 'A'. Heavy ground fire directed at K-Car.
3. Lynx c/s E4 (Flt Lt Mienie) does 2 x Frantan/.303 attacks West

to East in area 'A'. A5 does two bomb runs on area 'A'. K-Car calls for Hunters. Pink returns to Malapati for more troops.

4. Heavy fire still directed at K-Car now hit several times. Second Canberra (C5) on airborne standby bombs area 'B'.

5. Hunters strafe area 'A' along both sides of river. 4 more stops arrive. Para-Dak (F3) arrives from FAF 8 and drops Eagle callsigns in area shown. CTs return fire and K-Car hit several times. Cannon jams. K-Car pulls back H4 attacks W.

6. Second pair of Hunters on standby. Heavy fire directed at K-Car. At no time did K-Car/K-Car commander see 150 ters. Presume advance group of 30-40 contacted in immediate area.

7. Stop 2 tells K-Car heavy fire coming from open area to his (stop 2) north. Does not seem likely area but K-Car investigates. H4 (A/S/L Hatfield) relieves E4. 2nd pair Hunters arrive. F3 positions more troops at Groot Vlei (UL 180415).

8. K-Car is talked onto area by Stop 2 (area 'B'). Opens fire on a few (old abandoned) huts. No results. Still heavy fire at K-Car. Then K-Car sees approx. 6 ters in area 'B', opens fire. Ters E. 1 Frantan/.303 on target. (There were actually 11 ters in area 'B').

9. Hunters** attack target. K-Car cannon fixed. K-Car opens fire—cannon jams.

10. Pink Section troop in extra troops (now total of 16 stops). Pink 1 fired at by smallarms overshoots LZ. (Fire came from area 'B' prior to air attack.)

11. K-Car clears area. Eagle c/s 3 has contact with 3 ters. 3 ters killed (area 'C'). H4 drops 1 frantan/.303 N-S.

12. 2 more ters killed in subsequent follow up. Other 120 or so ters presumably legging it to Mozambique.

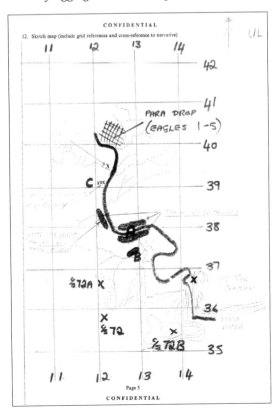

** Hunter strike using flechette proved very successful. Total of 11 dead found in area of flechette strike. Final tally 28 CTs killed of which 5 accounted for by stops.

This was the first use of flechettes; so OC SAS was present for yet another Air Force 'first'.

Preparing to attack external bases

BEFORE HIS POSTING TO COMOPS, Group Captain Norman Walsh had been Director Operations in Air Staff. Never one to sit and wait for action, Norman left his office as often as possible to seek out all available intelligence. During late November 1976 through to February 77 he and Peter McLurg always seemed to be in an awful hurry as they rushed between Air HQ, JSPIS at New Sarum and SAS HQ at Kabrit. During this time, Norman came to me regularly to keep abreast of weapons developments in which he was profoundly interested.

On one of these visits in January 1977, he and Peter laid a large-scale photograph across my desk. It was of ZANLA's main base and headquarters in Mozambique. Peter explained the layout of Chimoio Base and gave me a run-down on all available intelligence relating to it. Well over 6,000 ZANLA were known to be in residence with more trained personnel arriving daily from Tanzania and other countries. Norman warned that this was top-secret information and that my involvement was purely to assist him select the best weapons for a possible attack on the base. At that time Alpha bomb stocks were mounting but Golf bombs were not yet in production.

When he was posted to COMOPS two months later, Norman asked me to visit him regularly to keep him informed about weapons availability and run him through current project work. By that time Golf bombs were available and had already been integrated into his airstrike plans. Norman knew about the flechette dispenser system and the startling effects that could be expected from this weapon, so I suggested he consider them for use against large concentrations of exposed enemy forces, such as mass parades seen on some aerial photographs.

By June 1977, intelligence had established that there were 8,000 ZANLA in Chimoio Base and photographic evidence confirmed that the base was growing rapidly. Many miles to the north of Chimoio, inside the Tete Province, a second ZANLA base for about 4,000 CTs was also being monitored. Norman and his SAS colleagues linked this base, Tembue, with their attack plans for Chimoio. Realising that the threat from such large concentrations of trained CTs was overwhelming; they sought COMOPS authority to execute their plan.

General Walls and his COMOPS staff attended a number of

presentations at SAS HQ. These were made around large-scale models of the two targets. The operational proposals frightened those who listened because they were madly daring and very dangerous. Both proposals involved relatively straightforward air attacks that were to be followed with vertical envelopment by paratroopers and heli-borne forces. This was considered absolutely essential to ensure maximum results and to seriously disrupt ZANLA.

From the outset COMOPS totally rejected any idea of attacking Tembue due to its great distance from Rhodesia; but there was a softening towards the strike plan for Chimoio. Eventually, after many persuasive presentations and much lost time, the operational plans for both Chimoio and Tembue were approved. By then it was late October 1977 when Chimoio's numbers had risen to 11,000. Tembue was still reported to contain 4,000.

The task that Norman and his planning colleague Major Brian Robinson had on their hands was a daunting one. It was one thing to make operational proposals, but quite another to reduce them to the finest details that were so necessary to ensure effective execution.

The onset of the rainy season in November made it imperative that the attacks went in before large numbers of CTs launched into Rhodesia to take advantage of good bush cover with abundant food supplies. Had the attack been approved earlier any threat of bad weather affecting plans would not have been a factor, but now it was a critical issue and accurate weather forecasting was essential.

For some time a fundi in Salisbury had been providing the Air Force with weather information that he alone could receive indirectly from space satellites, using his own homemade equipment. Due to international sanctions Rhodesia was unable, officially that is, to receive satellite imagery of the weather patterns affecting southern Africa. How this man managed to tap into the Intelstat transmissions from Europe escapes me.

Cloud cover images were beamed down in digital form to the Intelstat receiver in Europe. Eight hours later, having been processed into usable form, the information was transmitted to a network of official receiver stations that subscribed to the service. Surreptitious interception of these signals in Salisbury obviously cost nothing but the data acquired had to be processed in a special way to get a printout resembling a photograph of cloud formations over southern Africa, as seen by the satellite. At around 10:00 every day this cloud-map arrived at Air HQ.

The cloud-maps were important to us because reports from weather stations to the north of Rhodesia were completely unreliable. Although the images we received were rather poor by modern standards, they were sufficient to warn of any major weather fronts that might affect operational planning. Nevertheless, they could not be relied upon to forecast localised orographic and thermal cloud situations that might affect long-range operations.

With the best will in the world, and using every available strike aircraft, the Air Force could not hope to produce the meaningful kill and serious wound rates we needed, because Chimoio was made up of so many camps spread over a vast area. There was no alternative but to use the very best available fighting soldiers to assault the targets immediately after a maximum-effort jet-strike.

Chimoio lay over ninety kilometres from the Rhodesian border and Tembue was almost three times that distance. However, Norman and Brian agreed that these distances favoured them in that they were both convinced neither ZANLA nor FRELIMO would seriously expect a combined air and ground attack so far from Rhodesia's border. Until now, all combined external operations had occurred very close to the border.

The Selous Scouts' attack on Nyadzonya Base in August 1976 had quite obviously taught ZANLA not to concentrate its forces, which is why Chimoio Base comprised so many small camps widely spread; and to a lesser extent this also applied to Tembue. Though the wide spread of targets compounded planning difficulties, it did not alter the planners' view that ZANLA felt perfectly safe from anything but air attack, particularly with FRELIMO's main base at Chimoio (previously Vila Pery) being so close by.

Planning the air attacks was simple enough and the selection of troops was obvious; the SAS and RLI would be used. But any idea of employing a mobile column to get a large ground force to either target was a non-starter as surprise would be impossible to achieve. Interference from FRELIMO would certainly occur early and involve heavy fighting most of the way to target, thereby giving ZANLA all the time in the world to vacate their bases. It was clear therefore that the ground force had to go in by air and be recovered the same way.

Our total airlift capacity was very small, which meant that very few troops would be taking on overwhelming enemy numbers, particularly at Chimoio. Only total surprise could turn ZANLA's numerical advantage to SAS and RLI favour, providing ongoing close-air support was available.

The general military principle of attacking an enemy with a force three times larger was a pipe dream. Even if every soldier in Rhodesia was made available, this could not be achieved. It had to be accepted that, at Chimoio, the troops would be outnumbered by at least fifty to one but OC SAS was not put off by these impossible odds, providing total surprise could be achieved.

Any idea of aircraft returning to Rhodesia for second-wave troops was discounted since this would take too long to have any meaningful effect on the ground in the critical first hour of fighting. In any case the trooper helicopters would first have to refuel inside Mozambique as soon as they had deposited the first wave of troops, thereby adding to the delay in getting back to Rhodesia for a second lift. If such troops were used it would also multiply post-operation recovery difficulties.

To meet all requirements in what would surely be a full

day of fighting, fuel and ammunition reserves would have to be available close to the battle sites at Chimoio and Tembue. Norman named these positions 'admin bases' into which a small force of protection troops, with all fuel and reserve ammunition, would have to be delivered by parachute at the same time that troops were landing in the target areas. No such luxury as a medical team could be considered. An Air Force officer would have to be at the Admin Base to co-ordinate all activities in and out of there.

There was no way of pre-judging the level or consequence of aircraft and troop losses that might occur in each battle or, heaven forbid, if an admin base was overrun. To cater for such unforeseen situations, and because every participating soldier would have to be airlifted back to Rhodesia, it was essential to retain a sizeable reserve of trooper helicopters as close to the action as safely possible. There were only thirty-two helicopters available. One would have to be specially prepared as a command helicopter with every radio frequency needed to control both air and ground actions. Another would be dedicated to the Admin Base commander, who would also carry all radio spares.

This left thirty helicopters; ten would carry troops to target, ten would take offensive action as K-Cars and the remaining ten would be held in reserve with back-up spares. The reserve helicopters would participate in the recovery of troops at the conclusion of operations.

Six Dakotas were available to deliver 145 SAS and RLI paratroopers, and another forty RLI could be carried to target in the ten trooper helicopters. Assuming that at least 1,000 ZANLA had been neutralised during the opening air strikes, just 185 men on the ground would face at least 10,000 armed ZANLA at Chimoio. Although assigned to their own specific targets, the ten K-Cars, carrying double loads of 20mm ammunition, could be called upon to assist troops where necessary. A civilian DC7 aircraft, flown by its owner Captain Jack Malloch, was made available to parachute-in the admin area protection troops, ammunition and fuel.

Norman Walsh planned to fly the command helicopter himself to control all air activity. Sitting with him would be Brian Robinson as overall commander of ground forces. Their helicopter would give them freedom to move about the target area to direct the ground battle or stand off if anti-air action made this impossible.

A specially equipped Dakota carrying General Peter Walls, Peter McLurg and a small staff would cruise around at height near the border to keep in touch with the command helicopter and provide immediate communications with COMOPS, Thornhill, New Sarum and the reserve helicopters.

Following their opening strikes, all jets would rush home to rearm and remain at immediate airborne or ground readiness to take on difficult enemy positions as they arose. This might include FRELIMO forces with tanks, should they choose to become involved.

Put very simply—that was the plan.

Op Dingo briefing

OPERATION DINGO WAS THE CODENAME given to the attacks on Chimoio and Tembue. Phase One was to be the attack against Chimoio on 23 November 1977. On completion, all helicopters were to move to Mtoko with their contingent of troops and the paratrooper element was to position at New Sarum preparatory to launching the long-range Phase Two attack against Tembue on 25 November.

I knew everything concerning Norman's airstrike plans because he had involved me in formulating them; but that was all I knew. He had not mentioned the use of ground forces until, at short notice, I learned that I was to be the Admin Base commander for both operations and was to attend a two-phase briefing at New Sarum on Tuesday 22 November. The reason Norman Walsh selected me for the Admin Base task was to give me opportunity to inspect the areas of jet-strikes so that I could analyse the effectiveness of our locally made weapons in live target situations.

One of 3 Squadron's hangars had been cleared and grandstands from the station sports field had been erected around a large-scale model of Chimoio Base. Present for the briefing were all the service commanders, senior staff officers from COMOPS and all active participants from the Air Force and Army. I remember the noise and excitement levels being incredible. Absolute silence fell when Captain Scotty McCormack of the SAS took centre stage to commence his target intelligence briefing on Chimoio. Having done this so many times for COMOPS, Scotty needed no notes for his excellent, smooth-flowing presentation. Much of what he had to say was new to me, even though I had known about Chimoio for months.

To assist in the briefing and to facilitate easy target identification during the operation itself, a single photograph of the entire Chimoio complex of camps was handed to every participant. This photograph incorporated grid lines bearing alphabetic letters for the vertical lines and numerical numbering for the lateral ones. The same grid was overlaid on the target model.

Norman Walsh followed Scotty and commenced the air briefing by saying H-hour for Chimoio was 23:07:45 Bravo. He then outlined the operational sequence with specific timings before giving a detailed briefing to each participating squadron.

He revealed that he had arranged for a DC8 jet-liner to over-fly Chimoio at H-hour minus ten minutes in the hopes that this would have every CT diving for cover. He expected that, by the time the lead Hunter struck, ZANLA CTs would have realised that they had over-reacted to a passing civilian airliner and would be mustering for the regular 08:00 parade.

Using a long pointer and giving grid references directly from the target model, Norman indicated old farm buildings on the western side of the main concentration of camps. These were the headquarters and living quarters of ZANLA's top commanders, Josiah Tongogara and Rex Nhongo. The first pair of Hunters, delivering Golf bombs against these HQ buildings, would initiate the air action spot on H-hour. Their Golf bomb detonations would act as confirming markers for a formation of four Canberras closing in from the west at low level to strike twenty seconds later. Smoke and dust from the Golf bombs would assist the lead bomber to ensure that the formation was correctly aligned with its targets commencing from the western edge of the HQ complex and stretching eastward.

Front-gun, Frantan and rocket attacks by Hunters and Vampires would follow the Canberras, striking against targets Norman indicated in sequence of attacks. At this time, the Dakotas would already be making their final run, three down the western flank of the main concentration of camps and three along the southern flank to drop the assaulting SAS and RLI paratrooper force in a single pass at H-hour plus two minutes.

Because of the noise factor, particularly over the flat terrain around Chimoio, the helicopters would be coming in well behind the quiet Dakotas. This meant that the paratroopers would already be on the ground before the command helicopter and K-Cars reached them at H-hour plus seven minutes. However, Hunter and Vampire strikes would still be in progress for much of this intervening time. Flying on the north side of the K-Cars would be ten trooper helicopters to place RLI in a stop-line along the north side of Chimoio Base.

With troops north, west and south of the primary targets, four K-Cars were assigned to 'close the gap' by operating along a line across open fields commencing at camps in the southeast all the way up to the left flank of the RLI stop-line. The other six K-Cars would take on satellite camps lying west of the main target and to the rear of the assault troops.

A single helicopter assigned to the Admin Base, carrying spare radios and me, was to break away from the trooper helicopters and land in the assigned Admin Base area. My first job was to direct the DC7 for its deliveries of the Admin Base protection troops, fuel and ammunition. Thereafter I had to oversee all activity including refuelling, repairs and casevacs for helicopters moving to and from the target that was a little under ten kilometres away.

The command Dakota carrying General Walls and his staff had all the equipment needed to communicate with the command helicopter on VHF and COMOPS via HF and teleprinters. This aircraft was to rove at height, up and down the Rhodesian border. Peter McLurg would provide the link through which Norman could bring in reserve helicopters waiting at Lake Alexander or jets from New Sarum and Thornhill.

To keep security as tight as possible, helicopters positioning at Lake Alexander, which lay twenty-five kilometres north of Umtali, were to fly from New Sarum and Grand Reef during the early hours, refuel and be ready for lift-off by no later than H-hour minus 90 minutes. Lift-off from Lake Alexander would be at H-hour minus one hour five minutes. Norman then gave details of how the DC7, Dakotas and jet aircraft were to launch from New Sarum and jets from Thornhill. Included were details of the ten reserve helicopters that would move from Grand Reef to Lake Alexander once the main force was clear.

Recovery of everyone back to Grand Reef, except for an SAS stay-behind force of ninety-seven men, had to be completed before nightfall. For this, all helicopters from the reserve pool at Lake Alexander would be called forward to assist the G-Cars and K-Cars already in the op area.

To be recovered were forty-eight RLI assault troops with parachutes, forty RLI troops of the northern stop-line, the admin area protection troops with parachutes, me and as many cargo parachutes as possible. No fuel drums, whether full or empty, would be recovered or destroyed.

The SAS stay-behind troops remaining in the target overnight were to be uplifted early next morning. Details for this recovery would be given at a separate briefing at Grand Reef. Norman concluded his briefing with details on VHF channels along with general and emergency procedures.

As commander of ground forces, Major Brian Robinson made his briefing in his usual crisp, clear manner aided by the target model, many charts and signals network diagrams. His in-depth briefing on all troop movements, all cross-referenced to Norman's briefing, completed the entire operational presentation. An operational order issued with maps and target photos assisted operators to follow the briefings and fully comprehend their tasks.

When these presentations ended and all questions had been answered, there was a noisy tea break in the Parachute Training School hangar before everyone reassembled for the briefing on Tembue. The venue and set-up for this briefing remained the same as for Chimoio, except that the centrepiece was now the Tembue target model, suitably marked with the same grid markings that appeared on photographs of the target.

The briefing followed the same format as for Chimoio but only took half as long to complete because radio networks and basic procedures remained unaltered. On completion, General Walls gave a short address before everyone rushed off to prepare for an early-morning start.

Chimoio attack

FLIGHT LIEUTENANT BILL SYKES WAS assigned to take me to the Admin Base. Our helicopter, together with twenty-one others, lifted from the 7 Squadron helicopter pad and headed for Lake Alexander. Different routes were used so as not to draw attention to unusually large numbers of helicopters heading for a single destination on the eastern border. The remaining ten helicopters were to move up later from Grand Reef.

Rough ground sloping up from Lake Alexander rose to a foresters' road running parallel to and some 300 metres on the south side of the water's edge. Full fuel drums had been laid out along this road during the night. This was not an ideal site because the helicopters were stretched out in a long line which necessitated quite a long walk for some crews to attend a final briefing which ended just as trucks rolled in with forty RLI soldiers.

OC 7 Squadron, Squadron Leader Harold Griffiths, who had to lead the formation of twenty-two helicopters, showed some concern because the weather was not as clear as had been forecast. Lake Alexander lay in high ground on the lee side of the higher range of mountains that formed the border between Rhodesia and the low ground of Mozambique. A moist air mass flowing from Mozambique was being forced to rise over the mountains, creating a continuous line of cumulus cloud whose base was at ground level along the borderline itself. Mountain-flying experience had shown that it was usually possible to remain visual under such cloud formation by following steep-sided river valleys and Griff had selected such a valley to break through into Mozambique.

When the time came to move, Griff led the way, heading for the valley but found his way blocked and had to turn about. Helicopters flying the loop caused by this diversion presented an impressive sight but timing was such a critical issue that the delay immediately became cause for concern. Fortunately, when he was heading north for a second valley, Griff spotted Mozambican ground to his right under a very small lift in the cloud base. This allowed all the helicopters to pass through before dense cloud reformed at ground level behind the last helicopter. All helicopters then descended to the low ground, initially over abandoned Portuguese farmlands for the run to target. With helicopters all around and flying low over exquisite countryside, it was hard to fully comprehend the fact that we were on a deadly mission with all hell about to break loose. Halfway to target I was surprised to see the DC7 cruise past on our port side looking quite splendid against the African backdrop. Almost immediately it turned to commence continuous orbits to stay behind the formation of helicopters.

Lake Alexander.

Helicopters passing over abandoned Portuguese farmlands.

Approaching Lake Alexander.

The main force had over ten minutes to run to target when Bill Sykes broke away, heading directly for the Admin Base. When we reached it, I was startled to find that this was not the fairly open area of ground that I had expected. Although undoubtedly the most suitable site for miles around, it was covered with fairly high grass interspersed with clumps of dense scrub that occupied almost half of the assigned area.

At about this time the reserve helicopters from Grand Reef were approaching Lake Alexander.

Bill Sykes and I did not see the airstrikes going in southeast of us but landed to prepare to take the DC7 drops. The rotors had not yet stopped turning when I spotted the big aircraft already running in from the east. It was two minutes too early, yet the Admin Base protection troops were already peeling out of the huge cargo door before I had a chance to call Squadron Leader George Alexander, who was flying second pilot to Captain Jack Malloch.

The DC7 lumbered past and rolled into a slow starboard turn to re-position for its second drop. On the ground and out of sight 500 metres away, the troops were gathering up their parachutes, well beyond the position I would have placed them; had I been given the chance. As the aircraft lined up for its second run, I called George by callsign, instructing "Red light on…" then waited for the position I wanted the first fuel drop to be launched. However, well before this position, the first pallet of drums was followed rapidly by three more. All were descending way, way short, just as first helicopters arrived over the Admin Base.

George Alexander, an excitable man at the best of times (he was part-Greek), cursed the helicopter pilots for being in the way of the DC7 that was, by necessity, staggering along close to stalling speed. I could see that all the helicopters were well clear but George who was used to Air Traffic Control separation was unaccustomed to seeing other aircraft so close to his. This was not Salisbury Airport! It was a piece of foreign bush supposedly controlled by a man, me, whose instructions were either not being received, or were being ignored because of George's stressed state. The helicopter pilots ignored his curses and landed next to me.

One of the trooper helicopters had taken serious hits that rendered it unfit to fly, even for a one-time flight to Rhodesia. The others could not take on fuel immediately, because my instructions continued to be ignored and fuel drops were going in where George chose to place them. When eventually the Chimoio operation was over, George claimed he had not received my instructions, even though the helicopter pilots had heard them clearly.

I had abandoned any hope of getting fuel and ammunition down where I needed them when Norman Walsh arrived, way ahead of time. His command helicopter was shot up and he needed to borrow another in a hurry. Both he and Brian were deeply frustrated by their unplanned absence from the action at the most critical time in the battle; but there was no aircraft immediately available.

Fortunately I had already arranged for the RLI protection troops, who should have been climbing a small feature next to the Admin Base to watch for enemy movement, to roll some drums clear of the drop zone so that helicopters could commence refuelling. The first machine to be refuelled was commandeered by Norman and Brian who rushed back to the action.

I inspected the command helicopter and the other damaged one. A complete main rotor head change was needed on the command aircraft and the other needed replacement of the entire tail cone. There was no hope of switching the complex radio system on the command aircraft, so I asked the 7 Squadron technicians present if they thought it possible to substitute the command helicopter's damaged main rotor head with the good one from the aircraft requiring tail cone change. "What a question, sir. We will have it done sooner than you think." With no rigging equipment or specialised tools, half a dozen technicians and two pilots descended on both aircraft with standard tools and plenty of energy.

George Alexander (right) is seen here with the American astronaut Walter Schirra. From left: Wing Commander Bill Jelley (OC Flying Wing New Sarum), Group Captain John Mussell (CO New Sarum) and Air Commodore Dicky Bradshaw (DG Ops).

Northernmost corner of Admin Base as seen from a K-Car.

I moved away from the repair party to attend to the removal of parachutes from drum and ammunition pallets lying in open ground so that helicopters could land next to them. This was important because parachutes blown up by rotor-wash could be drawn into spinning rotor blades with disastrous consequences. I was still dealing with this when the repaired command helicopter was flown in right next to me to be refuelled. I was happy to let Norman Walsh know his aircraft was ready for him. Being unable to communicate directly with the Command Dak, I asked Norman to arrange for a set of rotor blades and a tail assembly to be flown in from Lake Alexander. These arrived a little after midday and by 4 o'clock the damaged machine was ready to fly.

Many drums had landed amongst high bushes which necessitated manhandling them into positions where helicopters could land. There was no alternative but to use all available pilots and technicians as well as the RLI protection troops who, to their credit, never hesitated or moaned but got stuck into these onerous tasks. No sooner had they completed the work than I had to impose a lighter but equally onerous task on them. This was to flatten most of the low scrub for improved landing space, concentrate empty drums lying on their sides and position full drums standing up at twenty assigned spots so that crews coming in for fuel could differentiate between full and empty drums.

K-Car pilots and gunners arriving to refuel and re-arm reported that they were having a tough time with high volumes of small arms, anti-aircraft gunfire and more targets than they could handle. Flight Lieutenant Mark McLean, who had taken early retirement from the Air Force, was on call-up for Op Dingo. Sporting a beard he would not have been allowed to wear in regular service, he landed and removed his shattered bone dome. The graze and large swelling above his right eye bore witness to how close he had come to death from a vertical bullet-strike that had torn a section out of his protective helmet.

As with Mark's aircraft, every other K-Car had taken many small- and large-calibre strikes, but none too serious to keep them from returning to the fray.

Mark had been allocated a satellite target that was believed to be a camp for wounded veterans who had returned from Rhodesia to recuperate in Mozambique. It seemed to Mark that the intelligence on this 'soft target' must have been totally incorrect because there were far more anti-aircraft guns there than at any of the other satellite camps. In consequence he had been forced to call on two other K-Cars to help him neutralise the heavy-calibre guns.

During a few quiet moments at the Admin Base it was possible to hear the rumble of Alpha bomb and rocket strikes that Norman was directing against troublesome anti-aircraft guns and other points of resistance.

During his approach to Chimoio, the medium-level cloud he could see over the target area concerned Norman Walsh.

Fortunately this did not trouble Squadron Leader Rich Brand as he led his Hunters in for their initial strikes. He fired 30mm cannons at the Chimoio HQ buildings before Vic Wightman's Golf bombs hit the same target spot on H-hour. Squadron Leader Randy du Rand saw the Golf bombs exploding exactly where he expected them and led the four Canberras over the smoke and dust to deliver 1,200 Alpha bombs exactly as planned to cover an area of 1.1 kilometres in length by half a kilometre in width.

In spite of the shock effect of the opening air strikes, and those still in progress, some anti-aircraft guns took on the six slow-flying Dakotas as they passed in extended line astern at 500 feet, disgorging heavily laden paratroopers. During their short descent to ground, the paratroopers were surprised to see many CTs running towards them with some already passing directly below. Their drop line had been planned to be far enough from the campsites to ensure that all ZANLA within the primary target area would be contained before the paratroopers landed. As it happened, many paratroopers landed amongst fleeing ZANLA who, though armed, seemed to have only one thing in mind; escape!

Brian Robinson had been right in assuming that CTs would not move out along obvious escape routes but simply run in the direction they happened to be facing. He was wrong in assuming that he had planned an adequate distance from primary targets to the paratrooper drop lines because he had failed to cater for the Olympic speeds stressed CTs could achieve.

Paratrooper commanders had no time to organise their callsigns in the opening minutes, because officers and soldiers were taking on large numbers of ZANLA running from the ongoing air activities. Soon enough the CTs realised their way was blocked, though a few made the deadly error of attempting to fight their way through the troops in hope of gaining safety in the bush beyond.

Hunter and Vampire strikes and re-strikes were still continuing as the SAS and RLI soldiers killed hundreds of panicking CTs. The jets cleared back to base to re-arm as K-Cars moved into action, their cannons adding to the confusion of noise from smallarms and anti-aircraft gunfire.

Those CTs who realised that they were running towards certain death around the perimeter went to ground, allowing the assault troops time to organise themselves for their advance through the camps. The exposed breast of one dead ZANLA, still clutching an AK-47 rifle, confirmed intelligence reports that there were a number of Tanzanian-trained CT females present at Chimoio.

Brian Robinson had only just begun to give his orders when the command helicopter was hit, forcing Norman to clear to the Admin Base. The hiatus caused by the loss of their airborne commander might have been disastrous except for the calibre of men on the ground and in the K-Cars. Nevertheless, the return of Norman Walsh and Brian in the borrowed helicopter, albeit with reduced communication facilities, allowed organised movement to recommence.

Along the entire assault line, soldiers moved forwards continuously killing every ZANLA in their path. With so much ground to cover and with so many CTs in hiding, the fighting went on all day. Independently, K-Cars took on allcomers within and beyond the primary target.

The incoming and outgoing flow of communications to and from the command helicopter was relentless but rewarding. Norman ordered many Hunter and Canberra strikes against tough points to ensure that the roll-up action kept momentum. The gridded photographs of Chimoio allowed him to pass each target point to the striking pilots with pinpoint accuracy. Once his orders were issued, he could get on with other matters without having to oversee the strikes. At times there were as many as four targets lined up for near-simultaneous attention.

Brian Robinson had over sixty callsigns to deal with, a mind-boggling situation that he managed with incredible skill. His numerous actions as the Army commander in Fireforce actions had certainly prepared him well for this high-pressure situation.

Back at the Admin Base, with so much going on around me all at once over such a large area, I experienced moments of helplessness, even panic, when I felt I was not managing to do all that was expected of me. Fortunately our pilots and technicians got on with their work in typically efficient fashion, offering help or simply taking action without my having to ask them to do so. The RLI 'protection troops' were outstanding, having developed and maintained a smooth and cheerful routine.

A little after midday one SAS soldier who had been killed in action, Frans Nel, and a couple of casualties were delivered to me. I had been expecting many casualties throughout the day but these were the only ones that came to the Admin Base. This was incredible considering the very high number of dead ZANLA the K-Car pilots reported seeing in their own target areas and in the ground through which the assault troops had passed.

One of the Vampires was crippled by ground fire. Air Lieutenant Phil Haigh was flying the FB9 that sustained damage as it crossed over Vanduzi crossroads on return to base. This caused his engine to fail some way short of the border. Rather than attempt the notoriously dangerous act of abandoning an FB 9, Phil chose to glide across the border and make a forced landing in Rhodesia. This might have worked had the aircraft not run into the deep *donga* that wrecked the aircraft and killed Phil.

Phil Haigh (left) with Francois du Toit.

When Norman Walsh called me forward to inspect air weapons' effects, it was rapidly approaching the time for recovery to Rhodesia; in fact helicopters from Lake Alexander were already airborne en route to uplift troops. It was only in the air on the short leg to Chimoio that I realised just how late it was. With so much noisy activity and so much to do, eight hours appeared to have compressed into mere minutes.

There was too little time to inspect more that a portion of an Alpha bomb strike and one site struck by Golf bombs. Nevertheless this was more than enough to let me see what I needed to see. In fact I saw more than I bargained for and the experience shook me to the very core of my being.

The four-man SAS callsign assigned to protect and assist me were clearly amused by my discomfort at being on the ground. The real fighting was over and for these men Chimoio had become a quiet environment. Not so for one who felt safest in the air. I dropped to ground as bullets cracked overhead then raised myself sheepishly when I realised no one else had taken cover. The next time a flurry of cracks sounded around us, I remained standing when all four SAS had dropped to the ground. "Never mind, sir," said the nearest soldier, "it's the ones you don't hear that you need to worry about."

The air strike effects were very troubling. Analysing weapons efficiency and counting holes in dummy targets out on a prepared site at Kutanga Range was one thing. To see the same weapons' effects on human beings was quite another. I had seen many dead Rhodesians and CT killed in Fireforce actions and had witnessed the appalling carnage on civilians blown up by ZANLA landmines; but here I was seeing something more horrifying. Those who had been killed by the troops were greater in number, but somehow their wounds appeared to me to be so much more acceptable than those taken out by bombs.

The effect of an air strike.

The SAS men escorting me were used to seeing bodies mutilated by grenades, landmines and even heavy airstrikes. For me it was different. An airman's war tends to be detached. Even seeing CTs running and going down under air fire seemed

Helicopters in the Admin Base ready for lift-off to recover RLI and SAS troops back to Rhodesia. Note the extent of pathways and flattened vegetation created in eight hours.

remote. Never again did I accept airstrike casualty numbers as the means by which to judge our air successes without remembering the horror of what I saw at Chimoio.

It was a relief to lift off for the return flight to the Admin Base and thence back to Rhodesia.

The sun set as we crossed the border. In darkness we followed a long line of red rotating beacons as the largest-ever gathering of helicopters flew into Grand Reef. No cold beer ever tasted so good!

The Chimoio phase of Op Dingo was almost closed. In one day, ZANLA had lost in excess of 1,200 combatants dead with a much larger number missing or wounded. This had cost Rhodesia two servicemen killed, about six wounded (none seriously) and one Vampire.

The SAS stay-behind forces remained in ambush positions for the night and accounted for more CTs who thought all the Rhodesians had gone home. Early next morning, these men destroyed whatever buildings and equipment remained before helicopters recovered them along with selected equipment, and piles of captured documents.

Chimoio Base lay littered with bodies, burned-out structures and destroyed equipment. Hundreds of wounded ZANLA were pouring into FRELIMO's provincial town of Chimoio. The two ZANLA commanders we had hoped to take out, Josiah Tongogara and Rex Nhongo, were not in base and escaped as they had done before and would do time and time again.

We knew that, when they gathered courage to do so, ZANLA's leadership would visit the battle-site to ensure that all evidence of ZANLA's arms was removed. They must do this before calling international observers to witness the burial of 'Zimbabwean refugees' because ZANLA had registered Chimoio Base, along with all other military establishments, as a refugee camp.

We knew that particular attention would be given to showing

the UN High Commission for Refugees the bodies of a number of teenagers killed at Chimoio. These were the school children that had been forced, or enticed, to leave schools in Rhodesia to undergo military training in Mozambique. No doubt the chalk boards and timetables the SAS soldiers had seen in two classrooms would have been cleared of their Marxist slogans and instructions on weapons-handling. They were sure to have been adorned with make-believe items 'to prove their good works in teenager education'.

Phase One of Op Dingo was over. The countdown for Phase Two had already started as emergency repairs to the helicopters were hurried through with little time to spare.

Tembue attack

THE EASTERN SKY HAD ONLY just begun to light up on Friday, 25 November, as twenty-two helicopters lifted out of Mtoko and Mount Darwin on the first leg of the 320-kilometre journey to Tembue. The reserve force of ten helicopters was to follow one hour later with spares.

Reserve force.

Squadron Leader Rex Taylor, with a small team of Air Force VR and RLI troops, awaited the arrival of the helicopters at a 'staging base'. This base was sited at the eastern end of a long, flat, high feature known as 'the Train' lying between the Rhodesian border and Lake Cabora Bassa in Tete Province. The mountain was so named because, when viewed from the south, it resembled a steam engine with a long line of carriages travelling in a westerly direction. Our landing point approximated to the position of the guard's van.

Rex and his men had positioned the previous day to receive a large supply of fuel by para-drop. With plenty of time to spare, the fuel drums had been set out neatly throughout the open ground of the staging base and all parachutes were stacked out of harm's way. Everything seemed unhurried as the helicopters refuelled in the crisp, early morning air.

The 176-kilometre leg from here to Tembue would normally be the maximum range for an Alouette carrying a full load of laden troops inside Rhodesia. However, being only 2,000 feet above sea level in cold conditions, it was possible for the trooper helicopters to carry an extra ten-minutes' worth of fuel to cater for unexpected situations. Norman Walsh's command helicopter and the K-Cars with full fuel-loads could fly to Tembue and remain over target for a little more than one hour.

I enjoyed flying low-level over territory that was so familiar to me from my recce days. The countryside was quite breathtaking and not a soul was to be seen with so much noise from so many helicopters—anyone around had disappeared into hiding. The Cabora Bassa dam was about ten meters below its maximum level and I was astonished to see how much the water had eroded the banks along hillsides with long stretches of vertical walls at water's edge. Eight minutes from target, we heard the Hunter and Canberra radio transmissions as they made their airstrikes, dead on time. Earlier the six Dakotas had passed the helicopter force as they ran in to drop SAS and RLI paratroopers. My helicopter broke away from the others as they passed the Admin Base area. This site was populated by small trees and short grass but had plenty of openings for individual helicopters.

We landed in the centre of the selected location in the largest open space in the entire area. My immediate problem was to get the protection party down where I was and have fuel evenly distributed in the Admin Base area. George Alexander in the DC7, again flown by Captain Jack Malloch, responded perfectly to all instructions.

I had to climb onto the roof of the helicopter to see the DC7 early enough to give direction. "Red light on … five degrees right … steady … Green light." George was listening this time. Troops and pallets descended right where I wanted them on runs left, right, short and over my position. There was a tense moment when one pallet appeared to be descending directly onto me but, happily, it drifted enough to crash through a tree next to the helicopter.

The Admin Base was only six kilometres from the nearest edge of the target so we could hear the K-Cars firing quite clearly; otherwise the bush absorbed all sounds of smallarms fire. The Tembue Admin Base task was a cakewalk compared to Chimoio. All the trooper helicopters arrived and landed well clear of the cargo parachutes. The aircrews quickly disconnected them from the pallets, bundled them neatly and moved them centrally for easy recovery. Rolling the drums and standing them up in small clumps at each helicopter landing point was hot, sweaty work for the crews who completed the job before the first K-Cars arrived in the Admin Base.

The protection troops deployed in all-round defence and

were not seen again. There was only one drama in the Admin Base. Very few hits were sustained by K-Cars whose pilots reported fewer targets than they had seen in any part of Chimoio and a great deal less anti-aircraft fire. Nevertheless, one K-Car engine had taken a strike that necessitated its replacement. The technicians, using fuel drums as a working platform, made the engine change, and the helicopter that had flown it in completed the round trip from and to 'the Train' in less than six hours.

Awaiting para-drop of troops and pallets.

This Admin Base scene was repeated 360 degrees around.

It was late in the day when I went forward to be escorted by an SAS callsign through sections of the airstrike areas. The Alpha and Golf bomb effects were less gory than I had seen at Chimoio. However, my main interest at Tembue was to inspect the area of a flechette strike. During the planning phase of Op Dingo, I had asked Norman Walsh to consider using flechettes if he felt there was a target that suited them. Although he liked the idea, he decided against using flechettes at Chimoio because there would certainly be an international outcry following the inevitable inspection by the United Nations High Commission for Refugees. He chose rather to use one Hunter to drop a pair

PB's one-man Ops Centre at Tembue. All one needed was a parachute sunshade, radio in hand, a parachute bag to sit on and a planning board.

of flechette dispensers on the parade ground at Tembue. This was duly done.

Regrettably the daily parade had been postponed on this particular day; Sod's law—the base commander was suffering from a hangover so the parade square was vacant at the time of strike. A lone tree just short of the parade ground, on the right side of the attack line, was tightly embedded with flechettes from its uppermost branches all the way down to the base of its trunk. The entire parade site itself was crowded with partially embedded pink tail fins that had separated from steel shafts now buried below surface. Nobody, but nobody, would have survived the daily parade had it been held at the routine time.

FRELIMO, in their own base no more than three kilometres away from the ZANLA base, had no desire to come to the assistance of their comrades. This was pleasing because there was no external interference of troops who systematically winkled out ZANLA. Close-range firefights left many ZANLA dead with no casualties to the SAS and RLI. Out on the flanks, RLI stop groups accounted for CTs trying to escape past their positions.

Late in the afternoon, Canberras returned to attack ground surrounding an abandoned Portuguese store, thirty-five kilometres to the north of Tembue. This location had only come to notice when a captured terrorist revealed that there was a concentration of trained ZANLA residing there. The Canberra crews reported that their Alpha strike had been on target and later it was learned that ZANLA at that site had suffered many casualties, most having been seriously wounded.

Departure from Tembue occurred later than intended. On the way home one helicopter pilot reported being so low on fuel that he would not be able to reach 'the Train'. Norman Walsh instructed him to put down on a small uninhabited island in the middle of Cabora Bassa Lake and arranged for fuel drop by

a Dakota that had been on standby for such an eventuality.

Even before reaching Cabora Bassa, we could see a huge storm building up way to the south along the Rhodesian escarpment. Being so late, there was concern about having to pass through this after sunset, so helicopters arriving at 'the Train' refuelled and departed for Mount Darwin independently. The earliest ones, including mine, managed to bypass the heavy rain centres under heavy cloud. Tail-end Charlies were not so fortunate and I became really concerned when a fair number of the helicopters, including the command helicopter, were well overdue. As the night progressed, we received calls from various widely dispersed places reporting the arrival of helicopters that were remaining in situ for the night. All had been accounted for by 8 o'clock. Norman Walsh, who held back to ensure that the crew from the little island on Cabora Bassa reached 'the Train' safely, was forced to land at Chiswiti near the base of the escarpment.

He and Brian Robinson were thoroughly exhausted but very relieved that Operation Dingo was now behind them. Both phases had been totally successful and they had no intention of allowing their unplanned stop to deny them from celebrating their joint success. They found the local Army base pub and proceeded to drink it dry; or so we heard.

Next morning, helicopters returned to Tembue via 'the Train' to collect the SAS stay-behind force. Upon their return, Op Dingo ended.

For their superb planning and personal participation in these two operations, Group Captain Norman Walsh, BCR, and Major Brian Robinson, MCM, were made Officers of the Legion of Merit (Operational). They certainly deserved it. Harold Griffiths received the Jacklin Trophy from Air Marshal Mick McLaren on behalf of 7 Squadron for a year of astonishing successes, not the least being Op Dingo.

Effectiveness of Op Dingo

OPERATION DINGO COST ZANLA IN excess of 3,000 trained men killed and something in the order of 5,000 wounded, many too seriously to be of further use. Others lost all interest in fighting and deserted.

The two phases of Dingo involved the largest concentration of our air and ground effort for over four-and-a-half days and had cost us two dead, six wounded and a Vampire lost. But the successes achieved were astounding when compared to our gains inside the country during the eight-week period immediately preceding Dingo. At considerably higher costs in hours flown and weapons expended by jet, light fixed-wing and helicopter airstrikes, as recorded in 105 ASRs, only 283 CTs were positively known to have been killed with forty-two captured. There were almost certainly more CTs killed and wounded, both internally and externally, during this period but the combined figures could not compare with those of Op Dingo. Additionally, more servicemen were killed and wounded and one Lynx was lost inside the country during the same eight-week period. Two of those killed were Air Force men. They were Air Lieutenant du Plessis and Sergeant Underwood who crashed a Lynx in mountainous terrain whilst making a Frantan attack in support of Fireforce.

One important aspect of the Op Dingo successes was that it lifted moral amongst the forces and white population at a time when many civilians had lost all hope in the country's future. Emigration figures were alarming and the civilian Territorial Force was shrinking noticeably. This had less to do with terrorism and never-ending problems with Britain and the West as with doubts about South Africa's willingness to continue supporting us. The media said little about South African attitudes but, on their return to Rhodesia from visits to South Africa, Ian Smith's and his ministers' faces showed that things had changed. Gone were the smiles that were always evident after such visits. After the Portuguese collapsed our politicians looked drained and grim; the odd smile so obviously forced.

For months Ian Smith had been negotiating with local African leaders for an internal settlement that would raise Africans to political leadership under a Westminster-styled constitution. Joshua Nkomo and Robert Mugabe had been invited to participate. Both refused, preferring armed force to gain personal power. The need to end unnecessary loss of life by Rhodesians killing Rhodesians was not for them. In fact their craving for personal power stripped them of any sense of concern for the huge numbers of people they had wasted and those they were still prepared to sacrifice.

One man involved in the internal negotiations was Bishop Abel Muzorewa, the weak-kneed leader of UANC (United African National Council). Notwithstanding the recalcitrant attitudes of Nkomo and Mugabe, his reaction to the Chimoio and Tembue raids was to declare a week of national mourning. Although nobody seemed to pay the slightest attention to his call, it made whites wonder why Muzorewa, by then recognised as the most likely political figure to become first Prime Minister of a black majority government, could be mourning the loss of Mugabe's CTs when he had so openly declared them to be our enemies.

Ian Smith told the nation that the move to establish black rule in the country was to everyone's advantage, but Muzorewa's action did little to improve the confidence of those who had already lost hope. Nor did it stem the spreading gloom. Nevertheless regular force personnel were well pleased with the outcome of Op Dingo and remained steadfast in trusting Government to solve the political issues. Theirs was the job of containing the forces of two power-hungry and fortune-seeking demagogues.

Operation Virile

UNLIKE THE OPERATIONS HURRICANE AND Repulse areas where CTs had some distance to move through tribal lands before reaching white-owned farms, towns and strategic targets, Op Thrasher CTs entered directly into the commercial farming areas. Op Dingo had to a large extent blunted a westward drive from Chimoio that extended from Inyanga in the north down to Chipinga in the south. However, just prior to the attack on Chimoio, Selous Scouts had been cleared for an operation that aimed to stem the high flow of CTs moving into the Chipinga area. At the time ZANLA were able to travel unhindered from Chimoio along a primary roadway right up to the FRELIMO garrison town, Espungabera, sited alongside the Rhodesian border.

Operation Virile, another of Selous Scouts vehicle-borne fighting columns, should have launched three days before Op Dingo, but it was held over for fear that it would stir up FRELIMO and ZANLA to the detriment of the Chimoio operation. In addition, the nature of the Scouts operation made it plain that jet support might be needed but this could not be guaranteed whilst Op Dingo was in progress. In consequence, Op Virile was only launched on the night of 26/27 November.

Much had changed because clearance was given for Selous Scouts to destroy five bridges inside Mozambique and close air-support was included as a matter of course; a very refreshing reversal on earlier limitations. Because of the Chimoio and Tembue raids, it seemed that Vorster's obsessions with détente had fallen away and that Bishop Muzorewa had become South Africa's new hope. The usual 'political denial' had not been imposed because the bridges were of limited economic importance to Mozambique's overall economy. We really welcomed this change and saw it as the thin edge of a big wedge.

The objectives of this particular operation were to deny ZANLA vehicular access to the border by dropping five key road bridges between Dombe (near Chimoio) and Espungabera and destroy all motorised transport between the bridges.

As it progressed ever deeper into hostile territory, the large column enjoyed almost continuous daylight cover by a Lynx carrying Selous Scout Captain Athol Gillespie. His jobs were to give early warning of enemy vehicle movements, to provide the main force a continuous VHF radio link with its forward HQ at Chipinga and maintain communications with a rearguard force inside Mozambique, near Espungabera.

On the first day when the column was about halfway to its first objective, the bridge over the large fast-flowing Mabvudzi River, Air Lieutenant Chris Tucker flying the Lynx destroyed a Land Rover-sized vehicle that was moving towards the column. A pair of Hunters, flown by Rich Brand and Spook Geraty, had already cleaned up some larger vehicles farther east, but the weather precluded further Hunter involvement, forcing Chris to take on a number of targets on his own. By the 30 November the force was back in Rhodesia having successfully dropped the five bridges; a job made so much easier and safer by air support.

Black Friday

MANY FIREFORCE ACTIONS CONTINUED TO occur internally with variable results and limited RSF losses. This changed dramatically in a matter of hours in the Op Hurricane area on Friday 12 January 1978. Air Lieutenant Francois du Toit, the young officer I had trained in recce when he was still with SAAF, had been on helicopters for some time when he led a Fireforce action supported by another K-Car and three G-Cars. The Fireforce had been in an action initiated by the detection of an activated 'road-runner' (doctored portable radio).

The action became slightly confused by a second 'road-runner' signal emanating from the same general area. However, typical for the time of year, the bush was very thick and because the ground force of seventeen stops groups were largely inexperienced PATU men, only three CTs were

killed. The action was not yet over when K-Car 2, flown by Air Lieutenant Chaz Goatley with gunner, Flight Sergeant Ian (Flamo) Flemming, had to leave to refuel at Mtoko. On their way they came under heavy fire from dense bush resulting in the instant death of Ian Flemming. Francois in the K-Car immediately moved across and soon had G-Cars ferrying stops directly from the first scene to the new one. Then the airborne Army commander, Lieutenant Adams, was hit in the hand and was transferred to the lead G-Car flown by Air Lieutenant Mantovani, who took many hits as he lifted off. On arrival at Mtoko his G-Car was grounded.

A number of stops had already been deployed when a G-Car flown by Air Lieutenant Norman (Bambam) Maasdorp with gunner Flight Sergeant Henry Jarvie, came in with another load of troops. Just before touchdown they came under heavy fire and Henry Jarvie was killed. Norman and one soldier were wounded, and the aircraft was severely damaged necessitating a forced landing close to the CTs. The only remaining G-Car flown by Air Lieutenant Thorogood uplifted everyone from the downed helicopter and flew them off to Mtoko, leaving the two K-Cars and a Lynx, flown by Group Captain John Mussell, over the scene. By nightfall the only serviceable G-Car had brought in the last of the stops from the first scene, and Francois arranged all the callsigns into over-night ambush positions. One of these positions was attacked by about 20 CTs during the night and a soldier was killed.

During the frustrating and somewhat confused day-action the CTs had the advantage of unusually thick bush cover and, apparently, only lost two killed. We, on the other hand, had lost three killed and three wounded with two helicopters needing expensive repairs.

I had just returned to Air HQ from weapons testing at Kutanga Range and walked into the Ops Room as news came through about Henry Jarvie and Ian Flemming. News of this shocking loss stunned everyone, but none so badly as me. I suffered an assault on all my emotions, such as never before

Henry (left) and Flamo (right) seen here in Umtali at the 104 (VR) Squadron Mess with (left to right) Sqn Ldr Don Howe OC 104 VR Squadron, Phil Tubbs, Johnny Lynch and Mick Fulton.

and remember asking aloud, "Oh my God, why should such a terrible thing happen?"

The mainstay of our force undoubtedly lay with our technical men. As their OC on 4 Squadron, Henry Jarvie, the loveable clown, and Ian Flemming, the quiet good-natured armourer, had been two vitally important individuals. Following their transfer to helicopters, their personalities and talents benefited 7 Squadron greatly. But, that these two superb young men should die in the same Fireforce action was impossible to comprehend or accept. 12 January had been a very Black Friday for the Air Force.

Mini-golf bombs

I WAS SO AFFECTED BY THE loss of Henry and Flamo that I flew to Mtoko to talk to all the Fireforce participants. The problems they revealed were not new ones. Theirs had been the ongoing rainy season issue of not being able to see CTs, even when they had a fair idea of the general source of ground fire. I flew with Francois du Toit to view the contact area and whilst he was giving me a running commentary of the events, I came up with an idea that I guessed would turn similar situations to our advantage.

Had a pair of Hunters been immediately available to deliver four Golf bombs along the line of bush in which the CTs were

The bush density in this photograph is relatively low yet the trunks of trees plus limited overhead foliage could easily hide many men from aerial view.

known to be, the shock effect on survivors would undoubtedly have been significant. However, considering the time needed to bring in the jets from Thornhill, the casualties would already have occurred and the location of the stop groups would have disallowed the use of Golf bombs anyway.

John Mussell's Lynx flying in support of the Fireforce action had been of little value even though he was immediately available all the time. This made me wonder if my project team could produce

a weapon for the Lynx that would, in similar circumstances, provide severe shock effects with meaningful lethal range against CTs whose precise positions were not known.

By the time I reached Salisbury, I had decided what was needed and a new project was born to exploit existing Golf-bomb technology. My intention was to provide Lynx with a sizeable punch in the form of a 'mini-Golf bomb'.

As always, the project team engineers and Ron Dyer responded enthusiastically, and the requirement was discussed at length before we launched into Project Juliet. At the conclusion of this project, the weapon we produced was not nicknamed the Juliet bomb but became known by the term I had first used—the 'Mini-golf' bomb.

The Mini-golf took a great deal of time to develop because of numerous safety features that had to be built into the design to cater for low level release from the relatively slow-flying Lynx. It turned out to be an ugly tail-less beast that was designed for release at the end of a standard front-guns attack. The ANFO charge was contained in a thin-skinned steel cylinder surrounded by thousands of steel slugs entrapped by a 6mm steel outer-casing. Upon release, the bomb deployed a large parachute from its rear. The parachute's function was to retard the bomb sharply and pitch it to the vertical before it reached ground.

Simultaneous with the parachute deployment, an electric-switch device, housed in the sphere of an Alpha bomb outer casing, was released from its anchors in the nose cone. We named this device 'the seeker'. Para-retardation on the bomb forced the seeker to fly forward of the bomb, drawing out a five-metre electric cable. When this cable was fully extended, batteries were brought into alignment to complete a link between the electrical switch in the seeker and the bomb's detonator.

Early trials from 150 feet were frustrating because the speed and trajectory of the seeker was faster, and therefore shallower, than that of the retarding bomb until the electric cable was fully extended. This had the effect of bringing the seeker level with the bomb, until the bomb itself was facing vertically downwards. Only then did the seeker start to move forward of the bomb. This problem was overcome by simply increasing the release height to 300 feet to allow time for the seeker to reach its correct position before it contacted ground. On impact with the ground, the seeker's circuit closed to fire the bomb five metres above it.

The Mini-golf's high airburst was necessary to cater for CTs lying in ground depressions, *dongas* and riverbeds. To ensure the fullest possible effects of over-pressure, and to make certain that all shrapnel was directed laterally and downwards, the initiating Pentolite booster was installed at the rear of the ANFO charge. This forced propagation of the explosive wave in a shallow downward facing cone. The system worked well and gave effective over-pressure with dense shrapnel cover to thirty-five metres radius with random spike effects that extend as far as fifty metres.

Flight Lieutenant Spook Geraty used the first Mini-golf in action on 18 June. Two days later Cocky Benecke used four in a single action that accounted for seven CTs dead. Thereafter Mini-golfs were used frequently.

After one of the earliest Mini-golf deliveries into a bush area from which ground fire had come, but no CTs had been seen, troops located four dead terrorists and one who, though only slightly wounded by shrapnel, was found lying unconscious. He revived when an RAR soldier shook his shoulder. This particular CT was at the edge of the Mini-golf's effective range and had been well screened by trees standing between him and the point of detonation. When questioned by SB, the CT said he did not hear the bomb explode but was "suddenly overcome by a need to sleep". The ground troops who were more than 100 metres from the Mini-golf explosion reported being totally taken aback by the huge blast and shock wave.

This shock effect paid off in many actions according to K-Car pilot ASRs that reported two advantages accruing from Mini-golfs. One was that surviving CTs tended to remain where they were making it easier for ground forces to account for them and, more importantly, firing at aircraft either ceased or was substantially reduced.

Mini-golf was particularly useful against large enemy forces pursuing troops engaged on over border operations. In the first such action, east of the border village of Nyamapanda, Cocky Benecke (Hornet 20) was the pilot.

Ian Smith, Cocky Benecke, Dave Rowe and Brian Penton.

Cocky's ASR reads:

Hornet 20 was tasked to assist c/s 75 (4 man RLI callsign) who was being chased by over 50 CTs and called for assistance. On arrival overhead c/s 75,s position c/s 75A who was on an OP (about 5 kms to the West of c/s 75) informed me that the terrs were still chasing c/s 75. I identified c/s 75 and fired a few rockets into bushy areas immediately behind him. After a short while of orbiting around c/s 75 I was fired on by terrs using RPG 7, RPD and AK.
Using RPG 7 dust as an indicator I dropped a Mini-golf on that position. Mini-golf landed approx. 15 yds from RPG position. This

had a major effect on those ters who survived and allowed c/s 75 to make good their escape. No more fire was directed at the aircraft and no movement was seen from that immediate area after the bomb went off.
I continued to orbit the area and c/s 75A informed me that I was being fired on from another position 500 yards away but only from small arms. I could not see where the firing was coming from so did not attack. I then married 75 with 75A in an LZ and provided top cover until Black section arrived below Hornet 4 to uplift the c/s back to Kotwa.

Shown in this picture of Lynx armament layout are: (Left rear to forward centre) Frantans, Mini-golf with proboscis, grenade launcher, 37mm Sneb rockets, .303 ammo belts, Light-series bomb carrier with four 28-pound fragmentation bombs and white-bodied practice bombs. Twin Browning machine-guns above wing ahead of and either side of rear engine air intake.

The Mini-golfs had been in use for some time when, for safety reasons, it was decided to substitute the electrical seeker arrangement for a steel proboscis and accept a small reduction in killing range. Warrant Officer Bill Brown was one armourer who dreaded having to attend to early-model UXB Mini-golfs in the field. With live batteries and an electrical cable enmeshed in bush it was safest to simply rig up a delay charges to destroy such bombs.

ZANLA's changing tactics

ROBERT MUGABE IN TYPICAL COMMUNIST style, declared 1978 to be 'The Year of the People'. A few female CTs were with some groups entering the country and in the Op Repulse area there were clear indications that FRELIMO had become ever more involved.

Rhodesia saw a major change in government on 3 March

1978 following an internal political settlement signed by Ian Smith, Bishop Abel Muzorewa, Senator Chief Chirau and Reverend Ndabaningi Sithole (previously the leader of ZANU and ZANLA). The name of the country changed to Zimbabwe–Rhodesia and, incredibly, the white people calmly accepted this first move towards black majority government. For one year an interim government ran the country with ministerial portfolios shared by experienced white ministers and black co-ministers who were learning the ropes. This would end when blacks and whites cast their votes for the first majority government. Mugabe and Nkomo wanted no part in this arrangement and branded the black participants as sellouts—so the war raged on.

Now, as in many preceding months, ZANLA relied on *mujibas* (LTTs and local youth spies) to provide them with early warning on RSF positions and the movement of Fireforces. *Mujibas*, often posing as common cattle herdsmen, drove cattle through likely RSF positions. Their abnormal practice of driving cattle over high features clearly identified active *mujibas* who we counted as CTs. When caught in the act they were either captured or killed.

In most ZANLA affected areas high features abounded. *Mujibas* used these to establish an early-warning system in which whistled messages were passed from one high point to the next along the line of Fireforce and troop movements. At one stage *mujibas* started denuding high features of all natural vegetation in an attempt to deny RSF hidden OPs (observation points) but the practice was dropped when they realised they needed the same cover for themselves.

ZANLA's *mujiba*-warning system covered most of their operating areas other than half of the Op Repulse area where an extensive region of flat ground extended southwards from the Lundi River. Though crude, the warning system was very effective. A Fireforce flying at ninety knots could not hope to outpace the whistled warnings that passed ahead of their flight line at the speed of sound.

So troublesome was this warning system that selected troops moved into high points at night to kill *mujibas* when they took up positions at dawn. Visual recce from the air could not assist in these counter-*mujiba* operations because it was impossible to differentiate between RSF Op and *mujiba* path patterns. In spite of the *mujibas*, ZANLA continued to suffer greatly at the hands of the Selous Scouts pseudo teams who had learned to keep abreast of CT identification procedures. They knew what could and could not be eaten to fool the locals into believing they were bona fide ZANLA. Because of this the CTs were forced to find other ways of exposing Selous Scouts groups.

Individual CT leaders adopted a variety of short-duration identification methods. Sometimes this was to the detriment of genuine CT groups passing through or operating in adjacent areas. But, for a while, the Selous Scouts experienced setbacks. I recall one Scouts group being blown because the locals noticed that their weapons did not have barely visible scarlet thread tied to weapons' trigger guards. Another group was blown because

its members had not changed boot or shoelaces to the black ones the CTs had adopted. Switching cigarette brands was another of many ploys.

Norah Seear

DURING MARCH 1978 I WAS tasked to recce Chiweshe, Madziwa, Masembura, Msana and Chinamora Tribal Trust Lands extending in reverse order northward from Salisbury. I was pleased to do this as a break from my project work and more so because I was not encumbered with recce instruction. Whatever I located was passed on to JOC Hurricane at Bindura, but I only called for Fireforce once. On that occasion I had Norah Seear with me.

Norah was an excellent photo-interpreter with JSPIS (Joint Services Photographic Interpretation Services) based at New Sarum under command of Flight Lieutenant Bill Buckle. Two of Bill's male interpreters as well as Norah (a grandmother) and three younger women interpreters had on occasions sought my opinion on terrorist bases they were analysing.

Visiting JSPIS was always enjoyable and I found Norah's enthusiasm and open personality most appealing. She was especially keen to learn about visual recce. Not satisfied with all that I had told her, she asked if she could attend one of the many lectures I was called upon to give to Army personnel undertaking Air Orientation courses at New Sarum. Regrettably Norah pitched up at a particular presentation when I happened to be feeling really ill with a bad dose of flu. When the faces of the Army guys, who had been on a drinking spree in town the previous evening, showed that they were more interested in personal survival than in African toilet-path systems, I abbreviated my talk and left the room early, thereby disappointing Norah Seear. I still experience embarrassment when I recall the occasion.

Norah had obviously not been put off by my failure to teach her something new because she asked if she could accompany me on a recce of Chinamora Tribal Trust Land. I said I was more than happy to have her along for the ride but warned that the flight would be long and cold with no facility to relieve her bladder in flight. She assured me this was no problem because she had "the constitution of a camel".

Nora's presence in the aircraft was refreshing because of her never-ending questions which only dried up when I called Fireforce onto a group of CTs I found in a small base camp. The action that followed with RAR troops under command of Major André Dennison was very messy. (More about this officer shortly.) Nevertheless the Fireforce action had come at the end of our normal recce period so our airborne time was greatly extended by the action. At New Sarum, Norah showed she was not much of a 'long range' camel by making a headlong rush for the nearest loo.

This was the CT base Norah watched Fireforce react to during her flight with PB. Two feeding paths from four villages can be seen running toward the base from the main pathway running left to right under the only visible village. Two thin paths running toward the bottom of the photograph led to sentry outpost positions under trees. The base for twenty-five CTs is easily identified amongst trees at centre.

RAR Fireforces

WHEN FIREFORCES FIRST CAME INTO being they were manned exclusively by RLI. Throughout the war they were undoubtedly the finest of all Fireforce soldiers. Following the spread of the war and an increase in helicopter availability, RAR and Territorial Army units also became involved, but seldom did they perform as aggressively and efficiently as RLI. Certain of the Territorial Army units did well and the same could be said of RAR companies when commanded by the right officers and, even more so, when controlled by K-Car pilots.

From my own observations and the opinions expressed by other pilots, it was clear that the black soldiers of the RAR were good fighters who were too often severely encumbered by language difficulties between the white airborne commander and men on the ground. Most RAR soldiers spoke one or other of the Shona dialects and there were a few N'debele soldiers too.

Whereas they all had a fair understanding of English, the official language in battle, it was seldom sufficient for them to absorb fast-spoken instructions coming to them over crackling radios with the near-continuous presence of noisy helicopters during high-stress actions. It was noticeable that some white officers gained a great deal more from their RAR troops than others. These were ones who spoke calmly, clearly, slowly and used the barest minimum of simple words. Above all they remained cool-headed and never lost their temper nor showed any sign of irritation if asked to repeat instructions.

Officers who failed to get the best out of their black troops exhibited common characteristics. They were short-tempered and pompous. In the air they would instruct their men too quickly in sentences containing too many words. When these instructions were misinterpreted or there were requests for a repeat of instructions, the man on the ground received a verbal blast with accusations of ignorance and incompetence.

There was an occasion when one K-Car pilot was so annoyed by an RAR officer's inability to handle his men correctly that he surreptitiously muted the Army commander's radio link and took over control of the RAR men on the ground. Most K-Car pilots were every bit as good as the best of our airborne Army commanders, usually having seen more Fireforce actions. In this case the pilot directed the callsigns in 'Chilapalapa' that these particular RAR soldiers understood well.

The Shona word *Chilapalapa* is the name of a language developed on the gold mines of South Africa where it is known as 'Fanagalo'. This simple language continues to facilitate easy communication between mine management and thousands of mine workers coming from many African countries and language groups. Most Chilapalapa words come from Zulu, cautionary and swear words from Afrikaans and, simple words like left and right from English.

Anyway, the K-Car pilot directed the willing troops with ease and led them to success. Initially the Army commander frantically checked his radio leads for a fault he had no hope of finding. He gave this up when the air-gunner leaned across and shouted to let him know that

André Dennison.

the pilot and soldiers were managing fine and that the "headset failure" could only be rectified when they returned to base.

One RAR officer I got to know quite well at Mtoko was André Dennison, commanding 'A' Company of 1 RAR. He was an ex-British Army officer who performed with considerable courage in many ground actions with a weapon in his hands. As a combat leader on the ground he was first-class but his troops performed abysmally under his airborne control, even though they had done really well under previous airborne commanders. The reasons for this were very plain to many pilots, but André took no notice of the advice offered to solve his soldiers' "outright stupidity and inability to understand plain English". It was through officers like André that the RAR came to be regarded by many as second-rate soldiers. Those of us who knew how well they could perform thought otherwise.

André had a phobia about the Selous Scouts in general and Lieutenant-Colonel Ron Reid-Daly in particular. This led to a very unnecessary incident when, following two failed callouts by Scouts pseudo callsigns, André flatly refused to respond to a third one on the same day. Whilst all hell was breaking loose between Ron Reid-Daly, COMOPS and André Dennison, I arranged for Territorial soldiers operating fairly close to the Scouts callout position to prepare for immediate uplift for a Fireforce action. For this I had first sought COMOPS approval from Harold Griffiths, who was then working under Norman Walsh.

Away went the empty helicopters from Mtoko with their accompanying Lynx to pick up the TF troops who, though inexperienced in the Fireforce role, thoroughly enjoyed a small but successful action in the Msana Tribal Trust Land. André's frustrated anger switched from the Selous Scout CO to me for having "taken away my aircraft without my permission!" Such was the nature of the man as Fireforce commander! But with gun in hand and feet on the ground, André was a great soldier and leader of troops.

Bold actions—007 ideas

THE SAS CONTINUED WITH THEIR successful operations using minimum manpower for maximum results. During May 1978 eight SAS men made a parachute descent with canoes and plenty of explosives to take out a ZANLA barrack block in the FRELIMO stronghold town of Tete. In a typical SAS-styled night action involving moments of threat and doubts, they paddled heavily laden canoes down the Zambezi River right up to their target set high on the bank of the river. There

they set the charges that blew the barracks and its occupants to hell and back. Upon their return to Rhodesia the participants described the operation and spoke of their passage under the huge Tete bridge spanning the great river. They said how awesome the illuminated bridge appeared as they passed silently below FRELIMO guards and vehicles on the bridge deck high above them. The business of blowing bridges had become quite fashionable so it was not surprising that these men were considering how the Tete bridge might be dropped, if the need arose.

I was fascinated by the problems involved and went away with the subject turning over in my mind. As the SAS had said, dropping the bridge could be done easily enough if it was not located at a garrison town containing hundreds of well-armed troops. The question that exercised my mind was how the Air Force might deal with the problem, if given the opportunity. Looking forward in time and considering friendly Malawi's future interests in the bridge, there seemed no way Rhodesia would ever consider destroying such a vital road link. Nevertheless I could not get the subject out of my mind.

Tete bridge is a huge suspension bridge with two high support towers on each bank of the river. Over these towers two suspension cables pass from their deep anchor points on the south side to those on the north. These two enormously thick and powerful cables support the entire road platform by means of many vertical drop cables.

No available bomb or rocket would have any meaningful effect on this type of structure because assured destruction could only come from cutting through one or both of the suspension cables. The question was how this might be done. So far as I was concerned great accuracy would be required, so low delivery at high speed would be essential against this target sited at the edge of a highly defended town. It also meant that our fastest aircraft, Hunters, could make only one pass.

The system I conceived may sound too James Bondish but I have no doubt the project team could have developed it given time to perfect the explosive shearing device I refer to as a 'cable cutter'.

None of our team had any experience in high-energy shaped charges and explosive shearing devices so I went to Cambridge-trained ex-British Royal Engineers Captain Charlie Small with whom I had worked on the odd inter-force project. One of these projects had been to design a bridge and culvert destruction device to be mounted on a self-propelled vehicle that could be lifted by helicopter and placed on a safe section of the Maputo to Malvernia railway line. Once on the rails the vehicle was to be controlled remotely from the air and run to the target, bridge or culvert and usually defended, where it would be brought to a halt at the selected position for command detonation.

Charlie, who was then working with Selous Scouts, was experienced in the destruction of bridges as recently proven during Op Virile. His approach to dropping a bridge was to calculate the amount of explosive required for the job then double the quantity. Because of this, the rail vehicle became too heavy for carriage by one or two helicopters. Charlie's explosives alone required two Alouettes, another to carry the vehicle and a fourth one to transport engineers to assemble the unit on site. Though the feasibility work and designs were completed, the device was never put to the test.

Charlie's reaction to my plans to drop the Tete bridge was "it can be done". But he needed the cutting charge, 100kg minimum, to be in direct contact with the suspension cable and oriented so that the explosive 'cutting' wave faced the cable.

Arising from Charlie Small's advice, my concept involved two Hunters each carrying two 150kg bomb-shaped cable cutters under slung, and partially imbedded, within and under, 500kg inert bombs. One Hunter would approach on a line just inside the bridge towers at one end of the bridge whilst another did the same at the other end of the bridge approaching from the opposite direction. Both pilots would have to aim to pass thirty meters above the suspension cables at the relatively slow speed of 300 knots

To give them safe passage, another pair of Hunters would precede them by a few seconds flying at maximum speed directly over Tete town. This pair would then pull up into a steep, noisy, full-powered climbing turn away from the river to draw attention from the slower-flying Hunters approaching each other at low level along the river.

At half a kilometre from target the cable cutters would be released. As they fell away they would draw out a heavy twenty-metre length of super-strong stranded steel cable from a drum mounted inside the inert bomb. Just before the cable was fully withdrawn, as measured by the number of rotations of the drum, the 500kg inert bomb would release automatically from the aircraft.

The requirement was for the inert bomb to pass above the suspension cable and the cable cutter below it. Both units would have passed the suspension cable before their linking cable came taught against the bridge cable. The heavier bomb would continue on and the shock load on the cable (the reason for the slow attack speed) would be slightly damped by the inert bomb's flight line being drawn down. The cable cutter would pitch steeply upwards as it was brought to a rapid halt before changing direction back towards the suspension cable. As each cable-cutting device slammed up against the suspension cable it would fire its cutting charge.

If all four cable cutters succeeded in cutting right through their respective section of suspension cable that would be fine but it only needed one severed cable to drop the bridge. However, if neither cable was completely severed, the damage done would render the bridge unsafe, thereby necessitating many months for disassembly of the entire bridge before replacement of the custom-designed suspension cables was possible.

There was another unusual project explored but never put to the test. This was to have been a Hunter-borne, non-explosive, man-killing device. It all started with an article I read in some scientists' magazine reporting the potential of low-frequency noise to subdue riotous crowds or to actually kill large numbers of people if applied energy levels were high enough. The article told of a French scientist and his four assistants who were all killed in the wee hours of the morning when they conducted their first-ever test on an oversized, low frequency, 'whistle'. Disaster struck when they passed large volume airflow from a compressed air tank through the sound generator. Not only were buildings for some distance around subjected to severe damage, the autopsies carried out on all five victims revealed that their vital organs had been pulverised by the high energy, four cycles per second, sound force.

I was intrigued by this information and looked into the possibility of towing a suitable 'whistle' through the air behind a Hunter flying at high speed. Calculations, or should I say guesstimations, showed that the required amplitude of sound waves oscillating at four cycles per second could be achieved without danger to the pilot or anyone on the ground. Only in a sustained steep turn at the right speed would 'killer sound waves' focus for the few lethal seconds needed to cover a fair sized area within the orbit.

Had we had the time and found a suitable way of testing such a device, we might have produced an ideal low-cost weapon for a large variety of CT targets. I am left wondering if the concept was realistic, or not.

Katoog

DURING MY VISITS TO CSIR in Pretoria I became very interested in an aeronautical division project known as Katoog, which is Afrikaans for 'cat's eye'. This project looked to the future when a helicopter gunship pilot would be able to aim his power articulated guns by simply placing an illuminated spot in his helmet visor onto a target.

When I had checked on the project, back in February 1978, no noticeable progress had been made since my previous visit many weeks earlier. The South Africans were obviously in no great hurry as they knew that helicopter gunships and their rotating 'chin turrets', for which Katoog was intended, lay a long way off in the future.

For my part I could see immediate use for the Katoog system in a side-firing mode, so I asked if it would be possible to let me take the equipment, as it was, for a short-duration trial in Rhodesian operational conditions. The CSIR engineers were especially keen because this would give them early technical feedback; so a signal was sent up to Air HQ in which I made a proposal to borrow the equipment. Authority was given for me to pursue the matter with the South Africans.

Because Katoog was a top-secret project there was much to-and-fro communicating in Pretoria before the request was accepted in principle. However, the South Africans insisted on finishing an incomplete mounting for four .303 Browning machine-guns and conducting ground-firing trials before passing the system over. The gun mounting incorporated hydraulic servos to traverse and pitch the guns in direct response to Katoog's sighting sensor.

There was no hope of finalising a pilot helmet sight before the gun system itself was ready. So I requested that CSIR produce a simple mounting post on which to fix their angle-sensing device with a collimator-reflector gunsight affixed between two handgrips incorporating a firing button. The idea was that the guns would be operated by one of our helicopter gunners sitting in a sideways-facing seat set central to the front doorway of an Alouette. On his left side, the multiple-gun platform would be wholly accessible to him with gun barrels projecting through the rear doorframe.

By early May the system was working well and was transported with the senior project engineer to Salisbury on six weeks' loan. As soon as the whole unit had been fitted to an Alouette, firing trials were conducted with the CSIR project engineer making suitable adjustments to allow for direct aiming at targets with the guns offset for normal attack speed. Squadron Leader Ted Lunt and Corporal Thompson conducted these tests.

Ted Lunt.

Ted Lunt was the Squadron Commander of 8 Squadron, which had only just been created, ostensibly to lessen the burden on No 7 Squadron. Initially 8 Squadron operated Alouette IIIs, though none of us knew then that the true purpose of creating this new unit was to prepare for the on-take of larger helicopters.

We moved to FAF 4 at Mtoko and commenced work right away. The Alouette with the Katoog system was referred to as 'K-Car Alpha' to distinguish it from the 20mm K-Car gunships. The plan was for Ted to position at a safe place that was nearest to the area I was searching and wait for my call. In this way, and acting entirely on his own, he could respond very quickly.

We struck luck immediately when I called him to a large CT camp near an abandoned farmstead southeast of Mtoko. As Ted arrived, over thirty CTs broke cover and started running and splitting into small groups. I called for Fireforce as Corporal Thompson's first long burst downed six CTs. Five stayed where they fell.

Ted's specific instruction was to remain at 1,200 feet above

ground so that the Katoog aiming system and the four-gun mount could be compared directly with the established 20mm cannon performance. Whereas the first burst had been made from the correct height I could see that Ted was progressively dropping height to get at small groups now scattered and snivelling from cover to cover. So far as I could see CTs were dropping every time the guns fired but some rose again, staggering noticeably.

K-Car Alpha had run out of ammunition before the Fireforce took over. Most of the seventeen CT's accounted for had either been killed by Katoog or were so severely wounded that they were unable to escape the attention of the troops. Katoog had proven itself on its first live outing.

This poor-quality photo of K-Car Alpha shows how the four-gun fit looked when it came into squadron service with the name Dalmatian Fit. The essential difference from prototype is that, to make way for an airborne Army commander's seat (in which one armourer is seen sitting) the gun control yoke with gunsight was set high above and to the rear of the gun platform. Also seen in this photo is the pilot's armoured seat designed to protect head and body against enemy fire entering from the port side.

Ted was directed onto a number of unoccupied places before I put him onto a group of fourteen terrorists. Corporal Thompson knocked hell out of these guys who attempted to fire back at the helicopter until they realised they came short every time they stopped running in zigzag fashion. By the end of the action Ted had dropped right down to about 300 feet to get at three remaining survivors who made the mistake of going into cover under a small clump of bushes. They did not stand a chance. The whole group lay dead before troops arrived to sweep the area.

At this stage I brought in Hamie Dax, our successful PRAW recce pilot, to help cover more ground in an endeavour to locate a particular CT gang that was giving Centenary farmers a bad time. Squadron Leader Ted Lunt with Corporal Thompson responded to a call from Hamie.

This is what Ted wrote in his ASR of 23 June 78:

Gun trials on the Alpha fit continued daily with K-Car pre-positioning in areas as required in support of air recce.

PRAW crew (Dax and McCay) reported a likely camp at US400294 and requested a check out. No movement or signs of occupation were visible to the PRAW but in view of the pattern of camps found thus far, Dax indicated good possibilities. Run was made from NNE at tree top height in view of wind and terrain with last few hundred meters under direction of PRAW.

As the camp central complex was approached, K-Car Alpha observed an armed CT at very close range and opened fire. Immediately 8-10 CTs broke from the area scattering in all directions.

Targets were engaged with great difficulty and of necessity from close quarters at slow speed in view of the thick vegetation and rapid departure of CTs.

There being no Fireforce immediately available and PRAW not having seen CT's from height, many CTs unfortunately made good their escape. Several CTs were observed hiding in bushes and these were engaged and killed with very little trouble—indeed of those killed only two managed to get off a few rounds.

Upon initiation of the contact FF (from Mtoko) was called for and arrived within 30 mins or so. By this time no more CTs could be found and, having briefed K-Car 1 on the set-up and indicated the whereabouts of the 6 dead, K-Car Alpha withdrew to carry on with recce reactions, there being other camps to check in the area.

Under direction of FF Mtoko, paras were dropped to the East (1.5 km) then carried in by G-Car. A sweep line was formed consisting of 4 sticks (16 men) which moved from E to W towards a stop-line of 4 men. The camp was searched but only 6 dead located. No blood spoor was found and stops were uplifted and FF returned to Mtoko at last light.

ENEMY ACTION:

Nothing unusual—CTs remained within camp and only broke once engaged by K-Car Alpha. No attempt made to fire upon PRAW it seems, even though he was circling for some time prior to heli arrival.

DETAILS NOT FORMING AND INTEGRAL PART OF NARRATIVE:

4 of the 6 killed were fleeting targets—Alpha fit proved amazingly effective against these. This weapon proved itself to be far superior to the 20mm in this respect. 3 guns only were used, the 4ᵗʰ having jammed in the initial firing period.

Superb handling of the situation by the gunner Cpl Thompson.

I was asked to insert comments for the field commander and wrote this:

a. This report is written on behalf of OC FAF 5 at his request.

b. I was operating an area with PRAW pilot Dax. The Alpha K-Car was close at hand at Madziwa Mine with Lynx at immediate readiness at Mtoko.

c. This was another trial at air recce with immediate response, made possible by the need to test Katoog. Previously, recce information would be checked out the day after its attainment. This was failing as terrorists were obviously moving off after recce aircraft cleared the area. The plan on this day was to recce until a suitably fresh camp was located. Upon location the aircraft would remain overhead to keep CTs static and call for K-Car Alpha and the Lynx.

d. When Hamie Dax called, I moved over to him arriving some 4 minutes after K-Car Alpha. I then descended to 400 ft over the helicopter. All six terrorists had been accounted for before arrival of the Lynx, which was only 9 minutes after K-Car Alpha's first strike.

e. This action by an unsupported helicopter was not intended as the plan was for Lynx to link up with K-Car Alpha before moving to target. However, Squadron Leader Lunt moved quickly and being satisfied with my presence and the closeness of Lynx he proceeded to do battle. This type of action must be avoided in the future by adoption of a more flexible approach by the Fireforce. I am responsible for this situation, as I could have held K-Car Alpha back until the Lynx reached him.

f. Initial representation has been made to COMOPS (Gp Capt Walsh) requesting a follow-up by providing recce with immediate support. However, the potency of the Alpha K-Car is an essential ingredient if good opening results are to be achieved by a small element responding immediately to recce calls.

g. The stereotype employment of Fireforces has not produced acceptable results for over four months, making an altogether more aggressive approach essential. Recce will provide good results if Fireforces are positioned close to an area being covered by one or more recce aircraft; for instance Benecke and Dax. In turn, recce must work on the best intelligence available—as happened in today's work. Full Fireforce should not be used to make the initial checkout as this is cumbersome and slows down the whole procedure. One K-Car, a G-Car and a Lynx are all that is needed. If an action breaks, the remainder can be brought in at short notice. This system would also allow simultaneous check out on two camps, should the situation arise.

h. Another aspect that bears consideration is identifying specific terrorist leaders or terror groups requiring elimination. In today's strike we identified the terrorist group we wished to locate. The group was responsible for many actions against Centenary farms and this was having an adverse effect on farmers, their families and workers. The group contacted proved to be the very one we sought. Its leader, with size 10 boots and a frame to match, was amongst those killed.

j. Cost of ammunition expended—a mere $172.80.

On the night of 23 June 1978, probably whilst Ted Lunt was writing the ASR quoted above, a gang of CTs committed dreadful murder of seventeen innocent white missionaries and four of their children. This took place at the Elim Mission in the Vumba. The mission had previously been the Eagle Preparatory School that my brother Tony and I attended as founder pupils thirty years earlier. Rhodesians of all races were horror-struck by this senseless action, yet the rest of the world simply laughed it off, as they would do again when Air Rhodesia Viscount airliners were shot down.

The Katoog system continued to be used with considerable success, either acting alone or used as a component of Fireforce. Apart from the success of the sighting system, the density of fire from four guns using .303-ball ammunition proved many times more efficient, and a great deal cheaper, than single-barrel, slow-firing cannons with explosive 20mm shells.

Katoog was returned to South Africa at the conclusion of the six-week trial period. Six long months then passed before 7 Squadron received two systems, now referred to as either Dalmatian Project or Alpha Fit, for permanent use. Some of the 7 Squadron crews loved the weapon. However, most preferred the 20mm cannon because of the irritatingly high stoppage rate of .303 Browning guns.

Philippa Berlyn

PHILIPPA BERLYN (MARRIED NAME—CHRISTIE) was a Salisbury journalist who spoke fluent Shona. She was short, stocky and very plain in dress and looks but when it came to writing she was brilliant. Philippa had a very special interest in the wellbeing of black women and was particularly troubled by the hard times they were facing in the rural areas. However, since CTs disallowed newspapers in the areas they worked, Philippa could not get her messages and advice through to them. Because of this, she decided that she had to go to the women, and to hell with the risks that went with doing so.

I cannot remember the date she came to me at FAF 5, asking to be dropped off at a village some thirty kilometres northeast of Mtoko. She had already arranged to meet with a large number of local women and had been given clearance, in writing from Minister P.K. van der Byl, to make the visit. However the Army was unable to assist immediately and the Air Force had not been notified. Nevertheless, I sorted things out with Air HQ and clearance was given to deliver her at sunset for her all-night *indaba*, and collect her at sunrise.

The location to which Philippa was going happened to be a particularly hot spot, so the G-Car in which she flew was accompanied by a K-Car to cover the landing. The G-Car pilot who delivered Philippa was very relieved when he saw the large crowd of expectant women rushing to meet her as she climbed out, skirt flying, to meet them. But, like all of us, the pilot could not help being deeply concerned for the safety of this very brave white woman.

When the war ended, I learned from ZANLA that the local ZANLA commander had been fully aware of Philippa's impending visit and had instructed CTs not to fire at the helicopter but to keep a low profile. After dark and unbeknown to Philippa, ten CTs crept forward and remaining in the shadows surrounded the meeting place to listen to every word she spoke. So impressed were they by her fluency in Shona and the advice she gave the women that her departure by helicopter at sunrise went unchallenged.

Philippa's husband, law Professor Dick Christie, was not only good-looking, he differed a great deal from his softly spoken and very well-mannered wife. Whenever distanced from his professional environment he always let his hair down. Dick was an Air Force Volunteer Reserve officer who flew second 'dickey' in Dakotas. His favourite place for call-up was FAF 7, Buffalo Range. Dick Christie always celebrated his last night at FAF 7 by mixing a strange alcoholic concoction that included mashed bananas. There were never many takers for Dick's 'free drink' that went by some catchy name. In consequence, he drank more than he bargained for and got very happy, noisy and quite sloshed. It was in this condition that he became involved with others in 'roof-rattling' sleeping helicopter crews. Late drinkers often annoyed tired crew who had gone to bed at a sensible hour by throwing stones onto the noisy tin roofs of their billets. Dick joined in but, instead of throwing small sized stones, he heaved a brick that failed to make the height of the roof. Instead, it went through a window and broke the leg of a sleeping helicopter pilot. Next morning, a very sombre Dick was particularly embarrassed as he walked up the sloping deck of the Dakota past the unfortunate pilot who was lying strapped to a casevac stretcher. To add to his embarrassment, the pilot asked Dick if he was in a fit enough state to fly the Dakota.

Final tracker dogs trial

I HAD JUST BEEN AWARDED THE Defence Cross for Distinguished Service (DCD) for my project work when I was approached to try out dogs in a genuine track-down of CTs.

I learned that Flight Sergeant Terry Rubenstein, under direction from Wing Commander Rex Taylor, had resuscitated the radio tracker dog project. Rex and members of the Air Force Dog Section at New Sarum had been very annoyed by the Police Dog Training Centre's inability, or disinterest, in progressing the system to full operational status, so they trained two African handlers and their Alsatians for the task. Wing Commander Peter Cooke had tried them unsuccessfully in April 1978. The problems Peter encountered then were resolved but it was considered that I was the best man to make a final test.

DCD presentation by acting President Pithy.

Later with Beryl and son Paul who had, much to my astonishment and delight, successfully passed the gruelling selection process to become a member of the elite SAS.

I could not expect to be given an Alouette III for this task so Ted Lunt converted me onto an Alouette II because there were some spare at New Sarum. I had not flown this aircraft before even though most of the earlier helicopter pilots had undergone their initial helicopter training on this machine.

The Alouette II was not as pleasant to fly as its big sister, the Alouette III, but for me it was so much nicer than any fixed-wing aircraft. With two handlers and two dogs on board there was hardly room to move. Again I chose to base at Mtoko where I arranged ten 'volunteers' to walk a trail in the late evening. Next morning the dogs followed the trail without difficulty. Having satisfied myself that the dogs and handlers appeared to know their business it was just a matter of waiting for someone to come up with CT tracks to follow.

When a radio call came through reporting a night attack on a farm with fresh CT tracks confirmed, I called for the handlers and their dogs. Almost immediately I noticed how nervous the handlers were. As we lifted off one or both of them made their nervousness known by releasing wind which filled the cabin with an unwelcome stench.

The moment the dogs were put on the trail it became obvious to me that they were not going to run. After a number of failed attempts I landed back at the farm and questioned the two trackers. Neither one had ever seen action and both had heard horrifying stories of soldiers and airmen being killed in helicopters. I decided then that the dogs must have sensed their handlers' fear and that this was the reason they had reacted badly. I needed to prove this.

With JOC Hurricane's approval I arranged for a group of black soldiers to lay a trail from the same farm at the same time as the CTs had attacked it. Next morning I put down on their trail at the same time we had landed on the CT trail the day before. The dog handlers knew there would be no shooting at the end of the run and the dogs reacted normally, easily running down the soldiers ten kilometres from the start point.

The handlers' fear of potential CT fire and the adverse effect this had on their dogs had been proven. However, to give dog handlers airborne combat experience was an impossibility that threw the whole radio tracker dog concept out of the window. My own very biased opinion is that had I spent another year on helicopters back in 1969 this situation would have been foreseen and many successes might have resulted. The obvious solution was to train Air Force dogs to be handled by combat-experienced helicopter technicians or soldiers.

More enemy reversals

ZIPRA HAD BEEN PRETTY INEFFECTIVE inside the country because sporadic RSF actions had disallowed them from establishing themselves in the N'debele tribal areas as effectively as their ZANLA opponents had done in the east. So troubled were ZAPU's leaders about their waning image that they even resorted to claiming one of ZANLA's notable successes. This was an attack against the large fuel storage depot in Salisbury's industrial sites.

During the night of 11 December 1978, a small ZANLA sabotage unit fired RPG 7 rockets into three fuel-storage tanks, setting them alight. Such surprise was achieved that the CTs were gone before the Police protection detachment realised what had happened. The resulting fires radiated such intense heat that the tanks partially collapsed, spilling fuel in a chain reaction that destroyed twenty-two of the twenty-eight tanks in the complex. This attack dealt Rhodesia a near-crippling blow and it took three long months before the country's precious fuel reserves were restored.

In the meantime, ZIPRA agents and operatives in Rhodesia, obviously following ZANLA's lead, had been very busy recruiting in Matabeleland causing JOC Tangent great concern for the sudden high outflow of youngsters to Botswana. Most were being taken out at gunpoint! Nevertheless ZIPRA was still considered to be in a state of disarray following earlier SAS activities in Zambia. So, for the time being, ZANLA remained our primary concern.

During the latter quarter of 1977, the SAS was moved into the Gaza Province in an attempt to subdue that region in the manner they had tamed Tete. Unfortunately SAS was too small a unit to handle both provinces at the same time and the replacement troops sent to Tete did not operate in the same effective manner as SAS, simply because they were not trained for such specialised work. Consequently FRELIMO and ZANLA in Tete Province were let off the hook. Instead of being the hunted, they became the hunters again, which allowing CTs to pour into the Op Hurricane areas virtually unchecked.

In Gaza the SAS had good successes but they also had a very hard time. The FRELIMO Government had given greatest priority to assisting ZANLA with its main thrust into the southeast of Rhodesia. Because the Selous Scouts, SAS and air operations into Gaza had not been sustained on an ongoing basis, FRELIMO had been given the breathing space needed to build up substantial force levels to maintain the infiltration line for ZANLA.

Just before SAS was temporarily withdrawn from Gaza for the Op Dingo attacks on Chimoio and Tembue, a larger than normal SAS team dropped into Gaza Province on 1st November 1977. In an endeavour to mislead FRELIMO about the purpose of the para-Dakota's presence, the Dakota crew descended to low level to hand-launch Alpha bombs through the open cargo door along the general line of the railway. A very bad moment was experience when the Dakota inadvertently passed directly over heavily defended but blacked-out Mapai. The pilot bunted the aircraft in his endeavour to escape enemy 12,7mm, 14,5mm and 23mm fire that was ripping through his aircraft. In so doing, loose Alpha bombs and bodies floated in the air until forcibly dumped onto the floor when the aircraft levelled-off sharply too close to the ground for comfort.

Two days later, on 3 November, the SAS team brought a large convoy of FRELIMO vehicles to a halt when the lead vehicle struck the land mine SAS had laid as an initiator to their planned ambush. However, a series of explosions from ordnance on this vehicle made it impossible for the rest of the column to continue forward. Fearing air attack, the convoy backtracked a short distance and moved off the road.

The SAS had inadvertently hooked a much larger fish than the ZANLA convoy they had been expecting. They backed off immediately because the FRELIMO force was much too large and angry to engage. Through Giles Porter, (callsign C4) flying a Lynx with the SAS airborne liaison officer, Captain Bob MacKenzie, Air Force Hunters were called in for a dawn attack to destroy the vehicles, now hidden in the cover of dense trees and out of sight of the SAS men on the ground.

Vic Wightman and Dave Bourhill came in as Red Section. John Annan and Spook Geraty followed later as White Section. The term 'Bingo' in Vic Wightman's ASR means 'minimum fuel remaining'.

Vic's ASR reads:

Red Section arrived in the target area at approx. 0540B. C4 pointed out the burning vehicle which was about one kilometre up the road from where the hidden vehicles were believed to be. As no vehicles were visible either to C4 or Red Section, C4 suggested that Red Section descend to low level and have a look. Red Lead declined the offer on the grounds of fuel consumption and poor spotting capability at low level, whereupon C4, with a commendable display of moral fibre, descended to 50 feet and flew up the road from South to North. When he reached the assessed position of the hidden convoy a large number of twinkles from intense enemy fire appeared from the bush

to his left with airbursts assessed to have come from 37mm. As he broke away to the right Red Section turned in and fired long bursts of 30mm into the AA positions. After Red Section's first attack something (possibly a vehicle) was seen to be burning.

During the dive for the second attack, Strela smoke was seen heading northeastward. Another Strela was fired at Red Lead as he pulled up to perch for the third attack and the airburst was seen some way behind the aircraft. Red 2 also had a Strela fired at him as he pulled up. This is not the first time Red Lead has had Strela fired at him and there is no difficulty in identification.

Red Lead's third attack was guns only at the Strela site—Red 2 used 24 Matra. Since all 30mm ammo was used up and, at most, one vehicle was burning, Red climbed to FL 200 and called for another pair. While in the holding pattern several glints were seen which might have been reflections off windscreens. The position of one of these was noted. Red 2 ran short of fuel before White Section arrived but Red Lead was able to place 6 Matra at the position at about 0645B just as fuel reached Bingo for Buffalo Range. It was a lucky guess for the unseen vehicle burst into flames and started exploding.

At 0615B White Section was airborne. En route they were briefed by Red Lead and C4 on the situation and the AA. As they arrived overhead they observed Red Lead's final strike. C4 asked White Lead to strike along the left of the road in a northerly direction and White 2 along the right. Both used Matra and 30mm and were on target as observed by C4 who was by this time overhead at FL 120. As White 2 was pulling out of his attack he saw a group of vehicles just to the left of and about 2/3 along his line of strikes. He attempted to get White Lead's eyes onto target by clock reference from the burning vehicle.

White 2 observed White Lead's second strike to be at the left of the assessed position of the (unseen) group of vehicles and while pulling out White Lead also noticed them. Both he and White 2 attempted another strike but only saw the vehicles after ceasefire though White 2's second and third attacks appeared to rake through them. His subsequent attacks were to no avail as a 7.62 round had severed his armament circuits. White Lead was also having difficulty with intermittent firing. At this stage C4 assessed the targets as severely damaged and he recommended that no further Hunters be called for. White Lead was streaming fuel from his port 230 tank so diverted to Buffalo Range. White 2 returned to base.

As can be seen from the ASR, the Hunter pilots did not fully realise what damage they had inflicted. Giles Porter and Bob MacKenzie had been extremely lucky to survive the low pass in which unbelievably heavy fire, including flak and missiles, was directed at them; but this brave action had succeeded in finding the convoy. The SAS on the ground said the Lynx passed through the heaviest fire they had ever witnessed, making it all the more amazing that the Lynx suffered no hits.

During the night two days after the attack, a close-in reconnaissance revealed that the SAS had halted a mobile brigade including Russians who were aiming to establish this brigade's HQ in Mapai. Thirteen brand-new transporters and specialist vehicles had been destroyed along with spares for Russian tanks that were already in position at Mapai

Actions such as this should have been sustained but, with the SAS withdrawal from Gaza for Op Dingo, breathing space was again given to FRELIMO and ZANLA, allowing the rate of incursions into the Op Repulse area to increase. By now FRELIMO, incensed by Rhodesian forces' actions against them, increased their own numbers entering Rhodesia.

The SAS had expected to return to Gaza immediately following Op Dingo but their expertise was needed in Zambia and Botswana to counter renewed threats from ZIPRA's attempts to establish an effective front in Matabeleland.

In what was probably the most successful ambush of the war, ZIPRA lost large numbers of men and equipment in an SAS ambush in southern Zambia. After the ambush landmines were laid to take out ZIPRA hierarchy who were sure to visit the scene once they felt it was safe enough to do so. Three days later, in spite of Zambian Army assistance and a very precautionary approach to inspect the devastation, ZIPRA suffered the loss of its military commander, Alfred Nkita Mangena, and three senior men wounded when their vehicle detonated one of the landmines that awaited them. SAS had put ZIPRA on the back foot again, giving the overstretched RSF the respite they needed.

Deaths of du Toit and Nelson

AS STATED EARLIER, FRELIMO AND ZANLA had regained composure and control in the Tete Province following the withdrawal of the SAS. RLI teams were still there when, on 28 July 1978, two G-Cars with a Lynx in support were tasked to uplift callsign 74. This was about thirty kilometres north of the position where Cocky Benecke's Mini-golf bomb had relieved RLI callsign 75 eight days earlier. However, due to an aircraft un-serviceability problem, the RLI officer responsible for the external operation arrived to give the aircrew a briefing very late in the day. This unavoidable situation was a contributing factor to developments that occurred when it was too late to call for Hunter support.

Just before sunset and about three kilometres short of c/s 74, Francois du Toit was leading Air Lieutenant Nigel Lamb at about twenty feet above the trees when both helicopters came under intense fire from their left side. Francois, flying some 100 metres to the left of Nigel, was seen to flare indicating he was force-landing before disappearing from Nigel's view behind trees.

Still under heavy fire, Nigel had no alternative but to press

on to collect c/s 74 to bring troops back to check on the downed helicopter. As he did this, Nigel briefed Flight Lieutenant Mike Abrams flying the accompanying Lynx. When Nigel looked up for the Lynx he saw that "flak was bursting all around the aircraft." This was most likely RPG 7 rockets and Strela.

Due to high fuel weight, Nigel could only lift two men from c/s 74. Under supporting fire from the Lynx, he deposited the two soldiers, now called 74A, on the ground about fifty metres from the downed helicopter; but these two men came under intensive fire the moment the helicopter turned around to collect the remaining two members of c/s 74.

The weight of fire coming from a position just fifty metres from the crash site, which was over to 74A's right, showed the enemy's strength to be far too great for the two soldiers. Nevertheless they managed to get to within thirty metres of Francois' aircraft and reported that there was no movement whatsoever from the badly flattened helicopter. By then heavy fire, including RPG 7 rockets, was also being directed at c/s 74A and the Lynx from high ground 200 metres west of the crash site. Fire was returned by c/s 74A, the Lynx and the returning G-Car, but 74A remained pinned down.

Moving behind the cover of a low ridge, Nigel and his technician-gunner Chris Saint, dumped everything possible from their fully laden Alouette preparatory to rescuing c/s 74A. There was no time to dump the helicopter's refueller or the hot extraction gear. Fighting jangled nerves and uncontrollable shaking of his legs, Nigel flew back to recover the very distressed pair of soldiers. As he went he prayed for a safe LZ, a reliable engine and a very strong gearbox. Under heavy fire Nigel found a suitable LZ and Mike Abrams attacked to draw attention to himself whilst the two soldiers made a bolt for the helicopter. When the two panting men arrived, Nigel ordered them to abandon their packs before making a substantially overweight lift-off for Rhodesia. To have left the four RLI soldiers on the ground for the night was never a question, and it was too late to bring in other soldiers to the crash site.

The next day, with Hunters overhead, the RLI moved in and confirmed what was already known. Flight Lieutenant du Toit and Sergeant Nelson were dead, Francois having been mortally wounded in the initial ground fire. He died in his seat before he could complete the autorotative forced landing he had initiated. Either bullet wounds or the resulting crash killed his technician because both bodies were riddled with bullet holes. Many years after this incident, Nigel told author, Beryl Salt, "I have found it more comfortable to believe that these were inflicted before impact."

Like so many of our aircrew youngsters then engaged in operations, I hardly knew Sergeant Nelson (whose brother had leaped to his death from the burning helicopter). On the other hand I knew Francois very well; and Beryl had a particularly soft spot for this super young man with his ever-ready smile.

Second Tembue attack

I ONLY LEARNED OF FRANCOIS' DEATH when I was about to get airborne for another attack on Tembue, again as the Admin Base commander. It was early morning on Sunday 30 July when we set off for the Train to refuel in freezing cold weather before continuing on to Tembue. ZANLA had re-established Tembue base a relatively short distance away across the main road running from Tete town to Zambia to the east of the original base. This base was nothing more than a number of interconnected camp areas containing small bashas with no major structures such as kitchens, lecture rooms or latrines.

Two two-man Selous Scouts recce teams had been sent in but one was blown almost immediately forcing it to call for hot extraction. However, Schulie and his man remained in position and reported that, whilst CT numbers were way below expectation, there were certainly CTs present at the end of the base that they could see from their hide.

Airstrikes went in on time followed by paratroopers, helicopter-borne troops and K-Cars. The DC7 staggered over the Admin Base and put down the protection party, ammunition and fuel exactly where I wanted them dropped. This admin base lay in a vlei three kilometres to the west of the main road with Tembue 2, commencing some six kilometres away and stretching eastward for another six kilometres to Schulie's hiding place. Earlier admin area experience made the matters of parachute- and drum-handling run smoothly despite the discomfort given by the presence of many itchy buffalo-bean bushes. On this occasion I had a folding chair and a table on which to place my radio and keep simple records under a huge mahobahoba tree.

It was clear from the outset that very few CTs were being accounted for. Selous Scouts blamed the Air Force for dropping the paratroopers in the wrong place, forcing them to walk too great a distance to the CT base areas in which the embers of many night fires still glowed red. Unfortunately Selous Scouts had changed character a great deal by this stage in the war and were quick to point fingers when they themselves may have been at fault. Anyway, I have no doubt that Flight Lieutenant Dave Thorne, who led the four paratrooper Dakotas, placed the troops precisely where they were supposed to land.

At midday FRELIMO came to the party and commenced firing at helicopters crossing over the main road between the CT camps and the Admin Base. Explosions from the hills close behind us had me really worried until the protection troops said these were no more than echoes from the exploding RPG 7 and Strela warheads being fired at passing aircraft. Nevertheless there was now some concern for the safety of the helicopters and personnel in the Admin Base area, so SAS sticks were flown in from unproductive sectors of the CT bases to bolster the existing Admin Base protection party.

During the afternoon one helicopter coming in to land passed directly over another whose rotor blades were still slowing down after engine shutdown. This forbidden action resulted in the helicopter on the ground sustaining damage when its still turning blades flapped down into the tail cone. Moments later, a sound resembling heavy-calibre machine-gun fire in the centre of the Admin Base made everyone dive for cover before it was realised that another helicopter's rotor wash had drawn in a parachute that was being flayed by its fast-moving blades. Fortunately the only damage incurred was the destruction of the small plastic reservoirs on top of the rotor head; but these contained vital hydraulic fluid for the rotors damper systems and the aircraft could not be flown.

By late afternoon we had two machines awaiting repairs in the field and were almost out of fuel. Happily the FRELIMO force had moved off, probably having expended all its ammunition, but more fuel had to be flown in and it became obvious that everyone would have to remain where they were for the night. When the DC7 returned, its first drop was momentarily delayed beyond my 'green light' call resulting in a fuel pallet crashing through the mahobahoba tree under which I was standing and damaged my little table. What horrified everyone each time the DC7 passed 200 feet above us was the bright flaming of its ringed exhaust system that could not possibly be missed by Strela in the fast-fading light.

None of the aircrew had any type of bedding for the cold night ahead, nor did we have anything to eat. However concern for a possible FRELIMO attack put hunger in second place as we gathered up parachutes, rolled into them and lay quietly listening to every sound of the night awaiting to be overtaken by sleep. Around us the helicopter vision screens reflected starlight so brightly that they appeared like beacons to an unseen enemy. By this time however, there were fair numbers of SAS troops ranged around the Admin Base, which was very comforting. Lying on my back in moderate comfort and gazing at the bright stars so tightly packed in cold clear conditions, I couldn't help wondering why in the world war was so endemic to mankind when there was so much space for all to live in peace.

I was still pondering on this when I felt a snake move across my shoulder, over my chest, under the parachute and down to my feet. There it turned direction coming back between my legs heading for my chin. I dared not move nor even whisper a word to those around me. I felt the snake's head bump my chin then turn towards my feet again, this time outside the parachute. Then I felt a fluttering on my chest as the rest of the snake's body kept flowing upwards. When the tail was out, I gently lowered my chin to see what the creature was doing, only to find many little field mice milling around on my chest and stomach. These little blighters were responsible for my uncomfortable moments, having made a snake-like, head-to-tail journey through the warmth of my makeshift bed.

I rose at dawn in light, freezing fog to brew a cup of coffee. A little distance away I saw an old black man sitting by a small fire. He had been found close to the Admin Base the previous day and had been apprehended by the Army protection force to ensure that he did not go off to report our position to FRELIMO. The old fellow had been well fed with food he probably had not seen for years and seemed very pleased to be among us. Now however, in the cold dawn wearing only a pair of tattered shorts, he was very cold and his body shook in violent spasms that wracked his scrawny frame. I removed my anorak and took off the thick grey home-knitted jersey under it to give to the old man. Judging by the expression on his old face, nothing in the world could have brought him more joy.

The whole helicopter force lifted off early for the return flight to Mount Darwin, leaving behind the protection party, the old black man and two unserviceable helicopters with their crews. There were also stay-behind forces in the Tembue 2 camp complex.

It was only when we reached Mount Darwin that it dawned on me that the jersey I had given the old man had my nametag sewn inside its collar. Harold Griffiths, released from COMOPS for this operation, was returning to the Admin Base next day so I requested that he find the old man and remove the nametag from his jersey as a precaution against possible retribution by FRELIMO. When I saw Griff again, he handed me the nametag saying the old man had been sad to see everyone go.

I left Mount Darwin for New Sarum during the evening of our return from Tembue 2. To see me off was the New Sarum Station Warrant Officer, Barney Barnes, who was enjoying a spell at FAF 4. He was full of bounce and just as noisy as ever when he closed my Cessna's door and bid me farewell. So it came as a real shock to be told, only forty minutes later, that Barney Barnes had died of a heart attack as he entered the FAF 4 pub, having just seen me off.

Griff looking completely beggared upon his first return from Tembue 2.

Viscount disaster

SADLY, AIR RHODESIA HAD DONE nothing to protect their Viscount airliners against Strela, despite Air Force warnings and their knowledge of two failed attempts by ZIPRA to shoot down South African Airways aircraft on scheduled flights to Victoria Falls Airport. The price for this omission was paid on 3 September 1978 when a routine flight from Kariba to Salisbury met with a tragedy that had the people of Rhodesia reeling.

At this angle, Hunter exhausts became visible to Strela whereas the special paint rendered the airframe invisible. The Viscount on the other hand, having four large fully exposed exhausts plus a highly visible airframe was easily detectable for miles in any direction.

Captain John Hood and First Officer Garth Beaumont took off from Kariba Airport on Air Rhodesia Flight 825 climbing the Viscount out westward over the lake in accordance with standing instruction. This was a precautionary procedure to guard against possible CT ground fire that might pose a threat on the easterly climb-out over land. They turned southeastward for Salisbury and were still in the climb over Urungwe Tribal Trust Lands when a Strela missile exploded between the two starboard engines. Both engines failed and an intense fire broke out.

Having no option but to get the aircraft on the ground as soon as possible, John Hood put out a 'May Day' call but had insufficient time to give the Kariba Air Traffic Controller his exact location. Warning of an impending forced-landing was given to the passengers who adopted the head-on-knees posture to limit injury after touch-down. Following a relatively gentle landing on the best available open field, the aircraft rolled for some distance before pitching into an unseen *donga* that killed both pilots, destroyed the Viscount and ruptured fuel tanks that set the distorted cabin ablaze.

Forty passengers and crew died in the crash but eighteen miraculously clambered out to safety, most with injuries. Five of the passengers helped settle the injured before going in search of water and help. They were some distance away by the time a group of ZIPRA CTs arrived at the crash site. Initially the CTs told the survivors not to be afraid, but then opened fire killing ten of then. Three managed to make their escape under fire.

I flew one of a number of aircraft hurriedly gathered to search for the Viscount that was known to be down but whose fate was not yet known. Fortunately a Dakota, taking part in the search and assigned to the most likely area, was carrying SAS paratroopers fully prepared for deployment. It so happened that it was this Dakota crew who located the stricken airliner and the SAS parachuted onto site immediately. The horror of what they discovered and reported reverberated around the world.

Interviewed on BBC television that same evening, Joshua Nkomo responded with a big smile and a hateful belly laugh as he acknowledged that ZIPRA was responsible for the deliberate downing of the civilian aircraft. The Western world heard this quite clearly but chose to ignore the horror because Rhodesia continued to be a hindrance to the West's obvious desire to turn the country over to communists. So what if innocent civilians had been deliberately murdered!

Rhodesians had become accustomed to the attitude of so-called friendly governments; though none of us ever understood why they were so determined to destroy what Ian Smith termed 'responsible government'. They aimed only at appeasing black governments that had wrecked their once prosperous countries. This we had become used to, but the West's total disinterest in the Viscount disaster was sickening.

Dean of Salisbury's Anglican Cathedral, John de Costa, conducted a highly emotional memorial service for the victims of the Viscount disaster during which he expressed the feelings of all anti-communist Rhodesians in a sermon that highlighted the 'deafening silence' from our very kith and kin in the West. "Nobody who holds sacred the dignity of human life can be anything but sickened at the events attending the Viscount … this bestiality stinks in the nostrils of Heaven. But are we deafened with the voice of protest from nations who call themselves civilised? We are not! Like men in the story of the good Samaritan, they pass by on the other side."

Ian Smith had continued in his attempts to involve Joshua Nkomo and his ZAPU party in the new order of government. Following the Viscount disaster however, anger within his party and the Rhodesian people as a whole made further attempts

impossible. Everyone wanted Nkomo's blood together with those CTs responsible for mindless murder. One week after the Viscount disaster, a grim-faced Ian Smith addressed the nation and introduced martial law in selected areas. He also gave clear warning to neighbouring territories that they must bear the consequences of any defensive strikes we might direct at CT bases within their territories. This was no idle threat because over-border strikes into Mozambique and Zambia commenced one week later.

Before Air Rhodesia had completed preliminary work to provide Viscounts with anti-Strela shielding, a second Viscount was shot down on 12 February 1979, again by ZIPRA. For some reason the scheduled departure of this Viscount, again from Kariba to Salisbury, was running a little late. Inexplicably, instead of climbing out over the lake, the skipper decided to take off in the opposite direction. Turning for Salisbury in its climb over land, the aircraft was critically damaged by a Strela missile that sent it plunging into heavy bush in very rough terrain. No one survived this time.

Subsequent to the second disaster, Air Rhodesia succeeded in shrouding Viscount exhaust pipes and painting the aircraft with the appropriate low-radiation paint. The Air Force's modified Strela test-bed was unable to detect Viscounts flying above 2,000 feet. If any other Strela missiles were fired at Viscounts, they passed unnoticed.

Return to Chimoio

TEN MONTHS HAD PASSED SINCE Chimoio was destroyed, leaving ZANLA in a state of chaos until re-established in their New Chimoio complex east of the original site. SB had put together intelligence which, when linked to photo recce, revealed what was believed to be the whole of the target area.

Four white abductees were being held prisoner by ZANLA in this new base when Operation Snoopy was launched on 20 September 1978, again by SAS, RLI and Air Force. Photos of the base showed it to be more widespread than the original Chimoio base but an attack plan similar to Op Dingo was put into effect. Heavy haze conditions, covering Mozambique from ground level all the way up to 30,000 feet, had set in earlier than usual, but the jet pilots managed to find their targets for the opening strikes. When the troops and K-Cars moved in, it became obvious that the camps they were dealing with contained nothing like as many CTs as had been expected.

Then a Lynx pilot, conducting reconnaissance in depth, attracted very heavy fire from positions over thirty kilometres south of the attended area. Only then was it realised that

ZANLA camps were spread within an elliptically shaped area exceeding 200 square kilometres in extent. Immediately the whole complex became known as the 'Chimoio Circle'.

Troops were moved down from the northern sector of Chimoio Circle to the south where they came into contact with ZANLA in many different positions, resulting in some serious but unco-ordinated firefights. Jet and K-Car strikes criss-crossed over a multitude of targets that were surrounded by extensive trench systems incorporating many AA guns. Fighting and camp destruction operations continued into the second day before FRELIMO decided to enter the area with tanks, but apart from making a lot of noise and bumbling around in the dark, they were of no value to ZANLA who, though taking many casualties, were offering stiffer resistance than had been experienced on any previous occasion.

The haze problem worsened progressively due to huge amounts of smoke generated by hundreds of burning structures. So dense was the haze that an SAS-controlled Hunter strike, directed against the highest point of an adjacent granite hill, ended up on the same hill as the SAS callsign. Fortunately the Golf bombs detonated on the highest point over 100 metres from the callsign, but even this was too close and shrapnel mortally wounded Trooper Donnelly. The pilot, Vic Wightman, was very distressed by this unfortunate incident but, considering the amount of ordnance being put down in response to calls from the ground, it says much for the efficiency of pilots that no other soldiers were hurt in the awful conditions that prevailed. The error Vic Wightman made arose from the fact that the whaleback granite feature he was asked to attack looked much the same as any other of a number of such features within the Chimoio Circle, and they were all aligned in the same direction. Had the haze not so severely restricted visibility of the ground to a small patch directly below the aircraft, cross-referencing on river-lines would have eliminated any chance of this pilot error. The SAS quickly put the Air Force at ease by letting it be known that they fully understood the jet pilots' problems and accepted the attendant dangers.

Dave Bourhill.

For the Hunters and Canberras there were other dangers. Strela missiles were being launched and two of these found their mark. One Canberra crew was aware of a substantial bump on their aircraft as they were clearing target for New Sarum. Back at base they discovered this had been from a missile that detonated at the very rear of the jet pipe and sent a shower of shrapnel into the fuselage, rupturing one fuel tank. Dave Bourhill was in a climbing turn for re-strike when a missile narrowly missed his Hunter's jet pipe but exploded under the starboard mainplane leaving a huge hole in it. Back on the ground the damaged Hunter drew attention away from the damaged Canberra parked on the next concrete hard standing.

There was considerable disappointment in not finding the four white abductees the troops had hoped to rescue. However, amongst piles and piles of captured documents, SB came upon records dated three weeks earlier in which the four captured whites were listed as:

John HERNLEY. Place of residence—Bulawayo. Date of capture—5.2.78. (Note: ZANLA had erred in their spelling. It should have been Kennerley.)
Johannes Hendrik MAARTENS. Place of residence—Maringoyi Farm, Headlands. Date of captured—18.5.78.
Thomas WIGGLESWORTH. Place of residence—Odzani, Umtali. Date of capture—2.8.78.
James BLACK. Place of residence—Martin Forest, Melsetter. Date of capture—19.8.78.

Military ribbons and medals belonging to Thomas Wigglesworth were recovered from the personal belongings of a CT in Nehanda camp; the location known to have been where the abductees had been held. Fortunately, sufficient evidence was obtained for Red Cross International to bring about the release of these men from the Tembue area where they had been taken.

Here I divert for a moment. The Rhodesian's lack of knowledge concerning its enemy, particularly ZANLA, has already been touched upon, and I have told of my absolute fear and certainty of being killed if downed in Mozambique. The release of these men made me wonder if I might have been wrong in believing the press and some political statements that conveyed to Rhodesians the awful hardships the abducted men must be facing. Upon their release all these men said that they had been well treated, particularly by Josiah Tongogara. Since first news of their release came from press interviews in the Polana Hotel in Maputo, obviously attended by ZANU and FRELIMO officials, no notice was taken of their good reports. But then the Rhodesian Foreign Minister, P.K. van der Byl, introduced Maartens and Black at a press conference in Salisbury. This backfired on him to some extent because he was fully expecting to hear from these men what had been fed to the public. Instead Maartens, who was under no pressure to say the 'right thing', repeated what he had said in Maputo.

When relating to the return of his medals in a book he wrote about his time with ZANLA, Thomas Wigglesworth records that "truth is certainly stranger than fiction ..."

Returning to Op Snoopy. On Day Three of this operation all forces returned to Rhodesia. The Air Force was quite unable to sustain a longer stay and sufficient death, destruction and disruption had been imposed on ZANLA, for the time being.

World reaction to our external operations was nothing

like as damaging to Rhodesia as had been expected, and for the most part FRELIMO had not become involved. The benefits of going external, so long delayed, were proving to be much more cost-effective and infinitely more disruptive to both ZANLA and ZIPRA than internal operations. For the moment ZANLA was on the back foot, so attention switched back to ZIPRA.

Operation Gatling

BEFORE OCTOBER 1978, OPERATIONS INSIDE Zambia had not involved Air Force in anything more than a supporting role. The SAS had conducted superbly executed disruptive operations that succeeded in forcing ZIPRA to move away from the Zambezi River and ever deeper into Zambia. In the meanwhile Selous Scouts-controlled spies and SB agents had been very active inside Zambia gaining intelligence on ZIPRA because this was more difficult to gain than from ZANLA through scores of captured CTs. A clearer picture had emerged and Canberras were able to photograph defined positions for photo-interpreters to study.

With specific targets confirmed, and considering the experience gained in joint-force operations in Mozambique, it was time for the Air Force to become directly involved against ZIPRA in Zambia. It was payback time for the first Viscount disaster, which had occurred seven weeks earlier.

On 19 October, the Air Force engaged in three separate operations in Zambia, the first of which did not include any troops. This was because the target, previously white-owned Westlands Farm, was too close to the Zambian capital Lusaka. Lying just sixteen kilometres to the northeast of the city centre, this farm had become ZIPRA's military headquarters and training base. ZIPRA called it Freedom Camp (FC Camp). Being so close to Lusaka, ZIPRA considered the location to be immune to attack. However, with senior ZIPRA staff there and 4,000-odd CTs undergoing training in a relatively compact area, FC Camp made an obvious and very inviting target for airstrikes.

One thing that had to be taken into account was the possibility of Zambian Air Force fighters interfering with Rhodesian aircraft. There were also the matters of British Rapier missiles known to be somewhere in Zambia and civilian air traffic movements in and out of Lusaka Airport. To deal with the former issue, it was decided that the lead Canberra would forewarn Lusaka Airport by passing a message through the duty Air Traffic Controller to the Station Commander at the Zambian Air Force base, Mumbwa. This was to let him

know that Hunters were over his base with orders to shoot down any Zambian fighters that attempted to take off.

Timings were crucial because Canberras, Hunters and K-Cars allocated to the FC raid had to turn around after their strikes and link into a combined operation with the SAS against ZIPRA's Mkushi Camp. The third target, known to us as CGT 2, was to be handled by Vampires, Lynx, four K-cars, G-Cars and RLI paratroopers. CGT 2 was one of at least four ZIPRA bases established in rough country south of the Great East Road that ran eastward from Lusaka to Malawi. Not knowing ZIPRA names for these bases, they were named Communist Guerrilla Training (CGT) bases with identification numerals 1–4.

Diverting for a moment back to my JPS days. During the late 1960s South African, Portuguese and Rhodesian teams had been established for the Alcora Planning groups to consider mutual support in both regular and counter-insurgency warfare. Whereas I had been a member of the mapping committee, I was in the picture on most of the other committees' work. One of these dealt specifically with plans for strategic airfields. These plans involved the upgrading of existing air bases and the building of new ones suitably sited in South West Africa, Rhodesia, Mozambique and South Africa.

Each air base was to incorporate underground hangars and immediate-readiness fighter pens with intricate taxiways leading to two primary runways. The design allowed two whole squadrons of sixteen fighters to scramble simultaneously. However, the costs involved were so great that it was necessary to build the bases in stages. The first stage was to build one half of a total base with the end-plan taxiway serving as the first operational runway.

In Rhodesia, Thornhill and New Sarum needed no work as they both exceeded the needs of Phase 1, but three other sites had been selected. These were Wankie National Park, Fylde Farm near Hartley and Buffalo Range at Chiredzi. Buffalo Range already existed as an active airfield, needing only limited work to get it to Phase 1 status. Fylde had become operational before Op Gatling was mounted on 19 October and served as the base for Hunters and Vampires during this operation. At this stage work at Wankie was still in progress.

Green Formation of four Canberras left New Sarum a little after four K-Cars had taken off from Mana Pools on the Zambezi River. A total of six Hunters were involved. Two with Sidewinder air-to-air missiles headed directly for the Zambian Air Force base at Mumbwa and the other four followed a prescribed route to FC camp.

Squadron Leader Chris Dixon with Mike Ronnie as his navigator led Green Formation. Ted Brent with Jim Russell, Greg Todd with Doug Pasea, and Glen Pretorius with Paddy Morgan followed. The Canberras, flying low under Zambian radar, were loaded with a total of 1,200 Alpha bombs. The four Hunters of Blue Formation, led by Squadron Leader Vic Wightman with wingmen John Blythe-Wood, Ginger Baldwin and Tony Oakley, were also approaching target at low level and were some way behind the slower Canberra formation when they crossed the Zambezi River. Their speed would place them ahead for first strikes.

White Section, the Hunters orbiting Mumbwa, were flown by Rick Culpan and Alf Wild, who listened in to the attacking force transmissions whilst hoping the MiG 19 fighters would take to the air. In this they were to be disappointed because nothing stirred. Orbiting at height near the Zambezi River in the Command Dakota were General Peter Walls, Group Captain Norman Walsh and their communications staff who would remain airborne throughout the day to cover all three operations.

The Hunters struck dead on 08:30 taking out the FC headquarters buildings. The huge Golf bombs' plumes were not needed as markers to give Chris Dixon's bomb-aimer final

FC Camp. The Canberra Alpha strike was to cover the area from the treed camp area on the right, along the double path lines and beyond the parade area. Hunters were given HQ targets amongst the trees to the left of the parade ground. No anti-aircraft gun positions existed within the limits of this photograph.

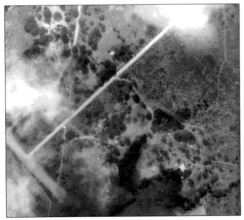

Hidden under smoke in this photo taken by a Hunter after re-strike are most of the destroyed HQ buildings.

confirmation of his line-up because Mike Ronnie could see the target during the formation's acceleration to attack-speed.

Chris's radio system was linked to a tape recorder in the cockpit for possible post-strike public relations purposes. On playback of the tape, we all heard the deep breathing of the crew building up during run to target and their comments about the precision of Hunter strikes. This was followed by excited shouting between Chris and Mike when they saw hundreds of CTs running in the treed and open areas through which the Canberra formation's bomb loads would run. On completion of their strike, Chris and Mike continued to communicate excitedly as, in the background, the calm voices of the Hunter pilots could be heard as they called, "turning in live" for their re-strikes.

When the Hunters cleared, the voice of Pink Formation leader, Squadron Leader Graham Cronshaw, showed that the K-Cars had arrived over FC camp. They were lucky that none of the anti-aircraft guns were manned as they set about attacking scattered survivors.

Chris Dixon had been instructed to contact Lusaka Tower before his strike, but something had gone amiss with frequency selection. He only made this call to a remarkably calm African controller whilst the K-Cars were active over FC camp. This was Chris's prepared message:

Lusaka Tower this is Green Leader. This is a message for the Station Commander at Mumbwa from the Rhodesian Air Force. We are attacking the terrorist base at Westlands Farm at this time. This attack is against Rhodesian dissidents and not against Zambia. Rhodesia has no quarrel—repeat no quarrel—with Zambia or her Security Forces. We therefore ask you not to intervene or oppose our attack. However, we are orbiting your airfield at this time and are under orders to shoot down any Zambian aircraft that does not comply with this request and attempts to take off. Did you copy that?

In response to a query from Lusaka Tower, Chris suggested that the departure of an aircraft be withheld for a short while. The controller was happy to oblige and even asked a Kenyan airliner, incoming from Nairobi, to hold off.

Chris had flown out of range when Dolphin 3, Norman Walsh in the Command Dakota, established contact with Lusaka Tower. Immediately after this the irritated Kenyan Airways pilot asked Lusaka "Who has priority here anyway?" to which the Zambian controller calmly replied, "The Rhodesians, I guess!" The Kenyan did not have long to wait. Norman Walsh returned Zambia's air space to the thankful controller once the K-Cars were well clear of the target.

Shortly after the air action, Lusaka's hospital became inundated with the inflow of wounded and dying ZIPRA personnel. All forms of transport kept bringing in more and more casualties way into the night. Zambian patients were incensed for being kicked out of their sick beds when all floor and bed space was taken up by the ZIPRA flood. Unbeknown to the Zambian medical staff, a Selous Scouts officer was sitting calmly in the waiting room, claiming to be there for an anti-cholera injection. He watched the never-ending stream of serious casualties in satisfied amazement having, himself, been responsible for locating FC camp. According to a ZAPU delegation report to a Pan African Congress held at Arusha, Tanzania in May 1979, 226 CTs were killed and 629 were wounded, most seriously.

The K-Cars returned to Mana Pools and the jets to their bases. The gunners, preparing their helicopters for the attack on Mkushi Camp, were full of enthusiasm having just returned from FC Camp. For the technicians at New Sarum and Fylde there was no time to find out how the Zambian raid had gone; and anyway the aircrew were too tied up to share their war stories. In spite of this the armourers, engine fitters, airframe fitters, electricians, radio men and refuellers went about their business with no less enthusiasm than their colleagues way up on the Zambezi River.

In most respects, the attack on Mkushi was conducted in the manner of the first attack on Chimoio with jet-strikes leading the action at 11:40. In this case six Dakotas dropped 120 SAS paratroopers in a semi-circle around the western and northern flanks of Mkushi base with K-Cars patrolling the Mkushi River, which formed the eastern and southern boundaries of the target. Forty-four SAS were landed by eleven G-Cars behind the cover of a small feature in the camp's southeastern corner. Eight kilometres southeast of target lay the Admin Base into which an RLI protection force was para-dropped with fuel and ammunition.

It was only when the ground fighting was underway, that the SAS realised Mkushi camp was occupied by women CTs with only a few male instructors. Our intelligence people had not known this. The women looked just like men in their camouflage uniforms and they bore their weapons with efficiency. Although some attempted to hide and take advantage of grass fires initiated by the air strikes and heavy firing, most fought back. The SAS could not help but be impressed by female aggression and fighting ability that kept the soldiers busy till late afternoon.

With the RLI protection force at the Admin Base was one unusual character. He was Sergeant-Major Standish who, as a grey-haired Territorial Army soldier on call-up with SAS, had managed to wangle his way onto Op Gatling. Stan Standish, who had been a paratrooper at Arnheim, claimed that only the Dakotas that had brought the force to Mkushi had seen longer service than he had. He thoroughly enjoyed his parachute descent into the Admin Base and gained the admiration of the aircrews who saw him set a great example to the RLI youngsters in matters of collecting parachutes and rolling fuel drums.

There had been some concern for the safety of helicopters parked on the Admin Base *dambo* (Zambian word for a small open grass area) because they presented a perfect target for any Zambian MiG 17 or MiG 19 pilot who might choose to attack them. As it happened, one MiG 19 did appear over the Admin Base but either the pilot did not see the exposed choppers or turned a blind eye and disappeared into the blue.

Mkushi was by far the best-organised base the troops had seen with many more facilities than in any ZANLA base. A red hammer and sickle emblazoned in red on one of the buildings emphasised ZIPRA's Russian orientation. When the fighting was over, the troops left everything just as it was for members of the press to view the next day.

The SAS referred to reporters as 'vultures' because they only turned up when the killing was over. There were certainly plenty of dead bodies, piles of captured matériel, stacks of ZIPRA documents and many Soviet manuals for the vultures to photograph and inspect. The SAS also had five ZIPRA prisoners for them to interview. Once the press had done their work and were on their way back to Rhodesia late on Day 2, all equipment and buildings were destroyed.

On Day 3 the SAS were in the process of recovering to Rhodesia when a lookout warned of the approach of a large armed force sweeping towards the main group. Hurriedly the SAS got into position and waited for the force to come to close range. They then opened fire on Zambian Army, Zambian Police and ZIPRA in a short sharp action that left forty-seven dead. Fortunately they captured a Zambian Army man and, incredibly, ZIPRA's senior Logistics Officer. His name was Mountain Gutu and his importance will become apparent. These two prisoners, together with the other five captives, were all flown back to Salisbury.

Well to the south of Mkushi, air attacks on CGT 2 were launched by four Vampires firing 60-pound squash-head rockets and 20mm cannons and four Lynx dropped Mini-golf bombs and fired 37mm boosted Sneb rockets. The RLI followed up in double Fireforce strength. I cannot recall any details of the ground action other than it occurred in difficult bush conditions resulting in the death of about sixty CTs. But this target turned out to be the toughest nut of the ZIPRA targets because it contained many very effective large-calibre anti-aircraft guns and missiles. Cocky Benecke took hits immediately, which forced him to withdraw with a holed fuel tank.

Nigel Lamb wrote, "huge easily visible shells arched lazily upward, then seemed to accelerate past us". Even climbing to 2,500 feet above target did not help so the helicopters beat a sensible retreat; but not before Mark Dawson's K-Car received an explosive hit which knocked out the instruments and wounded Mark in the leg.

The K-Cars split into two pairs running low level either side of a high ridge when Chaz Goatley was heard to shout to Mark Dawson that his tail rotor was slowing down. Mark knew his tail rotor drive-shaft had been severed before his machine started to spin in the opposite direction to the main rotor blades and, arching downwards, crashed through high trees which turned the aircraft upside-down. Fortunately there was no fire. The three K-Cars grouped over the downed machine before Nigel Lamb put down as close to the crash site as possible. Nigel stopped his rotors but left the engine running and hurried to the crashed aircraft with his technician-gunner Finch Bellringer. Immediately they found Mark's technician-gunner Roelf Oelofse who, having been thrown from the helicopter, was alive but completely incapacitated with a spinal injury. Mark was still in his seat, inverted, unconscious and blue in the face because his flak jacket was pressed tightly into his neck. Nigel quickly released Mark from his seat and, with his technician's help, moved him to his own helicopter. He wound up his rotors and climbed to join Ian Peacock's K-Car to give top cover whilst Chas Goatley and his technician, Mike Smith, landed to recover Roelf. Roelf recovered quickly but for six agonising weeks Mark Dawson lay unconscious in St Giles Nursing Home. After recovery it became clear that brain damage would disallow the frustrated young pilot from ever flying again.

Three operations in one day had ZIPRA reeling and the Zambian Government in a dither. ZIPRA's total casualties, according to figures given to the Pan African Congress in Tanzania, were 396 killed, 719 wounded and 192 missing. This had cost Rhodesia the loss of an SAS soldier, Lance-Corporal Jeff Collett, fatally wounded at Mkushi, and one helicopter that had to be blown up where it had crashed.

The Rhodesian Broadcasting Corporation gave news of the FC Camp raid as its lead report on the 8 o'clock evening news, but little was said about the other two operations in Zambia. Squadron Leader Alan Cockle, the Air Force PRO, arranged for the communiqué to include Chris Dixon's 'Green Leader' taped message to Lusaka Tower together with the controller's responses. Fresh in memory was ZIPRA's downing of the first Air Rhodesia Viscount sixteen days earlier, so news of the action against Nkomo's forces came as a much-needed tonic for waning morale, and 'Green Leader' became a national hero though few knew that he was Squadron Leader Chris Dixon.

Chris Dixon (left) with Rob Gaunt.

Mulungushi and Mboroma

MOUNTAIN GUTU, THE LOGISTICS OFFICER from Mkushi, turned out to be a vital man because he personally knew all the top rankers in ZAPU and ZIPRA as well as the location of ZIPRA's headquarters units, their camps and logistics sites. He was also able to confirm that most of ZIPRA's activities were geared to preparing for conventional warfare, though he could not give the reason for this. To us the Russian influence on ZIPRA was obvious.

A location that immediately drew special attention was ZIPRA's prison camp at Mboroma deep inside Zambia. Apart from ZIPRA dissidents and alleged spies, Gutu claimed that a number of Security Force personnel who had been abducted in Rhodesia were also held there. He willingly offered evidence and provided details of the ZIPRA personalities in charge of the prison camp. He not only gave the names and places in Rhodesia from which they originated but, in the typically African way, described their physical peculiarities. Whereas they were probably pretty average people, Gutu's descriptions made them appear to be a bunch of oddballs. Here are extracts of his written descriptions:

Camp Commander—Samson Dube. He originates from Kezi. Has a large scar on forehead as result of a knobkerrie blow prior to training. Approximately 35 years old.
Camp Commissar—Hobo Maqula. Originates from the Plumtree area. Approximately 42 years old and limps on left leg.
Chief of Staff—Takarayi Mbvizi. Has a very high-pitched voice and originates from Sinoia. Approximately 37 years old.
Medical officer—Kenni Malungu. After faction fight in Mozambique deserted and proceeded to Zambia. Is cross-eyed. Originates from Chipinga and approximately 31 years.
Logistics—Ndwini Sibanda. Subject is five foot five inches and bow-legged. Approximately 28 years old.

The Selous Scouts were given the task of moving on Mboroma with the prime objective of bringing all the prisoners back to Rhodesia. A close-in recce of the camp, conducted from high ground right next to its southern boundary, confirmed the presence of prisoners and established routines within the camp. Ron Reid-Daly wanted to conduct a pure ground action to simultaneously ensure the safety of prisoners and to allow the right moment to be selected before launching the operation. It would have been a simple enough matter to parachute the entire force into the remote countryside for an approach on foot to the target to meet Ron's objectives, but COMOPS disallowed this.

Instead, Scouts paratroopers enveloped the prison camp following a limited Hunter airstrike, but it resulted in the timing of the action being wrong—just as Ron had feared. Most of the prisoners were away on various foraging tasks, well away from target. In consequence only a quarter of the prisoners, thirty-odd, were flown back to Rhodesia a couple of days before Christmas 1978; so the Dakota effort allocated to uplifting troops and prisoners from a nearby Zambian airfield way exceeded demand.

The press had a royal time learning about the horrors of ZIPRA torture, starvation and general maltreatment of their unfortunate prisoners. Arising from this rescue mission, Selous Scouts, always maligned by the world press, were hailed as heroes and spirits were raised on that hot sunny Christmas Day.

Mountain Gutu had also confirmed that a main ZIPRA base for conventional forces existed in the old Federal Cadets Training Centre (later the Zambian National Service Training Centre) on the west bank of the Mulungushi Dam situated north of Lusaka. Selous Scout recce specialists, Schulie Schulenburg and his African partner, made a detailed close-in reconnaissance of the base to confirm what Gutu had said. This was done during the lead-up to the Mboroma rescue operation.

By the time he was uplifted back to Rhodesia, Schulie had set a record by being in hostile territory for two weeks without resupply. He reported that there were over two hundred men in camp who did not seem to have any concerns following the attacks on FC Camp, Mkushi and CGT 2 because they were so well dug in. Because of this, it was decided not to pursue the joint-force approach again, as we were likely to suffer unacceptably high casualties. Instead a Canberra formation attack was launched at the same moment that the Hunters were striking Mboroma on 22 December 1978. Results were pleasing.

Moatize hangar

EVER SINCE BUSH COVER STARTED receding in July the success rate of Fireforce actions had been mounting. It was in one of these in late November 1978 that a CT was captured by RLI troopies of the Mtoko Fireforce. Those who nabbed him did not know that ZANLA's High Command had made a big error in sending their high-ranking Secretary for the Tete Province on a staff visit to the Takawira Sector in Rhodesia.

SB was delighted to have this man alive considering that most of the CTs in the contact had been killed. Included in the wealth of information gleaned from him, SB learned of huge ZANLA weapons and explosives holdings in an aircraft hangar at the Moatize Airfield near Tete town. The information was passed to the SAS who came to the conclusion this was a job best suited to Air Force.

Five Hunters piloted by Squadron Leader Vic Wightman, Ginger Baldwin, Jim Stagman, Tony Oakley and Dave Bourhill were tasked to take this and other targets out in a single sortie. Though ZANLA's primary weapons holdings constituted the main target, a long ZANLA barrack building in Tete town was assigned for attention by Golf bombs after which vehicles and AA gun sites were to be destroyed.

On 8 December, four Golf bombs flattened the barrack block completely. Firing at the hangar had to be conducted from long range to avoid the chaos that tons of explosives detonating spontaneously would spew into the path of an attacking jet. It was the second pilot to fire at this target who had the satisfaction of seeing it mushroom in a truly massive explosion that necessitated a maximum 'G' turn to avoid flying through the cone of rising debris. When they had taken out assigned targets and had run out of ammunition, the aircraft climbed to 30,000. There the pilots looked back with satisfaction at the vertical pillar of smoke and dust rising more than 10,000 feet above Moatize Airfield where the hangar's shattered girders and cladding lay widely scattered.

Following this, the SAS moved in to blow up the Mecito bridge to ensure that ZANLA would not easily replenish their lost stocks or continue to move men to Tete by rail. This they timed to occur as a train passed over it on 15 December. Only five days later, with the railway line now out of action, ZANLA attempted to move ammunition up to Tete along their alternate route which was the main road running northwards from Chimoio along the low ground fairly close to the Rhodesian border. News of this impending movement was intercepted on the FRELIMO radio network.

An SAS ambush party struck the lead vehicles, forcing following ones to high-tail back the way they had come. Two pairs of Hunters flown by Vic Wightman, Jim Stagman, Ginger Baldwin and Brian Gordon destroyed the vehicles found hidden in an orchard by Cocky Benecke who had called for and directed their strikes. Following these, Cocky conducted a post-strike recce and confirmed that six vehicles, including a petrol bowser, had been destroyed, thus accounting for the entire resupply column.

Chapter

9

Posting to COMOPS

IN LATE NOVEMBER 1978, I was promoted to the rank group captain and replaced Norman Walsh as Director of Operations at COMOPS Headquarters. Of all the postings I might have been given, this was the only one I dreaded. Almost every man in the field thoroughly disliked this command unit and I did not relish the idea of serving under Bertie Barnard, now a major-general and still Director-General of Operations at COMOPS.

Lieutenant-General Peter Walls and his deputy, Air Marshal Mick McLaren, called me to their respective offices to welcome me but neither one gave me any specific direction other than to say I must start off by familiarising myself with COMOPS routines. At the time, General Barnard was away on long leave.

Unfortunately Wing Commander Dag Jones had also been posted out of COMOPS, leaving his replacement Squadron Leader Terence Murphy and me as new boys. We anchored on SAS Lieutenant-Colonel Brian Robinson who helped us settle in. Major Peter Burford, son of my old boss when I was an apprentice in Umtali back in 1956, was very helpful in running us through COMOPS procedures.

SAS Lieutenant–Colonel Brian Robinson with Ian Smith.

The tempo of external operations was increasing and occupied much of our attention, though Terence and I were little more than observers during lead-up planning for the Mulungushi and Mboroma actions. My first authoritative input came with the Moatize hangar strike. However, whenever time permitted Terence Murphy and I focused our attention on the internal scene.

For some months a force of auxiliaries (armed militiamen) had been building up as a counter to ZANLA and to provide protection for civilians in the rural areas. The black politicians, Bishop Muzorewa and Reverend Sithole both claimed that they had huge support amongst ZANLA personnel who would willingly come over in support of the new Zimbabwe-Rhodesia Government. Their claims proved to be little more than wishful thinking, because only a handful of genuine CTs responded to their much-publicised calls to 'come in from the bush'.

In an attempt to save face, both Muzorewa and Sithole gathered in many out-of-work loafers and crooks, claiming them to be ZANLA men. They fooled nobody but had succeeded in persuading COMOPS to arrange for the rabble to be given rudimentary training in arms. The task initially fell to Ron Reid-Daly's Selous Scouts who were horrified by the whole affair. Nevertheless they commenced training hundreds of undisciplined ruffians using old farmsteads as training bases.

Many dangerous situations were faced by the men assigned to training the auxiliaries, known as Pfumo re Vanhu (Spear of the People), because of a belligerent attitude induced in them by the few genuine CTs in their midst and by the black politicians who were, as always, vying for power. On one occasion a life-threatening situation developed necessitating

Combined Operations Staff – February, 1979

Listed here are only those whose names appear in this book. Seated: (from left) Mike Edden SB, Colonel Mac Willar (3), Major-General Bert Barnard (4), Lieutenant-General Peter Walls (6), Air Marshal Mick McLaren (7), Major-General Sandy McLean (8), PB (10). Standing middle row: (from left) Squadron Leader Terence Murphy, Squadron Leader Dag Jones (4) Squadron Leader Jock McGregor (8). Not present in this line was Lieutenant-Colonel Brian Robinson. Back row: Major Peter Burford (8th from left), Mrs Anne Webb (extreme right).

the full Fireforce action that destroyed one fully armed group of the Sithole faction.

By the time I entered COMOPS, there were Pfumo re Vanhu auxiliary forces in many of the collective villages and responsibility for training new auxiliaries had passed to Army and Police units, releasing Selous Scouts for to their rightful duties.

Some groups worked well whereas others treated the tribesmen in the same manner as CT thugs. On the whole, however, Pfumo re Vanhu succeeded in achieving many of their objectives. Only when our war was over did we learn of the very real threat they had posed to ZANLA.

Squadron Leader Terence Murphy, an ex-British Marine helicopter pilot, came to COMOPS fresh from Fireforce operations. With no specific task given to us, he and I conducted a joint study of internal operations and this led us to focusing on the auxiliaries.

Knowing the force levels already deployed and those in the pipeline, we worked out what we considered to be the optimum distribution of Pfumo re Vanhu forces to create maximum disruption and hindrance to ZANLA. Having done this, we

put our thoughts and plans to an assembly of Army officers and SB men. Also attending was Squadron Leader Jock McGregor. All agreed there was good sense and merit in our proposals. We had only just done this when General Barnard returned from leave.

Nobody seemed to have missed him whilst he was away but Bert Barnard had no time to listen to our plan claiming he had more important matters to attend. When eventually he did find time, he made continuity of our presentation almost impossible by interjecting after every statement we, the ignorant Blue jobs, made.

At one point a very irritated Terence Murphy, referring to his own Army training and experience, but without actually being rude, made it known that he had never known such arrogant interference from any senior officer during any of many staff presentations he had attended. Though surprised and somewhat taken aback by Terence's clever wording, I was pleased that he had made it possible for us to pick up on our thoughts and continue the briefing without further interruption.

At the conclusion General Barnard thanked us for what we had done but said our plan would not work. So it came as a surprise to learn from Squadron Leader Jock McGregor, who was one of two secretaries who attended all NATJOC meetings, that General Barnard had presented NATJOC with his personal plan for the deployment of Auxiliaries. Jock said it was identical to the presentation he had attended when Terry and I put our plan to him and other officers. I realised immediately that we should be pleased that the 'Barnard Plan' had been adopted rather than become thoroughly fed up with the whole affair. Nevertheless Barnard's underhandedness was galling.

ZANLA infiltration continued unabated and many CT groups were operating in depth in southern Matabeleland and the central Midlands. In one particular follow-up close to Ian Smith's farm at Gwenora, there was a contact with CT's that led to a serious air accident.

Flight Lieutenant Ray Bolton had been conducting helicopter conversions for non-Air Force pilots with a view to establishing if this was a viable way of bolstering operational helicopter pilot numbers. One of Ray's students was game-ranger Kerry Fynn who had been trained by the Air Force some years earlier. Ray and Kerry were at Thornhill when news of the contact came through and both flew troops to the scene and placed them down under direction of the unseen callsign on the ground.

Ray then saw the callsign but he could not see any CTs. Feeling certain that game-ranger Kerry stood a better chance of spotting them, he called Kerry over to look around. It so happened that the ground callsign then started giving a helicopter direction to turn 'right' to position over the terrorist group, but each pilot thought the direction was for him and both responded. Almost immediately Kerry spotted terrorists, rolled sharply to port to bring his gunner Corporal Turner into position to open fire, but collided with Ray's helicopter, which was crossing his path.

Both helicopters were crippled and crashed. Kerry and his technician died instantly, as did Corporal Cutmore, who was flying with Ray. Miraculously Ray survived the inverted crash because of the protection given his head and body by his armoured seat.

It was at about this time that we received a visitation in COMOPS from ex-RLI Major Alan Lindner, long-serving intelligence officer to Selous Scouts and now attached to Military Intelligence. He came to make a preliminary presentation of a detailed study he had undertaken. Alan made this presentation to General Barnard, Brian Robinson, Peter Burford, Terence Murphy, the COMOPS SB representative Chief Superintendent Mike Edden and me. Quite a bit of what he had to say involved the same matters Terence and I had considered in formulating our Auxiliaries plan. However, Alan's presentation went much deeper and moved through many steps before unfolding into a clearly defined strategy.

On his own and drawing from his experience with Selous Scouts, Alan had worked out the very military strategy that COMOPS should have produced many months earlier. His maps with well-defined overlays built up a picture that, because of its un-embroidered simplicity, unscrambled the multiplicity of problems facing us. It specifically revealed the most fundamental flaw in COMOPS operational management. Put simply, it showed that, in attempting to secure all internal ground and conducting external operations, our forces had been spread too thinly to prevent the cancer of CT encroachment into economically important areas that Alan called 'The Vital Ground'.

Vital Ground encompassed all commercial areas including white farms, isolated mines, main roads and rail routes. From those areas in which the CTs were strongest, the tribal areas, Alan's plan advocated almost total withdrawal of forces to make them fully available for external operations and to secure the Vital Ground in strength. Only then would Selous Scouts and high-density operations be mounted to progressively re-occupy adjoining TTLs with the odd probe into hot spots to keep abreast of developments and, more especially, to take out key CT groups.

External operations would obviously have to be stepped up and sustained to ensure that the CT presence in the semi-abandoned areas, some of which ZANLA had already claimed to be 'liberated areas', did not become too strong. Robert Mugabe had named 1979 *Gore re Gukurahundi* (Year of the Peoples' Storm) because his intention was to push in as many trained CTs as possible. We knew ZANLA had more men than they had weapons to arm them with but, at that time, we were unaware of just how serious this problem was.

Alan Lindner's plan was so convincing to those of us who heard it that an instruction was issued to all main players to attend a repeat presentation to the National JOC where Alan's proposals were accepted and put into immediate effect.

The virtual abandonment of the Tribal Trust Lands by the security forces did not affect the Sub-JOC locations as all of these lay in Vital Ground. However, many police stations remained in the unattended areas because, to its credit, PGHQ was determined to retain every single one of its many stations, no matter the dangers. This placed a few stations, particularly those close to the Mozambican border, in a very hostile environment often necessitating Dakotas to run the gauntlet to para-drop critical provisions to hard-pressed policemen and, occasionally, helicopters to change over personnel and undertake the evacuation of casualties. Nyamapanda, right on the border with Mozambique next to the main road to Malawi, was the most harassed and dangerous of all the police positions.

Protective villages continued to be manned by Guard Force with Pfumo re Vanhu auxiliaries in the consolidated villages. They could call upon Fireforce during daylight hours. Inevitably, however, ZANLA's many relatively ineffective stand-off attacks occurred at night.

One huge problem in leaving many hapless tribesmen to their own devices was that it caused streams of refugees to move out of the countryside to the safety of cities and towns. In consequence, shantytowns sprang up in untidy knots around many built-up areas.

Mozambican National Resistance

PRIOR TO HIS POSTING TO COMOPS, former Commander of SAS Lieutenant-Colonel Brian Robinson had been attached to an establishment specifically created to handle Special Operations. This Special Operations HQ had been under OCC control until COMOPS took over and brought special operations under its wing. Initially Brian was horrified at the prospect of working with Bert Barnard but he was able to conduct most of his work with Group Captain Norman Walsh with whom he had a good personal working relationship, as witnessed before and during Operation Dingo.

Although Brian enjoyed initial planning and tasking work, all of which was conducted in an operations room expressly reserved for top-secret operations, he sorely missed the nitty-gritty planning that SAS and Selous Scouts did back in their respective headquarters. Consequently, Brian spent much of his day prowling the corridors of COMOPS like a caged lion.

Having been so involved with Norman Walsh, Brian had a very high regard for Air Force opinion in all aspects of SAS and other specialist ground-force work. Having also been involved with me in earlier times, and whenever Norman had asked me to join in on special ops planning, Brian came to me first whenever he needed to bounce ideas off someone in COMOPS. We got on well, and were privy to every aspect of Special Forces operations other than Selous Scouts and CIO external undercover work. Whenever such detail as we needed was given, we kept it strictly to ourselves. One such undercover operation was revealed when the SAS and Air Force had to become directly involved in its development.

In late December 1978, I visited an isolated farm in the Odzi farming area east of Umtali. Here, at a top-secret Central Intelligence Organisation base, training was being conducted for a resistance movement that was intent on ousting FRELIMO from power. This organisation was variously known as MRM (Mozambican Resistance Movement), MNR (Mozambican National Resistance) and RENAMO. MNR was the term we preferred.

Milling around the helicopter I had flown myself on this visit was a scruffy but happy group of Mozambicans with huge smiles. A fair-sized force of these men was already operating in Mozambique and scoring spectacular successes against FRELIMO.

SAS were about to deploy with the resistance force to give them the training and direction that only the SAS could provide. Air Force would be needed for resupply and other supporting roles. Surprisingly, when the time came for the first para-supply by Dakotas, it was to deliver maize and vegetable seeds with only small amounts of ammunition and troop comforts included. The reason for this was that the MNR had little need for weapons or ammunition because they were capturing most of what they required from FRELIMO.

The willing support being given MNR by the local people bore testimony to the tribesmen's utter dislike of FRELIMO. However, willing as they were, these poor folk could not hope to provide all the food needs of the fast-growing resistance force. So, in response to SAS direction, MNR needed seed to grow its own crops for self-sufficiency within its safe havens in the forests and valleys surrounding Gorongoza mountain.

FRELIMO had antagonised the rural people in so many ways. They had kicked out Mozambique's white Portuguese and, in doing so, had brought about the destruction of the income base upon which rural families depended. Without the Portuguese, earnings by previous commercial, industrial and domestic workers had dried up. None of FRELIMO's pre-independence promises had materialised so the peasants, who had been forced into failed communal farming activities, were much worse off than at any time during their relatively stress-free existence under Portuguese rule.

The peoples' trust in MNR to return them to situations of 'the good old days' was reinforced by well-orchestrated radio broadcasts beamed from Rhodesia by Portuguese-speaking presenters. 'The Voice of Free Africa' services, whilst boosting the MNR image, incensed FRELIMO by emphasising the impotence of its leadership and slating communist ideologies that were failing to fill stomachs or keep people warm and children educated. The Mozambican peasants liked what they were hearing and MNR's popularity soared and spread.

The MNR might have substantially altered the course of our war had funds been available when they were needed back in 1976. This was another of many situations to which the 'too-little-too-late' tag might be pinned because, from the outset, MNR was very pro-white, pro-Rhodesia and violently anti-communist. This they demonstrated by providing us with some important intelligence on ZANLA's activities and locations. Of greater importance to Rhodesia was the fact that MNR activities were so troublesome to FRELIMO that earlier plans to pour more FRELIMO troops into the Op Repulse area were shelved. In fact many FRELIMO earmarked for Rhodesia were withdrawn to combat the MNR 'bandits'.

Whereas there had been no question of using the MNR to fight ZANLA CTs in Mozambique, FRELIMO sought ZANLA's assistance to combat the MNR. Had such a situation arisen two years earlier, combined Rhodesian and MNR action would have permitted our own forces to operate in depth against ZANLA and FRELIMO for as long as we chose, unencumbered by aircraft shortages and servicing cycles. Furthermore, with the MNR seeking as much credit as possible for anti-FRELIMO activities, the destruction of Mozambique's communications networks would have been made easy and would almost certainly have resulted in ZANLA's eviction from Mozambique.

The SAS enjoyed leading MNR and witnessed some very hairy fighting. They held back from each action to avoid compromising themselves and watched aghast when the first MNR leader, André, initiated ambushes and attacks by leaping to his feet, fully exposing himself with gun above head to shout the MNR slogan that triggered each action.

True or not, I cannot say, but I heard that FRELIMO soldiers were petrified of MNR. The story goes that MNR sometimes removed the heads of their victims and scattered them around to make matching them to bodies difficult. Every FRELIMO soldier hearing of this was worried that, should this happen to him, his spirit would remain trapped in his body if someone else's head was buried with it.

The SAS personnel operating with MNR were changed over regularly without difficulties until their operations spread southward to a new sector in the region of Chipinga. Here the MNR group resisted an SAS changeover fearing that they were about to be abandoned. At Gorongoza it was normal practice for the four SAS men assigned to the MNR to move miles clear of the base area to meet the team changeover helicopter. Whilst awaiting the arrival of the replacement team, the MNR remained inside their safe haven totally surrounded by loyal tribesmen. However, even having gained the confidence and open support of the locals for miles around, the relatively small MNR group camping in hills east of Chipinga only felt safe with SAS in their midst. In consequence, we at COMOPS were faced with an unusual problem when we learned that these MNR men were holding their SAS colleagues hostage to prevent them from moving off for a changeover the MNR leader feared might not take place.

At the cost of unnecessary flying hours, the situation was resolved by deploying the four-man replacement team miles from the MNR base for a long walk to effect changeover in the presence of MNR. But then, with eight SAS men making him feel doubly safe, the MNR leader attempted, unsuccessfully, to persuade the first team to stay on.

Luso Boma

IN SOUTH WEST AFRICA AND Angola, South African forces were involved in a war against SWAPO (SWA Peoples' Organisation) and to a lesser extent SAANC. As a result of their intelligence, we learned in late January 1979 that a large concentration of ZIPRA men were undergoing training under Russian and Cuban instructors at Luso Boma in Angola.

Photo-reconnaissance confirmed the site of the large base in central-east Angola, and a preliminary feasibility study was conducted to establish if we could undertake an air attack against it. Clearly the target lay at too great a range for Hunters with under-wing stores. For the Canberras it was possible but the range left no reserve of fuel for possible Inter-Tropical Convergence Zone weather problems on the day. Initially it was decided to postpone the attack until weather conditions improved in May. However when the second Viscount was shot down by ZIPRA on 12 February 1979 it created a need for another high-profile retaliatory action and Luso was the best target we had at the time.

OC 5 Squadron, Squadron Leader Chris Dixon (Green Leader), was brought in to discuss the matter. He immediately said his squadron could meet the task and advocated operating out of Victoria Falls Airport for a normal climb to 30,000 feet.

The disused Portuguese aldeamento *and ZIPRA barracks (top) surrounded by anti-aircraft gun positions, half of which are seen here (and ringed). The ZIPRA and SAANC barrack lines are barely visible at the top of the photograph with white fields on either side. Below the barracks are the various buildings that served as headquarters, classrooms and accommodation for Russians and Cubans.*

One engine would then be closed down for the cruise to target. Both engines would be used for the descent, attack and return to height where, once again, one engine would be closed down for the return to Victoria Falls.

This was all very well, but Luso Boma base was too large to be covered by the formation of only four Canberras we could be certain of having on the day, when in fact six Canberras were needed to cover the whole target. An approach was made to the South Africans who had a vested interest in the same target because some SAANC were also training at Luso Boma. If we did not attack the base, the South African Air Force would probably do the job anyway. But, since we wanted to smack ZIPRA ourselves, an opportunity existed to undertake a combined formation strike. Air Commodore Norman Walsh was in favour of using an extra Canberra to drop 1000-pound bombs with variously set time-delay fuses to confuse and delay the enemy's post-strike mopping up operations. In consequence, seven Canberras were used.

To launch aircraft from South West Africa and

Ted Brent.

Rhodesia for link up in Angola was feasible but unwise in view of the need for joint planning and briefing of crews. So three SAAF Canberra B9s positioned at remote Fylde Air Base to keep their presence secret. After briefing, our four Canberras positioned at Victoria Falls. The SAAF aircraft, with modern engines and higher fuel capacity, had no problems with the longer range they had to fly from Fylde. Rudie Kritsinger, Roley Jones and Willie Meyer captained these bombers. Although Hunters had been discounted from the strike itself they were to be on station at height armed with Sidewinder air-to-air missiles to counter interference from the Zambian Air Force or, less likely, Cuban-operated MiG 19s and MiG 21s based at Henrique de Carvalho in Angola.

When the time came for start-up on 26 February 1979, Chris Dixon with Mike Ronnie in the lead aircraft of Green Formation could not get one engine started. Chris immediately handed the lead to Ted Brent and Jim Russell who, as was standard practice, were fully prepared for such an eventuality. The other two Canberras were crewed by Glen Pretorius with Paddy Morgan and Kevin Peinke with, I think, J.J. Strydom.

The Rhodesian formation was still climbing and had the SAAF formation visual when Chris Dixon reported being airborne five minutes behind. Ted continued with the formation of six until he was well inside Zambia. Near Mongu he went into a shallow orbit to await Chris. At this point our radio-intercepting service picked up a call from Mongu reporting the presence of 'enemy aircraft' to the Zambian Air Force base at Mumbwa.

When Chris caught up, he instructed Ted to retain the lead and the formation continued on its way. The Non-Directional Beacon at Luso Airfield was expected to assist the formation but, typical for Africa, it was on the blink. Nevertheless the formation navigators all map-read whenever there were gaps in near continuous strata-cumulus cover along a weaving route between cumulonimbus storm clouds. Fortunately the low cloud cover ended before Luso.

When Ted spotted the airfield at Luso, he instructed the Rhodesian pilots to fire up their cold engines as he commenced a fast descent for a wide port turn to pass low over the airfield on heading for the base which was close by. A huge storm stretched right across the run-up path to target but the Canberras had come too far to be put off by this difficulty. Three Rhodesian and three SAAF bombers moved into formation for the low-level attack. The fourth Rhodesian Canberra levelled off at 1,500 feet above and behind the main force.

With six aircraft correctly stationed in their wide flat Vic positions, the formation entered heavy rain at full attack speed with all pilots holding heading and height on instruments.

When he judged the moment was right, Ted called "Bomb doors, go." Almost immediately the formation burst through the rain and there, dead on the planned strike-line, lay the target. The formation swept through, releasing 1,800 Alpha bombs onto a target sodden by the very storm through which

Some of the few CTs that came out of cover after the rainstorm can be seen lying on the ground. Less easy to see are those lying or running through the scrub on the left side of the photographs. Note the dirt thrown up between trees top left of nearest barrack block in top photo followed by early stage of detonation in lower picture. Note also the wide spread of Alpha bomblets where dirt showers appear in the bottom photos after the full detonation to the left of the upper line of barracks in the upper photo. Note: Single round white marks at left centre of photographs are filing punch holes.

it had just come. Immediately the formation was through, the seventh Canberra unloaded tightly grouped 1,000-pound delay bombs into the main CT barracks.

The Canberras opened up into battle formation remaining low level for a while before climbing. The three SAAF aircraft pulling ahead because of their superior thrust and were soon lost from sight. Two Zambian MiG 19s that had searched the southwestern skies of Zambia for 'enemy aircraft', were already back on the ground and all Canberras reached base safely. One of the 1,000-pound bombs had failed to release over target but had detached itself later with quite a bump as it fell onto the closed bomb-bay door. Once on the ground the bomb-bay doors were opened gently, sufficiently to get a hand in to make the fused bomb safe. Thereafter, with the aid of acquired army and police mattresses, the bomb was allowed to fall free.

Unfortunately for us, the inclement weather had driven many CTs into buildings, giving fair protection against those Alpha bombs that did not actually come through their roofs—many did.

At my request, one of the Canberras had been fitted with a camera in its bomb bay to record its own strike. The resultant photographs revealed battle tanks, row upon row of barrack buildings and swastika-like figures of men running for cover or lying down with bomblets bouncing and bursting around them.

According to ZAPU's briefing to the Pan African Conference in Tanzania, ZIPRA's casualties were 174 killed and 533 seriously wounded. They mentioned fourteen civilian cooks and bottle-washers killed and three wounded, but said nothing about the SAANC and Cuban casualties or the loss of large quantities of explosives and equipment that we knew (from radio intercepts) had been inflicted.

Considering the weather situation and the size of the formation, the Canberra boys had conducted a fantastically cool-headed strike. At the time they did not recognise the degree of disruption they had caused, nor could they guess how this action would set ZIPRA's plans back sufficiently to cost them dearly in time to come. Back on the ground, Ted Brent was heard to say, "Fear I knew not; but terror, yes." He was commenting on his participation during downloading of the 1,000-pound hang-up. For armourer Warrant Officer Bill Brown, this was just another potentially dangerous situation requiring a cool head and technical expertise gained over many years in the RAF and in Rhodesia.

Vanduzi Circle

BACK IN MOZAMBIQUE, ZANLA HAD recovered from their late-September mauling in the Chimoio Circle and had moved closer to FRELIMO's Chimoio town into a new site we named the 'Vanduzi Circle'.

From captured CTs who had been at this location during the early stages of its construction, we learned that the many camps making up the entire ZANLA complex lay between two easily identified hills. Photo-reconnaissance confirmed the existence of the new base area but from photos alone it was impossible to determine key points. To find this out, the SAS was tasked to go in to gain a clearer picture. This was necessary at the time because the Fireforces were reaping such important rewards in securing the internal Vital Ground that there could be no

question of withdrawing them for another joint-force operation in Mozambique. If the SAS could pinpoint worthwhile and clearly definable targets within the Vanduzi Circle, jets would have to take them on to help keep ZANLA off balance.

After an aborted first recce attempt, the SAS broke from their four-man team to test the viability of using just two lightly loaded men to move into the intensely active enemy base area. Whereas a total of six men were deployed in early March 1979, four established a secure base from which Richard Stannard and his companion, 'Jungle' Jordan, worked forward.

These two men succeeded in scaling the difficult feature Monte Bassa, one of the two features between which the Vanduzi Circle lay. From a lofty position they watched a great deal of ZANLA activity just below their OP. For two days they monitored all movements until they were sure they had the place they had been sent to find. Hunters, Canberras and K-Cars moved in. The jet strikes were over when the helicopters arrived and drew fire from many heavy AA positions the SAS had not seen because of the density of the bush. This proved that the base was much larger than they had thought.

When everything was quiet FRELIMO turned up, as had been expected, and for which the Hunters were busy rearming back at Thornhill. Richard and 'Jungle' Jordan, still unnoticed in their lofty hide, watched ZANLA's dead and wounded being loaded onto a large truck whilst an armoured personnel carrier with FRELIMO troops prowled around.

When the Hunters returned, Richard was able to direct them onto the personnel carrier, which was taken out along with most of the FRELIMO troops surrounding it. As this happened a Strela missile was launched unsuccessfully, again at Vic Wightman who whipped around and blasted the launch point.

Having suffered losses due to the return of Hunters, FRELIMO realised there must be Rhodesians close by. Their radio messages were picked up in Rhodesia, passed to COMOPS, and relayed through SAS HQ to Richard who commenced his move-out after dark.

Unfortunately the two-man team was spotted next morning and a hot pursuit by angry ZANLA resulted in Jordan being wounded and having to call for hot extraction. Not long after this Richard Stannard was back on Monte Bassa from where he again directed jet-strikes and, again, he called Hunters back to strike ZANLA and FRELIMO whilst they were gathering casualties from the first strike.

Thanks to Richard's successes, ZANLA was forced by FRELIMO to move away from them. The Vanduzi Circle of bases ceased to exist and it would be four months before we would find ZANLA's new location close to our border.

Cost comparisons

PRIOR TO HIS DEPARTURE FROM COMOPS, Wing Commander Dag Jones, acting for General Barnard, instructed MID (Military Intelligence Department) to conduct a survey on the cost-effectiveness of internal versus external operations. By the time this lengthy study was completed much had changed. Nevertheless, it served as a rough guide for planning.

The MID assessment used the months January and February 1979 from which to draw figures and make comparisons. The task was difficult because they were trying to compare apples with oranges, except where costs were concerned. These are condensed details of Fireforce (FF) versus external operations, for what they are worth:

INTERNAL:

Fireforce	Army Unit	Deployments	Kills	Areas of Operation
A	1RAR	56	23	Northeast – ex Darwin
B	RLI	40	81	Northeast – ex Mtoko
C	2RAR	53	59	Eastern – ex Grand Reef
D	2RAR	40	43	Eastern overlapping SE
E	RLI	48	56	Southeast – Buffalo Range

Considering that January and February had been very quiet months between major external offensives, MID's choice was hardly an ideal time frame for comparisons. Besides, there had been considerable internal movements of forces into the Vital Ground, adversely effecting Fireforce activities in which 60% of calls proved to be 'lemons' because bush cover was at its thickest.

In these two months only 262 CTs had been killed in Fireforce actions, according to physical body counts that is. The cost per terrorist killed translated into high expenditure in Rhodesian terms. (I do not remember the actual cost comparison but can recall that it was in the order of one tenth of the American figure for Vietnam.)

EXTERNAL:

On the other hand, according to FRELIMO radio intercepts, 103 ZANLA CTs were killed in Mozambique by jet-strikes and landmines previously laid by Special Forces. In Angola 174 ZIPRA were killed with 533 seriously wounded. Since we did not have these figures at the time, they were not included in the cost-comparison study.

Ignoring those dead and wounded CTs in Mozambique, about which we knew nothing, the cost per terrorist killed externally (according to the study) was in the order of one-third of the internal cost. Within the next ten months this would reduce to less than a quarter in spite of greatly improved internal successes.

Externally things were going to hot up and prove just how seriously political restraints had increased costs and greatly expanded CT numbers.

ZIPRA plans revealed

DURING MARCH 1979, ACTING ON intelligence from their agent in Botswana, the Selous Scouts mounted an ambush on the main Grove Road linking Botswana with Zambia. This road ran close to Rhodesia's western border where the Scouts established their ambush position. Their targets were two well-known, high-ranking ZIPRA officers.

One was Dumiso Dabengwa (the 'Black Russian'), second only to Nkomo and head of ZIPRA Intelligence. The other was Elliott Sibanda (the 'Black Swine'), ZIPRA's senior intelligence officer for the 'Southern Front' whose office was in Francistown, Botswana. These two men were transferring brand-new ZIPRA vehicles, purchased in South Africa, to Zambia.

When the Selous Scouts sprung its ambush, Dumiso Dabengwa escaped unharmed but Elliott Sibanda was seriously wounded and captured. Following stomach surgery that saved his life, Elliott Sibanda willingly gave the most important information we had received to date concerning ZIPRA's future plans and dispositions.

We knew that ZIPRA indulged in a mix of conventional and irregular training and that the larger proportion of men had been preparing for conventional war. However, until Elliott opened Pandora's box, we thought ZIPRA's low level of activity was largely due to our external ops. Sibanda disabused us of such comforting thoughts.

Nkomo's Russian advisors had persuaded ZIPRA to retain a limited force of active irregulars to keep Rhodesian eyes off the main intention, which was to invade Rhodesia. When the moment was right, the irregulars were to commit defined acts of sabotage in conjunction with a full-scale invasion by regular forces, supported by armour and air, in two drives via Victoria Falls in the west and Chirundu in the north.

Beira fuel refinery

WHILST SIBANDA'S INFORMATION WAS STILL being digested, the Selous Scouts were actively attempting to assassinate the elusive Joshua Nkomo in Lusaka and the SAS embarked on a daring operation to boost the MNR's growing image by destroying the enormous fuel storage facility in Beira.

During Federation of Rhodesia and Nyasaland days and continuing for three months after the imposition of economic sanctions on Rhodesia, crude oil had been pumped from Beira to the Rhodesian fuel refinery at Feruka just west of Umtali. For this, Beira's fuel storage capacity had been increased well beyond its original requirement, which was to service central Mozambique and Malawi. In consequence the target was huge.

In happier times it had taken only three hours for Rhodesian holidaymakers to motor from Umtali to the popular seaside resorts of Beira town. The Canberra that carried the SAS commander on a night reconnaissance to check the refinery's lighting arrangements took a mere forty minutes from Salisbury. For the SAS and MNR attack group it took many days along a very circuitous route. Nevertheless they reached their target and, in a spectacular action, ignited the fuel tanks, severed the main fuel transfer line to spill crude into the docks and cut off the main electrical power-lines serving Beira town. They had completed their noisy job before FRELIMO defences woke up to what was happening.

During a running withdrawal under heavy FRELIMO gunfire, one MNR man was killed outright but was left where he lay. His body, plus many MNR leaflets and paraphernalia deliberately scattered around, convinced FRELIMO that the attack had been a purely MNR affair. The effects of this action really frightened the FRELIMO Government, which until now had been confident that the MNR was not powerful enough to target vital installations, particularly in built-up areas. In truth they were not; the SAS was responsible for the planning and its own specialists made up more than 90% of the attack force. All the same the world was awakened to the MNR's existence and South African fire-fighters had to come to Mozambique's aid to put out the raging inferno.

Assassination attempts on Joshua Nkomo

BACK IN RHODESIA, DETAILED INTELLIGENCE given by Elliott Sibanda made it clear that ZIPRA's invasion plan had to be stopped in its tracks—urgently.

A host of possibilities were discussed in COMOPS HQ. The courses to be taken were broken into four categories—assassination of key men—destruction of ZIPRA's concentrated weapons holdings—attacks on ZIPRA regular force bases and—destruction of Zambia's communication lines. It was clear that all of these things would have to be done, but priorities had to be established.

Consideration was given to eliminating ZIPRA's Russian advisers who were all known in detail, including their home locations. However this was discarded as the benefits to be gained would be short-lived and the consequences to Rhodesia potentially damaging. Joshua Nkomo's early demise made much better sense as it would cause major disruption to ZAPU's leadership and profoundly affect morale, thereby giving us more time to produce detailed dossiers on all other targets.

Even before Elliott Sibanda's information had come to hand, Selous Scouts had attempted to assassinate Nkomo using a car bomb. But, no matter where it was positioned, Nkomo always followed another route home; so another option was adopted. This was to kill the ZIPRA leader in his home, which necessitated having a Selous Scout in Lusaka to watch for the right moment. This was no easy matter as Nkomo spent a great deal of time on overseas and local travel. Once home however, he would remain there for the night. But, since there was no certainty he would be in his high-security house the following night, action had to be taken immediately Nkomo was known to have returned home. Three times Ron Reid-Daly received the codeword sent from Lusaka via a contact man in South Africa to say Nkomo was home, and three times the assassination group launched into Zambia.

The first group went in by helicopter for a night walk-in approach to RV with the agent. But the agent failed to turn up with transport to take them to target. This was because heavy rain had washed away a vital bridge between Lusaka and the assault group.

On the second occasion, the Scouts assault team was helicoptered to a drop-off point much closer to Lusaka. However, they encountered such heavy jesse bush that they were unable to reach the agent and his Toyota Land Cruiser, this time waiting at the RV point. Instead, the assault force found itself in the middle of a Zambian Army exercise and had to make a hasty retreat for helicopter recovery.

The third attempt probably gave the Scouts their best chance of success. This was a parachute descent onto the same road the agent had been using, but very close to Lusaka. Following their para-descent, which was to be controlled from the ground by the Scouts agent, the Dakota was to mask the purpose of its presence by flying straight on to drop pamphlets onto a known ZIPRA base.

Unbeknown to the Scouts, however, their agent had been arrested by Zambian police just after he had passed the codeword that launched the assault force into the air. In consequence, with nobody at the drop-zone, the troops had no alternative but to remain aboard the Dakota for the leaflet-drop and an unhappy ride home.

Though certainly not for want of trying, Selous Scouts had experienced such unbelievable bad luck in their attempts to kill Nkomo that our COMOPS planning team recommended to General Walls that he should pass the task to the SAS. The general agreed.

When he learned of this decision, Ron Reid-Daly burst into COMOPS in a rage. He took the COMOPS decision as an insult to himself and his men. He could hardly be blamed for believing that the Selous Scouts were being badly rated by COMOPS, or for worrying about the profound effect this would have on the morale of his force. So it was with some difficulty that General Walls assured Ron that his COMOPS planning staff had simply recognised that such a run of bad luck had to be broken and a fresh start made.

When Ron had calmed down, he suggested that Selous Scouts should be given one more try. He advocated flying the assault team directly to the golf course that lay just over the road from Nkomo's home. This was an intriguing idea which, being so utterly crazy and brazen, would almost certainly have worked—but considering the Scouts' run of bad luck, Nkomo would probably be away on his travels anyway. "No, Ron," said General Walls, "the SAS have the task—and that is final!" But the Selous Scouts' commander would not let go.

In an endeavour to reach some sort of compromise, Ron asked the general to let the team he had sent to Zambia participate with the SAS. This was flatly refused but, recognising Ron's deep desire to have some level of Scouts' inclusion, General Walls decided that SAS would take one white Scout who knew Lusaka backwards, he having been the agent with the car bomb. In addition, a black Scout who could speak Zambian languages would also join the SAS team to do any talking, should this become necessary.

The SAS were already in an advanced stage of planning when General Walls ordered them to include these two Scouts. To say that the SAS officers were incensed by this instruction would be understating the case. I recall that they were as mad as hell at such high-level interference in specialist planning that already included a navigator for Lusaka. The black Scout seemed a good idea but this, it was felt, should have come to them through Brian Robinson as a 'useful suggestion'. But then, orders are orders!

Two SAS men were dropped from an operation considered by some to be 'an exciting opportunity'. However, the men whose names were taken off the list had no idea of this because the plan was only known to a handful of officers right up to the moment the operation was launched.

Whilst this was happening, the Canberras were tasked for a second raid on ZIPRA's Mulungushi camp. It was supposed to be another offset bombing raid in which Schulie would be setting up the RAMS flares. As it happened, Schulie called Ron Reid-Daly at Selous Scouts HQ late in the day to say the attack should be postponed because he had only seen a few ZIPRA in camp. Air HQ received this message but, with COMOPS concurrence, decided the raid should go ahead because the moon conditions were favourable for a visual attack. Ron Reid-Daly was unable to pass this decision to Schulie who had switched off his radio for the night and had set off for an even closer inspection of the target.

Why these vital changes in plan had failed to pass from Air HQ (the tasking agency in all air matters) to the Canberra boys I cannot say. They got airborne on the night of 10 April and, working to their original Air Task, proceeded to target fully expecting Schulie to ignite the outer flare at 19:00.

Ted Brent received no response to his calls to Schulie and

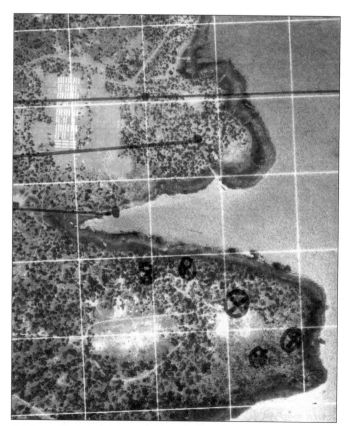

Mulungushi barrack lines top left. ZIPRA HQ, stores and senior accommodation lie either side of the small sports field - bottom right. X marks, so far as I can recall, are positions of Russian tanks.

no ignition of the inner flare occurred when he transmitted the RAMS coded signal. Though agitated by this turn of events, Ted could not avoid taking his formation directly over the target and drawing heavy fire from Mulungushi's AA guns. He was blissfully unaware of Schulie's close-in recce as he brought the formation around for the run onto a target whose specific location was readily identifiable from the source of tracer streams that continued to rake the sky.

On the ground close to target, Schulie and his mate experienced a mixture of angry disbelief and fear when the changing position of the Canberras sound made it obvious that the jets were coming around again for a visual strike. All they could do was lie flat and pray until bomblets passed over them and detonated too close for comfort. ZIPRA on the other hand had been given so much warning that the casualties they sustained that night were low. According to intercepted Zambian radio traffic, only three ZIPRA were killed and twenty were wounded.

The Canberras returned to the same target at 08:30 the next day in hopes that senior ZIPRA officers would be doing their usual thing of visiting the base following a night attack. As it turned out this did not happen because, unbeknown to COMOPS at the time, all the CT brass was tied up in some special meeting in the Mulungushi Hall at Lusaka's International Conference Centre.

That same afternoon at 17:30, Canberras and Hunters struck a ZIPRA training base known as Shilende Camp. After this attack, a Zambian Army unit's communiqué to Army HQ in Lusaka reported having found 134 ZIPRA dead and over 200 wounded. Two days later, 13 April 1979, Nkomo was reported to be home for the night and the SAS assassination team was unleashed from its waiting position on the waters of Lake Kariba.

As usual during all our special ops, Brian Robinson and I remained in COMOPS with the duty staff through the whole night. We sat chatting and drank endless cups of coffee whilst awaiting codewords relayed from Lieutenant-Colonel Garth Barrett (SAS had changed from 'squadron' to 'regiment', hence the OC's rank). Garth was with Wing Commander Peter McLurg in the Command Dak flying over uninhabited ground inside Zambia. The codewords would let us know the progress of the vehicle-borne force during its route to Lusaka and back.

Apart from the Command Dakota, there was nothing the Air Force could do to assist the SAS during the night. Nevertheless, Hunters at Thornhill and helicopters at Kariba would be waiting at immediate readiness before dawn in case the SAS had need of them. Two of the Hunters were armed with Sidewinder missiles to take on Zambian Air Force fighters posing any threat during the SAS exfiltration phase.

Because SAS had chosen to conduct a vehicle-borne operation using their own specialist Sabre Land Rovers, it gave opportunity to increase the force level and objectives for the foray into Lusaka where a number of worthwhile ZIPRA targets existed.

Serious consideration was given to including a team to release the Selous Scouts agent from Lusaka Prison; but this highly emotive issue, was dropped for two reasons. Firstly, if the rescue attempt failed and Zambians were killed—a real possibility—the agent would be identified for what he was and he would be left to pay a horrible price. Secondly, it would divert effort away from our main objective, which was to counter ZIPRA's invasion plans.

Final selection was made for two additional targets. One was Zambia's National Stores in which ZIPRA had amassed large quantities of war matériel alongside that of the Zambian Army. The second was Liberation Centre, the joint HQ for co-operative planning by senior officers of ZIPRA, South African ANC and SWAPO (South West African Peoples Organisation).

With the advent of landmines, SAS specialist Sabres (modified long-wheel-base, four-wheel-drive Land Rovers) had been withdrawn from active service—but they were just the vehicles for this operation. Seven Sabres and the three assault teams were waiting on the vehicle transport vessel Sea Lion. Then the signal came through to move from their starting point out on Kariba Dam's deep waters where they had been waiting well away from prying eyes.

The force made an uneventful landing on the Zambian shore just before darkness fell and set off through rough country on an old disused road. Numerous difficulties were encountered in navigating at night along this indistinct track. Negotiating muddy rivulets with steep approaches made the going tough. One of these muddy ravines caused the loss of one vehicle through engine failure. The consequence of this was that critical equipment on the stricken Sabre forced National Stores to be dropped from the target list.

Because of its difficulties, the convoy was running late when it turned onto the main tar road to Kafue Bridge and Lusaka. The bridge was considered to be the greatest threat point of the entire mission. But, as it happened, the large Zambian Army protection force that was expected to be there simply did not exist, much to the relief of all concerned, and the convoy continued on to Lusaka without incident.

Whereas the attack on Nkomo's home was scheduled for 02:00 it went in almost one hour late. Odd hiccups occurred in breaking through Nkomo's elaborate security ring but these made no difference to the ultimate outcome. Following the elimination of moderate resistance by ZIPRA security guards and the destruction of the house, a thorough search failed to find the unmistakable fat body of Joshua Nkomo.

Considering the efficiency and completeness of the attack, there was great disappointment, even anger, for the SAS operators and the staff at COMOPS. But it was clear to us in COMOPS that Nkomo had been tipped off. The big question was, 'by whom?'. This issue will be dealt with later. But one thing needs to be said for the benefit of many people who believe that Ken Flower, Director of Central Intelligence, was the mole who gave early warning to Britain and CT leaders. In the case of Nkomo this was not possible. He was in COMOPS the whole time from launch to return of the SAS group. At no stage did he use a telephone of any signalling equipment. I have to say that I have always considered Ken's number two in CIO to be the more likely culprit.

Not far away the team assigned to Liberation Centre put in its attack the moment they heard firing from Nkomo's house. Having completed their noisy work and set explosive charges to blow Liberation Centre's offices, armoury and many vehicles sky high, the team was preparing to depart when a ZIPRA vehicle came charging towards the SAS men. The vehicle was hit by a hail of bullets but careened on down the street and away into the night. The SAS did not know it at the time but they had come very close to killing ZIPRA's second commander, Lookout Masuku. I will give Masuku's account of this incident later.

The two task teams then linked up and the convoy travelled back to the rough bush track without incident. Behind them the President of Zambia was red-faced over such a commotion in peaceful Lusaka because it had disturbed the sleep of 300 guests engaged in the OAU Conference he was hosting.

Long after sunrise, the mission commander called for a helicopter to collect three soldiers who had been wounded during the attack on Nkomo's house. This was to save them the agony of a very bumpy ride down the final tortuous stretch of track to the lake. By midday, the force was back on Sea Lion and the exhausted expedition commander was debriefing us in the COMOPS Op Room by mid-afternoon.

The next day I was surprised to find General Walls, Air Marshal McLaren and Brian Robinson laughing their heads off in the passageway next to Mick's office. I took this to be normal because Brian was usually very humorous. He saw me and beckoned me to come over to share the joke. No wonder there was such mirth. Brian had brought the news that Nkomo had told reporters he had been at home when the SAS attacked but managed to escape through his toilet window. Anyone hearing or reading this had to be amused by the thought of the enormously fat Nkomo going through an incredibly small window—but the same picture painted in Brian's words caused us long-forgotten laughter pains.

Kazungula ferry

AT THE SAME TIME THAT the SAS force was moving towards Lusaka, a smaller SAS team was engaged in another clandestine operation. This was at the point where the borders of Rhodesia, Zambia and Botswana meet at Kazungula. The target was the Kazungula ferry owned by Zambia and serving as a vital road link to Botswana across the Zambezi River. For Zambia, it was one of only two active links to Botswana and South Africa, the other being the Victoria Falls rail and road bridge.

Despite Rhodesia's repeated warnings to both Botswana and Zambia not to allow the ferry to be used for any activity aimed against Rhodesia, ZIPRA was known to be using it freely. Whereas neither Botswana nor Zambia openly sanctioned ZIPRA's use of the ferry (in fact these two countries forbade it) there was clear proof that ZIPRA was employing clandestine methods to move large amounts of men and equipment into Botswana via Kazungula.

Sneaking men and matériel onto the ferry for the easy road route to Francistown was a much quicker and safer option than walking the long, slow and dangerous overland routes through northern Matabeleland. From Francistown it was a simple enough matter to move to any location in Botswana to launch small forces across the ill-defined border with Rhodesia. JOC Tangent in Bulawayo had repeatedly urged COMOPS to take any action that would put an end to this state of affairs.

COMOPS had been giving consideration to destroying the Kazungula ferry long before Ian Smith warned neighbouring

Nkomo's house, after the attack.

Joshua Nkomo.

countries, following the Viscount disaster, that they must face the consequences of supporting ZIPRA and ZANLA. In fact a Danish airline that had been flying ZAPU recruits from Botswana to Zambia took the Rhodesian threat to intercept and shoot down its aircraft seriously. The flights ceased immediately; but the ferry remained available.

Whereas it had been considered a simple enough task for SAS specialists to destroy the ferry, the economic consequences of disrupting the route had been assessed as too damaging to South Africa, Botswana, Malawi and Zaire. This all changed when ZIPRA shot down the second Viscount and its invasion plans had become known.

The SAS team moved to the border fence with Botswana after dark. Part of the force eased its way to the ferry's landing point on the Botswanan shore where it submerged a large explosive charge directly under the position the ferry would dock. The charge was then rigged for a command detonation by radio when the ferry was docked above it.

Well before sunrise on 13 April 1979, all members of the team were hiding next to the border fence inside Rhodesia to wait for the critical moment. Flying out of hearing distance, a Lynx stood by as back-up to the ground party, just in case the ground party's radio transmission failed to activate the explosive charge. For technical reasons the ferry did not cross the river at its scheduled time of 08:00. It remained on the Zambian bank of the Zambezi for another two agonising hours before setting off for the Botswanan bank where many vehicles and people awaited its arrival.

Considering that there were people to be dropped off on the south bank and others waiting to get onto the ferry, the SAS had a very small time-window in which to blow the ferry when it was empty. This they achieved with a perfectly timed vertical thrust that broke the huge ferry in two.

It was only when the Selous Scouts objected strongly to COMOPS for having destroyed the ferry that I learned how important it had been to undercover agents moving to and from Zambia. Obviously General Walls and others knew this, but ZIPRA's invasion plans took priority and the 'need to know' principle had been strictly applied.

This eventful week rounded off on 21 April when the country went to the polls to vote for its first black government. For some reason, Josiah Tongogara had instructed ZANLA not to interfere with voters and, for the most part, his instruction was heeded. ZIPRA tried to interfere but with limited success and an amazing turnout of 63% of voters occurred. Six weeks later Bishop Abel Muzorewa became the first black prime minister of Zimbabwe–Rhodesia.

Cheetahs

AIR COMMODORE NORMAN WALSH HAD made a secret visit to the Middle East, probably in late 1978, to arrange for the purchase of second-hand Bell 205 helicopters. This helicopter had given excellent service to the Americans in Vietnam where it was known as the 'Huey'.

Seven of these machines arrived at New Sarum in a somewhat dilapidated state. However, our ever-brilliant technical staff stripped the machines completely, removing many kilograms of sand in the process, and in no time had them spick and span and performing well. This was a particularly noteworthy achievement considering that Warrant Officer Johnny Green and his team had no technical manuals from which to work.

Air HQ gave the Bell 205 helicopter the name 'Cheetah' and all seven aircraft passed to No 8 Squadron. Although the Cheetahs were sometimes used on Fireforce work, in which they could carry two Alouettes-worth of troops, they became almost exclusively earmarked to support increasing levels of external operations.

Opportunity was taken during the earliest Cheetah test fights to conduct para-trooping trials. Though these were entirely successful, Dakotas continued to be a more cost-effective method of deploying paratroopers on over-border tasks.

Uncomfortable times in COMOPS

FOR SOME TIME IT HAD been clear that ZAPU and ZANU were receiving forewarning of some of our cross-border operations. It was also clear that the warnings were being given very close to the times of attack. Nkomo's absence from his home was the last straw. We later learned that the warning had reached him from someone in CIO at about the time the attack force was crossing the Kafue Bridge. Nkomo apparently called for a doubling of the guard before he and his wife moved away to the safety of President Kaunda's State House. He seemed untroubled by leaving his staff to a fate he failed to warn them about.

Probably prompted by Ron Reid-Daly's opinions, General Walls made it known that he suspected there was a mole in COMOPS. We were all stunned by this accusation, each considering it a personal affront. The entire staff became very angry that such an opinion existed, never mind that it had been aired in an unnecessarily brazen manner. This occurred immediately after Brigadier Peter Rich was posted in to replace General Barnard as Director General Operations. In discussions with Peter Rich, the COMOPS staff suggested that he should ask General Walls to exclude anyone but COMOPS and the operators from any knowledge of the timings of impending externals. General Walls accepted the idea.

Although CIO and appropriate agencies were always kept in the picture on what was being planned, selected operations were launched earlier than these agencies expected. Every time this was done, we gained maximum surprise because no forewarning to the enemy had been possible via the unknown mole; and General Walls' trust in his staff was restored.

Unrelated to the mole issue, COMOPS had acquired such a bad reputation amongst Army officers that this made being a member of COMOPS staff distinctly uncomfortable. However with Brigadier Peter Rich as DG OPS, the situation soon changed because COMOPS directives, instructions and queries were all processed through the correct military HQ channels. By mid-year many old tensions had fallen away and co-operation improved noticeably.

When I first joined COMOPS, General Barnard had made some snide remarks about the Air Force taking time off work to suit themselves whilst the Army slogged on. Initially I was perplexed because this could not possibly apply to Norman Walsh, Griff, Dag, Terence or me who regularly worked long hours, seven days a week. Then it dawned on me that his remarks had been aimed at Mick McLaren who played golf every Wednesday afternoon.

Mick McLaren seemed to me to have become a very secluded man who worked quietly in his office on specific tasks and only appeared amongst the planning staff for special operations' briefings. He attended all the NATJOC meetings chaired by General Walls where he showed irritation over general ramblings and recurring deferrals on matters that needed urgent resolution.

Just before lunch one Wednesday, I was alone with the air marshal in his office when he told me that Wednesday afternoon golf was essential to keep him sane in a job where, in spite of his position as Deputy Commander of COMOPS, he was neither fish nor fowl. He lacked the authority and job satisfaction that he had enjoyed as Air Force Commander.

It was obvious to COMOPS staff that Mick's disposition has changed radically and his frustration ceased whenever, in the absence of General Walls, he was in charge. On these occasions he played no golf and was to be seen everywhere in COMOPS. His style of dealing with staff was friendly but forceful, and his chairing of NATJOC meetings was completely opposite to that of General Walls.

Invariably Mick was faced with long lists of matters that had been repeatedly deferred; a situation he could not abide. I attended a few of his NATJOC meetings to give briefings on various matters and witnessed the marked difference in atmosphere to meetings chaired by General Walls. In his strong South African accent, Mick opened one meeting by pointing out that the only establishment represented at NATJOC with no outstanding items was the Air Force. He insisted that this had to be equalled by all establishments before the next meeting.

Deferred subject after deferred subject was addressed directly to the appropriate head, giving the length of time that had elapsed since the matter was first raised, together with all the reasons previously given for deferrals. In most cases Mick offered his personal opinions on resolutions then directed that the matter be cleared immediately or, at the latest, before the next meeting. He concluded by saying "Gentlemen, I want action. Let me emphasise, yet again, that a wrong decision can be turned around or modified, but no decision is inexcusable."

By the time General Walls returned to chair a NATJOC meeting, no pending matters remained. Unfortunately, however, new subjects needing decisions started to pile up; and Mick returned to playing golf every Wednesday afternoon.

So far as I was able to judge from general opinion amongst COMOPS officers and those in Army, Air Force and Police HQs, Rhodesia's forces would have been better off with Mick McLaren as the supremo and Brigadier Peter Rich as his Director-General of Operations. Under such leadership, COMOPS would have fulfilled the purpose for which it was created, and correctly handled directives and instructions would have been dealt with in a manner that avoided the unnecessary antagonisms and mistrust that had been created.

Black government

THE ADVENT OF CHANGE FROM white government to a black majority government had little effect on the management and execution of military aspects of our war—we continued as before. It seemed strange however to have Bishop Abel Muzorewa attending meetings in COMOPS in place of Ian Smith. This dapper little man wearing a dark suit, dog collar on purple clerical vest and outlandish black and white Mafia-styled shoes was very different to the PM we had all come to know well. In his hand, Muzorewa carried a colourful beaded stick that was to be his personal hallmark in the manner of President Kaunda's white handkerchief and President Kenyatta's bull-tail switch. Apart from the PM, I only had personal dealings with one black minister.

Minister Francis Zindonga was thickset and enormously pleased with his newfound authority. He had already proven himself to be the only politician with the guts to go into troubled areas to address the tribal folk and tell them about the principles and thoughts of the new government. He had gained a good reputation at COMOPS before I accompanied him to meet white ranchers in the Nuanetsi District Commissioner's offices in the southern lowveld.

Muzorewa in typical dress seen here with that despicable rat Lord Carrington; ultimate architect of Rhodesia's demise.

At the time, cattle rustling in the south had become a major problem along with the wilful destruction of miles and miles of fencing. Because of this martial law had been applied to the region. It so happened that Zindonga had been plagued with the same problems himself on his own ranch in the Wedza district. Consequently, he fully sympathised with the ranchers who were up in arms about CT-inspired theft of their highly bred herds.

Zindonga listened to many ranchers tell of how herds were being driven so fast and so far that many of the cattle were found dead along the drive trails. In some cases the herds had been deliberately stampeded to flatten fences resulting in serious injuries that necessitated the destruction of many suffering animals.

When he had heard all that had to be said, Minister Zindonga rose and told the farmers just what they wanted to hear. There were too many cattle rustling events that, together with calls to CT targets, made it impossible for Fireforce or troops to respond to all situations. Because of this, Zindonga gave ranchers the authority to take the law into their own hands and shoot rustlers on sight. The new government would fully support such 'self defence' actions in these critical times. From COMOPS' point of view this dangerous talk highlighted the difference in approach to problems between the old and new orders.

Civilian convoys and rail protection

BY NOW ZANLA GROUPS WERE actively attacking trains on the southern route to Beit Bridge. Even prior to the main offensives, the precaution of escorting all civilian traffic along the route had been taken following deadly ambushes in 1976 on a pair of South African motorcyclists and a lone car. Thereafter nobody was allowed to travel alone, day or night. All civilian vehicles accumulated at the starting points (Fort Victoria—southbound and Beit Bridge—northbound) at published starting times for two convoys a day in each direction, all in daylight hours.

When proceeding to South Africa on holiday with my family in 1976, the convoy commander adjudged me to be driving the slowest vehicle because I had our large Turner Swallow caravan in tow. Because of this I was instructed to be the pace-setter behind two armed Land Rovers. At the rear of 150-odd civilian vehicles were another two armed Land Rovers and another two that roved up and down the three-kilometre convoy length for the three hour–twenty minute drive to Beit Bridge. No pee-breaks were allowed!

The convoy system became a way of life for locals and visitors alike and there were few difficulties or incidents on the roadway. This was because CTs preferred to attack at night to give themselves ample opportunity to move well away before sunrise. Close by on the railway line, things were not so comfortable because it was impossible to confine all rail traffic to daylight hours and flexible response to attacks was not possible for trains in motion.

The greatest threat to rail traffic came from track sabotage, though surprisingly few incidents of this nature went undetected before a train reached any point of damage. Ambushes proved to be more troublesome until ex-Air Force 20mm Hispano cannons were mounted on special wagons—three per train. These armed railway wagons switched from northbound to southbound trains when gun crews were changed over.

Most of the gunners were coloured soldiers, nicknamed 'goffles'. They did a good job of silencing or limiting CT ambushes, providing they opened fire the moment an ambush was sprung. Sometimes, however, these soldiers were not as wide-awake as they should have been. Following two particularly damaging attacks, it was established that the goffles had picked up prostitutes to provide them 'comfort' on their usually uneventful and boring rides. But female distractions resulted in the CTs having sufficient time to lay down damaging fire before cannons responded. In consequence, the armed rail wagons changed name from Cannon Wagons to 'Nanny Wagons'.

British Conservative government

ON 3 MAY 1979, THE BRITISH public voted the Conservative Party into power and Margaret Thatcher became the UK's first female prime minister. Having been so badly let down by a communistically inclined Labour Government, there was good reason for Rhodesian morale to be uplifted. Margaret Thatcher's statements concerning the need to forget the past and judge the Zimbabwe–Rhodesian situation in the light of the present situation reinforced our hopes in her. She even intimated that Zimbabwe–Rhodesia had done enough for the Conservatives to grant the country recognition and remove sanctions. This all came as a breath of fresh air giving hope that communist ZANU and ZAPU would not be coming to power. Unfortunately history proves that we were wrong. We had yet to learn that the Conservatives were bigger 'snakes in the grass' than their predecessors who, it has to be said, did not speak with forked tongues.

Flechette success

IN EARLY MAY I RECEIVED an urgent message from the Duty Officer at JOC Thrasher to say that a TF callsign of 4RR was

asking for an immediate jet-strike. The callsign was in an OP on a prominent mountain ridge overlooking a known CT entry route that ran from the Revue Dam area in Mozambique into the Burma Valley, Rhodesia. This callsign had noticed high levels of activity in four villages with many women moving to and from a section of bush lying between the villages carrying bowls and dishes on their heads. The callsign commander told JOC Thrasher he was 100-per cent certain that a large group of ZANLA CTs were being fed and, since he was FAC trained, he could talk jets directly onto the target.

It so happened that a pair of Hunters had just been scrambled for an internal target. I cannot recall who was leading but know for certain that the wingman was Ginger Baldwin. My gut feeling was that the Mozambican target deserved priority, so I requested Air HQ Ops to divert the Hunters to the Burma Valley area. The pilots were unprepared for this change and did not have large-scale maps of the target location. Fortunately Burma Valley was very well known so it was easy enough to give the TF callsign position as the third border peak on the south side of the valley.

When the Hunter section made contact with the callsign, they received a very crisp and concise description of the target, so much so that they were able to visually identify the exact section of bush thirty seconds (slant-range about four nautical miles) from target. As the lead Hunter commenced its attack, the TF callsign was instructed to pass correction on leader's strike to the second Hunter. When the first 30mm cannon shells exploded, the TF called the correction, "Drop 50—Right 20." Ginger Baldwin then fired his cannons on the correction and received the call, "On target!" whereupon he released two flechette dispensers at the end of his cannon run.

Back in COMOPS I was perplexed to learn that flechettes had been dropped in Mozambique—something we were not supposed to do by our self-imposed ruling. However, because Ginger Baldwin had set out for an internal target with flechettes, and because Air HQ imposed no restriction for the external scene, he did not hesitate to use them.

Although this happened to be a genuine mistake it resulted in Rhodesia's singlemost devastating air action against ZANLA. But I only learned this after the war had ended. From ZANLA's top brass I learned that they feared the 'Racist South African nail bombs' more than the other South African weapons. They were in fact talking about Flechette, Alpha, Golf, and Mini-golf systems. Since we had not used flechettes externally, other than one pair of dispensers dropped at Tembue and the pair delivered by Ginger Baldwin, I thought ZANLA was talking about flechette successes inside Rhodesia. "No," they said. "We know about some comrades nailed inside Zimbabwe, but it was the death of our twenty-six top commanders at Revue that made us fear these weapons most."

The whole situation came about because of ZANLA's growing concern over the Pfumo re Vanhu auxiliaries who had become a serious hindrance to their operations in most sectors. Josiah Tongogara decided there was only one way to find out exactly what was happening. He sent twenty-six senior commanders to Rhodesia to investigate the matter and return with detailed reports and recommendations—but none of them even made it into the country!

As the TF callsign had said, Mozambican villagers were feeding these commanders preparatory to their night entry into the Burma Valley. Once through this valley they intended to disperse to undertake independent analyses of the widespread auxiliary threat.

They did not count on Ginger Baldwin's 9,000 flechettes, which eliminated every one of their numbers together with the unfortunate Mozambican women who were feeding them. The description given of this strike intrigued me. The body of the leader bore twenty-six flechette wounds and the least number of hits seen on any commander's body was six. What shook the ZANLA HQ team investigating this incident was the fact that every single feeding pot and plate had been holed by not less than one dart.

If only we had known about this success six months earlier we might have used more flechettes externally; but not a single radio FRELIMO intercept exposed ZANLA's grievous loss!

ZIPRA's NSO

ELLIOTT SIBANDA, THE ZIPRA MAN captured by Selous Scouts in Botswana, had undergone successful stomach surgery before revealing the existence and location of ZIPRA's Department of National Security and Order (NSO). This fancy name was for ZIPRA's central intelligence organisation that was structured and controlled by Moscow's KGB. Commanding NSO was Nkomo's number-two man Dumiso Dabengwa (the 'Black Russian'), who was reputed to be a KGB colonel.

The SAS was given the task of taking out the NSO, situated in a suburb of Lusaka southeast of the city centre. Planning commenced immediately to meet the following requirements:
1. Capture Dumiso Dabengwa, his deputy Victor Mlambo and the counter-intelligence officer Gordon Butshe.
2. Capture all radio and cipher equipment.
3. Capture all documents and
4. Destroy everything else.

The SAS planners were acutely aware that their return to Lusaka so soon after the attacks on Nkomo's house and Liberation Centre was fraught with perils. The Zambian Army and Air Force were expected to be alert and better prepared and ZIPRA would surely be fully primed to repel attacks at every one of its many facilities in and around Lusaka. Surprise

alone was the key. The biggest question was, "What if the unidentified mole in Rhodesia lets the cat out of the bag?" So many ideas were explored on how to get to target secretly and safely. Consideration was given to many modes of transport such as a furniture removal pantechnicon with motorbikes aboard, railway wagons, hijacked cars, maybe Sabres again, parachuting in and so on. However, CO SAS, Lieutenant-Colonel Garth Barrett, who would command the operation, discarded these in favour of going in and coming out in our newly acquired Cheetah helicopters. Consequently, Squadron Leader Ted Lunt, OC 8 Squadron, was brought into the planning to assess the feasibility of doing this.

Running a Canberra photo-recce of the NSO target was discounted, as this would warn the enemy of an impending action. Instead, old survey photographs were dug up which showed NSO buildings and surrounds to be just as Elliott Sibanda remembered them. So, despite Brian Robinson's concerns, there was no alternative but to use them for planning. The photographs showed a house and two office blocks surrounded by a security wall with a road running past the front gate. Unoccupied plots surrounded the rear and sides and, according to Elliott Sibanda, Dumiso Dabengwa and his men actually lived in the house and should be there when the attack went in.

Johnny Green (second from left) seen here when the first Cheetah was rolled out of the refurbishment hangar. Squadron Leader Ted Lunt is 6th from left. Note Strela screening and turned up exhaust.

Ted Lunt, who would lead the Cheetah formation, was satisfied that there was plenty of space to land the four helicopters allocated for deployment and recovery of the force. His main concerns centred on fuel endurance, night navigation for a dawn attack, and air defences that included MiG jets and British Rapier missiles. The Director-General Operations at Air HQ was Air Commodore Norman Walsh who, unlike his predecessors, involved himself deeply in the detailed planning, would be flying in the Command Dakota with Wing Commander Peter McLurg and SAS Major Graham Wilson.

By this time the Cheetahs had been stripped down to their last components and painstakingly rebuilt by a team of 8 Squadron technicians under Warrant Officer Johnny Green. To repeat what has already been said—considering that they had no technical manuals for this difficult task, it says much for dedication, ingenuity and technical expertise that all seven helicopters had been standardised and that all of Ted Lunt's pilots were trained and ready.

Preparations for the operation, codenamed 'Carpet', included full-scale rehearsals using old buildings on an isolated farm west of Salisbury. Although the Cheetahs partook in these rehearsals, this could not prepare the pilots for formation without the aid of navigation lights and flying low level in very dark conditions. This they had to manage when the time came in the early hours of 26 June 1979. Included with the SAS assault and defence parties was Elliott Sibanda. Elliott's job, using a loud-hailer, was to call upon the men inside the NSO to surrender themselves to the troops. He would then identify whoever responded.

Ted Lunt and his pilots did a great job of navigating their way from Makuti in Rhodesia to a point well to the northeast of Lusaka where they then flew west before turning south for the run to target. A diversionary attack by Hunters against FC camp, now reduced to a small ZIPRA contingent, was planned to occur a little after first light when the helicopters would be approaching that location from the north. The purpose of this attack was twofold. Firstly it was intended to draw any armed reaction to the northeast of the capital and away from the NSO in the south. Secondly, Rhodesian helicopters seen flying south from that location would appear to have come from the attack on FC camp, thereby obscuring their true mission.

Navigating the route did not work out perfectly. Probably due to an incorrect wind forecast, Ted had flown further north than planned and map-reading was almost impossible as he struggled to establish his exact position in marginal light. Because of his uncertainty, Ted asked Norman Walsh to put in the Hunter attack on FC camp on time, in the hopes the Golf bomb flashes would give him a position fix. Norman politely disallowed this, preferring Ted to be at the right point before the Hunters attacked.

The formation was running late, which was just as serious for the ground force as it was for helicopter fuel states. Norman Walsh and Graham Wilson were actually considering cancelling the operation when Ted positively identified his position. A quick assessment was made and the go-ahead was given, even though the troops would be landing twenty minutes behind schedule. The Hunters did their trick and the helicopters, now seriously low on fuel, passed FC heading for the NSO.

As the NSO came into view, everyone saw that there was a new building there, but otherwise the layout was correct. However there were more defence positions than expected, these having been established after the raid on Nkomo's house.

Whilst the Cheetah pilots concentrated on landing in their pre-planned positions, they had to put up with closing-range fire from ZIPRA and very noisy return fire from SAS troops in the cabins behind them.

As soon as the troops deplaned, the helicopters lifted off and headed south. Ted located an isolated *dambo* only eight minutes flying time from target and set his formation down in a box pattern with machine-guns facing out in an all-round defence posture. Engines were run down but the motors were left at idling rpm as precaution against potential starting problems. Fuel was transferred to main tanks from drums the helicopters had carried to this point. Being much lighter now than when they left Rhodesia, the helicopters were set to carry higher loads from NSO than they had delivered there. Out on the cold *dambo*, the helicopters waited patiently for Norman Walsh's call to return to target.

Unbeknown to the helicopter crews, things had not gone according to plan at NSO. Some of the explosive charges intended to blow access holes through the outer security wall had failed to function causing delay in the assault on buildings. All resistance had been overcome by the time the assault force commander, Captain Martin Pearse, threw in a delayed-action bunker bomb to blow down a wall to gain access to the guard room. He had moved around the corner of the building, where he should have been completely safe from the explosion, but the quality of the building was so poor that the wall behind which Martin was sheltering collapsed on him. The death of this truly superb and much revered officer stunned everyone, though it did not prevent them from continuing to work with typical SAS efficiency.

Upon their recall to target, the helicopter crews were greeted with the sight of flattened buildings and huge piles of bags filled with NSO paperwork. These bags and all the men they had brought to Lusaka were quickly loaded together with one protesting prisoner who claimed to be an innocent local visiting a friend.

Because of the early-morning delay, fuel remained a problem but there was just sufficient to get all the machines back to

The nine participating pilots. From left: Brian Gordon, Justin Varkivisser, Guy Dixon, Siggy Seegmuller, Dave Bourhill, Steve Kesby, Vic Wightman (OC 1 Squadron), Ginger Baldwin, Tony Oakley.

Hunter formation passing over Thornhill Air Base upon its return to base.

account of this matter later. In the meanwhile, Elliott Sibanda blew the cover of the prisoner, who continued to claim he had been a local visitor. He was in fact a high-ranking Russian-trained ZIPRA intelligence officer by the name of Alex Vusa. His capture substantially reduced SAS disappointment at missing the three big fish because Vusa's information led them straight into their next big hit.

The SAS were also disappointed that, because of the lateness of their arrival at target and the poor building standards, they had been unable to locate a bunker in which ZIPRA was reported to hold its most important files and a safe containing a large quantity of American dollars. But, because of the rubble from destroyed walls, discovery of the bunker's entrance coincided with Lieutenant-Colonel Barrett's order to withdraw. Fortunately, however, a master index of files amongst the recovered documents showed that the SAS had collected all but a handful of NSO's material.

The information gleaned from the captured documents not only confirmed all of Elliott Sibanda's facts, it expanded on them. Of importance too were lists of names of individuals and a host of overseas organisations supplying ZIPRA with intelligence on Rhodesian affairs. Details of this information were not immediately made known to COMOPS staff because other agencies would be following up on them. Alex Vusa's verbal information was our priority concern!

Xai Xai

UNRELATED TO VUSA'S INFORMATION, A very real opportunity to kill both Joshua Nkomo and Robert Mugabe presented itself when we learned that these two leaders and their party hierarchy would be meeting in the Chongoene Hotel in the coastal village of Xai Xai.

Rhodesian soil. A reserve Cheetah waiting at Makuti brought forward a whole load of drummed fuel to link up with the formation that waited on the ground close to the south bank of the Zambezi River. Once refuelled the force returned to base.

The helicopters were still refuelling near the Zambezi when nine Hunters made a formation fly-past over the parade that marked the opening of Parliament for the first black Government. We had not yet received replacement Hunters and had only nine, four of which had been seen over Lusaka that morning.

The precision flypast was widely publicised with supporting photographs which, when added to reports of the morning strikes in Zambia, caused quite a stir since it was thought that we might have more Hunters in service than the nine the West had on record. Outsiders could not guess that 100% serviceability was possible in a fighter squadron lambasted by sanctions. This is because they had no idea of the astounding capabilities and dedication of Rhodesian Air Force technicians.

The SAS failed to capture any of the ZIPRA men they had hoped to find because none was present at NSO. Following the attack on Nkomo's house, all had taken the precaution of sleeping elsewhere. I will deal with Dumiso Dabengwa's

On 22 June Maputo sent this message to Xai Xai: "Do all the preparations in Chongoene Hotel in order to receive the participants to the conference of the five Patriotic Front and representatives of ZANU foreseen for next July." Three days later, Zambian Air Force HQ informed Lusaka International Airport that, "ZAF transport to route Lusaka–Beira (refuel)—Maputo to stop over for seven days—return Lusaka. Aircraft to convey Nkomo plus party of ten leaving Lusaka 280400 June 1979."

Rhodesian operations against ZIPRA in Zambia may have prompted this meeting. Additionally, or alternatively, the new British Government or Frontline presidents may have insisted on ZANU and ZAPU coming together. Whatever the case we recognised that, potentially, we had a great opportunity target on our hands, though there were important issues to take into account.

The meeting at Chongoene Hotel was likely to commence on Saturday 30 June or 1 July but because ZANU and ZAPU seldom saw eye to eye, there was always the possibility that one party would walk out on the other. With six days apparently set aside for the meeting, Sunday 1 July was selected as the best time to strike.

Hurriedly we took aerial photographs of the hotel and managed to get detailed plans of its two-storeyed layout and construction. Six Hunters dropping Golf bombs and four Canberras each delivering four 1,000-pound high-explosive bombs from relatively low level were considered more than sufficient to destroy the entire hotel and everyone in it. The big question on our minds was, "Who is everyone?" Who besides ZAPU and ZANU might be at the conference?

The heads of state for Mozambique, Zambia and Tanzania seemed likely participants as they all had a vested interest in seeing ZAPU and ZANU settle their differences so their operations might at last be co-ordinated to mutual advantage.

We did not think the death of Samora Machel would rock the political boat too much. But the death of Kenneth Kaunda or Julius Nyerere, heads of British Commonwealth countries, by an overt Rhodesian Air Force strike would seriously upset Margaret Thatcher's Conservative Party when there seemed to be an improvement in attitude towards Zimbabwe–Rhodesia.

The intelligence people made every effort to establish what these leaders were planning for 1 July, and to pick up on any clues concerning members of the OAU. The only positive information gleaned showed that President Seretse Khama of Botswana was to open a two-day conference in Arusha for Front-line States' foreign ministers and overseas development representatives of major donor nations.

Nyerere should have been attending a mini-summit in Khartoum during 24 and 25 June to discuss Western Sahara issues, after which he was to meet with the Nigerian leader, Olesgun Obasanjo—probably in Nigeria. At short notice, he cancelled this trip and sent a representative instead. No reason for this change of plan could be established, but the timing was suspiciously close to the Xai Xai meeting and Kaunda's

movements could not be established at all; so, we had no alternative but to turn away from the opportunity.

Nevertheless, plans to assassinate Mugabe and Nkomo remained COMOPS priorities.

Attempts to assassinate Robert Mugabe

WE KNEW THE LOCATION OF Robert Mugabe's home on Avenida Dona Maria Segunda in the once-plush suburb of Maputo and a CIO undercover agent had been watching this house for some time, studying Mugabe's movements and habits. Unlike Nkomo, Mugabe's routines were easy to monitor and were highly predictable. So a small SAS team was assigned to take on the task of assassinating the ZANU President.

Opting for a sea approach to a beach that had been well known to holidaymakers during Portuguese times, the SAS used inflatable rubber dinghies, powered by silent motors to avoid having to move through populated areas. Twice the team arrived at Mugabe's house around midnight but on both occasions it was vacant, despite the fact that the agent had watched Mugabe arrive home a few hours earlier. This made it blatantly clear that someone 'in the know' in Salisbury had tipped off Robert Mugabe in time for him to get away to safety.

Both times the disappointed SAS team left the house untouched and returned silently to their hidden dinghies. The next day ZANLA and FRELIMO security personnel were observed to check out the rooms and garden before Mugabe himself returned home.

Though substantially annoyed by this, the SAS and COMOPS staff could not help being impressed by the fact that, unlike Nkomo, Mugabe had taken the trouble to get his entire household and security personnel to safety. We were also impressed by the fact that FRELIMO had not been called to ambush the house, obviously to safeguard their mole in Salisbury.

Having established modus operandi, thought was given to paying a third visit; this time to plant high explosives in the roof of Mugabe's house that apparently had not previously been checked by security guards. The existence of these explosives would be withheld from CIO until the agent advised that Mugabe had re-entered his home when they would be activated by a highflying Canberra. This might have worked, had other priorities not overtaken SAS.

ZIPRA loses war holdings

ALEX VUSA, THE INTELLIGENCE OFFICER from ZIPRA's NSO, told of a large build-up of arms and equipment at a location west of Lusaka. He had not been to this location himself but during his regular visits to JZ training camp he had noticed many large ZIPRA vehicles, all heavily laden, moving westward past JZ camp. He believed there had to be a storage site in the countryside close by because, after a short time, specific laden vehicles that had passed him earlier were seen to be heading back towards Lusaka empty.

We already knew that flights were coming in from Angola at night to deliver large amounts of ZIPRA equipment—but why at night? Why was ZIPRA not using Zambia's National Stores in accordance with Zambian Government instructions? Putting two and two together, it became obvious that Nkomo was not only intent on hiding his build-up from us; he was also hiding it from the Zambian Government.

The location of JZ camp was known, so a Canberra recce was flown over the area that Vusa had indicated. Photographs showing multiple tracks covering a huge area in which plies of equipment lay stacked under bush cover immediately confirmed Vusa's story. There could be no doubt that these were ZIPRA's main stores for its invasion plan.

There was urgent need to get troops to this location as the possibility existed that ZIPRA might move everything to a new site, particularly with NSO records and Alex Vusa in Rhodesian hands. Again the task fell to the SAS. At the very time that we had planned for the now-abandoned strike against the Chongoene Hotel in Xai Xai, Operation Chicory was launched.

Cheetahs carrying men and demolition equipment.

On 1 July five Cheetahs, carrying a force of fifty men laden with demolition equipment, lifted off from Bumi Hills.

Being a Sunday, ZIPRA's defending force was expected to be pretty relaxed and probably reduced in strength. Religion had little to do with this. In southern Africa it was almost standard practice for Sunday to be a time for visiting, resting and drinking. Nevertheless, we decided that an opening airstrike was essential to soften defences and create distraction whilst Cheetahs landed the SAS force.

Considering there was so much high explosive on the ground, I remember being somewhat concerned for the safety of the Canberras if Air HQ chose to make a low-level attack with Alpha bombs. With Norman Walsh overseeing the air plan this was simply not something to be worrying about and the strikes went in without problems. Five Cheetahs landed the troops during Hunter re-strikes then turned back for Bumi.

The shortest day of the year had only just passed so nightfall was quick in coming; not that this limited the SAS. By the time the Cheetahs came in to collect them in fading light, everything had either been destroyed or was rigged for destruction.

The ground force had enjoyed an exciting time with rockets zooming out of large fires with huge bangs and pressure waves emanating from ground through which the fast-moving line had passed. The destruction of weapons, explosives, vehicles, tents, bulk fuel, boats and so on was right up SAS's street. As they flew back towards Kariba, they were able to look back with satisfaction as timed charges continued to set off massive explosions that lit up the clouds and bush for miles around.

This was another very bad day for ZIPRA—their invasion plan was doomed. They had not only lost all they had been hiding from the Zambian authorities, they were red-faced by Rhodesia's exposure of their underhandedness.

Political turmoil

IT WAS VERY FRUSTRATING TO be tied to COMOPS where I lost close contact with the goings-on in Air HQ, the messes, the squadrons and FAFs. Air Strike Reports were seldom seen; not that these were withheld in any way. I could have gone up to Air HQ to read them but the tempo of work in COMOPS prevented me from doing so.

By now almost all young pilots and technicians were unknown to me. I knew they were out there performing fantastic work, but reading daily Sitreps (Situation Reports) from the JOCs failed to put names and faces to actions and incidents. Planning, reviewing, listening to operational debriefs and tasking new ones was all very well, even exciting, but one always saw the same people attending planning and debriefing sessions. All were familiar personalities from happier days in the field though few were blue jobs. This really niggled me giving emphasis to a grim sense of being separated from my own force.

Being mid-winter, the Fireforces were rattling up great successes against ZANLA which, when added to the mayhem being meted out to ZIPRA, should have put smiles on our faces; but political issues tended to darken the long hours and weekends in COMOPS.

In early June, US President Jimmy Carter, contrary to British Government's perceived intentions, ruled against the lifting of sanctions by the USA. Then in early August, Margaret Thatcher dashed all hopes of granting Zimbabwe–Rhodesia recognition when, at the Commonwealth conference held in the Mulungushi Hall in Lusaka, she reneged on her earlier promises. She moved instead for an all-party conference to be held in London.

What was particularly galling to Rhodesians was the fact that Maggie had been pressurised into this by the Australian prime minister who, considering his own country's record in dealing with ethnic folk, had absolutely no right to go against our wish to retain responsible government. Rhodesia's constitution sought to bring the black folk into government in a controlled and progressive manner. There was certainly nothing racist as with Australia's approach to colour. One only needs to consider that component of the Australian Constitution, which reads, "… make laws for people of any race for whom it is necessary to make special laws".

This was another overt move to push Rhodesians towards the communist take-over we were still thoroughly determined to prevent. Neville Chamberlain's failed policy of appeasement in his dealings with Hitler was forgotten after Winston Churchill returned British political drive back to one of strength. However, once Churchill and the British Empire had gone, Britain became embroiled in misguided guilt for her colonial past thereby weakening her ability to counter fascism and communism. Retaining favour with Africa's corrupt and ineffective dictators had become more important to British politicians than supporting a country intent on holding to a western-styled democratic government, without sacrificing efficiency and self-sufficiency.

To add to these concerns, Sithole was not acting in unison with Government and James Chikerema withdrew his support from Muzorewa's ruling party. It was not as if we did not expect to see infighting and incompetence in the new government order because all along we knew that relinquishing control too early would not work; but circumstances had made this the only option to attracting Western approval and circumvention of the Marxist alternative.

By now the title appended to the increasing exodus of whites seeking safer pastures changed from 'chicken run' to 'owl run' because many considered it the wise thing to do. Yet, for most

white Rhodesians, the desire to remain in God's own country remained strong. Like everyone else in COMOPS I had one aim in mind. This was to support the government in power, weak though it was, and work flat-out to destroy the enemies that sought to remove it.

The saying that every dark cloud has a silver lining was applicable to these times. South Africa was embroiled in what became known as 'The Information Scandal'. I do not remember the details but know that it forced a change in national leadership. Vorster was out of the driving seat and P.W. Botha took the wheel. With this change came a marked improvement in political attitudes towards Zimbabwe–Rhodesia and the inflow of goods returned to normal.

Operation Uric

FOR THE MOMENT ZIPRA WAS hobbled but ZANLA, with ever-mounting assistance from FRELIMO, was increasingly active in the south. Terrorist numbers in the Op Repulse area had grown to the point where over 50% of ZANLA's deployed force, estimated at 11,000, was in that area in early August 1979. In a show of support to the Muzorewa Government, South Africa committed a Fireforce comprising Puma helicopters, Dakotas and troops to the south of the country. Fielding as many fighting troops as all of our Fireforces put together, there were great hopes that this force would make great inroads against ZANLA and FRELIMO, but it was not to be. As we had come to know only too well, the flat lands of the region rendered intelligence of the type needed to bring Fireforces into contact almost impossible.

At the same time an impending multi-party conference in London was making world headlines; but President Machel of Mozambique saw some danger to ZANU's position if the talks took place. He turned his full attention therefore to assisting ZANLA push for an early outright military victory. To achieve this meant cutting Rhodesia's road and rail links to South Africa and countering ZIPRA's limited encroachment into southern Matabeleland.

More radio-equipped FRELIMO forces were added to those that had been operating inside Rhodesia for some time and some elements had even penetrated into ZIPRA areas. Externally, FRELIMO forces deployed along the well-established communication lines through Gaza Province from the coast to the Rhodesian border were now given instructions to strengthen their bases and give maximum support to ZANLA. By mid-August ZANLA was receiving overt assistance to the extent that they had become fully integrated with FRELIMO in their bases, defences, and transport systems. With over 15,000 trained CTs poised to move through Gaza, the dangers to Rhodesia were escalating rapidly.

This situation meant that any actions we took in Gaza would involve deliberate confrontation with FRELIMO, which until now had been avoided wherever possible. Now, however, the FRELIMO Government's undiluted involvement with Mugabe's ZANU party brought about a substantial change in political thinking. Major economic targets, which had hitherto been safeguarded by 'political considerations', no longer enjoyed such protection. This was all possible because of new thinking by the black government of Zimbabwe–Rhodesia and changed attitudes within the SA Government.

In COMOPS there was little to ponder on how to stem the impending flood. Norman Walsh's operational plans, shelved for 'political reasons' in 1977, had to be put into urgent effect. They involved in-depth destruction of road and rail communications, specifically bridges, and first priority was given to Gaza Province.

Whereas the railway had already been put out of commission by the Scouts and SAS in numerous short-duration operations, FRELIMO had not been neutralised—quite the opposite. They had in fact acquired considerable combat experience and determination in countering RSF forays against their ZANLA brothers. They had also put together sufficient road transport to fully compensate for the loss of rail transport.

In particular, FRELIMO had been given so much breathing space between operations that they had been able, with considerable assistance from Russian advisors, to build up a formidable military base at Mapai incorporating heavy ground and counter-air defence networks. In addition they had installed defensive positions around all strategic and economic key-points. All in all this made a job that might have been a cakewalk two years earlier complicated and extremely dangerous.

The first phase in this operation was to cut the transport line running from the Aldeia da Barragem road–rail bridge that formed part of the Limpopo River irrigation system all the way northwestward to our border. It involved cutting the huge Barragem bridge plus four lesser ones, mining main and secondary roads and destroying all transport north of the Limpopo. Equal in importance to destroying ground communications was the destruction of Mapai itself. This was considered essential to drive FRELIMO out of Gaza and force ZANLA into adopting the safer northern routes through Mozambique that would channel them through hilly terrain best suited to Selous Scouts and Fireforce operations.

There was some division in COMOPS thinking concerning operational priorities and actions to be taken in Operation Uric. Together with Brigadier Peter Rich and Brian Robinson, I saw Mapai as the key target around which to focus all other operations. Air Commodore Walsh supported this line of thinking, though he had no direct say in the ground planning.

The SAS, RLI and Army Engineers were earmarked for the destruction of bridges and mining of roads, so we recommended that a strong Selous Scouts vehicle-borne force with Air Force jet support should move on Mapai at least three days ahead of these actions. The object was not to attack Mapai directly but to subject it to siege and harassment to soften up and hem in the garrison force. We knew this force relied heavily on daily supplies of road-transported water, a commodity that was very scarce in that arid area. So denial of water would be the Scouts' prime objective.

The planning sessions became somewhat heated and were incomplete when Op Uric was launched prematurely. This became necessary when an agreed date for the commencement of an all-parties conference at Lancaster House in London was

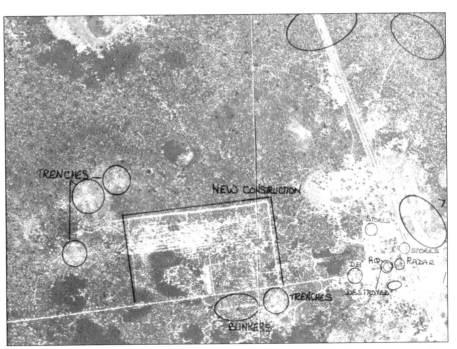

Mapai comprised the old railway town in bottom right-hand corner and the large base area nearby. The nearest available water can be seen in the shallow pan at top left side.

suddenly thrust upon us. It was less than two weeks away.

Because of the political time factor, General Walls hurriedly ruled out Mapai, as he believed destruction of communications had to take first priority and, if successful, this would effectively force Mapai's collapse. He also wanted to ensure that all air support would be available to the SAS, RLI and Engineers operations.

On D-Day minus one, 1 September 1979, fuel, explosives, ammunition and most participating troops were parachuted into the forward Admin Base located in remote ground 200 kilometres inside Gaza. Then, on D-Day, a heavy *guti* (low cloud with heavy drizzle) came down, forcing a postponement. Luckily the miserable weather only lasted one day instead of the usual three days.

Mapai knew something was afoot and sent out many armed patrols to seek out the Rhodesian forces they knew were active somewhere to their east. They had no idea how many Rhodesian soldiers were there or what their mission was.

On D-Day, now 3 September, a helicopter force comprising SAAF Pumas (thanks to the South African Government favouring Prime Minister Muzorewa) with five Cheetahs and twenty-four G-Cars left Rhodesia at first light. They all had full fuel tanks to avoid having to refuel at the Admin Base before uplifting troops to their assigned targets. Whereas all the Rhodesians were functioning under the codename Operation Uric, the SAAF participation was titled Operation Bootlace. This was to reduce the risk of being accused by the international community of joint involvement with Zimbabwe–Rhodesia.

The helicopters were still approaching the Admin Base when a FRELIMO patrol comprising twenty-four men happened upon the base. In a sharp exchange twenty-two FRELIMO lay dead. Another was captured wounded but one managed to escape.

What with the delay due to weather, Lancaster House talks only seven days away and discovery of the Admin Base, General Walls was in a bit of a quandary. He was flying in the Command Dakota with Air Commodore Walsh and staff. Time had become more critical and some operational adjustments had to be made on the run.

SAS made up the largest component of the ground force and were flown to the huge Aldeia da Barragem target just 150 kilometres northwest of Maputo. They landed under cover of Hunter strikes against the main FRELIMO defences. Thereafter, the SAS fought through the surviving elements of the enemy force, capturing a couple of heavy anti-aircraft guns that they later put to good use. One SAS soldier was wounded during multiple encounters and a Cheetah was called forward from a secondary refuelling point just six minutes' flying time to the north of target.

As Flight Lieutenant Dick Paxton approached for the casevac he was inadvertently routed over a FRELIMO strong point and suffered a direct hit from a missile that exploded on the main rotor gearbox. In the ensuing uncontrolled crash, technician Aircraftsman Alexander Wesson was killed outright. Dick was injured but was extremely lucky to be dragged from the wreckage by a very brave SAS Sergeant, Flash Smythe, before burning fuel engulfed and consumed the Cheetah.

By late afternoon, the SAS had completed the difficult and stressful task of setting up the charges on the road and rail bridges. Charges had also been set on at least one of the four irrigation canals' sluice gates. Having detonated these charges, the SAS team was to hold its position until next day to confirm that both bridges were wrecked before their planned extraction.

Surprisingly, the forces at the other four bridges had been unopposed. They completed their work, confirmed their bridges destroyed, knocked hell out of all enemy transport in their immediate areas, and then flew back to the Admin Base—as intended. RLI mine-laying teams worked throughout the day along main and secondary routes.

Back at COMOPS we thought everything was running to plan. But as night fell, we learned that the SAS Barragem force and most of the RLI mine-laying teams were being recovered to the Admin. Base. This struck us as very strange indeed because they should have been on their tasks until at least the end of D-Day plus 1.

The reason for the withdrawals came as a real shock. General Walls had decided to change direction and attack Mapai. We could not understand our commander's thinking. All along it had been agreed that conventionally defended Mapai was too strong a target to take on directly; hence the inclusion of Selous Scouts during initial planning. A prolonged period of softening and harassment had been considered of paramount importance to demoralise and weaken the defenders. But now a small force of just 200 men, mentally unprepared and armed only with light infantry weapons, was under orders to attack a much, much larger fresh force that was alert, dug-in and armed with vastly superior weapons.

The Air Force, having at most eight available Hunters and five Canberras, could not possibly hold a cab-rank to provide the ground troops with 'on call' heavy support. Most of the time the aircraft would be out of the area—a frightening thought indeed. There was absolutely nothing we could do about this in COMOPS other than hope and pray that General Walls knew something that we did not.

As it happened our mutually expressed fears were well founded. The nightmare that followed next day started off with the downing of a SAAF Puma well short of Mapai itself. An RPG rocket exploded behind Captain P.D. Velleman instantly killing him and his crewmen, Lieutenant N.D. Osborne and Sergeant D.W.M. Retief. There was no hope for the twelve Rhodesian soldiers aboard as the helicopter smashed through trees and broke up in a line of flaming wreckage.

The only casualty I knew well was the Army engineer Captain Charlie Small whom I had worked with on projects of mutual interest to Air Force and Army. Before his death he had played a big part in preparing the SAS for the intense bridge demolition work yet to come.

Hunters and Canberras struck and re-struck Mapai before ground forces, now depleted by 6%, landed near the target. From the outset it was clear that FRELIMO was too well established to simply pack up and run. Close-quarter contacts in the face of intense enemy fire from every conceivable type and calibre of weapon proved the Rhodesian troops' abilities to cope with heavy enemy fire, but the target was just too large and complicated to be quickly overrun by such a small force armed only with light infantry weapons.

The intensity of anti-aircraft fire directed at attacking jets amazed even the most battle-hardened soldiers. Equally amazing, and extremely discomforting, was that these heavy weapons were turned against the troops whenever the jets were not around.

General Walls soon realised that Mapai could not be taken without committing the troops to a long period of sleepless close-quarter combat—possibly another three days. However, the inevitability of unacceptably heavy Rhodesian casualties forced him to decide on a withdrawal—not a pleasant situation for Rhodesia's top general. Just another command cock-up in the endless list of failures by senior British generals! By nightfall the Mapai force was back in Rhodesia. The next day, remaining RLI mine-laying teams were collected and the Admin. Base was wrapped up.

Op Uric had fallen short of its primary aim of denying FRELIMO and ZANLA easy access through Gaza. One reason for this was that the road bridge over the irrigation barrage had not been rendered totally unusable because the engineers who built it had laid greater quantities of steel reinforcing than was revealed in the design plans. Had the SAS remained on target, as originally planned, they would have finished the job. The second reason was that the Hunters, wholly occupied in supporting the ground force at Mapai, had not been given opportunity to destroy vehicles trapped between the downed bridges.

This was the first occasion the RSF had failed to overrun the enemy. It was an issue that dampened spirits even more than knowing that our Government was about to face difficult times in their talks, commencing 10 September, with the devious Brits and our communist enemies. Neither ZAPU nor ZANU were any happier because they too utterly distrusted the British Government—not that this gave any comfort to us.

The international press inferred that a ceasefire followed by all-party elections in 'Zimbabwe' would be the outcome of the talks. Such ceasefire and political preparations for 'one man one vote' elections were envisaged for early 1980. Nkomo was in a worse position than Mugabe if such elections were to take place so early. ZAPU was sitting high and dry because Rhodesian forces had rendered all hope of an effective ZIPRA invasion impossible, whereas ZANU was well placed with thousands of ZANLA CTs in the country and many more immediately available to flood across the border.

In London, ZAPU and ZANU presented themselves as the 'Patriotic Front'. This apparent coming together of bitter enemies may have impressed the British and the OAU but it certainly did not fool Rhodesians. We knew only too well that ZAPU and ZANU would be at each other's throats

the moment the conference ended, no matter the outcome. Nevertheless, more to counter ZANLA than to challenge the Muzorewa Government, it was obvious to us that ZIPRA urgently needed to get as many trained men into the country as possible to prepare the ground for the envisaged election.

With all fronts likely to explode in our faces, it was clear that we were in for a massive increase in the intensity of over-border operations. Knowing that events in and around Rhodesia would influence the political standing of opposing parties at Lancaster House, we needed to indulge in operations that would strengthen the hand of Prime Minister Bishop Abel Muzorewa and his delegation. To do this meant taking no-holds barred actions in both Mozambique and Zambia.

Enhancing MNR's image

THE MNR CONTINUED TO BE a vitally important force for the eventual overthrow of the FRELIMO Government. For the moment however, we needed to direct their activities to impose limits on ZANLA by severely affecting Mozambique's infrastructure. This had to be done in a manner that would continue to improve the MNR standing with the civilian population at the greatest possible cost to the Mozambique Government.

Two specific targets were chosen. The first was the vital telecommunications relay centre east of Beira known as the Troposcatter and the second was Beira itself. The Beira mission will be covered shortly, but the importance of destroying the Troposcatter needs to be understood. Essentially it was to improve our intelligence-gathering capability. Most sensitive communications on the FRELIMO political and military networks relied on the highly sophisticated coding equipment of the Troposcatter, but this prevented us from eavesdropping on all enemy communications. With the advert of MNR, it was logical to destroy the facility and force FRELIMO to rely entirely on the HF networks we were already monitoring successfully.

Extra SAS men were flown in to meet up with the MNR liaison team and, together with an MNR force, they made a successful attack on the Troposcatter station two days after the Lancaster House talks started.

Attacking this target on the top of Monte Xilvuo right next to the main Beira to Chimoio road was no easy matter. However, drawn by the sound of the fighting and explosions that carried for miles from this elevated but successful attack, FRELIMO moved tanks and hundreds of infantry in an endeavour to cut off and destroy the mixed SAS–MNR force.

Whereas the range of our Cheetah helicopters allowed for the timely long-range recovery of most of the force, three men were left behind. Without a radio they had become separated during a firefight through one of the FRELIMO ambush points. For two days Cheetahs and Lynx searched for these men in the hopes that they were still alive and free.

Heavy anti-aircraft fire helped aircrew identify the positions of the pursuing FRELIMO forces and this gave proof that the lost men were still alive; but hours of searching failed to find them. Fortuitously the crew of the last Lynx to fly search at the end of the second day spotted the hard-pressed men's heliograph and wood-smoke signals, resulting in rescue. Only six days later the SAS and MNR were on the move again, this time to Beira.

Tony and me at Beira, as youngsters.

Here I divert to give one of the reasons the SAS–MNR force was visiting Beira.

As youngsters, my brother Tony and I occasionally went by train to Beira to visit my godfather and his wife, Alan and Sheila Martin. Alan was managing director of the Beira Boating Company and had at his disposal a fleet of launches and barges. My deep love of ships was developed in Beira docks where Tony and I had free access to the launches and boarded many ships. One point Alan made clear to us was that although Beira appeared to be a good harbour it was not a natural one because the entire Pungwe/Buzi estuary was extremely shallow. Because of this, the two dredgers we saw working daily were absolutely essential to keep the channel, specially cut for large ships, free of the sand and silt that relentlessly flowed in from the Buzi.

Many years later in less happy circumstances at COMOPS, I raised the matter with Brian Robinson who immediately saw the dredgers as key to putting an end to Beira's shipping. Now, on the night of 18 September 1979, the SAS–MNR had the two dredgers, *Matola* and *Pungue*, as two of their specified targets.

To avoid walking through miles of highly populated ground around Beira, the force was dropped off for a night approach to Beira docks. Coming in from the sea in quiet motor-driven inflatable dinghies, they sailed up the wide estuary of the rivers Pungwe and Buzi, heading for the dredgers and a dark landing point near the docks.

Subsurface limpets and other explosive devices sank both dredgers. At the same time the sea gates of Beira's only dry dock were wrecked, rendering that facility unusable. Whilst the dredgers and dry dock were being rigged for destruction, two other forces were busy on separate tasks. The larger of the two forces aimed to enter the town of Beira to destroy the central telephone exchange and break into Beira's prison to release all its political prisoners. The other force aimed to destroy ZANLA's war matériel stored in a dockside warehouse.

Unfortunately, intelligence concerning the telephone exchange security arrangements and civilian activities within the town and around the prison proved to be badly understated. Beira was alive with hundreds of people and FRELIMO had become so concerned about MNR activity, that they had substantially increased guarding levels on all likely MNR targets, including the telephone exchange. Although the force dressed in FRELIMO uniform reached both targets, the SAS commander was forced to move his men into hiding to think things through whilst awaiting an abatement of the unexpectedly high civilian activity. But then a suspicious civilian spotted the luckless team and reported its presence to FRELIMO who sent a patrol to investigate.

Following the death of some of these unfortunate investigators, the SAS–MNR force made a running retreat to the waiting dinghies distributing MNR pamphlets as they went. During the retreat, the demolition team assigned to blow up ZANLA stores was ordered to abandon its task. Notwithstanding failure to release prisoners, destroy the exchange or blow up ZANLA holdings, the main objectives of the operation were achieved. The dredgers had been sunk, the dry dock was out of commission and FRELIMO's fear of the MNR had been heightened.

The use of fixed wing and helicopters during the Troposcatter operation exposed Rhodesia's direct involvement with the MNR. Although we had hoped to avoid this it turned out to be an advantage. This was because FRELIMO concerns about the MNR forced President Machel to realise that either the war with Rhodesia had to end or ZANLA had to get out of Mozambique to save his country's economy from total destruction. But in COMOPS we planned to do just that. Operation 'Manacle' was the elaborate plan for SAS and RLI demolition teams to destroy every worthwhile bridge between Maputo and the Zambezi River.

Air Force jet support was to be given throughout against FRELIMO forces guarding all the bridges. These were then to be secured by SAS–MNR protection teams before demolition parties and their explosives were para-dropped directly onto target. After destroying each bridge, helicopters would recover the demolition teams to Rhodesia to prepare for their next targets. At the same time helicopters would move the SAS–MNR securing teams to their next assigned bridges.

Whilst these plans were being finalised, other external operations in both Zambia and Mozambique were underway.

Search for New Chimoio

FOR MANY MONTHS AN ONGOING operation, codenamed Bouncer, sought to ambush likely roads used by ZANLA's top commanders. Ideally we hoped to capture or at least kill Josiah Tongogara and Rex Nhongo. However, in spite of many Bouncer deployments by SAS and Selous Scouts, all attempts failed though many high-ranking CTs were killed in the process.

In late September an SAS–MNR team was flown to an unpopulated start position for a twofold task. One was to locate ZANLA's elusive 'New Chimoio' base, which captured CTs implied had moved well away from the Chimoio and Vanduzi Circle areas. They claimed it was now well established and much closer to Rhodesia on the west side of the main Vanduzi to Tete road. Since Tongogara and Nhongo were reported to be living in the base, the team's second task was to make yet another Bouncer attempt on them.

Having walked through the night, the SAS–MNR team came upon an unmarked but well-used vehicle track that was in current use. Feeling certain that this led to the ZANLA base, which the team commander thought was still some distance off, the team moved into an elevated daytime hiding place. The intention was to observe the surrounds before setting up an ambush late in the afternoon in hopes that one or other of two Toyota Land Cruisers driven by Tongogara and Nhongo would pass their way.

Whilst in hiding the team was surprised by the high level of general activity around the area but then became very concerned when a large force of ZANLA passed along the vehicle track, quite obviously checking for mines and human tracks. Realising that this must have been prompted by the sound of the helicopters dropping them off the previous evening, the commander guessed the base must be much closer than expected. So, instead of going ahead with the ambush, the commander wisely decided to remain in hiding that night and send his MNR men out early next morning to have a chat with the locals. When the MNR returned, they reported that the base was very close by.

Having established this, the commander decided to go ahead with the ambush. The team did not have long to wait before two vehicles came their way. As they came into view, the ambushers saw that they were both Toyota Land Cruisers. These they took out in a slick action that killed all the occupants. Fires raging in both vehicles were so intense that it was impossible to get close to them. However, one SAS soldier reported glimpsing what he thought was a white man's body in the flames. Later this was confirmed when radio intercepts revealed that three

Russian advisors were amongst the fifteen-odd dead.

The team cleared the area only to find they had been so close to the enemy base that hundreds of ZANLA were closing in pursuit, so a call was made for hot extraction. Under continuous and heavy fire, the team managed to survive a long running-battle before being whipped away to safety by the Air Force.

Now that we had a fair idea of the base's actual location, thought was given to photo-recce. Initially it was considered that if this was done, ZANLA would move because we had received vague information about ZANLA's unique air warning system. Two tame baboons Jamie and Amie, having been subjected to many airstrikes, were said to be ultra-sensitive to the sound of jets. Apparently they gave early warning by screeching and leaping about long before ZANLA heard sound of the aircraft that so terrified these two animals. Even a high-flying Canberra passing quietly over a noisy camp might get the baboons excited.

It was decided, therefore, to put in another ground recce. The SAS were fully committed on other tasks, so the Selous Scouts deployed one of their oft-proven two-man recce teams. This time no helicopter was used and the team walked in from the border. Unfortunately, it was detected in the early stages of its passage through the base and was forced to call for hot extraction. By now, however, captured CT's were indicating that the base was highly prepared with sophisticated heavy anti-air and ground defences specially sited by Russian advisors. The deaths of three Russians certainly gave weight to these reports. The captured CTs also said ZANLA felt too strong to be frightened off the present base position by the passage of any aircraft.

The rainy season had started early this year but a photo-recce flight was made immediately a gap appeared in the weather. Even though the JSPIS photo-interpreters had poor-quality photographs to work from, they immediately identified elaborate defences including many heavy-calibre gun positions and extensive trench works linking and surrounding each of at least four bases. Typical for this time of year, cloud cover masked much of the ground in which we believed there must be additional bases. They needed to be pinpointed and analysed but bad weather thwarted further attempts to photograph the area.

Fortunately, two high features at the northern end of a line of rugged mountains contained the bulk of the defences, and these had been exposed. Since there was need to get on with the job, planning for an operation codenamed 'Miracle' was formulated on the basis of what was known and a fair amount of reasoned guesswork on what could not be seen.

The SAS were preparing to go external against two large bridges in Zambia and another three in Mozambique, but this was not the only reason the Selous Scouts were earmarked for the job with RLI in support.

Operation Miracle

INTELLIGENCE INDICATED THAT ONLY ZANLA occupied the New Chimoio base and that FRELIMO had sent them far away from Chimoio town to prevent Mozambican civilians from becoming involved in future RSF raids. Captured men also indicated that if CTs were forced to leave the base, they would move towards Rhodesia because FRELIMO had forbidden them from going in any other direction.

Ron Reid-Daly recognised that this suited Selous Scouts pseudo work perfectly, so he decided to deploy a large number of pseudo callsigns to the north, west and south of the base. Once in position, and under Ron's direct command from his own forward HQ set high on a border mountain, the callsigns would interrupt ZANLA's supplies and, coupled with Air Force bombardment, induce fire-fights that would have CTs in a jitter. Ron expected that the CTs would not know who was pseudo and who was genuine, thus forcing them to indulge in attacking one another on sight. To the east of the base, RLI paratroopers would form a line of ambushes to take on any CTs breaking east in contravention of FRELIMO orders.

The plan was wonderfully unconventional and would certainly have prevented the imminent launching of large numbers of ZANLA intent on influencing the Lancaster House talks. However, General Walls rejected the idea, initially preferring to employ well-proven operational methods. This soon changed because there was considerable apprehension over Soviet advice and planning for ZANLA's defences. Those that we could see were clearly superior to any ZANLA defences encountered before.

Besides, we remembered how in 1967–8 Soviet studies of Rhodesian tactics and operational methods had led ZAPU and SAANC to use difficult crossing points over the Zambezi River where gaps existed in our border control. The reader will recall that large groups were deep inside Rhodesia before Ops Nickel and Cauldron got underway. More recently, we had seen the effectiveness of Soviet planning at Mapai; so now we wondered if those Russians killed by the SAS had prepared a deadly trap for us at New Chimoio. It occurred to the planning team that the well-proven vertical envelopment of bases by paratroopers and helicopters might be exactly what the Russian advisors would expect, particularly as the base was less than twenty kilometres from the border and a mere fifty kilometres northeast of Umtali. We simply could not take the risk of running our helicopters and slow fixed-wing aircraft into a well-laid Soviet trap.

Consequently it was decided to go conventional by employing Selous Scouts in their vehicle-borne fighting role with large-calibre guns and jets in support. Since this would involve moving many men and vehicles into position before launching Op Miracle, there was concern that the CTs in nearby New Chimoio would be fully prepared for the attack. So, to mask our true intentions, it was decided to mount high-density operations to create as much noise and movement as possible in the Mutasa and Holdenby Tribal Trust Lands whose eastern boundaries were the international border nearest to New Chimoio. As the HD Op got under way on 27 September, Selous Scouts pseudo teams moved in amongst the African population along and across the border to prepare for the expected westerly breakout from New Chimoio.

The high-density operation ruse undoubtedly worked, but it cost us dearly when three fine men and a K-Car were lost. Air Lieutenant Paddy Bate was flying down a river-line in the Mutasa TTL when his K-Car was pulled to the ground by power-lines he had not seen. Paddy, his gunner Sergeant Gary Carter and RLI Major Bruce Snelgar were all killed.

Wilky crash.

This was the fourth incident of helicopter crashes through cable- and power-lines that I can recall. In November 1973 Squadron Leader Eddie Wilkinson and Sergeant Woods were returning from an action flying low level directly towards the setting sun. Eddie spotted troops waving madly next to a stationary vehicle. He thought they were in distress and turned back to investigate. Blinded to some extent by the sun, Eddie failed to see the telephone lines that snagged his nose wheel as he came into the hover. Feeling himself being drawn downward he increased collective to climb but this simply resulted in the aircraft being somersaulted into an inverted crash. Though he and his technician were lucky to escape alive, Eddie was annoyed with himself when he learned that the soldiers had only been waving in friendly manner at the passing helicopter.

Then in December 1975, SAAF Lieutenant van Rensburg was the only survivor of the Vumba cable incident in which General John Shaw and Colonel Dave Parker died. In March 1977, Mike Mulligan suffered head injuries in a crash following collision with power-lines near Mrewa. According to fellow pilots this brought about a substantial change to Mike's character. This was because he had ended up inverted and, as would happen later to Mark Dawson, choked on his armour vest.

Returning to Op Miracle. Two days later, in the early hours of 29 September 1979, the Scouts fighting column commenced the difficult task of crossing the Honde River border into Mozambique. This constituted the only major obstruction between Rhodesia and the ZANLA base. The mobile force of Selous Scouts, Armoured Car Regiment and Rhodesian Artillery comprising one command vehicle nicknamed "the Pig", nine Eland armoured cars, twelve infantry vehicles carrying 320 infantrymen, and six 25-pounder artillery guns.

In the absence of suitable bridging equipment, crossing the Honde River proved more difficult than expected. A bulldozer had to be used to pull every one of the vehicles through deep water and heavy mud resulting in a delay of almost seven hours. Whereas the column should have reached target to coincide with the first airstrikes at 07:00, they did not get there until mid-afternoon.

Ron Reid-Daly in his elevated command post on the border was no less frustrated by the delay than Air Commodore Norman Walsh and Lieutenant-Colonel Brian Robinson in the high-flying Command Dakota. They need not have worried! ZANLA did not budge in the face of air attacks and were well prepared for the first ground actions that occurred too late in the day to produce any meaningful results.

The jets revisited target a few times before the vehicle column eventually reached the western outskirts of the huge base. Extremely heavy and accurate fire greeted every striking aircraft, though miraculously none was hit. In the meanwhile, RLI paratroopers had been dropped well to the east of target and had walked in to set up a series of ambushes to cut off any CTs breaking eastward. Because breakout was expected to be westwards, the RLI was very thin on the ground. Events were to show that this was a major tactical cock-up because, whilst the mobile column was digging-in for the night in the face of a fair deal of enemy attention, the RLI was actively killing many CTs breaking their way.

From the outset it had been clear that the high mountain features overlooking the bases would be key to the outcome of Op Miracle. At the northernmost end of the range lay a prominent domed granite mountain stronghold the Scouts nicknamed 'Monte Casino' after the famous, strategically important defences on the Italian mountaintop monastery that the Germans defended so aggressively during WWII.

Monte Casino not only gave the defenders an excellent view of the Rhodesians below, it contained the majority of heavy guns and mortars defending the entire area of bases that swept in an arc from west through north to east. Within the area of bases there were many other anti-aircraft guns, all well sited and widely dispersed.

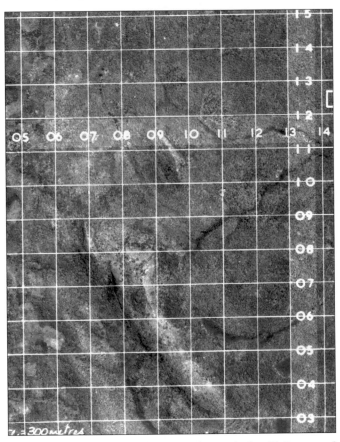

The base and defences lay between the vertical grid lines north to south 11 to 05 and the lateral grid lines west to east 06 to 12. Rhodesia lies to the left of this photograph.

Just to the northeast of Monte Casino was a small isolated hill feature lying between two of the bases. This was nicknamed 'Ack-Ack Hill' because it contained a cluster of concentrated anti-aircraft gun positions. Then, to Casino's south, a high ridge running southward gave a number of other anti-aircraft gunners and mortar teams superb visual command of all ground approaches to the base and to Monte Casino itself.

Early on the morning of Day Two the troops came under heavy and accurate fire from Monte Casino, making progress very slow. Low cloud disallowed air support; but then the same cloud lowered and blinded the defenders. This allowed the Elands to move closer to provide assault troops support from their incredibly accurate 90mm guns.

It was past midday before the Hunters could return to target, by which time a good assessment had been made and troublesome positions were pinpointed for their attention.

By mid-afternoon one particularly troublesome promontory

(photo grid 070050) near the western CT base had been overrun by Scouts, but not before it had been hurriedly vacated, weapons and all. Nevertheless this vantage point gave improved observation of Monte Casino (photo grid 085065), allowing accurate direction to be passed to Hunter pilots, the mortars and Elands firing against enemy emplacements that had survived earlier attention.

Following one concentrated bombardment of Monte Casino, an attempt to overrun its heights was thwarted by intense fire from Ack-Ack Hill (photo grid 095110), together with hand-grenades lobbed down from the unseen defenders above. Meanwhile, widespread fighting continued all day as troops laboriously worked through two large bases lying closest to Monte Casino (centred on photo grids 065098 and 060115).

By nightfall of Day Two, Rhodesian forces had established themselves for a renewed attempt against the main defences the next day. Otherwise a situation of stalemate appeared to exist in the target areas with both sides settling to wait out the long night. Meanwhile the RLI had another busy night shooting an increased number of CTs fleeing east. To the west, the Scouts pseudo teams waited patiently, but nothing came their way.

Captain Peter Stanton, having transferred from the Special Branch to the Selous Scouts, spent the night interrogating a captured CT who turned out to be the man responsible for ZANLA's base defences. Again the Rhodesians had managed to secure a key man at a critical time. From him, Peter Stanton acquired all the details of the ZANLA defences, which were then passed to unit commanders before they launched into action on Day Three. The first of these involved clearing all the defences of a long ridge south of Casino (commencing at 072039 and extending well off the photograph through 077028).

Also revealed by the captured CT was the fact that Rex Nhongo had been at the base when the first airstrikes went in on Day One. He had crashed his Land Cruiser (around photo grid 050110) in his hurry to get away. He had then taken another vehicle and departed for Chimoio. The Selous Scouts found the crashed vehicle exactly where Peter Stanton said it would be and, following temporary repairs, it was brought back to Rhodesia at the conclusion of the operation.

Hunter strikes were placed on each defended position before Scouts moved in to secure them. In a series of surprisingly smooth-flowing actions, the entire ridge was cleared. Ack-Ack Hill was all but neutralised by Hunters delivering Golf bombs before troops overran it. These actions made it possible to mount a second attempt on Monte Casino.

When the assault took place, however, the troops were amazed to find the mountaintop deserted. Survivors had left behind many of their dead in trenches and crevasses. Wrecked guns lay strewn about the pulverised ground, which had been totally denuded of vegetation. The fact that the trees immediately outside of the anti-aircraft gun sites were still standing bore testimony to the accuracy of ground and airstrikes.

Incredibly, the soldiers came upon Jamie and Amie off to one side of the devastated area. The two baboons immediately settled down when the Scouts took them into their care. Also taken into care were a few surviving anti-aircraft guns that had been moved but then abandoned.

A small sector of the Monte Casino gun emplacements.

Some of the guns captured in the camp areas.

Following sharp actions that neutralised odd pockets of resistance, all the bases had been overrun by the end of Day Three. As they progressed through the bases burning and destroying all structures, the troops could see how well the defences and bunker systems had been prepared. Huge quantities of cooked food, found uneaten in the large kitchens, confirmed the estimated occupancy on Day One to be somewhere between 6,000 and 10,000 male and female CTs.

The great majority of ZANLA had left the area in what appeared to be an ordered easterly withdrawal. Had this been anticipated, more troops would have been positioned east of the base. As it was, the gaps between the RLI ambush locations were too wide to prevent the outflow, though many CTs had fallen to the sharp-shooting soldiers.

Thought was immediately given to mounting a new operation as it seemed certain there would be many vehicles moving along the main tar road running north from Vanduzi to collect fleeing ZANLA. The Selous Scouts' mobile column could be expected to have a fine time if diverted to this new task, but it was too late to do this as Day Three drew to its close.

During the night of Day Three, an early-warning callsign posted to the south reported FRELIMO tanks with deployed infantry advancing towards them along the narrow vehicle track leading to the base. The 25-pounder guns were given appropriate co-ordinates and commenced firing. Following two corrections, the guns straddled the tanks with a full salvo. This had the desired effect. The infantry scattered and the tanks, one trailing smoke, high-tailed back from whence they had come.

Unfortunately no details were available to undertake a follow-up operation on fleeing CTs with any degree of certainty. In the meantime, our eavesdropping services reported considerable FRELIMO radio traffic that showed FRELIMO was moving in strength towards the ZANLA base. The risks involved in pursuing ZANLA outweighed the advantages to be gained because, by driving ZANLA from its main base and substantially disrupting its incursion plans, Op Miracle's primary objectives had already been achieved. It was decided instead to recover forces in daylight on Day Four with small stay-behind parties remaining in hiding to watch for opportunity air targets.

The stay-behind units remained on the high ground around the base to observe activities throughout the following week. During the morning of 3 October 1979, Day Five, they reported the presence of a large FRELIMO armoured column that had interrupted its northbound journey towards Cruzamento village to give Monte Casino a thorough going-over with accurately placed cannon fire.

At Cruzamento village the armoured column based up and was joined by additional FRELIMO forces that came in from the east. There was a great deal of activity amongst the men and vehicles of the concentrated force, which appeared to be preparing to launch a night-time retaliatory attack against the nearby RSF permanent base at Ruda. In COMOPS we decided it was important to break up the force to drive FRELIMO back east. The Air Force was tasked to do this.

First strikes went in at around 13:00 against concentrated men and vehicles. First over target were Canberras flying low and fast to deliver Alpha bombs against exposed personnel. Next came Hunters attacking with Golf bombs, Matra rockets and 30mm cannons. The strikes inflicted high casualties with the destruction of a number of vehicles, but this only had the effect of bringing about a limited dispersion of the force.

A heavy haze lay over the entire area due to smoke still drifting from the ZANLA base and dense black smoke rising from burning vehicles. Although these conditions made observation of FRELIMO's activities difficult, the Scouts OPs could see enough to establish that FRELIMO was regrouping in preparation for their planned action. The Air Force returned as soon as the jets had rearmed; but this time disaster struck in consequence of poor visibility caused by smoke and heavy haze.

It started when Flight Lieutenant Kevin Peinke and his navigator, Flight Lieutenant 'JJ' Strydom, struck one section of FRELIMO forces that were straddled either side of a section of road. They were on top of the first men and vehicles before seeing them but managed to release half of the bomb load amongst others ahead. Kevin decided to reverse direction and, using the dust and smoke from his first strike, bomb that part of the target he had seen first. This was an unusual and fatal error of judgement. Other enemy elements concentrated close by had seen the Canberra turning back and were fully prepared with every gun when the bombs were released.

The Canberra lost both engines, forcing Kevin to convert excess speed to height for a powerless glide towards the border. It can only be assumed that Kevin waited for 'JJ' to get from his bomb-aimer position in the aircraft nose back to his ejector seat, but time was too short. Both men died when the Canberra crashed short of the border.

Brian Gordon.

Hunter pilots flying that afternoon said they had experienced great difficulty in judging their height above ground due to the appalling haze. This is possibly why Air Lieutenant Brian Gordon was seen to fly into the ground when making a rocket attack against armoured vehicles. His recovery from the dive was either made a fraction too late or he may have been hit. The sad facts were that we had lost another fine airman and our Hunter fleet was now reduced to eight aircraft.

Op Miracle had been successful but the cost to Rhodesia was unacceptably high. Two airmen and an RLI officer had been lost, together with an Alouette, in the high-density operation performed in direct support of Op Miracle. One Selous Scout was killed whilst clearing trenches on Day One. Another was killed and three seriously injured on Day Three when a captured weapon exploded as it was being made safe. Then on Day Five the Air Force suffered the loss of three officers, a Canberra and a Hunter.

Chambeshi bridges—Zambia

PRIOR TO MY ARRIVAL IN COMOPS, plans had been made to pressurise Zambia into making better use of its southern rail route through Rhodesia to the ports of South African. Although an economics issue, it fitted well with military plans to deny ZIPRA the rail and road facilities needed to transport war equipment from Dar es Salaam to Lusaka. The plan involved the destruction of the Tanzam rail and road bridges across the Chambeshi River situated a great distance northeast of Lusaka. Whereas the SAS had been fully prepared for this task, it had been shelved because 'political repercussions' remained a big concern at that time.

By August 1979, there had been substantial changes in political thinking and, because world reaction to our recent external operations had been less than expected, Operation 'Cheese', was on the action board again. Although there were other externals on the go, Op Cheese was the most exciting one to follow because it was so audacious and was the longest-range operation ever undertaken by any of our ground forces. The two Chambeshi bridges, lying half a kilometre apart, were almost 800 kilometres from the still-secret Air Force base at Fylde from which the operation was launched.

We were still getting over the shock of the Canberra and Hunter losses that day when Jack Malloch set off from Fylde to drop a four-man SAS free-fall pathfinder team from his DC7 into the target area. Things did not work out as planned near the bridges because one parachute failed to open, costing the team the loss of its canoes. In consequence, there was a long walk to recce the bridges and an equally long walk back to the rendezvous point to take the night drop of another twelve men.

This drop was successfully conducted when the DC7 returned around midnight on 8 October. From there the sixteen-man team had to make its way upstream to the bridges in heavily laden canoes and a powered inflatable dinghy. The Chambeshi River was flowing more swiftly than expected and

this delayed arrival at the targets until the night of 11 October. Once there, the bridges were rigged for demolition in the manner the SAS had pre-planned and practised. Whilst the explosive charges were being placed, two of the team members set up a roadblock to hijack a suitably large vehicle. This was necessary to transport the whole team with canoes and dinghy to a remote position in far-off Luangwa Game Reserve for uplift to Rhodesia by Cheetah helicopters.

The hijacking of a twenty-ton truck driven by its white owner was successful but became complicated when the brother of the driver, noticing that the twenty-tonner was no longer following his own truck, turned back to investigate. This man refused to leave his brother.

In the meanwhile, a third white man stopped, believing the twenty-ton truck had broken down. As if this was not bad enough, a ten-year-old white boy was accompanying one of the brothers, his uncle, as a special birthday treat. Consequently, for security reasons, the SAS had to hold captive the three white men, two black co-drivers and the ten-year-old birthday boy. Once the charges were set and fuses lit, the twenty-ton truck carrying twenty-two people with canoes and dinghy set off down the main road towards Lusaka. Some way from the bridges the satisfying sound of a single huge explosion reached the men; but they had no way of knowing if the bridges were down. When dawn was breaking a little short of the small town of Serenje, the truck turned south down a secondary road towards the Luangwa Game Reserve.

Unhappily they came upon a power station in the middle of nowhere and the SAS were forced to shoot security guards who came to investigate their presence. From there they managed to bundu-bash their way to a position where the Cheetahs collected them, captives and all. By this time the SAS team was relieved to get the news via their HF radio that Canberra reconnaissance had confirmed both bridges were down.

The hapless Zambians were noticeably apprehensive about their own safety right up to the moment they were ushered into the Cheetahs. Thereafter they relaxed and were treated to Rhodesian hospitality until suitable arrangements were made for their safe return to Zambia.

Moatize bridges

THE OP MANACLE PLAN TO destroy all Mozambique's bridges was initiated with the downing of three rail bridges on the line north of the Zambezi River. Apart from denying ZANLA any rail transport for men and munitions from Beira to Tete Province, severing the line at this particular time complemented the cutting of the Tanzam rail at the Chambeshi River. With this rail line also cut, Zambia would have no Mozambican outlet as an alternative to the South African ports.

Ten months had passed since the SAS destroyed the Mecito bridge and the train that was crossing it. No attempt had been made to repair the bridge or recover the engine that remained nose down in the riverbed, but trains were being run to each side of the river to transfer passengers and porter goods from one train to another. The destruction of another three widely separated bridges would put an end to this practice.

Dakotas delivered three SAS teams to the bridges during the evening of 12 October 1979. Early next morning, Cheetahs brought in the heavy explosive packs and the three bridges were dropped in daylight on the same day.

FRELIMO guards at the biggest bridge had fled when their fire was answered with overwhelming aggression. Apart from this, no opposition occurred save from a swarm of bees. Stirred to anger by detonation pressure waves, thousands of bees attacked all the members of one team, causing two to be hospitalised. Also stirred to anger was the FRELIMO Government.

Improved methods of packaging and laying demolition charges had worked so well for the SAS on the five bridges in Mozambique and Zambia that the same principles were adopted and tailored for each of the bridges assigned for destruction during Op Manacle. When all was ready however, the Mozambican op was postponed at short notice. The SAS were about to launch from Chipinda Pools in southeast Rhodesia when analysis of intelligence confirmed the imminence of a ZIPRA invasion. Understandably the SAS Regiment was incensed by the eleventh hour deferral of an operation for which they were so well prepared. It had happened many times before but, in this case, there was a general belief amongst the SAS officers that there were sinister reasons for calling off their biggest job which, for the first time ever, involved every available member of the SAS.

Encounter with conventional ZIPRA forces

FOR SOME TIME SELOUS SCOUTS teams had been operating inside Zambia on recce and disruption tasks south of the main road from Lusaka to Livingstone. Helicopters were used for all deployments and recoveries and a limited amount of assistance was given to Scouts by Lynx pilots making visual recce sorties to assist in the selection of unpopulated routes.

First indications of a ZIPRA conventional force in the remote dry country northwest of Kariba came from one Lynx pilot who reported encountering heavy anti-aircraft gunfire when he was returning to base from a recce task. Little notice was taken of this until two helicopter pilots were subjected to the same treatment from precisely the same location.

The Canberra tasked to photograph the spot did so at midday on 10 October when the sun was directly above the aircraft. The Kariba area had remained completely dry in spite of heavy rains in the eastern areas of the country. In consequence, the dry white soil of the region reflected the sun's rays so strongly that images on the photographs blended all features in a manner that made distinguishing between rocks, scrub and open ground difficult—even through stereoscopic viewers.

Apart from a single vehicle track leading to the area, the JSPIS photo-interpreters could find little of interest on or near the prominent ridge the pilots reported as being the source of enemy fire. So one of the pilots was called in to view the photographs to clarify what he had seen coming from where.

Bill Buckle was considering re-tasking a Canberra recce for 10:00 the next day to overcome the glare problem by bringing shadows into play. Whilst he pondered this with others, Norah Seear was taking another close look at the southern end of the ridge where the pilot said at least two of the guns were positioned. Vaguely, very vaguely, Norah saw lines that might be trenches—but she could not be sure.

In COMOPS we knew that the pilot reports were accurate and that ZIPRA had certainly been where the anti-aircraft fire had come from. It was decided therefore to send in the SAS to investigate rather than run another photographic sortie, which might cause ZIPRA to move away.

Captain Bob MacKenzie moved to Kariba and, on 18 October, launched two SAS patrols by helicopter. One patrol landed well to the north of the ridge to ambush the track and the second team was put down well to the south of the ridge. Once they were down, Hunters and Canberras put in strikes. As the jets cleared, a high-flying Dakota ran parallel legs each side of the ridge, dropping incendiaries in a failed attempt to burn vegetation and deny the enemy bush cover. Orbiting high over the ridge in a Lynx piloted by Air Lieutenant Trevor Jew, Bob MacKenzie took a good look at his area of operations.

Apart from the main north/south ridge-line, a lesser ridge ran parallel to it two kilometres to the west with a bone-dry water pan surrounded by thick bush occupying much of the space between them. The vehicle track from the north passed the pan on its eastern side. Bob came to the conclusion that the main base, if occupied, was on the low ground around the dry pan with primary defences high on the ridges.

Bob and all the pilots saw trenches but no sign of people or anti-aircraft fire. The SAS patrols agreed that not a shot had been fired at any aircraft. So, all in all, it looked as if ZIPRA had vacated the position. Nevertheless, Bob MacKenzie instructed his teams to continue as briefed. This was to move closer to the base then listen and observe from ambush positions—a classic SAS task.

The southern SAS patrol had only just established its ambush after sunset when a ZIPRA patrol came their way moving through thick bush in extended formation. One ZIPRA man was killed before the main group scampered into deep cover. Blood spoor showed that others had been wounded and dragged to safety.

Because of this action, Bob ordered both patrols to break ambush and commence a move towards the main ridge. They were to link up on the high ground at first light before descending into the suspect base area. Faced with thick jesse bush conditions on a dark night, the southern patrol opted to move along the vehicle track. In doing so it ran into a ZIPRA ambush in which one of the SAS men, Lance-Corporal McLaurin, was fatally wounded. In consequence, and because another soldier was down with severe heat fatigue, the patrol moved to safety and held position until a helicopter casevac was made at first light.

Because both patrols were still well short of the ridge, helicopters moved the troops closer to their objective. At the time, the commanders of both groups were sure that ZIPRA must have pulled out of the area following afternoon and night encounters. They were seriously mistaken!

Unbeknown to the Rhodesians, a large conventionally trained and highly disciplined ZIPRA force, dug in on the ridges and pan area, awaited them. All command posts were linked by landline telephones that allowed the progress of the two SAS patrols to be relayed by those who could see them to others who could not. Not a sound could be heard by the SAS as they climbed the steep-sided ends of the ridge.

As they were nearing the top, the southern group came under unexpected intense and accurate fire from a host of weapon types. The group was pinned down and could not move in any direction without attracting angry attention. Jet support was called for.

Trevor Jew and Bob MacKenzie immediately got airborne from Kariba in a Lynx. They aimed to establish the position of the pinned-down group as well as the ZIPRA elements containing them. They arrived ahead of the jets and picked up the flash and dust of a ZIPRA recoilless-rifle firing at the trapped soldiers. In an attempt to relieve the hard-pressed soldiers, Trevor turned in with the intention of neutralising the enemy position with Frantans. Showing great discipline, the enemy had patiently withheld their fire against aircraft the previous day; but now they opened up with a vengeance the moment Trevor commenced his attack dive.

The weight of fire was too great to continue the attack and, as the Lynx pulled up and turned, it took critical strikes which forced Trevor to turn for home. On the way his damaged front engine quit and at Kariba he was forced to make a relatively high-speed belly landing because severed hydraulic lines had disabled undercarriage and flaps functions.

In the meanwhile Hunters drew all enemy attention to themselves when they put in attacks on the pan area. This

allowed the southern patrol sufficient breathing space to make a hurried withdrawal. Both patrols were then recovered to Kariba, but not before the northern group had a short contact near their helicopter pick-up point. Three ZIPRA were killed and one was captured. Miraculously, as had happened before, the captured man turned out to be a key figure. He was the logistics officer for the base.

From this important man a number of issues came to the fore. The base contained part of a battalion of ZIPRA's 1st Brigade from Mulungushi comprising over 200 conventionally trained men with another 100 men expected to arrive soon. This particular base had been established recently as the forward element for an intended invasion of Rhodesia across the Kariba dam wall. The logistics officer said the present force would definitely not abandon its position even knowing an attack was coming. Whilst plans were being made for this, the commander of the southern SAS patrol was redeployed with a smaller callsign to keep an eye on ZIPRA developments from an OP on a prominent hill feature.

Operation Tepid

WE HAD STUMBLED UPON THIS forward base at a time when disturbing intelligence was reaching COMOPS. It concerned the movement of large numbers of ZIPRA's conventional forces from Luso Boma in Angola and from Mulungushi in Zambia. Most appeared destined for CGT 2 base, which was obviously another forward launch-point for the impending invasion. In addition, large quantities of arms and equipment, including MiG 21 fighters, were reported to be arriving in Zambia.

Joshua Nkomo was obviously pulling out all the stops to get his large invasion force into Rhodesia before the Lancaster House talks progressed to a point where this might no longer be possible. Those forces he had in the country were small and ineffectual whilst the forces of his rival, Robert Mugabe, already dominated all of the Shona tribal areas and large sections of his own Matabeleland. Considering the imminent possibility of a ceasefire agreement to be followed by all-party elections, this was not a happy situation.

There was also the probability that, following a ceasefire, Kenneth Kaunda would prevent Nkomo from expatriating his weapons and equipment—particularly after having been caught out for hiding the war materials that the SAS destroyed in July.

After the war was over, we learned that Joshua believed his only hope was to launch all his forces immediately with a view to overrunning Salisbury in two fast-moving drives. If successful, he hoped to secure Rhodesian forces to his cause so that, together, the RSF and ZIPRA could destroy the common enemy ZANU. Thereafter, an interim government would be established to prepare the country for all-party elections that excluded ZANU.

At COMOPS we obviously knew nothing of this. All we knew was that we had to stem the flow of ZIPRA men and equipment to the border areas, and secure the three permanent bridges at Victoria Falls, Kariba and Chirundu. But first the troublesome base near Kariba had to be taken out in an operation codenamed 'Tepid'.

Lieutenant-Colonel Ian Bate.

The RLI and SAS were assigned to Op Tepid. Since the RLI outnumbered the SAS, command of daytime operations from a high-flying Lynx was given to OC the RLI, Lieutenant-Colonel Ian Bate. Command at night vested with OC the SAS, Lieutenant-Colonel Garth Barrett.

The basic plan was for two RLI assault groups, both moving from the north, to drive the enemy off both ridges. Once these were secured, an SAS assault force would move, also from the north, through the main base below the ridges with RLI giving supporting fire from their elevated positions.

The assault forces were choppered in at dawn on 20 October. Once they had moved forward to their start positions, SAS and RLI mortar teams were brought in to the west of the western ridge. There were tense moments when the helicopters came in to land within sight of the enemy. ZIPRA had made an excellent appraisal of likely helicopter LZs and had prepared their long-range mortars for the very positions the helicopters landed. The enemy must have enjoyed the sight of Cheetahs making a hurried departure and the mortar teams scurrying for cover.

No attempt was made to prevent ZIPRA breaking out to the south because the whole aim of the operation was to drive ZIPRA from its base and, hopefully, to force the abandonment of heavy equipment. In the event, the RLI force on the eastern ridge only reached the centre of the feature at its highest point when it was stopped dead in its tracks. Troops became pinned down by accurate fire from both their own ridge and from the western ridge. Before long, the western assault force was also bogged down through intense fire from both ridges.

The distance between the two assault forces was almost two kilometres but the enemy gun positions responsible for holding them up were less than 200 metres from each force. In consequence the use of Golf bombs was impossible, yet only Golf bombs would have been effective against the entrenched enemy who had good overhead protection.

The Rhodesians were at a distinct disadvantage. They were exposed and only had light infantry weapons, whereas ZIPRA were dug in with vastly superior heavy weapons. It was just like Mapai all over again, and a situation of stalemate existed. Yet, even though the Rhodesians were out-gunned and could not move forward, ZIPRA preferred to remain in their defensive positions, fearing to expose themselves to the jet-strikes we could not have made so close to our own forces.

Attempts to outflank enemy gun positions on the eastern ridge resulted in a number of RLI soldiers being wounded. On the western ridge, an RLI trooper had been killed. Hunters, limited to 30mm cannons and 68mm Matra rockets, were employed on numerous occasions, but no strike was really successful. ZIPRA simply dived under cover when a Hunter turned in, accepted the explosions above them and immediately emerged to continue firing at anything that moved. By sunset nothing seemed to have been achieved and the RLI was ordered to make a tactical withdrawal, under cover of darkness, to re-group.

When Garth Barrett took command that evening, nothing suggested that ZIPRA had been rattled. Everything pointed to the Rhodesians having to reorganise, bring in extra troops with heavier weapons and make another push next day. Garth realised that, even though ZIPRA seemed too strong to even consider moving out, he should position a force for this eventuality and ordered the positioning of ambushes on the vehicle track south of the base.

Between nightfall and midnight the area was quiet, but then ZIPRA unleashed a full-scale mortar bombardment on likely Rhodesian positions and even fired two 122mm rockets to add to the noise and excitement. At the time the Rhodesians had no idea that this was a cover-up to an orderly withdrawal of the entire ZIPRA force. During its move southwards, the enemy force was allowed free passage by one of the RLI's southern ambushes because the unit commander realised his force of twenty men was too weak to take on nearly 200 closely grouped ZIPRA. For this he was strongly criticised!

After the war I learned from ZIPRA that the reason for the withdrawal was that their positions had become known to the Air Force and that the Rhodesian ground forces were known to have moved some distance away. This being so, the ZIPRA commander felt certain all his positions would be annihilated by the Air Force the next day using their 'silent bombs'. This was the name given to Golf bombs because men who had been just beyond their lethal range claimed they had not heard the bombs go off. They had only experienced high over-pressure and suffered temporary deafness.

Follow-up operations got under way at first light, but only limited kills were scored against the ZIPRA force, which had taken the precaution of splitting into small groups. Nevertheless the aim of driving ZIPRA from its base had been achieved.

Operation Dice

LANCASTER HOUSE TALKS HAD BEEN on the go for six weeks when Op Tepid wrapped up, and General Peter Walls had been called to London. Before his departure, the general listened to his COMOPS planning team's ideas on how best to counter a ZIPRA invasion. We specifically argued against ambush and harassment tasks in Zambia because this would have limited effect in stemming any large-scale flow and would almost certainly lead to clashes with Zambian forces. Yet to await ZIPRA's move and deal with each crossing-point on the Zambezi River, from Rhodesian soil, was obviously ridiculous. Not only would ZIPRA make its crossings at night to minimise interference from the Rhodesian Air Force, their powerful Soviet-supplied equipment would easily drive off any protection force during the critical stages of establishing a bridgehead on Rhodesian soil. Thereafter we would be forced to destroy some of our own bridges to hold up the enemy for Air Force attention in daylight.

Only the destruction of Zambia's road bridges and culverts on all routes to our border made sense because this would prevent any large-scale movement. Our plans to cut the Great East Road from Lusaka to Malawi, the southern route from Lusaka to Chirundu, and the southwestern route from Lusaka to Livingstone were already complete.

General Walls needed no persuading. He realised only too well that Rhodesia's David could only beat ZIPRA's Goliath in this way. However, he was at pains to make us understand that the destruction of a Commonwealth member's bridges would wreck any hope of the British Government showing any sympathy to the Muzorewa Government's cause.

Whilst, from his understanding of the goings-on at Lancaster House, he doubted that any such empathy existed, we could not rock the boat just yet. General Walls said he would be in a better position to judge all issues once he got to London. In the meanwhile the SAS, Selous Scouts and RLI were to get on with the job of harassing ZIPRA movements. In consequence, Operation Dice started out with ambushing tasks to make access to Victoria Falls, Kariba and Chirundu difficult.

Masses of bridge demolition gear prepared for Op Manacle in Mozambique lay begging to be used when it was all too obvious to the frustrated SAS that only the destruction of bridges could meet our Zambian objectives. So, even though they had been told Op Dice only called for harassing work, SAS moved all the demolition gear to Kariba; just in case. It is just as well these explosives were immediately available. Without any forewarning during the night of 15 November, a signal

from General Walls to COMOPS ordered the immediate implementation of our plans to destroy Zambian bridges.

Ian Smith had returned home from the Lancaster House talks on 11 November. On his arrival at the airport he told reporters that the British had manoeuvred the Muzorewa Government into accepting a bad agreement. He said there was now no alternative but to make the best of a bad deal. Without actually saying so, he implied (in my mind) that the British Conservative chairman of the conference, that poisonous snake Lord Carrington, had deliberately set the stage for a communist party take-over.

Lancaster House talks, 11 November 1979.

Thirteen times Rhodesians had celebrated Rhodesia's Independence Day on 11 November but this was now a thing of the past—there was no longer anything to celebrate. This is why, even if General Wall's 'green light' on the bridges seemed at odds with what Ian Smith had said four days earlier, we were delighted that Rhodesians were not going to take things lying down.

Whilst lawyers in London settled down to preparing written agreement for all parties' signatures at some time in December, the SAS moved in on the bridges with RLI troops in support. We all knew they had to act fast before any political change in direction occurred. In four days, nine primary road bridges and one rail bridge were dumped. The SAS demolition teams had become so expert in their tasks that bridges were downed even before their Cheetah transport had reached their refuelling points back in Rhodesia. This not only resulted in the ground teams having an unnecessarily long wait for recovery, it put our COMOPS planners back to work revising methods, movement plans and time-scales for the destruction of Mozambican bridges in Op Manacle.

Eight of the Zambian bridges had been specifically selected to curb ZIPRA's movements to the border. Another two across the Mubulashi River were not. Whereas we were disallowed from taking any action against railway bridges on the line from Lusaka to South Africa, the rail bridge on the Tanzam rail line and an adjacent road bridge over the Mubulashi River were taken out. This was to complement the downing of the Chambeshi bridges on the same line five weeks earlier and to deliberately pressurise the Zambia Government. If this over-stressed Kenneth Kaunda's economy, it was nothing compared to what was planned next. The same SAS commander who had taken out the fuel refinery at Beira in Mozambique was about to launch a purely SAS raid to destroy Zambia's large fuel refinery at Ndola. Simultaneous with this, Op Manacle was to go ahead on the Mozambican bridges. This was all very exciting stuff but it came to an abrupt end on 22 November when General Walls signalled COMOPS instructing that all external offensive operations were to cease forthwith. The war in Zambia and Mozambique was over. ZIPRA was out of the game, but General Walls instructed that internal operations against ZANLA were to be intensified until the expected ceasefire came into effect. He said this might occur before Christmas.

Chapter

10

Ceasefire

A TOTAL CEASEFIRE WAS TO come into immediate effect when all parties to the Lancaster House agreement signed the enacting document. As soon as this happened, the warring forces would cease hostilities and all BSA policemen were to revert to normal policing duties. The RSF were to return to barracks whilst ZIPRA and ZANLA forces were to move into sixteen (later increased to seventeen) assigned Assembly Points (APs) inside Rhodesia. The APs were to be under the control and protection of a Commonwealth Monitoring Force (CMF). Nothing was said of the Pfumo re Vanhu auxiliaries though, ultimately, they also remained in their bases.

In addition to his main duties, the Commanding General of CMF was to head a Ceasefire Committee. This committee of eight, comprising two officers each from the British Army, the RSF, ZIPRA and ZANLA, was to facilitate inter-force co-operation and deal with any ceasefire violations that might occur.

When Lieutenant-General Walls returned to COMOPS from London, he called me to his office to tell me that, when the time came, I was to be his personal representative on the Ceasefire Committee. He said, "I refuse to sit with those bloody Brits and communists or give them any sense of equal rank with myself or any of the service commanders." Because I held the rank group captain (Army equivalent colonel) he decided to lend weight of rank to RSF representation by recalling Major-General Bert Barnard from retirement, but only to attend committee meetings. All executive functions were to be handled by me. My lack of faith in Bert Barnard caused me some concern but, in the event, we got on fine.

In addition to Ceasefire Committee work, it would be my responsibility to act as the liaison officer between ZIPRA, ZANLA and COMOPS. This meant I had to establish a close personal relationship with the top commanders with a view to providing General Walls feedback on all relevant matters. In addition, I was to do whatever I could to ensure that the senior men were adequately cared for and give them whatever assistance I considered reasonable. No funds or other guidelines were given.

It was such an anticlimax returning to routine operations, though my time was taken up to some extent in preparing for the early arrival of CMF military contingents. From early December, RAF C130 transporters arrived daily at Salisbury Airport and New Sarum ferrying in tons of equipment and Commonwealth soldiers from UK, Australia, New Zealand, Kenya and Fiji. Puma helicopters and large trucks came in by USAF C5 (Galaxy) heavy transporters.

On 12 December 1979, the British Governor and his wife, Lord and Lady Soames, arrived to strains of 'God Save the Queen'. This all seemed so unreal to us who were once such ardent royalists. Rhodesians did not leap to attention as in times before UDI but simply looked on in stunned silence. The long years of sanctions were over, but it was impossible to fully comprehend that the country was now effectively in British Government hands, for the first time in history.

After the Governor's arrival came two senior ZANLA commanders, Rex Nhongo (deputy commander) and Josiah Tungamirai (chief political commissar) who landed at Salisbury Airport to rapturous applause from thousands of black folk who had been forcibly 'bussed in' to welcome them. Later, at the same airport, the arrival of Joshua Nkomo with ZIPRA's commanders, Lookout Masuku and Dumiso Dabengwa turned out to be a low-key affair.

I first met the CMF Commander, Major-General John Acland, at a cocktail party given by him to introduce his staff officers to General Walls, his staff officers and their wives. Being a purely military affair with no political overtones, it was a surprisingly easy-going occasion. One of the officers we met was married to a lady whose name was to become well known. He was Lieutenant-Colonel Parker-Bowles.

Following the signing of the Lancaster House Agreement in London by Muzorewa, Mugabe, Nkomo and Lord Carrington, the ceasefire came into effect at midnight on 23 December. The next morning, the first of the ZANLA and ZIPRA men trickled into the Assembly Points that had been made ready by CMF teams during the preceding two weeks.

Even before this I had been in daily contact with ZIPRA and ZANLA commanders and their staffs who were billeted in the Audio-Visual Centre of the University of Rhodesia. From day one I found it easy to communicate with ZIPRA's Lookout Masuku and Dumiso Dabengwa. Both smiled easily and acted in a friendly manner. Their ZIPRA staff members were smart, efficient and courteous. Being the commander of ZIPRA, Masuku dressed in camouflage uniform and wore a Russian officer's peak cap with no badge or emblem on its red band. Dabengwa wore smart-casual civilian dress.

ZANLA was very different. It took ages before Rex Nhongo and Josiah Tungamirai opened up to any degree, possibly because they suffered major daily hangovers from heavy drinking. From the moment of our first meeting, Rex pressurised me to arrange for the return of his Toyota Land Cruiser taken by Selous Scouts at New Chimoio. The uniformed ZANLA commanders and men were surly and slovenly. Visits to ZANLA at the Audio-Visual Centre were initially made uncomfortable by particularly mean-looking individuals who delighted in cocking their AK-47 rifles as I passed. Once he got to know me better and having been promised the return of his Land Cruiser, Rex Nhongo put an end to this nonsense.

On Christmas Day we received news that ZANLA's top commander, Josiah Tongogara, had been killed in a vehicle accident in Mozambique. He was due to arrive in Rhodesia a few days later, having completed his briefing of all ZANLA forces still in Mozambique. At the time I was unaffected by this news because I thought Tongogara would be no easier to deal with than Nhongo and Tungamirai. I now know I was wrong to think that way.

Josiah Tongogara.

Rex Nhongo and Josiah Tungamirai seemed unmoved by the loss of their commander whereas ZIPRA's hierarchy was visibly shaken and depressed by the news of Tongogara's death. Masuku told me angrily that this had been no accident—it was nothing more than a deliberate assassination of a powerful military leader by radical members of ZANU's political wing. Explanation for this was to come later but some time passed before a highly qualified mortician from Doves Morgan Funeral Services in Salisbury was sent to Maputo to view Tongogara's body. Having done this, Ken Stokes concluded that Tongogara had died as the result of a vehicle accident and that no foul play was involved. You will see shortly why ZIPRA agreed with the vehicle accident aspect, but not with the 'no foul play' conclusion.

Meetings of the Ceasefire Committee were held every Monday and Thursday in a small natty conference room in an outbuilding in the lovely gardens of Government House. General Acland sat at the head of the long table with Brigadier Gurdon at the other end. General Barnard and I were on one side of the table with General Barnard closest to General Acland. ZIPRA and ZANLA sat opposite us. ZANLA's Rex Nhongo sat closest to General Acland with Tungamirai next to him. Then came Lookout Masuku with Dabengwa sitting nearest to Brigadier Gurdon.

In this photograph taken at the start of a Ceasefire Committee meeting, Dumiso Dabengwa (left) and Rex Nhongo decided to pose as heads of their military wings whilst Lookout Masuku and Josiah Tungamirai watched from behind the camera. Next are the British Army officers, Brigadier Gurdon and General Acland. Rhodesians are General Barnard and Group Captain PB. The man in the background (left) is Lieutenant-Colonel Parker-Bowles.

To begin with no staff accompanied General Barnard and me, whereas ZIPRA and ZANLA always had six or more seated and standing behind them. Later we had one intelligence officer and a very good-looking female secretary, Miss Gardener, sitting behind us to record proceedings.

General John Acland conferred the title 'general' on each of the 'guerrilla' commanders in an obvious endeavour to give them equal status with himself and General Bert Barnard. In these circumstances I was the most junior man on the committee yet, almost from the start, I became aware of the fact that both ZIPRA and ZANLA looked me in the eye when making any contentious statement or responding to any query concerning cease-fire violations. I found this distinctly uncomfortable as any question from, say, General Acland, would be answered directly at me. Explanation for this took some time in coming.

Most ceasefire infringements were levelled against ZANLA because, from the very beginning, it was obvious that ZANLA had kept the majority of its forces in the field and sent thousands of *mujibas* to the Assembly Points under control of a handful of genuine ZANLA juniors. ZANLA managed to fool the British who were only interested in the 'number of ZANLA soldiers' inside the APs. However, this situation incensed General Walls and the National JOC, the only Zimbabwe–Rhodesian authority able to challenge the Brits to hold to the rules set out in the Lancaster House Agreement.

Most ceasefire violations resulted from election campaigning rifts between ZANLA and the Pfumo re Vanhu auxiliaries of Muzorewa and Sitole, whereas a few were undoubtedly generated by Selous Scouts who had kept some men in the field to monitor the extent of ZANLA violations. In the three months preceding elections, only a handful of problems were raised by or against ZIPRA whose forces within the country had moved into the Assembly Points in accordance with the London agreement. We knew however that over 10,000 ZIPRA men had remained in Zambia.

ZANLA, on the other hand, had withheld some 17,000 men in Mozambique and used the forces in the country to force a Mugabe victory at the polls through viciously applied intimidation on the civilian population together with selective murder. Their line was, "ZANU started the war and only Mugabe can stop it. If Mugabe does not win the elections, the war continues and you will pay for it with your lives". This was an impelling reason to vote for Mugabe. It was also precisely what we expected from him having known from the start that he would flout any agreement, particularly with Britain.

Although this was in direct contravention of the London agreement, and in spite of overwhelming evidence to prove it, Lord Soames refused to rule against ZANU's participation in the elections. Unfortunately General Walls, being a military man, seemed out of his depth in dealing with Soames and a Conservative Government that continued to rely on the manipulations and lies engineered by the British Foreign Office.

Meeting after meeting Rex Nhongo and Josiah Tungamirai whispered to each other in their Shona vernacular. Most of the whispered communications held up proceedings whilst they conspired to find a way out of every accusation levelled at ZANLA and to conjure up counter-accusations. Both ZANLA men seemed particularly concerned not to be overheard by ZIPRA who would understand what was being said, but they were quite unconcerned about the four whites who they were quite certain could not understand their language. They were wrong! I understood all I heard.

Some time in late February or early March, I foolishly let loose on Rex Nhongo in his own tongue challenging his past and present whispered lies. This had an electrifying effect on the meeting and obviously tickled the ZIPRA commanders who did nothing to suppress their mirth. Thereafter the whispering ceased, but I continued to be the one to whom every difficult communication was directed.

The general elections were due to take place over three days commencing 27 March. Thereafter the new government would rely on the military to oversee the integration of all armed forces. It was obvious to me that my liaison tasks between our past enemies and COMOPS could not adequately prepare the ground for such a complex process. I conveyed this opinion to General Walls and suggested that a joint headquarters be established to prepare for integration and the calling-in of arms and equipment. It was a relief to learn that he recognised this need and had already earmarked a recently built wing at Army HQ for the purpose, though the move would not take place until the election results were known.

Dinner with ZIPRA

ZIPRA COMMANDERS TOLD ME THEY had no difficulty in opening up to any Rhodesian but they strongly distrusted ZANLA and the Brits. Both Masuku and Dabengwa said they could not talk to me freely at the Audio-Visual Centre or in the grounds of Government House—the only places we met. So, when I suggested they come to my home for dinner, they immediately agreed. The reason I did not offer dinner at a hotel or restaurant was that I had no funds to meet expenses that I could better afford at my own table.

The look on Beryl's face when I told her that the ZIPRA commanders were coming to dinner was one of utter disbelief. When Beryl relayed the news to our Shona housekeeper-cook Sarah, her eyes widened in horror whereas our N'debele gardener Obert was delighted. Sarah's fears were calmed and she was asked to provide a three-course meal, including roast beef and Yorkshire pudding, just as she would do for any of our regular friends.

Accompanying Lookout was his wife Gift and Dumiso came alone. Beryl drank brandy and ginger ale and I had beer even though the three visitors asked for cool drinks. Before and during dinner, Debbie and Paul were with us and the general conversation was very easy-going. The visitors were at pains to greet Sarah and later praise her for an excellent meal.

Throughout the evening it was very noticeable that Gift kept her right hand covered with the shawl she was wearing, even when eating. After dinner the children had gone off to their rooms when Beryl asked Gift how she felt about being with us. Following a moment of hesitation, Lookout suddenly uncovered Gift's hand and placed his palm directly on hers. "Look we are whole," he said raising they hands, "Five fingers." We knew Lookout had a finger missing on his left hand, but had not realised that Gift hid her hand to cover the loss of a thumb. By showing that her missing thumb and his missing finger were obscured by the presence of the other's hand, Lookout was handling Gift's hesitation and expressing in this strange way that all was well. He then told us how he and Gift had lost their digits.

When he heard explosions during the SAS attack on Nkomo's home in Lusaka, Lookout awakened his sleeping wife and two children, got them into his car and rushed off to a safe house with his bodyguard in tow. He made the mistake of routing via Liberation Centre just as the SAS force was withdrawing from it. Having driven through a blinding hail of gunfire, Lookout pressed on to a friend's house close by and only just reached there when his damaged engine seized. The bodyguard was dead, Gift and both children were severely wounded and Lookout had also been hit. The whole family was flown to Moscow where they recovered to health after many weeks of medical attention. The only externally visible signs of the ordeal were the missing thumb and finger.

A few days after their first meeting, Beryl bumped into Gift who was very distressed because one of her children, who had survived the shooting, had drowned in a private swimming pool in one of Salisbury's posh suburbs.

Dumiso carried on with the subject of Nkomo's house attack to tell how Joshua and his wife left home in a hurry for Kaunda's palace immediately upon receiving a late-night warning of the impending attack. Whilst on the subject, I asked him about the NSO attack. Dumiso confirmed that he and other senior men had kept well clear of the NSO for fear of a Rhodesian attack, which he thought would only take place at night. He had taken up night-time residence with a girlfriend and returned daily to the NSO no later than 06:00. On the day of the attack, he intended to do the same but his girlfriend said she had dreamed of jets attacking at dawn. She insisted he remain at home for at least two hours to relax with a cup of coffee and listen to the radio. Dumiso obliged.

As it happened, Hunters attacked FC camp at dawn, but Dumiso did not know this at the time. The first he knew of any hostile activity was when he heard explosions and firing at NSO. He claimed that this was not the only occasion that dreams had saved him from RSF attacks.

I asked Dumiso and Lookout why, when difficult issues were raised during ceasefire meetings they and the ZANLA commanders always addressed me. The answer was surprising. They said ZIPRA's reason for doing this was identical to ZANLA's. Both insisted that the Air Force was superior to the Army. They considered themselves to be on an equal footing

with the Army because they used similar equipment and fought on their feet. The Air Force was quite different. In their minds it was this complex high-tech force that had been responsible for the devastation visited upon their own forces. Because of this I was held in highest esteem at the Ceasefire Committee meetings.

Breaking away from the after dinner chat for a moment—Rex Nhongo had much the same to tell me later. But when I challenged him on the issue and said that the RLI had knocked hell out of his forces, he asked, "When did that happen without Air Force direct support and fire power?"

I tried again. "What about the SAS, they knocked the socks off you guys?" "Yes", he said, "but they are Air Force troops!" I told him he was wrong. "Rex, SAS are Army troops." His reply was typical. "Comrade Group Captain PB, the war is over so you do not have to lie to me any more. You know, and I know, that the SAS are Air Force troops. They live over the runway from Air Force, they are always with Air Force, they wear wings and blue belts, their badge has a helicopter rotor blade (in the illustration it can be seen that this is actually a dagger) and, just like the Air Force pilots, they only attacked my men, never civilians."

Returning to the after-dinner chat, Dumiso and Lookout happily answered many questions and I answered theirs. They confirmed ZIPRA's intention to launch an invasion but this was stymied by the destruction of bridges during Op Dice. Worse still, it removed any hope of joining up with the RSF to bring about the destruction of ZANLA.

They had a lot to say about the efficiency of Rhodesian-made air weapons and told me they had recently learned that I was the prime mover in developing them. Rather than being annoyed by this they were deeply impressed because, like ZANLA, they had previously believed the weapons were South African products.

We then came to the matter of ZANLA's Josiah Tongogara. I asked them why they had been so distressed about the news of his death. The story went back a long way to a time before Tongogara and his DARE had been imprisoned following the death of ZANLA's Operations Chief, Herbert Chitepo. From those early days right through to Lancaster House, ZIPRA had found Tongogara to be open and scrupulously honest. He was the only ZANU or ZANLA man in whom they had implicit trust.

During the Lancaster House Conference, Josiah Tongogara made telephonic contact with Lookout and Dumiso from his hotel room. Tongogara said there was urgent need for a serious discussion on proposals he wished to place before them. He offered to meet at any place of ZIPRA's choice. Dumiso and Lookout said they were happy to meet Josiah at his hotel, in his own room.

On arrival, they found that Tongogara had Josiah Tungamirai with him. They were not at all happy about this knowing that Tungamirai headed ZANLA's political commissariat, a communist affliction ZIPRA used but which the seniors of ZIPRA could not abide. Anyway Tongogara seemed unperturbed and, working from notes, he got straight down to business.

He started off by expressing the hope that the conference would succeed because he was not prepared to see a continuation of war and the loss of more young lives simply to satisfy greedy politicians. He said he feared that either Mugabe or Nkomo, possibly both, would walk out of the conference. If this occurred, he for one wished to take matters out of political hands but he needed help to achieve this. If ZIPRA agreed with his wish to withdraw all forces from contact, it would then be essential to get to General Peter Walls before he left London and draw him into also taking joint action. Tongogara then spelled out a plan that was unconditionally accepted by the ZIPRA commanders.

For me it was really quite incredible to learn that Josiah Tongogara, the man we took to be our radical archenemy, was a man who really sought peace and stability. Recorded here are the points of agreement he made with ZIPRA—as I recall them.

First was the matter of setting up a military triumvirate of the RSF, ZIPRA and ZANLA, initially in London. Their joint task would be to bring into immediate effect a disconnection of forces. Tongogara had no difficulty in accepting that General Walls should head the triumvirate whose headquarters would be established in Salisbury and separated from existing RSF establishments. ZIPRA and ZANLA would order all their forces to move into military camps on home soil at locations agreed by General Walls.

Under direct control of the military triumvirate, a process

Sir Humphrey Gibbs.

of weeding-out and disarming undesirables would be implemented. Those who wished to retire or return to their homes would be free to do so. Thereafter integration of the three forces would commence. Since Tongogara believed this would take at least five years to complete, he expected that many more willing volunteers would leave the ranks during this time.

The military triumvirate would impose on 'Zimbabwe' a 100-seat interim government of national unity represented in equal part by the parties currently headed by Muzorewa, Smith, Nkomo and Mugabe. Overseeing this government would be an 'Executive Governor' who Tongogara believed should be Sir Humphrey Gibbs because he was the only person who would be acceptable to all parties, including the British and African governments.

Selection of ministers to administer existing civil services was to be established by majority vote for approval by the Governor. Existing RF ministers, if not returned to their positions by popular vote, would be asked to assist new ministers for a period of at least one year.

A general election would be withheld for five years or be undertaken after the military integration process was complete; whichever was the longer period. No direct British interference or participation would be tolerated. If South Africa objected to the new order, African ports would be used to the mutual benefit of central African states. Mandatory sanctions could be expected to fall away automatically and the South African Government's stranglehold on the country would no longer be an issue. (I was surprised to learn that Tongogara knew of this.)

No active support would be given to any nationalist party or force acting against South Africa. This was to guard against any external aggression from that quarter.

It would be the military triumvirate's urgent task to settle any fears within the population, black and white, and seek their backing and assistance to make Zimbabwe a prosperous and happy place again. Tourism was to be actively promoted and anyone wishing to leave the country should be allowed to do so without any restrictions or penalties being applied so as not to induce doubt or panic in others.

This was the basic plan that may very well have come into being if Mugabe, having walked out at Lancaster House, had not been forced to return to the talks by President Machel. Mugabe was at Heathrow Airport intending to fly off to New York when Machel told him to get back to the Lancaster House talks immediately or else withdraw his forces from Mozambique.

ZIPRA believed Mugabe relied heavily on Tongogara's strength and backing and that he would have been in a stronger position had Tongogara returned to the country. However, the radical political members of ZANU saw him as a threat to their own futures, having obviously been given the details of Tongogara's discussion with ZIPRA by Josiah Tungamirai.

Whatever their reasons, they hired a well-known East German assassin to kill Tongogara. This particular assassin specialised in 'vehicle accident'.

Lookout said that the assassin, whose typically German name I have forgotten, arrived in Maputo ten days before Tongogara's death. Three days after the fatal vehicle 'accident' and immediately prior to his departure for Europe, Enos Nkala met him at Maputo Airport to make payment, in American dollar notes, on behalf of himself, Simon Muzenda, Dr Herbert Ushewokunze, Edgar Tekere, Edison Zvobgo and a couple of others, for services rendered.

Visits to ZANLA Assembly Points

THE SEVENTEEN ASSEMBLY POINTS IN which ZANLA and ZIPRA personnel were being housed and fed by the CMF were given the name of the place upon which each was established. For simplicity's sake, alphabetic identification was also used. These were A to R. (the letter 'I' is not used as a military abbreviation to avoid confusion with the numeral '1')

Sequentially identified around the border areas in a clockwise direction were the APs commencing with the first ZANLA group located at AP Alpha near Hoya in the northeast. AP Romeo at Rukomechi Mission in the north was the last ZIPRA point. All APs were to be visited by the Ceasefire Committee.

Because we would be the first senior RSF officers any of our former enemies would be seeing in the flesh, General Barnard and I were apprehensive, but not to the same extent as the ZIPRA and ZANLA commanders who were about to visit each other's armed forces.

We set out for AP Alpha early one morning in an RAF Puma helicopter. The crew of this helicopter, like many of their colleagues, had experienced difficulty in map-reading their way around the country with no familiar navigational aids to help them. I told the skipper not to worry as I would be keeping an eye on our position from the rear cabin and he could call me forward if he needed to do so.

I sat with Rex Nhongo and Mugabe's deputy Simon Muzenda because we would be traversing areas that Rex had walked eight years earlier. I found it both strange and surprisingly pleasing to show Rex such places as his original base on the escarpment next to St Albert's Mission, the route he had taken from the Musengezi River up the escarpment and the location of Altena Farm where his first action triggered Operation Hurricane.

The visits to AP Alpha and Bravo went off well enough, though it was patently obvious that most of the men in the camps were anything but bona fide ZANLA. The few regulars were easy to spot because they carried standard issue AK-47 assault rifles that were in fair condition. The rest carried old beaten-up SKS rifles that had been out of use for over ten years save for the few issued to LTTs in 1972. At Marymount Mission (AP Bravo) I saw half a dozen sophisticated Swiss sniper rifles. They were obviously brand spanking new, never having been exposed to the rigours of the bush, but none had ammunition.

I stayed very close to Rex Nhongo wherever he went, just in case anyone decided to take a pot shot at me. I noticed that Lookout and Dumiso were doing the same and that Generals Acland and Barnard, accompanied by Brigadier Gurdon, kept close to the CFM officers.

Of all the ZANLA APs we visited I remember AP Charlie best. It was situated at the disused Nyagoma School in the extreme northeast. Here the ZANLA inmates were accommodated in British Army tents set in lines under a forest of superb trees that formed a continuous overhead canopy over many acres.

This photograph was taken late in the visit during a refuelling stop at Kariba. From left: Rex Nhongo, unknown standing in for Tungamirai, General Acland, Lookout Masuku, Brigadier Gurdon, PB, General Barnard and Dumiso Dabengwa.

During our briefing in one of the classrooms by Australian CFM officers, a landmine detonated in the Cordon Sanitaire some five kilometres to our east. A few minutes passed before a second mine detonated causing the AP's senior ZANLA man to rise from behind me and move to Rex who was sitting directly in front of me. He bent down and whispered in Rex's ear, "*Madora wa tuka.*" This annoyed Rex who, in a loud voice, asked the man if he thought he was deaf. Of course he had heard the mines explode, "They must have been triggered by baboons."

After the briefing we strolled through the camp to an open

patch of ground where over 1,500 armed men stood five lines deep along three sides of a box formation. We positioned at the centre of the fourth side and Rex Nhongo moved to the centre of the square to give the gathering the same message he gave at every assembly point. This was to say the war was over and everyone had to work together to establish the new Zimbabwe. He had brought two senior RSF 'comrades' with him to prove that he was already working with his previous enemies. He said nothing about the Brits.

Having completed his talk he signalled me forward to address the gathering and introduced me in Shona. "This is Comrade Group Captain PB, once our enemy in the sky but now my friend. He will tell you why he has come to see you." I asked Rex if I should speak in the vernacular. "Certainly not," he said, "I do not want these people to know you understand their language. I will interpret what you say." So I made a series of short statements in English and Rex passed these on in Shona.

Right to left: General Barnard, General Acland, PB, Dumiso Dabengwa and Lookout Masuku.

At one point Rex misinterpreted what I had just said, deliberately I think, so I asked him to correct this. He immediately told the men that I was not satisfied with his interpretation and corrected the error. I nodded in agreement and completed what I had to say in mediocre Shona. Only in Africa could such anomalies pass without fuss. Rex then led the gathering in song, as was ZANLA's custom at the conclusion of every meeting.

Only people who have experienced massed African voices in the open will understand the power, richness and purity of sound that comes from a people who harmonise perfectly without training or effort. I hated the *chimurenga* lyrics but the sheer volume and beauty of voice overrode the objectionable racial hatred expressed in the words.

Having left our position, every head was turned to watch us passing behind one echelon when I spotted a face I recognised. I immediately broke away from the official party and strode

through five lines of perplexed men, mostly armed *mujibas*. The man I was moving towards turned away abruptly.

When I reached him, I asked, "Hey Timothy, what are you doing here?" There was no reply and he remained facing away from me looking down at his own feet. Accepting this rejection, I said, "Behave yourself Timothy. Visit me when you get to Salisbury."

The official party had come to a halt to see what I was doing. As I returned to Rex's side, he asked me who it was I had spoken to. I said I knew him as Timothy. Our servants in Salisbury had told Beryl and me about a youngster who was sleeping in a toilet in the suburb of Hatfield where we lived. He had lost his parents in the Mtoko area and, though tended by an uncle, was living a miserable existence. We decided to take him on as an assistant to Obert, our gardener. Timothy was given a warm comfortable bed, clothing, food and spending money. He was fine for many months and we were about to send him for schooling at our expense when he began to give Sarah and Obert a hard time. He had been warned to behave himself, but this did not work so we got rid of him. A year had passed since last I saw him.

Rex listened to my story then expressed his mirth with his typical deep belly laugh rolled into his rough smoker's voice as he said, "He will be in for a tough time now! Everyone here has seen you and heard you talk. First they may wonder why you went to Timothy, but will then come to the conclusion he was passing information on ZANLA's activities to you in Salisbury."

The implications of this were frightening, so I asked Rex to make sure no harm came to the young man. "Do not worry," said Rex, "he will not be hurt too badly. After what you did for him he deserves a bit of rough treatment for letting you down." (In July 1980 Timothy was disbanded and visited us in Salisbury. He was well and confirmed that he had been severely harassed, "but not too badly hurt.")

Of all the Commonwealth Monitoring Force teams in the ZANLA bases, only the Fijian team at AP Hotel appeared

ZANLA mujibas.

to be popular with the inmates where there was a modicum of order and discipline. This probably had a lot to do with the colour of the Fijian's skin. Otherwise all ZANLA APs were packed with scruffy, ill-disciplined *mujibas* who scowled and slouched about. As already mentioned, there was very little evidence of men possessing the calibre and looks that typified the ZANLA operators we had either killed or captured in operations. Other than the Swiss sniper rifles, weapons were old and dilapidated. The operational weapons inside Rhodesia were very obviously still in the field with many hundreds of ZANLA's regulars involved in electioneering work.

Unlike General Barnard and me, General Acland and Brigadier Gurdon seemed impressed with what they saw, whereas Lookout Masuku and Dumiso Dabengwa were horrified and their disdain for ZANLA showed clearly in their facial expressions.

No notice whatsoever was taken of our comments about the types and state of weapons until these Brits saw how ZIPRA's men were armed.

Visits to ZIPRA APs

AFTER ZANLA, ZIPRA LOCATIONS WERE like a breath of fresh air. It certainly opened the eyes of the Brits and might even have made them realise why we insisted that all ZANLA APs were full of *mujibas*. The reason Rhodesians preferred ZIPRA was immediately apparent to General Acland and Brigadier Gurdon. They could see that the ZIPRA men were dressed in clean, crisply pressed uniforms; they moved with purpose, smiled easily, displayed good discipline and acted with courtesy.

It was possible to walk around without an escort, which I enjoyed. Wherever I went I was saluted and greeted in a friendly manner and also drew men who wanted to walk and talk with a Rhodesian Air Force pilot. It was only at AP Romeo, the very last Assembly Point to be visited, where Lookout Masuku had unusual events planned.

As our helicopter was making its long descending approach to Rukomechi Mission, one could not help but notice, from about five kilometres out, that many anti-aircraft guns were tracking the Puma helicopter. Lookout Masuku had forewarned the RAF crew of the guns so the helicopter captain was perfectly happy to maintain direction and descent.

Because nothing had been said to any of us in the rear cabin, the sight of those tracking guns put fear in the eyes of Simon Muzenda, Rex Nhongo and Tungamirai's deputy. I was also feeling uncomfortable until I saw the smile on Lookout's face as he winked at me.

When we alighted from the helicopter, the bush that surrounded the small LZ came alive as hundreds of armed ZIPRA men rose from the cover they had used to camouflage their presence. The Brits seemed impressed and ZANLA shrugged it of as unnecessary bravado.

Guard of honour.   *This style of marching, both fascist and communist.*

A guard of honour awaited our arrival and General Barnard was invited to inspect the men dressed in East German fleck-camouflage uniforms. Their goose-step march-past made my skin crawl, but one could not miss the fact that we were watching trained soldiers.

This style of marching, both fascist and communist, made my skin crawl.

After the usual briefing, this time by ZIPRA officers, we were invited to a parade to be followed by a weapons demonstration. Some 2,000 ZIPRA soldiers were formed up in tiered lines from ground level to the top of the long earth embankment that served as a grandstand for the mission's football field. The visiting party formed up in a line facing the assembly with CMF and ZIPRA officers behind.

Lookout Masuku moved forward and gave a short message to his troops. He then said that he would introduce the members of the Ceasefire Committee individually. Lookout gave place of honour to the Rhodesians and for reasons already known to me I was introduced first. I simply took one pace forward, saluted and stepped back into line. General Barnard followed me. Next Lookout introduced General Acland and Brigadier Gurdon before ZANLA.

Rex Nhongo was standing right beside me. As he stepped forward to salute, he was greeted with the menacing metallic sounds of heavy weapons being cocked. Being so close to him I went cold, expecting to be shot at any moment. Rex ignored the deliberate insult, saluted and stepped back. When Tungamirai's deputy stepped forward, weapons were cocked again. ZIPRA's hatred of ZANLA had been shown in a very graphic but typically African way!

Formalities over, we were asked to turn around to watch anti-aircraft crews deploy and fire their weapons. In the absence of an air target, a prominent white rock on a large hill about three kilometres away to our left was declared to be the target.

Whistles were blown and out of the bush to our right emerged three crews pulling wheeled guns to a position some thirty metres to our front. One 23mm and two 14.7mm guns were set up quickly, and one of the 14.7 pieces commenced firing but jammed after expending about ten rounds. The others then opened fire, creating one hell of a din. Green and red tracer rounds raced away with the red 23mm rounds travelling noticeably faster than the green ones. The accuracy was impressive.

The senior ZIPRA commander of AP Romeo insisted that I should take a close look at the guns. He boasted that these had shot down some of our aircraft at Kariba. I did not argue with him because he seemed so pleased about something that never happened.

COMBINED OPERATIONS HEADQUARTERS
FEBRUARY 1980

Back row: S. Karoulis, K. E. Wainer, Pte (RWS) C. A. Brooking, H. F. Dixon, WO2 J. Knight, C. Gardiner, C/Sgt (RWS) M. S. Finch, Cpl (RWS) K. M. Anderson, M. M. Partington. Centre row: A. Webb, Lt N. Dunn, Lt-Col B. G. Robinson OLM MCM, Maj A. M. Linder OLM, Maj A. B. C. H. Dalton OLM, Sqn Ldr R. R. MacGregor, Col H. Meyer, Wg Cdr C. J. Dixon DCD, A. J. Barthorpe, I. Young, S. Stevenson, Sgt R. D. Williams, W. Ackhurst. Seated: C Supt R. H. H. E. Harvey, Lt-Col J. M. Templer, Lt-Col P. J. Burford MLM, P. R. Cocksedge, Brig L. Jacobs MLM, B. Page MLM, Lt-Gen B. P. Walls GLM DCD MBE, Air Mshl M. J. McLaren CLM, Maj-Gen A. B. Campling DCD, Gp Capt P. J. H. Petter-Bowyer MLM DCD, Asst Cmmr G. E. Hedhes, C Supt A. J. Worden, Col E. M. Willar (Rtd) MLM DMM.

Elections

UNTIL A NEW GOVERNMENT WAS elected into power, management of the country vested with the British Government in the person of Governor Lord Soames, though law and order remained in the hands of NATJOC. In terms of the Lancaster House Agreement, Lord Soames had the responsibility of preparing all polling stations and ensuring voters enjoyed total security and freedom of choice. Of greater importance was his responsibility to ensure that no political party indulged in the intimidation of voters during the lead-up to elections. Any party found guilty of intimidation was to be disqualified wholly or in part by proscribing specific electoral zones.

In this task Lord Soames failed dismally. Mugabe's ZANU party not only disregarded its undertaking to get all ZANLA into the APs, it kept 90% of its forces in the field with orders to indulge in cruel electioneering methods including murder of important members of black opposition parties. Soames knew this was going on but refused to invalidate Mugabe's party either wholly or in those areas where intimidation was greatest. The British had neither the courage nor integrity to stand by the very agreement they had brought upon the four contesting parties. Appeasement in the face of threats from the OAU and black Commonwealth leaders was obviously more important to Britain's long-term objectives than the future of the people of Zimbabwe–Rhodesian. When Henry Kissinger met Ian Smith many months later he explained the paradox like this. "The politics of convenience has little to do with truth or logic!"

We had become accustomed to British duplicity but could not abide what we perceived to be total inaction by our NATJOC in forcing Lord Soames to act on British undertakings. The NATJOC's attention seemed wholly distracted by other matters.

For some weeks a team had been assembled in COMOPS to monitor loads of incoming data to pre-determine the final outcome of elections. Information poured in from all provinces giving voter numbers and their political leanings. As I recall it, the opinion being expressed to NATJOC was that Ian Smith's RF party would secure all twenty white seats and Joshua Nkomo was sure to get at least twenty N'debele seats. Muzorewa and Sithole only needed to win eleven seats to allow a coalition between these parties to block Mugabe's ZANU party. The team advising NATJOC was adamant that Muzorewa alone would do better than this.

I was having a drink in the small COMOPS pub one evening when, inevitably, the elections became the topic of conversation. Some time earlier I had come to the firm conclusion that, short of proscribing ZANU, there was absolutely no hope of stopping Mugabe coming to power. I expressed this opinion but had no chance to qualify it because a fiery COMOPS lieutenant-colonel was so put out by my words that he leapt across the bar counter intending to strike me with his fist. Major Peter Burford quickly came between us and told his colleague not to be a bloody fool. "I think the Groupie may be right. Give him an opportunity to tell us why."

My contention was this. The electorate could be counted on to give Smith and Nkomo a total of forty seats. For a number of reasons I thought this left the remaining sixty seats open to Mugabe. In terms of the Lancaster House Agreement, Mugabe should already have been ruled out of the elections for blatant and widespread intimidation and murder. But, the Brits were obviously not going to do this and, from what we could see, the NATJOC seemed either misinformed or too weak to force the issue, even though the Lancaster House Agreement had placed it in control of all security matters. NATJOC was specifically tasked with ensuring that the entire election process was conducted in a free and fair manner. With intimidation peaking and time running out, this made the NATJOC's perceived inaction all the more intolerable.

Muzorewa had shown himself to be weak and indecisive, whereas Mugabe had told the people that only he could stop the war. In Harare Township the urban people, who had been on-side throughout the war, were now openly singing Mugabe praise songs. To my way of thinking, the writing was on the wall. Eighty per cent of the black electorate lived outside Matabeleland, and all of these would vote 'for peace'. They had suffered most and were now thoroughly sick and tired of a war they genuinely believed could only be stopped by Mugabe. That was my contention, but General Walls and the NATJOC obviously saw things differently.

Possibly because he believed the information being fed to him and wished to uphold the morale of his forces, General Walls called a meeting of Army and Air Force officers at the New Sarum Sports Club. As I recall, no member of COMOPS staff was included.

Since I did not attend the meeting addressed by General Walls, I cannot say exactly what was said. I do know, however, that he gave the assembled officers his personal guarantee that he would not allow Mugabe to come to power. I also know that the general's speech left most officers with a clear understanding that military action would be taken against ZANU in the 'unlikely event' that it gained a majority at the polls. This notion, however, was very much at odds with what General Walls had told his own staff. In COMOPS we had been informed, categorically, that no unconstitutional action would be considered. General Walls said, "There is no question of Rhodesians indulging in a military coup."

The 'whites only' election was held on 14 February and went off smoothly with Ian Smith's RF party gaining all twenty white seats, as expected. On 27, 28 and 29 February the 'common roll' voters went to the polling stations where ill-prepared London Bobbies and other Commonwealth observers watched the long lines of voters 'to ensure that no intimidation was taking place'. They had no idea that ZANLA had told harassed tribesmen that the reason for three days of voting was simple. Day One was for all people voting for Mugabe; Day Two was for Muzorewa and Day Three for Nkomo. Anyone not voting on Day One would be dealt with very severely.

The observers, most on African soil for the first time, were blissfully unaware of subtle intimidation going on right under their noses or of blatant intimidation against people approaching from beyond their sight; this was at its worst during Days Two and Three. But Rhodesians who watched could clearly see ZANLA's underhanded methods. Intimidation was rife and people were told that voting for Mugabe had been extended to include all three days. "The spirits and special spies will reveal any individual who did not place his mark in favour of ZANU."

The news coming in from all around the country seemed to undo any false hopes amongst members of the NATJOC. High levels of frustration were evident with much toing and froing between COMOPS and Government House. General Walls sent an urgent signal to Margaret Thatcher in an attempt to stop the rot. He received no reply until elections were over, and there was not the faintest hint that any action would be taken by Britain against ZANU.

Whilst this was going on, I continued to spend most of my time with ZIPRA and ZANLA. ZIPRA knew what was going on in the field and were thoroughly depressed. ZANLA knew what was going on in the field and were elated. Throughout the day of 3 March, results of the elections kept coming through but no clear-cut trend emerged until late that night. Things looked bad when I eventually retired to bed.

I recall sitting at my desk the next morning when a sensation of overwhelming panic struck me just as a cup of tea was placed before me. Even though I thought I was fully prepared, final confirmation over the radio of Mugabe's whopping fifty-seven seats victory floored me. It must have been really awful for those who had been so confident that Muzorewa would get more than eleven seats because he only gained three! During the afternoon the Ceasefire Committee held its closing meeting and a final photograph was taken on the steps outside the conference room.

In a stunned state I wandered up to Air HQ to be near friends and to gaze out of the window of the office I once used for my projects work. Salisbury's streets and avenues were filled with celebrating blacks. Open lorries were parading about, filled with excited people, flapping their arms and uttering the sound of a cockerel crowing at dawn—ZANU's election symbol.

Front row: General Barnard, Rex Nhongo, General Acland, Dumiso Dabengwa, PB. Middle row: Brigadier Gurdon, the pretty Rhodesian lady (half hidden) Miss C. Gardener who took notes for COMOPS, Lt-Col Parker Bowles, Lookout Masuku.
Back row: Left: Rhodesian Army intelligence officer (face remembered but name forgotten). Not present: Josiah Tungamirai who had not yet returned from ZANLA's pressure-electioneering campaign.

Because I was a member of the Ceasefire Committee with continuing liaison duties between COMOPS, ZIPRA and ZANLA, it is not surprising that I was totally unaware that SAS and RLI were on immediate standby to take out ZANLA's hierarchy in the event of a Mugabe victory. However, high hopes following detailed planning and rehearsed tasks, which included the employment of tanks and other heavy equipment, turned out to be a damp squib. The secret codeword to launch this top-secret operation was never given. Incensed by General Walls's assurance that Mugabe would not be allowed to come to power, the disgusted SAS named the situation 'Rhodesia's Walls Street Crash'.

At all of Salisbury's major road intersections vehicle-borne troops waited for trouble whilst trying to put on a brave face for passing civilians—but nothing happened. Overhead, helicopters orbited, watching for any breakout of looting—but this did not occur. An air of depression and uncertainty hung over all who opposed ZANU as well as many who had been coerced through fear into voting for Mugabe' party. Many

people went home, shops closed and almost all work had ceased by midday.

Radio and television stations ran some regular programmes, but for the most part Mugabe's victory held prominence. Repeatedly listeners and viewers were reminded that Robert Mugabe would address the nation at 8 pm.

When he came on air, Mugabe projected himself as a decent chap, preaching reconciliation and the need to put the past behind us. He was at pains to give hope and asked every citizen of the new Zimbabwe to move forward with faith and determination to build on its vibrant economy in a non-racial society. Whilst he was speaking, I sensed considerable relief. However, when he had finished, I thought things through.

When released from prison in 1974 to participate in the Zambian–South African sponsored talks in Lusaka, Mugabe had broken solemn undertakings by escaping into Mozambique. He had failed to meet any promise made to Nkomo. Yet now, having blatantly broken every agreement with Britain and three other parties at Lancaster House, he was projecting himself as an honest and fair-minded man. I could not accept this. The Mugabe leopard was not about to change his spots; he was a Marxist through and through and could be counted on to change direction whenever it suited him.

Within an hour of the speech my mind was made up. I had to resign from the Air Force and decide if I should stay in Zimbabwe or sell up and move my family away from a Marxist government that would undoubtedly become a one-party dictatorship, just like the rest of black Africa. Personal enrichment for Africa's leading politicians had deprived their peoples of pre-independence wealth and their pathetic management had destroyed previously strong economic foundations. Zimbabwe would be no different!

Joint High Command HQ

SETTING UP THE JOINT HIGH Command Headquarters commenced on 6 March. Whilst COMOPS HQ was being wrapped up I, together with a handful of officers, commenced furnishing new offices in a newly built wing at Army HQ. Unfortunately Brigadier Peter Rich had retired and Brian Robinson was no longer with COMOPS so those of us remaining no longer enjoyed any spirit of fun and laughter. Brigadier Leon Jacobs replaced Peter Rich but I hardly ever saw him.

Air HQ was already inundated with resignations. So, knowing that the notice period would only take effect at the end of the month, I did not tender mine right away. I had in excess of 300 days' leave due, though only 184 of these attracted leave pay, but this was more than sufficient to cover the mandatory three-months notice period meaning that I could withhold my resignation to the end of March and leave the service immediately. As it happened, I stayed on until the end of May.

The ZIPRA and ZANLA commanders moved into their offices as soon as they were ready. Progressively other offices filled and Zimbabwe's Joint High Command HQ started to function under command of Lieutenant-General Walls who had been appointed to the position by Prime Minister Mugabe.

My job was to continue as the linkman with ZIPRA and ZANLA, initially to prepare for the integration of forces. Since most of this involved Army matters, Lieutenant-Colonel 'Fluff' Templer worked with me. Amongst the many issues to be thrashed out was the question of bringing in all ZIPRA and ZANLA arms and equipment from Zambia and Mozambique. Though it took some time, ZIPRA handed me their ordnance schedules and, as agreed, Fluff Templer let them have sight of the Rhodesian Army's schedules. I did the same by showing those of the Air Force.

Rex Nhongo insisted on seeing all these schedules, even though he was not forthcoming with his own. This was largely due to the loss of Josiah Tongogara and utter confusion in Mozambique. Besides, most records were lost to ZANLA during multiple operations against the various Chimoio bases and finally as a consequence of the Monte Casino raid. Nevertheless, I refused to show ZANLA anything until they were in a position to reciprocate.

ZIPRA's lists were neat and well presented. They revealed larger numbers of battle tanks, APCs and other fighting equipment than we had expected. I had already left the service when ZIPRA's equipment eventually came into the country via Victoria Falls, but was told that the equipment matched the lists, whereas ZANLA, as expected, never made any submission.

ZANLA continued to claim having more equipment than ZIPRA. We knew this was pure bluff, which was later confirmed by a senior ZANLA officer. In a drunken state he let slip that there were no reserves in Mozambique and that, had the war continued, ZANLA would have collapsed around mid-1980. This was mind-boggling news making us realise that, had Op Manacle taken place, ZANLA would have been out of the game before the Lancaster House Talks were concluded. Bloody sickening! Nevertheless we were stuck with a political failure and had to make the best of the situation.

Fluff Templer and I spent many hours in discussion with the ZANLA and ZIPRA commanders and provided them with every single idea on many matters relating to the integration of forces. Along the way, agendas were raised for repeat discussions with General Walls, the Commanders of the Army and Air Force, the Commissioner of Police and Ken Flower who continued to head CIO.

Nothing that Fluff and I recommended was accepted in these long drawn-out meetings that covered the same ground but resulted in totally different agreements. I felt we were wasting our time but General Walls insisted that Fluff and I should continue because we were exposing ZIPRA and ZANLA to many issues and complications that prepared them better for the high-level meetings.

When I submitted my resignation to Air HQ, the only real resistance to my leaving service came from Air Commodore Norman Walsh and Group Captain Hugh Slatter who both tried to persuade me to stay on. At Joint High Command ZIPRA and ZANLA received the news badly. All four commanders, individually, begged me to remain because they said they knew me better than any other RSF officer and had come to trust me above all others. This was the continuing issue of preferring Air Force to other services.

My situation became especially difficult when Rex Nhongo said that he and all ZANLA and ZIPRA commanders wanted me to take overall command of all forces. He said Mugabe had supported this. I told Rex this was an absolute impossibility. Not only was I five rank-levels below the rank he was considering, I was totally unprepared in experience for such a position. His reply showed how differently he thought. "When the sergeant is better than the lieutenant-colonel, the sergeant becomes the full colonel."

This situation was altogether unexpected and I saw great danger in it. In Rhodesian terms, I knew I was totally unprepared for such a responsible position, and even less so for what promised to become a political post. Why I even thought the matter through I couldn't say because my heart was already set on getting out of uniform. Strangely, I was helped in making a final decision by one of ZANLA's field commanders who warned me that Zimbabwe would soon be driven by ideologies that would fail to fill peoples' stomachs. He was certain that the ordinary man would fail to realise any of the 'freedom' promises made by politicians whose future actions would all be driven by personal greed.

On Tuesday 27 May 1980, four days before my last day in office, I was leaving home for work when I spotted a stationary grey Land Rover with a long HF aerial. It was parked just beyond our garden gate on the other side of the street. Immediately I became suspicious and, as I passed by and looked towards the driver, I saw a white man of about sixty years of age flick his head away and raise a newspaper high enough to prevent my seeing his face through my rear-view mirror. Day and night for the next 730 days my movements were monitored from grey CIO Peugeot 504 sedans with long HF aerials.

Air Marshal Mick McLaren had retired four months earlier and became Director of Shell and BP Subsidiary Companies. When I retired, he offered me a position as general manager of one of these companies. Within eighteen months I was managing two more and became a member of the Board of Directors of Subsidiary Companies.

This must have been a headache for the CIO who monitored all my movements. From early morning until about midnight, one of four vehicles was always in one or other of three shaded parking spots outside my house. But what really floored me was that the other three vehicles were waiting at the three companies, all manned by elderly white men whom I deliberately ignored. My business telephones were fine but my home telephone was tapped whenever I was at home. About one second after line connection, a distinct click was followed by a dull background noise that persisted for the duration of each call.

I can only assume that my reasons for refusing to stay on with the Zimbabwe forces were treated with suspicion, something along the line "If he is not with us he must be against us!" Funnily enough I became so used to being monitored that, when surveillance was lifted on 27 May 1982, I experienced a strange sense of nakedness knowing that I was no longer important. In November and December I went overseas to explore a business opportunity. Upon my return, full surveillance of my movements was reinstated, but only for one week. This made it safe for me to move out of Zimbabwe.

In April 1983 I left the country of my birth for good. Beryl stayed on for another five months to wind up her hairdressing business and sell our home. Both our children had moved ahead of us to South Africa. Debbie was nursing at Groote Schuur Hospital and Paul was at Rhodes University in Cape Town doing Chemical Engineering.

There was much pain in leaving such a beautiful country, but we had decided that Rhodesia no longer existed. This had nothing to do with the change of the country's name or the fact that blacks were in power. It had everything to do with a top-heavy government bent on establishing a Marxist-styled one-party dictatorship that would almost certainly destroy our country. Anyway Mugabe's promises of a country in which all could live in harmony and peace were already showing serious cracks.

Many officers and men stayed on with the Air Force of Zimbabwe, all enjoying hugely accelerated promotion to fill gaps left by senior men who chose not to serve under the new political order. Those who remained were all fine men who gave their all to maintaining the Air Force they loved. But then things took a nasty turn on Sunday 25 July 1982 when South African-based saboteurs launched an attack against aircraft based at Thornhill.

What these saboteurs hoped to achieve one cannot say but the repercussions of the incident were horrifying. Determined to find someone to blame for the embarrassment of losing four brand-new Hawk Mk60 fighters, Hunters and a Lynx, Mugabe's bullyboys turned on Air Force officers who suffered arrest, foul torture and false accusations. This hysterical action by ignorant political thugs showed that ZANU did not understand that Air Force men could never have considered destroying the very aircraft they loved so much.

I have to say that this horror made me pleased I had left the service when I did. But knowing my friends were in prison I sought to see what I could do to help. The Commander of the Air Force of Zimbabwe, Air Marshal Norman Walsh, told me to stay well clear of these matters, as they were very sensitive. He himself was under twenty-four-hour surveillance and did not require any more help than he and the imprisoned officers were receiving from lawyers Mike Hartmann, Rhett Gardener and Mike d'Enis.

More than a year passed before the officers were acquitted and released by a black judge on 31 August 1983. Outside the court they were immediately re-arrested and another long year followed before all were eventually released and deported from Zimbabwe, their service pensions having been denied them.

How those guys managed to put on a brave face on the few occasions they were seen during trial baffled me until I learned how Air Force technician-turned-chaplain, Boet van Schalkwyk, and the men's wives had given so much support, love and spiritual guidance.

Barbara Cole's book *Sabotage and Torture* tells the full sad tale of torture and trumped-up evidence against these unfortunate victims caught up in a wicked political game.

One of the few officers who remained in service with the Air Force of Zimbabwe was Ian Harvey who, with twenty-two years of service to Rhodesia, was a flight lieutenant from 1967 to 1980. Even before I moved to COMOPS, Ian had recorded 4,000 flying hours on Alouettes but then went on to exceed 6,000 hours; a world record I thought until I learned Mark Smithdorff had many more from his military service and fire-fighting operations in America.

Following another twenty years in service with Robert Mugabe's Air Force, Ian finally retired in the rank air vice-marshal. For this he received no more than his Mercedes staff car.

From left to right: Air Lieutenant Barry Lloyd, Wing Commander John Cox, Air Lieutenant Neville Weir, Air Commodore Phil Pile, Wing Commander Peter Briscoe and Air Vice-Marshal Hugh Slatter. (Not seen here was Nigel Lewis-Walker who was being held in Gweru (Gwelo) Prison. He was the last to be freed.)

In much happier times, Ian receives congratulations from Group Captain Mick Grier on completing 4,000 hours on Alouette lll.

Epilogue

RHODESIA CAME INTO BEING IN November 1890 and ceased to exist in April 1980. In only ninety short years Rhodesians transformed raw bush into a highly developed state—the breadbasket of Central Africa. Though always a member of the British Empire, self-governing Rhodesia never came under direct British rule. This suited Britain's many governments because, unlike many members of the Empire, Rhodesia needed no support from British taxpayers. White Rhodesians, and many black ones too, were staunch monarchists who willingly gave support of arms to King and Queen in every British war fought in South Africa, Europe, the Middle East and Far East. Rhodesia's contributions and status were always recognised and lauded until the mid-1960s.

By this time dismemberment of the British Empire had brought about the steep decline associated with party political handling of everything British. With this also came an end to an Englishman's word being his bond; politically that is. So too had Britain's political might been substituted by weak-kneed policies of appeasement in which Rhodesia was another stepping stone down Britain's road to self-destruction.

Establishing Britain's Empire did not occur without some serious flaws, even unashamed exploitation of peoples and natural resources. But not one country so affected failed to enjoy massive development and a legacy of efficient infrastructure. This is plainly visible in those British colonies that were granted independence but retained responsible government in white hands. They continue to prosper whilst those that find it necessary to use colonialism as an excuse for their own failings, particularly in Africa, have suffered serious and ongoing decline. In spite of this, successive British governments have shamefully led Britons into feeling ashamed of their colonial past.

It was the British Government that created the Federation of Rhodesia and Nyasaland by linking two British colonies to self-governing Rhodesia. Having in this way given three unequal countries equal status, Britain's policies of appeasement kicked in to destroy its own brainchild after only ten years; this despite the fact that union of the three states had been an unqualified success. In appeasing the wants of power-seeking black politicians, common sense and the interests of ordinary citizens were forsaken. Remember Henry Kissinger's words, "The politics of convenience has little to do with truth or logic!"

In compensation for agreeing to the dissolution of the Federation, Britain's Conservative Government promised independence to each of the three states but only honoured its pledges to Northern Rhodesia and Nyasaland. The solemn promise of independence given Southern Rhodesia was ignored because of the newfound obsession to appease Africa's black governments, no matter their corruption and total lack of management skills. Taking full advantage of Britain's whimpering 'apologies for her colonial past', black governments followed the Soviet Union's lead by introducing racism as a whipping tool. In turn this led Britain into creating the political mess that perfectly suited communist aspirations and led Rhodesians into a thirteen-year-long civil war.

Rivalry between Britain's two main political parties has created seesaw situations within Britain itself, but none has been so damaging as suffered by Britain's colonies. Every state granted independence experienced the intrigues and lies that had become the post-WWII hallmark of British political expediency. It was these traits that forced Ian Smith's Rhodesian Front party to declare UDI in 1965 after all options were rendered intolerable by both Labour and Conservative governments constantly moving the goal posts they themselves had set.

It can be argued that UDI was a mistake, but I know for certain that we would have become a communist state that much earlier had UDI not been declared. The question is: was it all worthwhile? Again I feel Ian Smith had to do what he did to gain time in hopes that the West would come to understand that Rhodesian plans to progress gently towards responsible black majority rule was a much better option than the hurried Marxist take-over we all feared and fought so hard to prevent. Argue as one might, the facts are that racism became the main political issue and Britain rejected white-led democracy in favour of black Marxism. In his bid to justify the horrific policy of apartheid, Prime Minister Vorster of South Africa used Rhodesia as his political pawn, thereby undermining all efforts to gain Western support. Even our hopes in Margaret Thatcher were dashed when we came to realise that 'the Iron Lady with more balls than the men' had succumbed to the policies of appeasement expounded by her gutless male colleagues.

Every living white Rhodesian was, and remains, incensed by the duplicity—particularly by Vorster—that led to Rhodesia's unnecessary demise. Whereas the black folk did not recognise the dangers of voting ZANU into power, today they know better. But this late realisation cannot circumvent the unnecessary suffering and bloodshed they will surely face for bringing to power an unbelievably selfish, power-crazy,

Marxist demagogue. Too late they have come to understand that ZANU's promises of utopia in 'liberated Zimbabwe' were only for the good of Mugabe and his fat cats—certainly not for theirs. Even the CTs who fought and died to bring about the promises made to them by Mugabe are losers.

Yet, angry and sad as I am for the destruction of my own dreams, I look back on my days in Rhodesia as God-given and wonderful. Nobody can take away memories of life in 'God's own country' amongst wonderful people of all races and creeds. Most white Rhodesians, now spread across the world, share this opinion and the vast majority of black folk trapped in Zimbabwe look back longingly to the days they lived under paternal white government. Harold Macmillan's 'winds of change blowing across Africa' have for these unfortunate Zimbabweans proven to be nothing short of winds of destruction.

Twenty years on at the turn of the century, I am sad to say that I realise how successive British governments have continued the downward spiral in which their winds of destruction have turned to sweep across Britain. The deliberate destruction of Britain's TSR2 bomber development programme by order of Harold Wilson was an early case in point. This really shook Rhodesians because the Labour Government's order included the destruction of all data, rigs, jigs and moulds. If a British prime minister was prepared to destroy Britain's lead in world aeronautical affairs thereby creating loss of prestige, loss of jobs, loss of huge foreign earnings and forcing English engineers to move to other countries, it is hardly surprising that he was so hell-bent on meeting other socialist communism wants, including the destruction of responsible government in far-off Rhodesia. For the Conservative Government to follow suit was mind-boggling.

That is all behind us now. President Robert Mugabe is the only one to have benefited from the policy of appeasement. But in Britain the same policy has led to appalling declines such as permitting children to enjoy power over their elders and allowing the finest rail system in the world to degenerate to its present situation. Illegal immigrants are afforded preferred treatment over British-born citizens. Major companies pass business to the Far East to escape disadvantages stemming from ongoing governmental mismanagement of the county's affairs. Brussels sets the rules for UK trade. The euro might soon replace Sterling thereby destroying British independence and power forever.

I am a Rhodesian, first and foremost, yet I often find myself wondering why I am still proud to be British having seen the destructive forces of misguided rule by successive British governments. My simple conclusion is that, like most Rhodesians, I was brought up to be the royalist I am today. It is the British Crown that anchors us to our history and our successes. British royalty sets us apart from all other nations even though the UK Government and British media find cause to undermine it at every turn. But it seems to me that the unique position the royal family holds in ordinary British hearts is going to make political suicide just a touch too difficult for destructive politicians and pressmen.

Only a substantial change of the direction in political leadership and national thinking can save Great Britain and recover her to her rightful position of strength and self-respect.

But above all I say, "Please God, save the Queen."

Glossary

A/S/L	Air Sub-Lieutenant
AD	Accidental Discharge (of a weapon)
AFA	African female adult
AFJ	African female juvenile
AFS	Advanced Flying School
ALO	Air Liaison Officer
AMA	African male adult
AMJ	African male juvenile
amsl	above mean sea level
AP	Assembly Point
ASI	Air Staff Instructions
ASR	Air Strike Report
ATC	Air Traffic Control
ATOPS	Anti-terrorist Operations
AVM	Air Vice-Marshal
B of I	Board of Inquiry
BCR	Bronze Cross of Rhodesia
BFM	Belt Feed Mechanism (20mm Hispano cannons)
BFS	Basic Flying School
Bravo	Rhodesian time zone (Greenwich Mean Time is Zulu) Earlier hour zone going east is Alpha then Bravo and so on
BSAP	British South Africa Police
casevac	Casualty evacuation
CFS	Central Flying School (RAF)
CMF	Commonwealth Monitoring Force
CSIR	Council for Scientific and Industrial Research (South Africa)
CSM	Company Sergeant-Major
CT	Communist Terrorist
DCD	Defence Cross for Distinguished Service
DGSS	Director General of Supporting Services
DI	Drill Instructor
DZ	Drop Zone (paratroopers and para-supplies)
EFJ	European female juvenile
EMA	European male adult
EMJ	European male juvenile
FAC	Forward Air Controller
FAE	Fuel-Air Explosive
FASOC	Forward Air Support Operations Centre

FIS	Flying Instructors' School
FL	Flight level
FRELIMO	Front for the Liberation of Mozambique
GAC	Ground to Air Controller
GCV	Grand Cross of Valour (Rhodesia's equivalent to the VC)
GSU	General Service Unit (equivalent to RAF Regiment)
GTS	Ground Training School
HALO	High Altitude – Low Opening (free-fall parachuting)
HF	High Frequency (radios)
IF	Instrument Flying
ILS	Instrument Letdown System
INTAF	Internal Affairs
IP	Initial Point (starting position of jet run-in to attack)
ITCZ	Inter-Tropical Convergence Zone (meeting of warm Congo air and polar air)
JOC	Joint Operations Centre
JSPIS	Joint Services Photo-Interpretation Services
LTT	Locally Trained Terrorist
LZ	Landing Zone (applicable to helicopters)
MID	Military Intelligence Services
MLM	Member of the Legion of Merit (Operational or Non-operational)
MNR	Mozambican National Resistance
NDB	Non-Directional Beacon
OAU	Organisation of African Unity
OCC	Operations Co-ordinating Committee
OCU	Operational Conversion Unity (advance pilot training for weapons)
OFEMA	Français D'exportation de Matériel Aéronautique
PAC	Pan African Congress
PAF	Portuguese Air Force

PATU	Police Anti-Terrorist Unit
PJI	Parachute Jumping Instructor
PMC	President of Mess Committee
PR	Police Reserve
PRI	Photo Recce Interpreter
PRAW	Police Reserve Air Wing
PTC	Pilot Training Course
PV	Protected Village
QFE	International Civil Aviation code for altimeter setting that will read zero feet at the selected ground position.
QHI	Qualified Helicopter Instructor
RAMS	Radio Activated Marker SSB
RAR	Rhodesian African Rifles
R&R	Rest and Re-training/Rest and Recuperation.
Ratpack	Ration Pack
RP	Rocket projectile
RSF	Rhodesian Security Forces
RSM	Regimental Sergeant-Major
RSO	Range Safety Officer (air weapons ranges)
SAAF	South African Air Force
SAAFCOL	SAAF Staff College
SAANC	South African African National Congress
SACP	South African Communist Party
SAM	Surface-to-Air Missile
SAP	South African Police
SB	Special Branch (of Police)
SCR	Silver Cross of Rhodesia
SOP	Standard Operating Procedure
SSB	Single Side-band radio
SSQ	Station Sick Quarters
SSU	Short Service Unit (refers to pilot training scheme prior to 1960)
Strela	SAM 7 anti-aircraft missile
STO	Station (or Senior) Technical Officer
SWA	South West Africa
SWAPO	South West Africa Peoples' Organisation
SWO	Station Warrant Officer
TF	Territorial Force
TNT	Trinitrotoluene (explosive)
TTL	Tribal Trust Land
UANC	United African National Council
UDI	Unilateral Declaration of Independence
UXB	Un-Exploded Bomb
VHF	Very High Frequency (radios)
VNE	Velocity Never to Exceed (maximum allowable flight speed)
VR	Volunteer Reserve
ZANLA	Zimbabwe African National Liberation Army (ZANU's military wing)
ZANU	Zimbabwe African National Union
ZAPU	Zimbabwe African Peoples' Union
ZIPRA	Zimbabwe Peoples' Revolutionary Army (ZAPU's military wing)